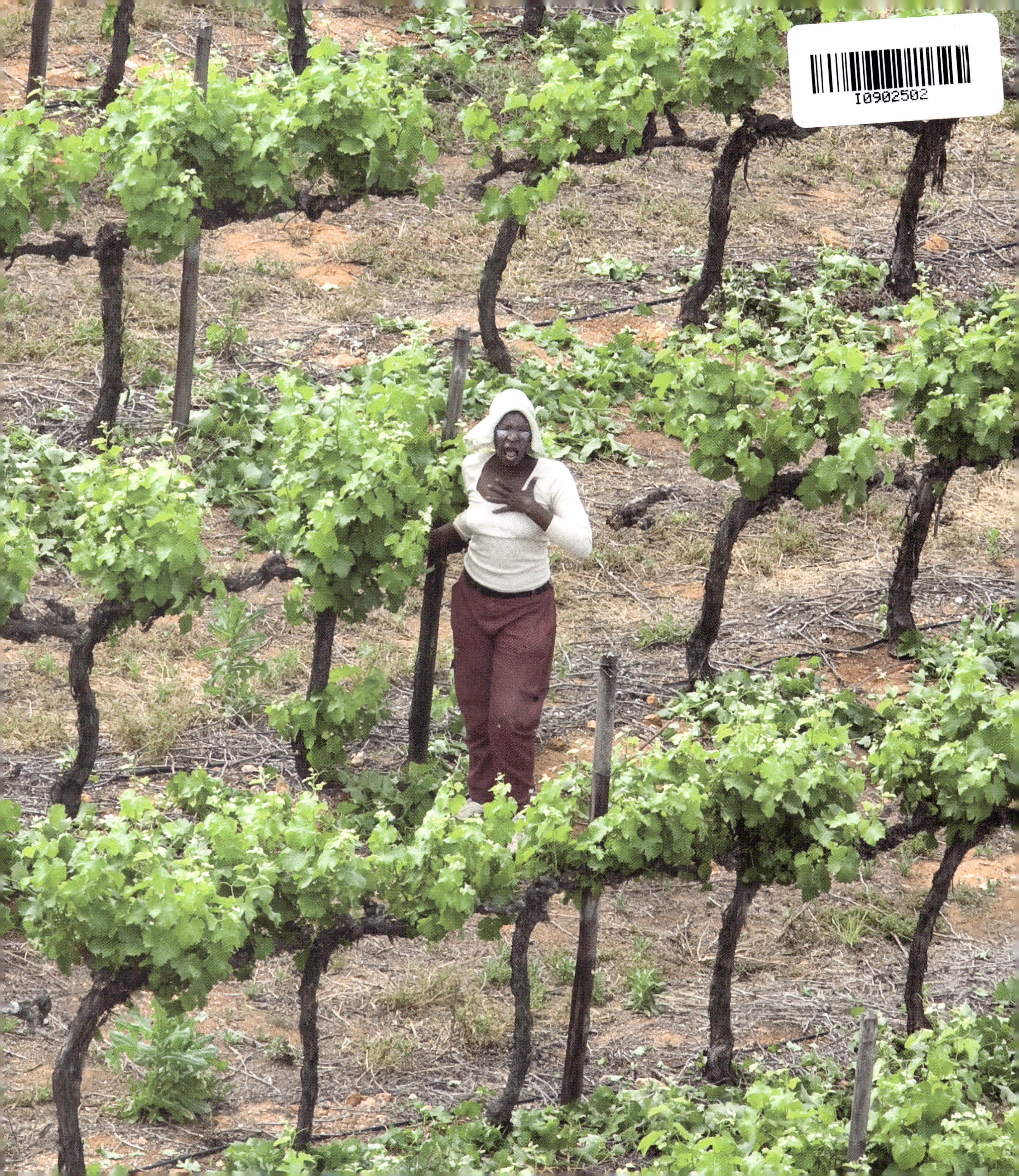

Karel Tomeï

FLYING OVER SOUTH AFRICA

Karel Tomeï

FLYING OVER SOUTH AFRICA

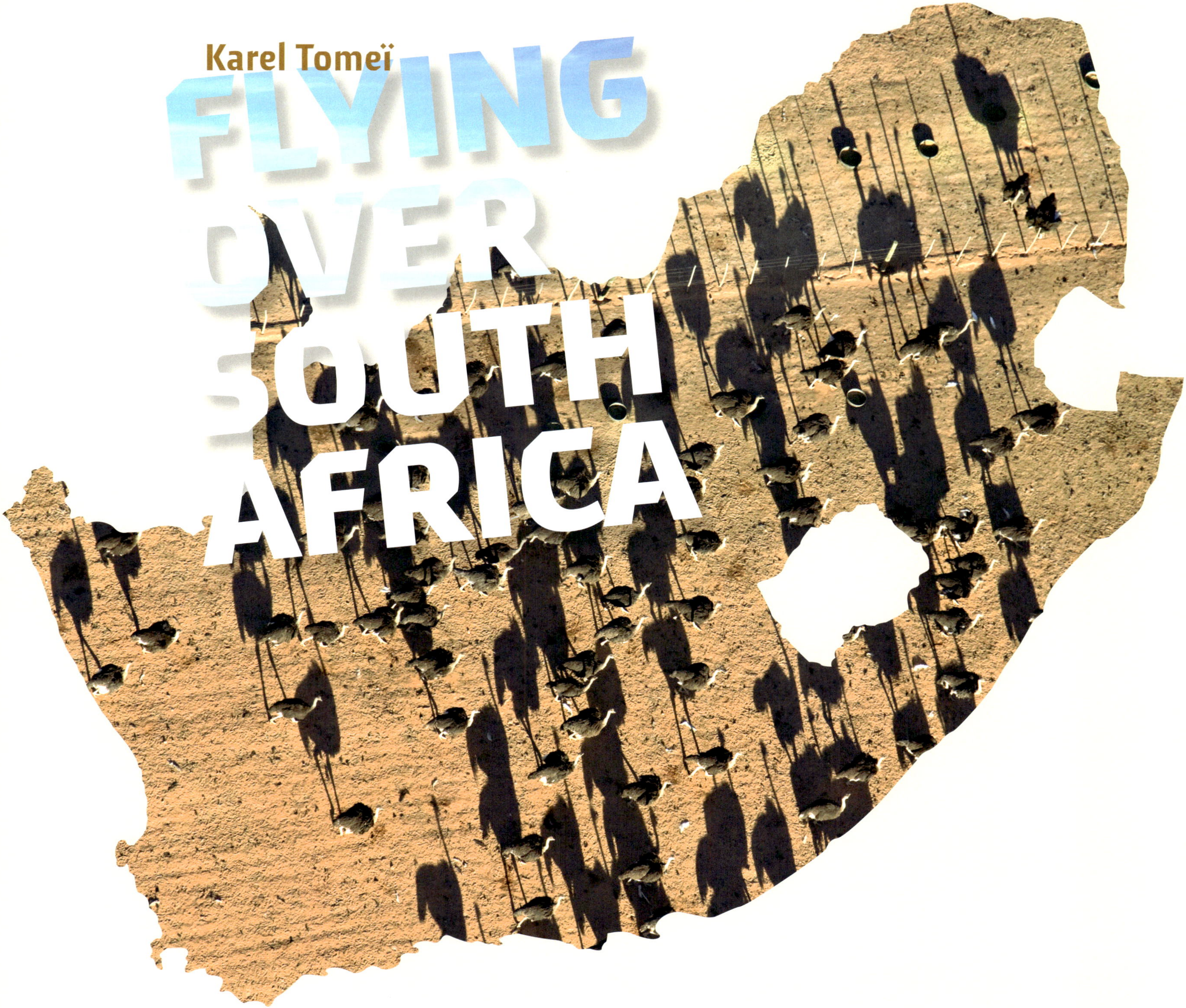

Scriptum

For 40,000 summers the San (Bushmen) people roamed the plains of Southern Africa. For them, borders were dictated by rivers and the need to hunt and survive, not by politics. They lived among the animals, sharing their habitat. As the life of the Bushmen demanded that they be constantly alert, small hills known as 'koppies' were a favourite place for gathering. The high vantage points provided excellent protection. In the Richterveld, several koppies were 'factories' where these diligent hunters would make stone and hunting tools. Their superb hunting skills and their ability to live in semi-desert areas – they would, for example, bury ostrich eggs filled with water for later use – ensured their survival through the centuries. Within their society, there was great respect for the animals they hunted, and the Bushmen were thankful to the animal for giving its life for their survival. Blending with nature was so important that the elders deemed it important for a true Bushmen to die 'a small death' before he could blend in with his surroundings. Today, we would call this 'giving up our ego'. Modern man could perhaps do with a few more 'small deaths'.

A modern rock painting

These fascinating people, with their small stature and distinct features, roamed the southern tip of Africa, observing their habitat, wondering at the moon at night, leaving behind footprints and precious rock paintings, and narrating tribal history and tales of their experiences around the camp fire, talking in their own clicking Bushmen tongue. And for 40,000 years they did all this without doing any damage to the world that provided them with sustenance.

During all those centuries, their view of the Earth was from ground level. Aerial views were for the birds that spread their wings and floated on the thermals created by the African sun. The soaring eagles and their fellow aviators, large and small, were alone in enjoying the view that can only be seen from the sky.

In this aerial documentation, Karel Tomeï has captured the eagle's view of South Africa. But he has also captured the way the 'cultured' human beings who moved to this region have influenced and changed it. These were people driven by greed, taking more, much more than they actually needed. Land was confiscated, Bushmen were jailed for cattle theft, a concept that they had never known in all those 40,000 years. Modern man is now coming to recognise the effects of his 'carbon footprint'; he could learn a lot from the Bushmen. But to do that, they will have to look to the past. For the visitors from the North who came first in ships and later in silver birds managed to destroy the Bushmen's habitat in just three centuries. It should make us humble.

Karel, with your artist's eye and critical vision you have captured South Africa in a way that will inspire the reader to think more deeply about the beauty that you have so aptly transformed into a work of art.

A modern rock painting.

Frans Grotepass

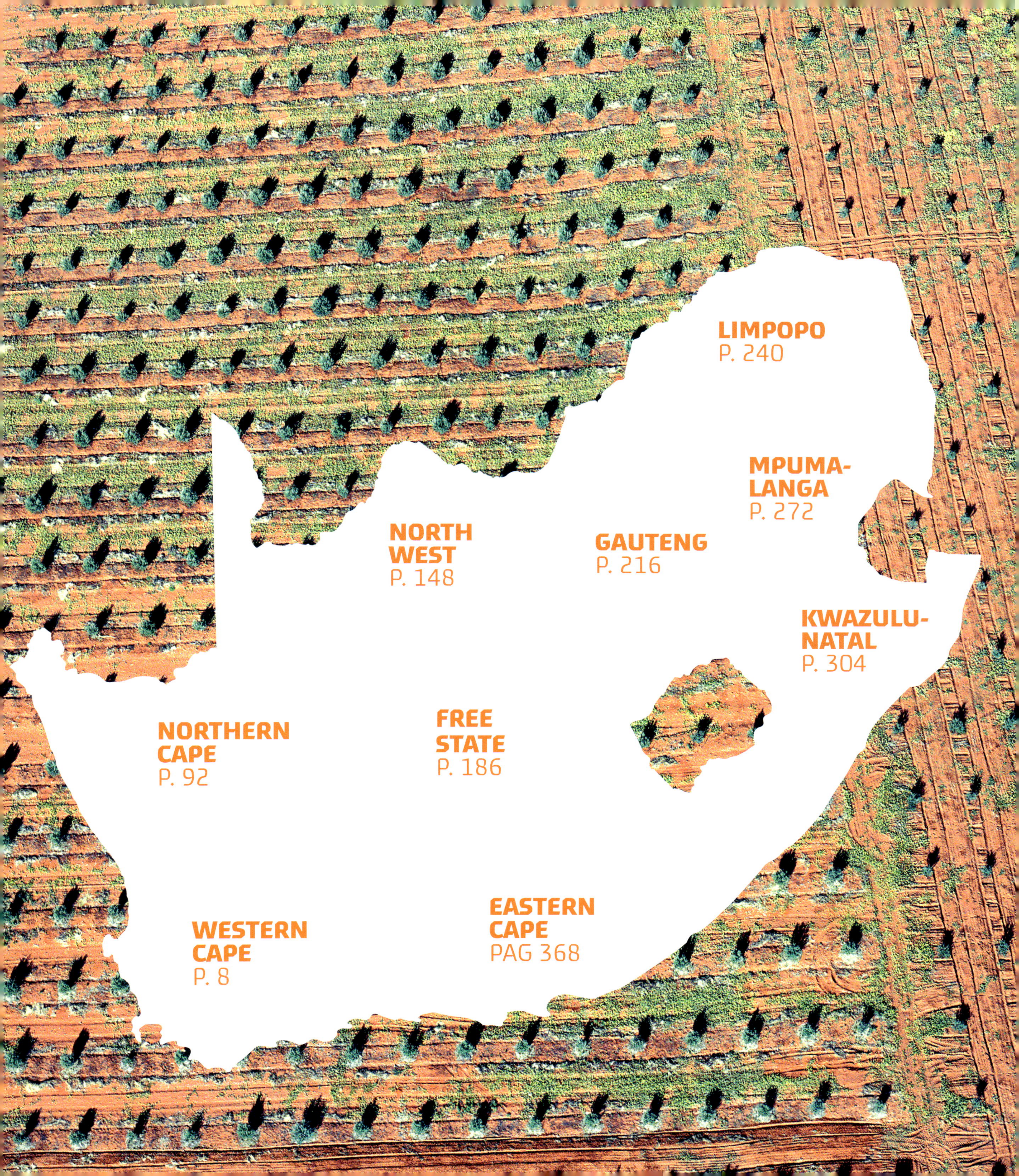
LIMPOPO
P. 240
MPUMA-
LANGA
P. 272
NORTH
WEST
P. 148
GAUTENG
P. 216
KWAZULU-
NATAL
P. 304
NORTHERN
CAPE
P. 92
FREE
STATE
P. 186
WESTERN
CAPE
P. 8
EASTERN
CAPE
PAG 368

Getting to know a country starts by looking at it. Because you see a lot more from a higher viewpoint, I have the habit of climbing a hill or some other high vantage point whenever I visit an area that I do not know, so that I can get a good impression of the surroundings. I've used this method in many countries and employed it some fifteen years ago when I first visited South Africa, a country that – thanks to its many mountain ranges – invites the visitor to view it from above.

A magnificent country from a different viewpoint

For many years, whenever I visited, I would climb the nearby mountains to study the landscape, until a friend invited me to make a flight in his aircraft. I love flying, because it gives a surprising twist to my view of the world and inspires me in my work as an aerial photographer. When I'm in the air, areas that I thought I knew well often turn out to look completely different.

That happened during my first flight above South Africa. From the aircraft, because I could see farther than when I was standing on top of a mountain, the impressive landscapes I had seen before took on a new dimension. The flight was what you would call an eye opener. I became inquisitive about other parts of South Africa and so, during my subsequent visits, I rented a plane and pilot to fly over a different area each time. I became fascinated by the enormous diversity in this vast country, where each region has its own characteristic beauty.

A plane allows you to get up close to even the most inaccessible places. South Africa has a host of interesting places that are almost impossible to reach by car, or even on foot. This makes the air traveller a privileged individual. He visits places that others rarely or never see.

My intention to compile these impressions in a new photo book slowly took shape when I learned that the last book of aerial photography on South Africa, 'South Africa from the Air' by aerial photographer Herman Potgieter, had appeared in 1992 and that after his death in an air crash in Nairobi in 1998, nobody had continued his work, except perhaps the makers of aerial photographs for brochures and postcards.

I decided to take up the challenge and produce a book that, through aerial photographs, would show today's South Africa. Its cities, its coastline, its wildlife and its landscapes, natural and industrialised. But I would work in a different way than Potgieter. I didn't want to shoot from a plane but from a helicopter. I always found this the best way of working when producing my previous aerial photography books. Thanks to its slower air speed and greater manoeuvrability, a helicopter allows the photographer to approach the subjects from different viewpoints and show them in greater detail. A plane forces you to take a greater distance into account. You are forced to choose a wider view, you have to leave out details or simply miss them because of the distance. And it is exactly in the details that I often find the eloquence I want to give to a photograph.

Bearing in mind the many mountains and the often capricious weather conditions for which some places were renowned, I looked for an experienced pilot who was also so familiar with the country that he could act as my guide. One day I happened to run into Glen Brown, a very experienced helicopter pilot who had crossed South African airspace in all directions in his Robinson R44 and spoke the language and several dialects fluently. Glen proved an efficient and reliable partner. He was the ideal companion on my journey, which took up about five months over the course of a year. In that time, we flew more than 15,000 kilometres. I owe many special shots to Glen's sharp eyes and extensive knowledge of nature. The most memorable examples are the photographs of thousands of dolphins chasing sardines, a breathtaking spectacle which I consider one of the absolute highlights of our journey. Despite the thorough preparation and the meticulous planning which preceded each flight (sometimes the rear seats were removed from the helicopter and the space crammed with jerry cans of petrol because we were flying over areas that were practically uninhabited), we were nevertheless on several occasions forced by bad weather to make a landing and wait in some isolated spot until the storm had passed. We once roughed it for a week on the Wild Coast of the East Cape Province in a 'resort' that consisted of nothing more than a few ramshackle huts, after we had finally succeeded, with considerable difficulty, in landing our helicopter. Dozens of cockroaches infested my camera bags and the weather refused to clear up, and yet I experienced my stay there as a dream. It was the sort of place that is becoming all too rare in our world: deserted, quiet and unspoilt. You could be alone there with the wind and watch in amazement the antics of the dolphins in a river estuary. The beach was an unusual type of black sand, which I later learned was rich in titanium.

Several hundred kilometres to the north along the same coast, the dune landscape has been thoroughly ravaged by titanium mines, because in South Africa, economy often wins out over ecology. Fortunately, initiatives are being developed to restore the landscape. After being forced to land by a second storm, we met a group of artists who lent us a car so that we could do some shopping. They told us they would show us their work when we returned, but when we drove into the grounds later that evening, everybody was lying in an unusually deep silence and the heavy scent of whisky hung in the air. As a gesture of thanks, we left the car there with a full tank of petrol. The cordiality and hospitality that we encountered during our journey here and at other places gave our efforts a special added value. When you stay in one place for a longer period, you start being treated like one of the family and the stories begin to flow. On a farm in Mpumalanga, which looked so impoverished that it seemed impossible to me that people could eke out a living there, I found a school exercise book in which the farmer's daughter had described how a tornado had razed this once prosperous farm to the ground after a long period of drought. Her story, written in a childlike way, was all the more poignant because it clearly demonstrated how resilient people can be. Just as time carves rough traces in the mountains, difficult living circumstances do not fail to leave their mark on the hearts of the inhabitants. And yet I have often concluded that, despite all adversity, their determination and love of life has remained unbroken.

The people of South Africa have their own story, and perhaps deserve their own book. In the lonely places we visited, we met the most eccentric people, often with animals as their only companions. There was, for example, a very elderly bartender who shared his bedroom with all his pets; when he went to bed at night, he would be followed by a complete parade of animals. There was also a farmer who tried – with little success – to cross zebras with horses. And a cook who kept a parrot which would squawk directions at him in the kitchen.

And of course there were the monkeys. They would appear in the most unexpected places. For example, in a hotel in Johannesburg, where they first stole our breakfast from under our noses and then grabbed the keys from the car's ignition. The keys to the helicopter were on the same keyring. I have never laughed as much as when Glen shouted to the waiter: 'Follow that ape!'

This hilarious incident clearly shows that wild animals still have a place in what has become a cultivated and regulated country. The wildlife simply had to be included in this book. I have tried to put together a selection of photographs that give the broadest and most characteristic impression possible of modern South Africa, a country where, despite all the progress, nature is still an indispensable factor. I hope you enjoy getting to know this special country and hope that you have as much pleasure viewing the photographs as I had in making them.

Karel Tomeï

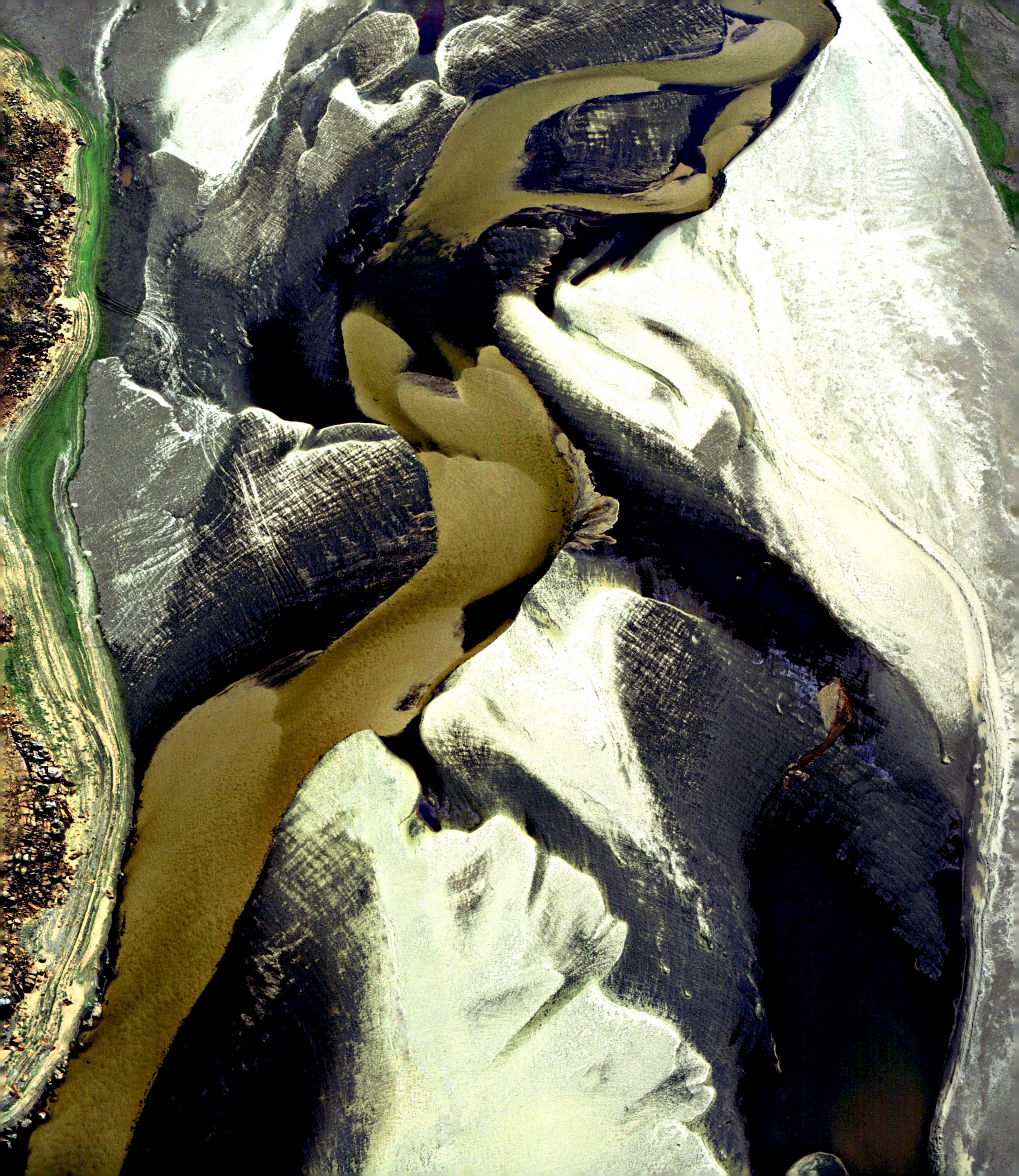

WESTERN CAPE

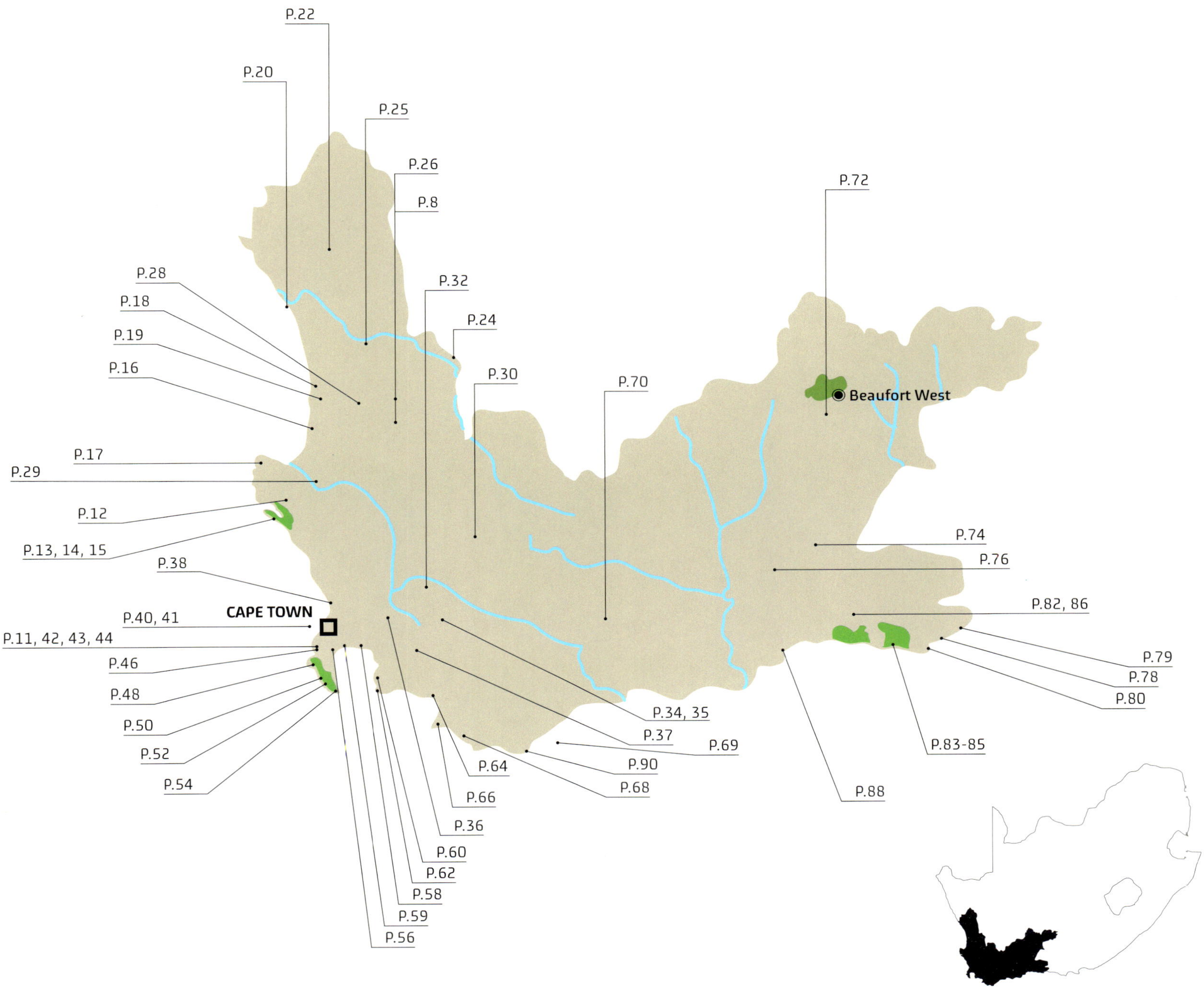

The Murderer's Karoo. A sparsely populated, semi-desert area in the interior of the Western Cape Province. Nobody knows how the area earned its remarkable name. Some claim that in former times, runaway slaves, cattle thieves and other criminals sought refuge here, far from the inhabited world and the reach of the strong arm of the law. Others say that the bone-dry Murderer's Karoo simply owes its name to the murderous heat of the sun that rules here in summer.
But fortunately – or so the story goes – there is one who can break the power of the sun. When drought persists for too long and the heat becomes unbearable, the mountain tortoise seeks shelter under overhanging rocks and kneels to pray for rain. And so he remains, on his knees, motionless, until the wind brings the scent of water.

Of whales, ostriches and mountain tortoises

Some 300 kilometres to the south west of the Murderer's Karoo lies Cape Town. The mother city of South Africa. In 1652, the Dutch United East India Company founded a staging post here. The inhabitants of the settlement would barter with the Khoisan natives to supply Dutch ships with fresh food and water for their long voyage to the East. Nearly a century and a half later, in 1795, the Cape Colony fell into British hands and the role of the Company came to an end. But the legacy of this first Dutch multinational can still be seen everywhere: from the Company Gardens and the Castle in Cape Town to the Dutch Colonial architecture in Swellendam and Tulbagh, and from the vineyards around Stellenbosch to the Shipwreck Museum in Bredasdorp.

In terms of population, Cape Town, including the gigantic, densely populated townships of Khayelitsha and Mitchell's Plain, is the second largest city in South Africa. The mother city is dominated by Table Mountain. The thousand metre high mountain, with its flat top, offers a beautiful view across the modern metropolis. And of course to Robben Island, now an impressive museum, but not so very long ago one of the most infamous prisons in South Africa.

The inhabitants of Cape Town are known for their incorrigible chauvinism. And to be honest, they do have a lot to be proud of. On the east coast, for example, nestled against the Indian Ocean, lies the ever whispering, green rainforest of Tsitsikamma with its extremely rare African Forest Elephants. The west coast, on the other hand, is a rough world where the Atlantic winds keep the trees and shrubs bent and stunted; a world in which everything revolves around catching lobster – the red gold of the west coast. On the south coast lies Hermanus where, in the spring, the whales come in almost to the rocks. And Cape Agulhas, the most southerly point of the African continent, where the Atlantic and Indian oceans meet.
And there is more in the interior: a broad band of unique Cape fynbos, more than one hundred kilometres wide, which is home to nearly 6,000 species of plant that are found nowhere else; the rugged Ceder Mountains, where the world famous rooibos tea is grown; the Kleine Karoo, the capital of which – Oudtshoorn – has been the centre of the world trade in ostrich feathers for nearly a century; and Devil's Peak near Cape Town, which owes its name to the pipe-smoking contests between Dutch sailor Jan van Hunks and the Devil in the 17th century. And, of course, the Murderer's Karoo, where the mountain tortoise patiently prays for rain...

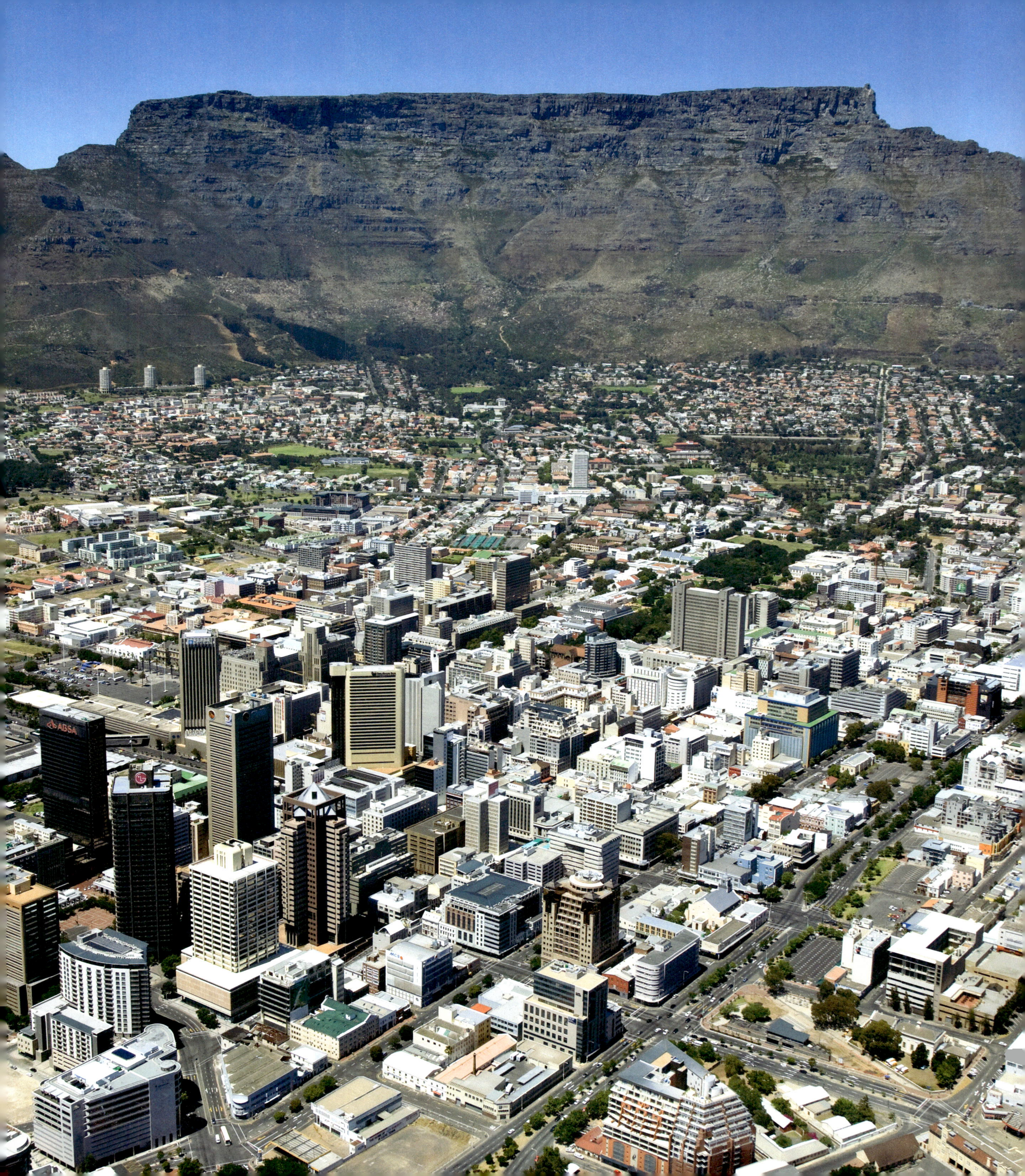

↓ Saldanha Bay
→ Langebaan Lagoon

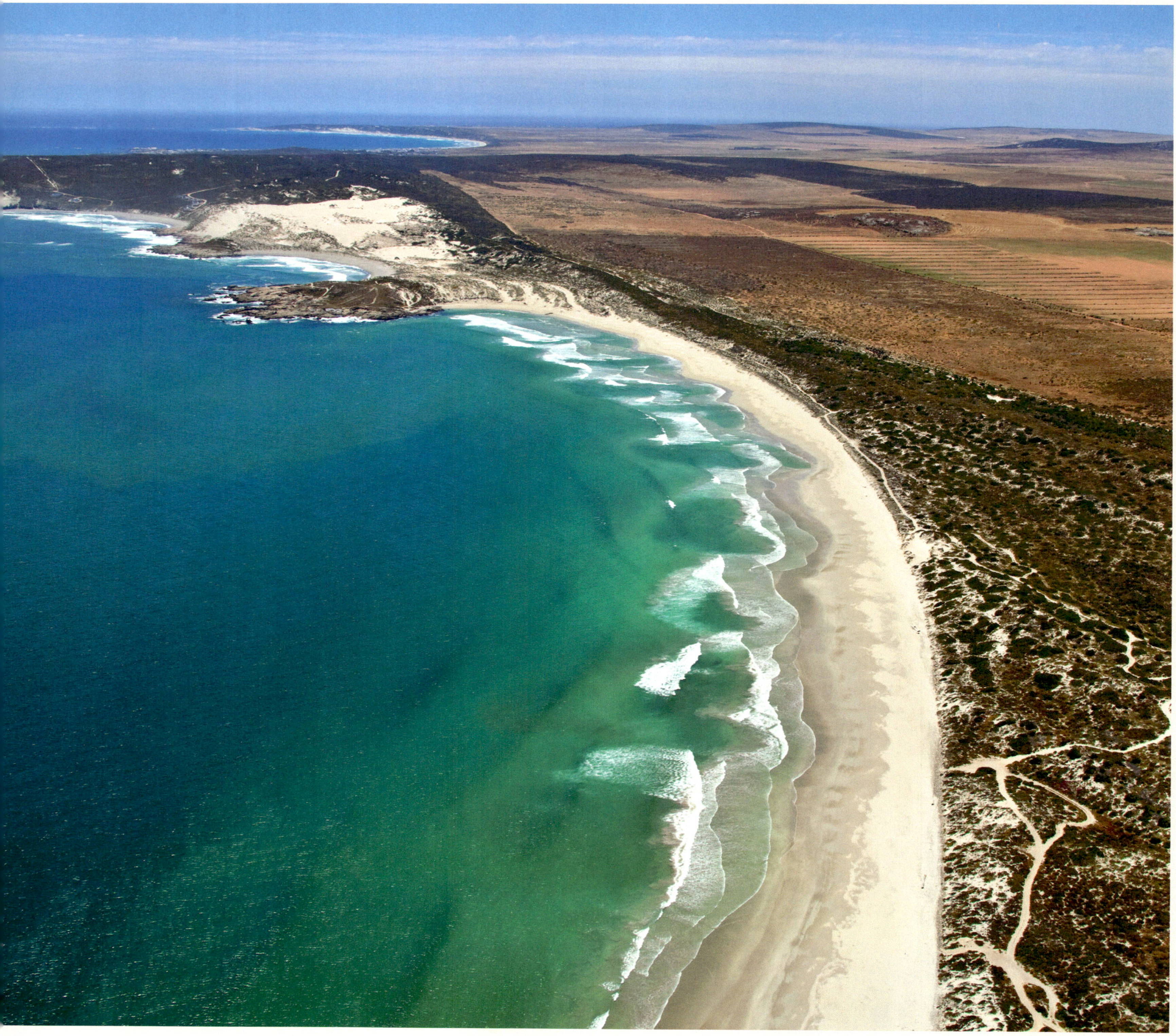

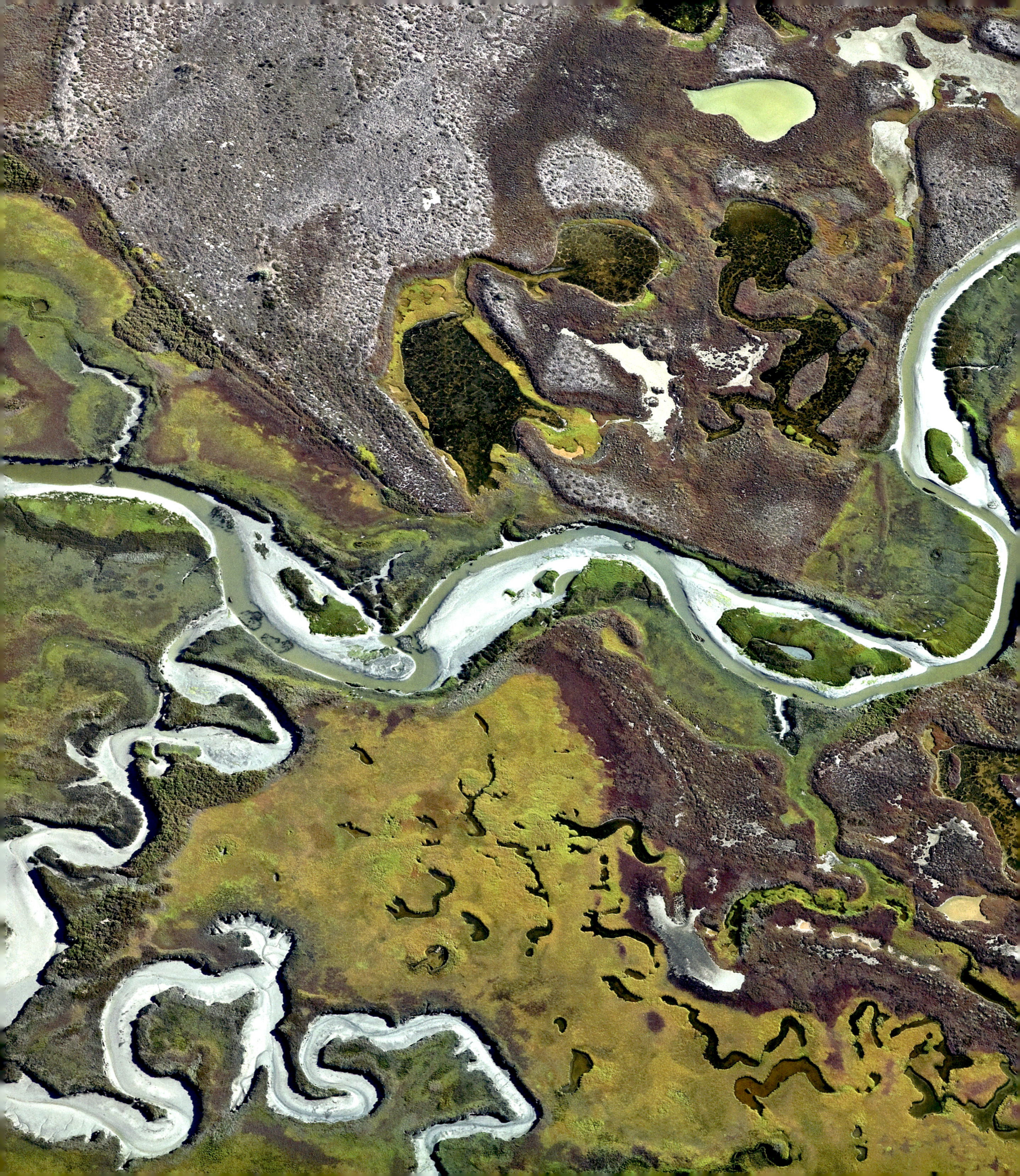

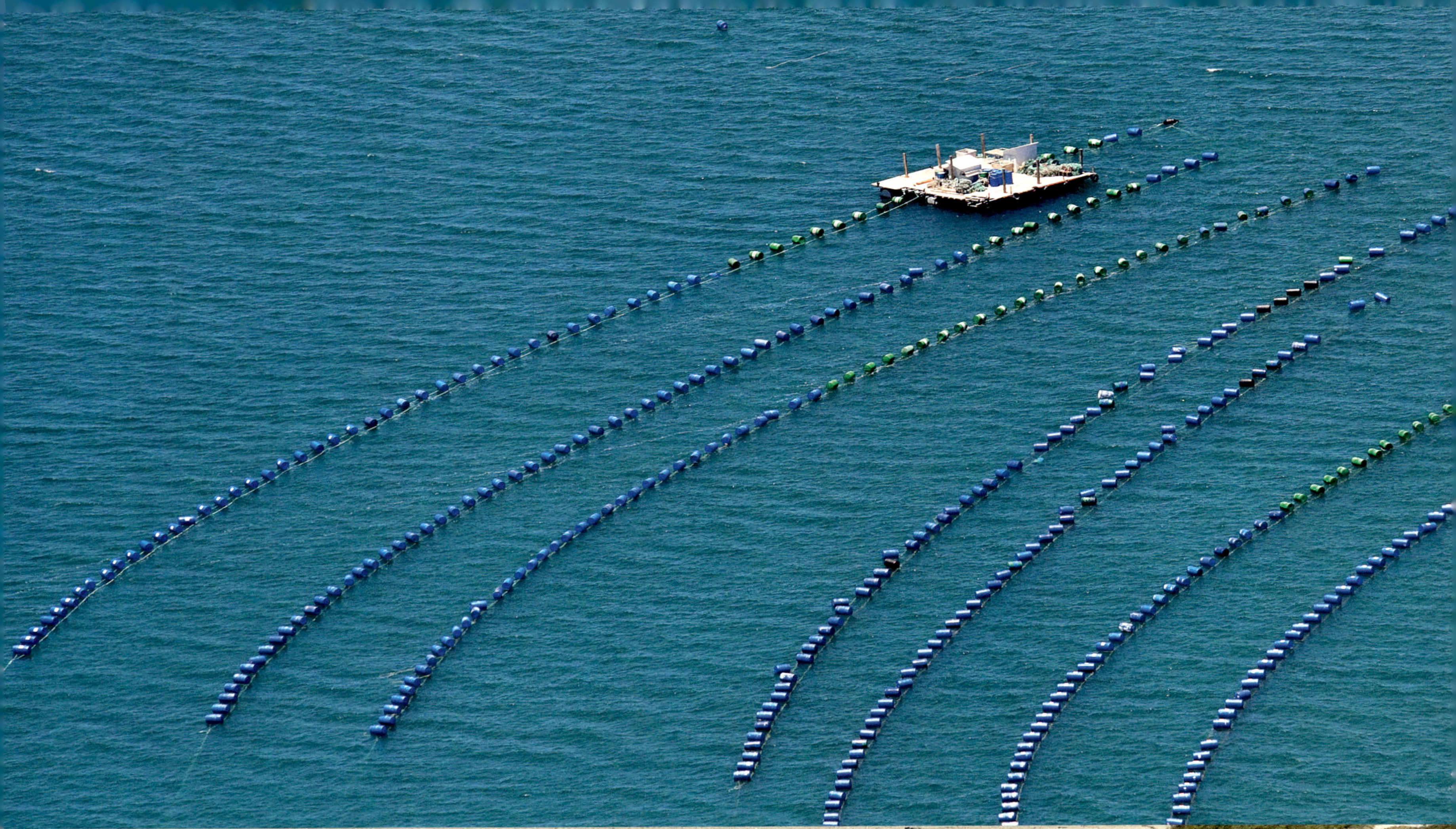

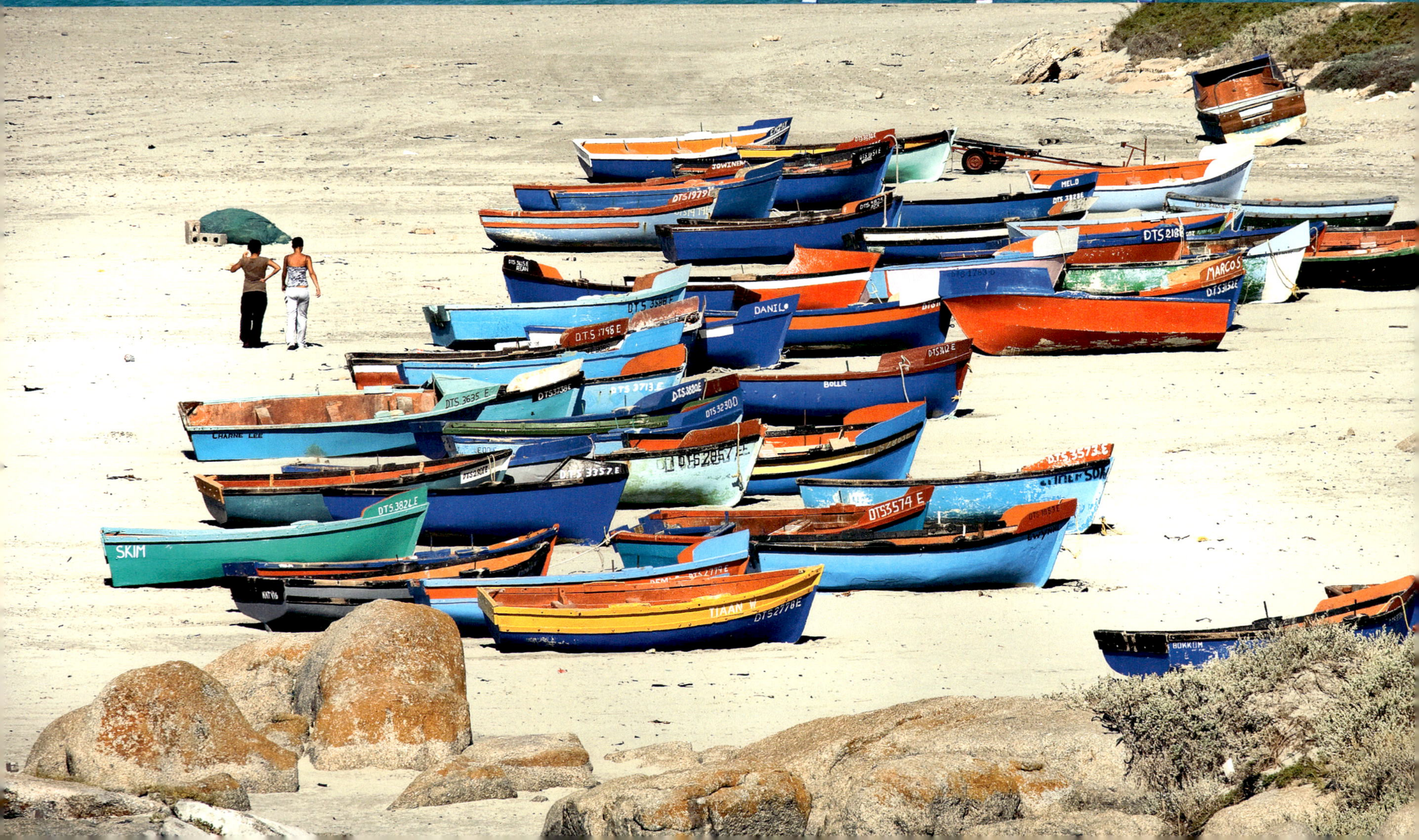
SKIM
MARCOS
DANILO

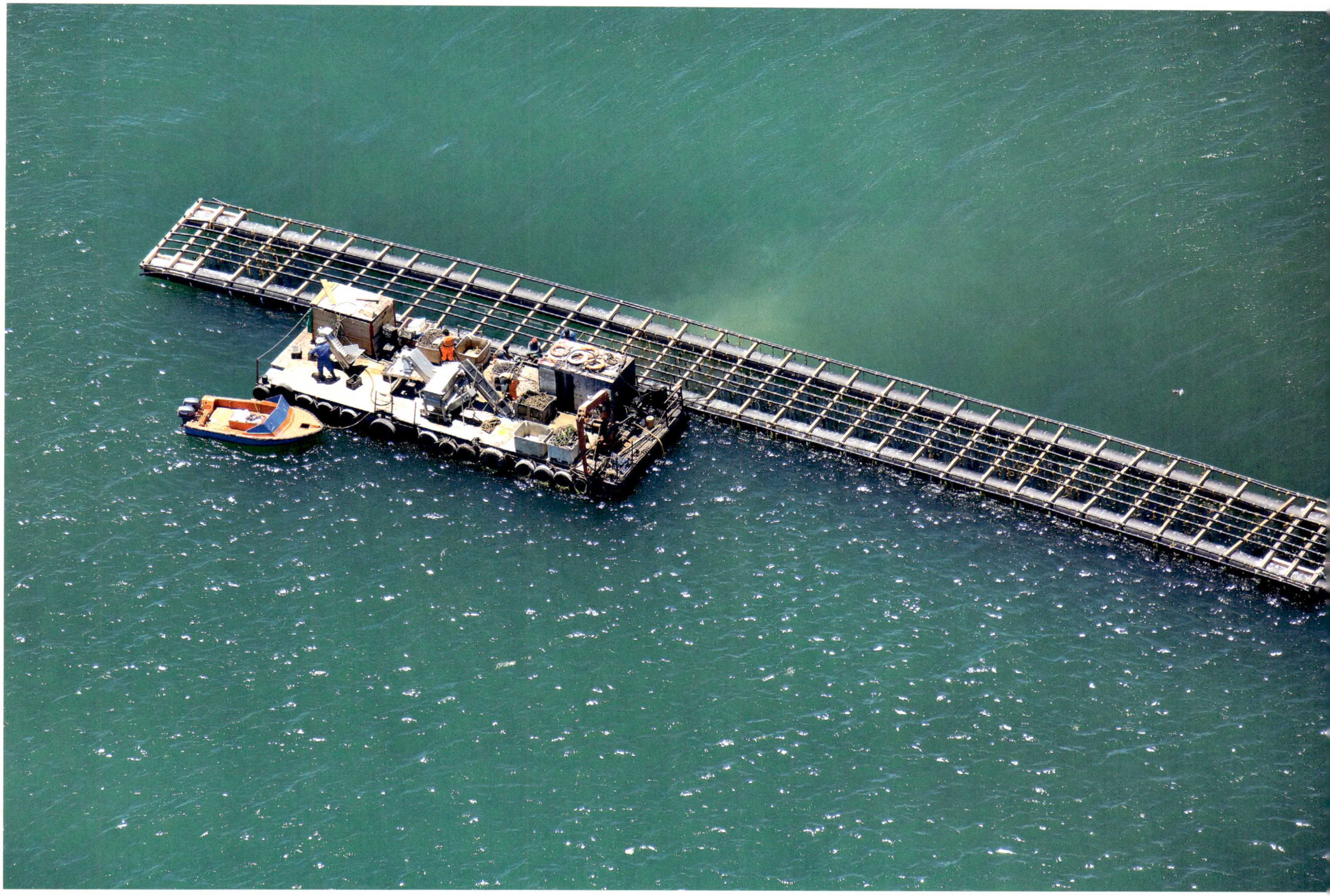

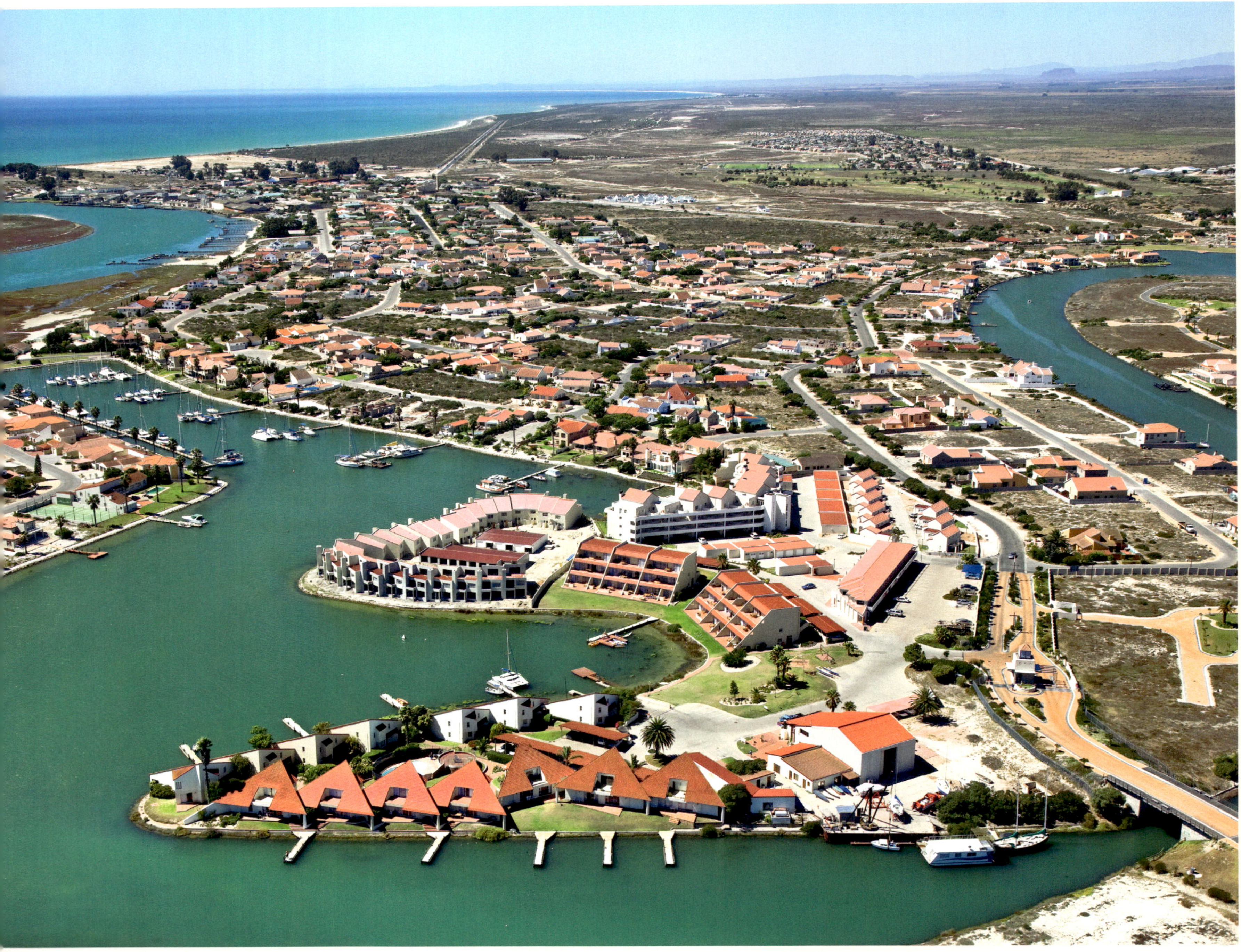

← Velddrif
↓ Cape St. Martin

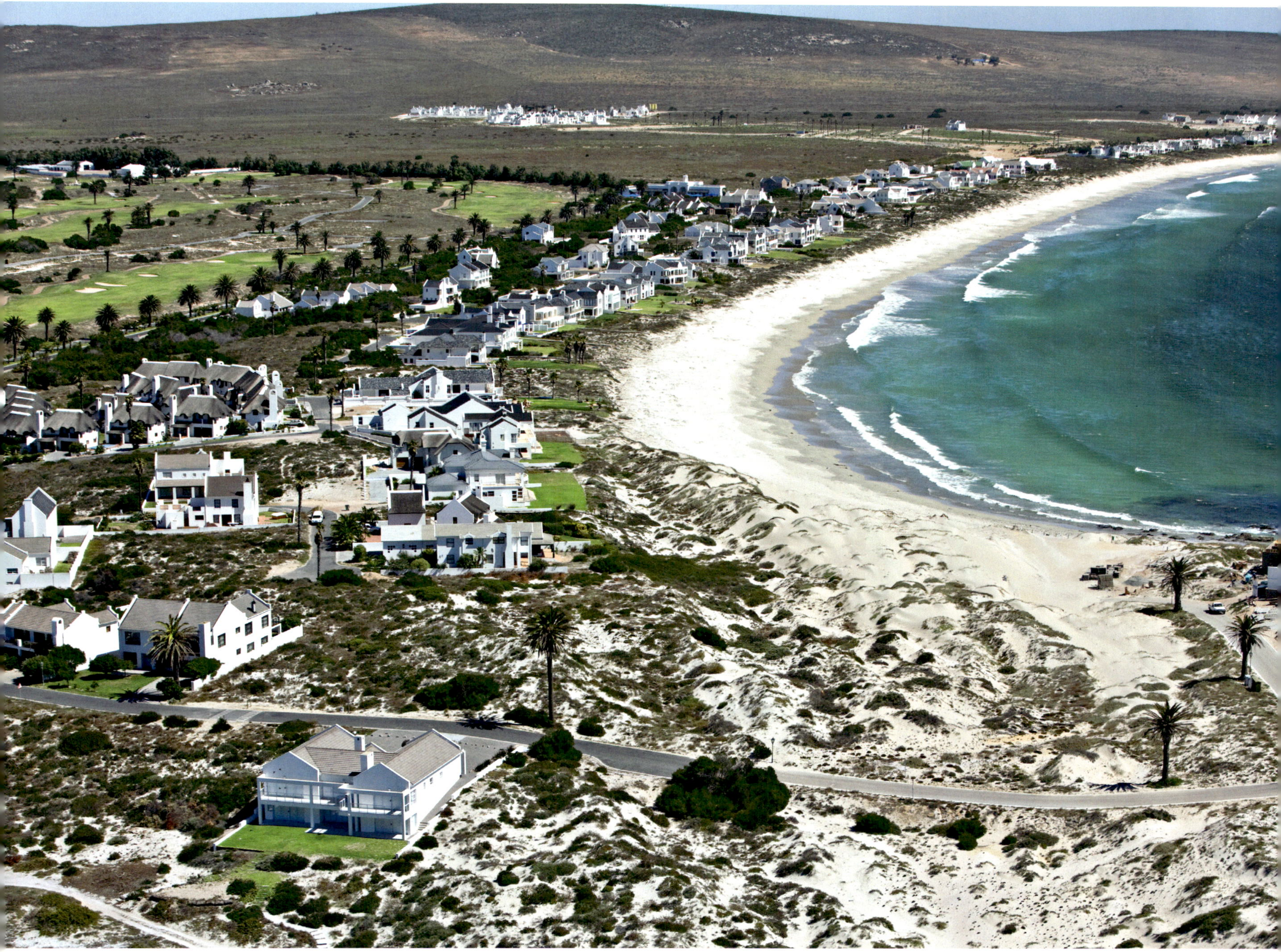

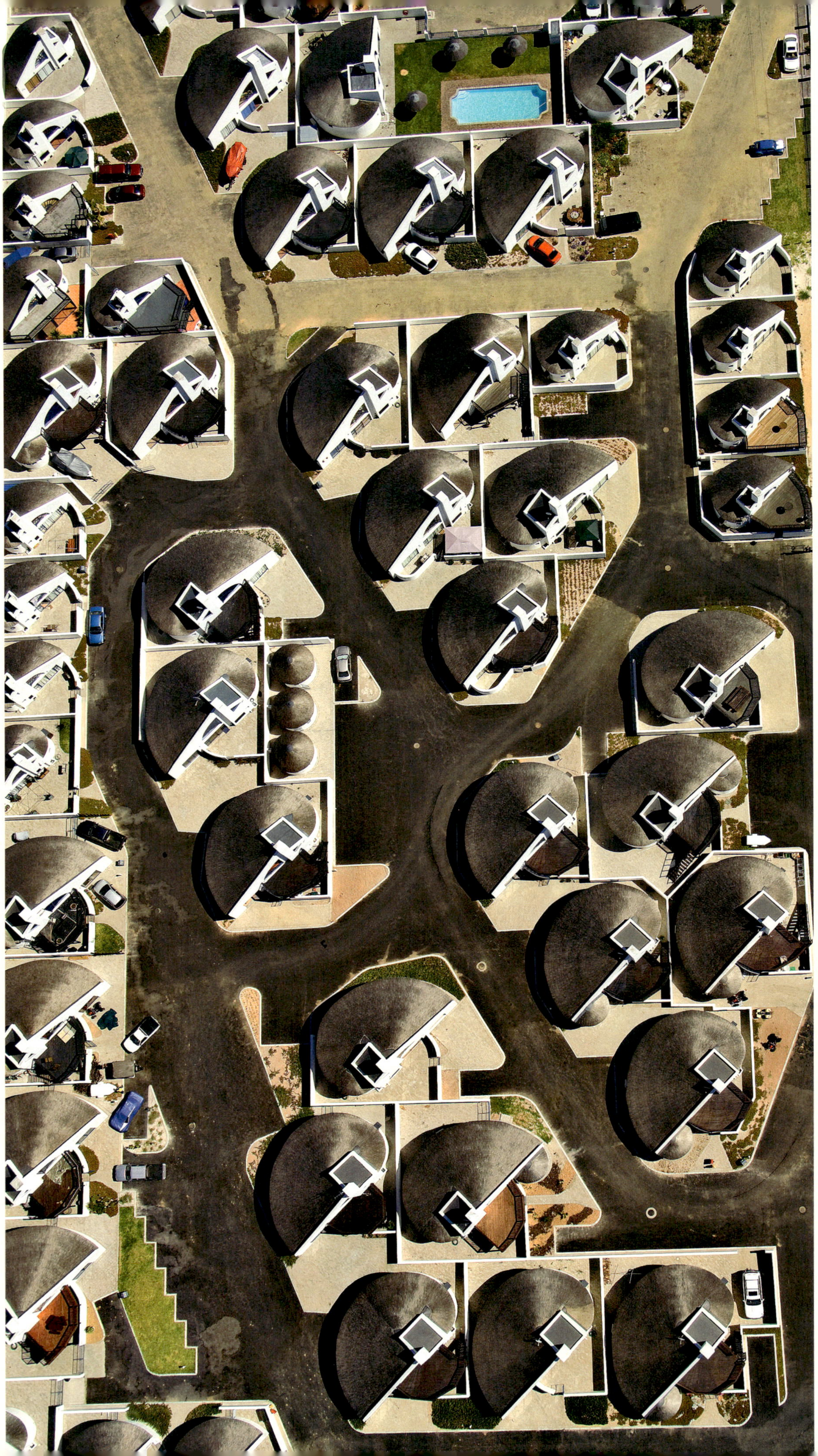

← Dwarskersbos
↓ Salt plant 'Sandveld'

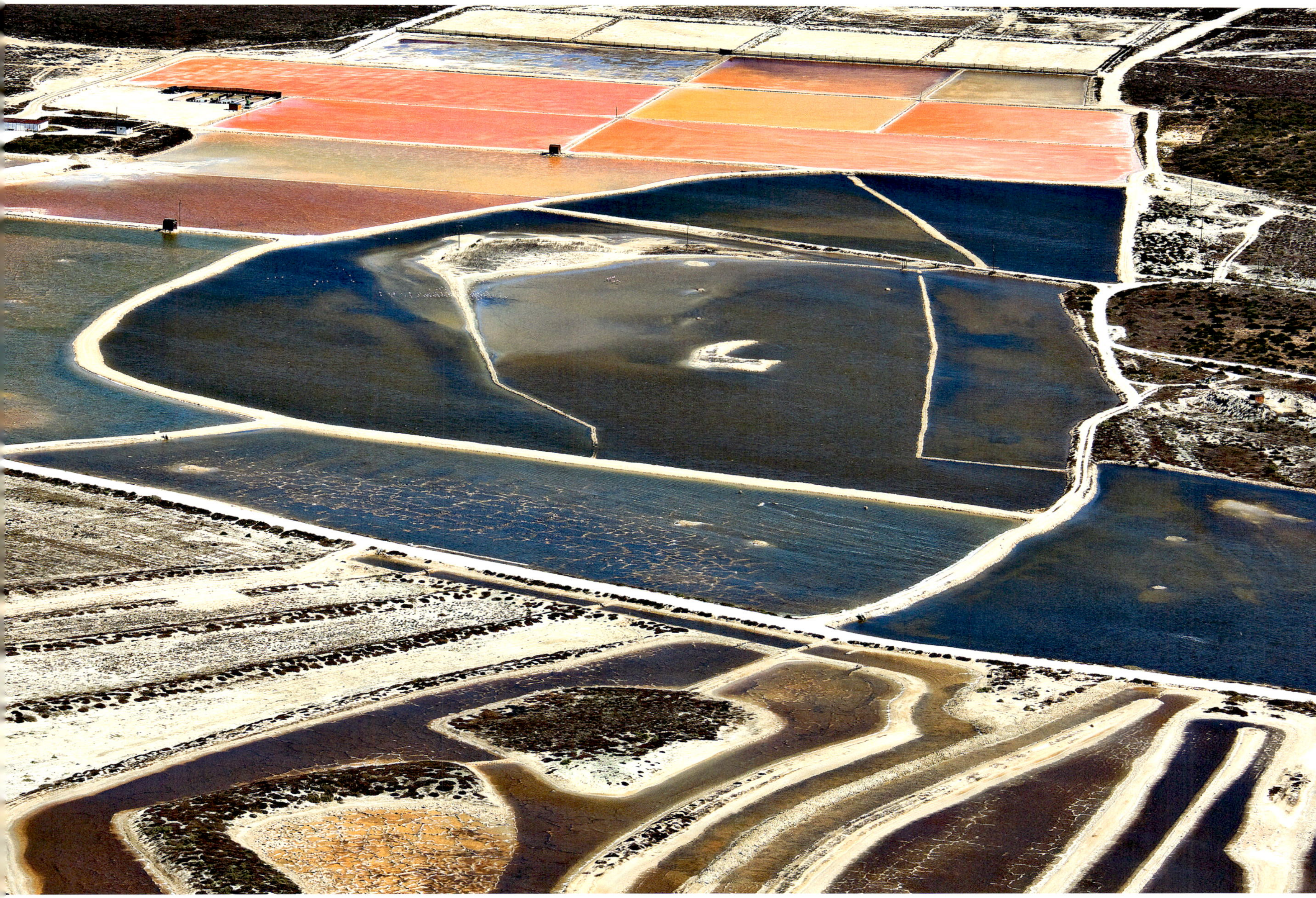

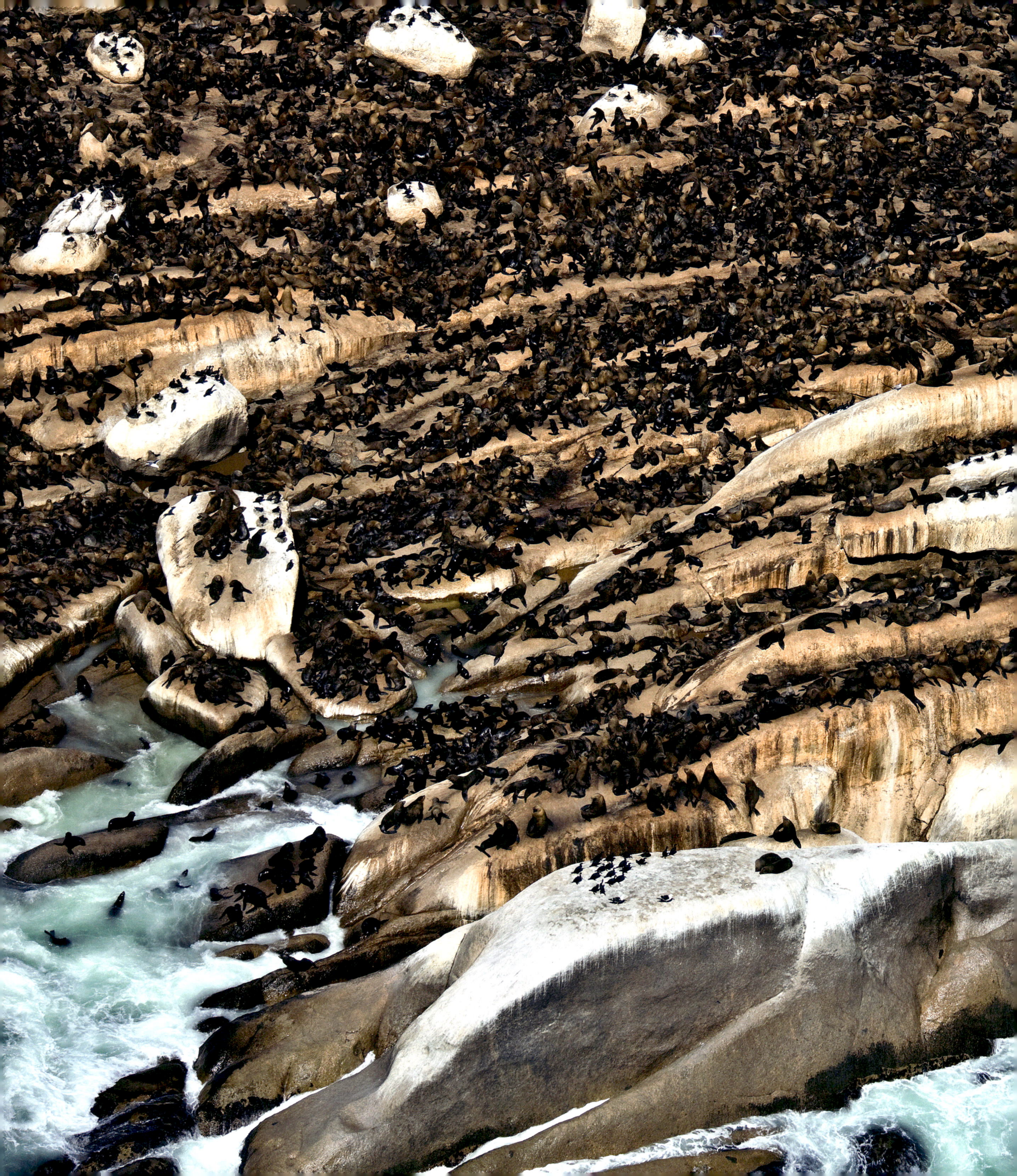

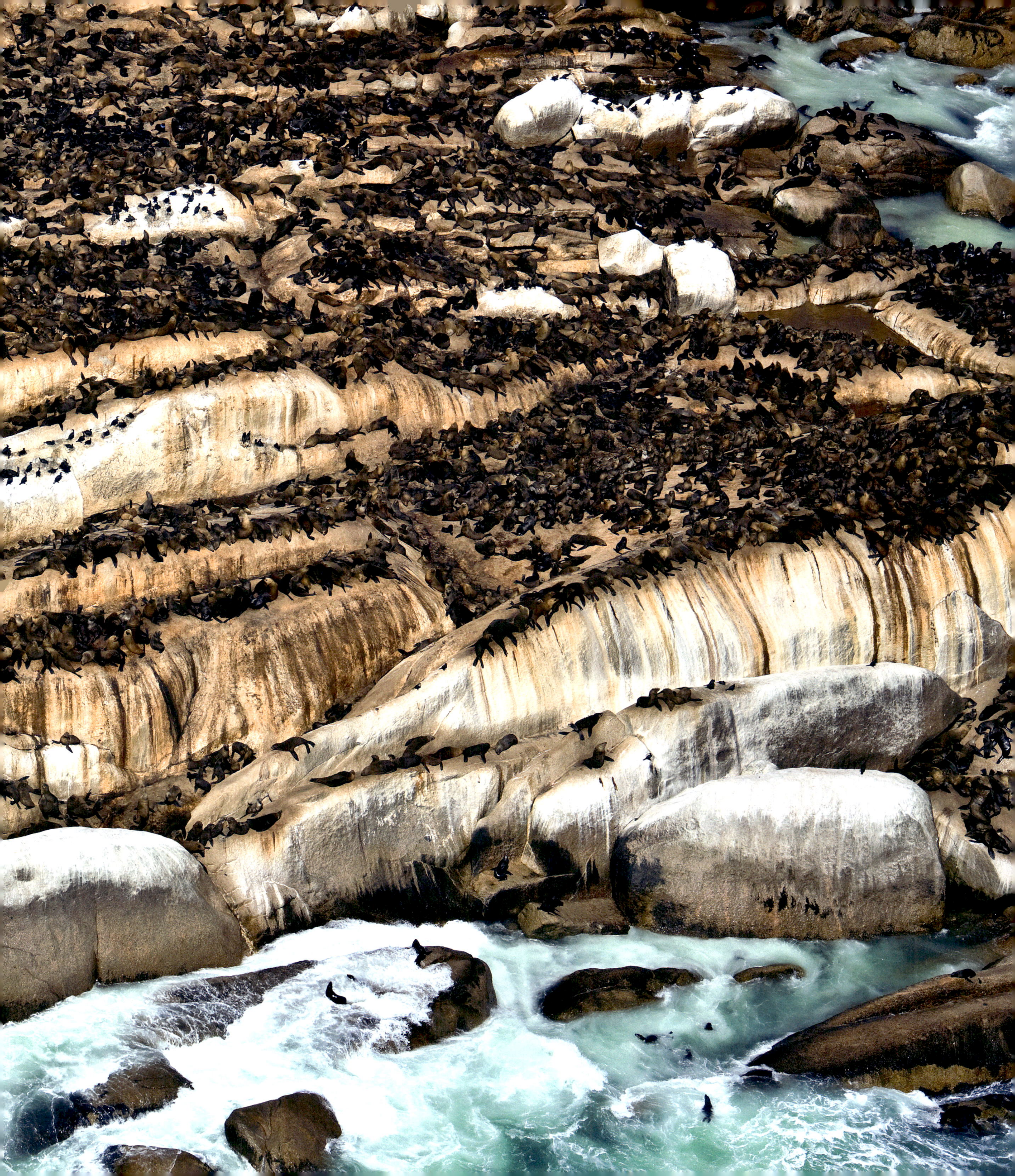

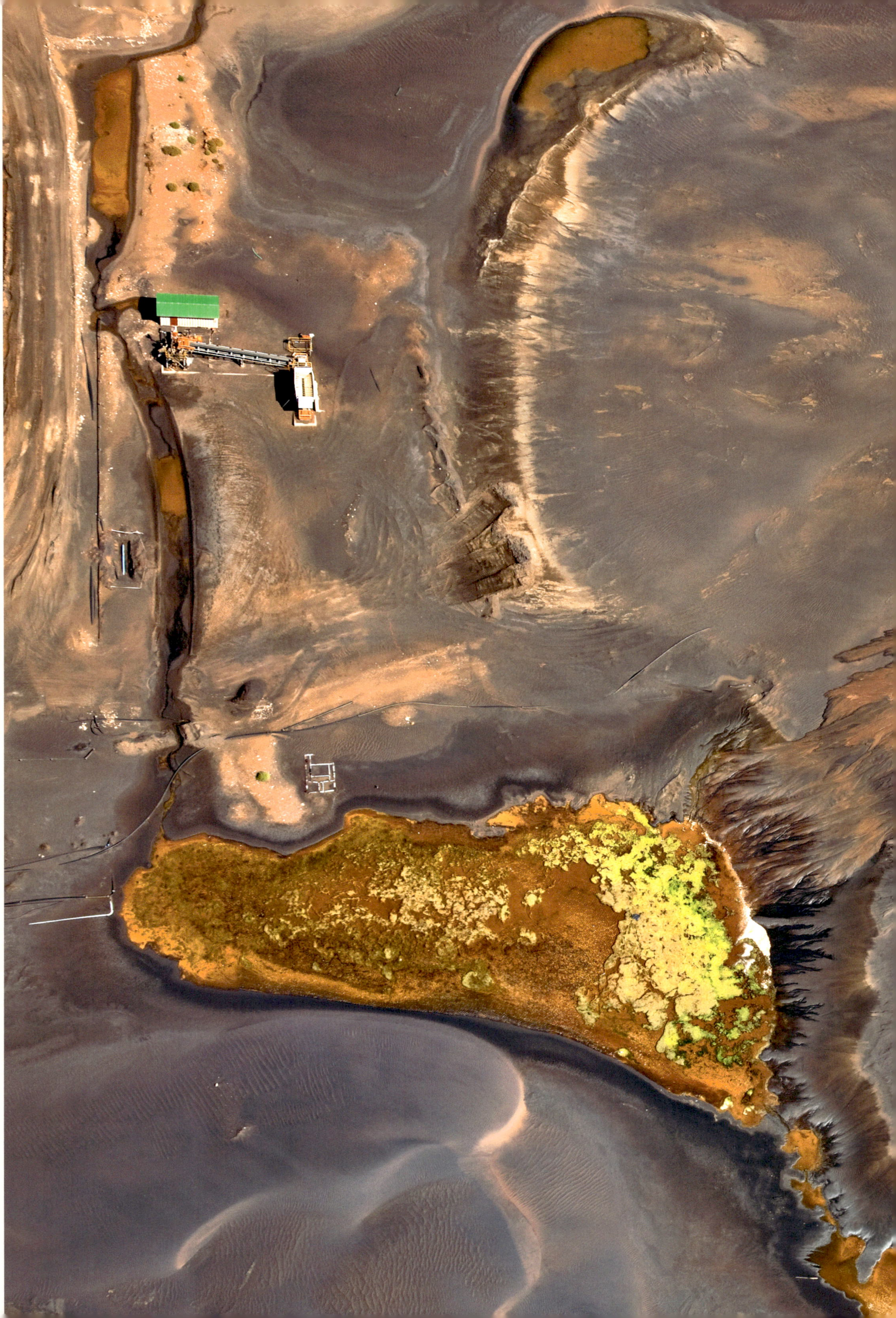

← Seal Island
→ Vanadium mine

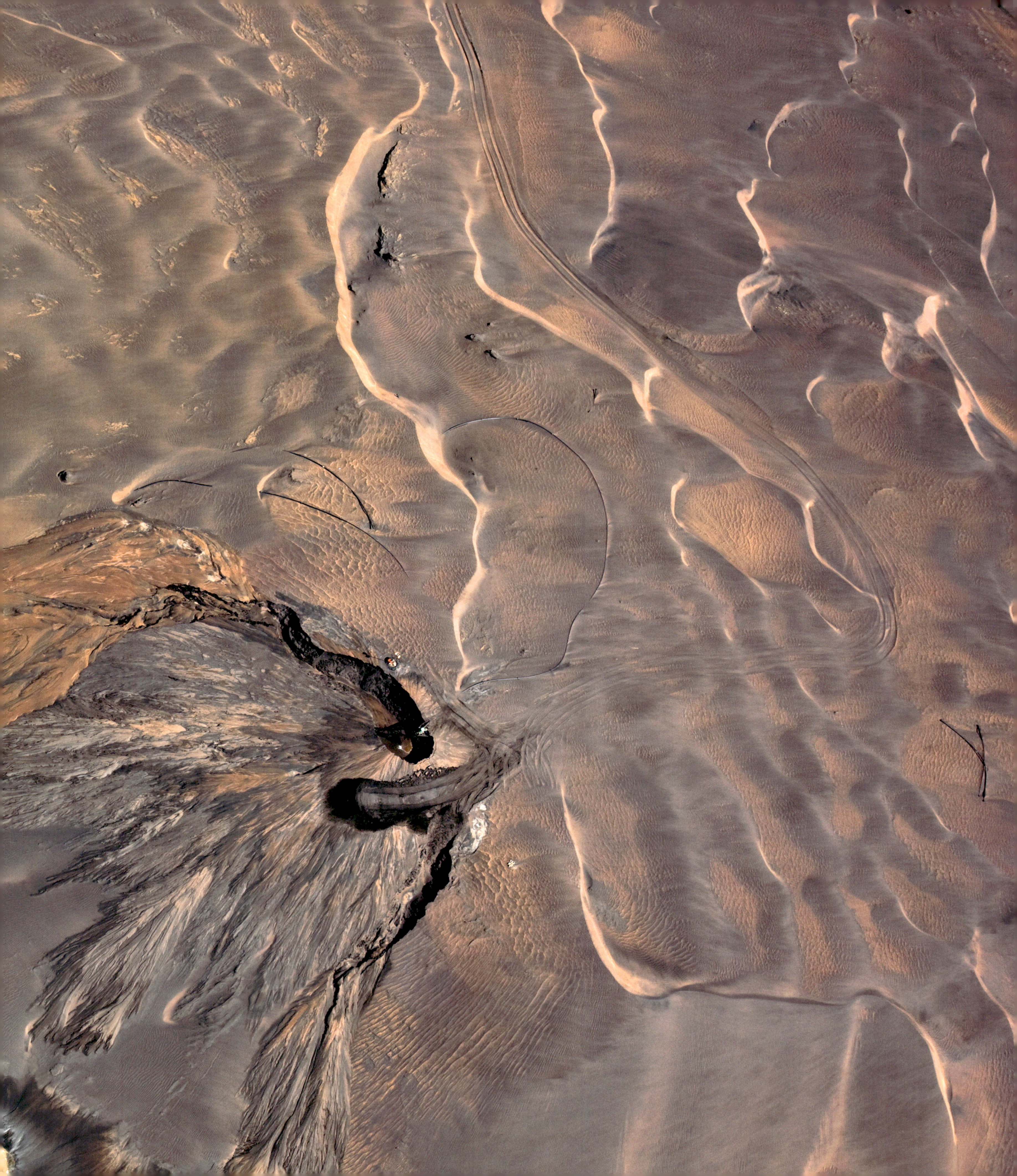

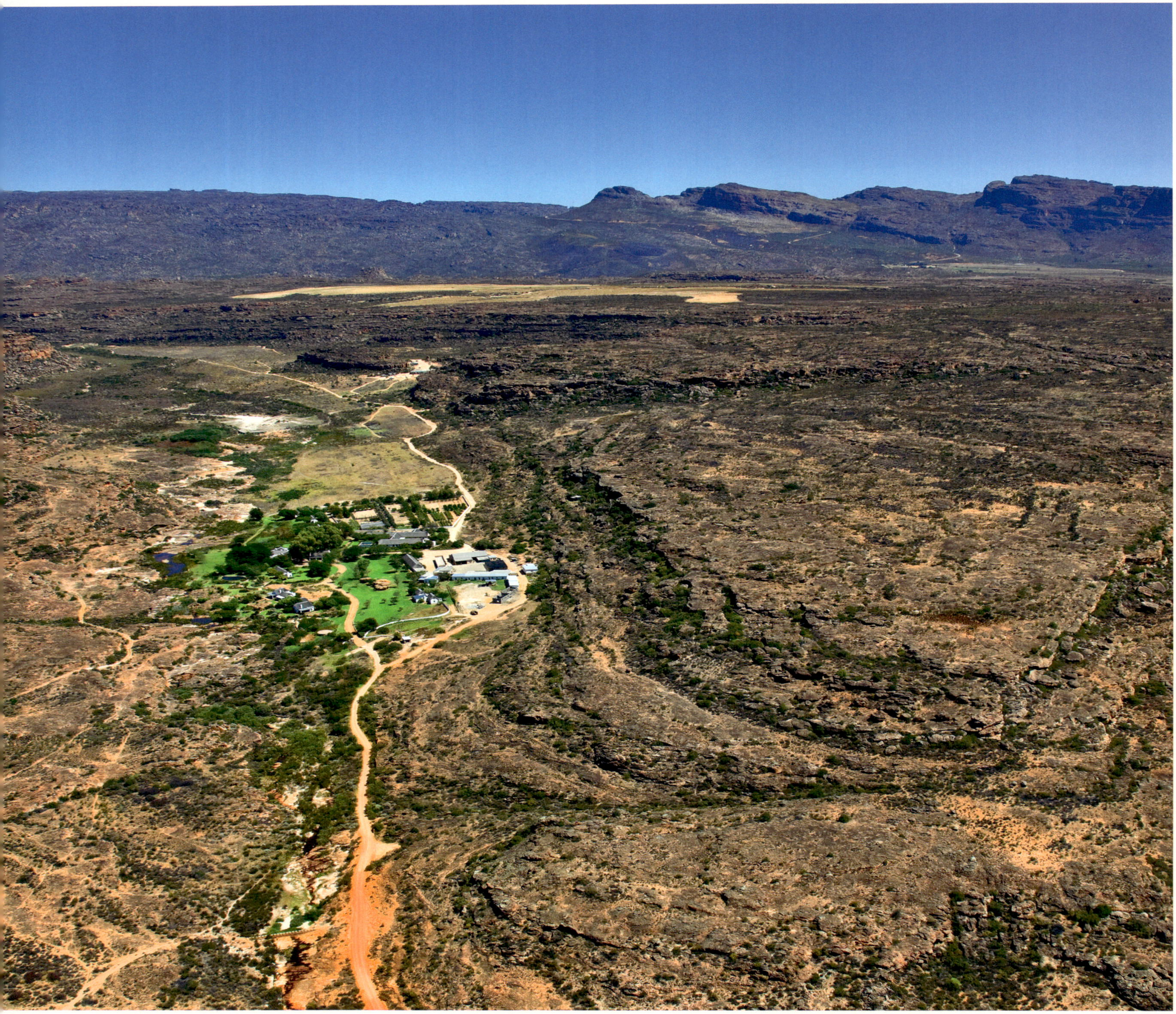

↑ Farm near the Cederberg Mountains
→ Clanwilliam Dam

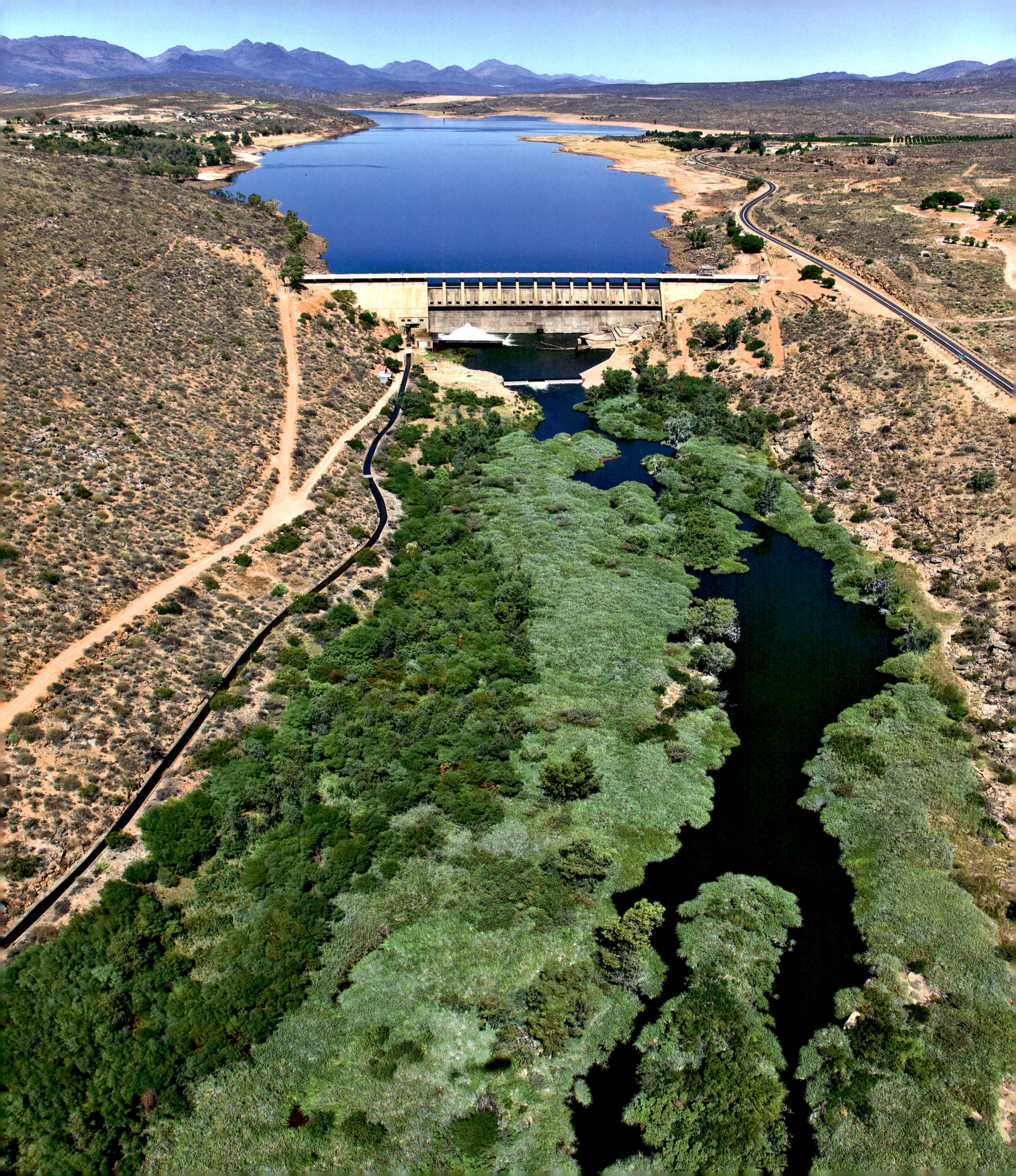

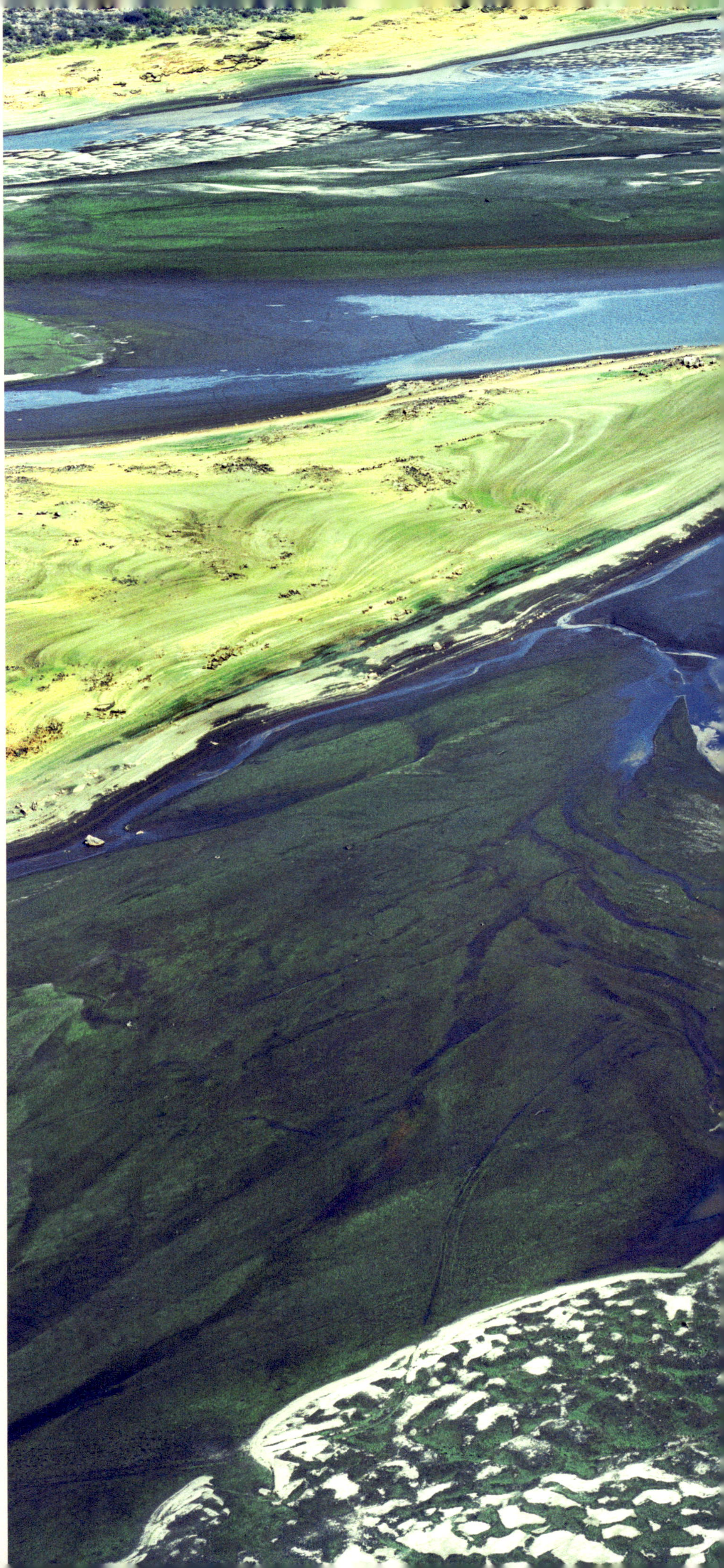

→ Elephants River, near Citrusdal

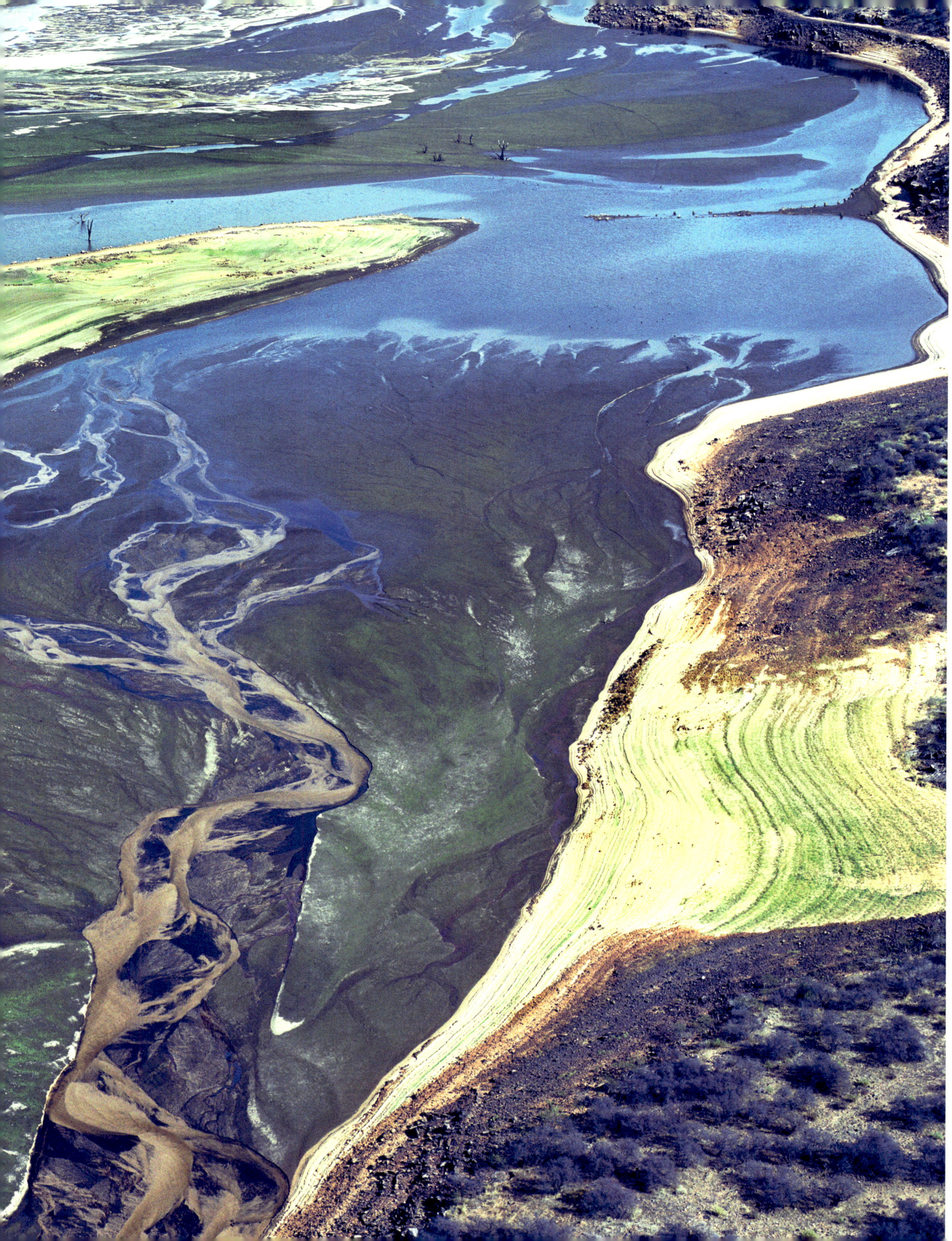

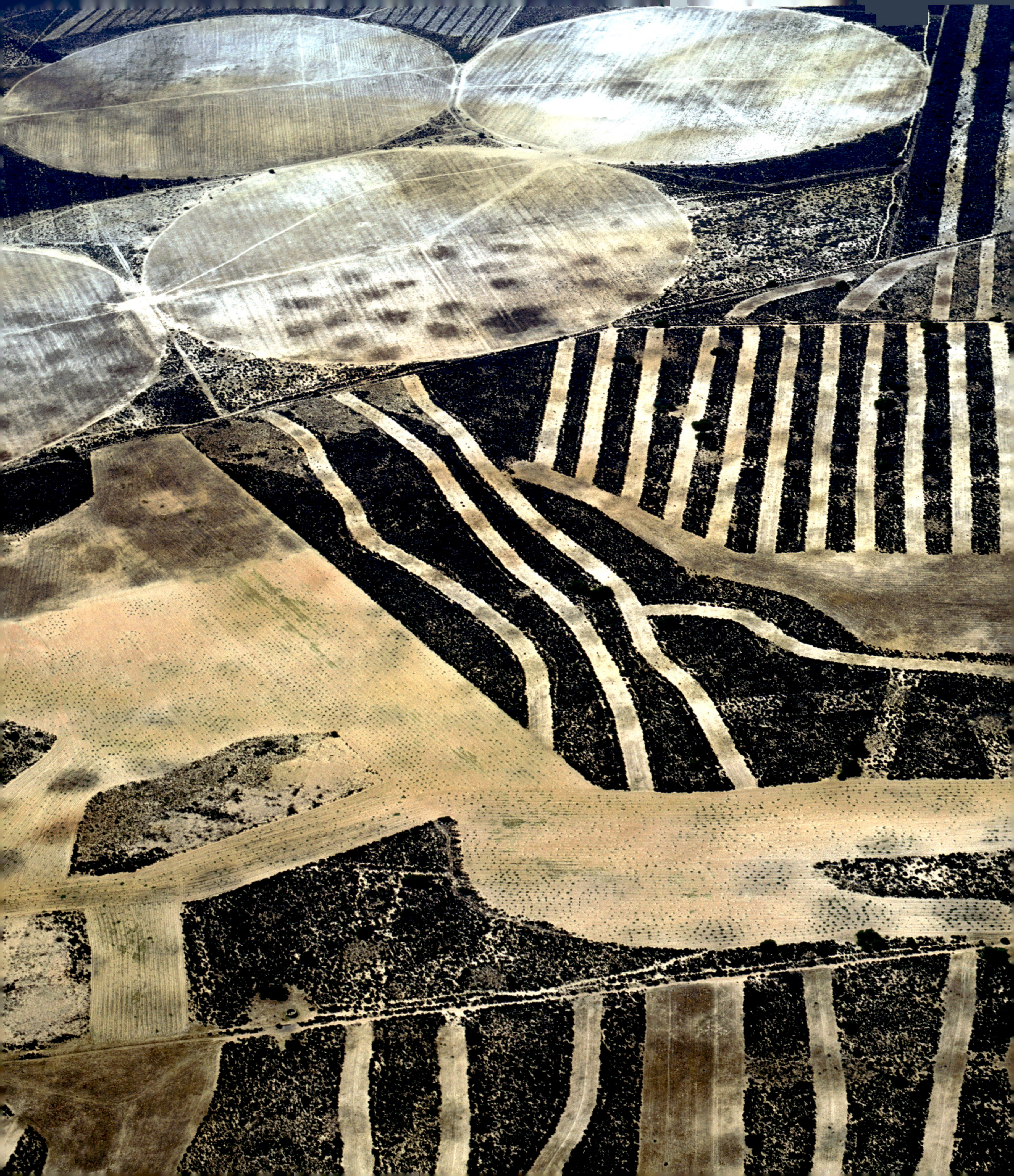

← Potato fields near Piketberg
↓ Salt plant behind Great Berg River
→ Agricultural area, Worcester

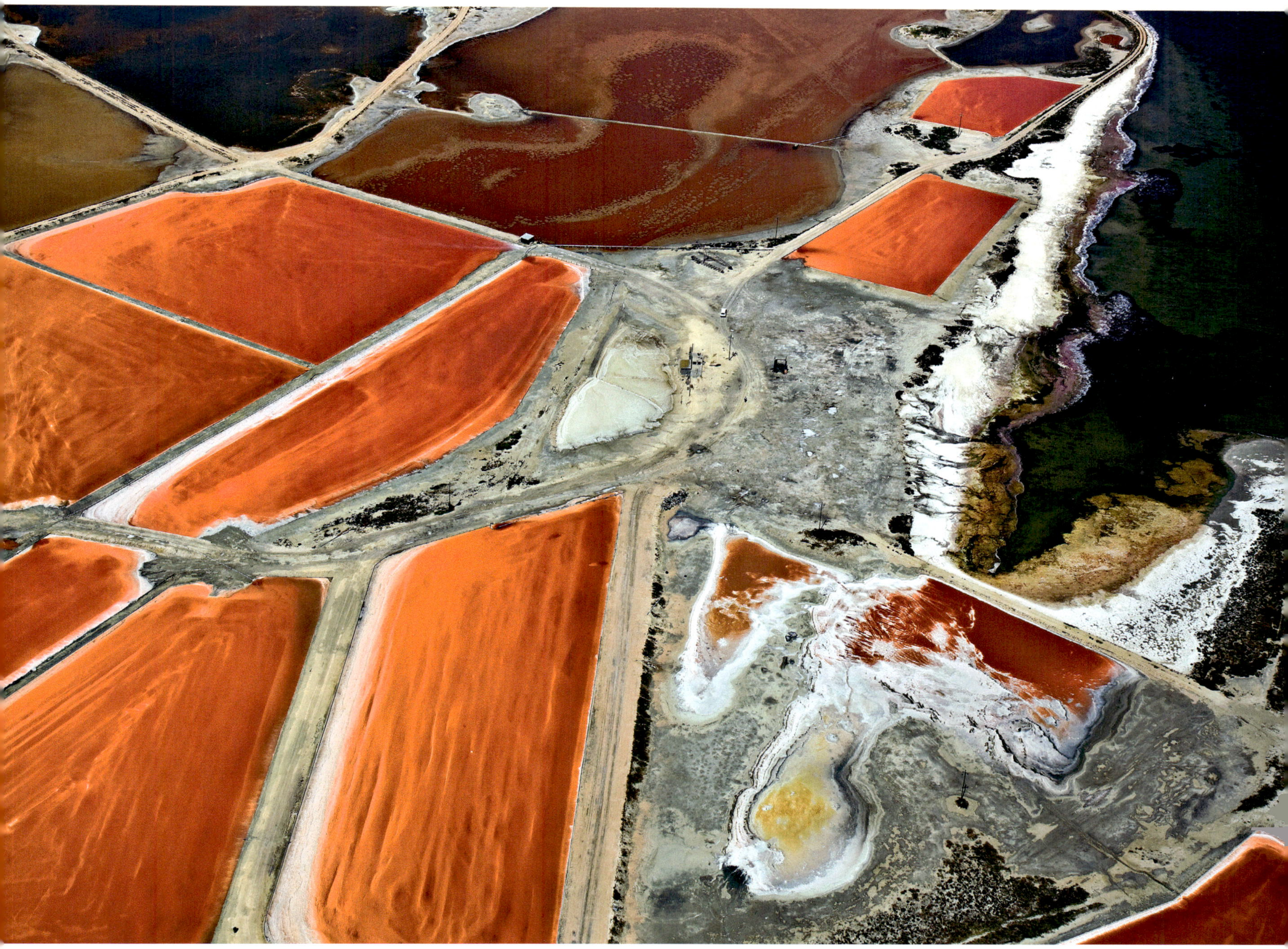

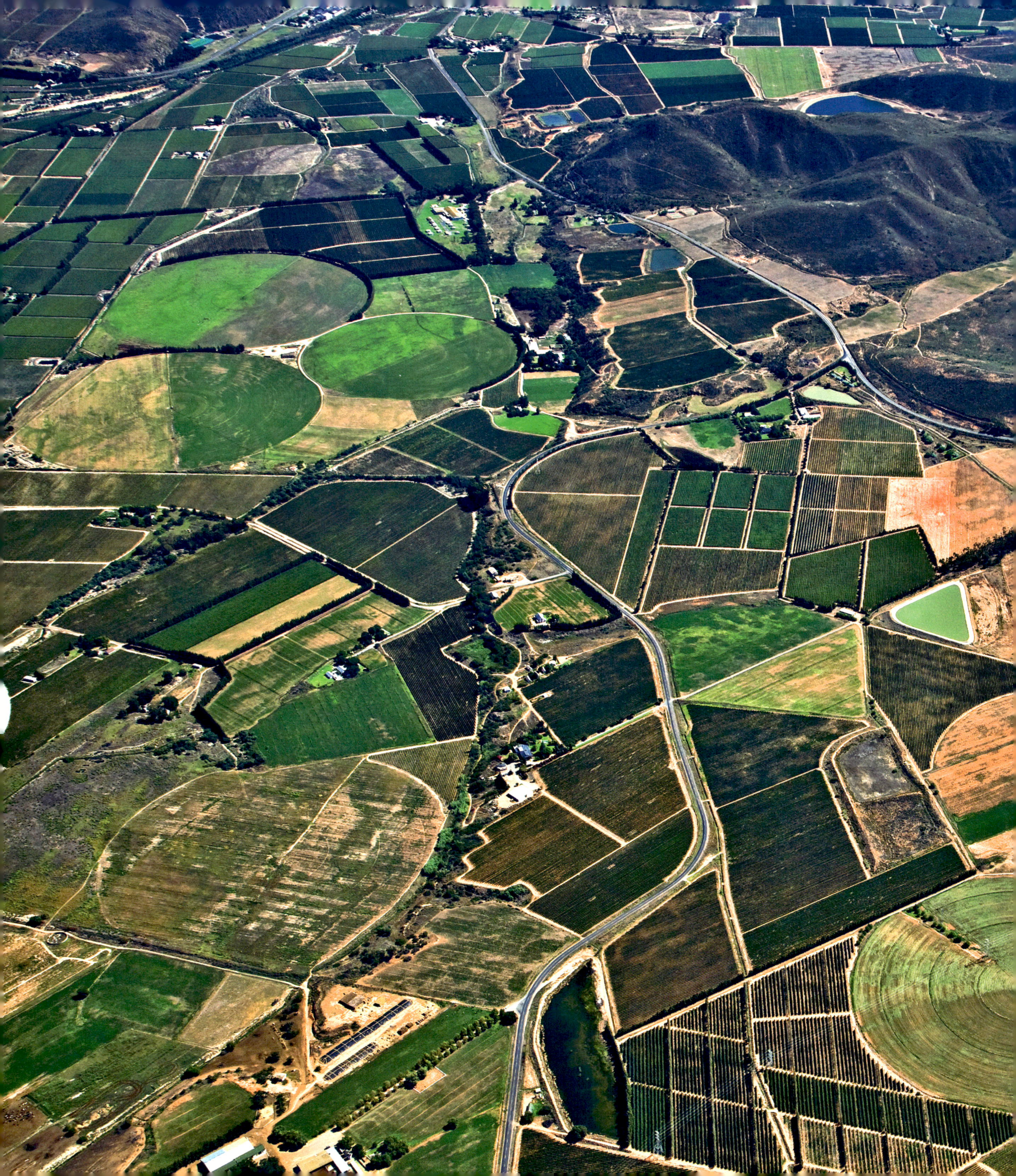

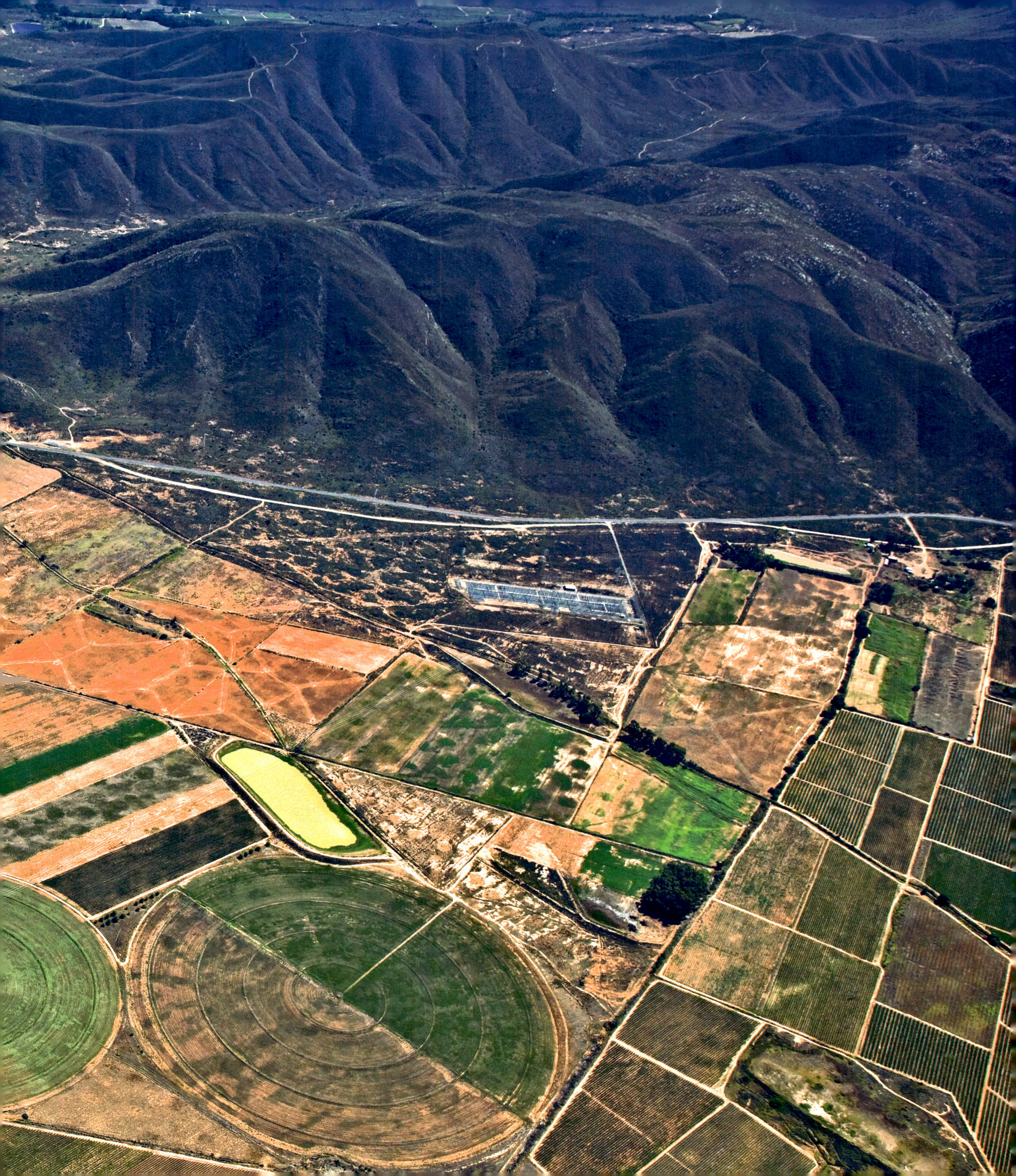

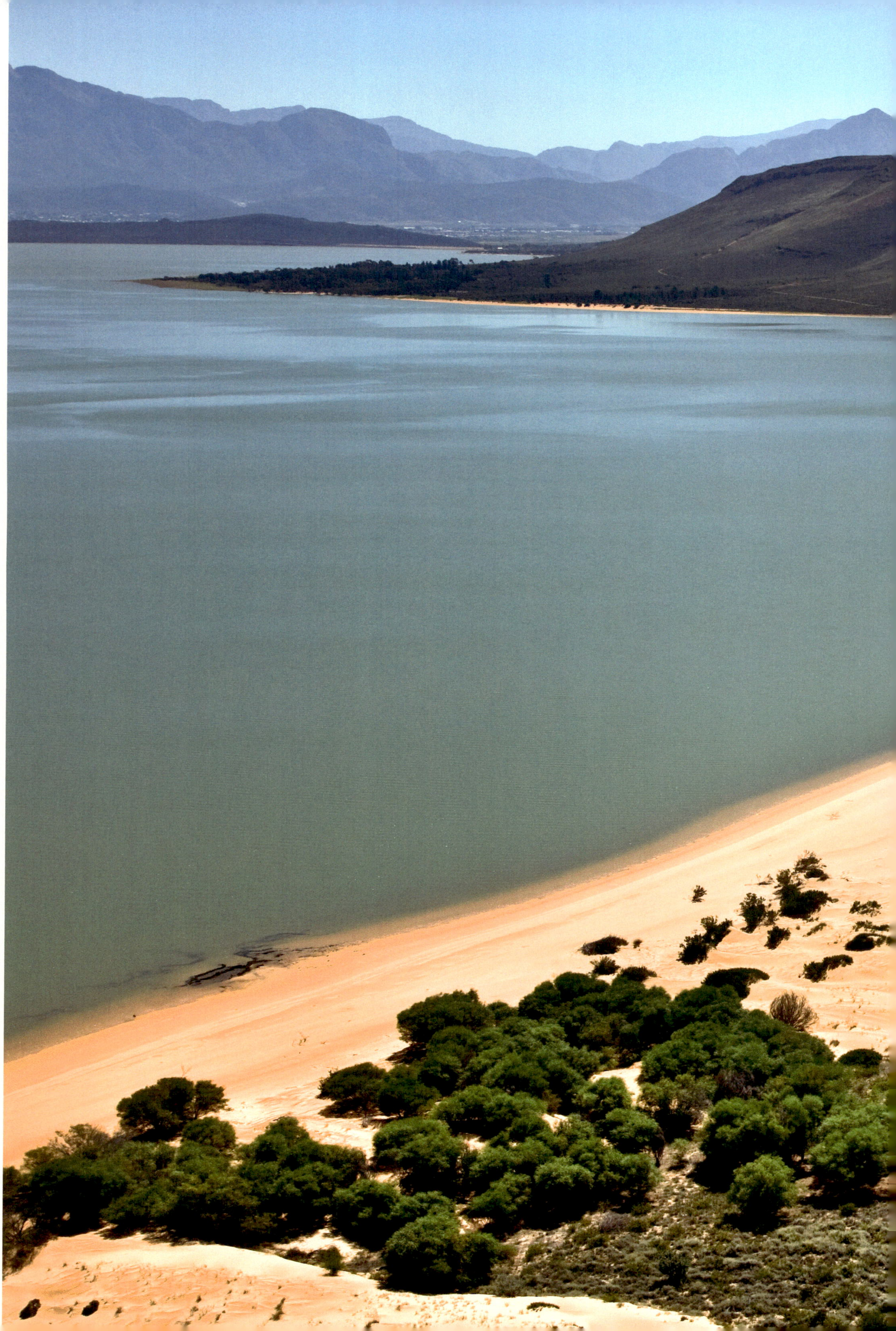

→ Brandvlei Dam,
south of Worcester

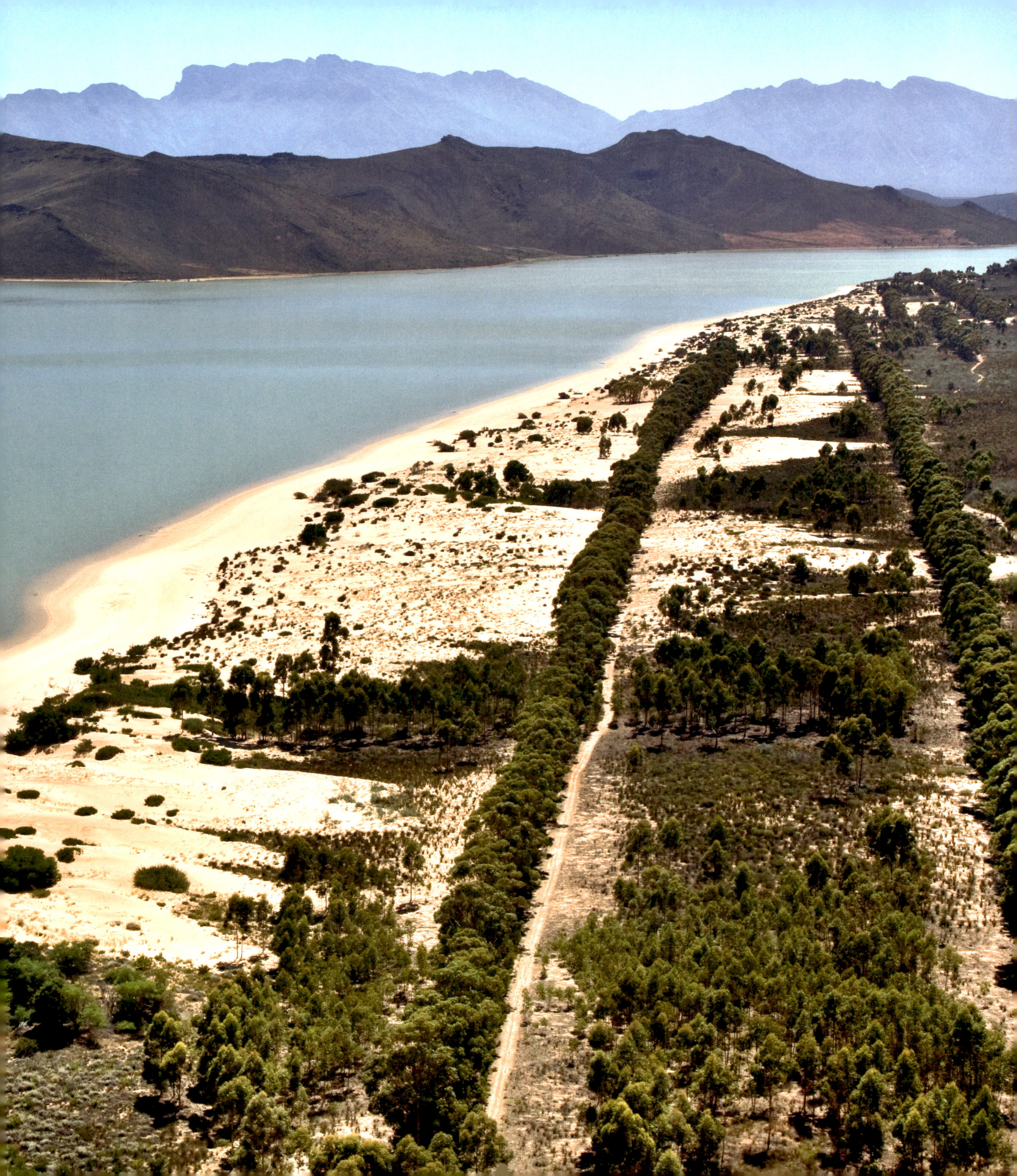

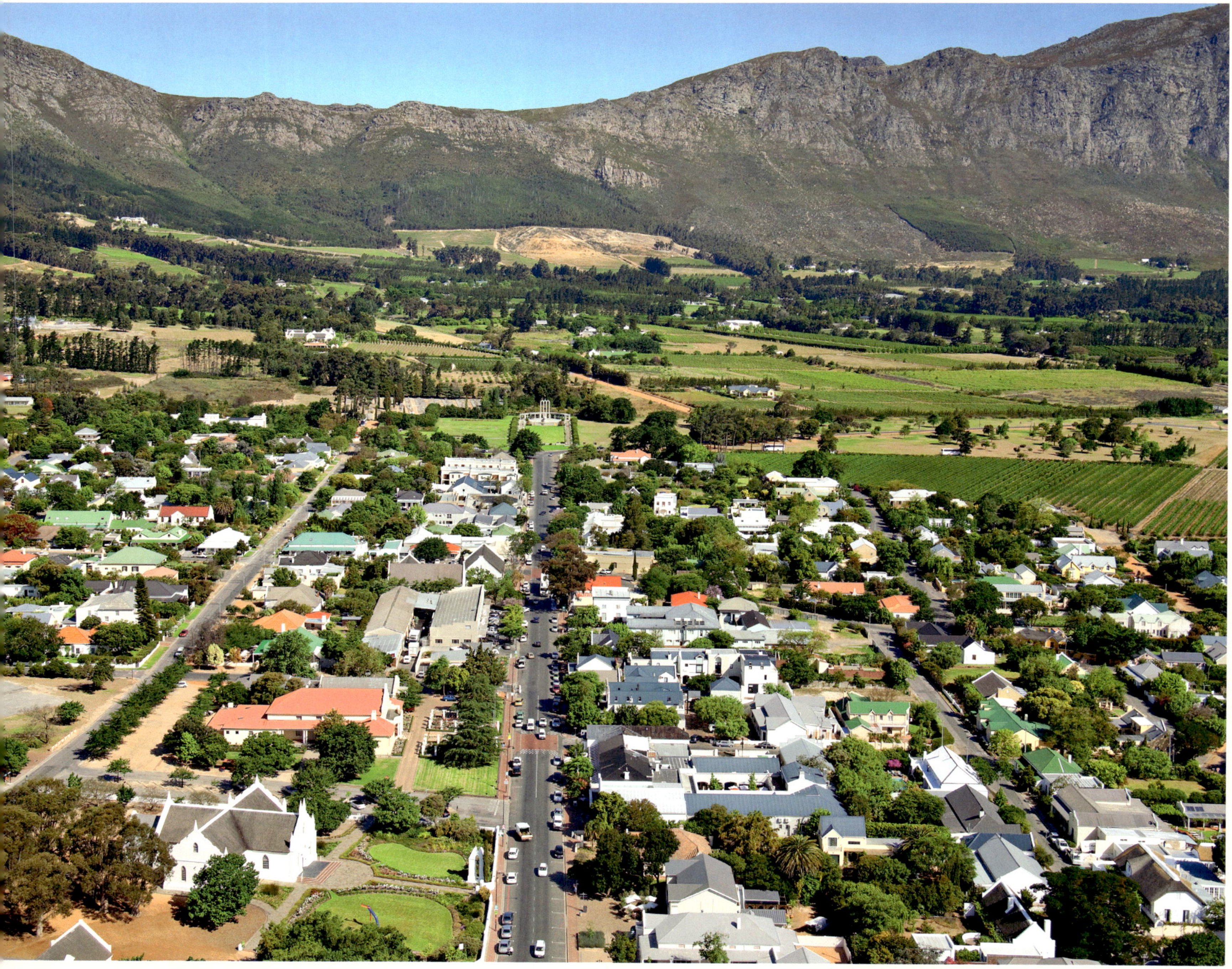

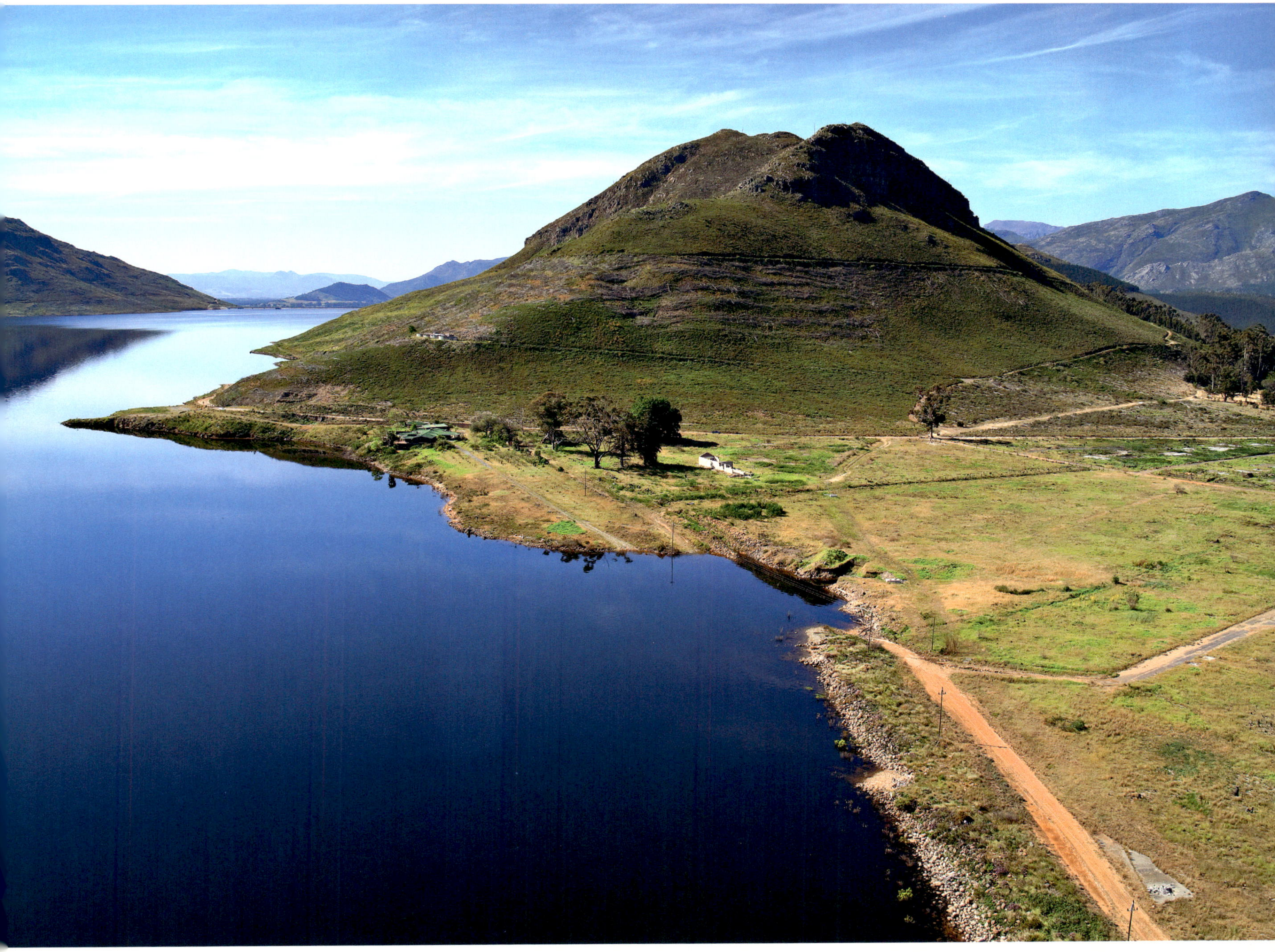

↓ Tokara Wine Estate, Helshoogte, Stellenbosch
→ Somerset West

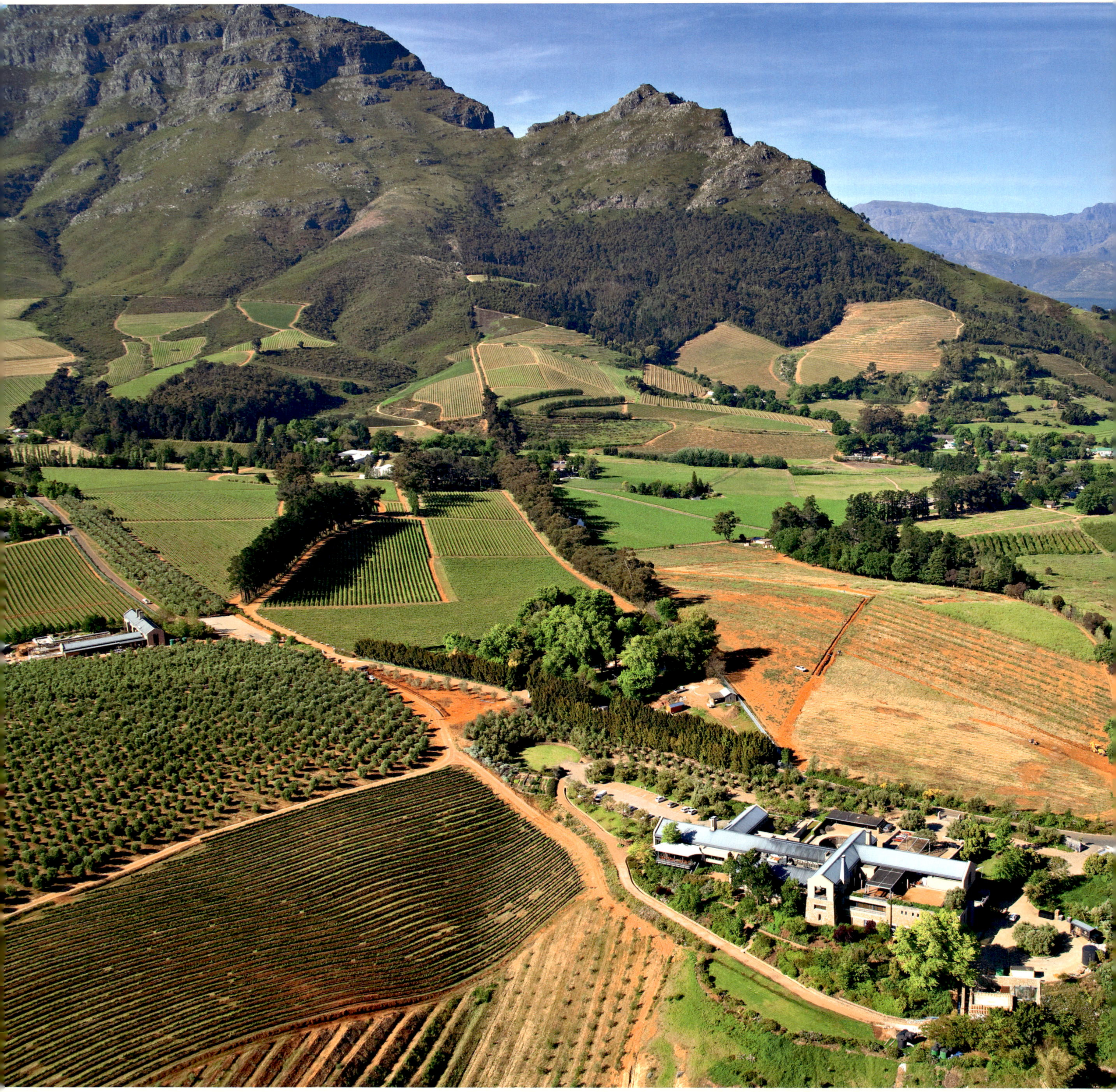

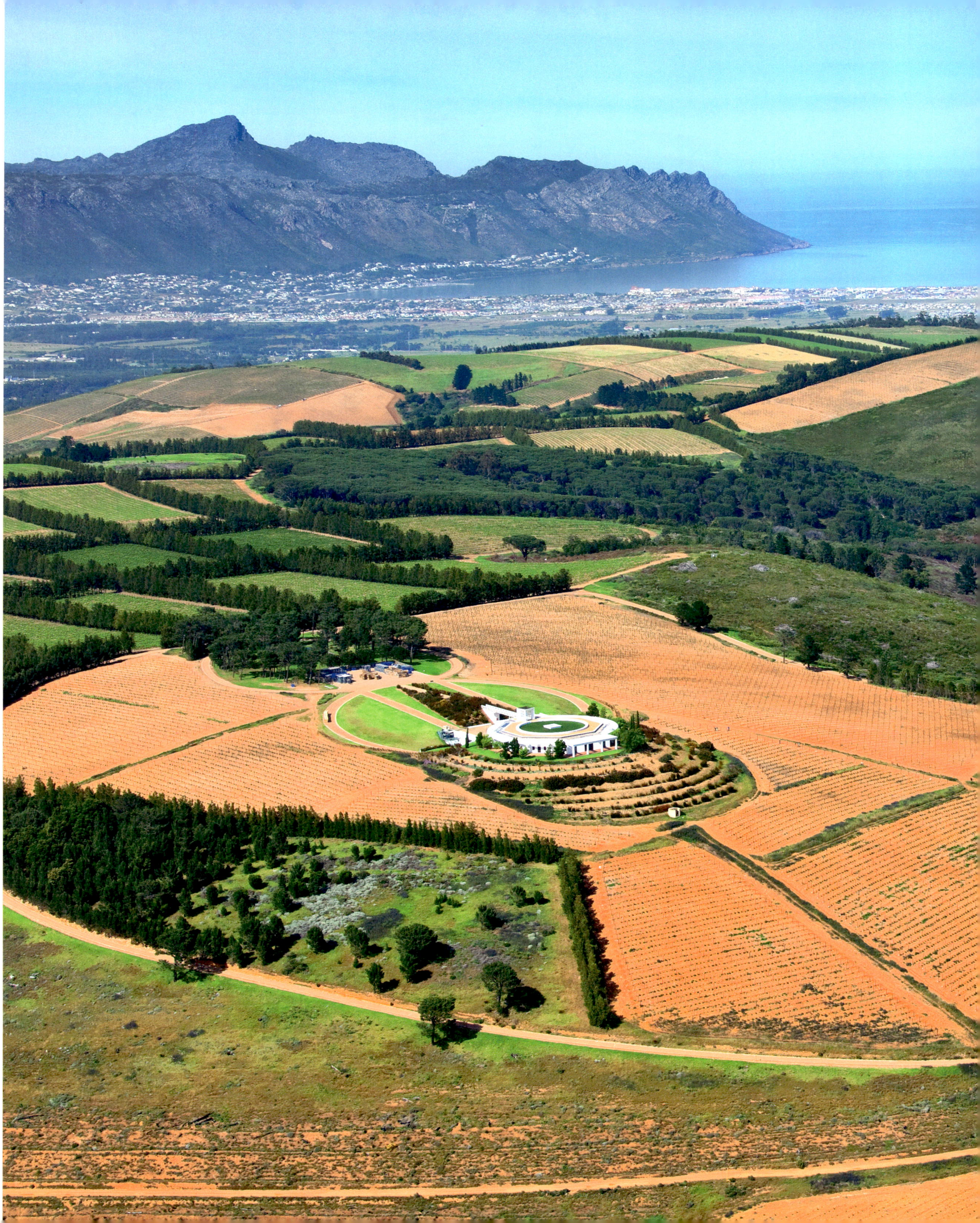

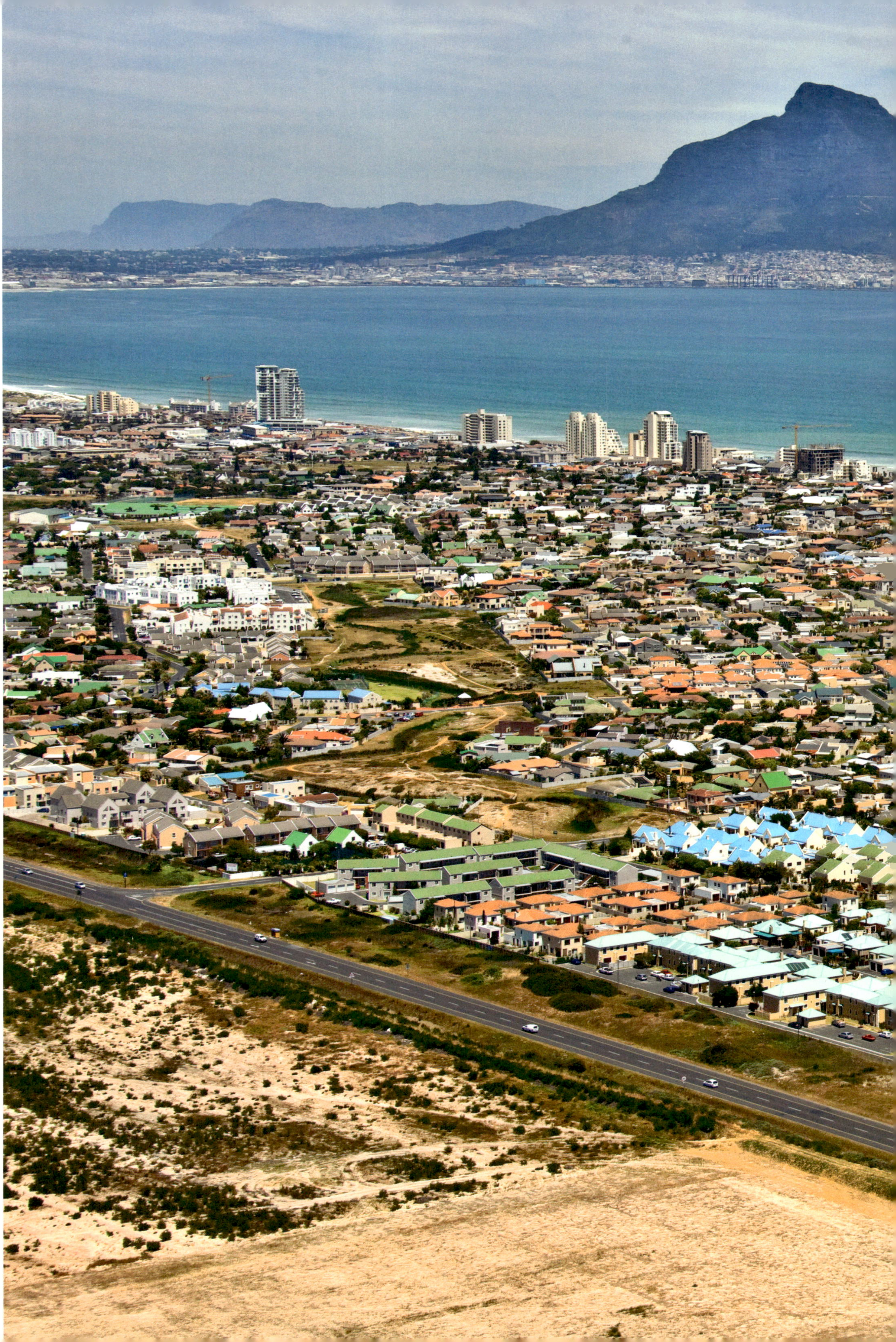

→ Bloubergstrand

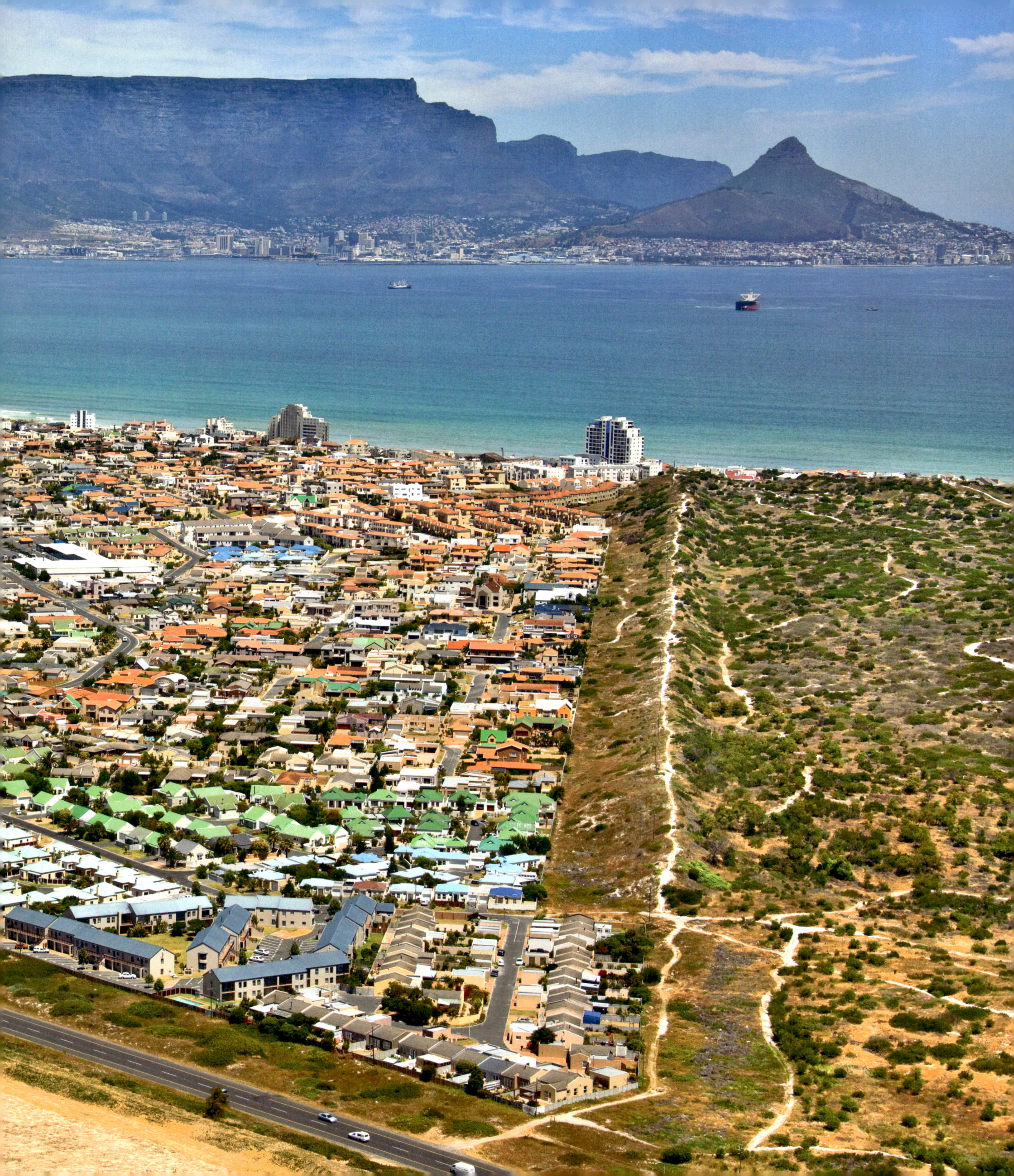

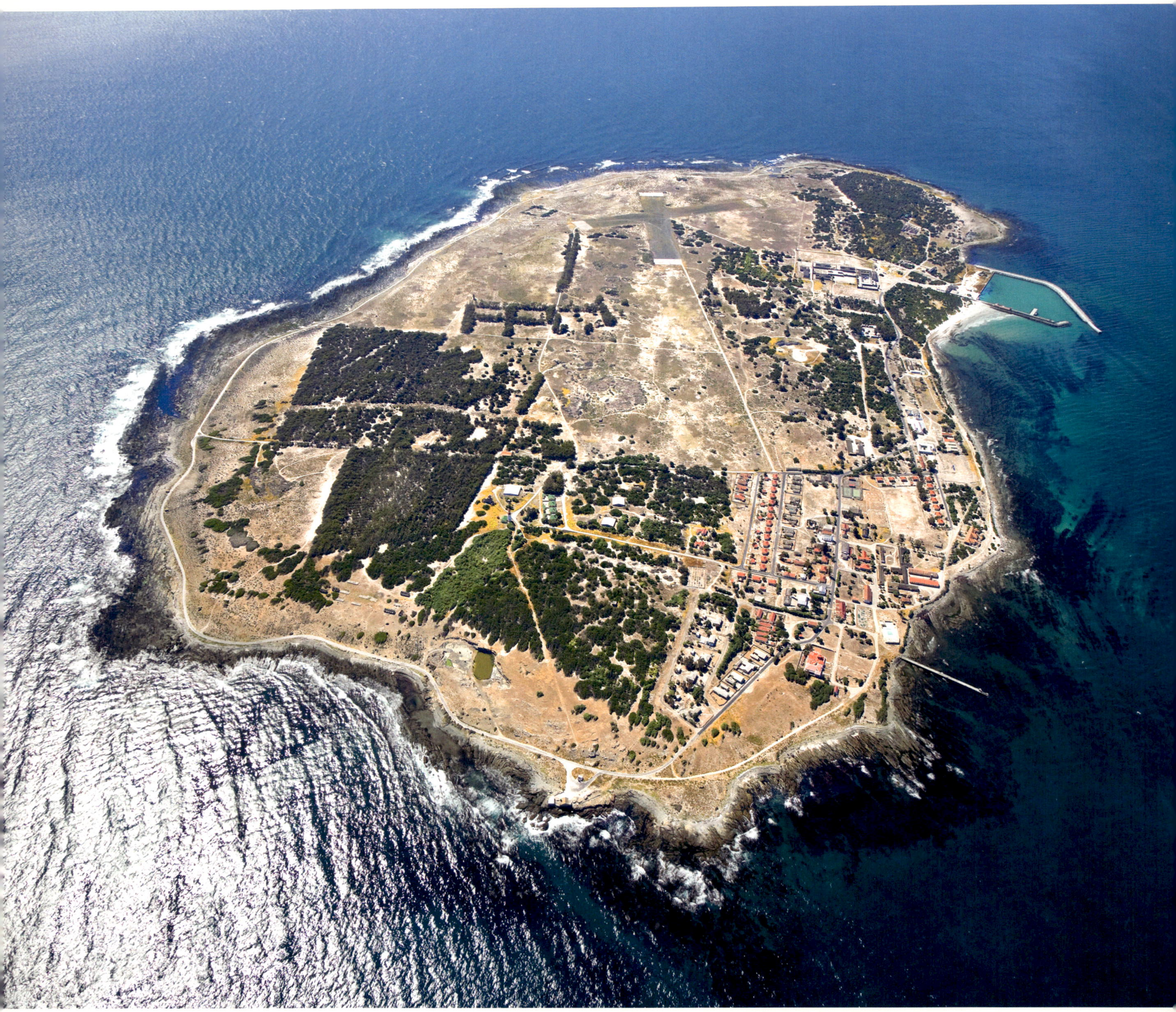

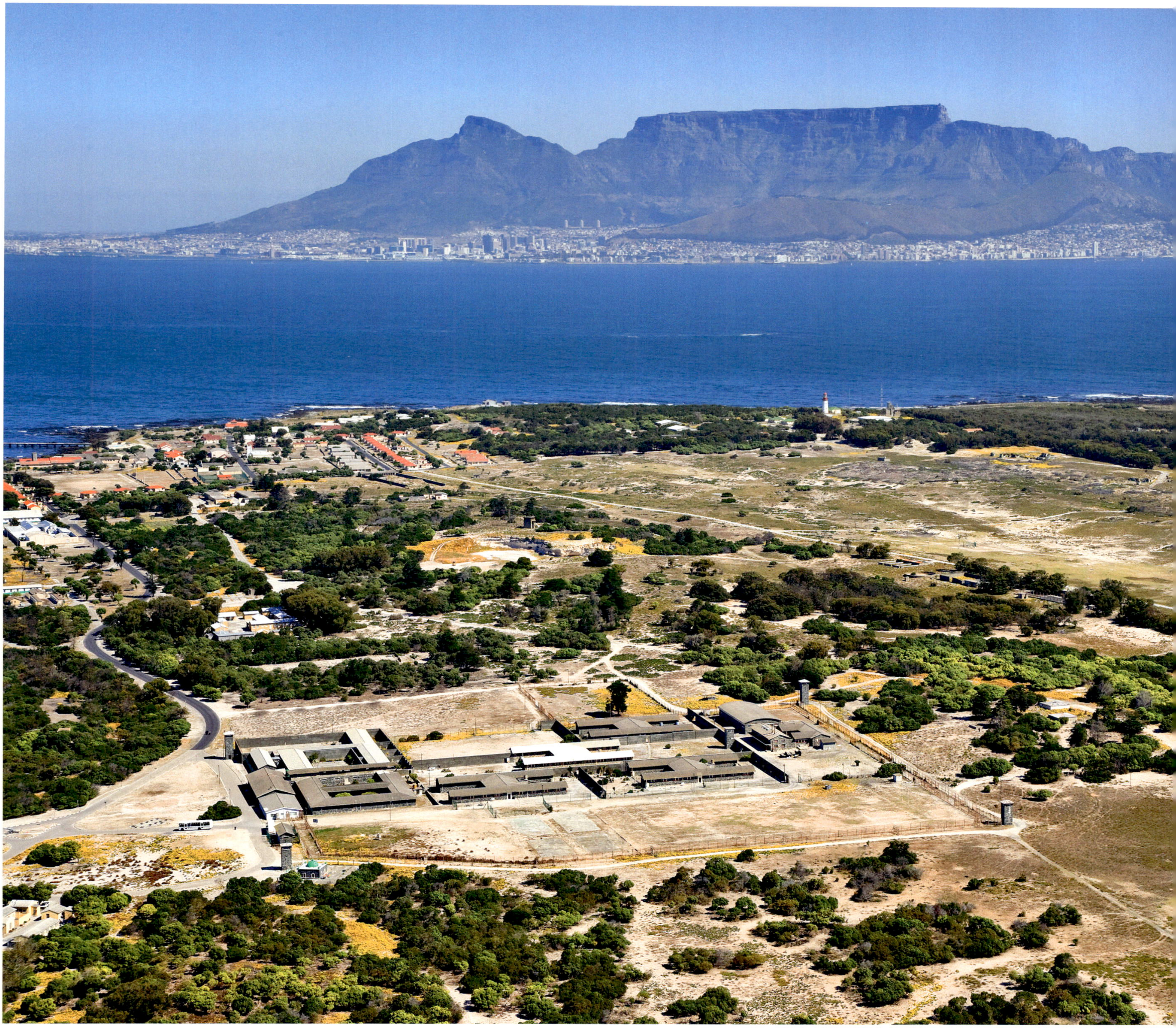

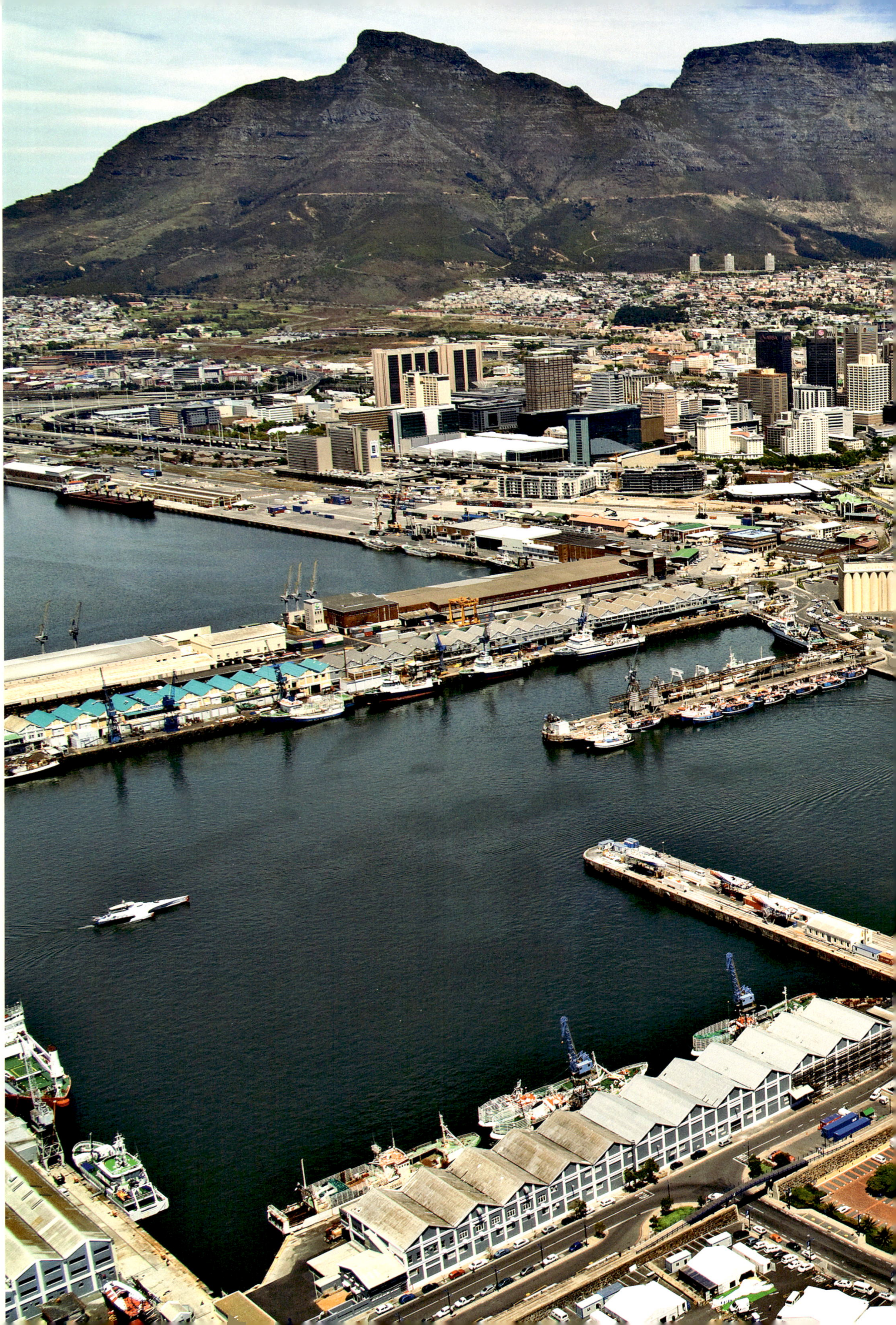

→ Cape Town from the Waterfront with the Table Mountain

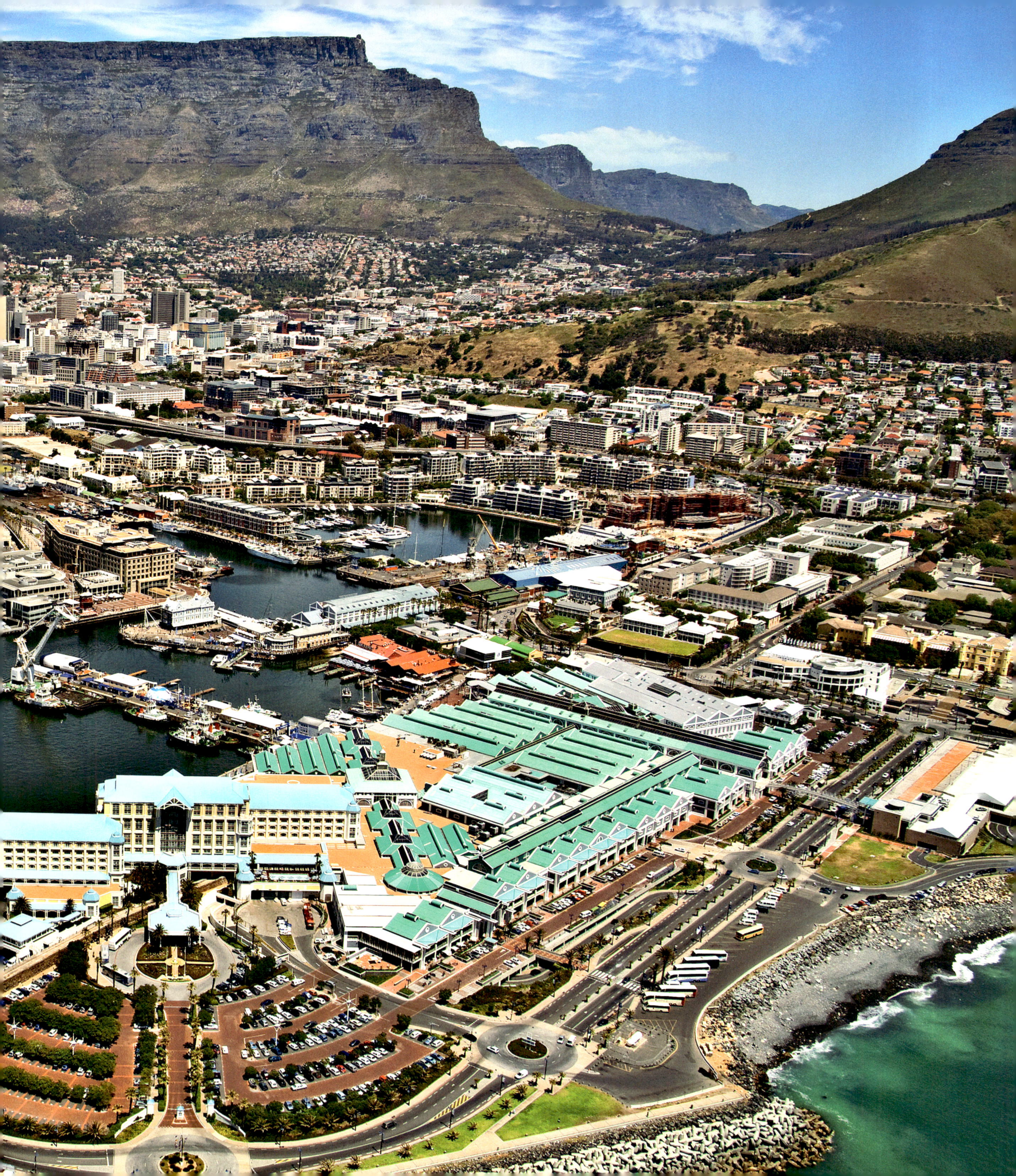

↓ Castle of Good Hope in foreground, Cape Town
→ Heerengracht, Cape Town

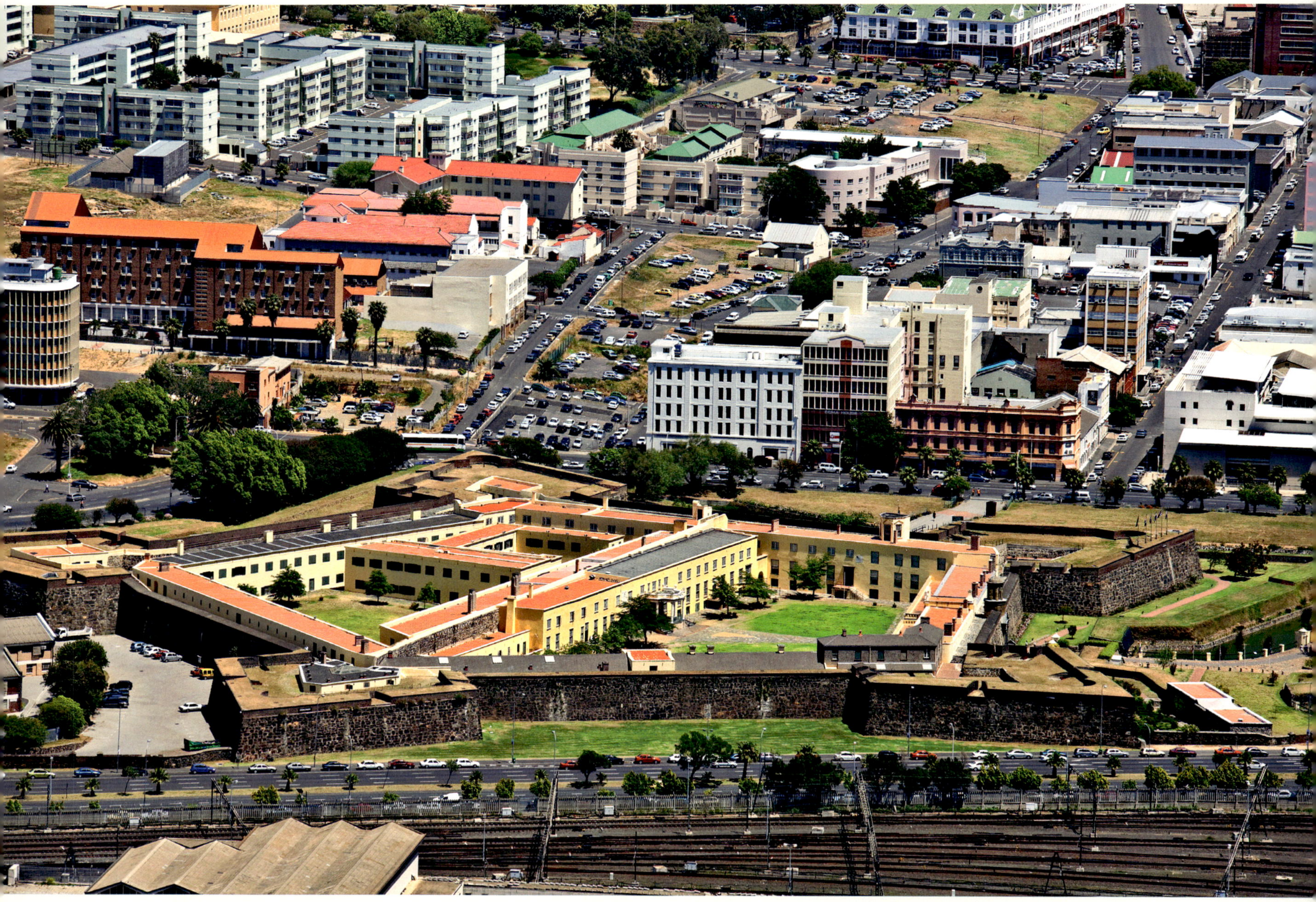

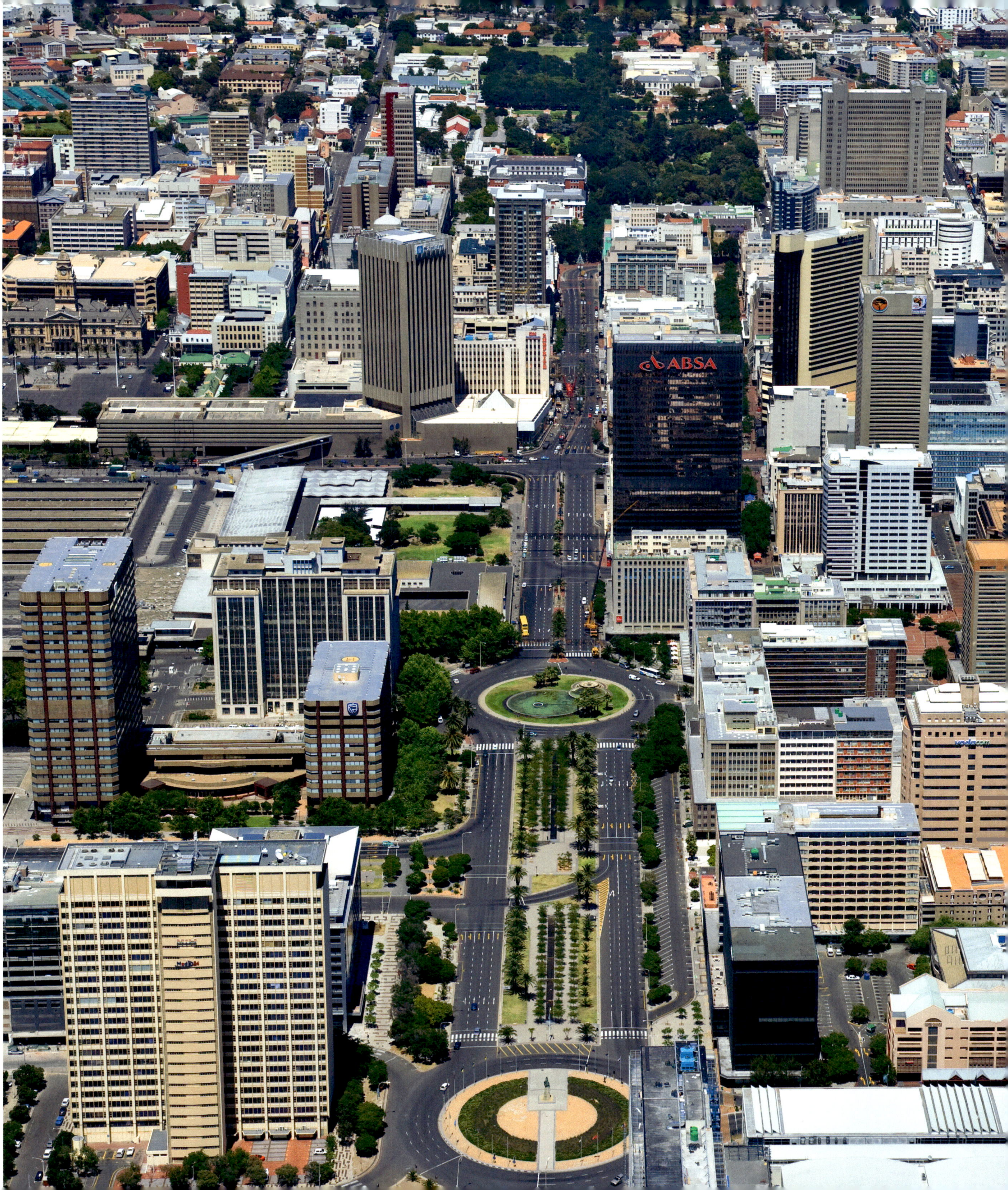
ABSA

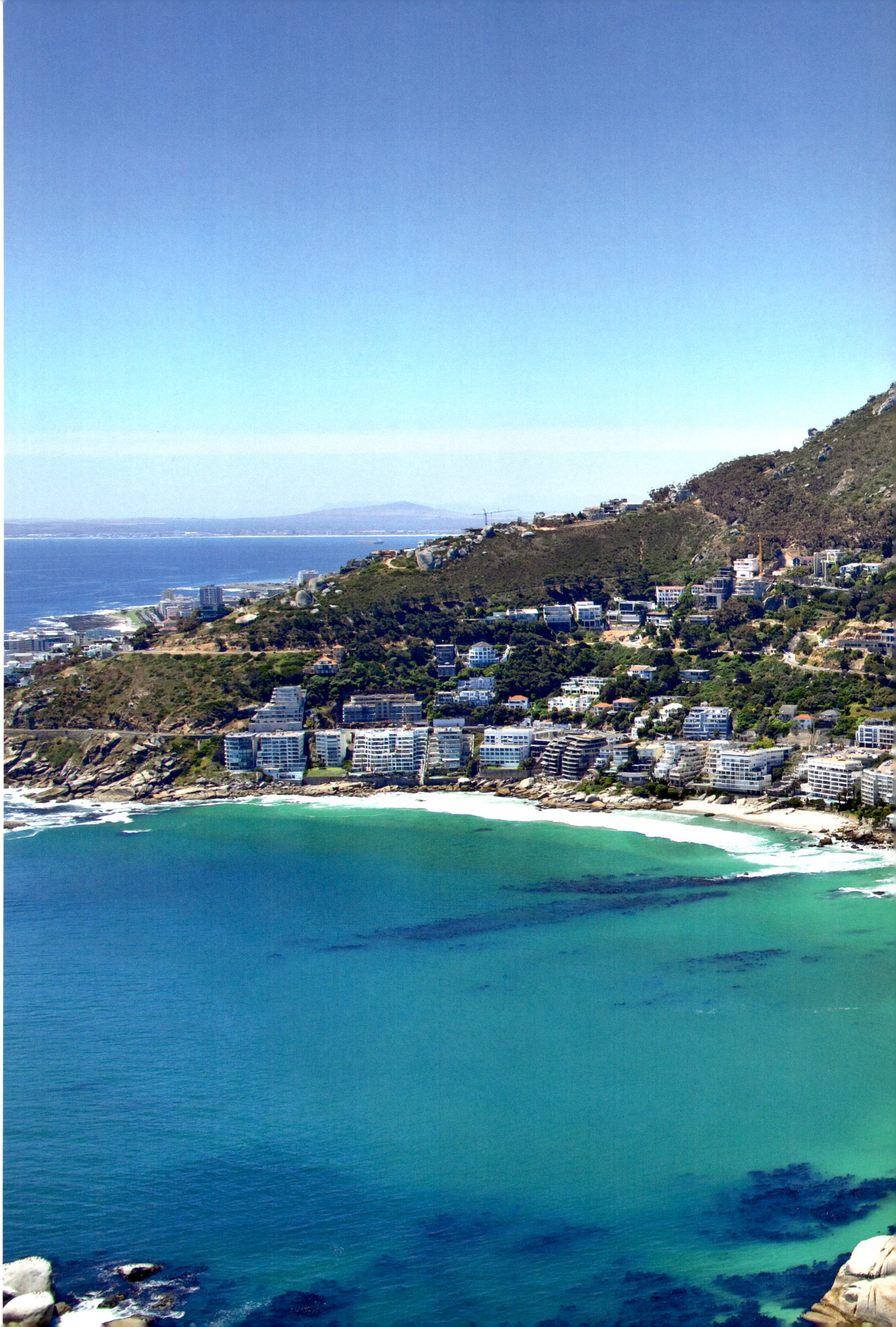

→ Clifton Beach, Cape Town

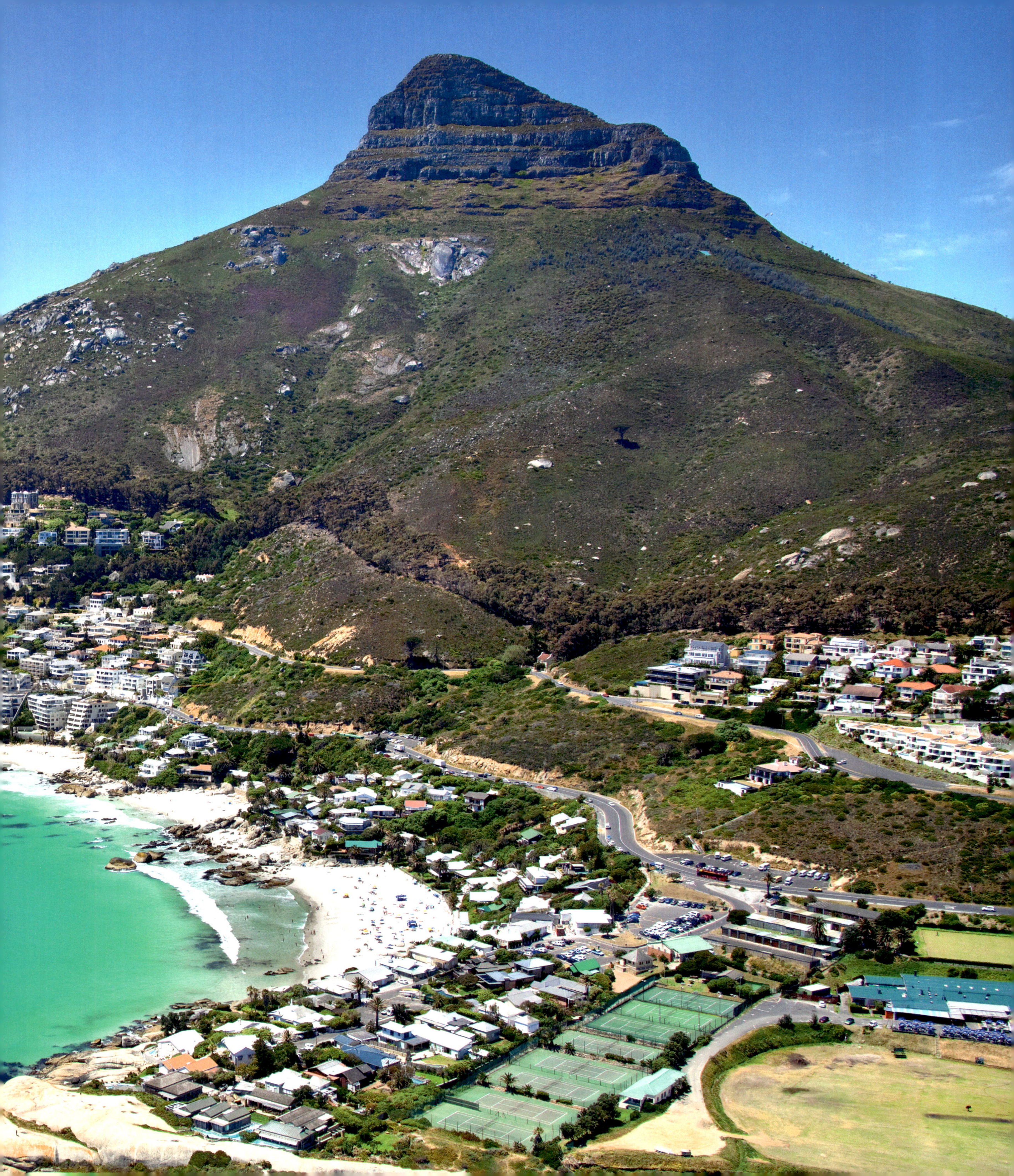

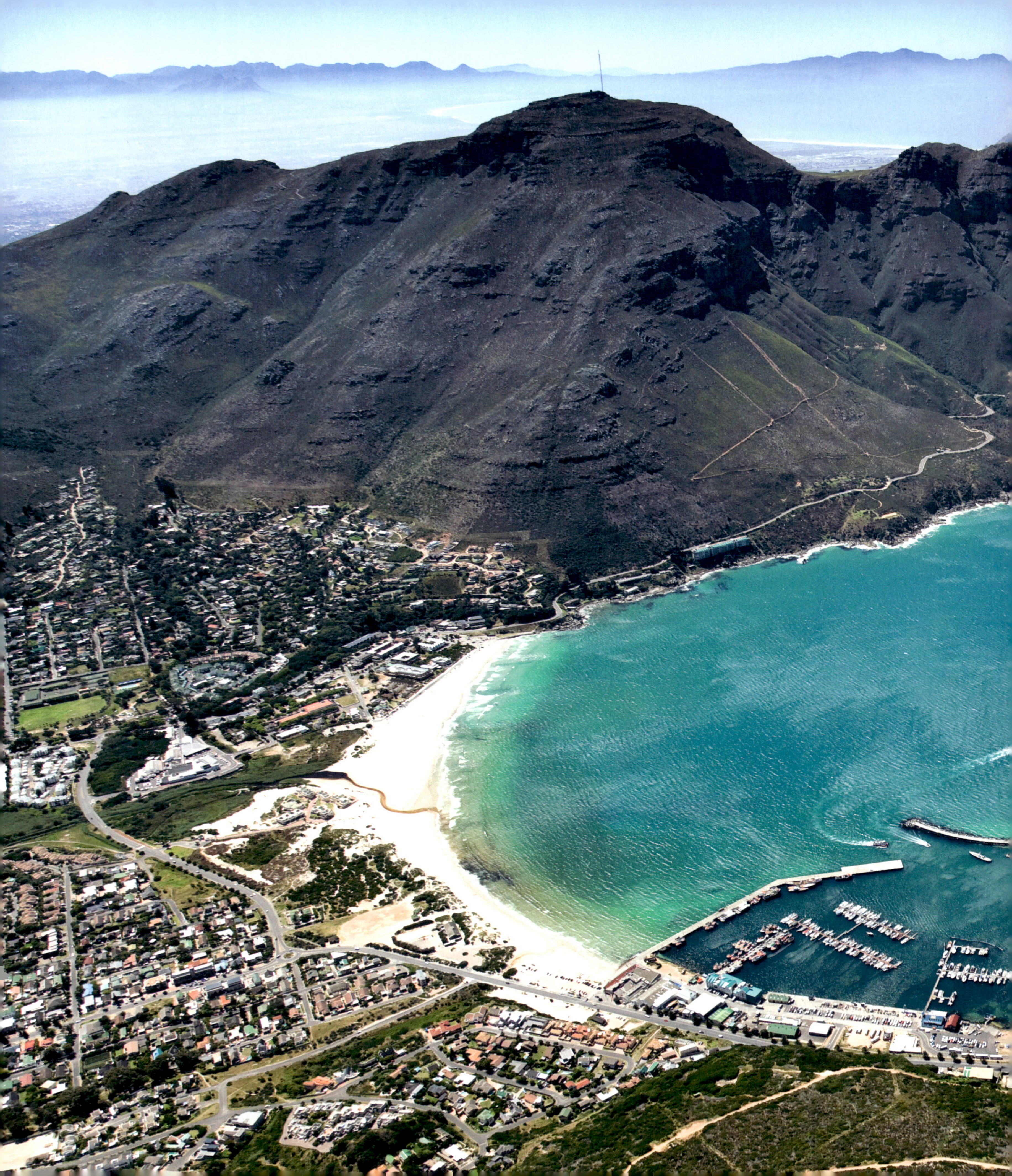

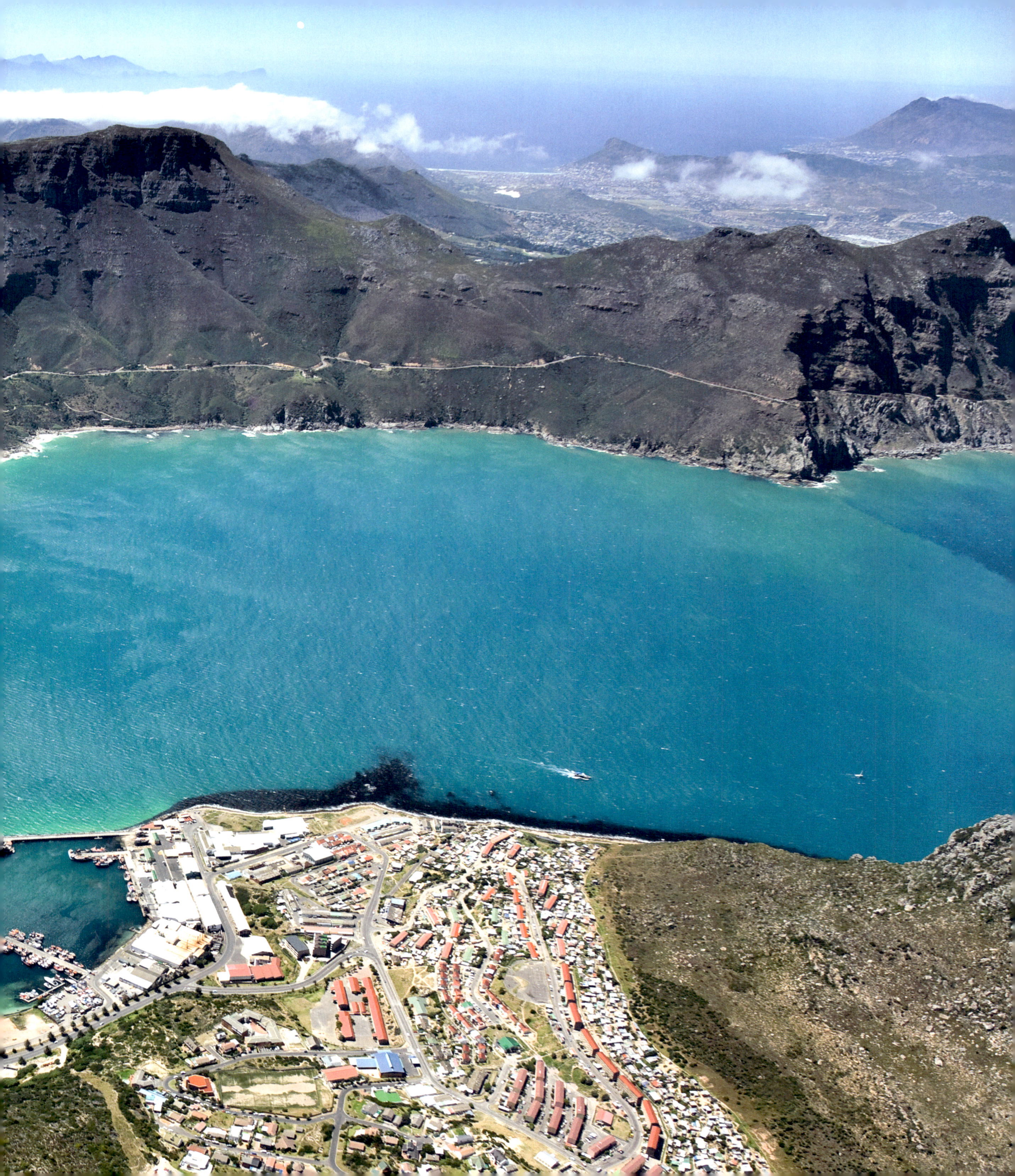

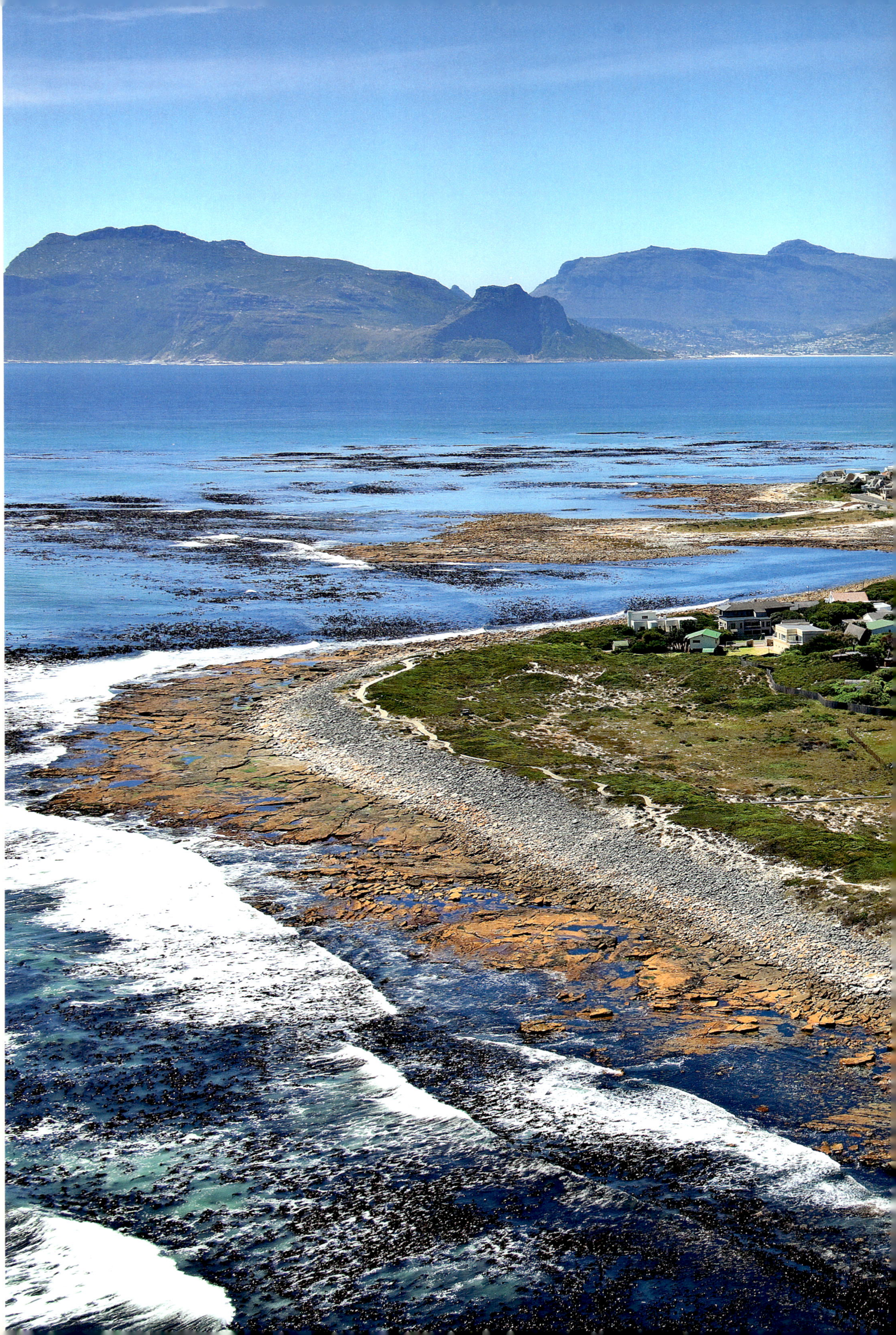

← Hout Bay
→ Slangkop Lighthouse, Kommetjie

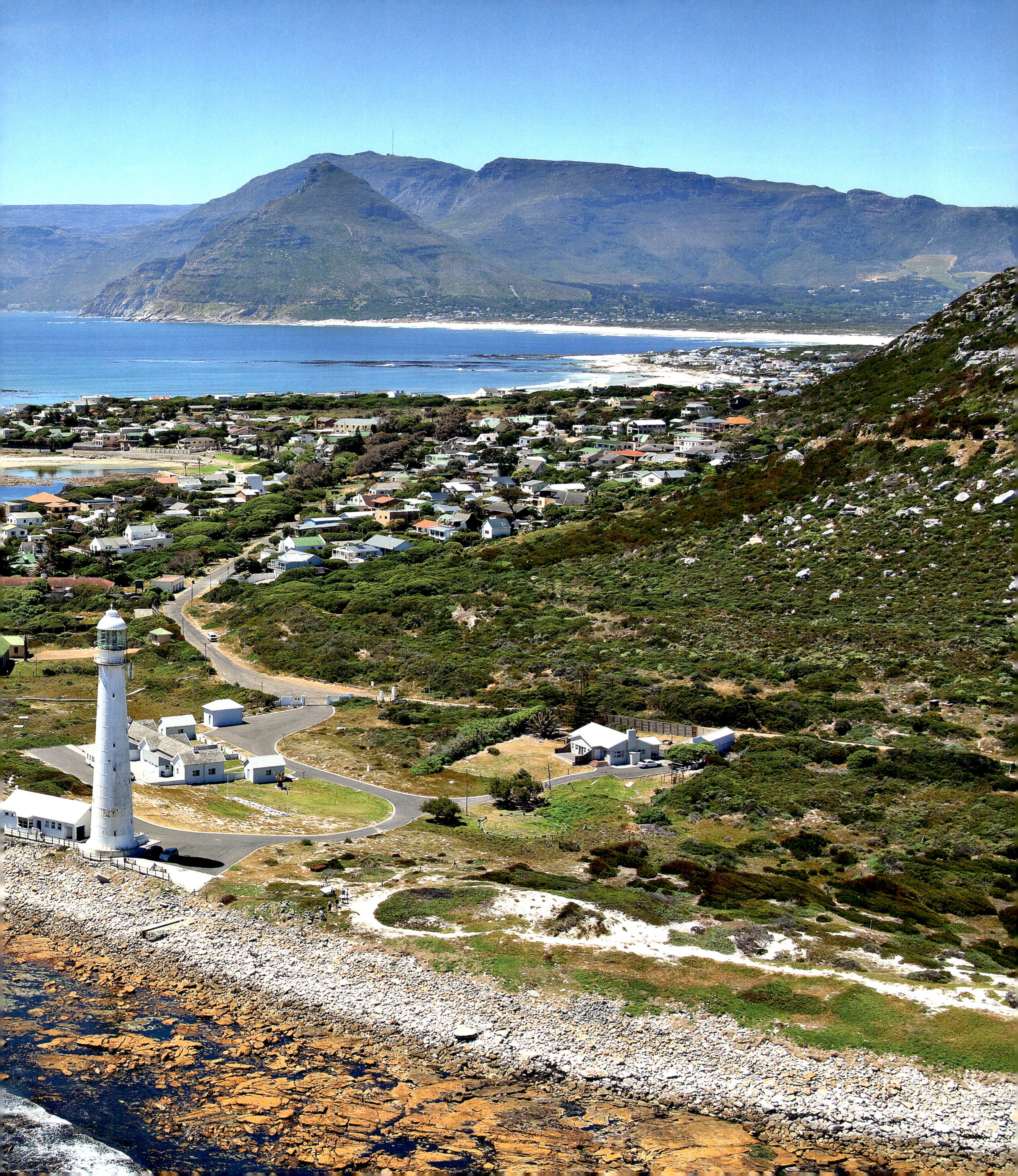

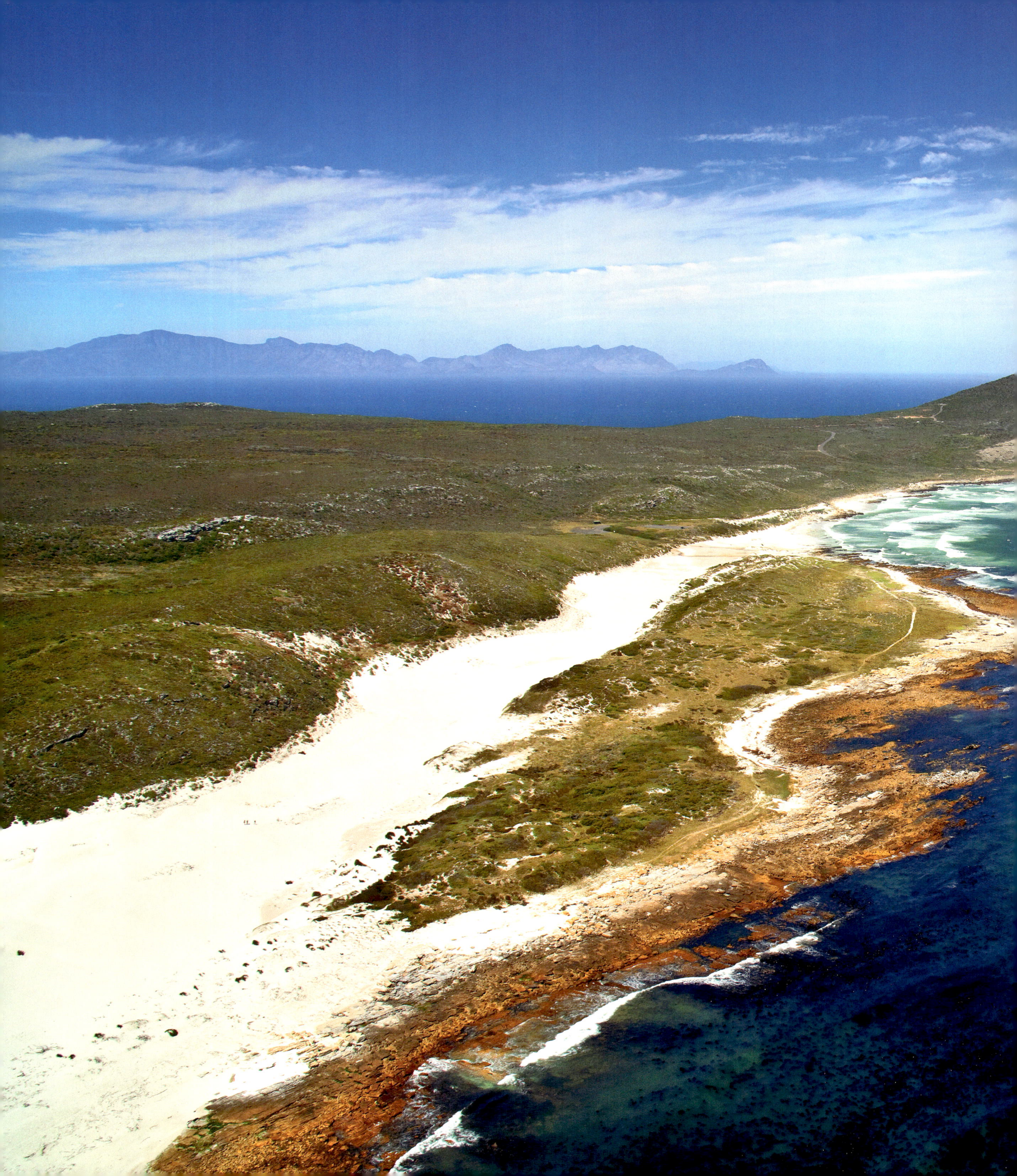

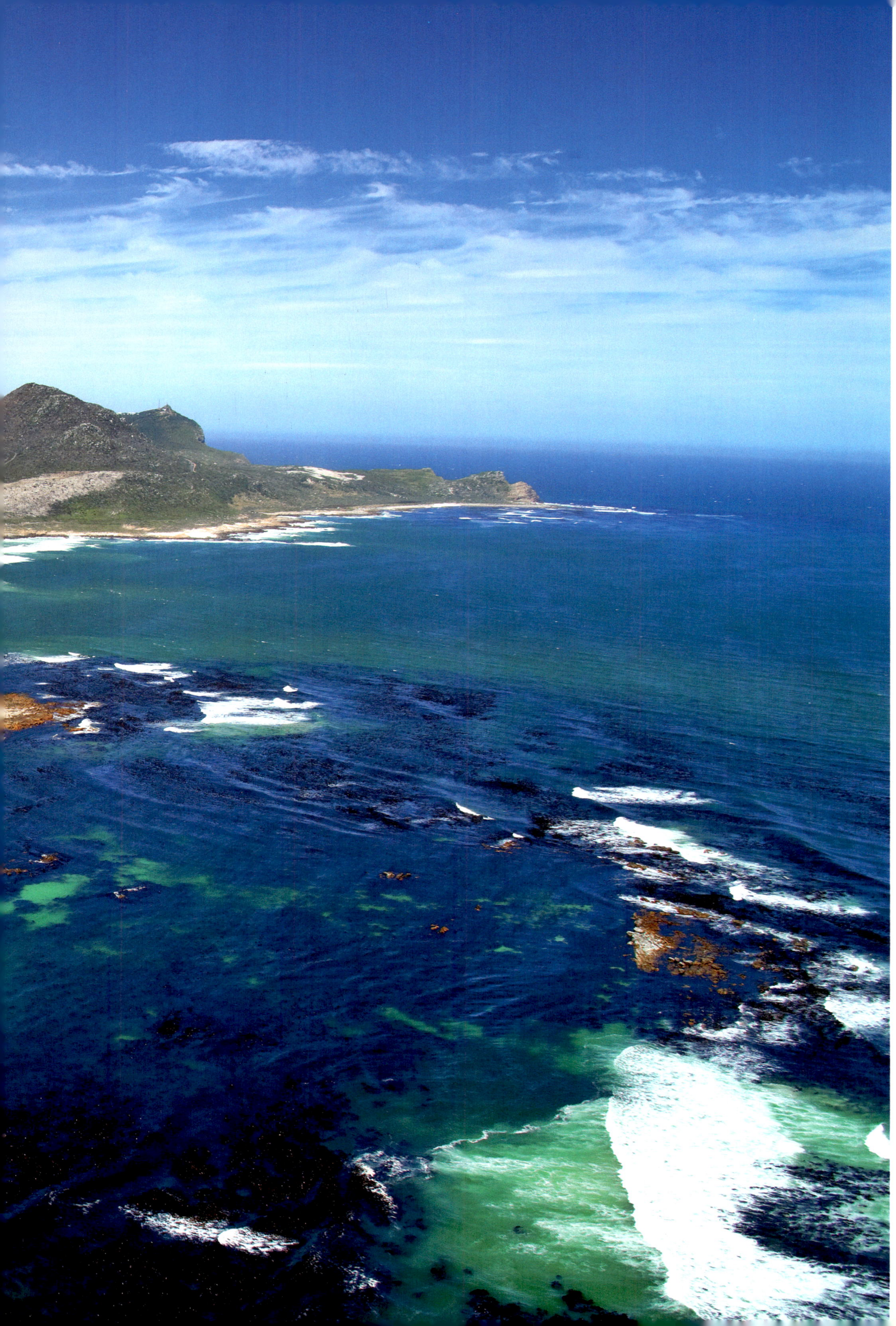

← Neptune's Dairy with Cape of Good Hope

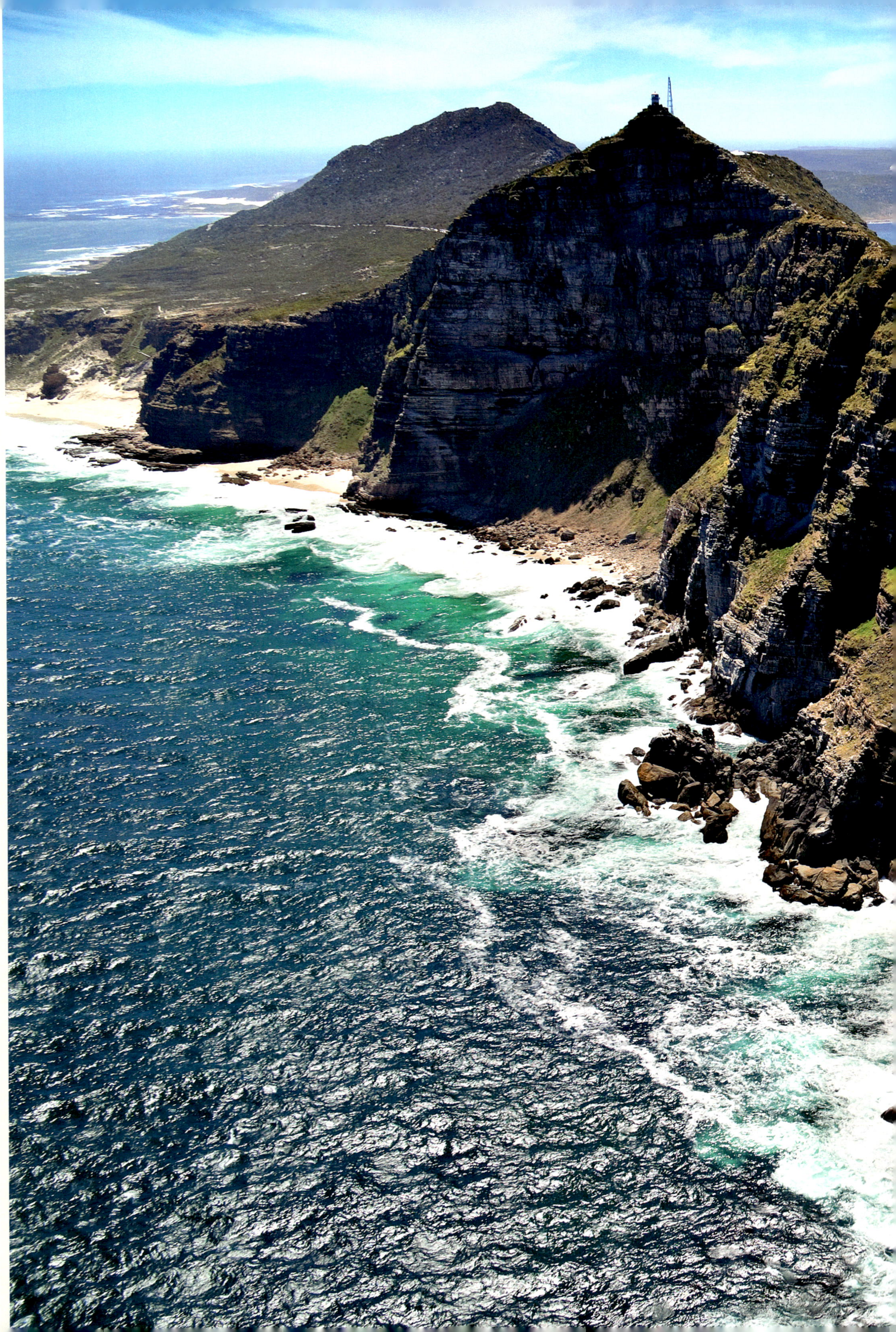

→ Cape Point

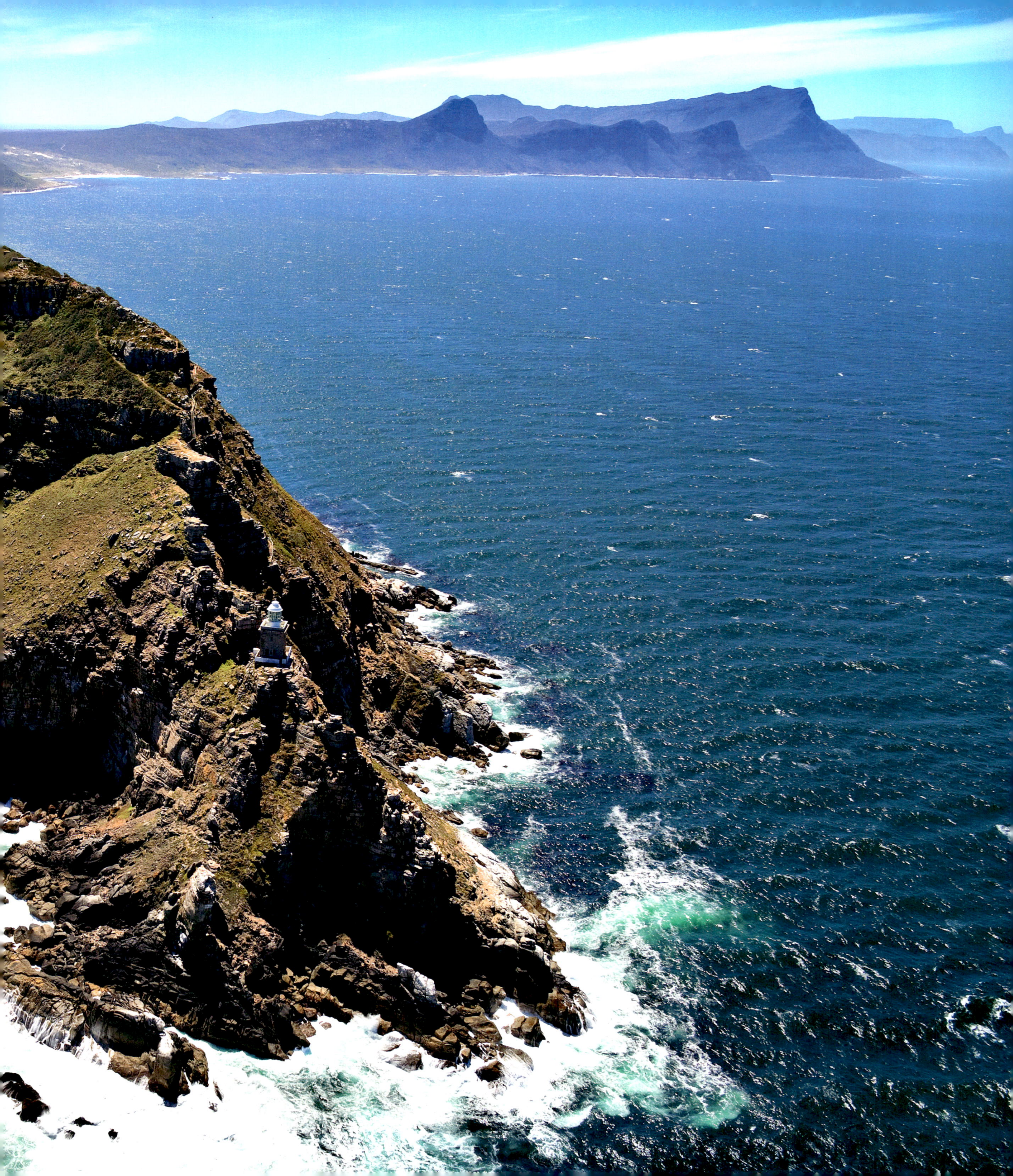

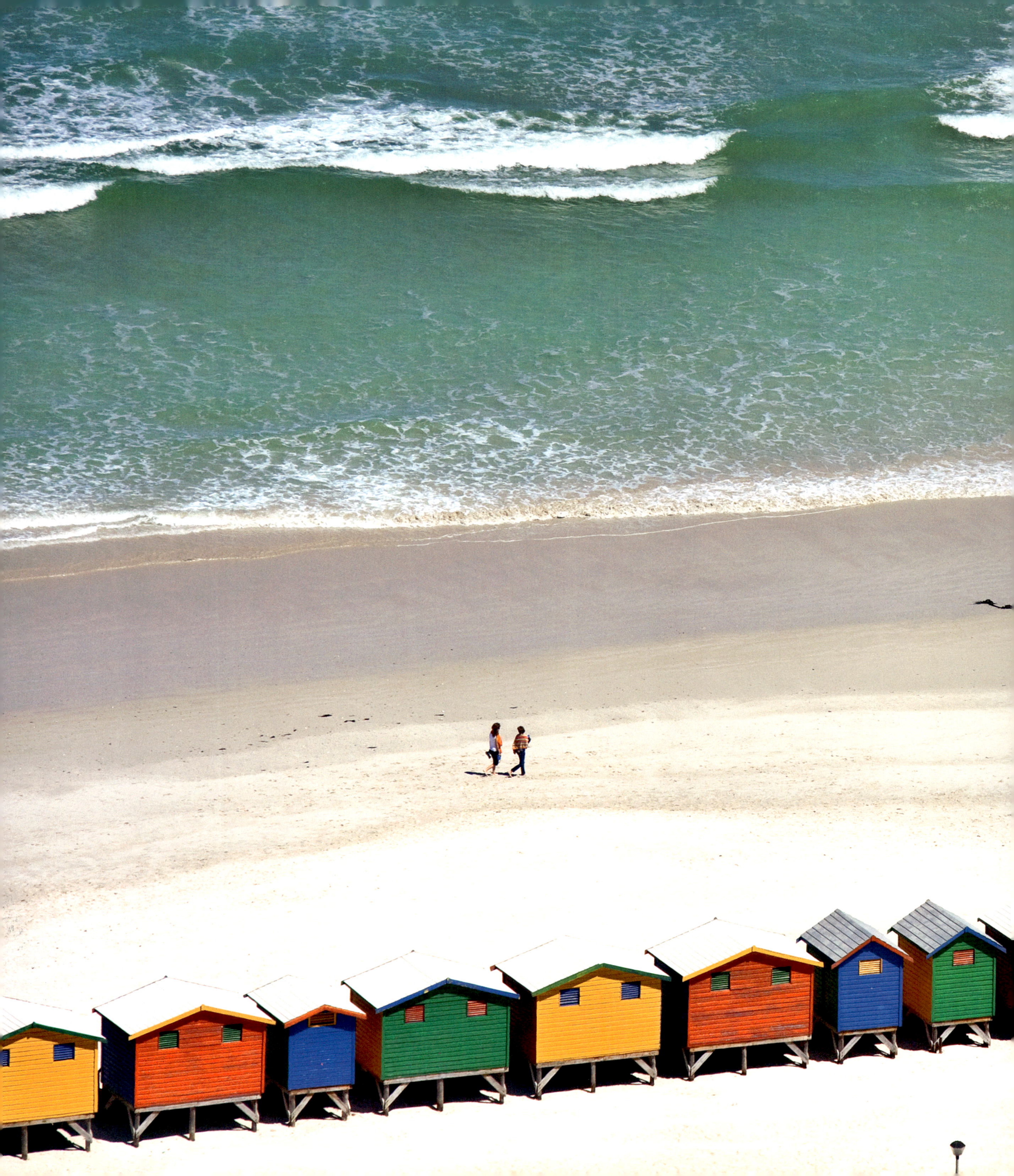

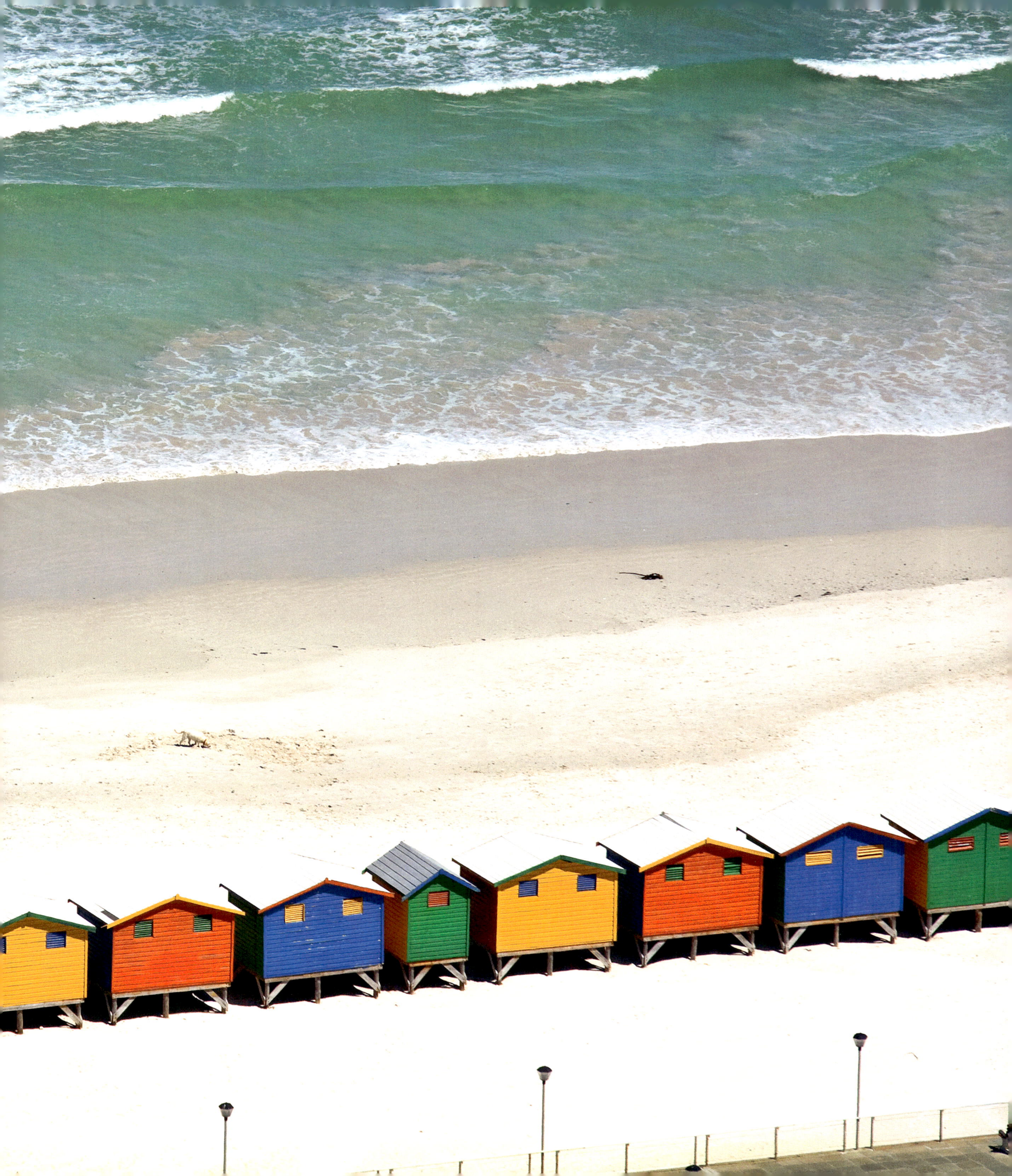

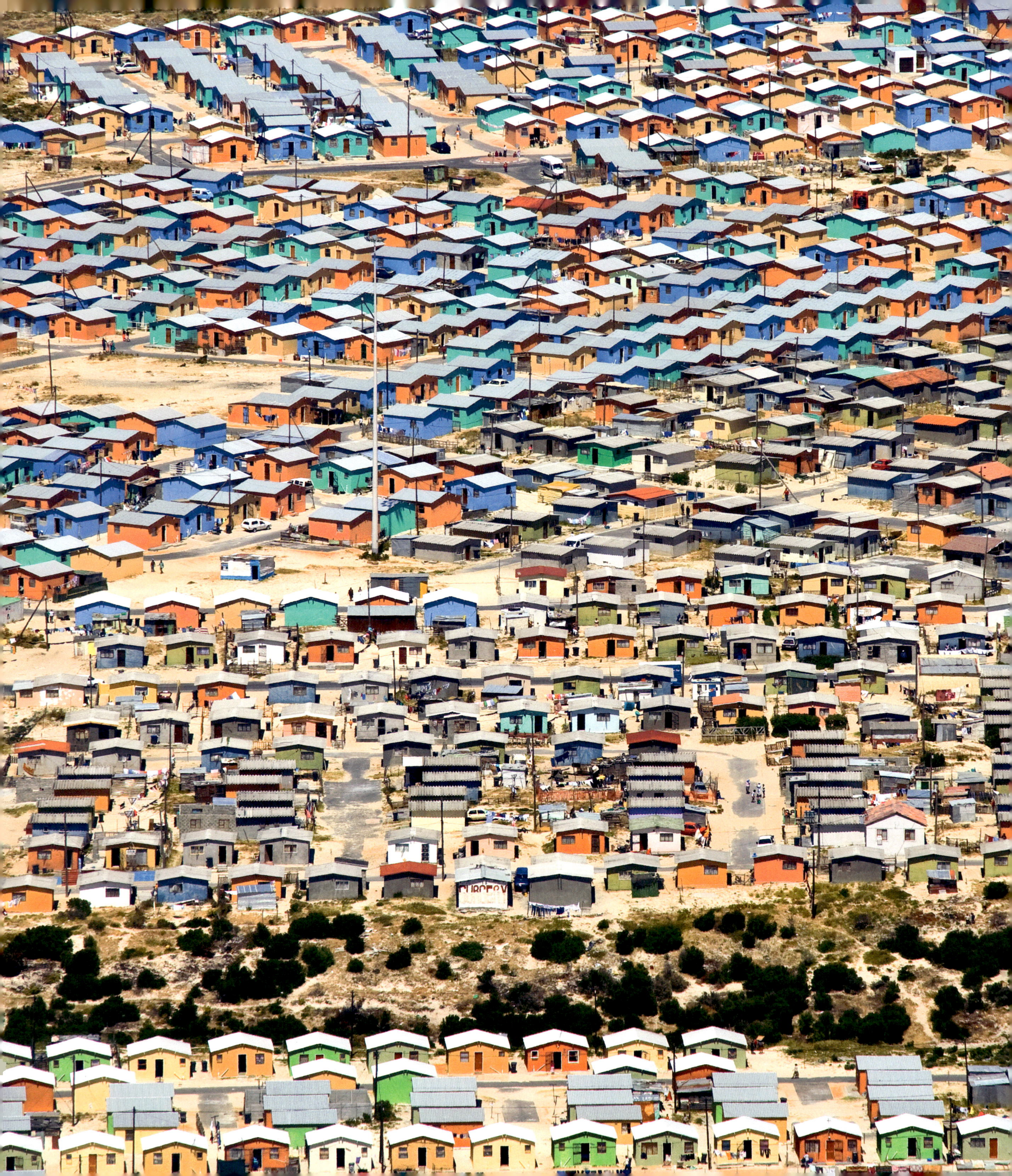

←← Muizenberg
← Khayelitsha
↓ Mitchell's Plain, southeast from Cape Town

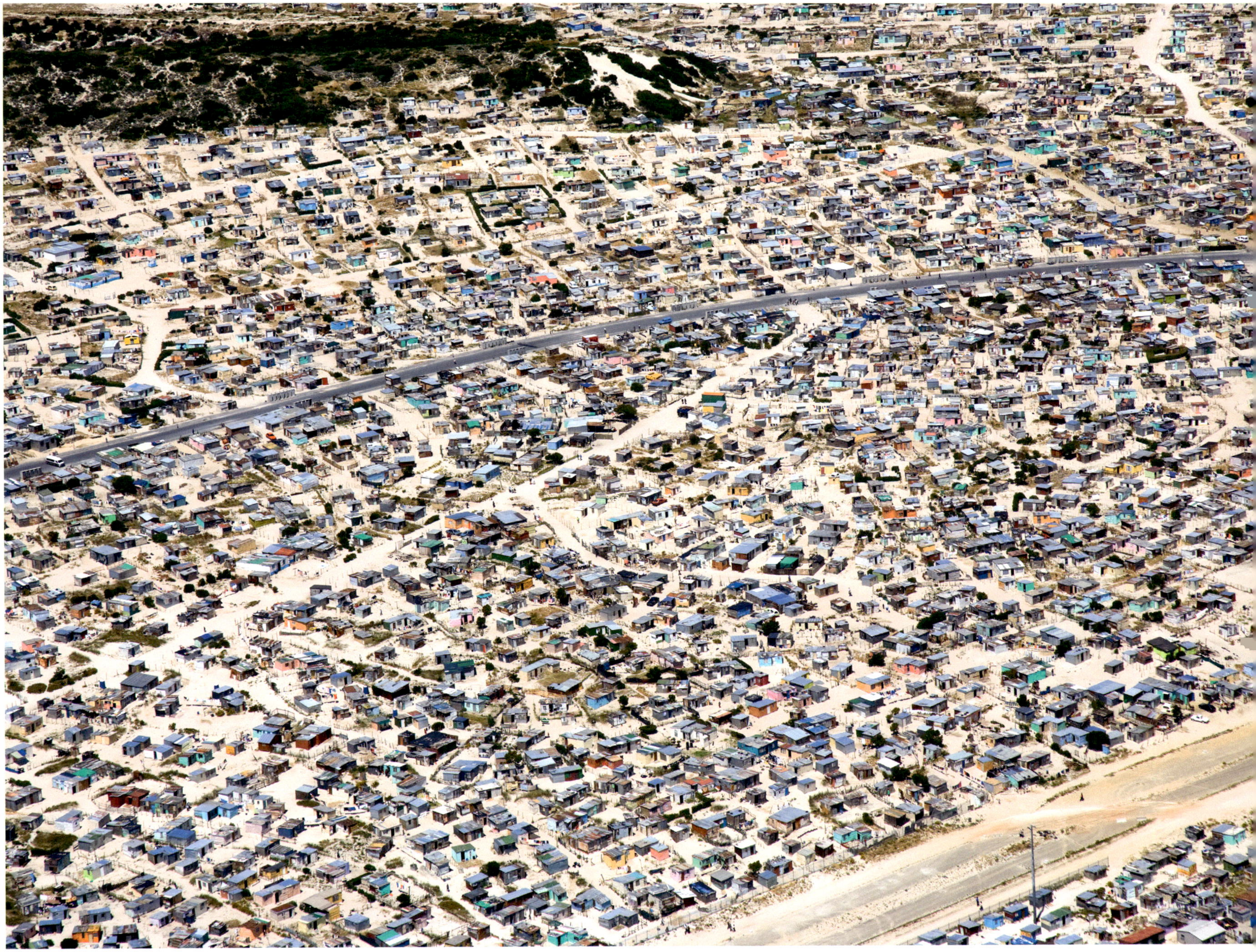

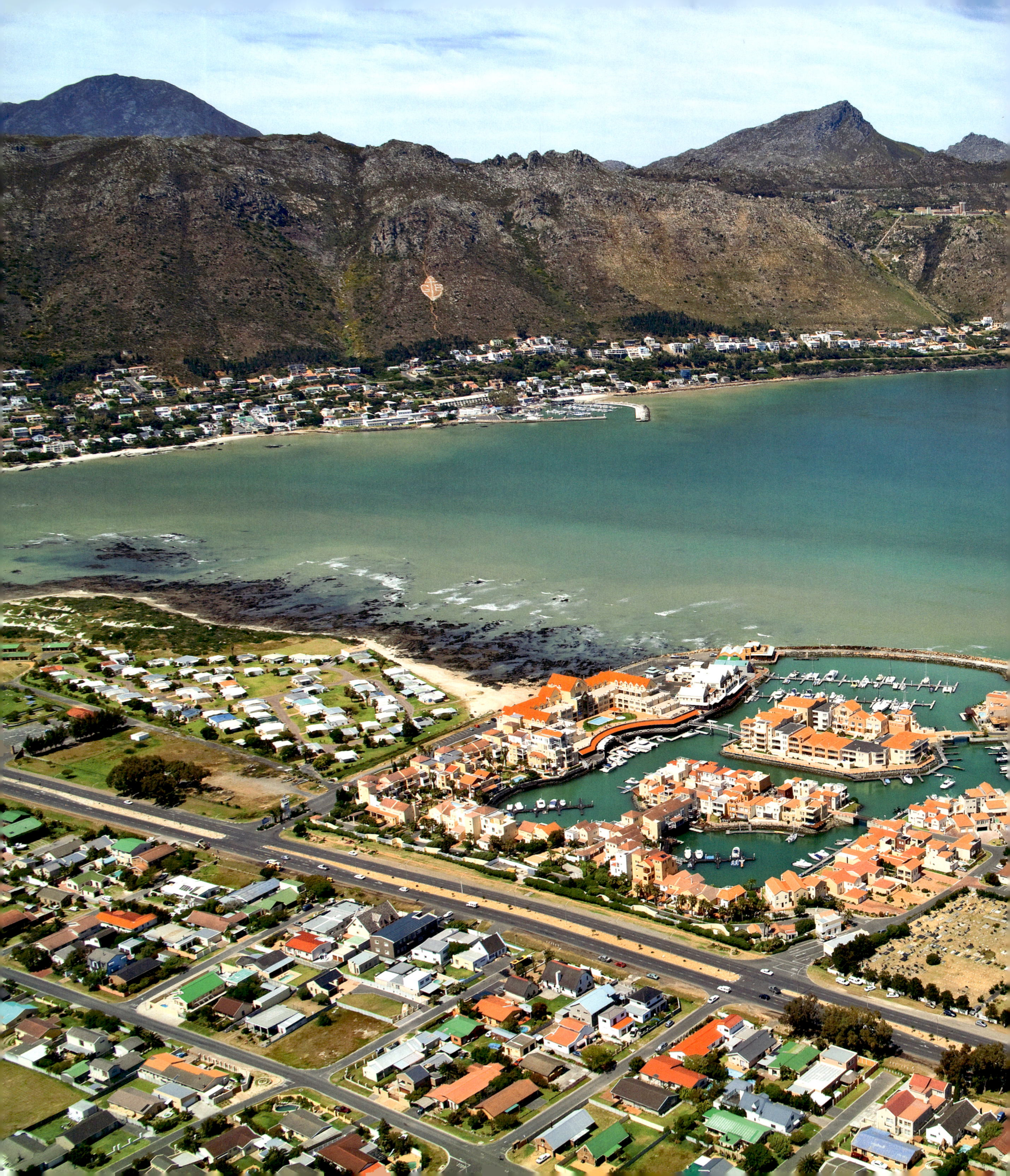

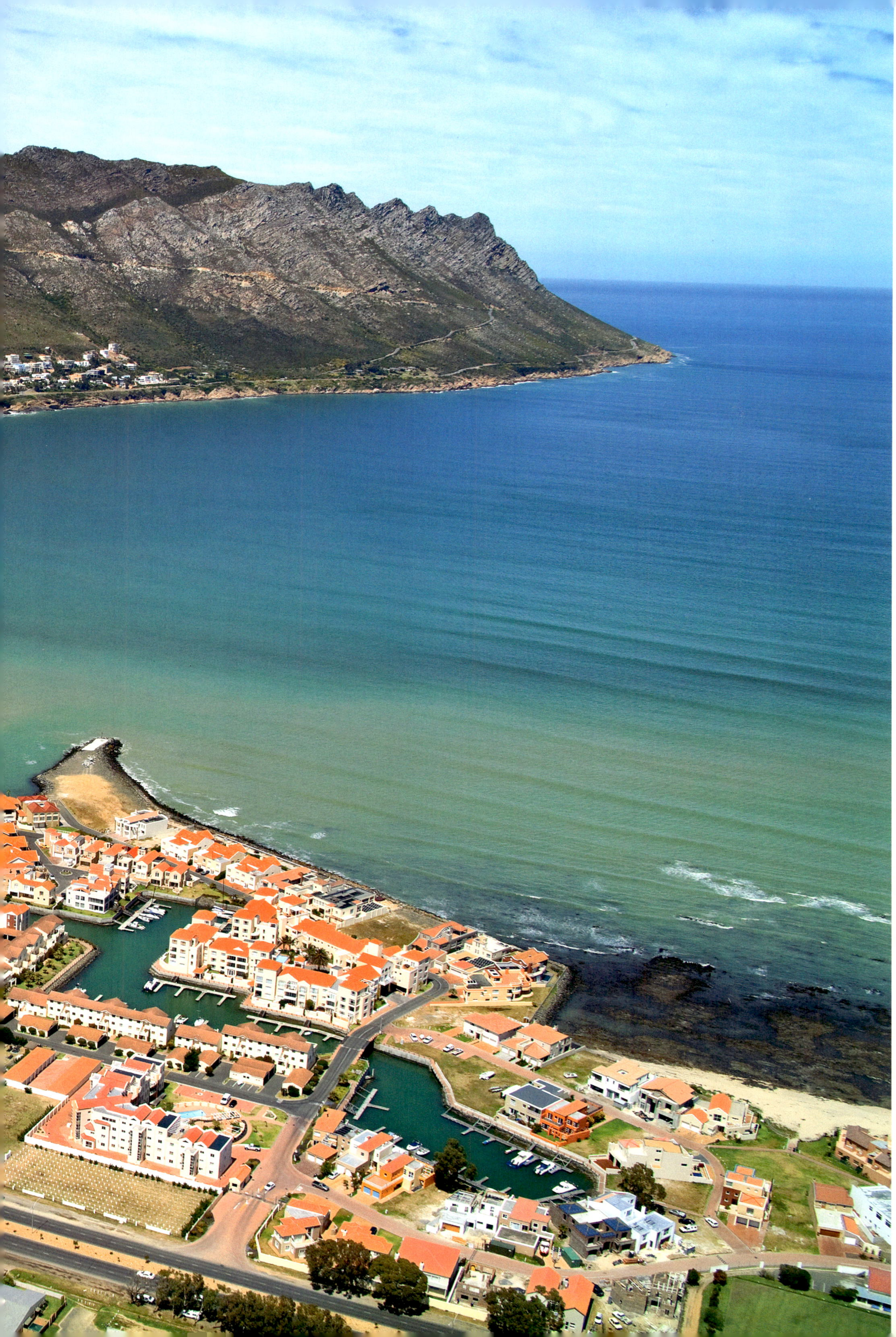

← Gordon's Bay

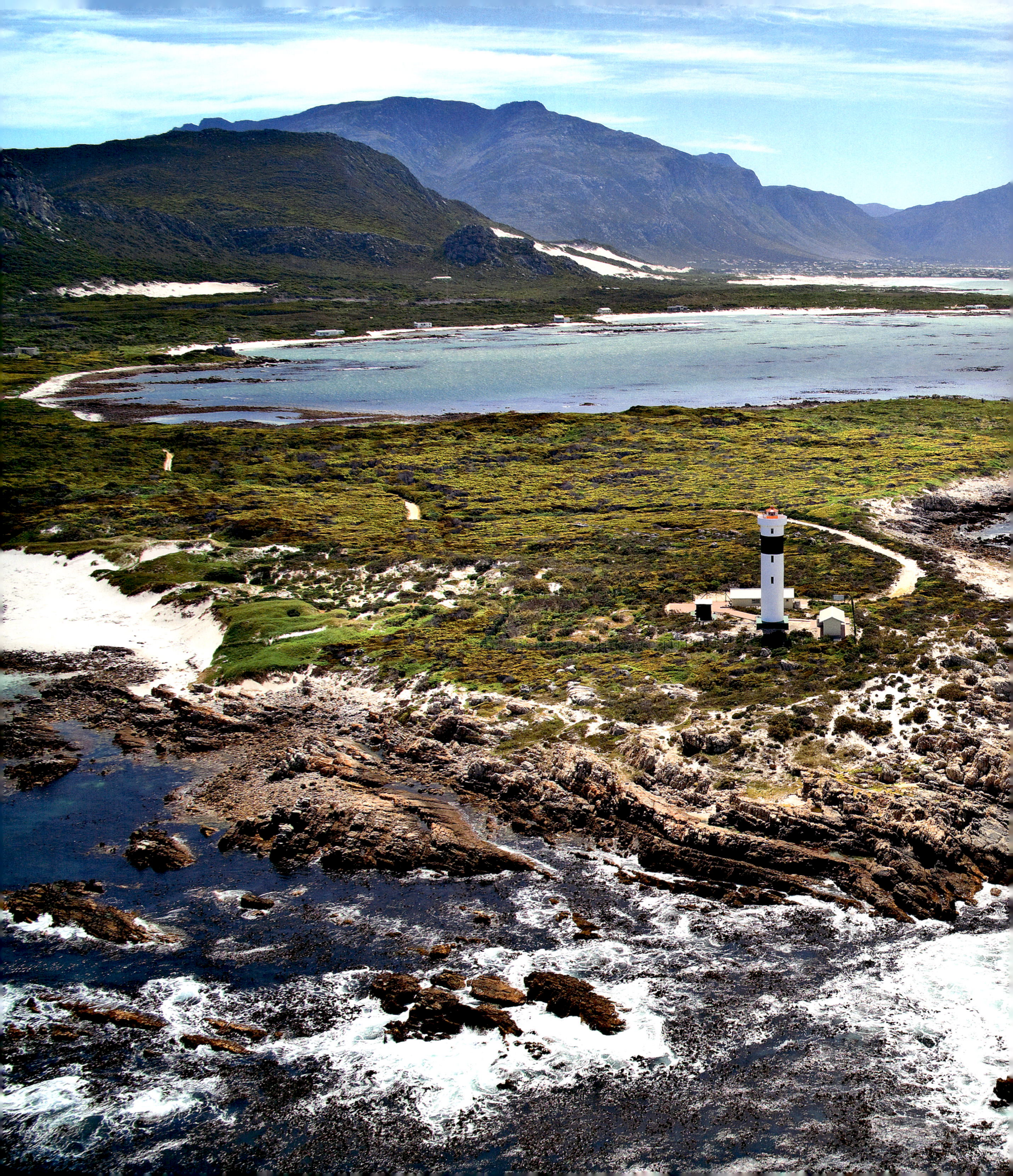

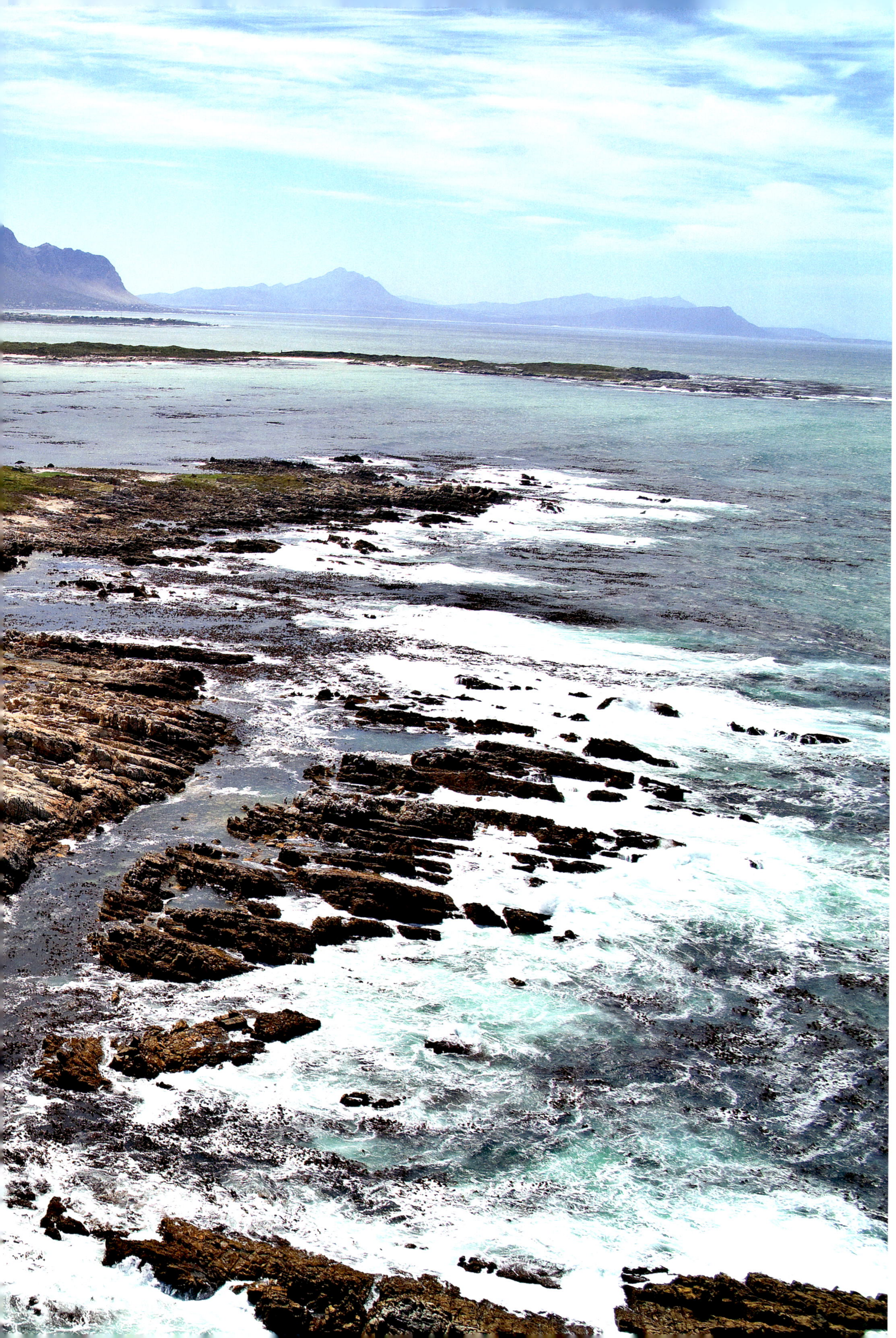

← Cape Hangklip

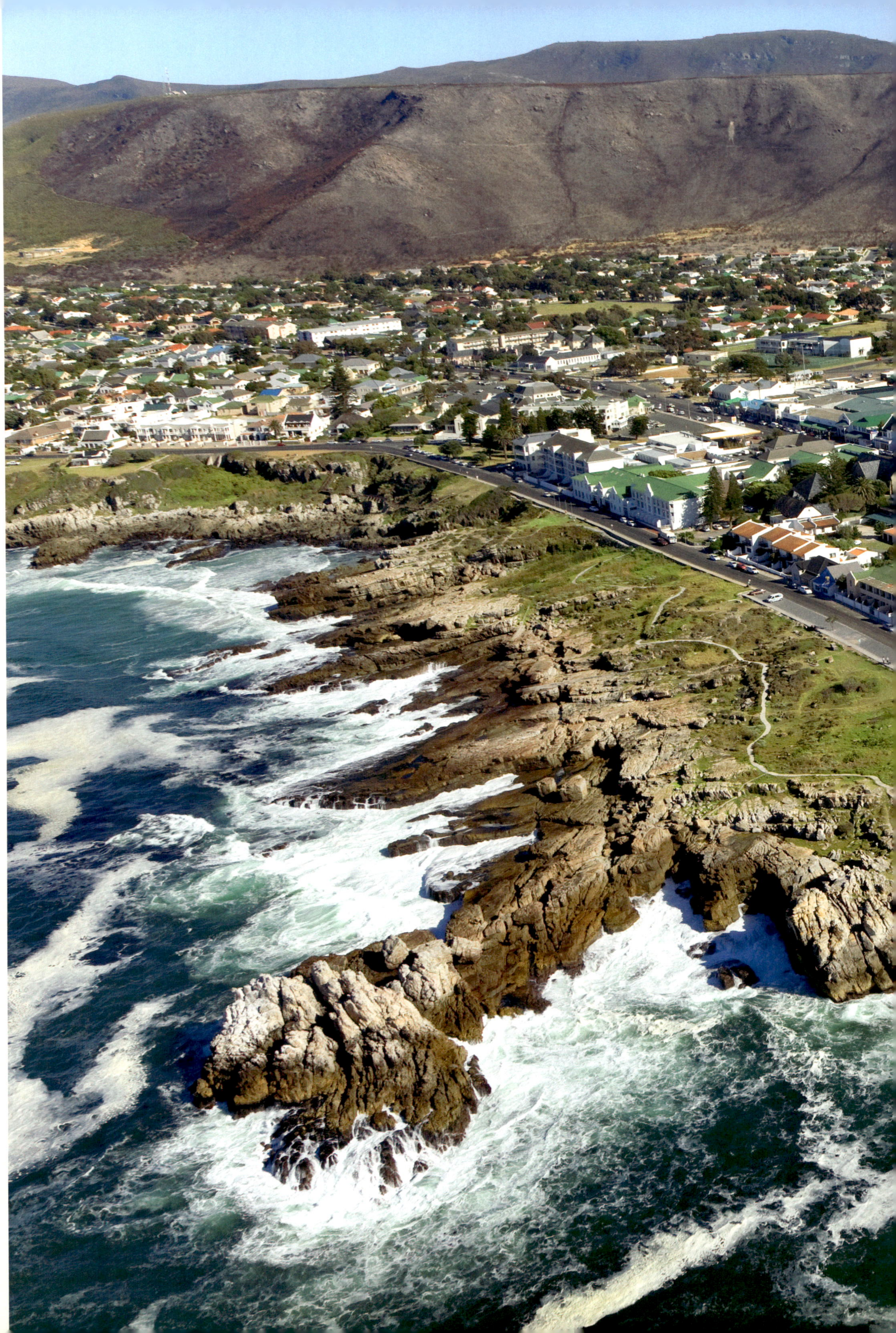

→ Hermanus

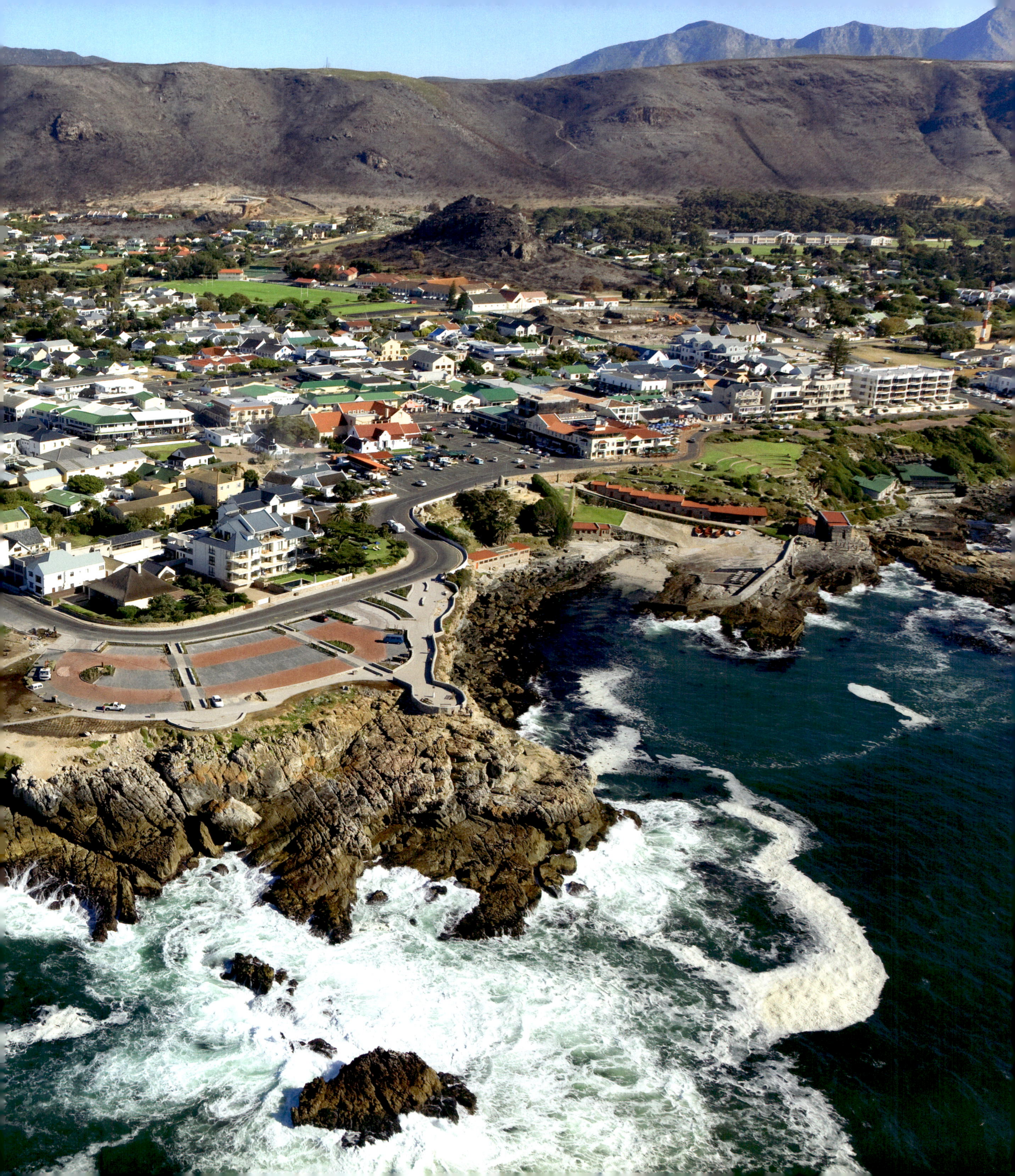

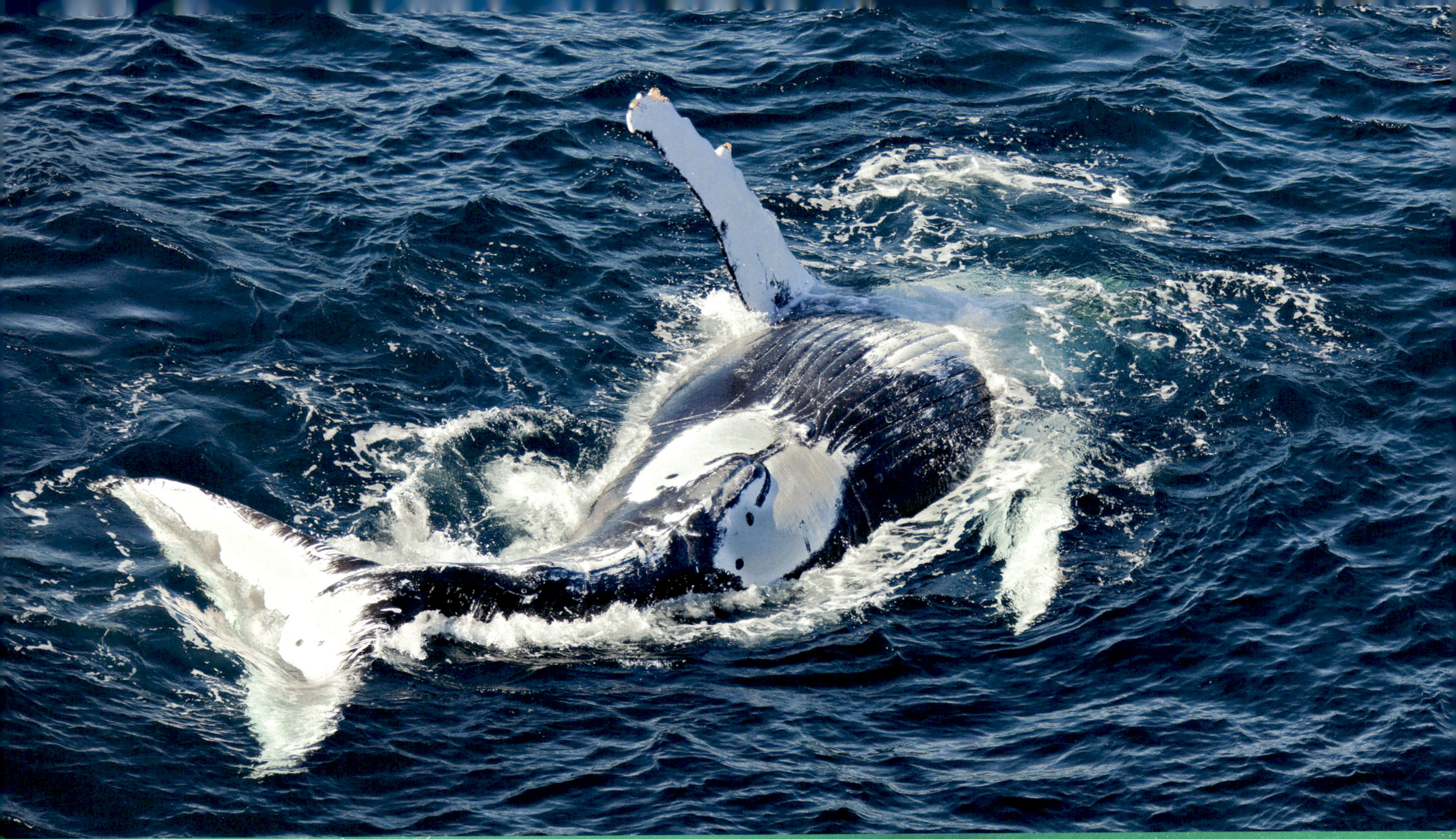

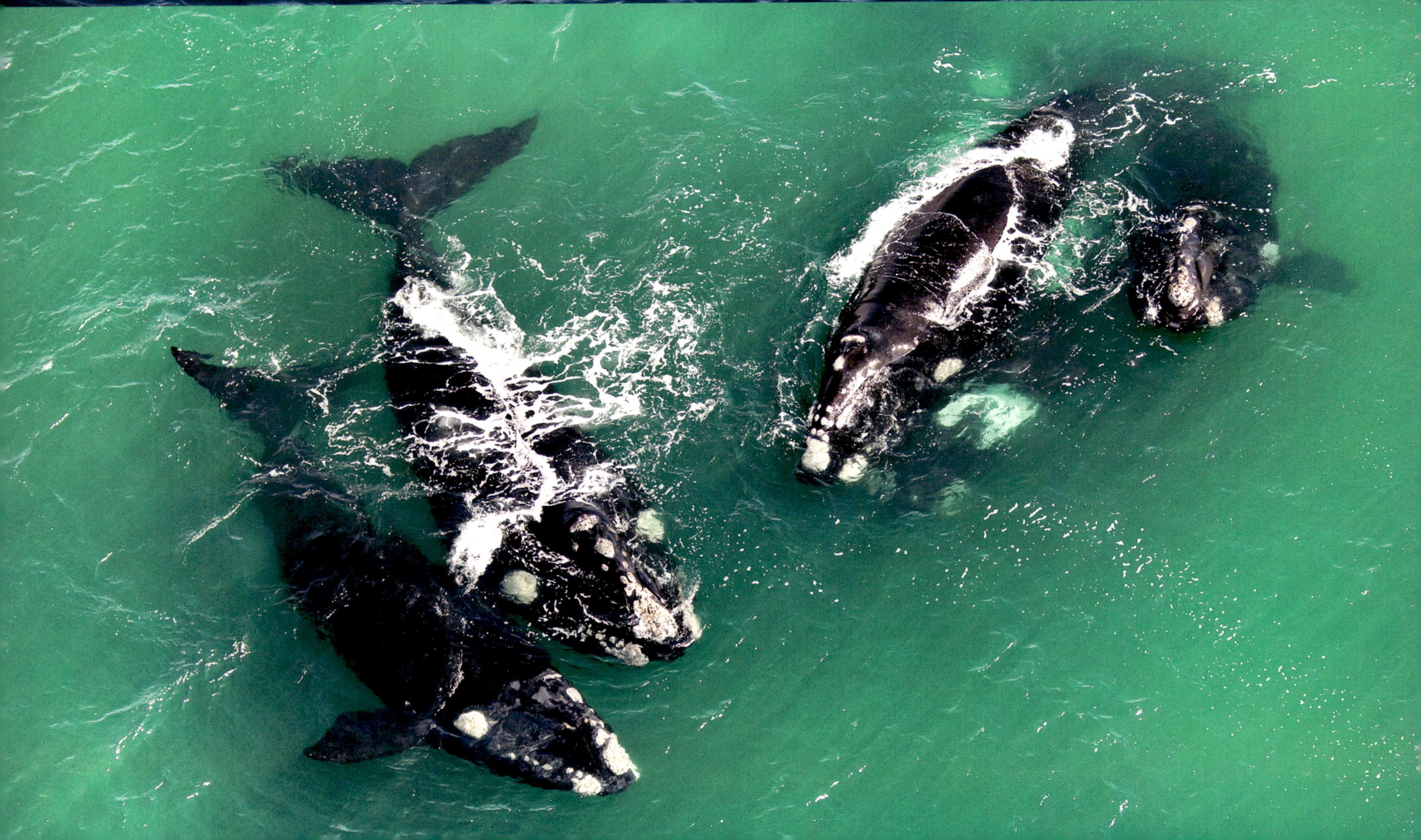

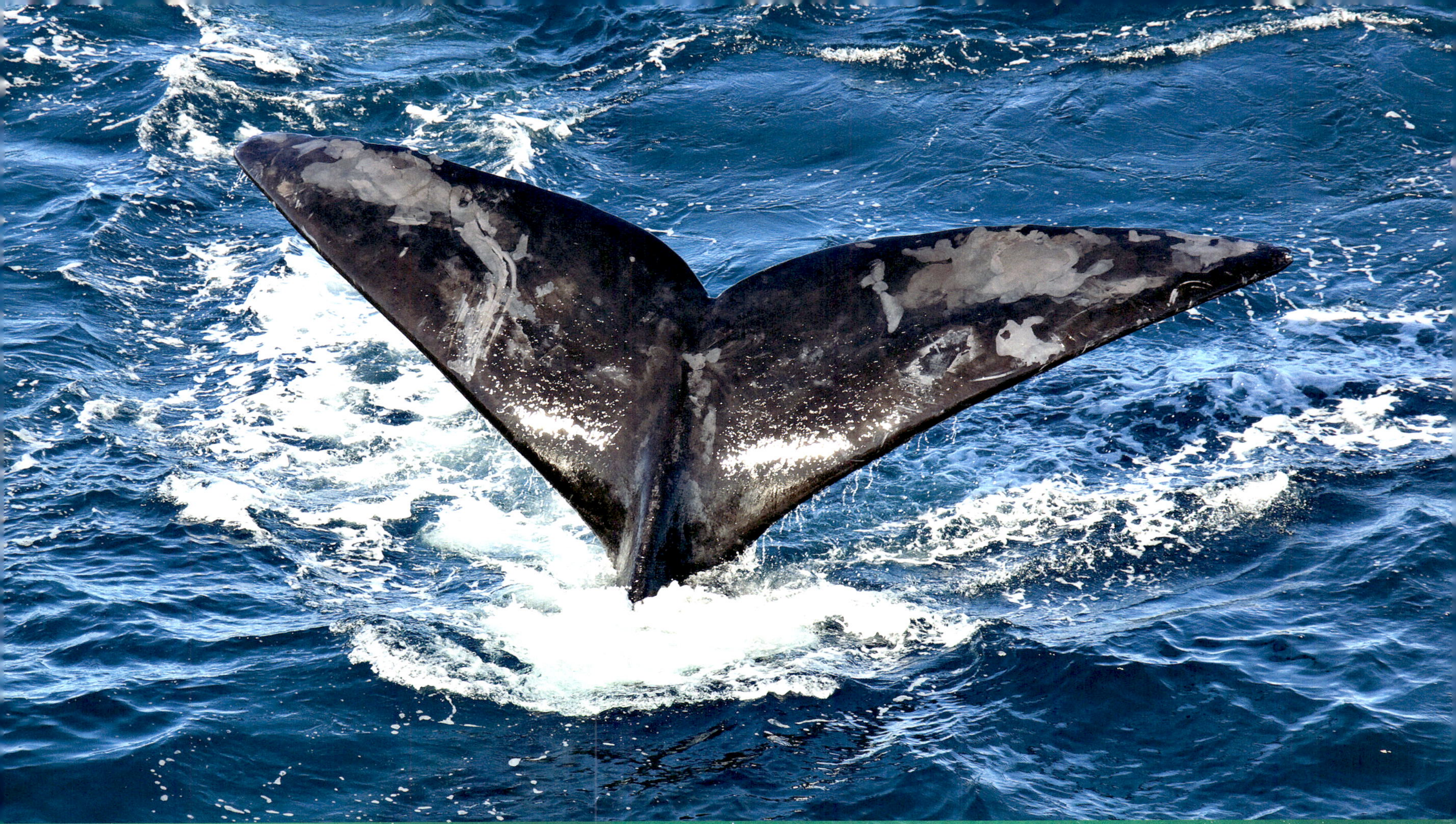

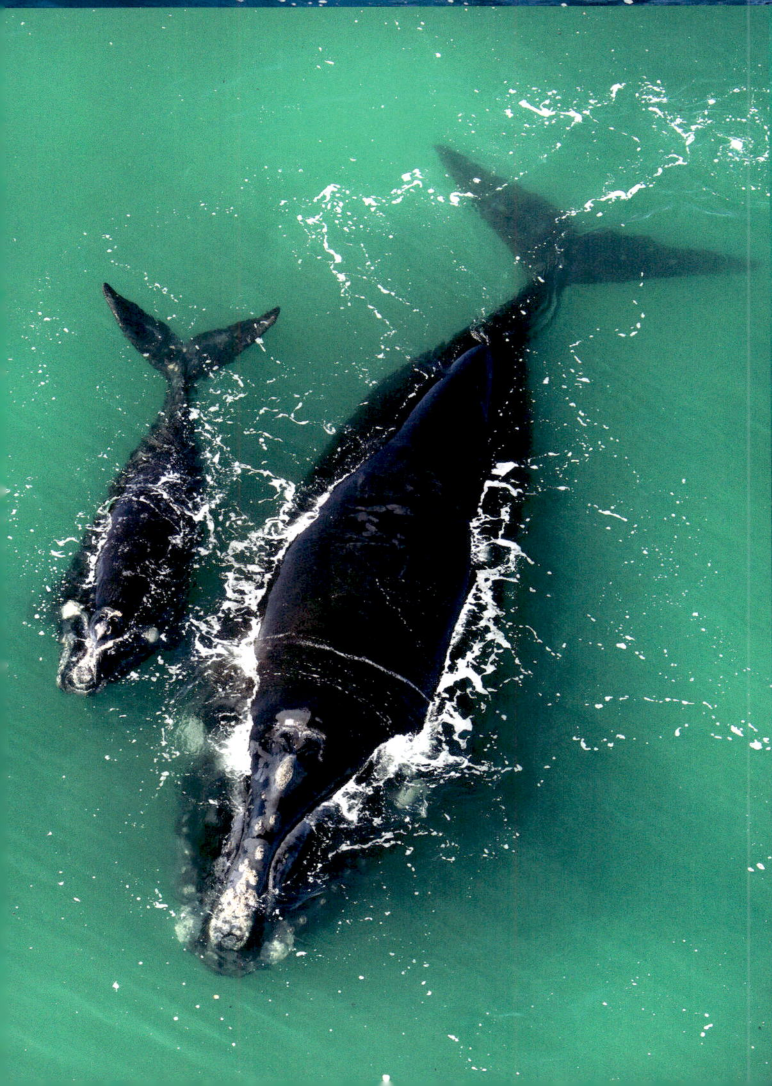

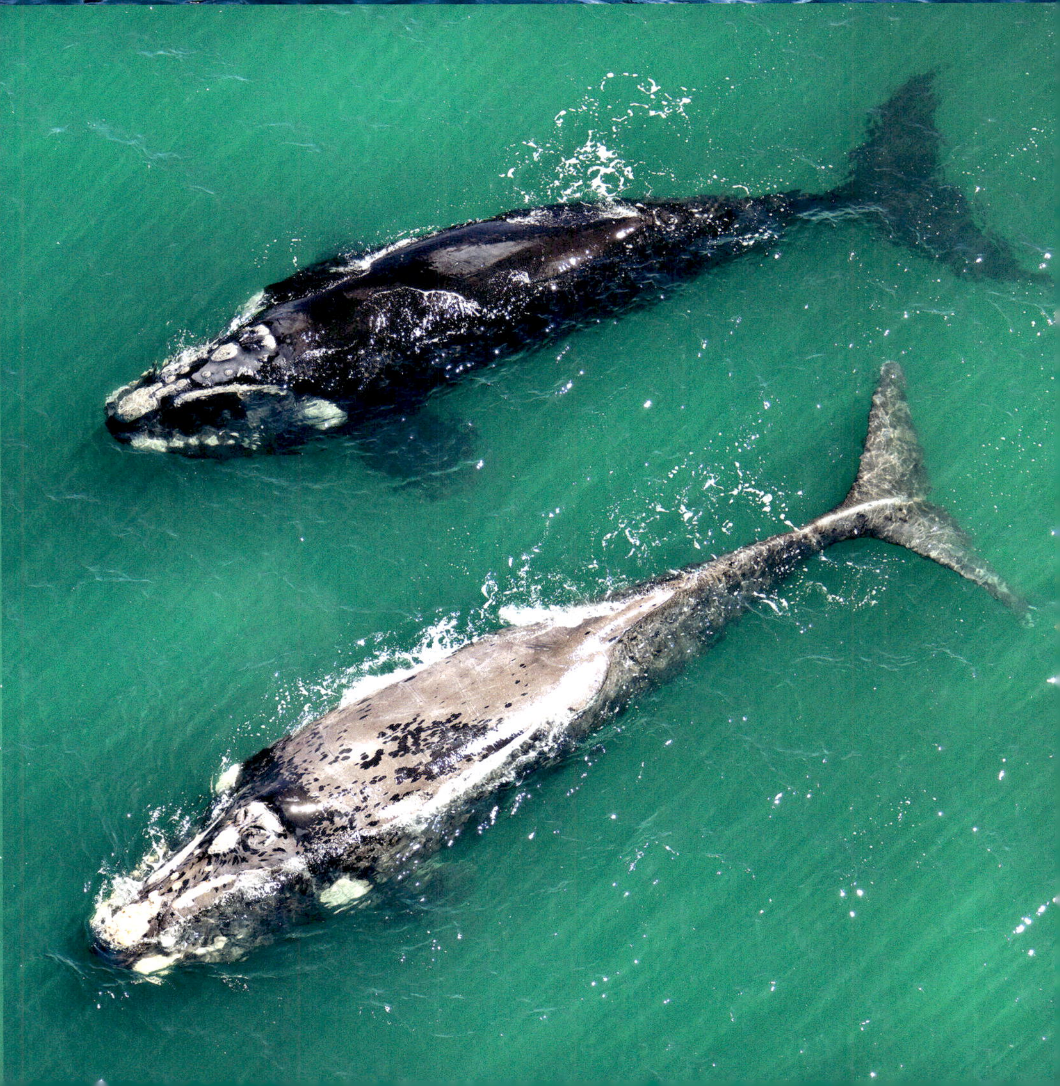

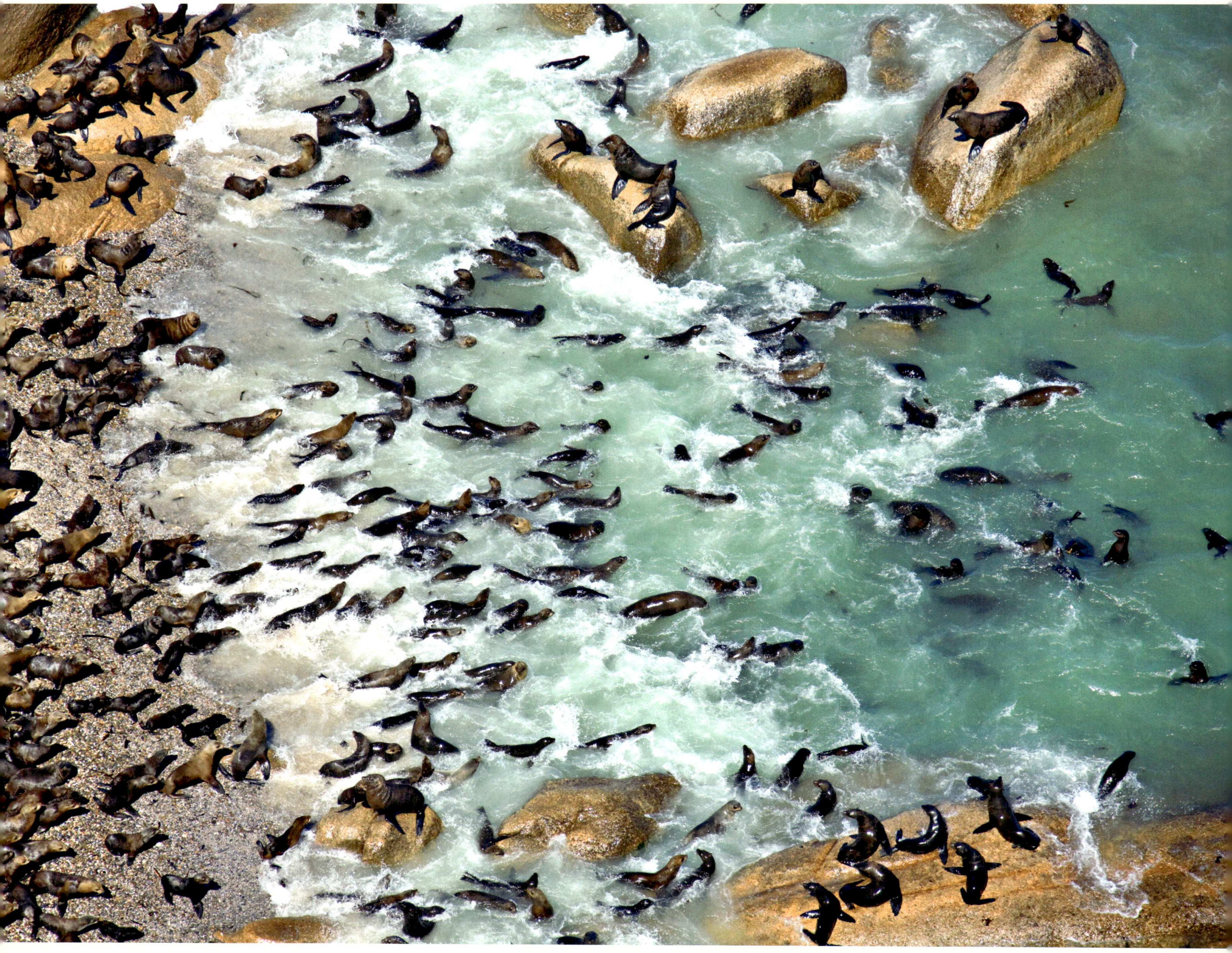

←← Whales close to the shore
← Seal Island, Atlantic Ocean
↓ Seaweed fishermen, Pearly Beach

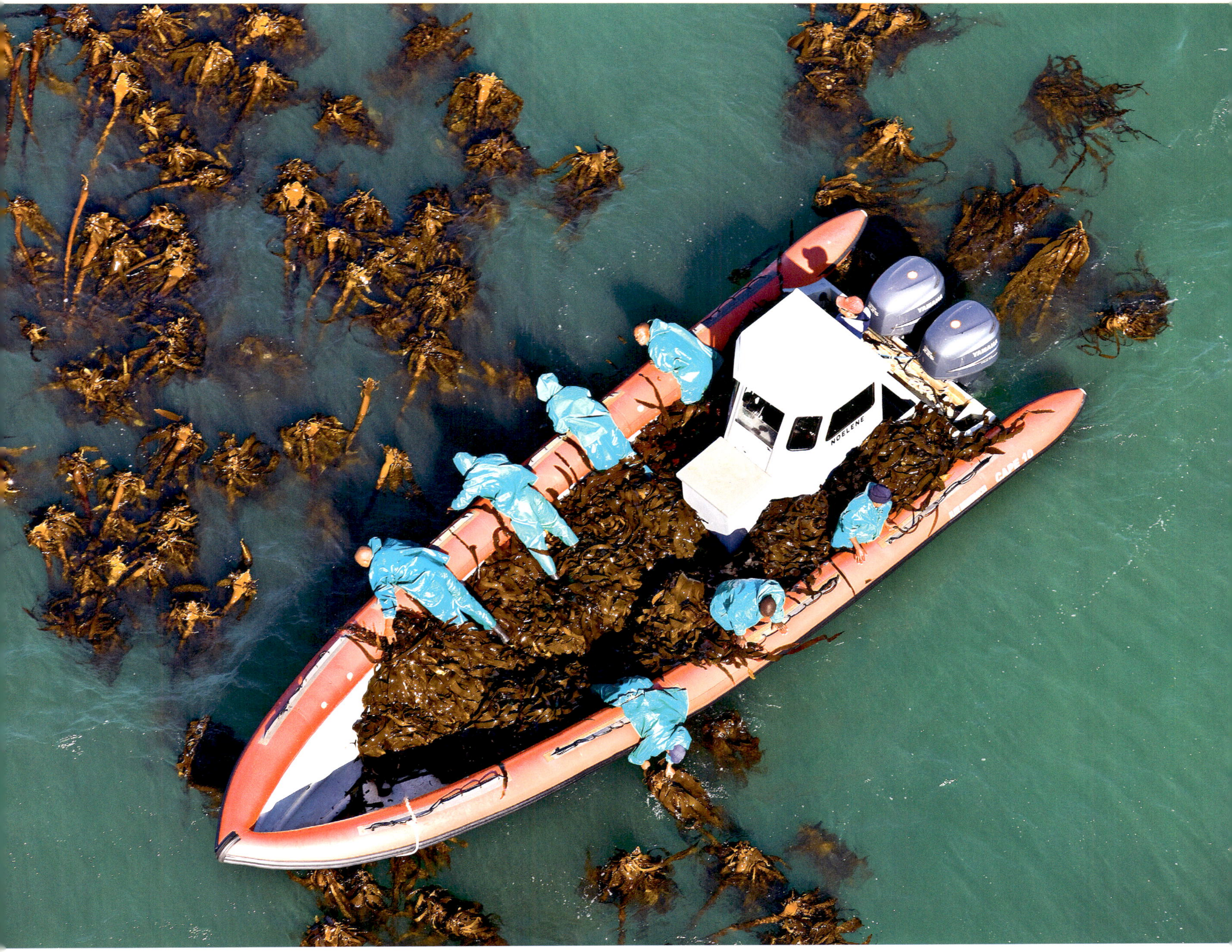

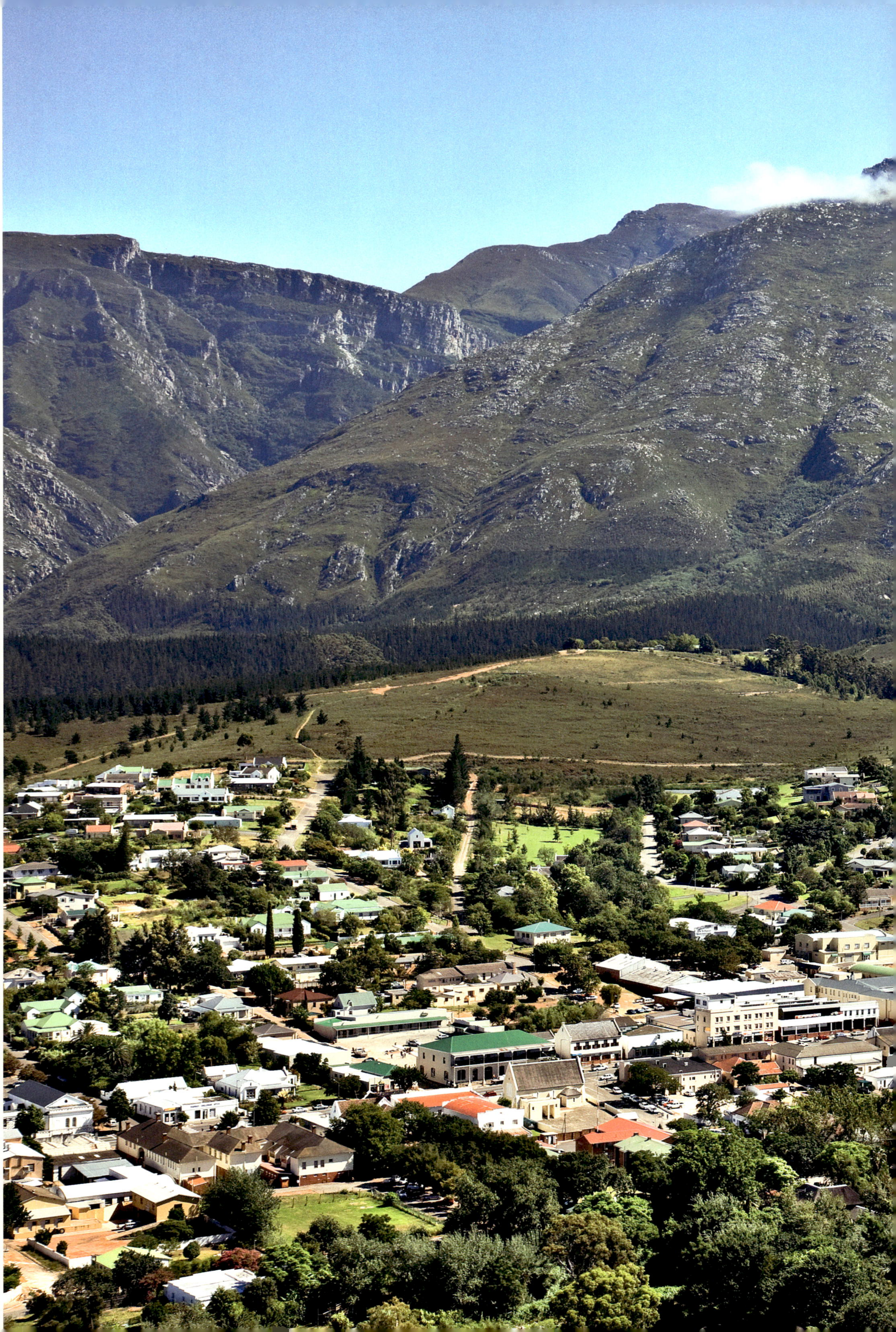

→ Swellendam

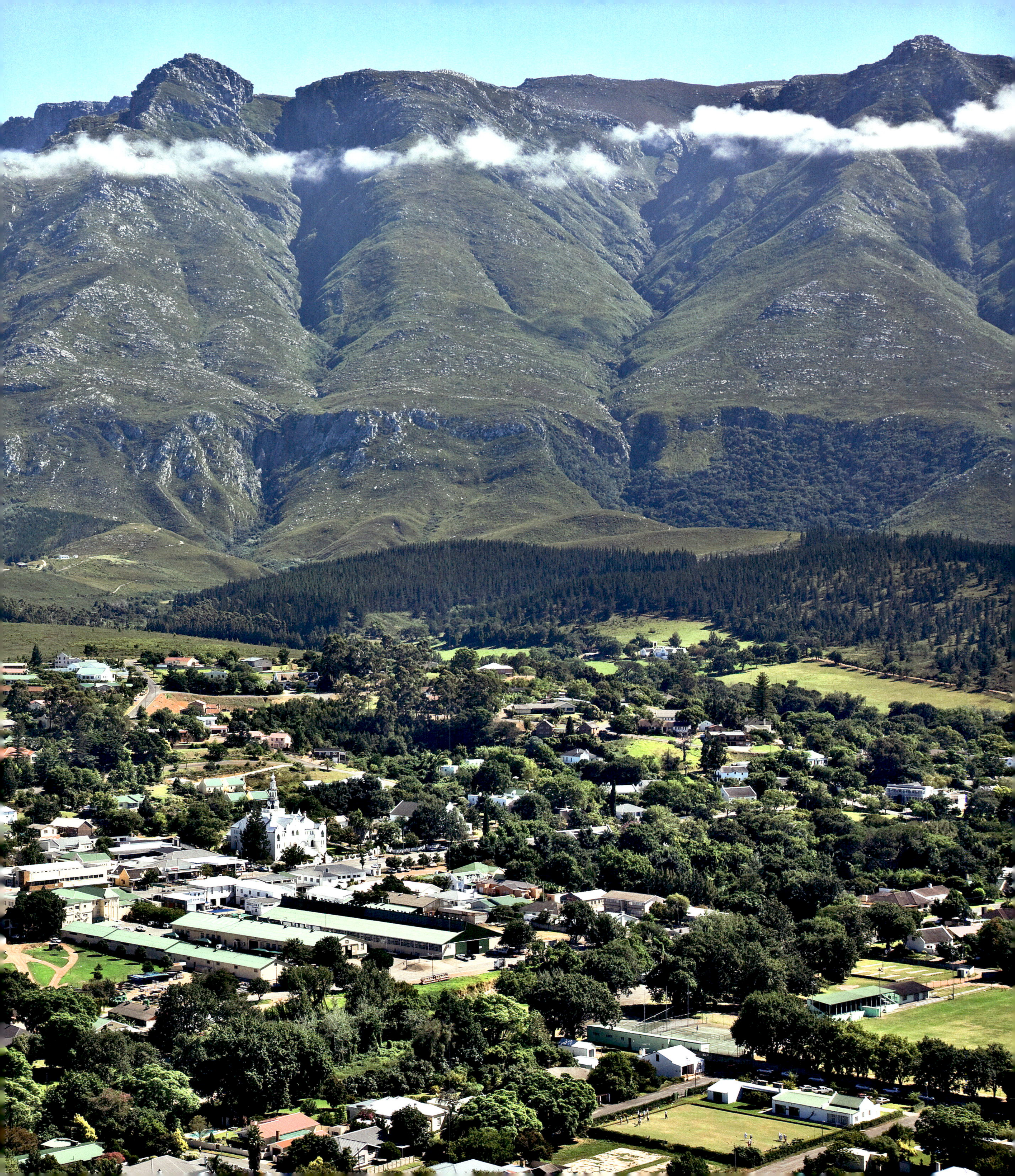

↓ Dam, Beaufort West
→ Beaufort West

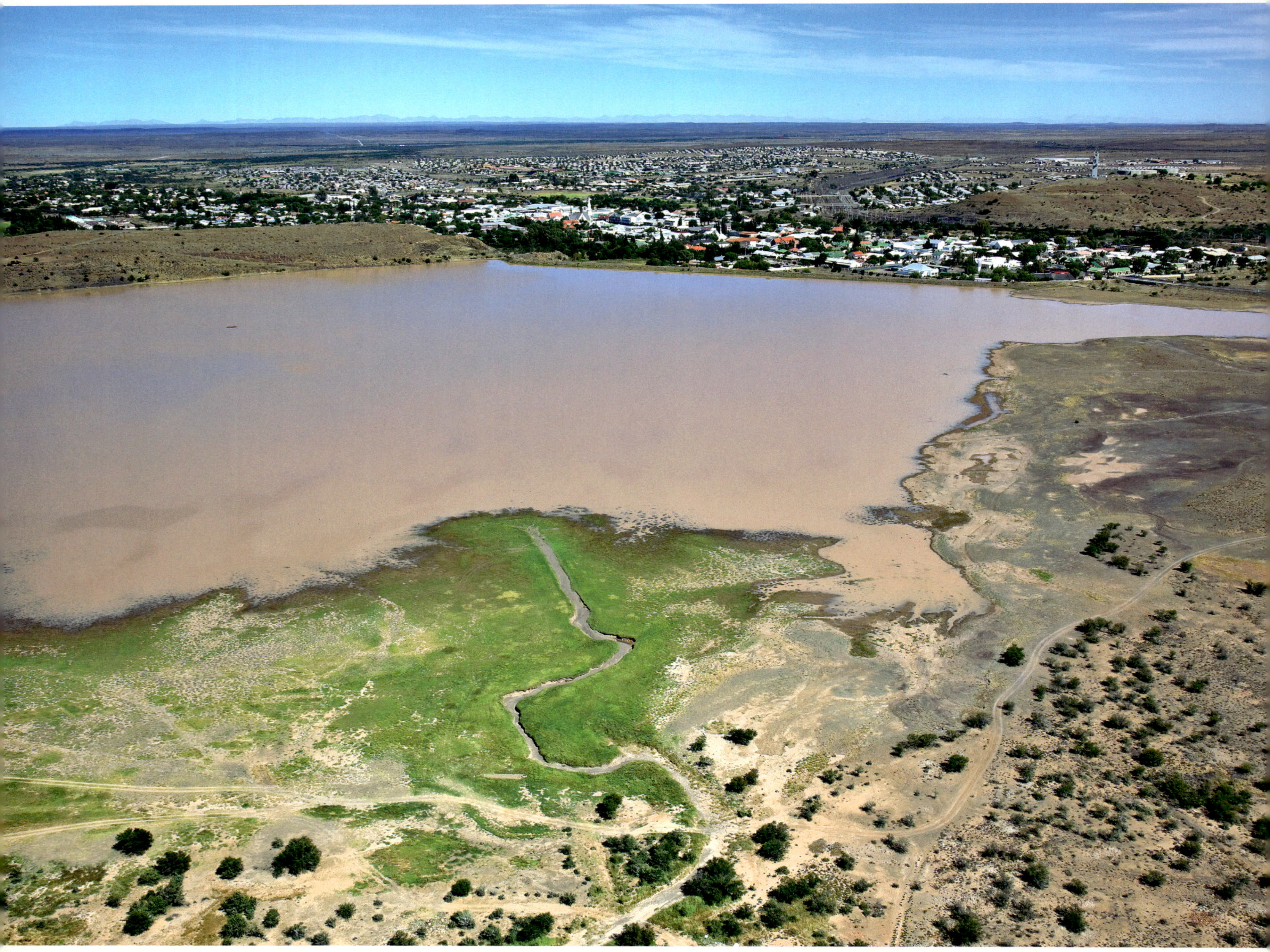

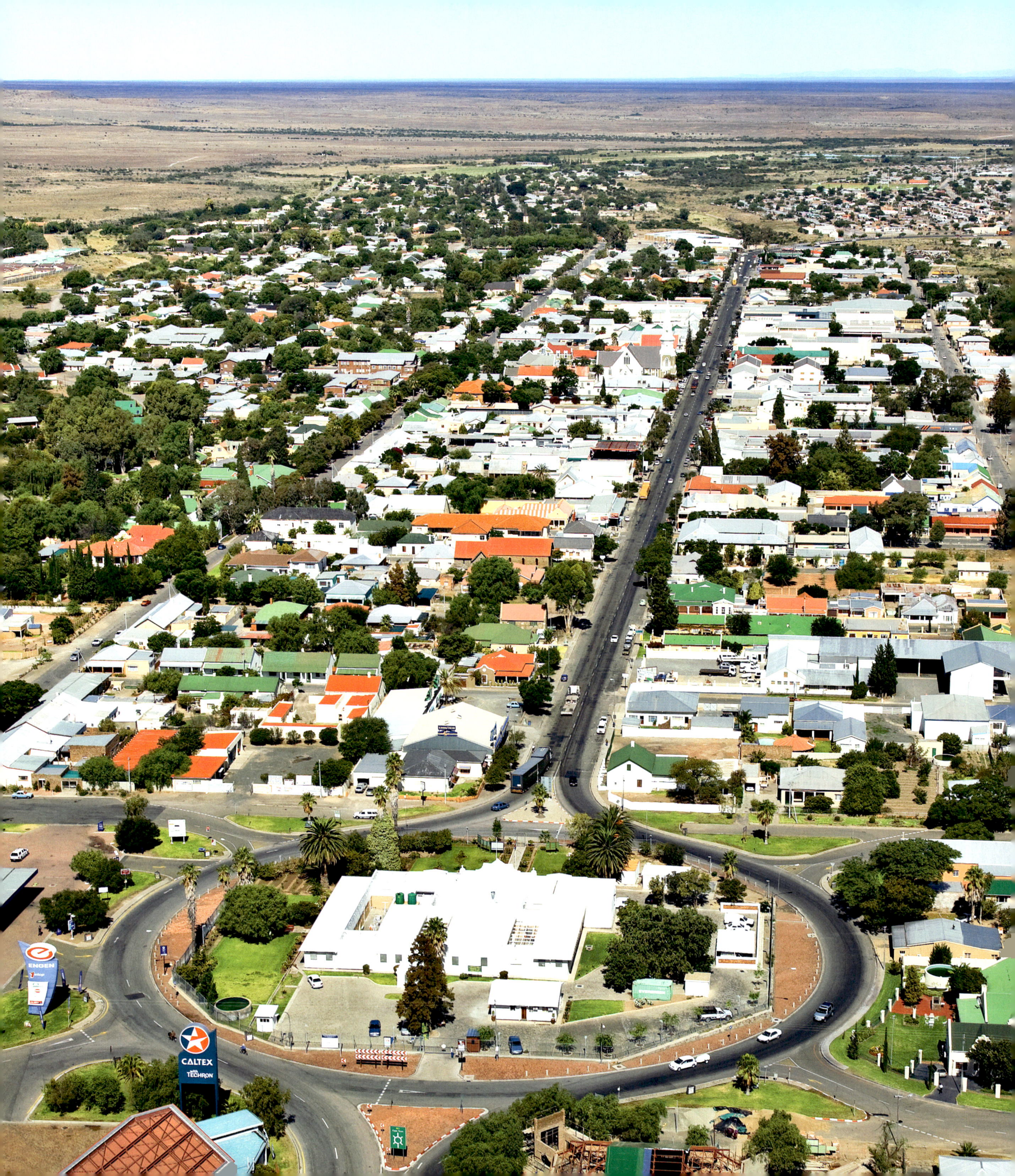
ENGEN
CALTEX
TECHRON

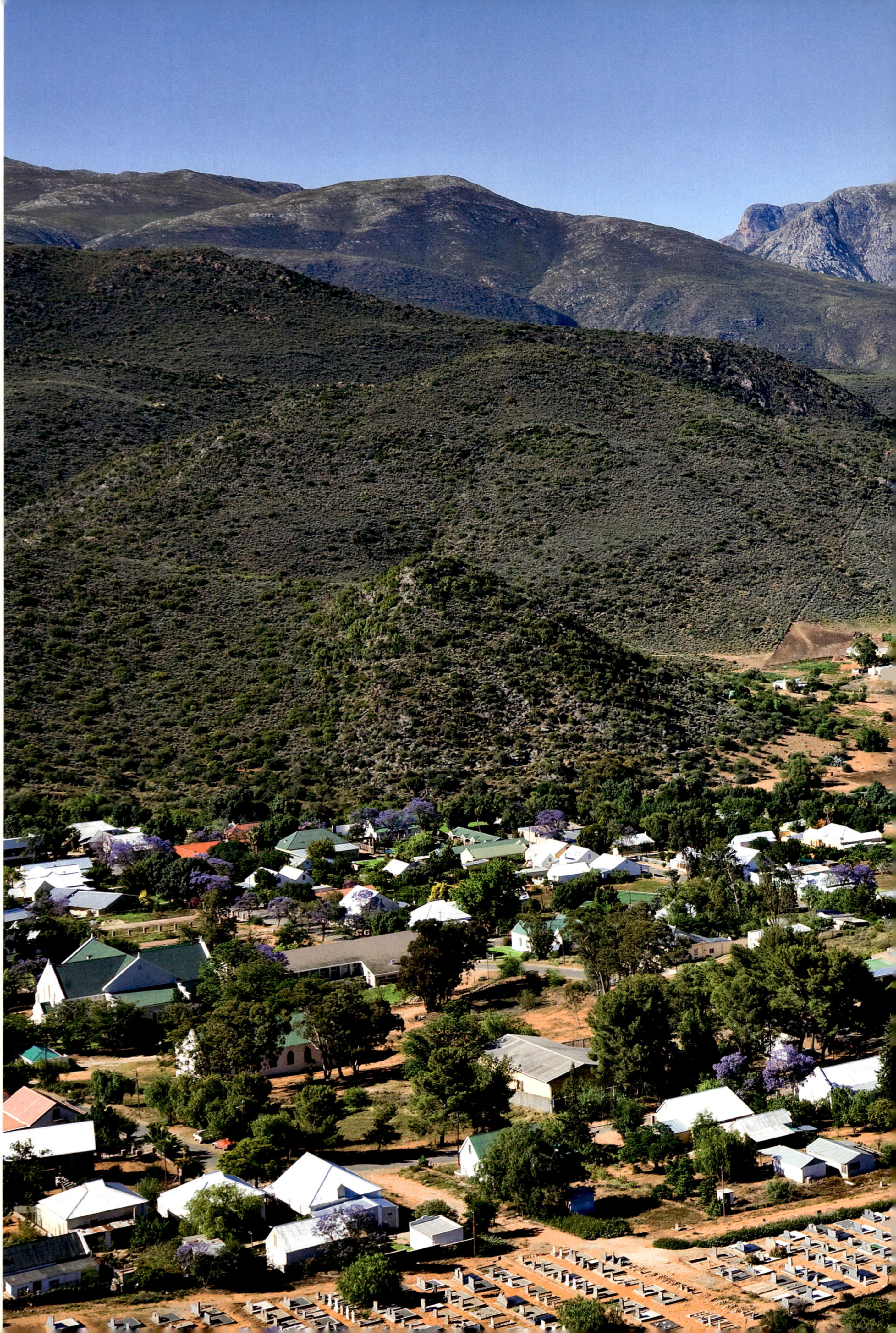

→ De Rust near Meiringspoort

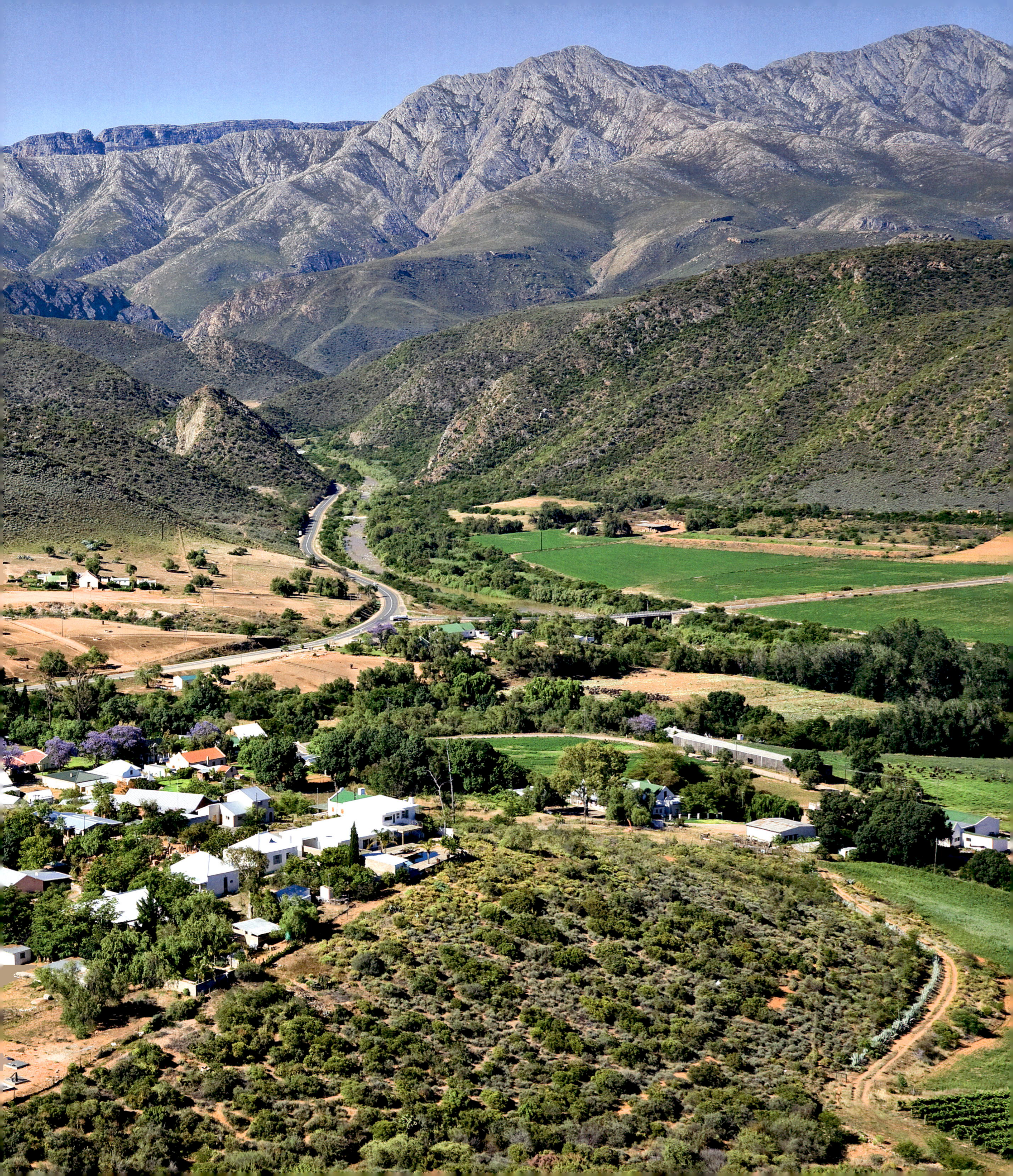

↓ Art festival, Oudtshoorn
→ Ostrich farm, Oudtshoorn

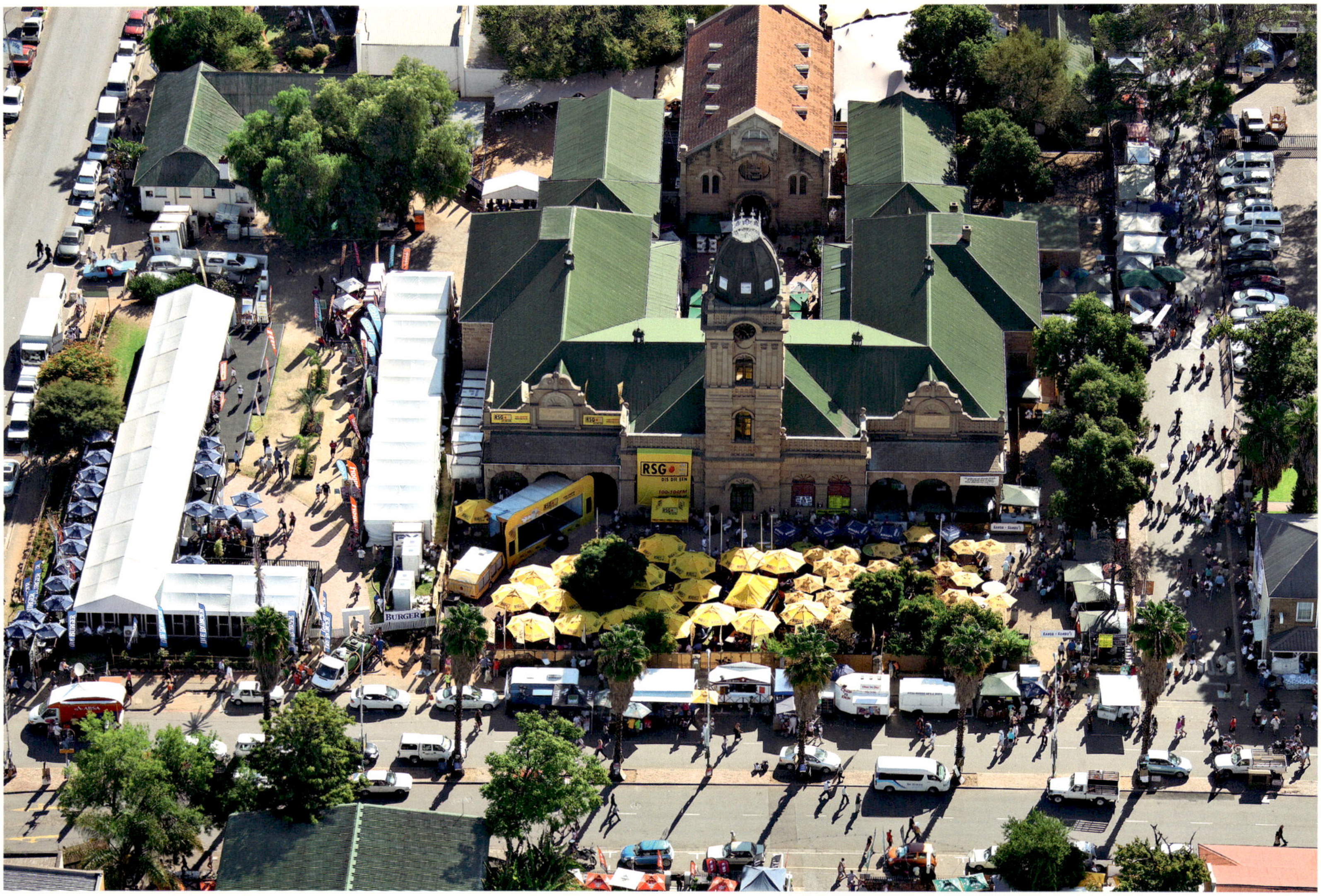

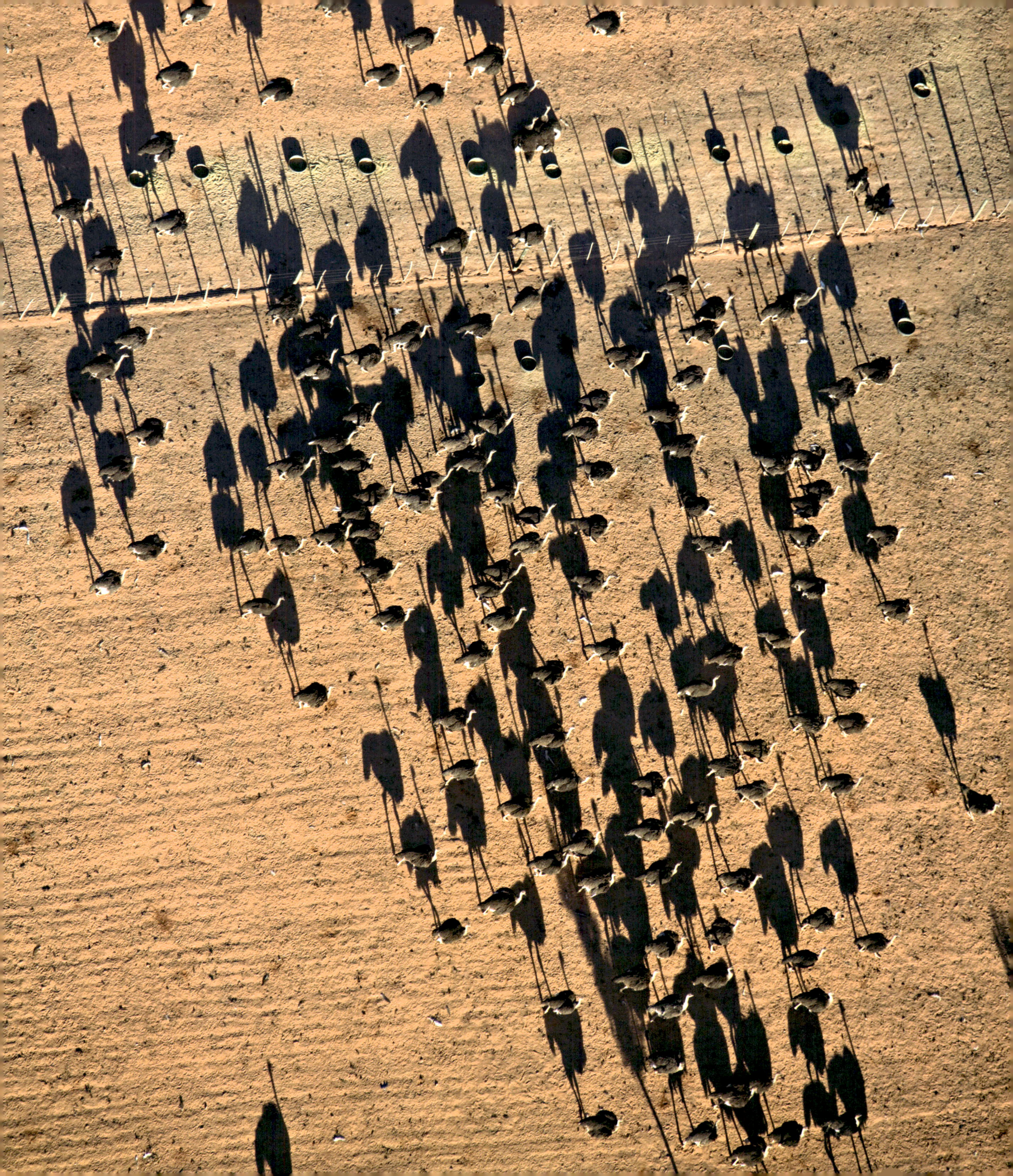

↓ Storms River

→ Ottertrail near Tsitsikamma

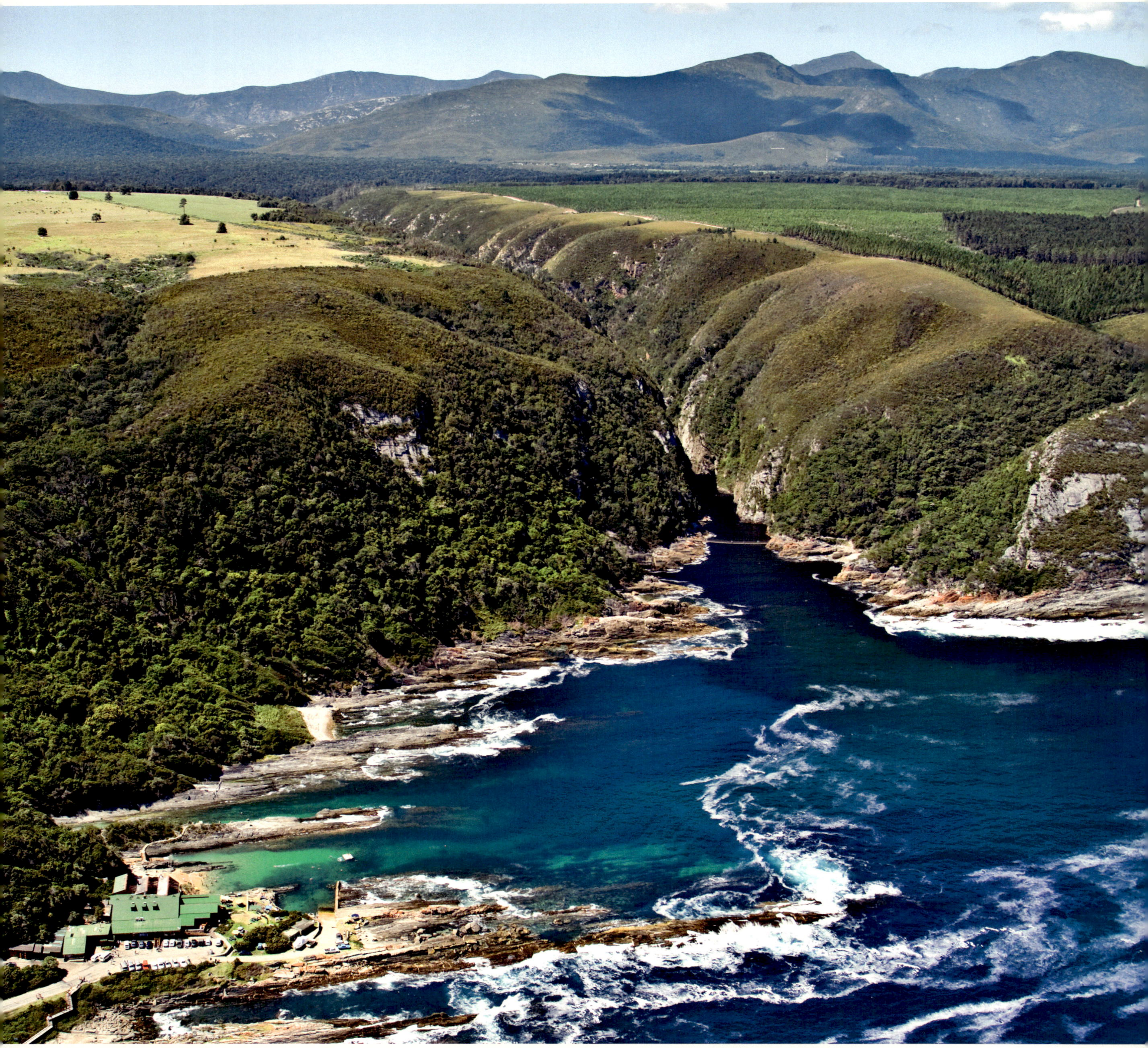

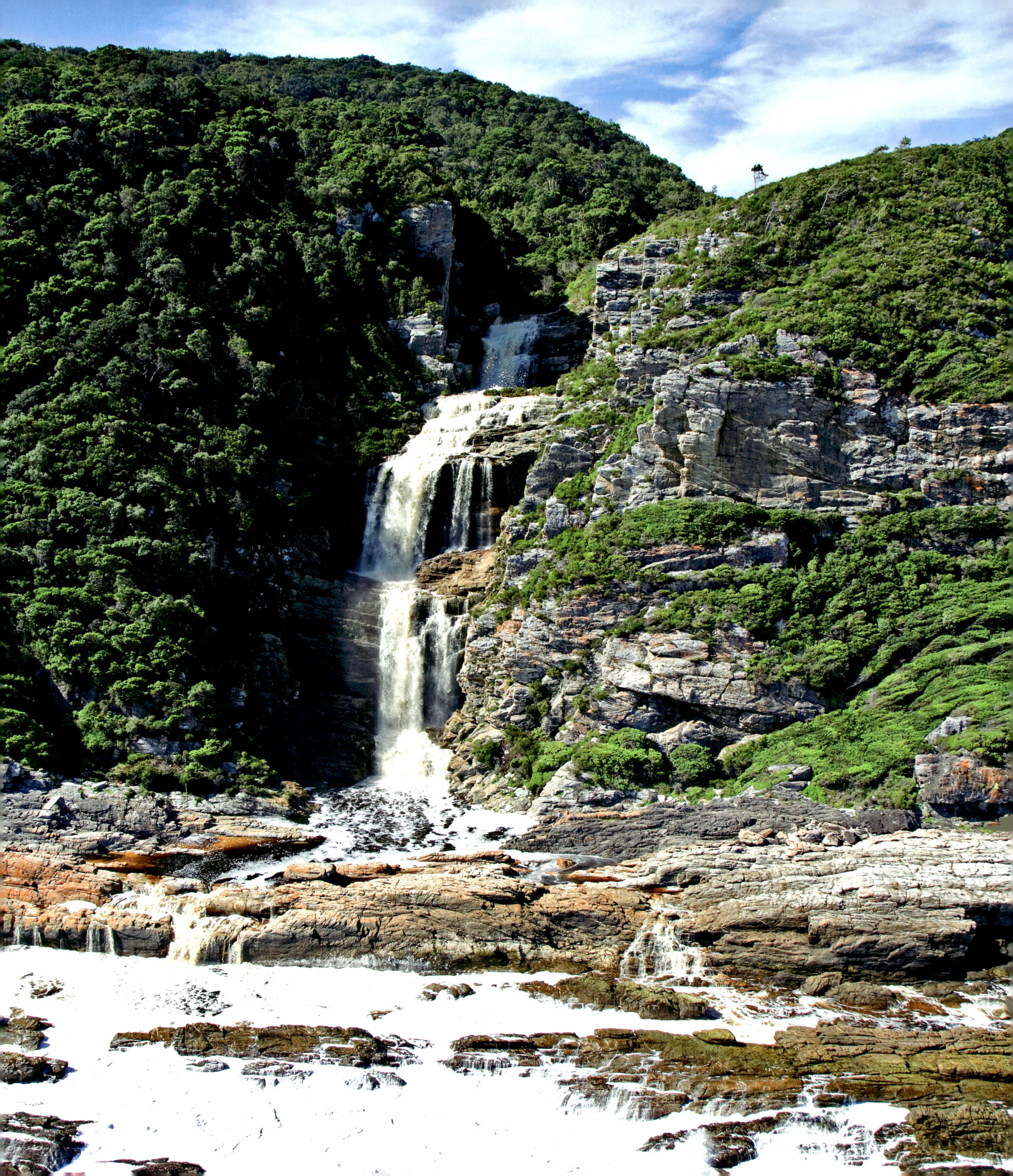

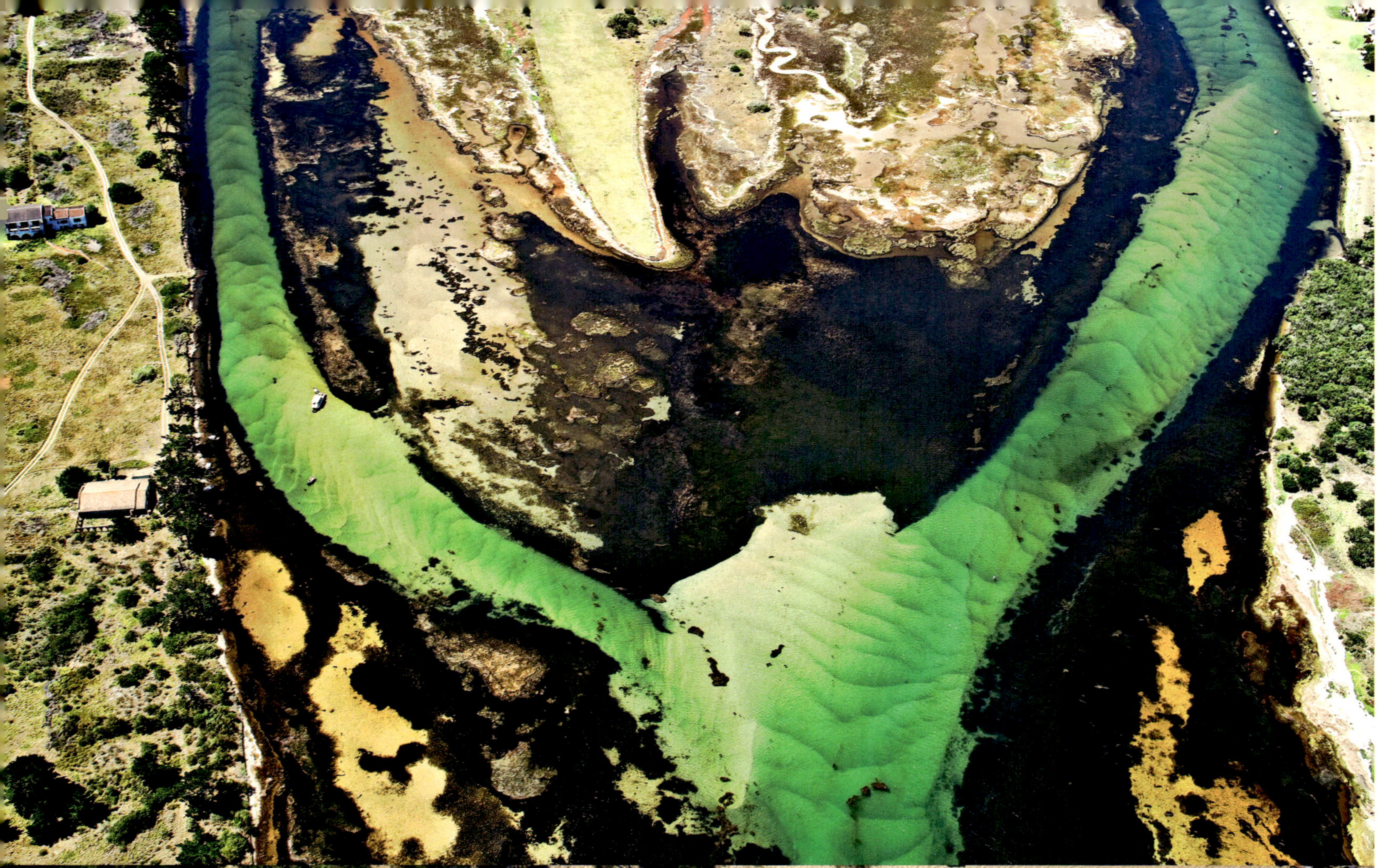
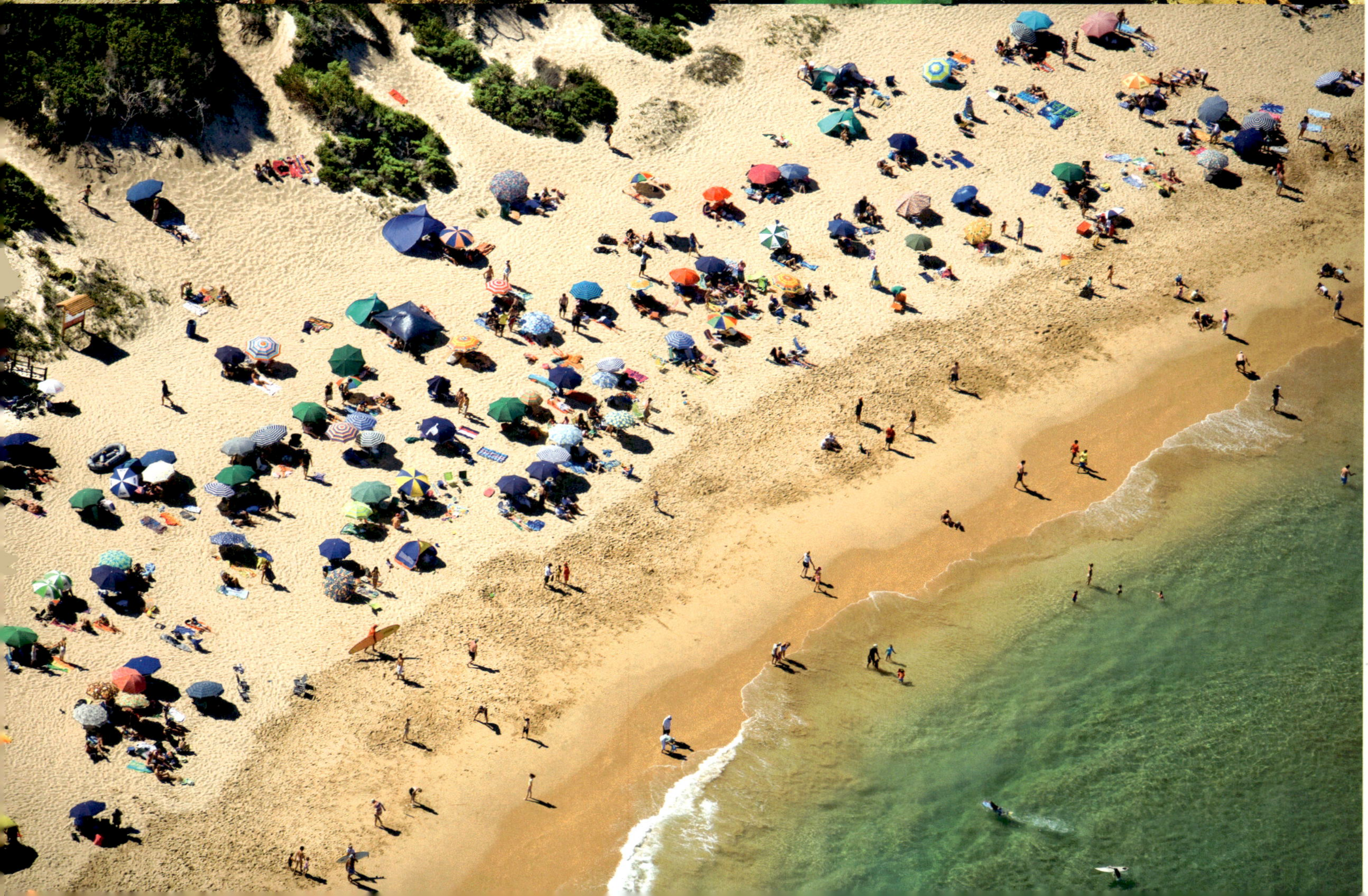

← Keurbooms River
←↓ Plettenberg Bay Beach
↓ Golf course at the mouth of Keurbooms River

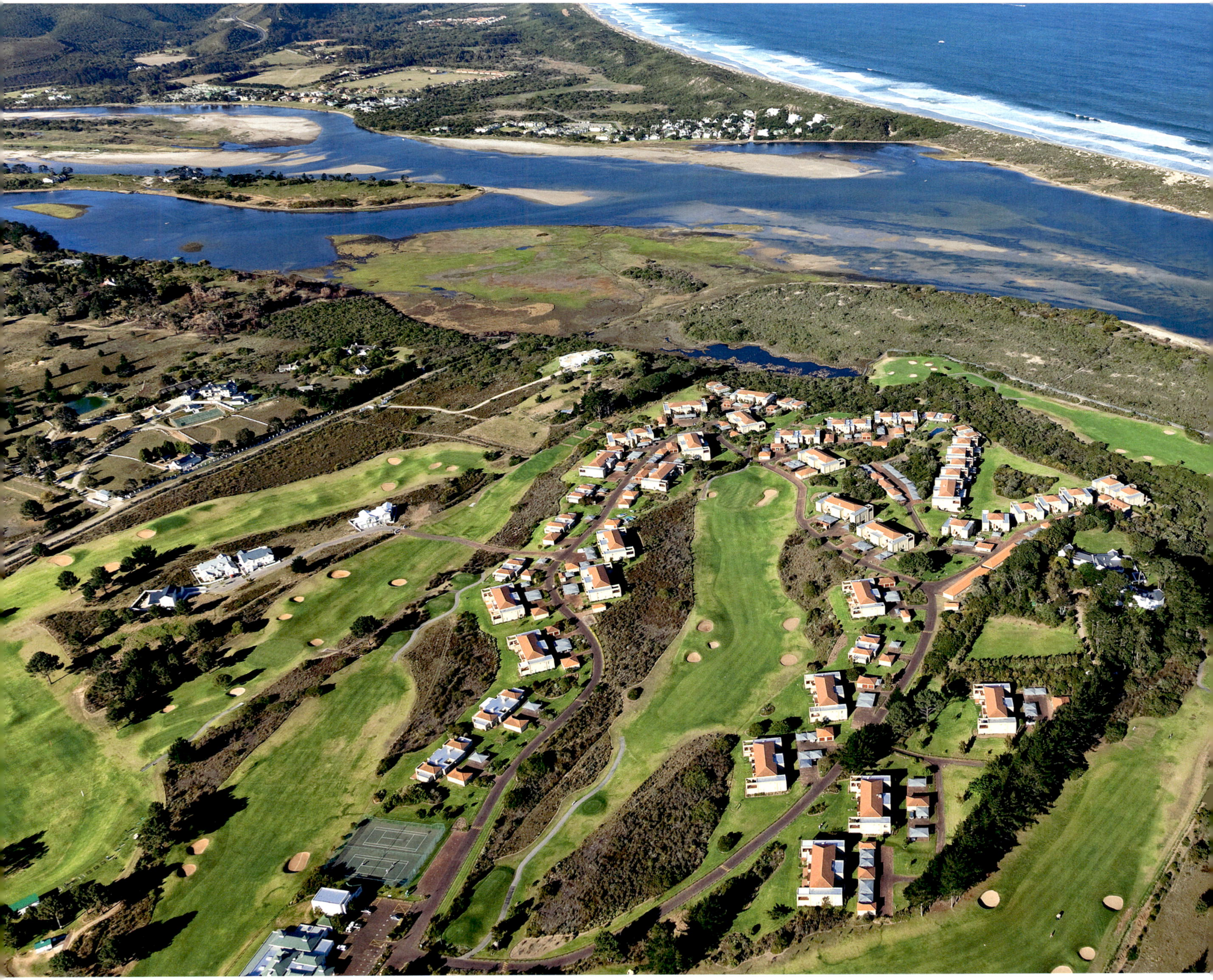

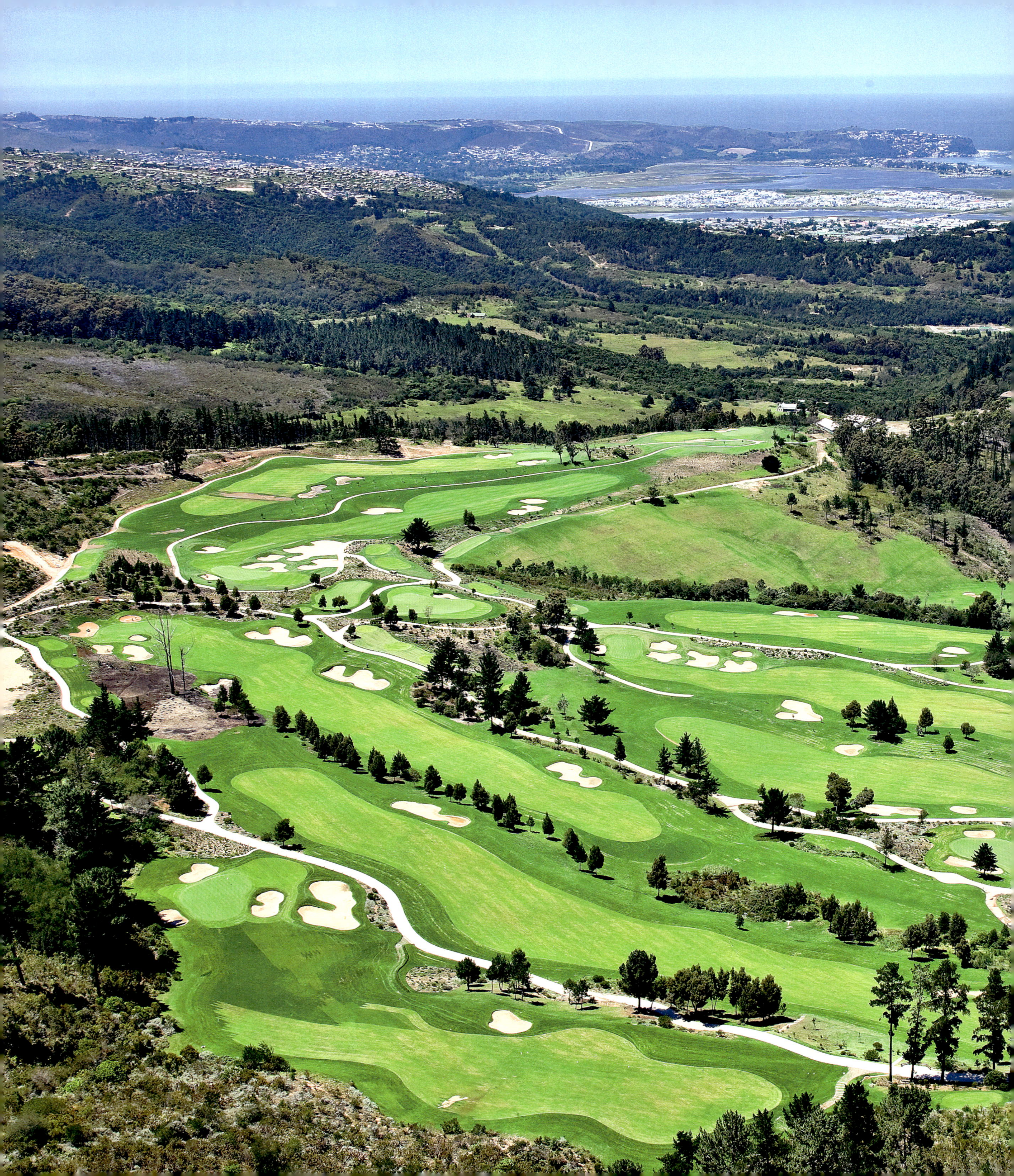

← Simola Golf Estate, Knysna
↓ The Knysna Waterfront

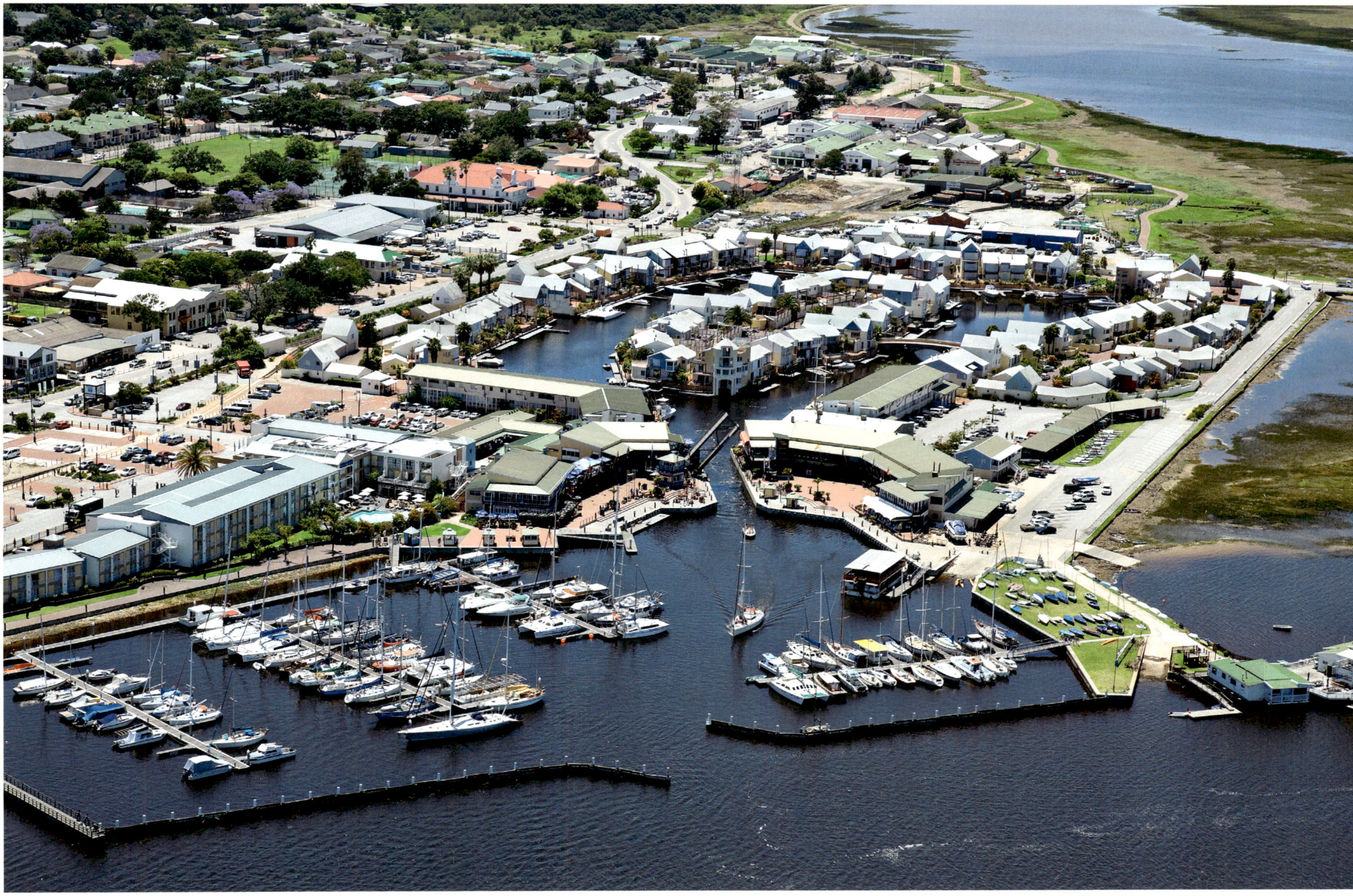

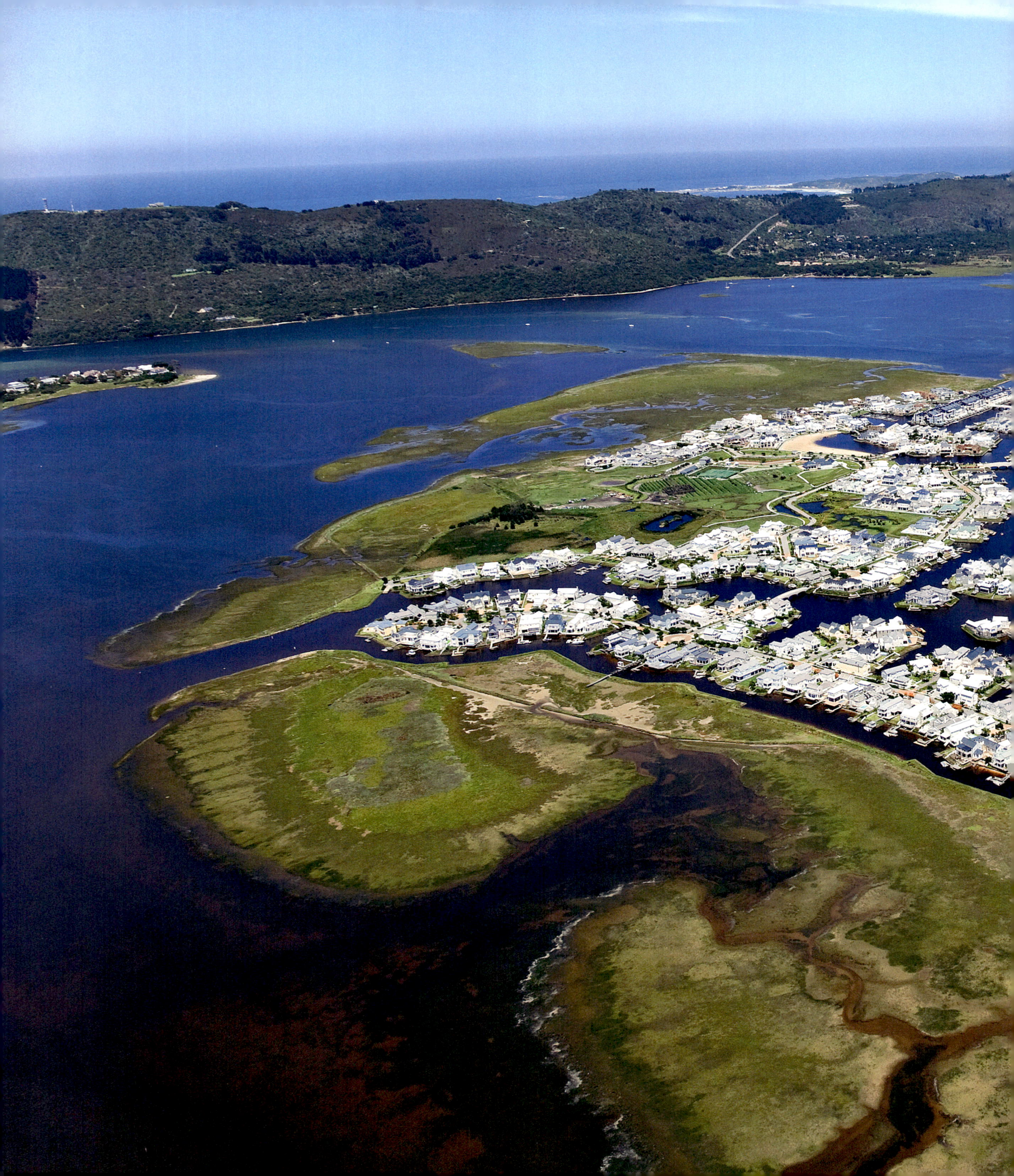

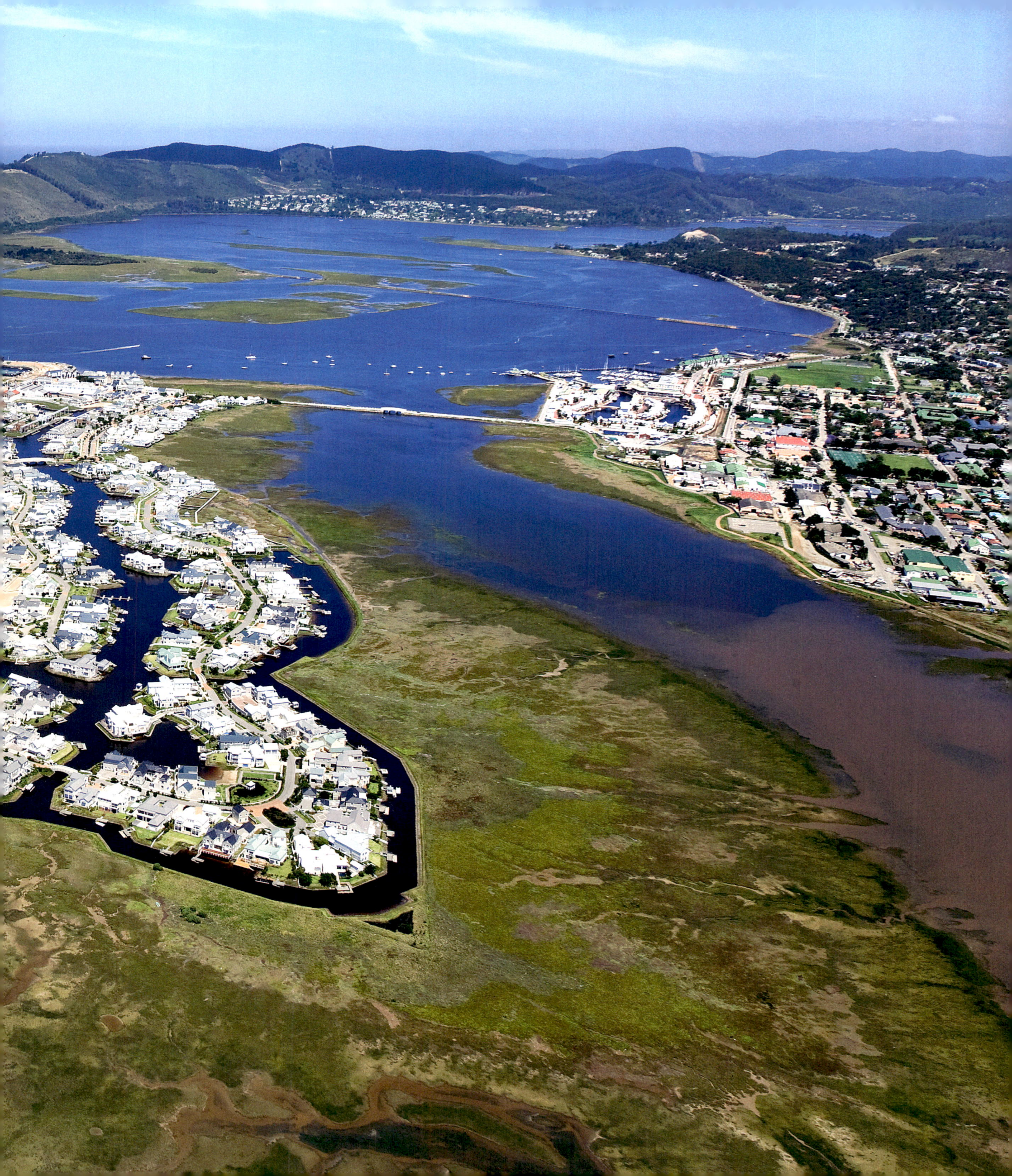

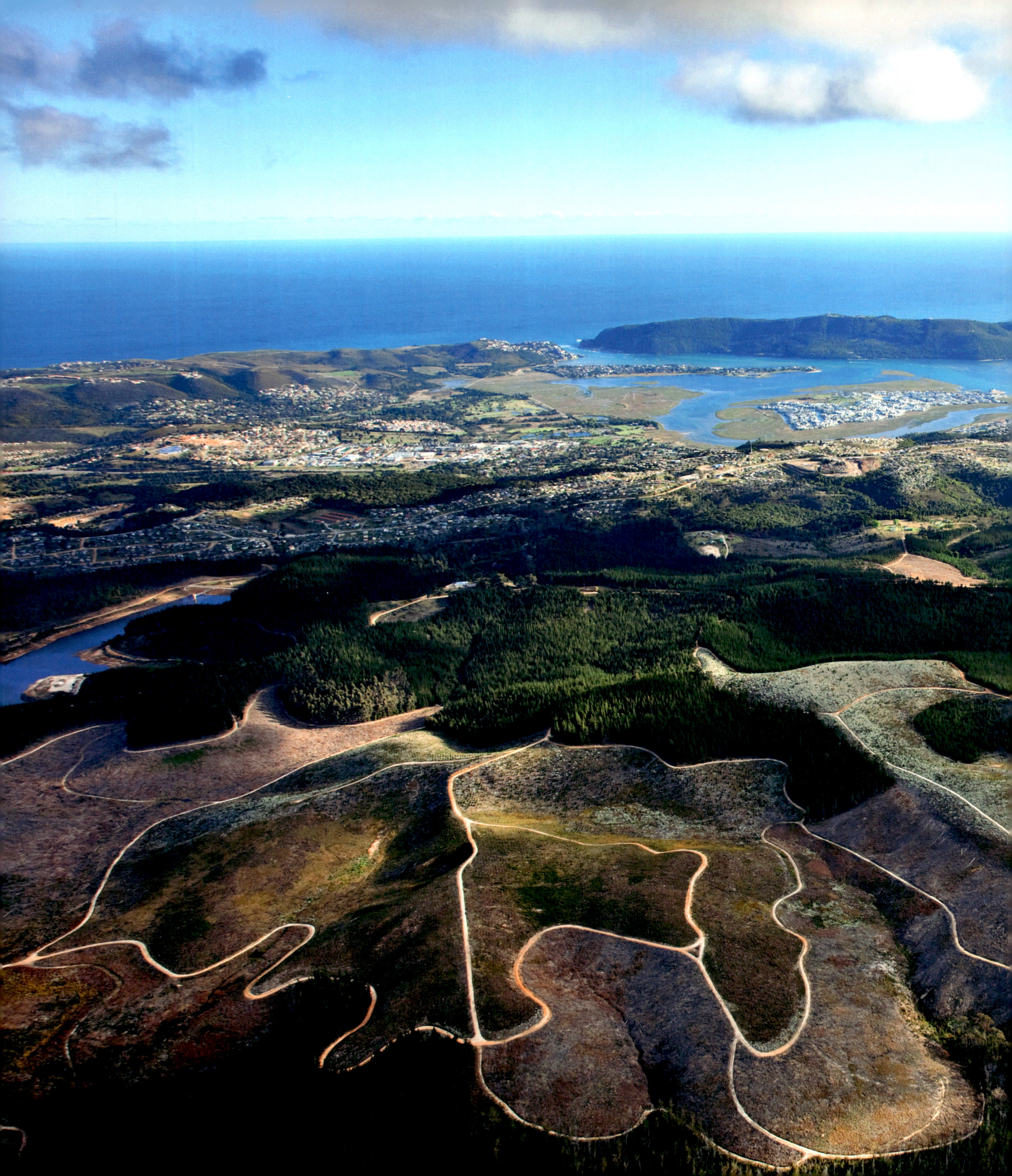

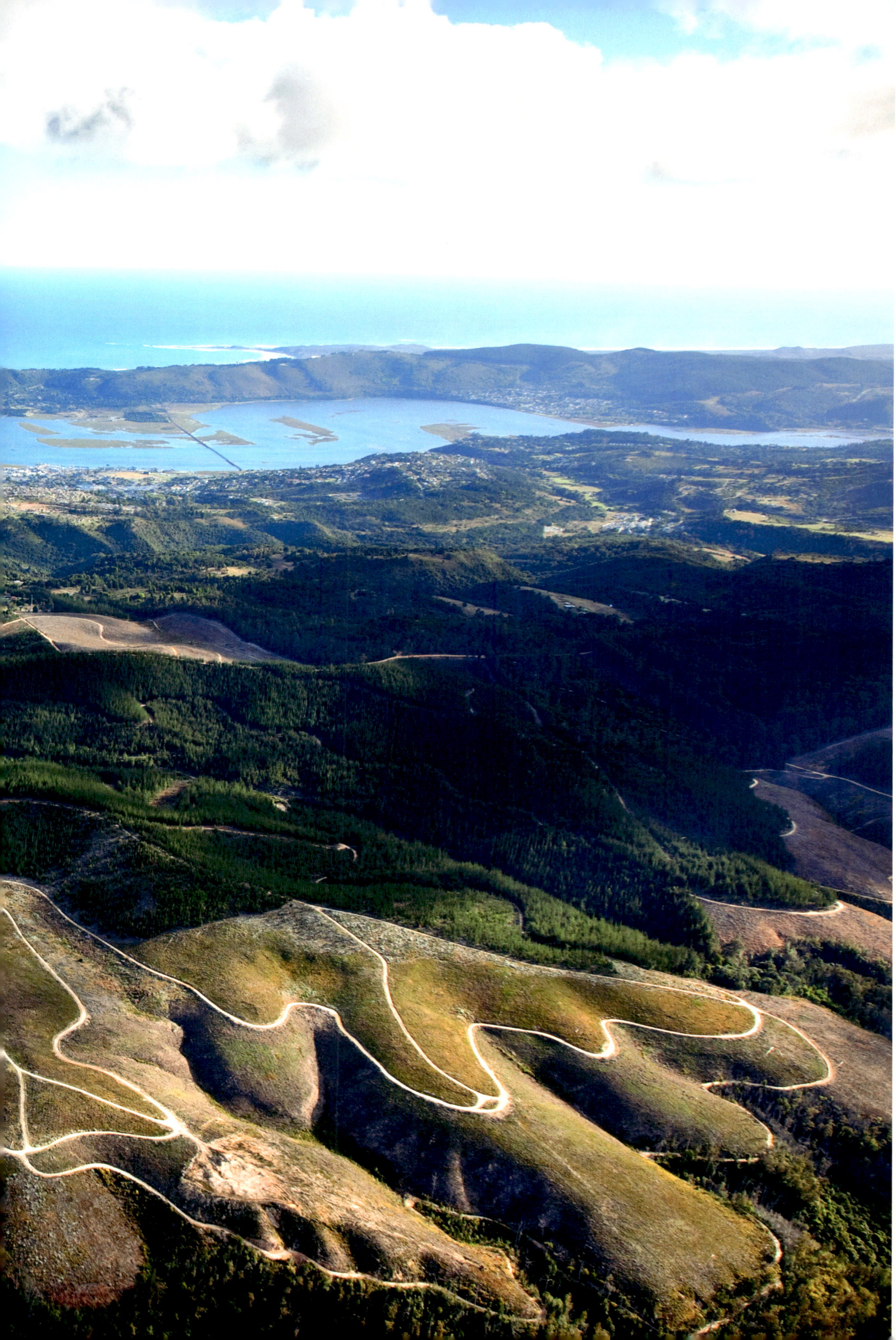

←← Knysna Lagoon with Thesen Island
← Mountain view of Knysna

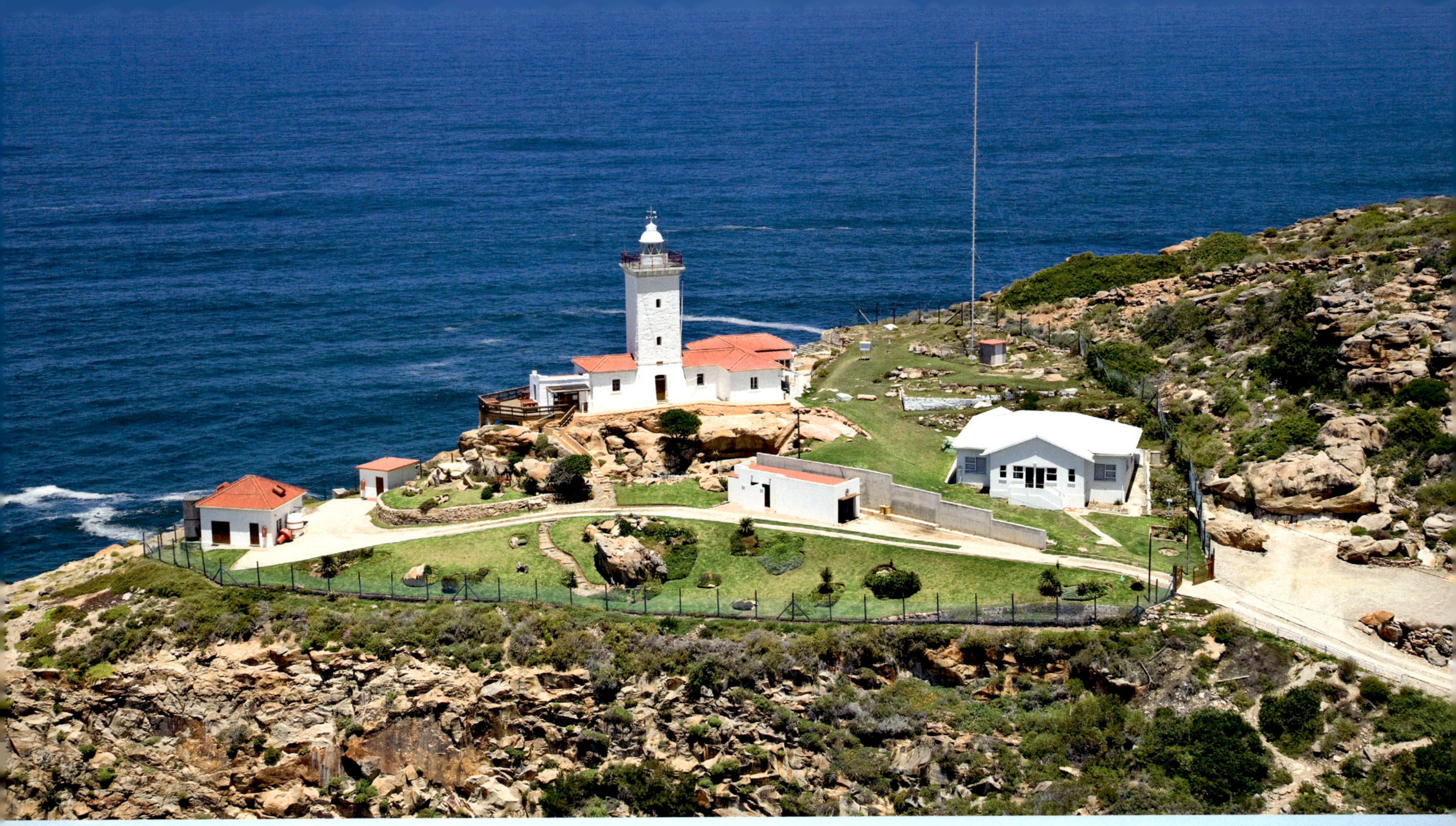

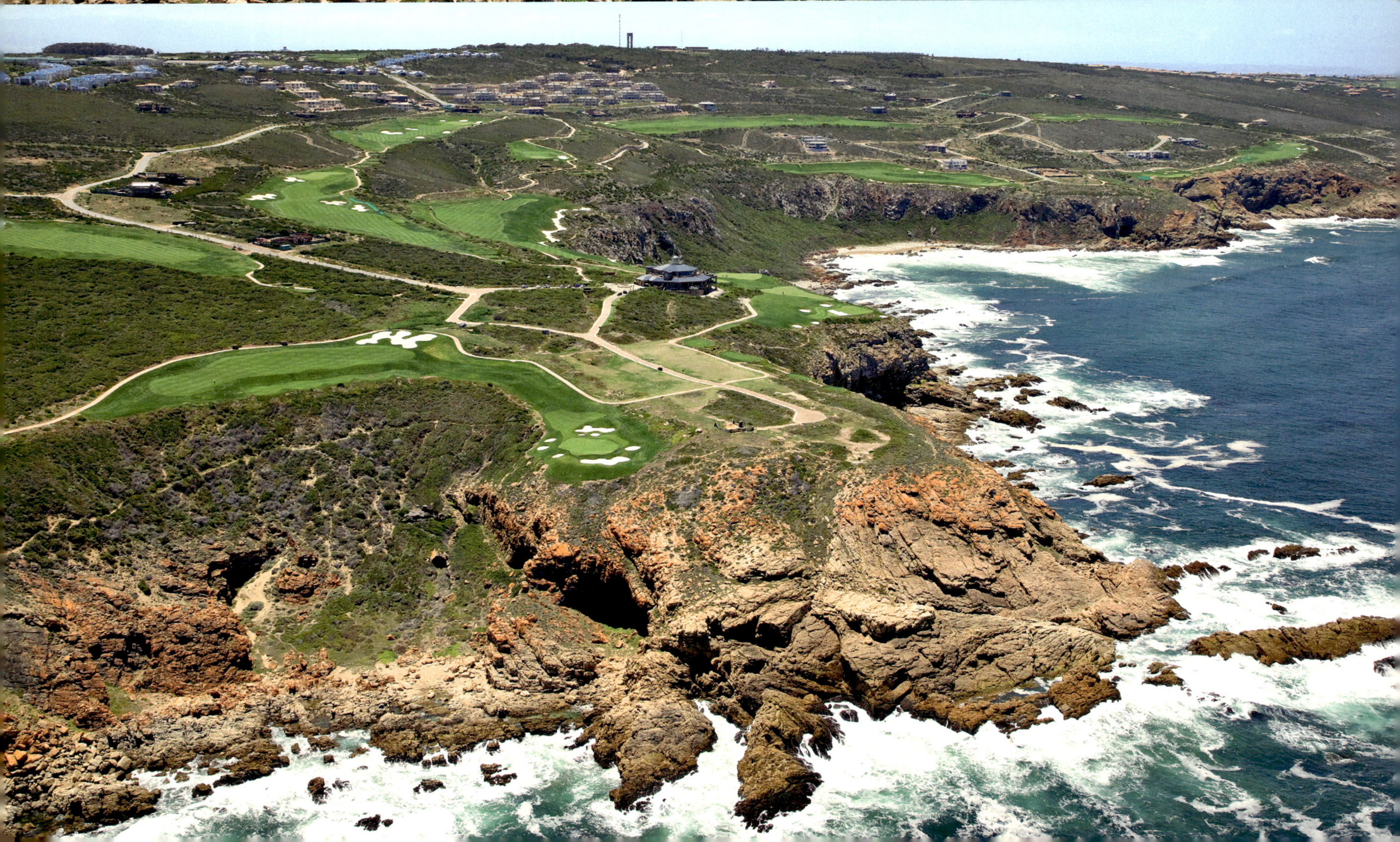

← Cape St. Blaize, Mossel Bay
←↓ Golf course on Pinnacle Point, Mossel Bay
↓ Boat racing, Mossel Bay

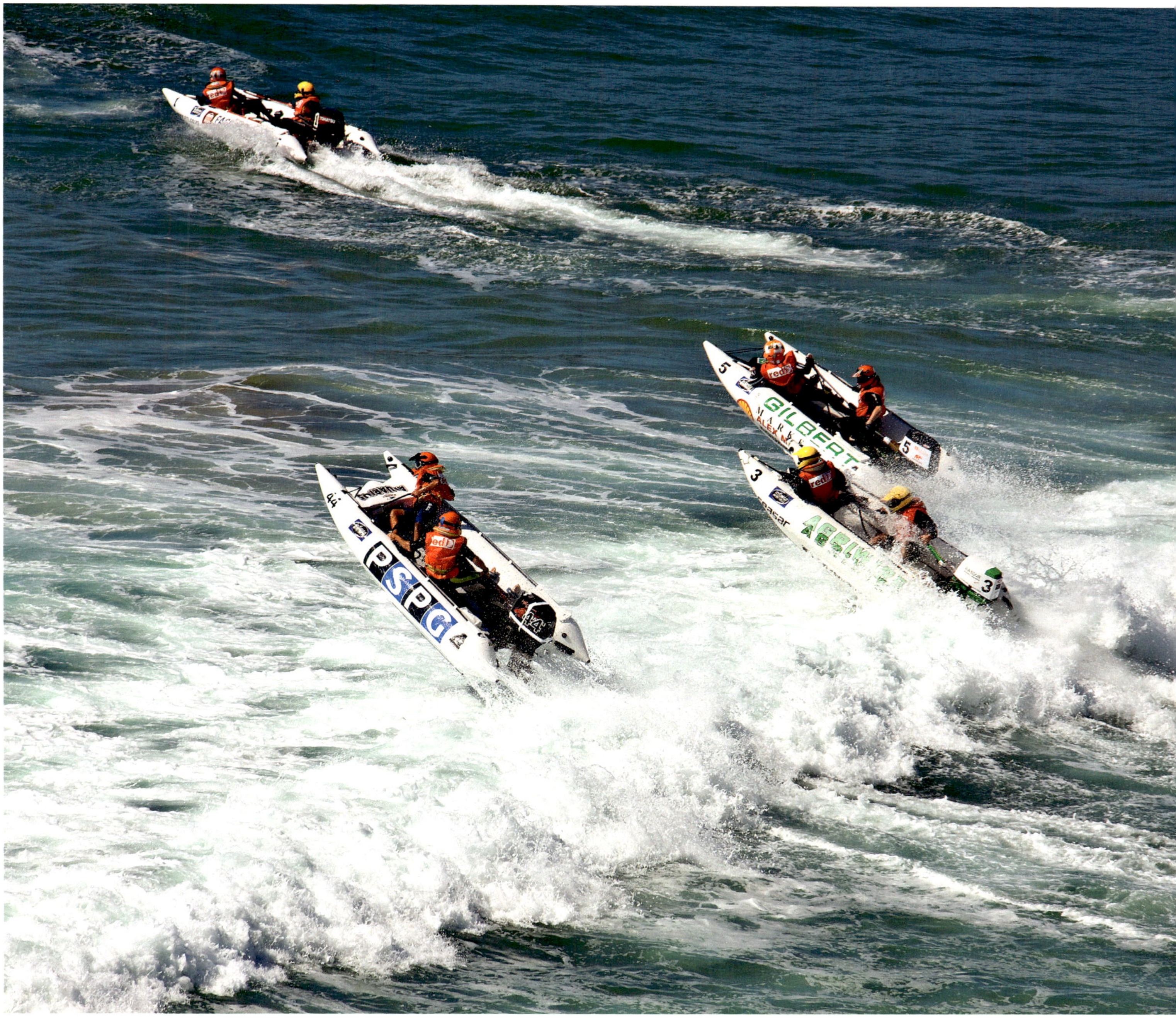

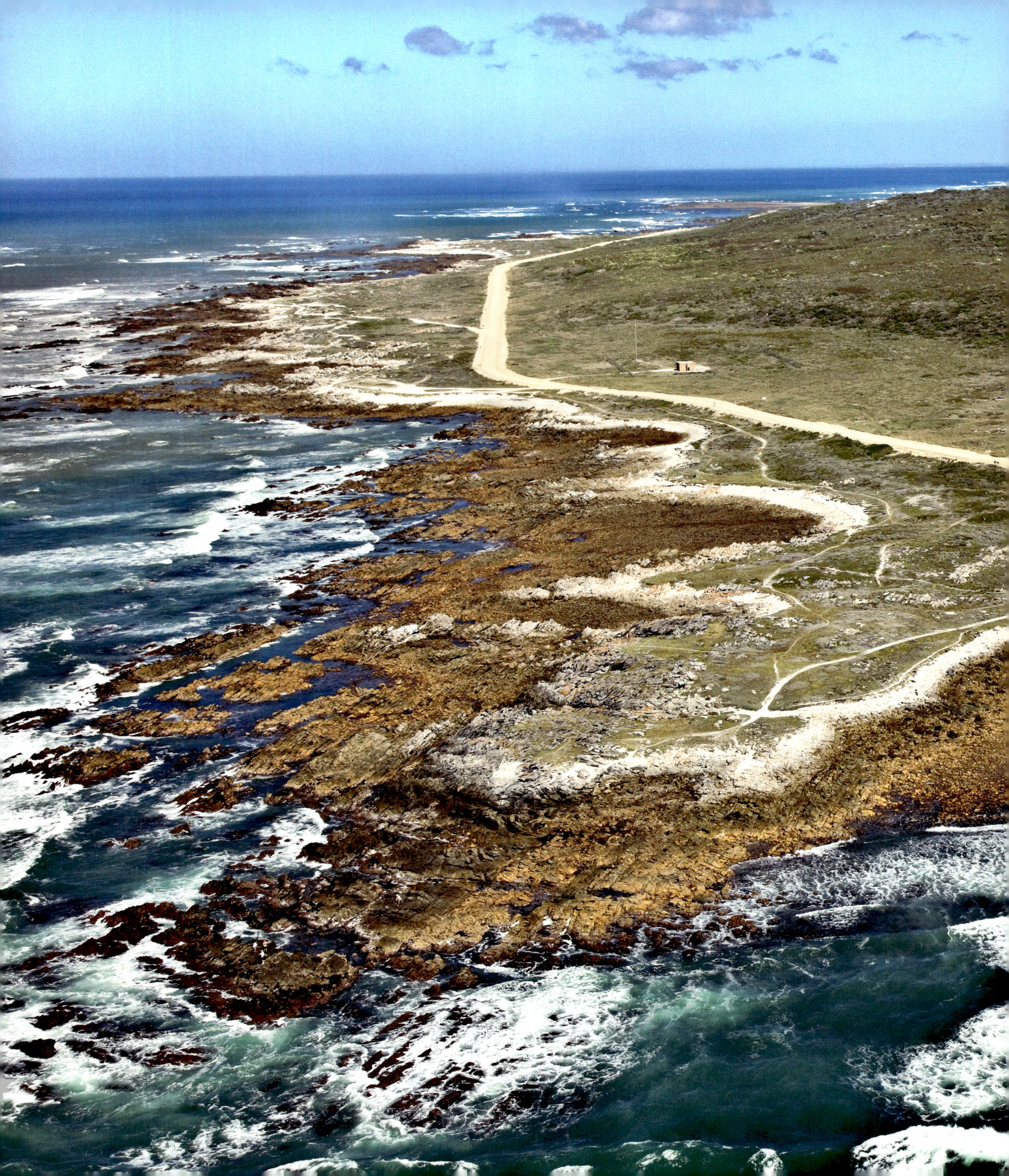

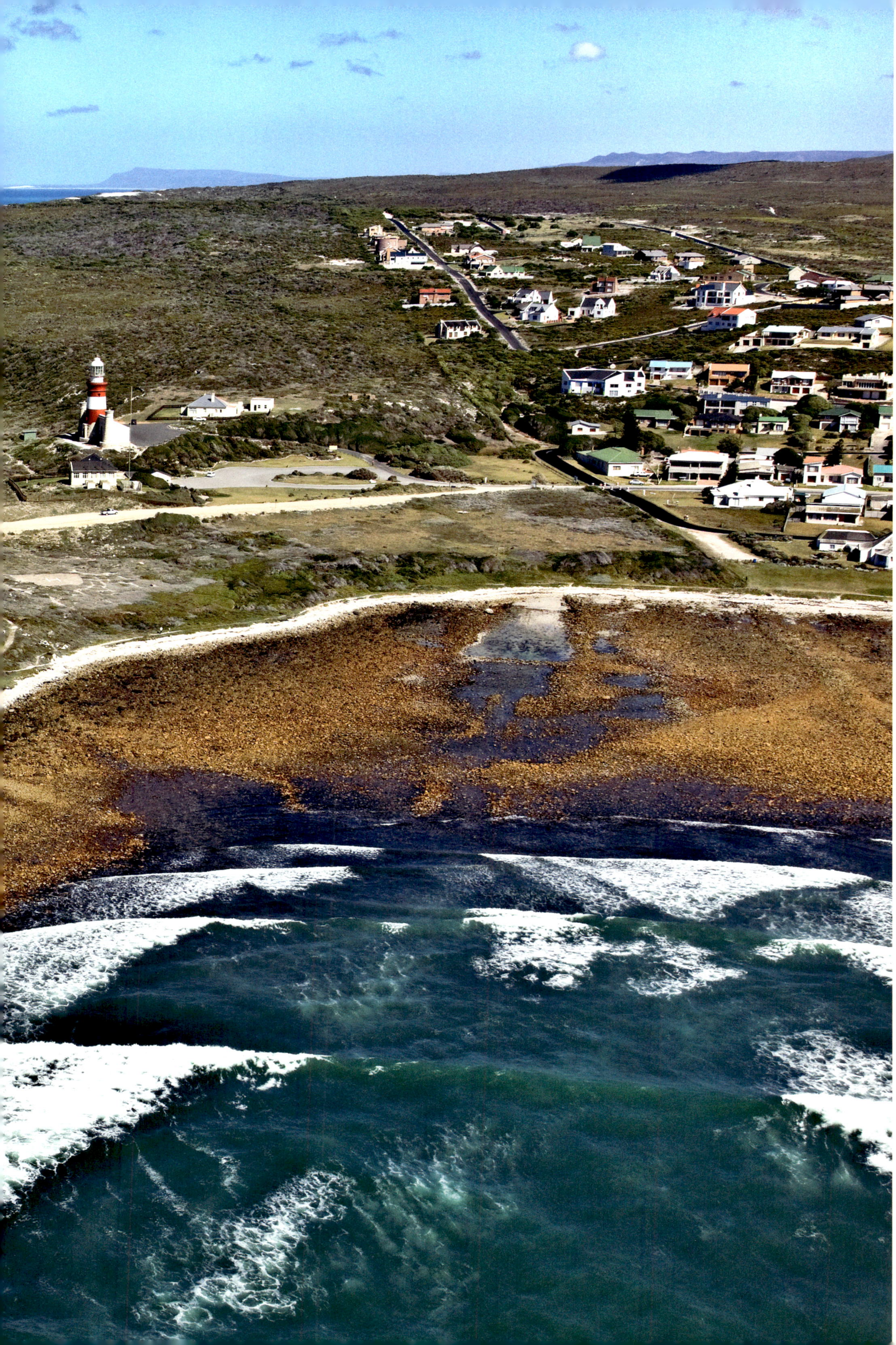

← Cape Agulhas,
southernmost tip of Africa

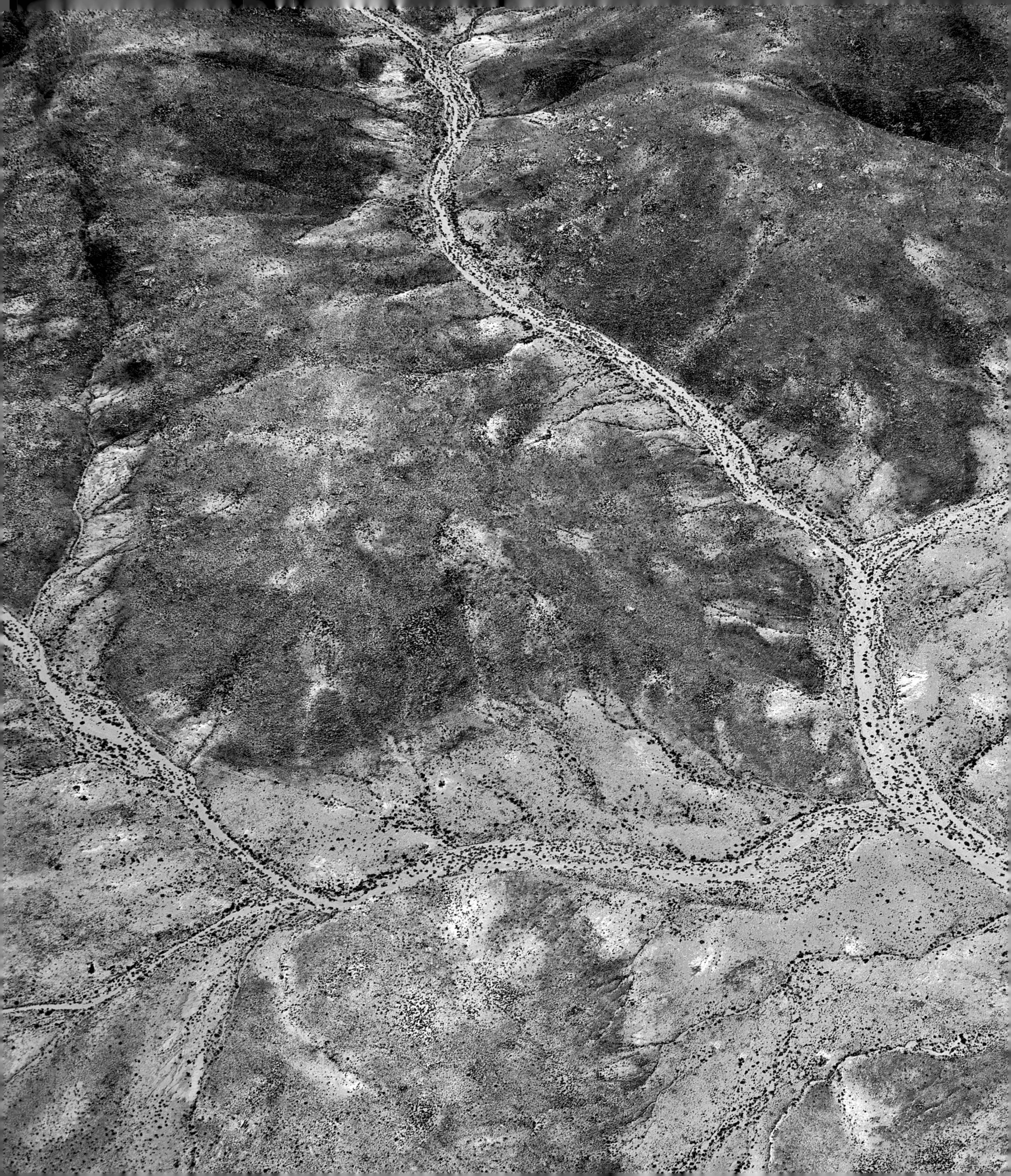

NORTHERN CAPE

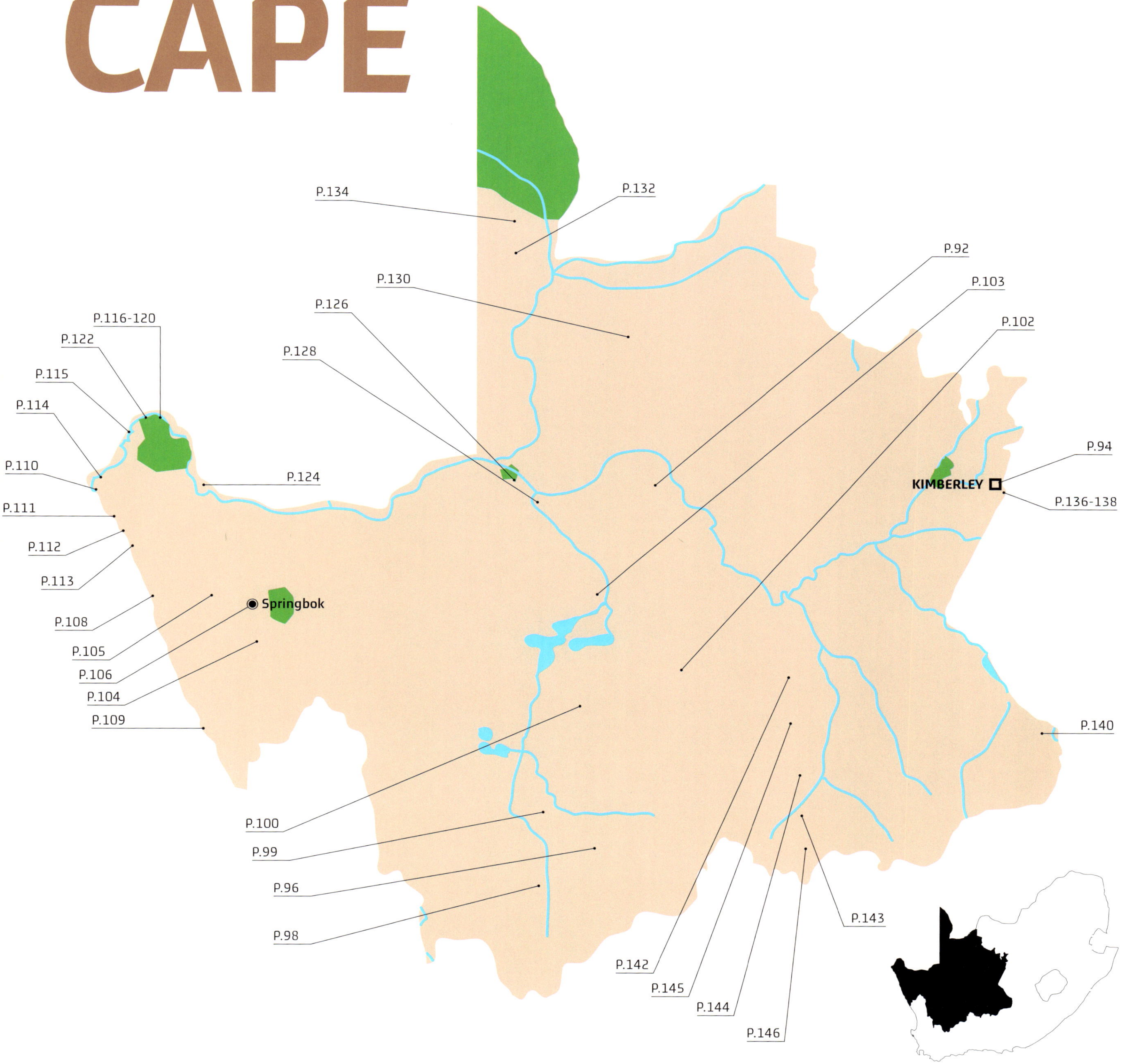

Some say you have to be born here to love it. The emptiness. The silence. The desolation. The ice-cold nights. The horizon that is only broken here and there by the silhouette of a solitary tree or a slowly revolving wind pump.

South Africa's Jewel Box

But anybody who has visited the expansive Northern Cape will come to regard the sparsely populated province as one of South Africa's crown jewels. A land that is a treasure chest of stories of the original inhabitants, the Khoisan. Such as the story of the halfmens (half human), a tree whose crown always points to the north. According to legend, the halfmens dates from the time when Nama-speaking shepherds were driven by rival Khoisan tribes from the fertile pasturelands in the south to the dry north, to what is now known as Namaqualand. Those who looked back during the flight were turned into halfmense and were forever doomed to look to the north.

The Gariep or Orange River is the artery of the Northern Cape. Over the past fifty years, large tracts of land along its banks have been developed into vineyards. The Orange River Wine Cellars Cooperative, founded in 1965, is the largest wine producer not only in South Africa, but in the whole southern hemisphere.

The Northern Cape's reputation as a crown jewel is partly due to its capital Kimberley, where a rough diamond of more than eighty carats was found in 1871. In the years that followed, a hole measuring seventeen hectares and more than 200 metres deep was dug there. Although this enormous open-air mine has long since been decommissioned, Kimberley still advertises itself as diamond capital of the world and the Big Hole is the city's most important tourist attraction.

Today, diamonds are mainly mined in and around the little village of Alexander Bay, where the Orange River flows into the cold Atlantic Ocean. Here there are many stories – true or not is hard to say – about smugglers who concealed rough diamonds from the authorities in hollow shoe heels, behind hub caps and even in biltong, the dried meat that is considered a delicacy in South Africa.

But it is in the far north of the province, in the parched lands of the Kalahari, that the traveller discovers why the Northern Cape fully deserves to be called South Africa's crown jewel. Here is the Kgalagadi Transfrontier Park, a colourful, tranquil world of red sand dunes, pure sparkling white saltpans and clumps of grass, bleached faded green by the sunlight. A world where diamonds are not found in the ground but in the sky. Spend a night in Kgalagadi, and you find yourself in a stargazers' paradise. Far removed from any air and light pollution, the Magellan Cloud and the Southern Cross are visible to the naked eye. And, with a decent telescope, you can even see a sparkling array of stars in that same Southern Cross. An array of stars that astronomers have dubbed the Jewel Box.

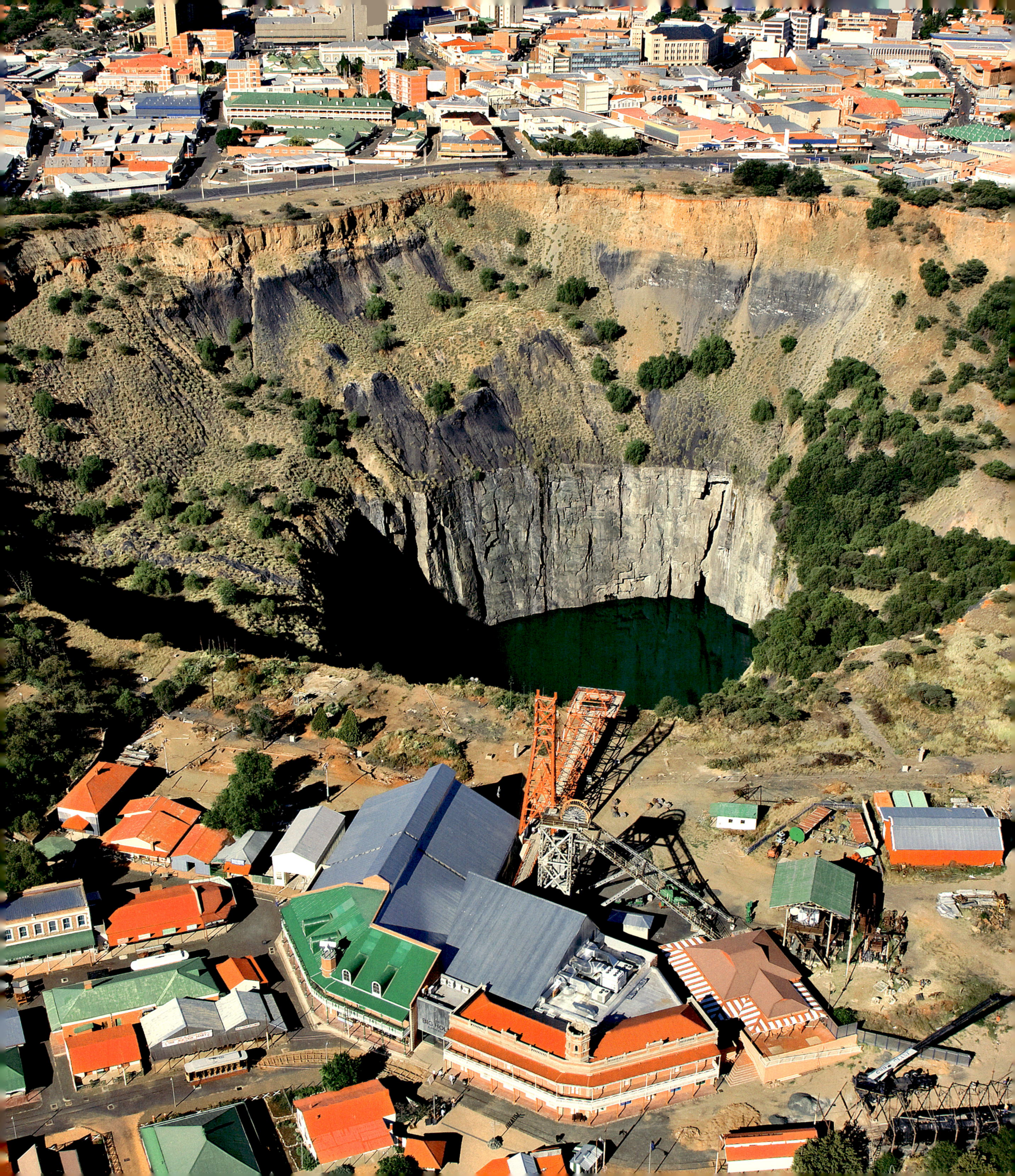

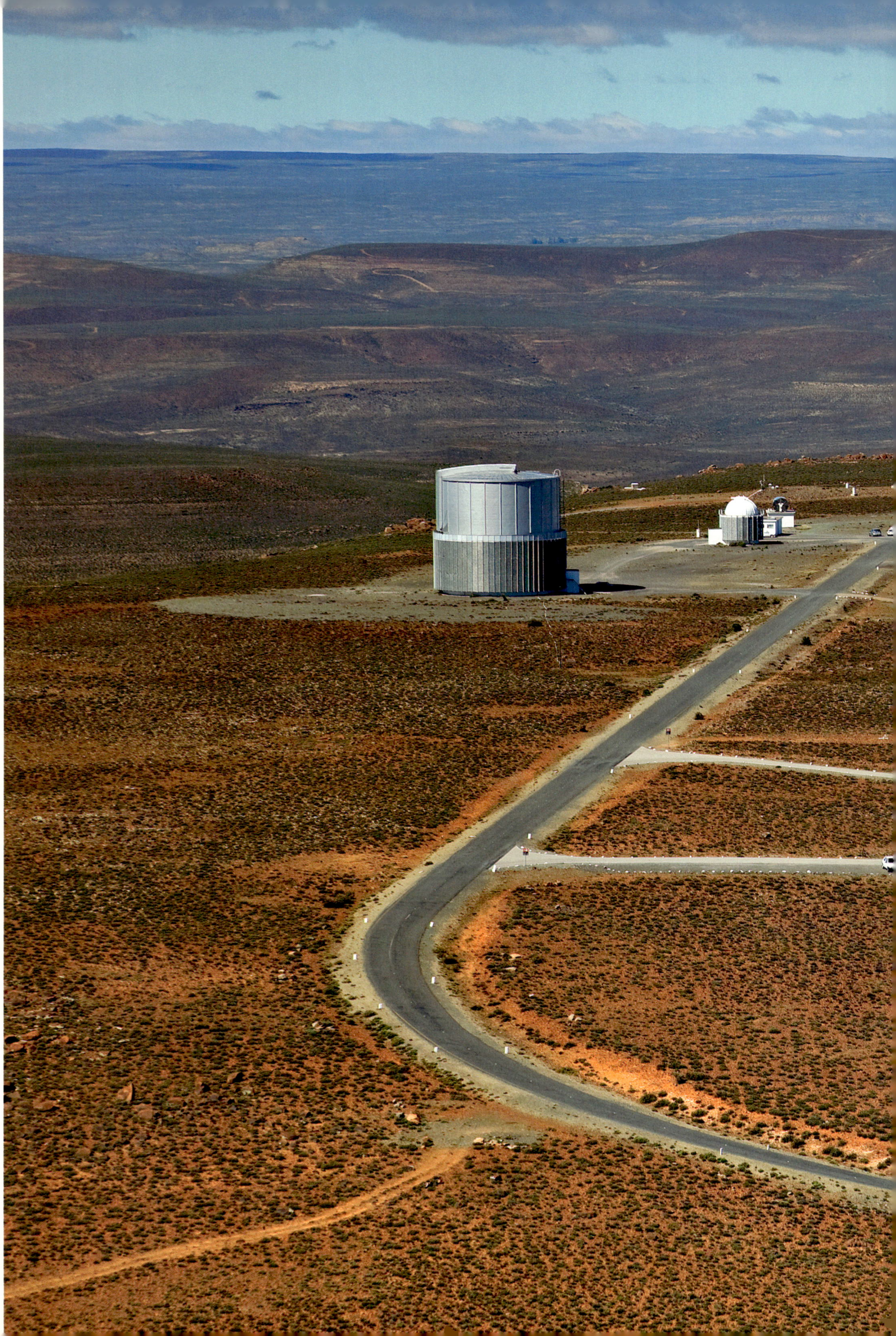

→ South African Astronomical Observatory

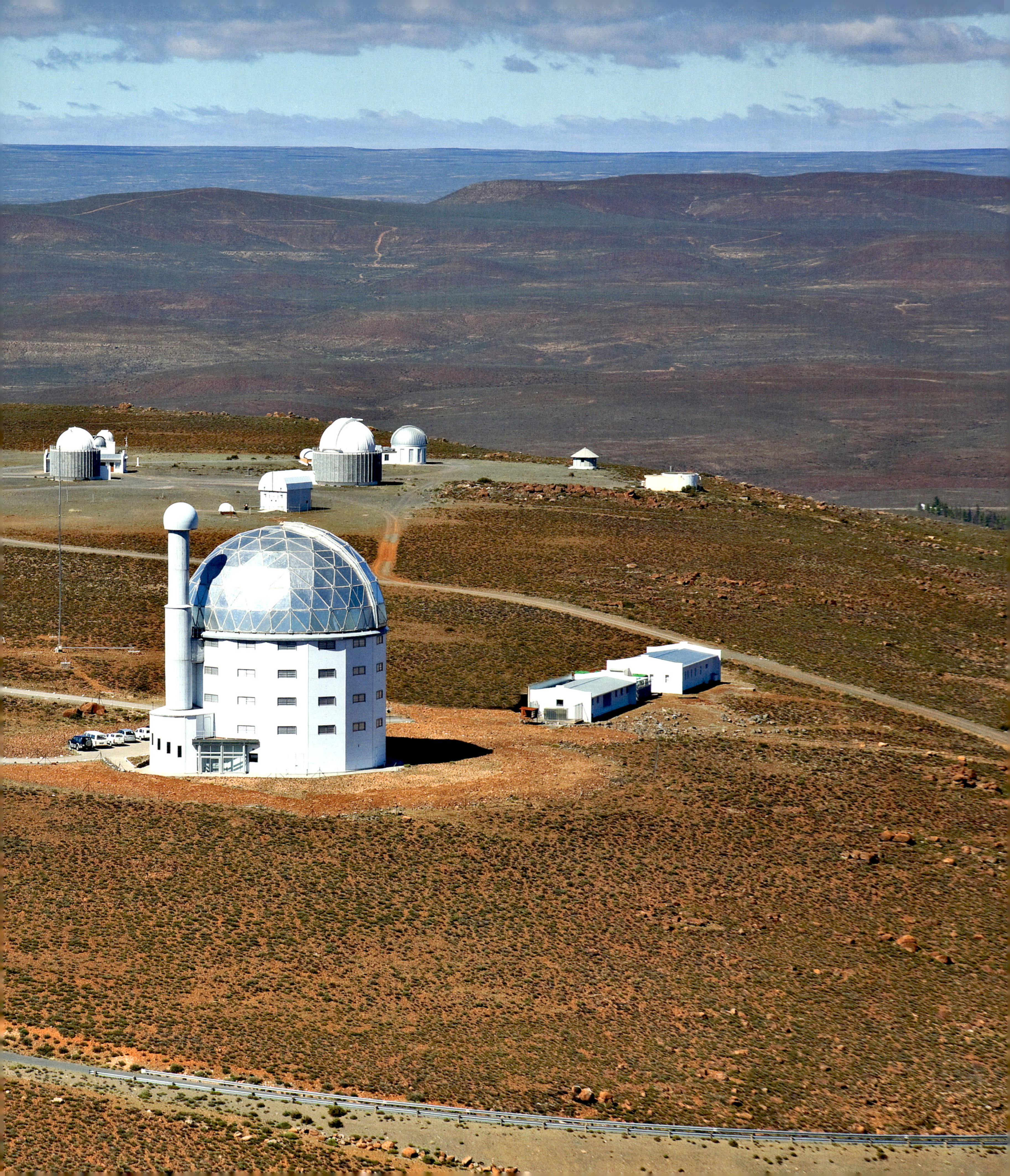

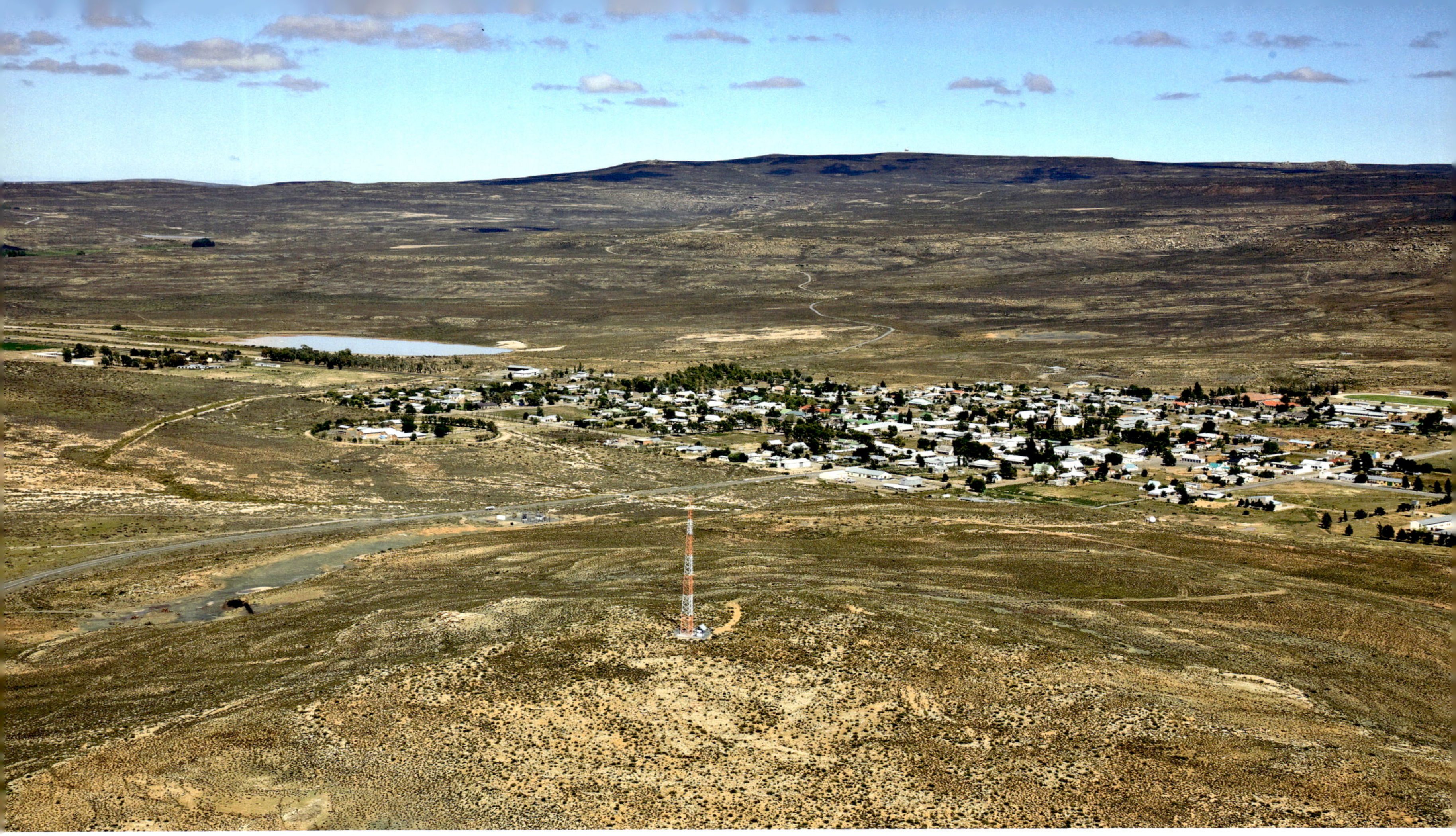

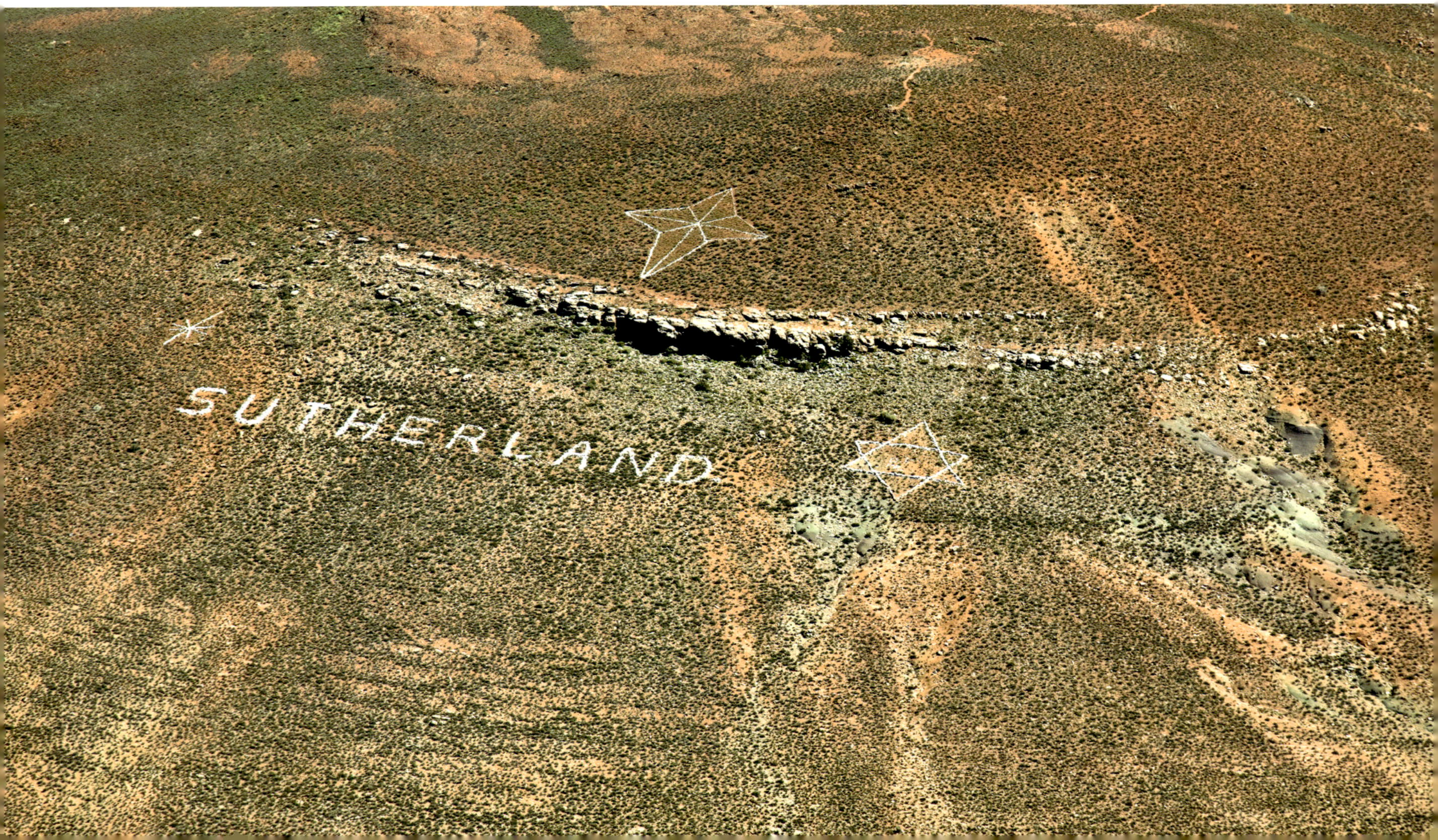
SUTHERLAND

←↓ Sutherland, coldest place in South Africa

→ Aviation beacon at 6000 Ft

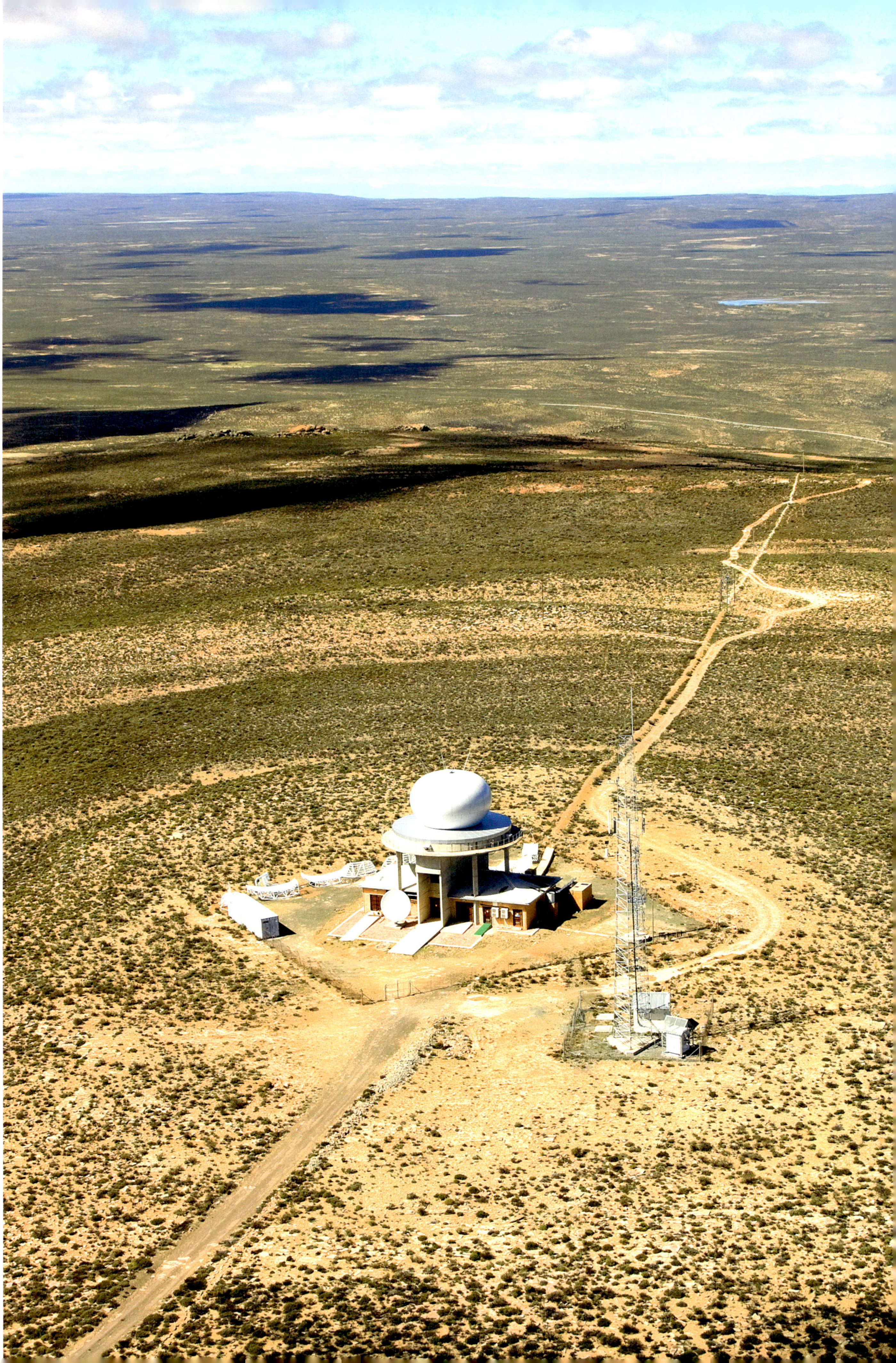

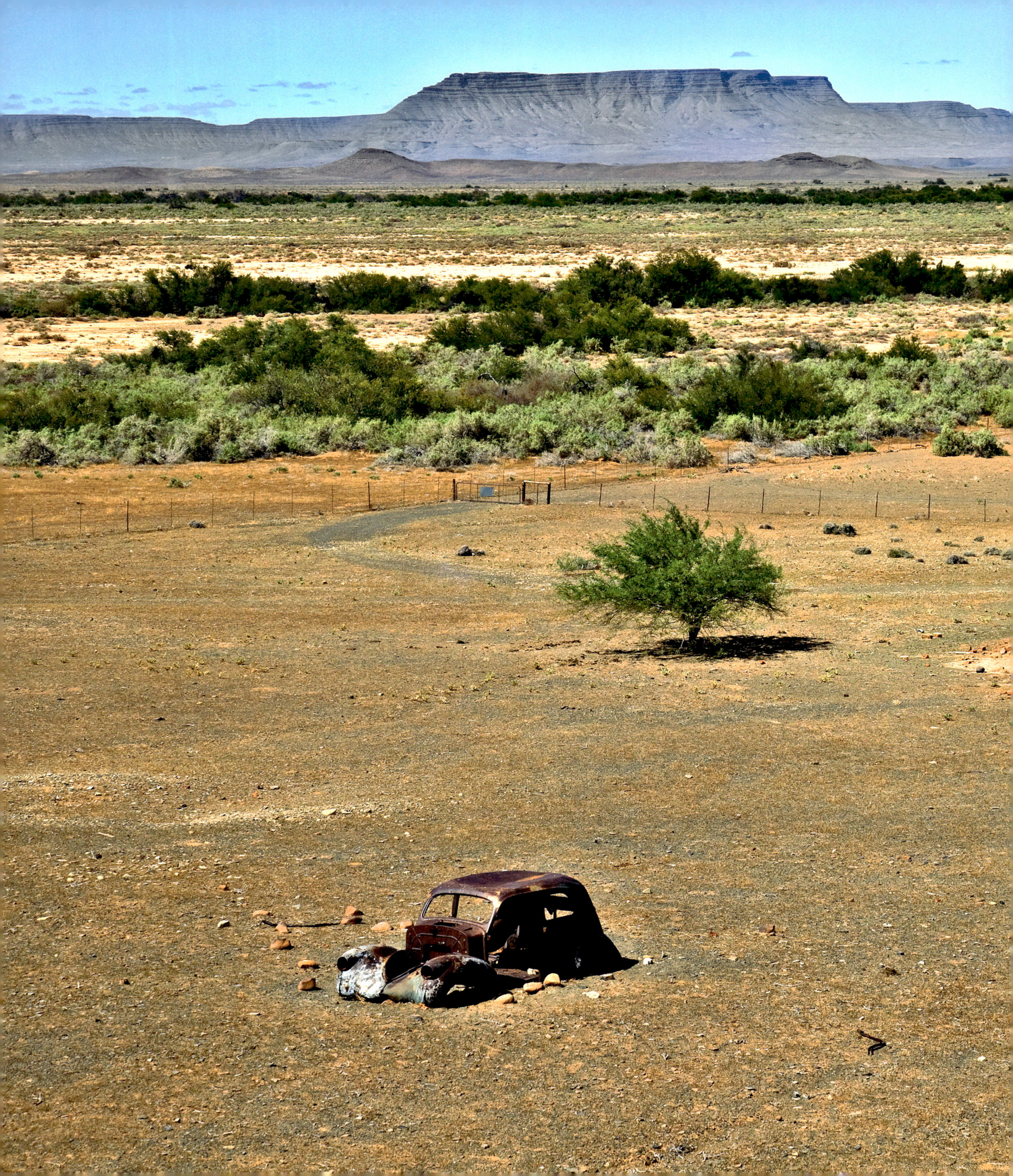

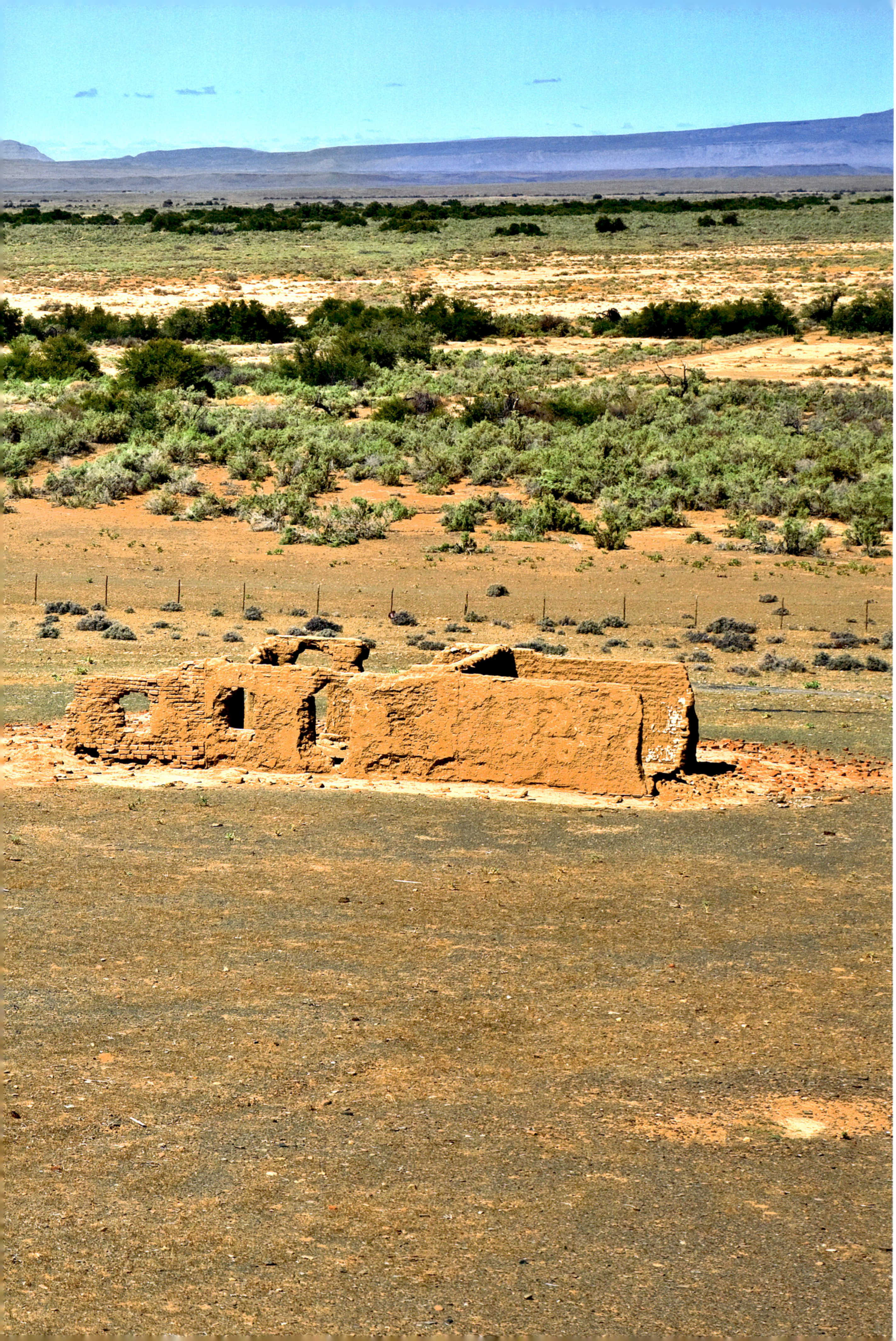

← Abandoned farm in Tankwa Karoo

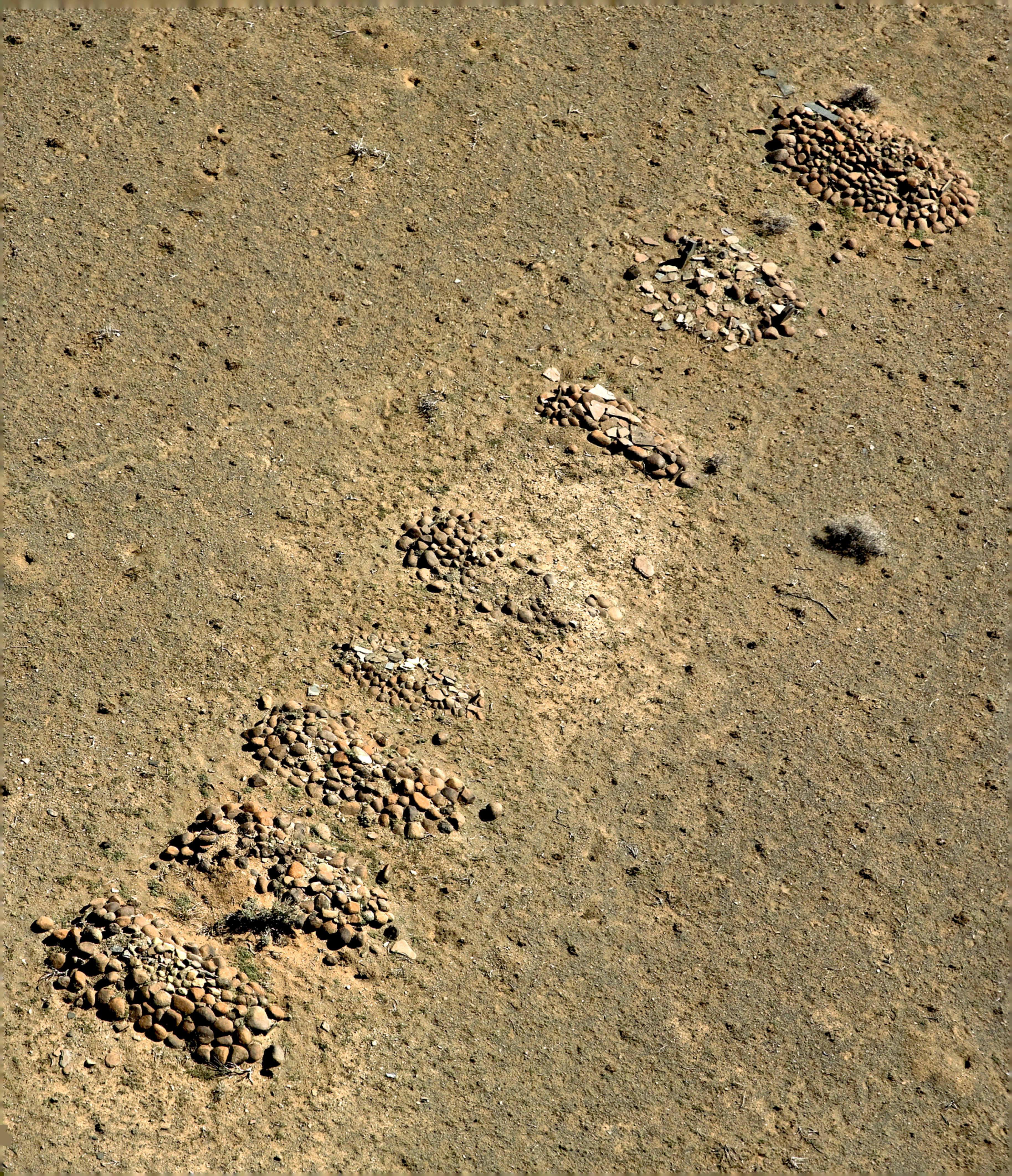

← Graves on an abandoned estate
↓ Farm, Kolkenburg

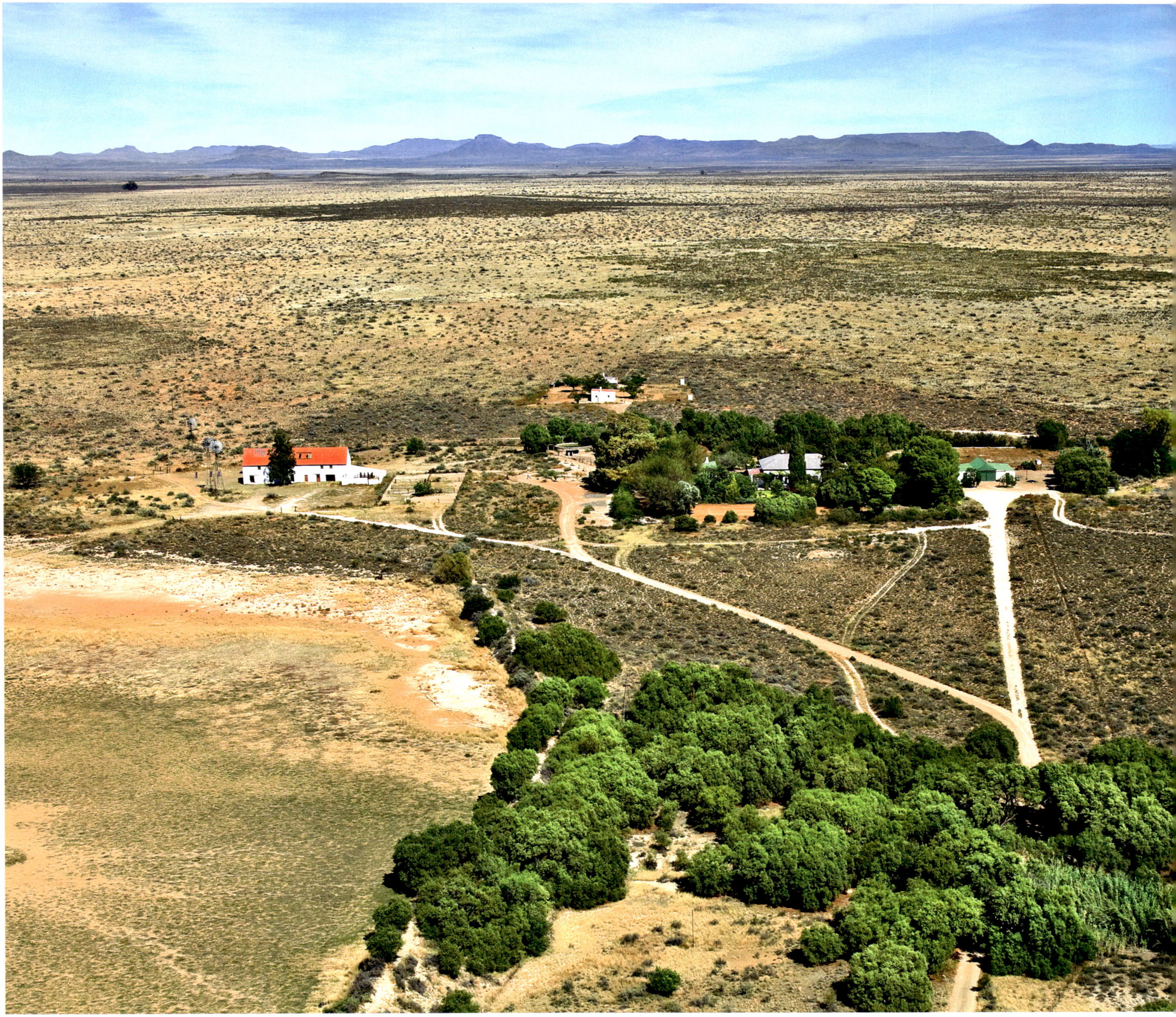

↓ Namaqua Game Lodge, south of Springbok
→ Namaqualand

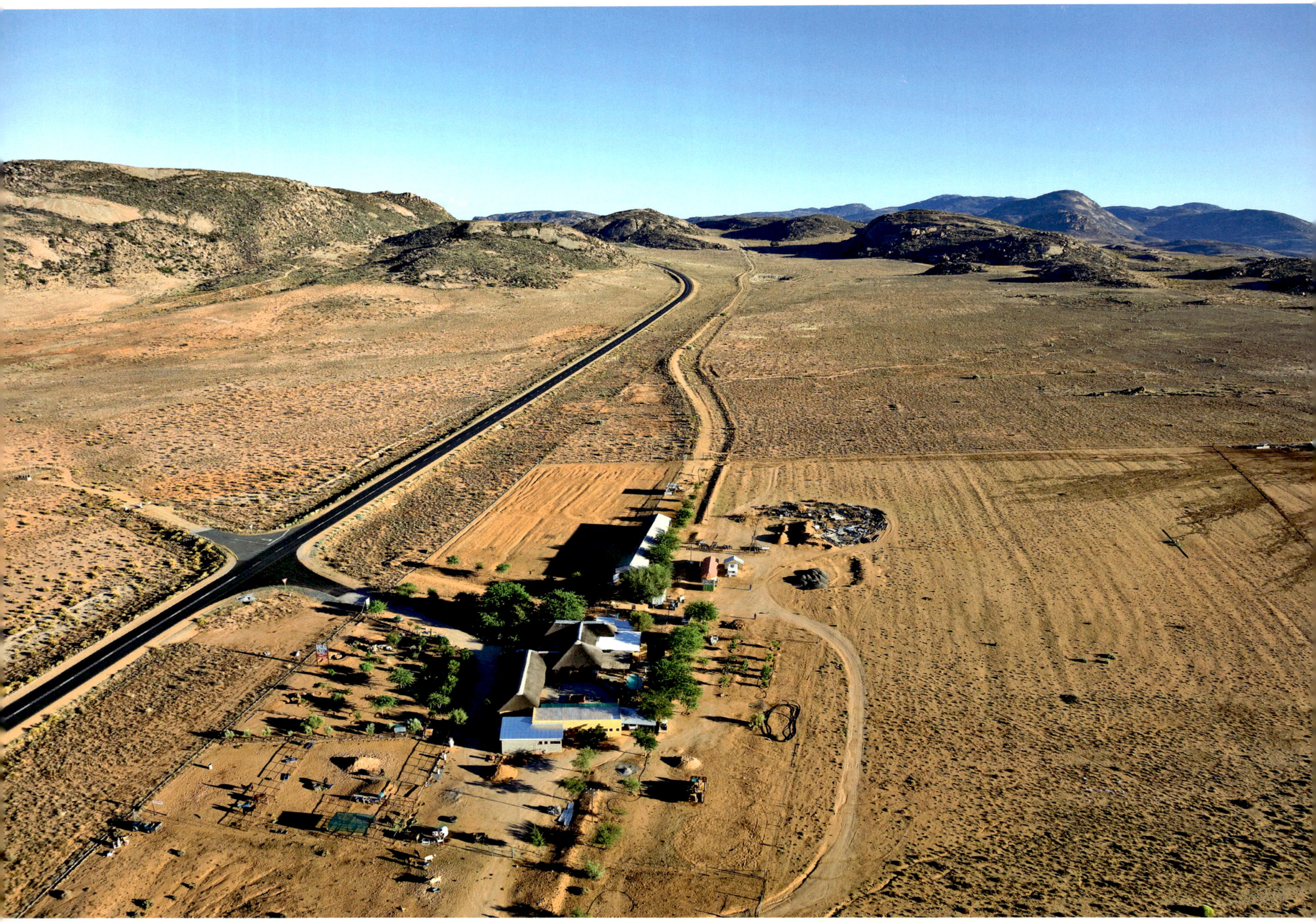

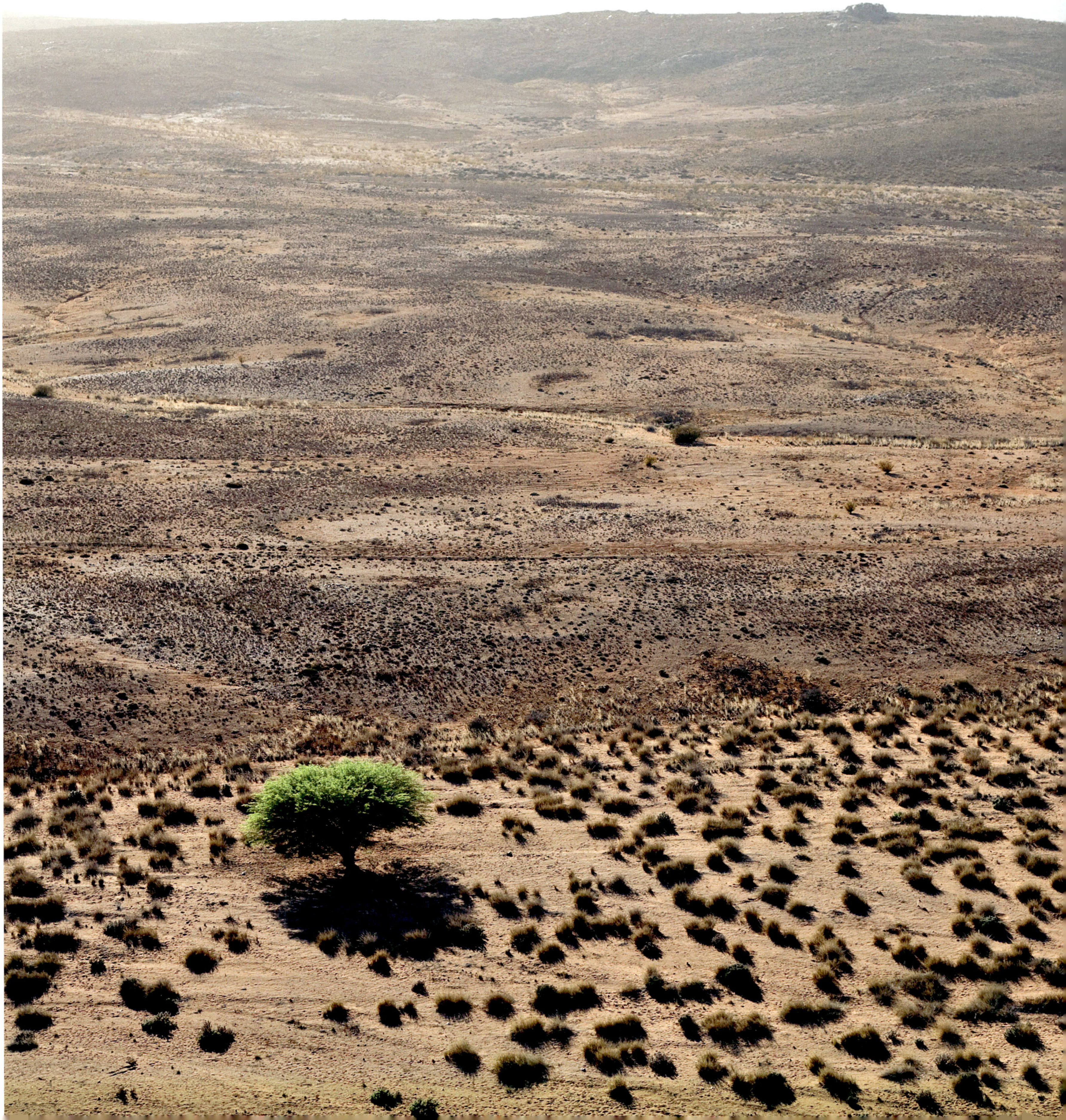

↓ Springbok
→ Copper mine shaft, Springbok

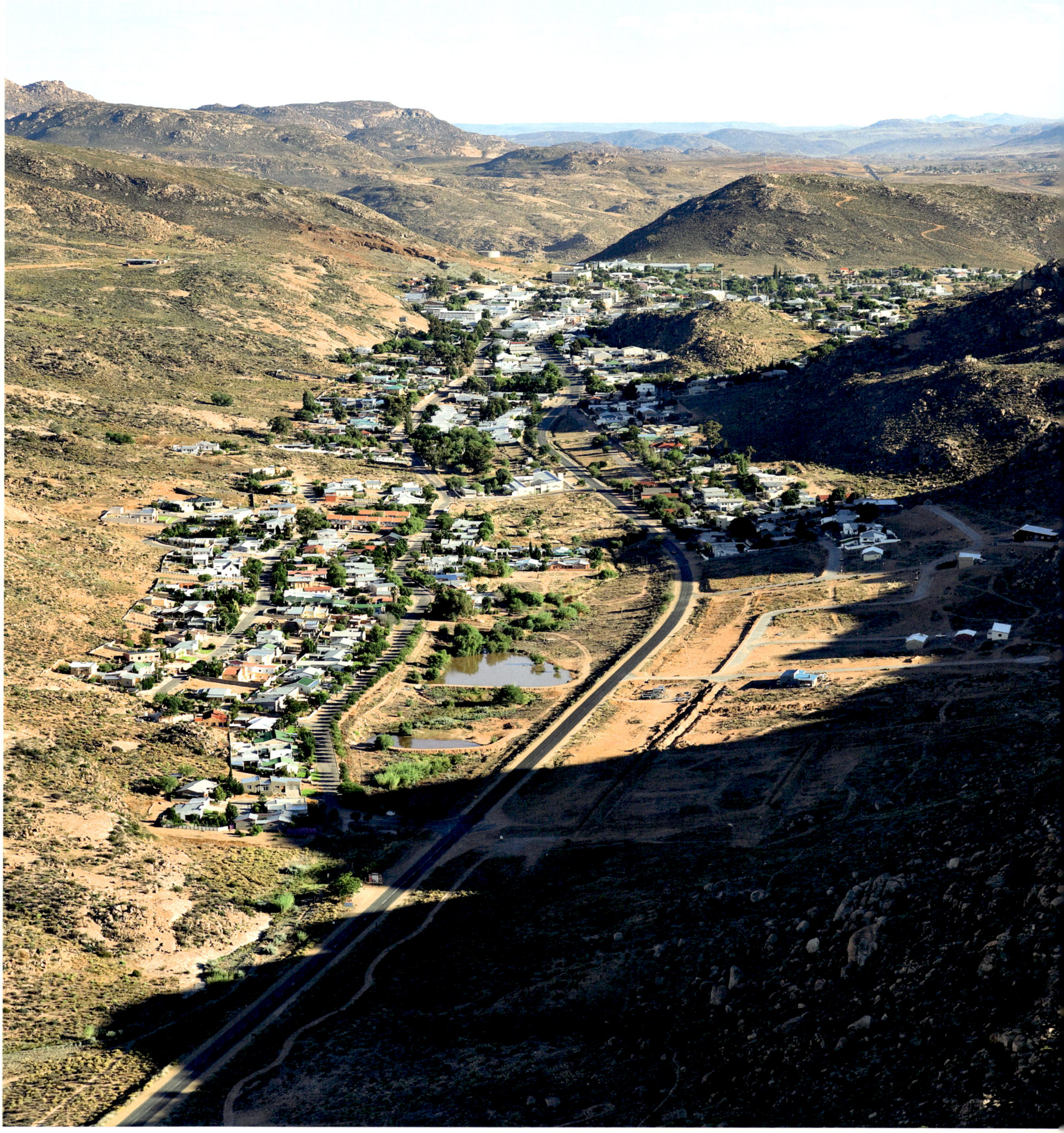

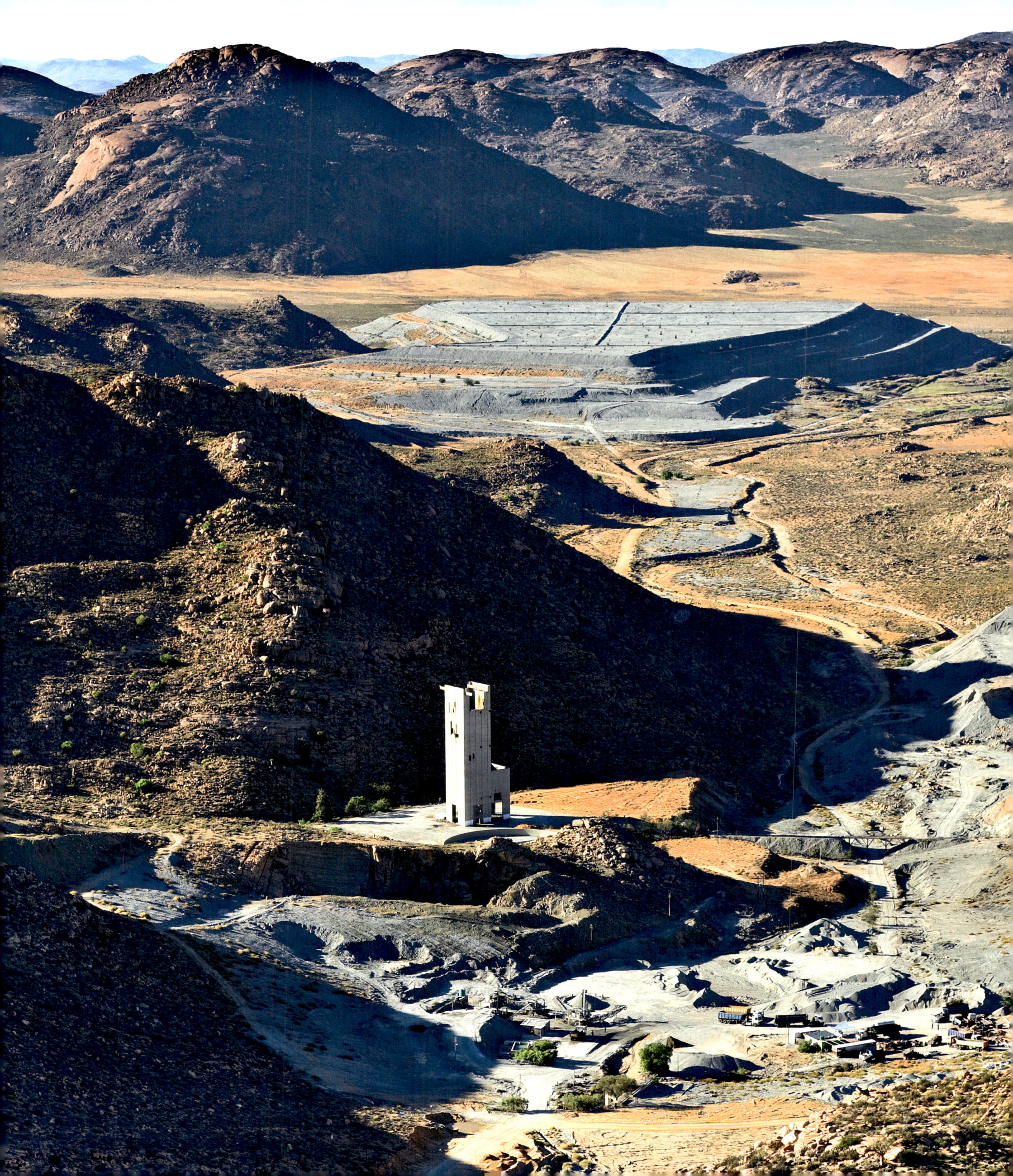

↓ Open mine, Kleinsee
→ Diamond mine, Hondeklip Bay

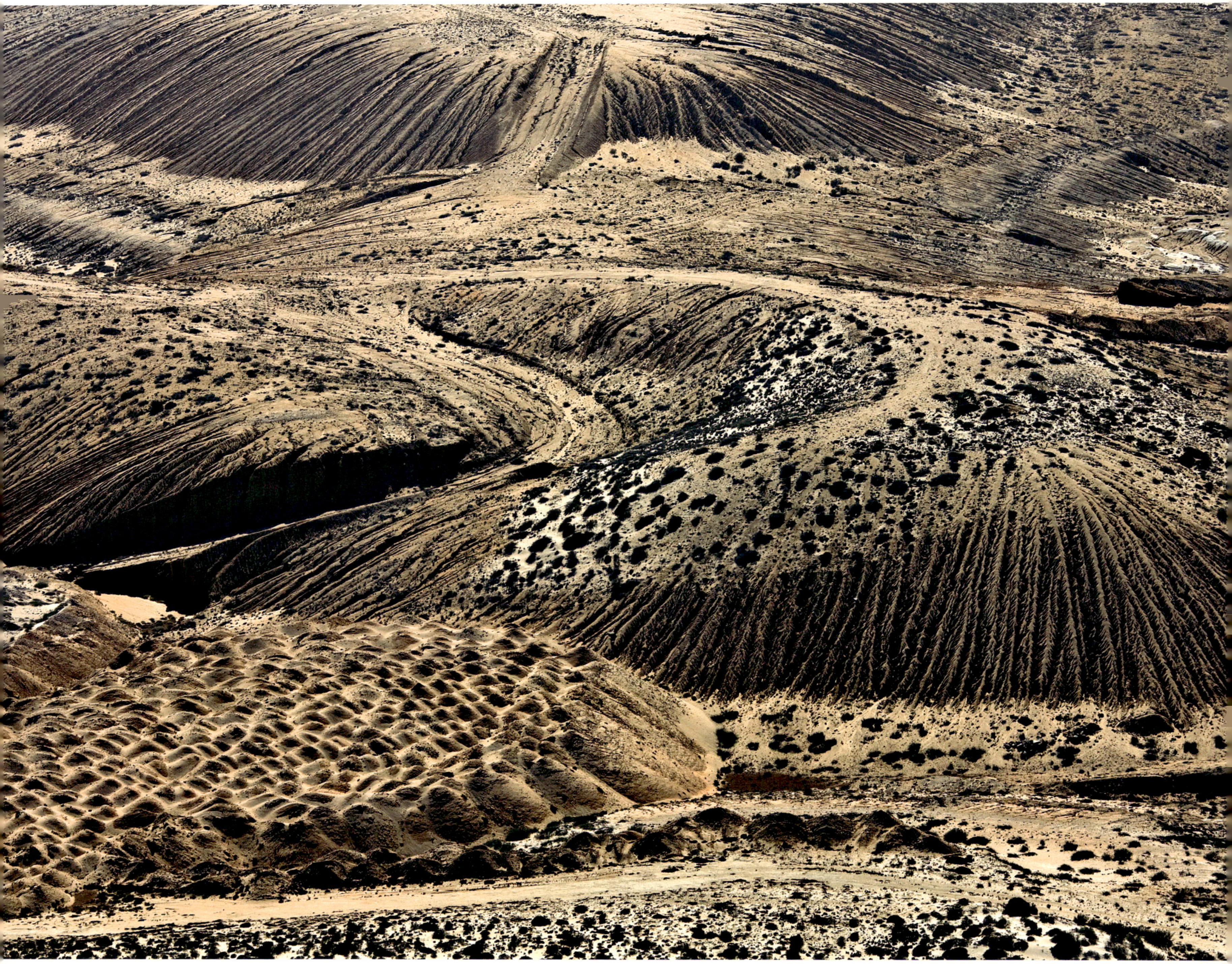

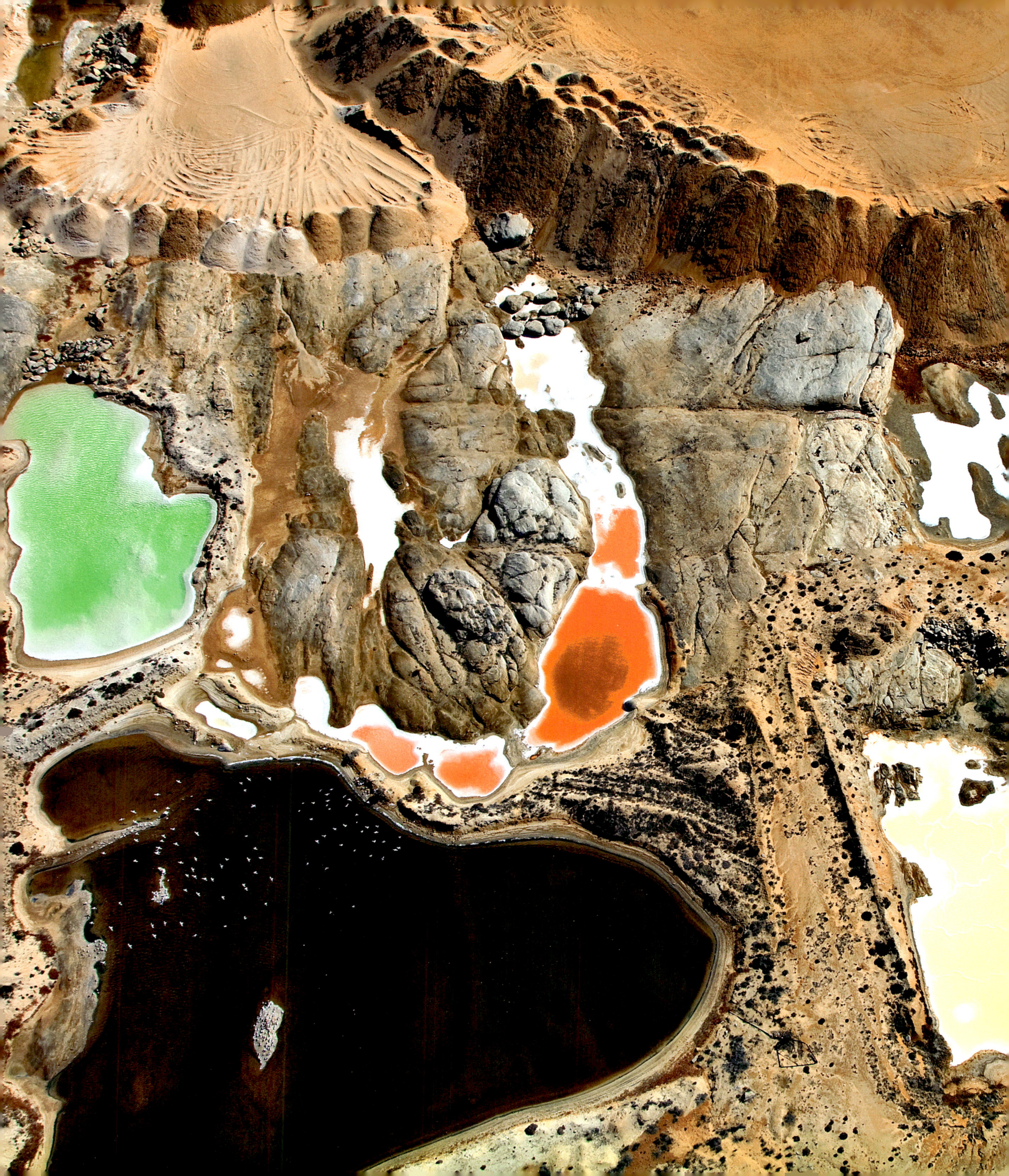

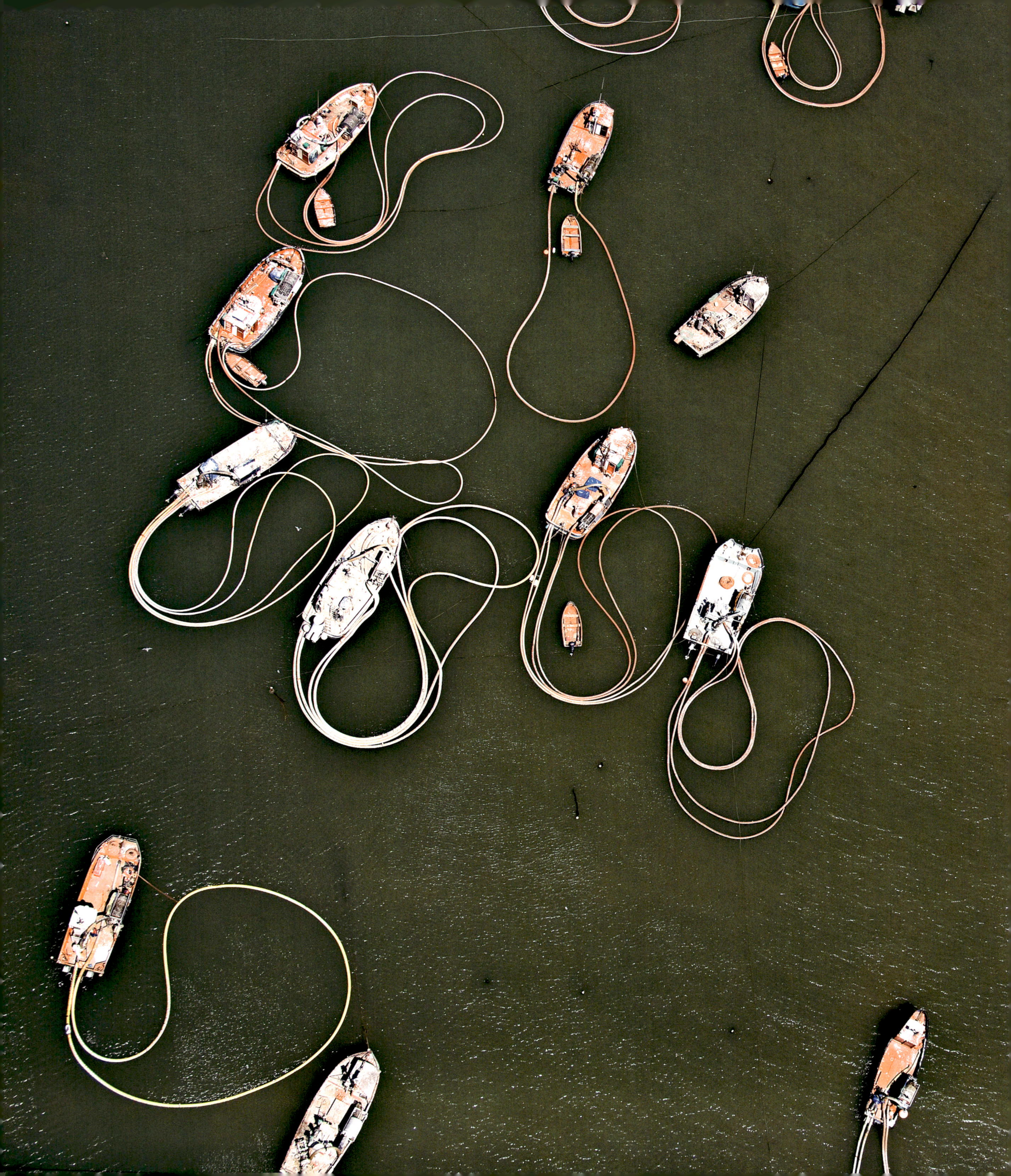

← Diamond boats, Alexander Bay
↓ 'Wreck point', Atlantic coast

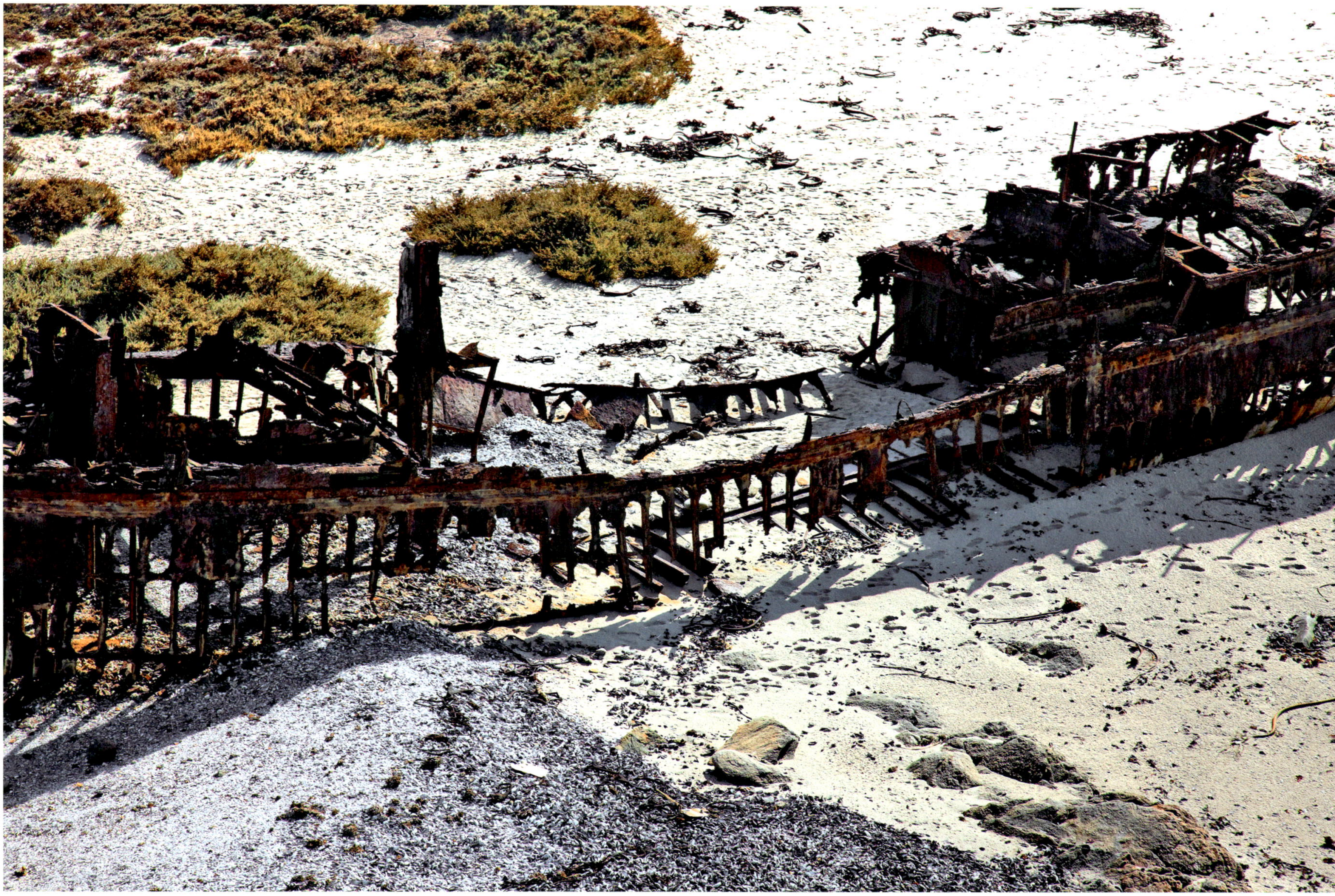

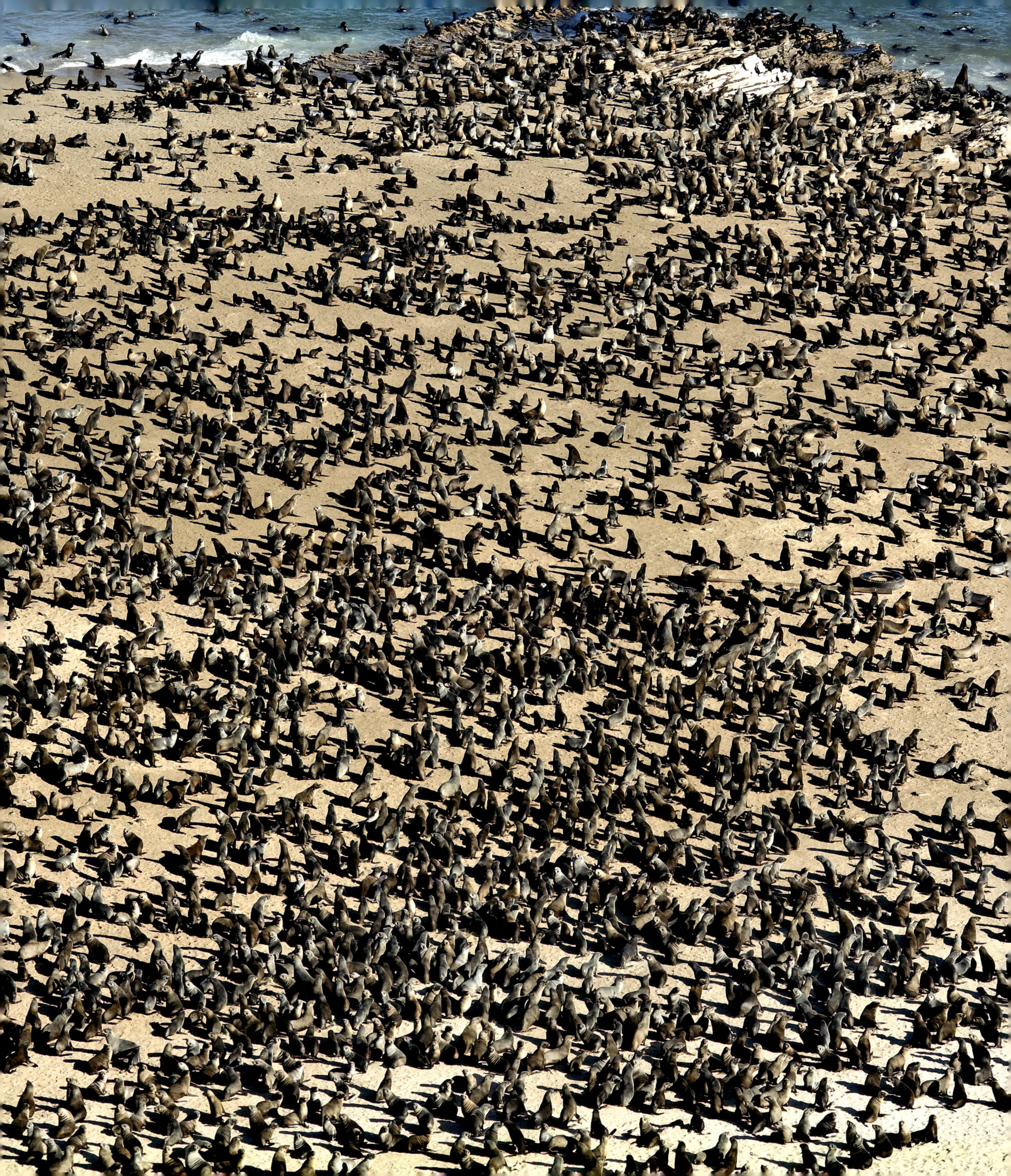

← Seal colony, Port Nolloth

→ Ostriches enjoying the view

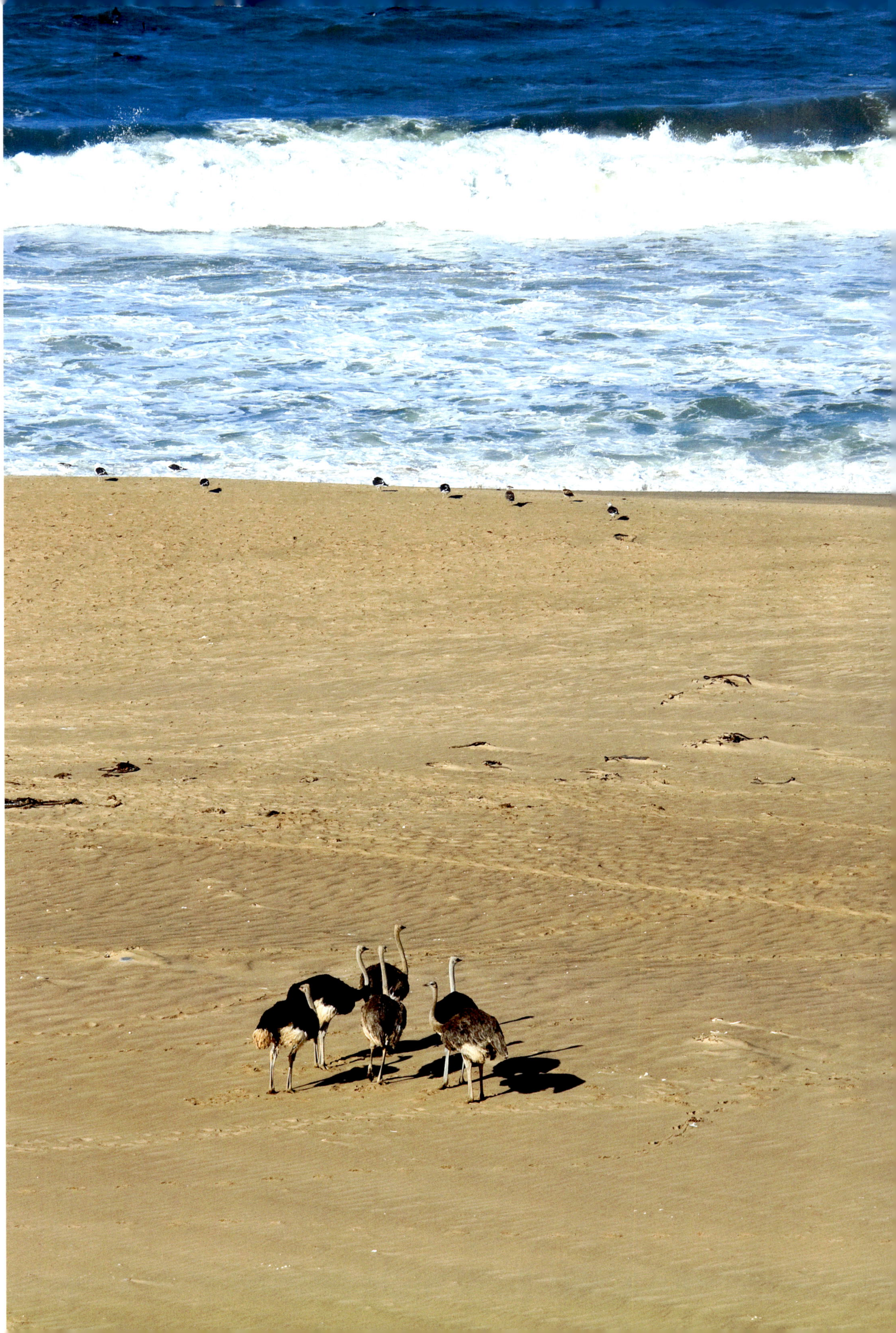

↓ Red sand dunes, west of Richtersveld
→ Orange River mouth, Alexander Bay

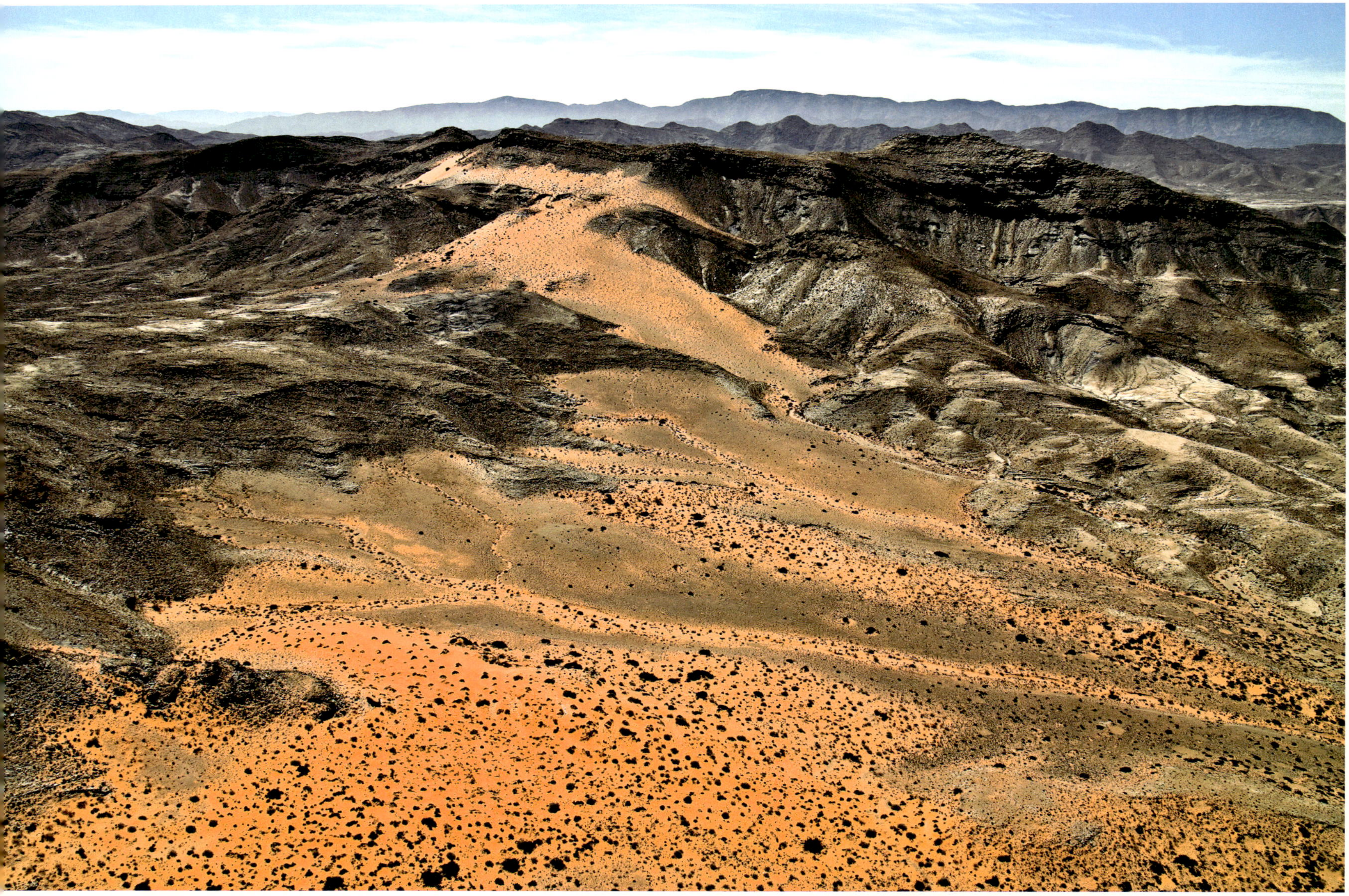

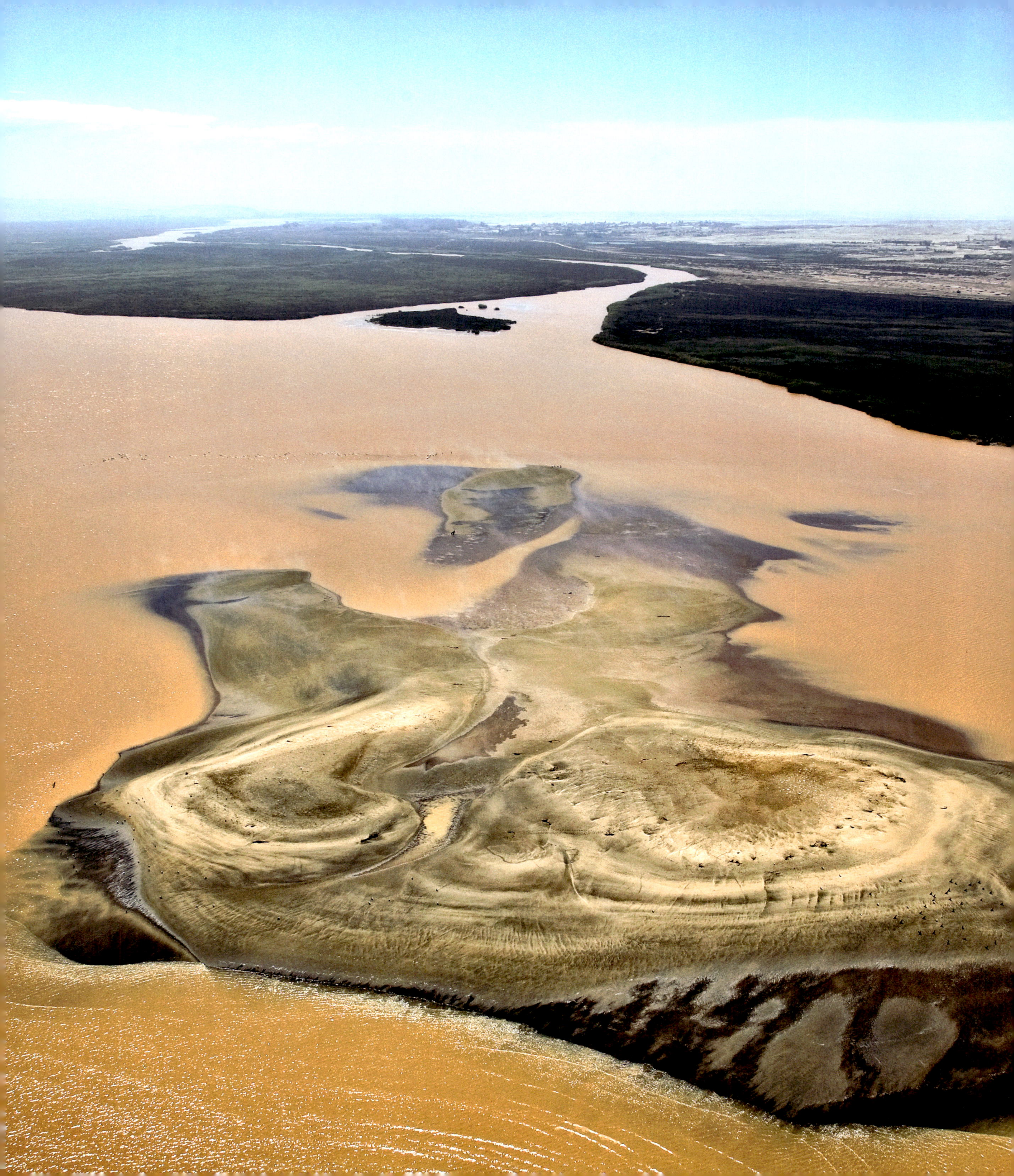

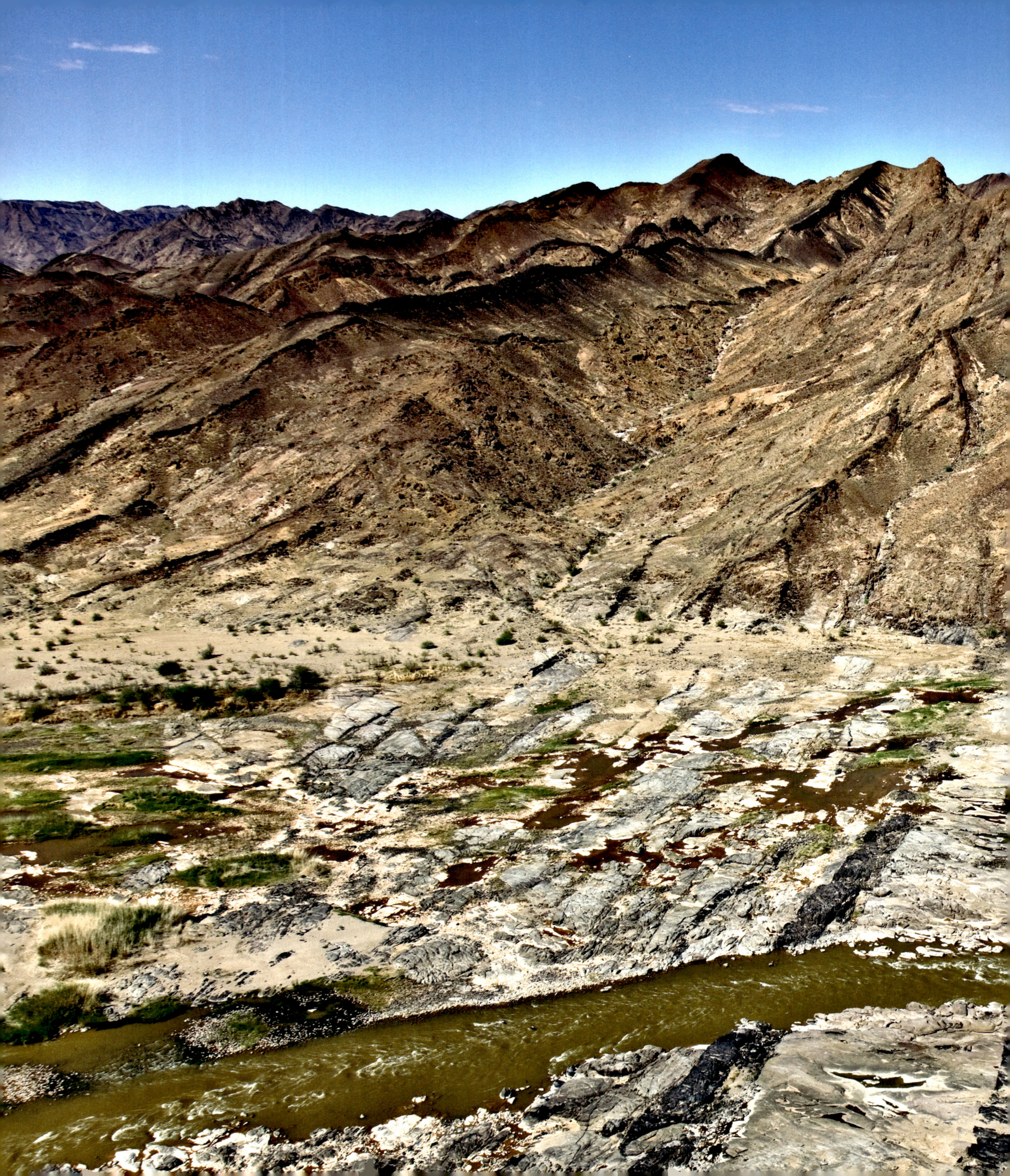

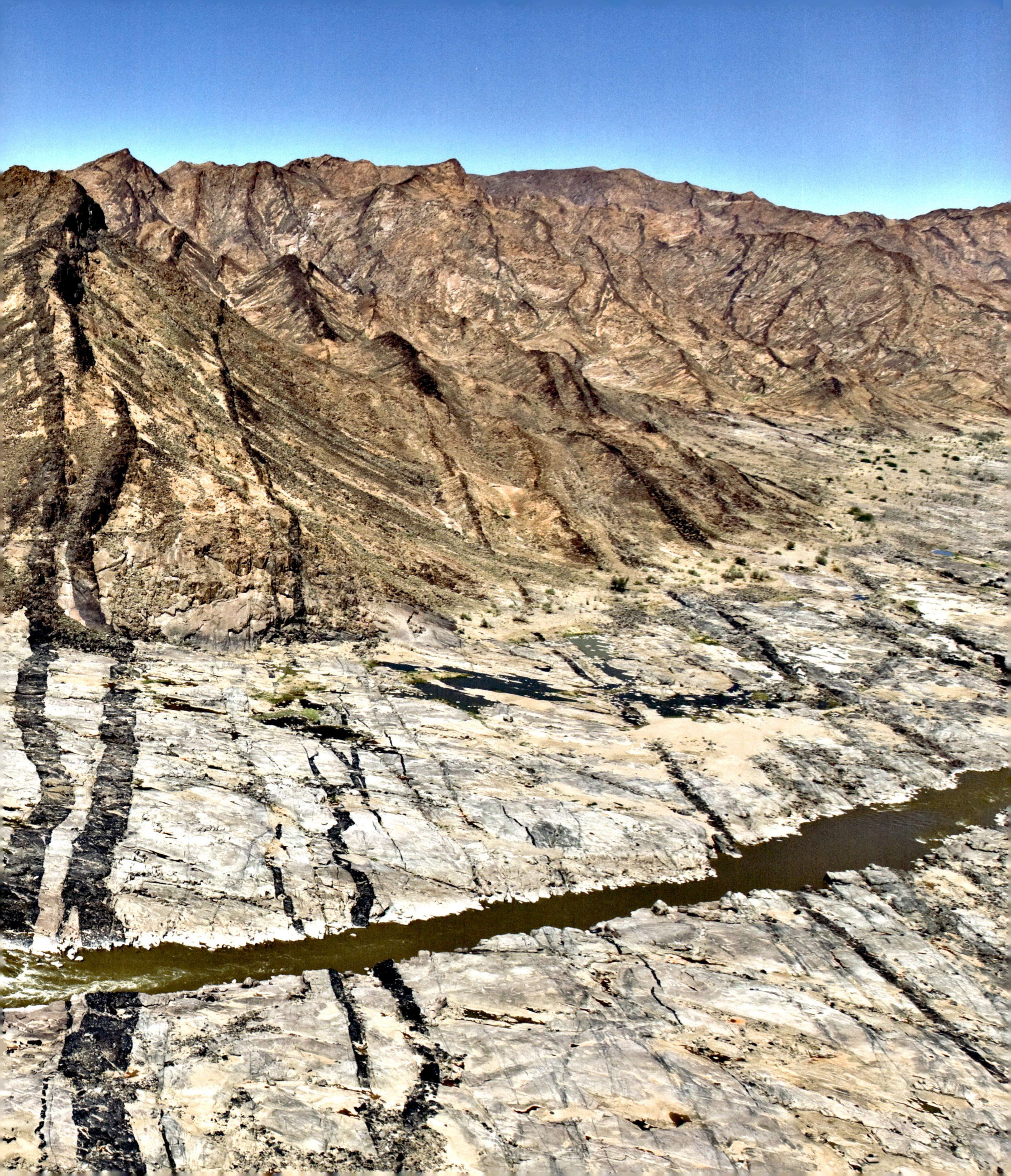

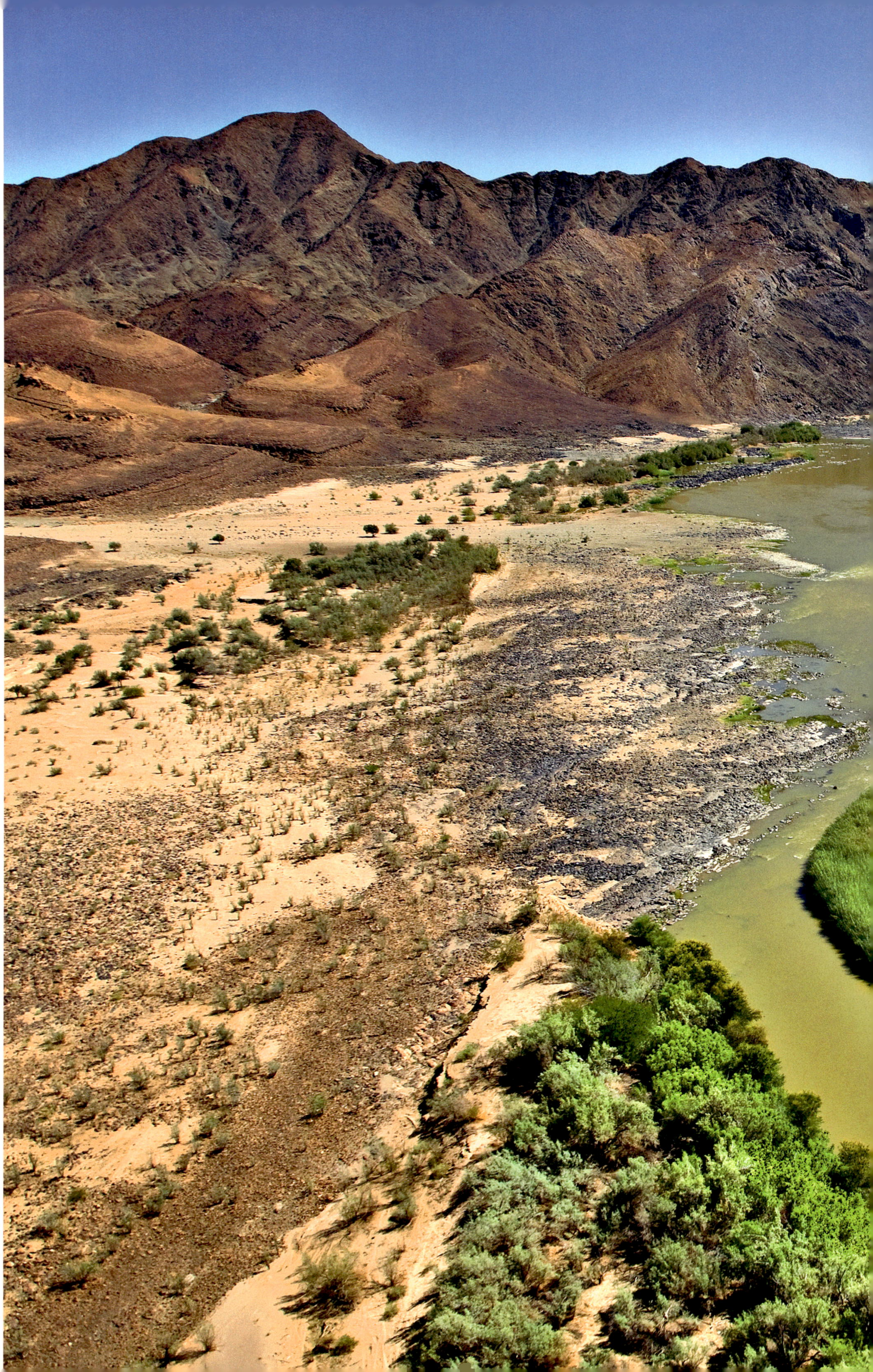

←→ Richtersveld National Park

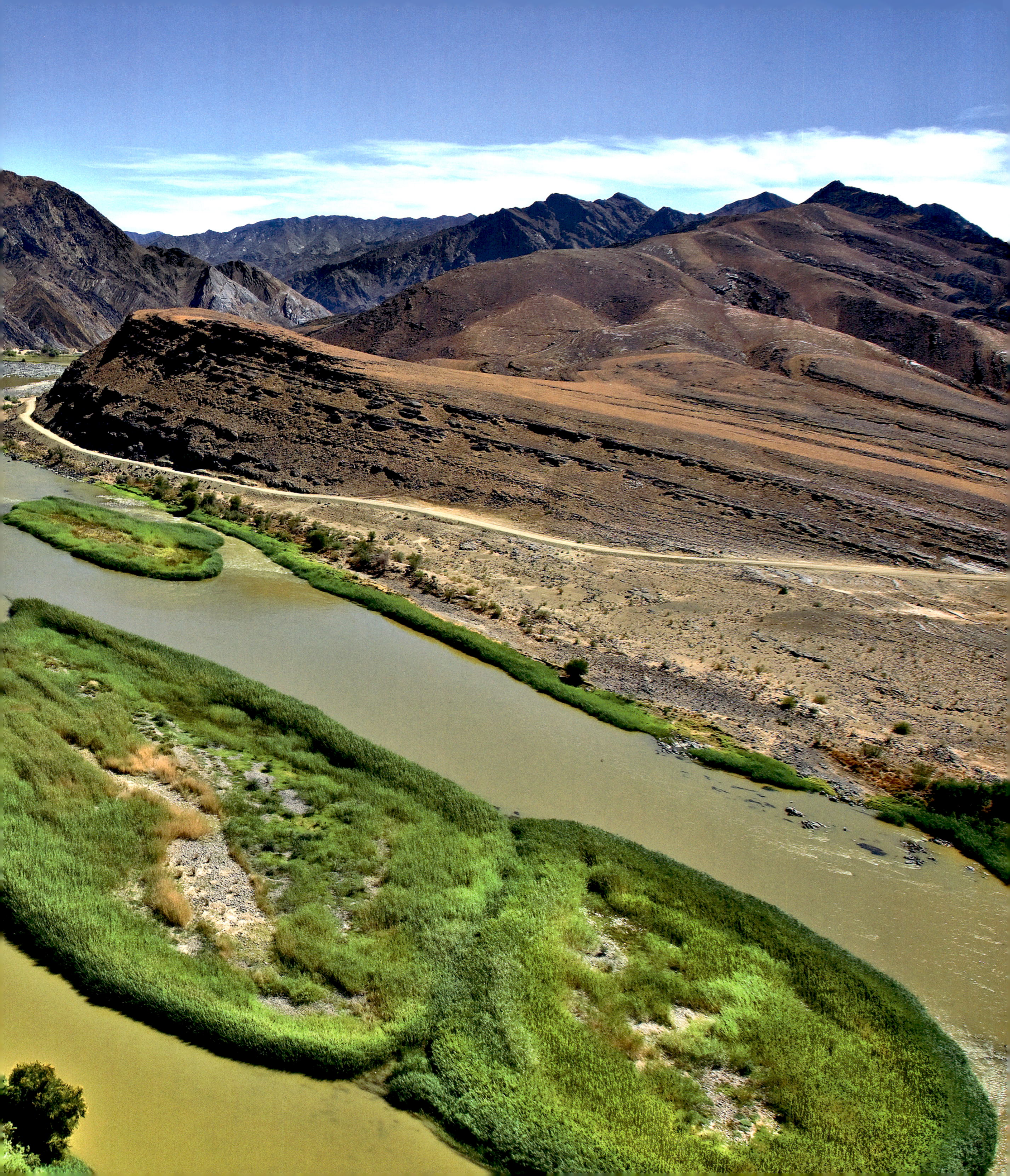

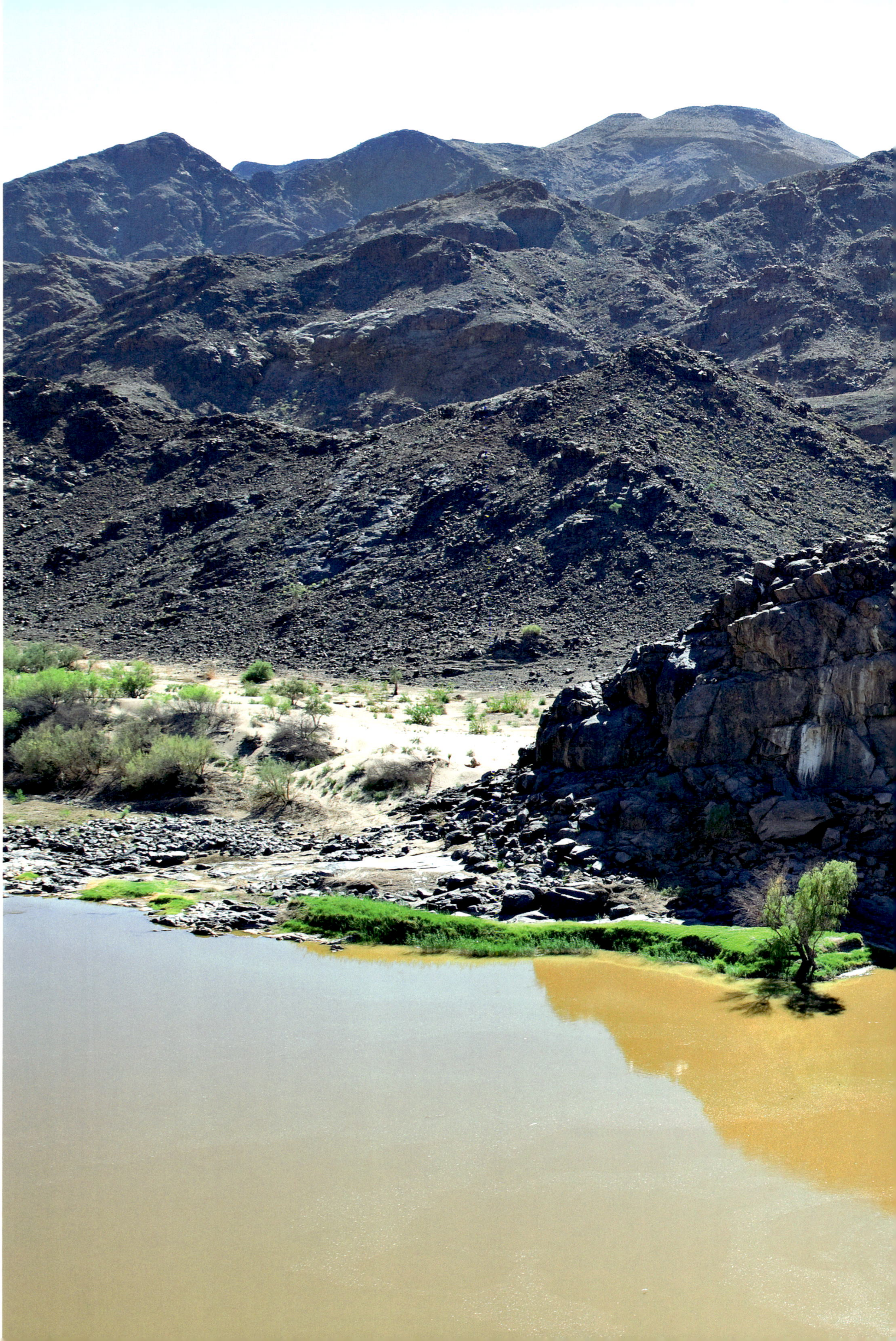

→ Orange River, Richtersveld

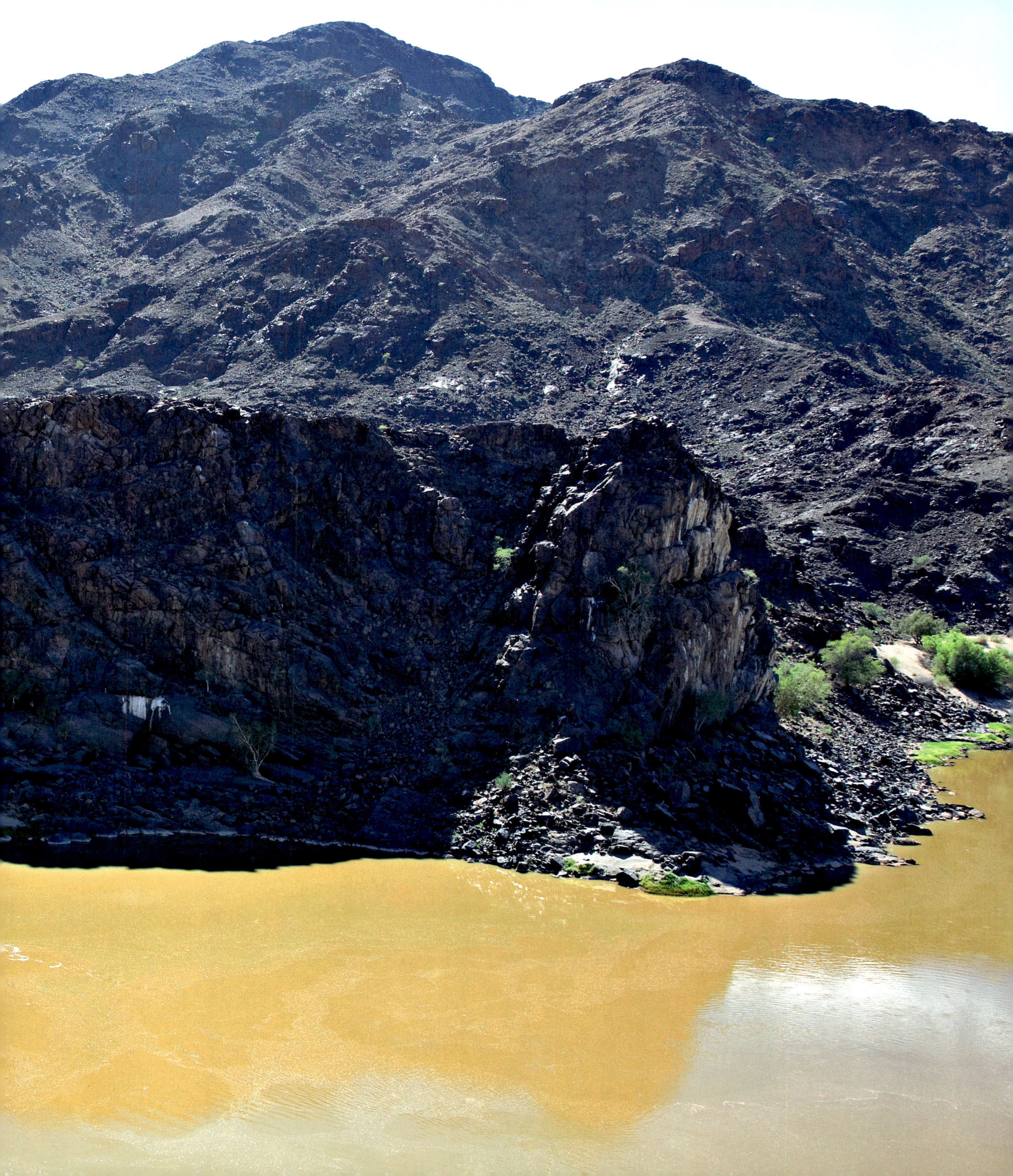

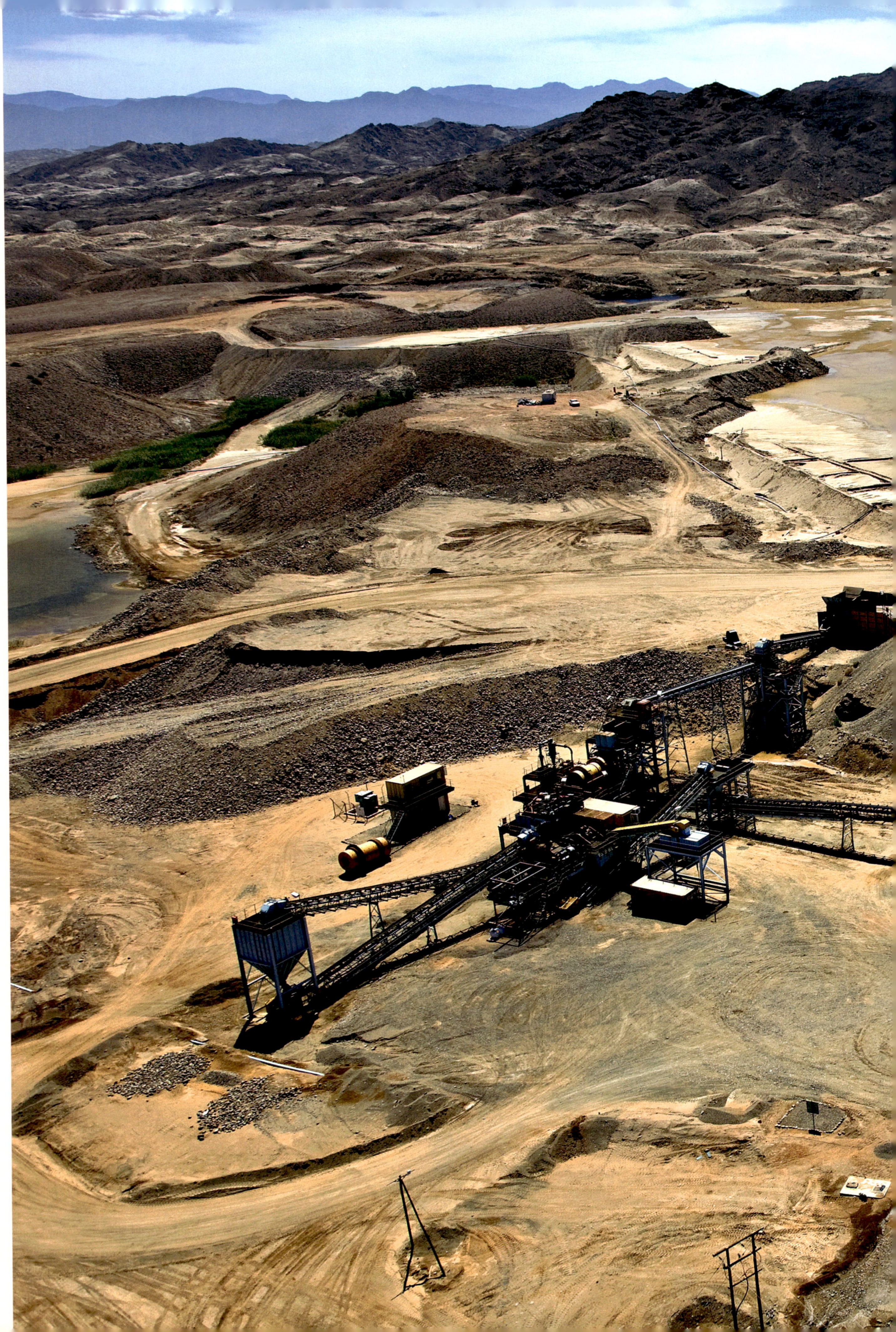

→ Diamond mine, Richtersveld

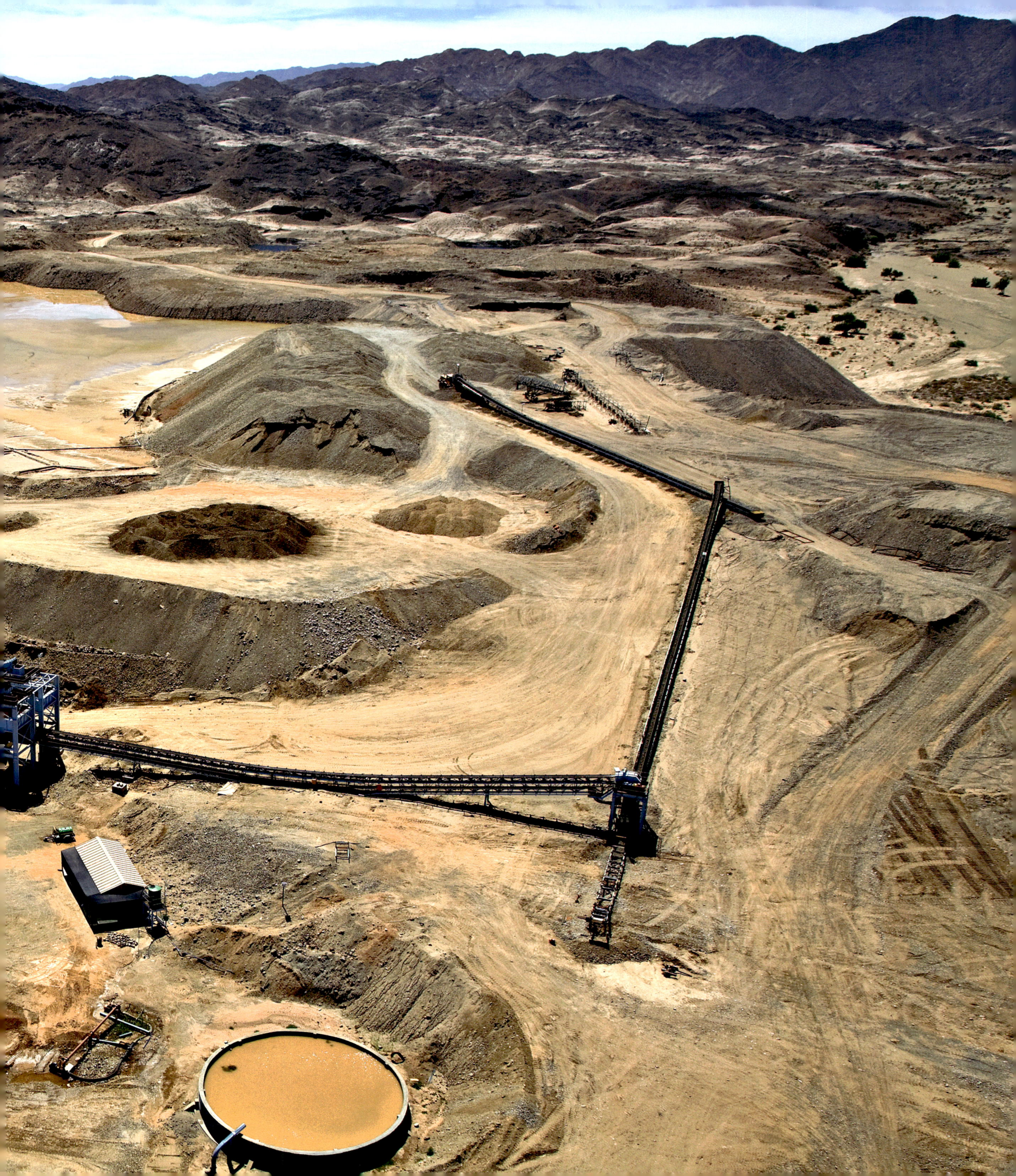

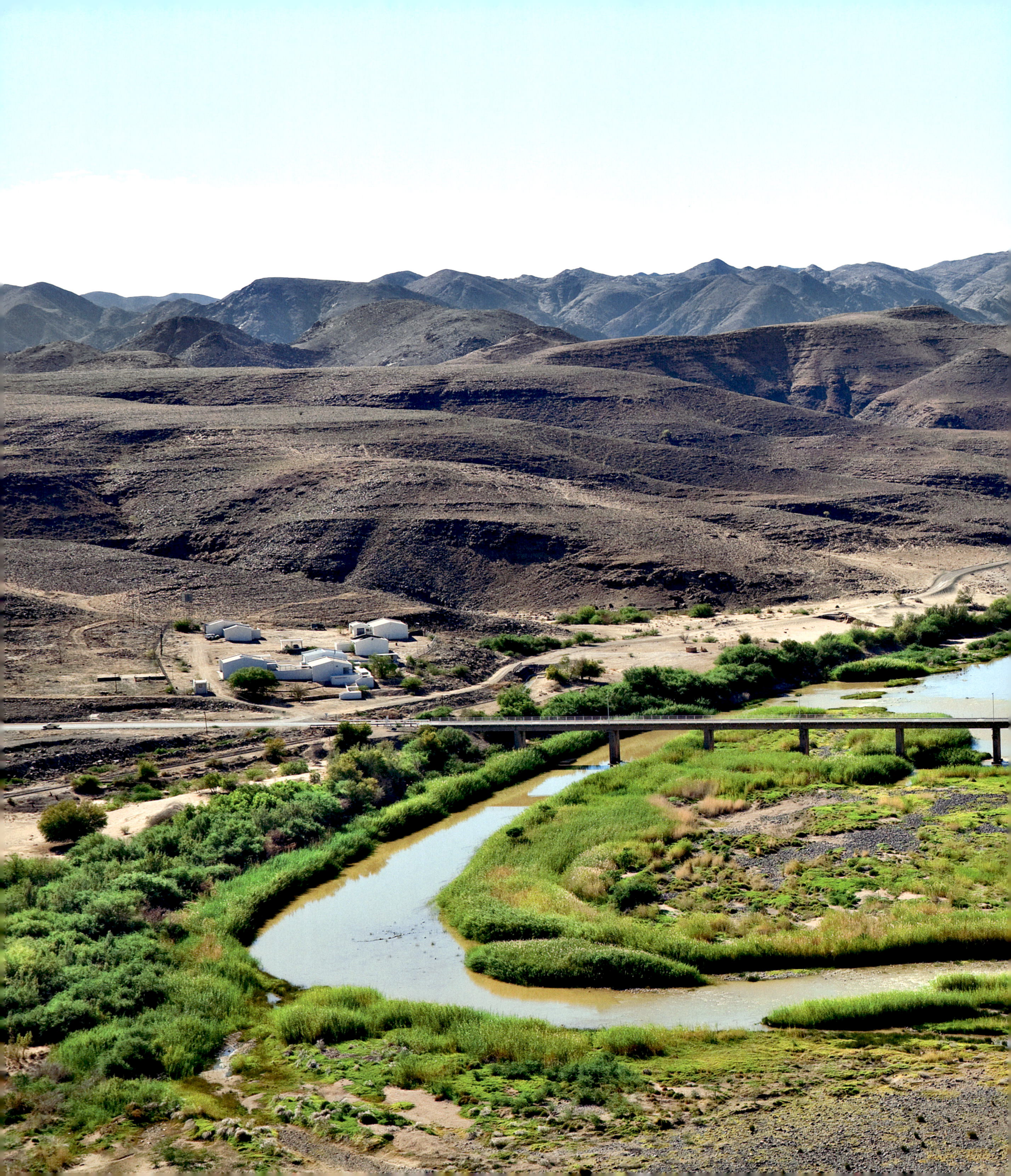

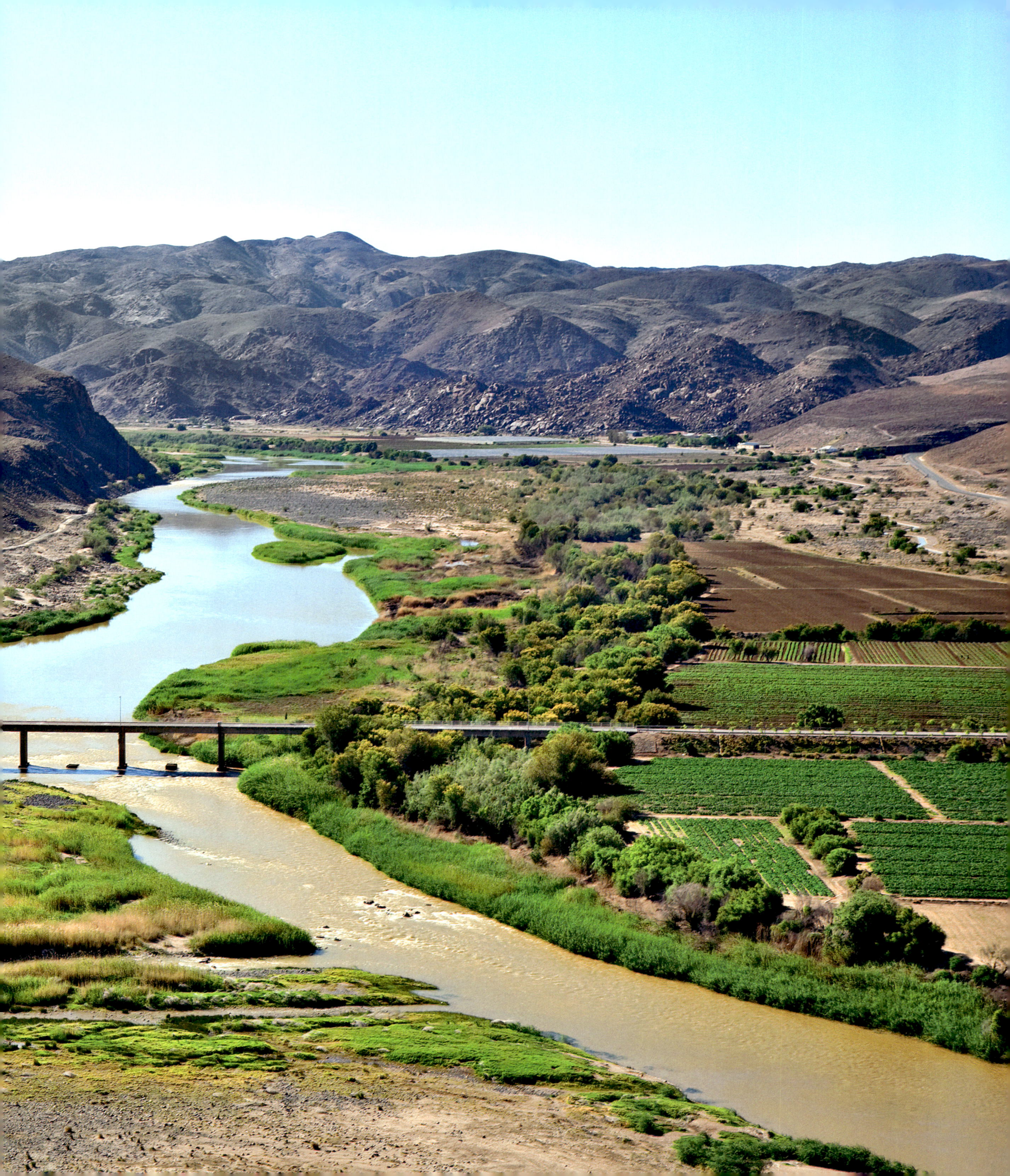

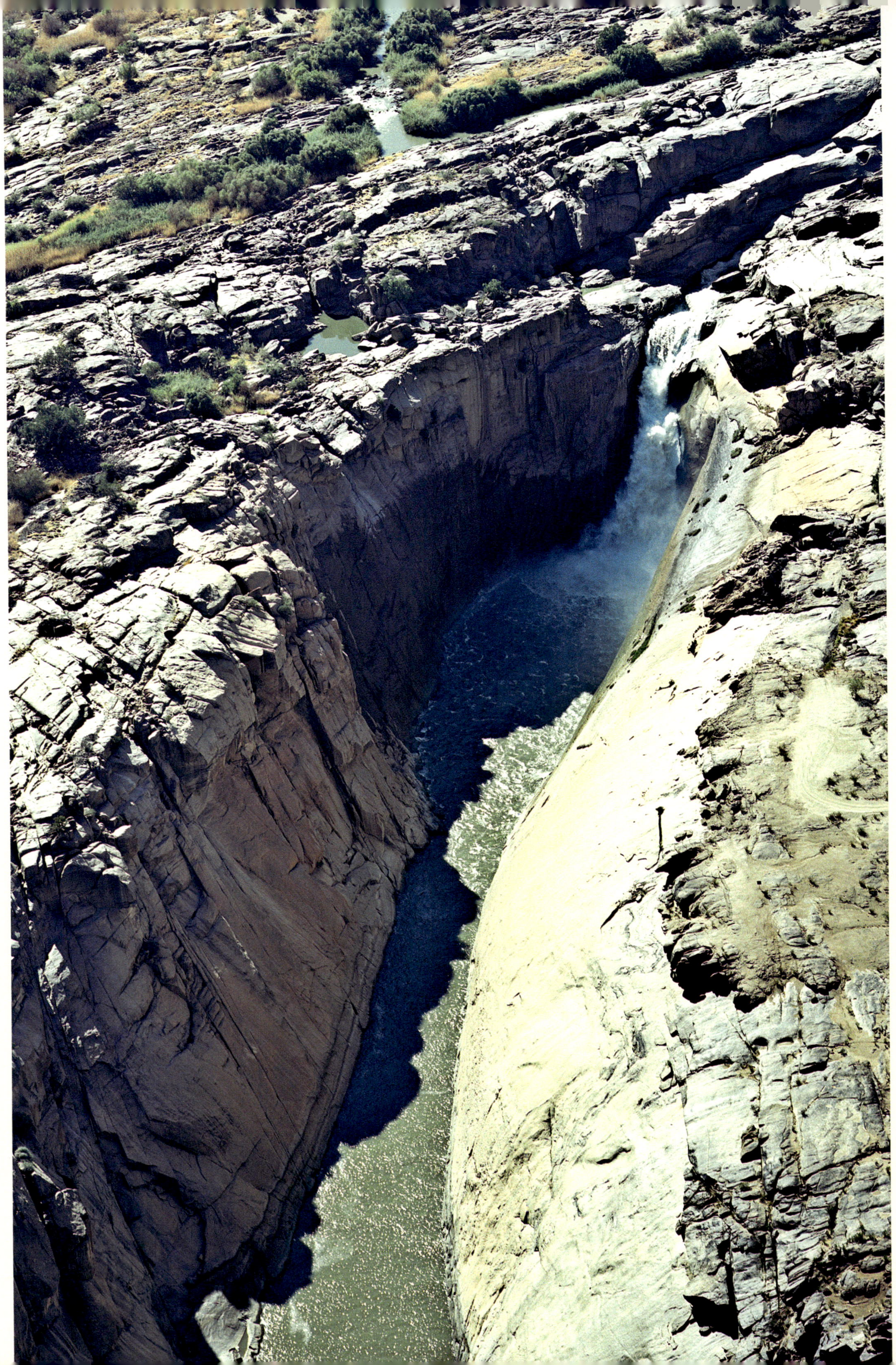

← Border between South Africa and Namibia, Vioolsdrif
→ Augrabies Falls National Park
→→ Drying place Sultana grapes

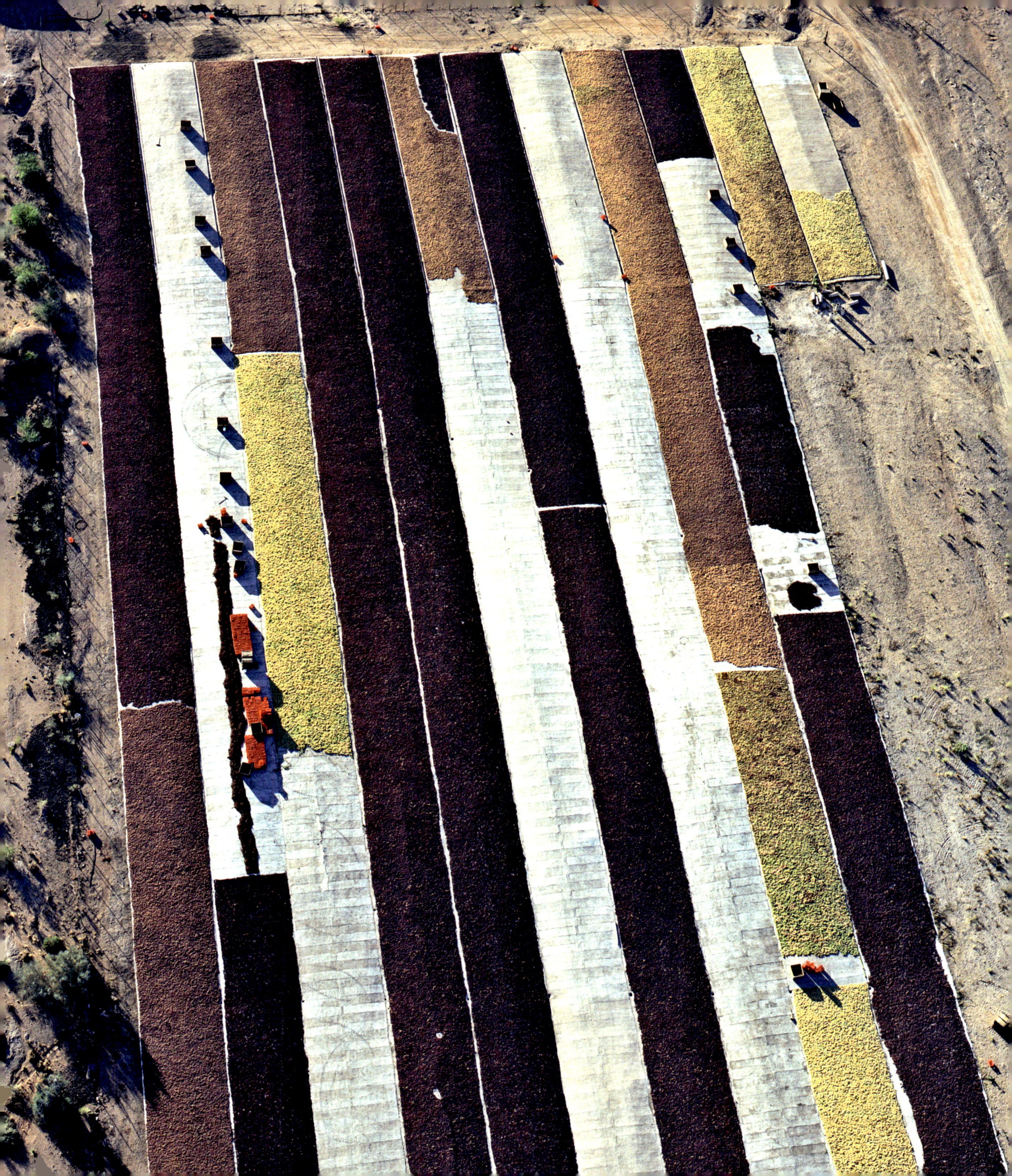

↓ Sultana grapes drying in the hot sun, Kakamas
→ Olive tree plantation, Kakamas

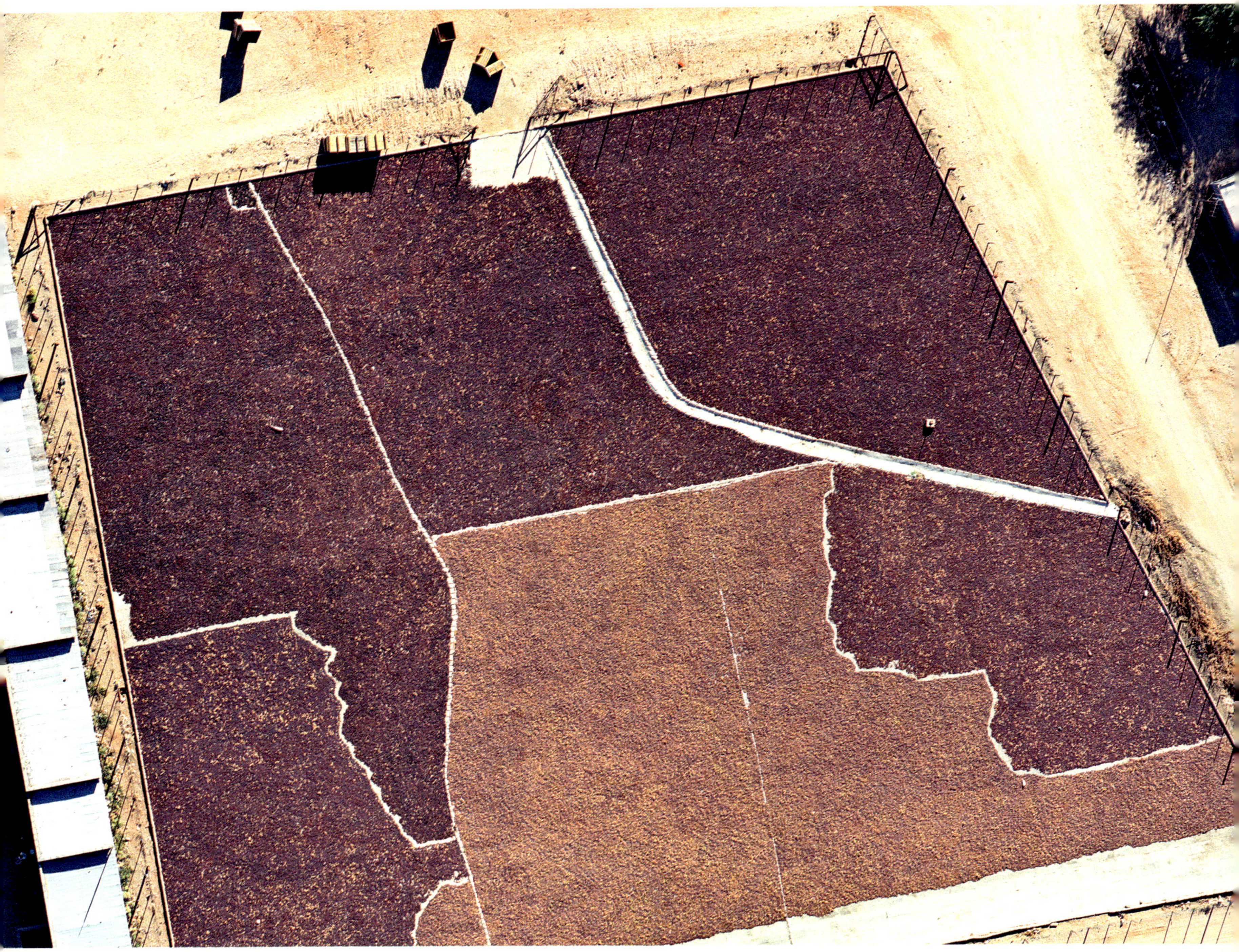

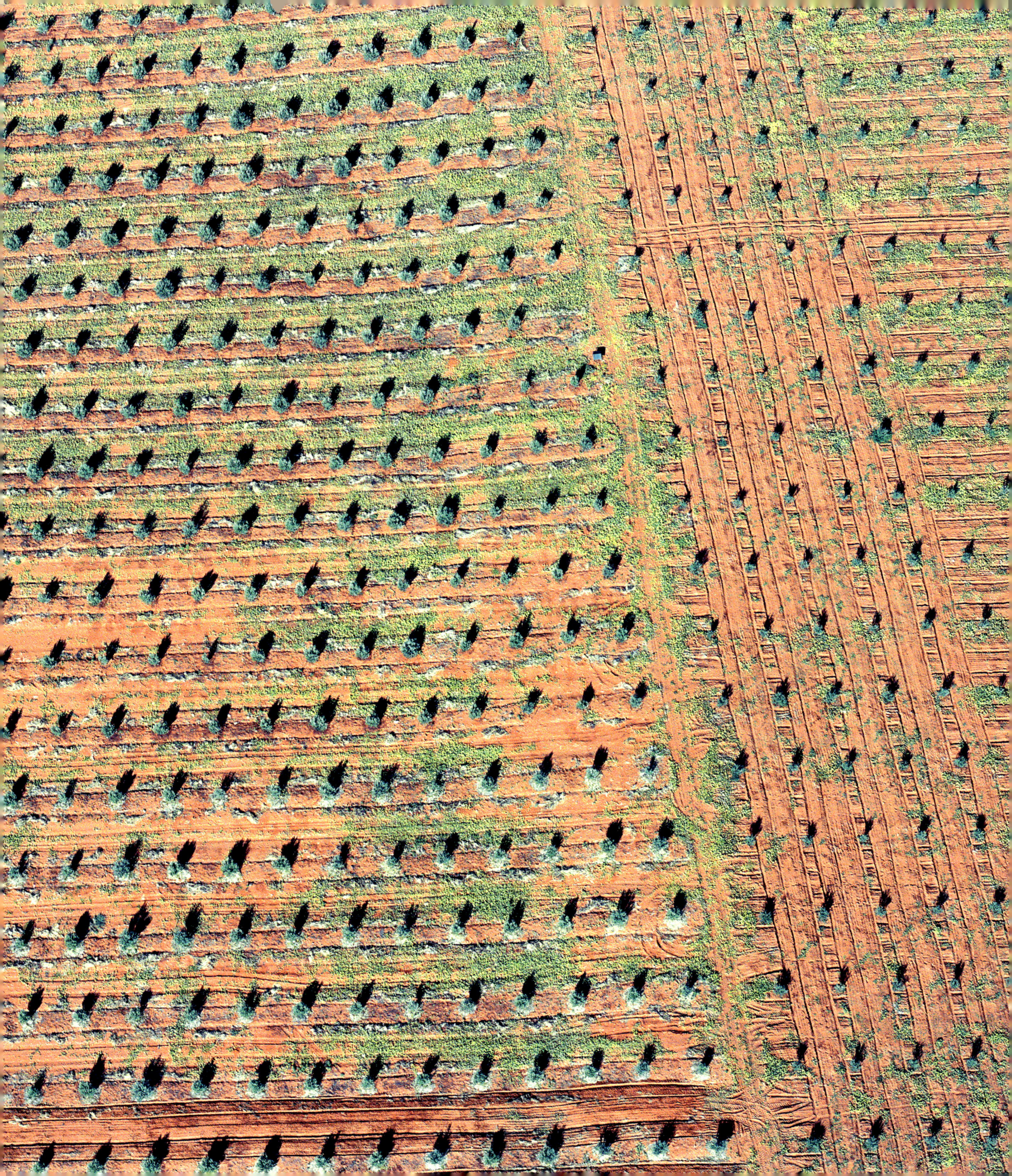

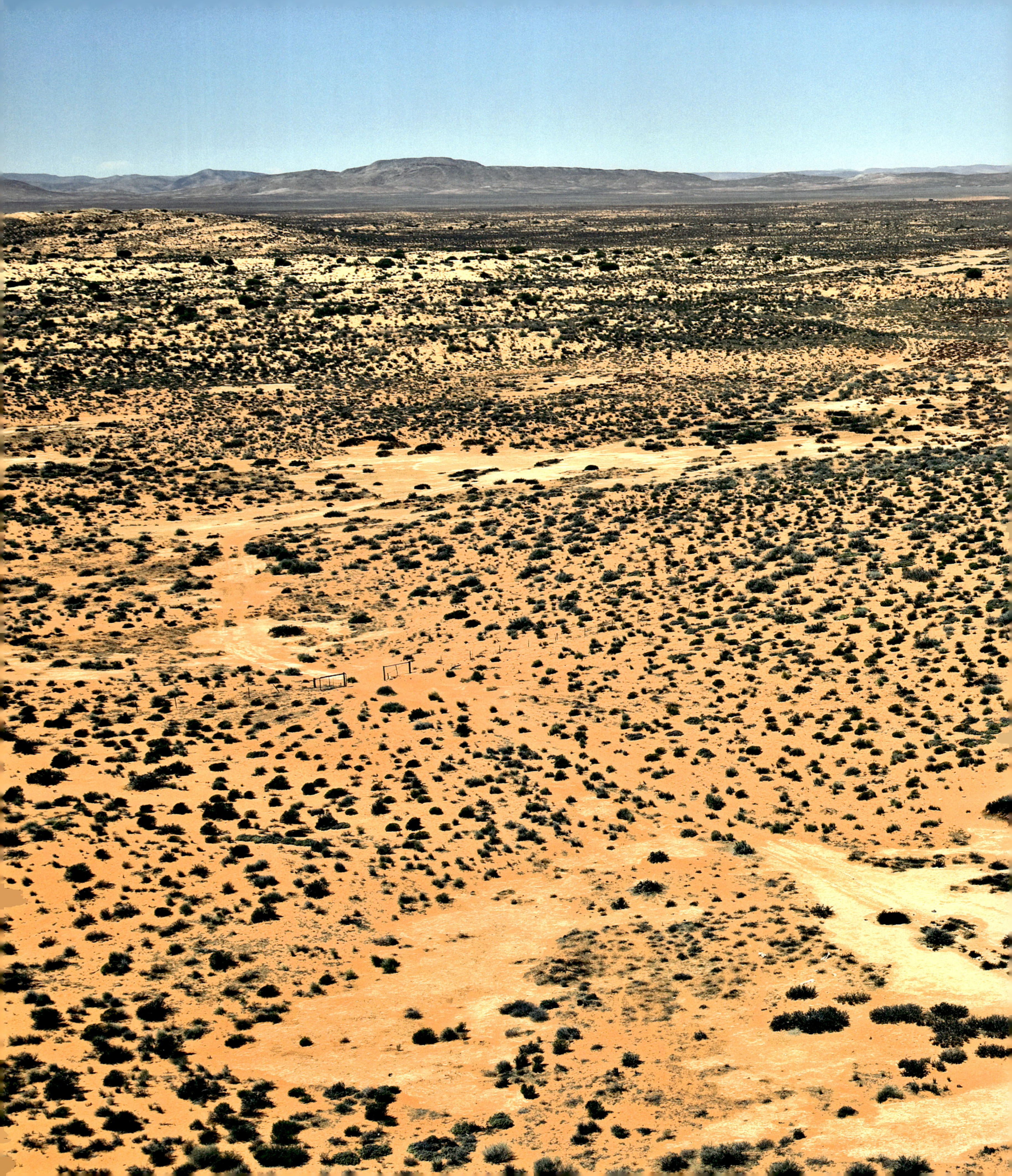

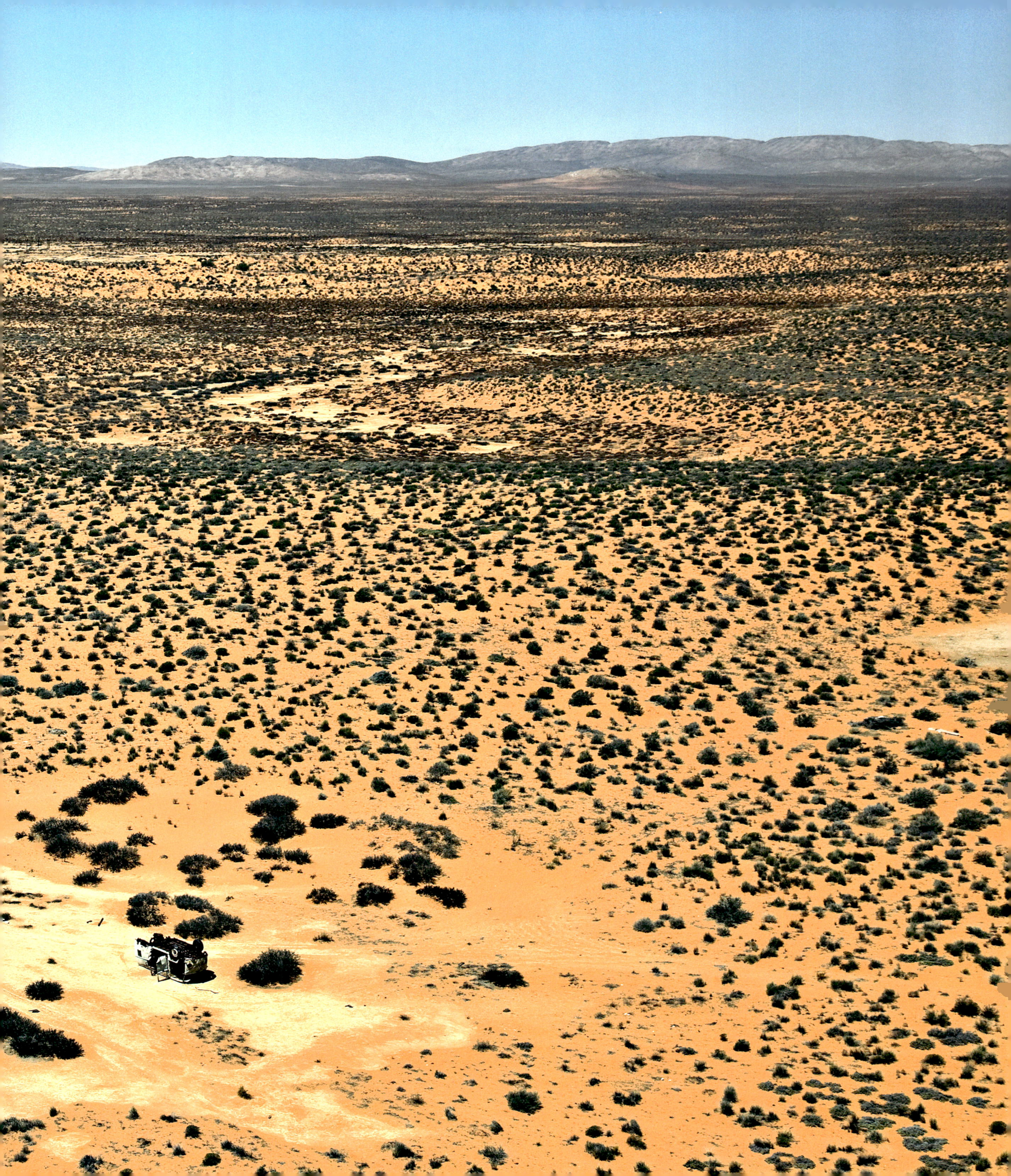

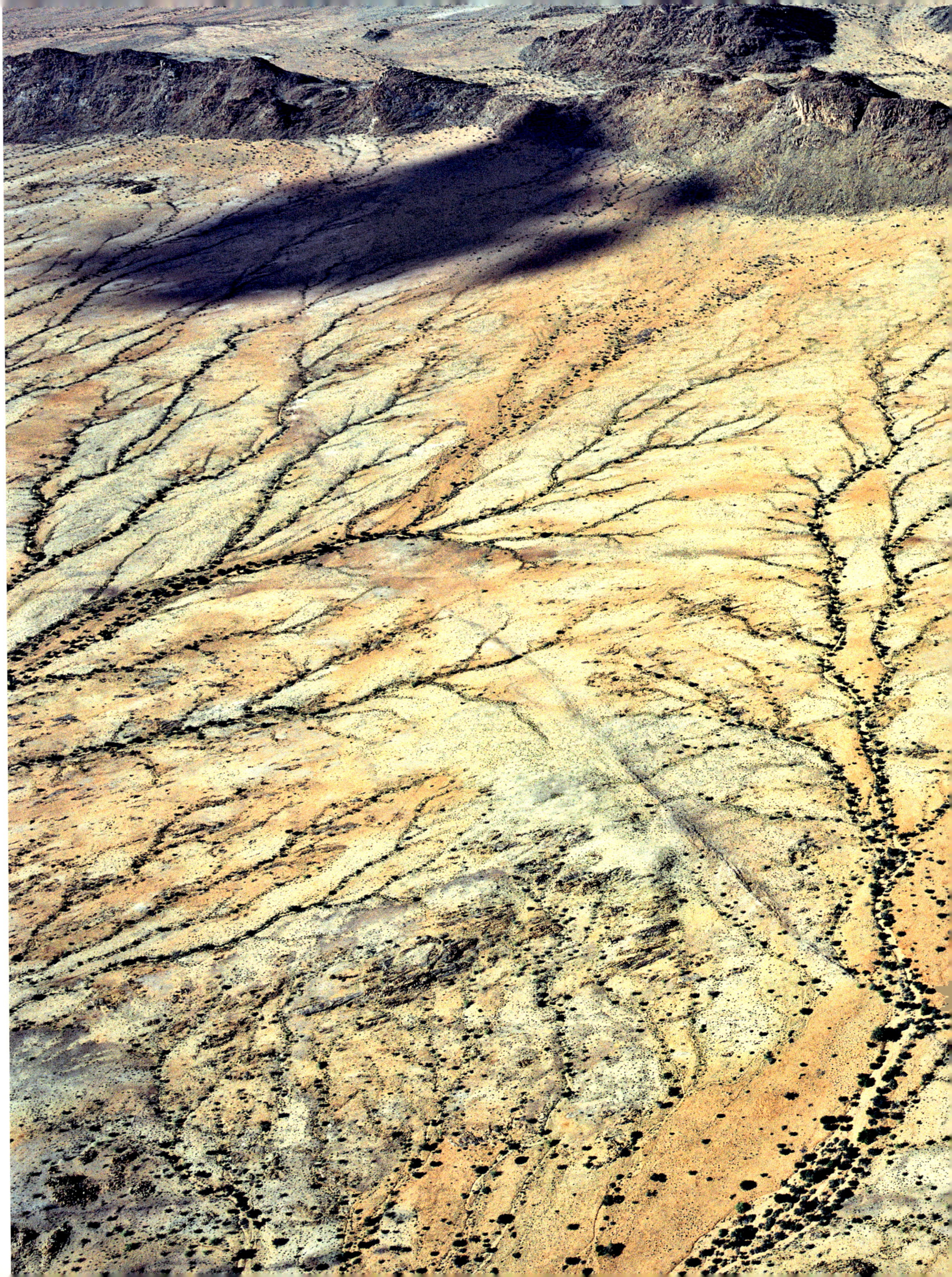

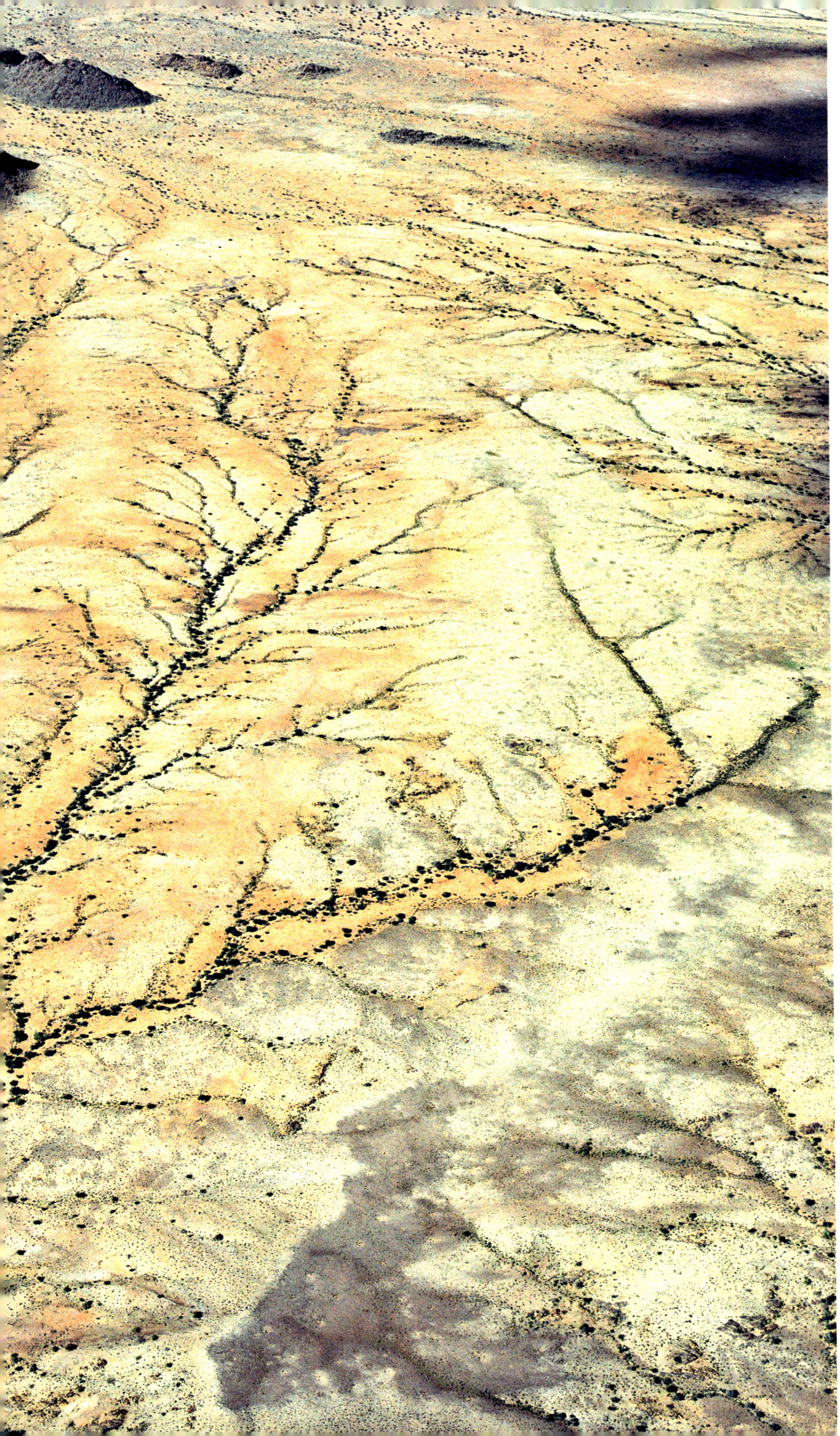

←← Peace and quiet in the desert
← Landscape between Namibia and Botswana, south of Kgalagadi Transfrontier Park

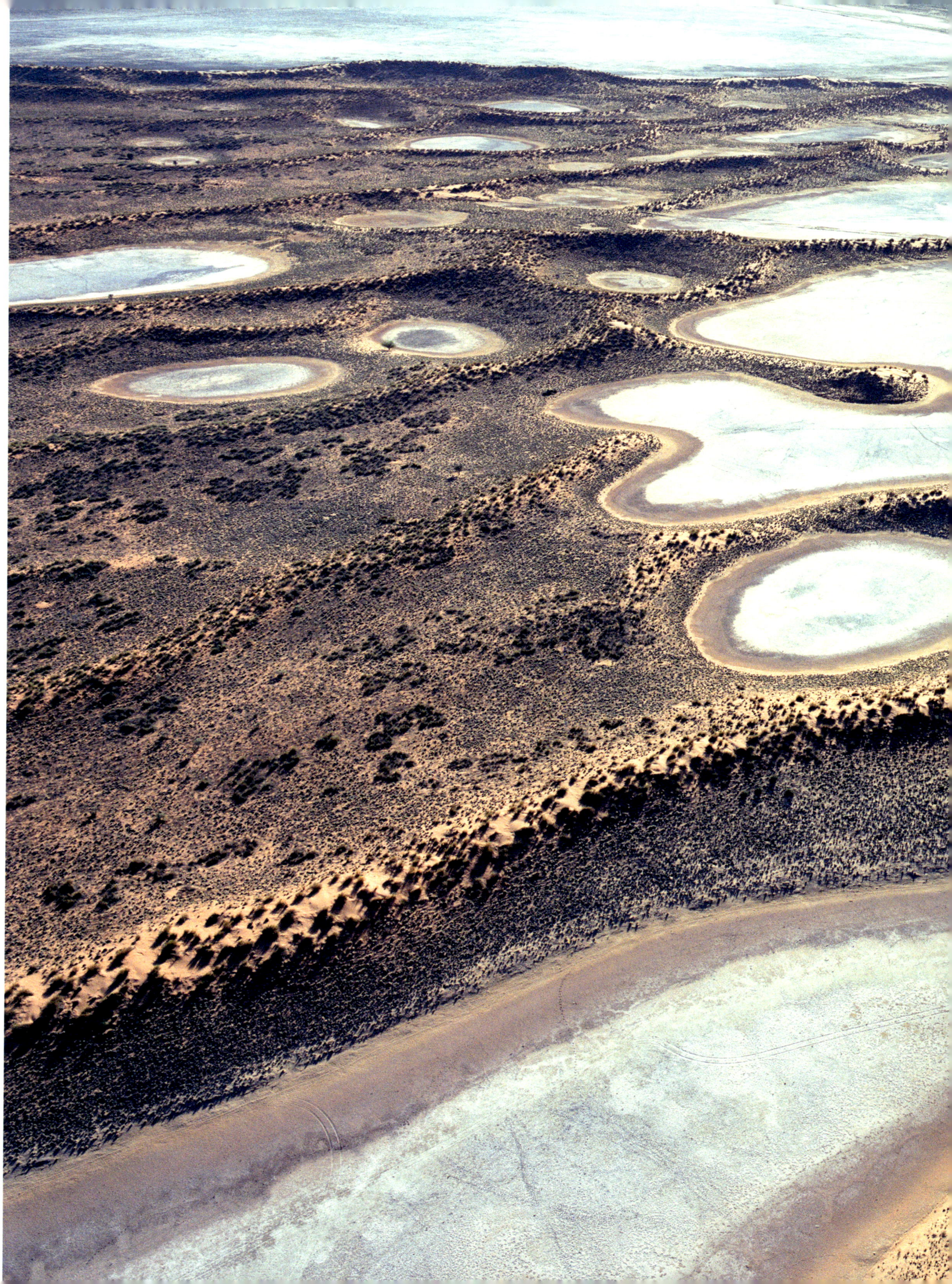

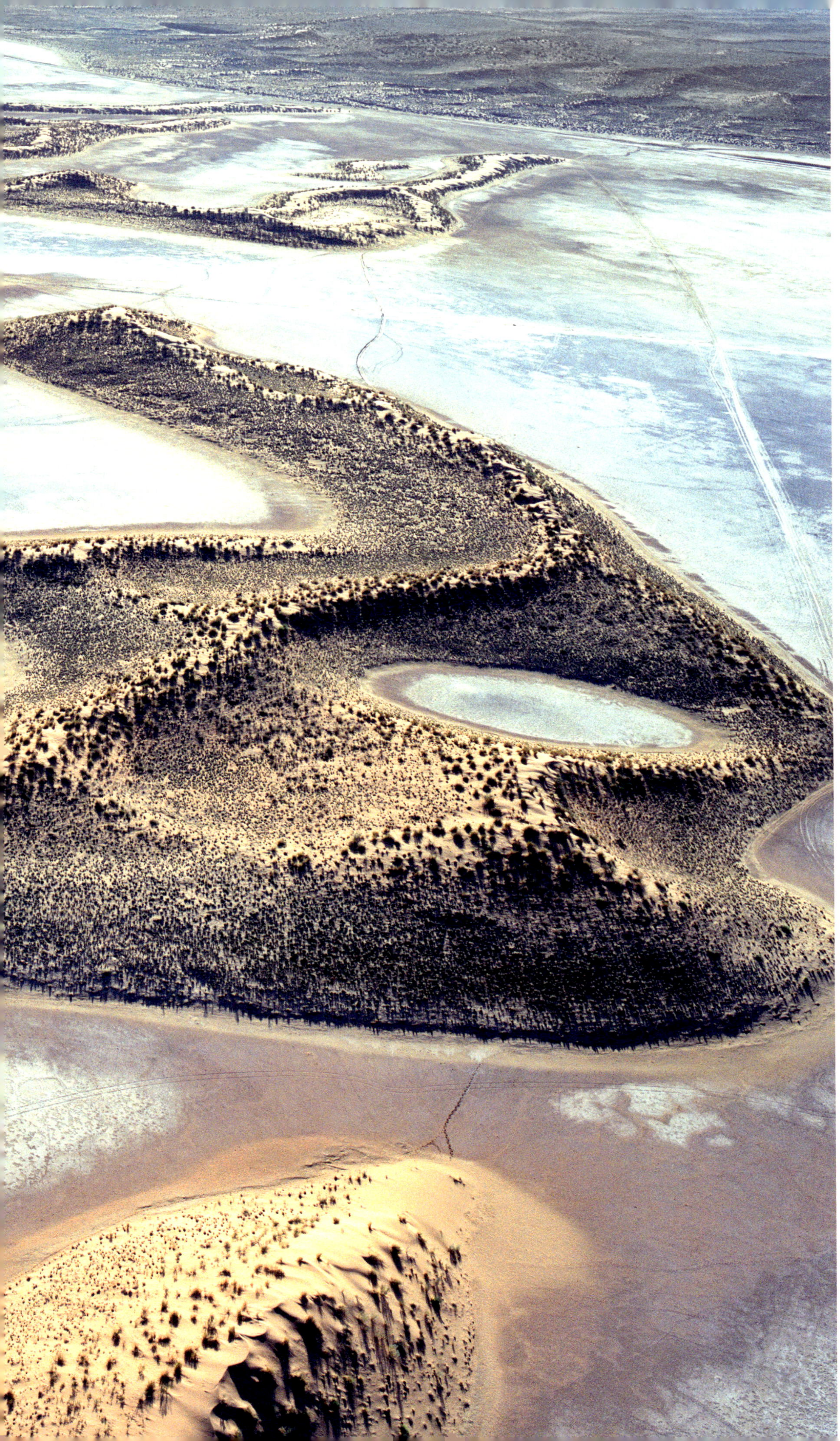

← Koppierkraal Pan,
between Namibia, Botswana
and South Africa

→ Flamingo Island, Kimberley Dam, protected breeding area

→→

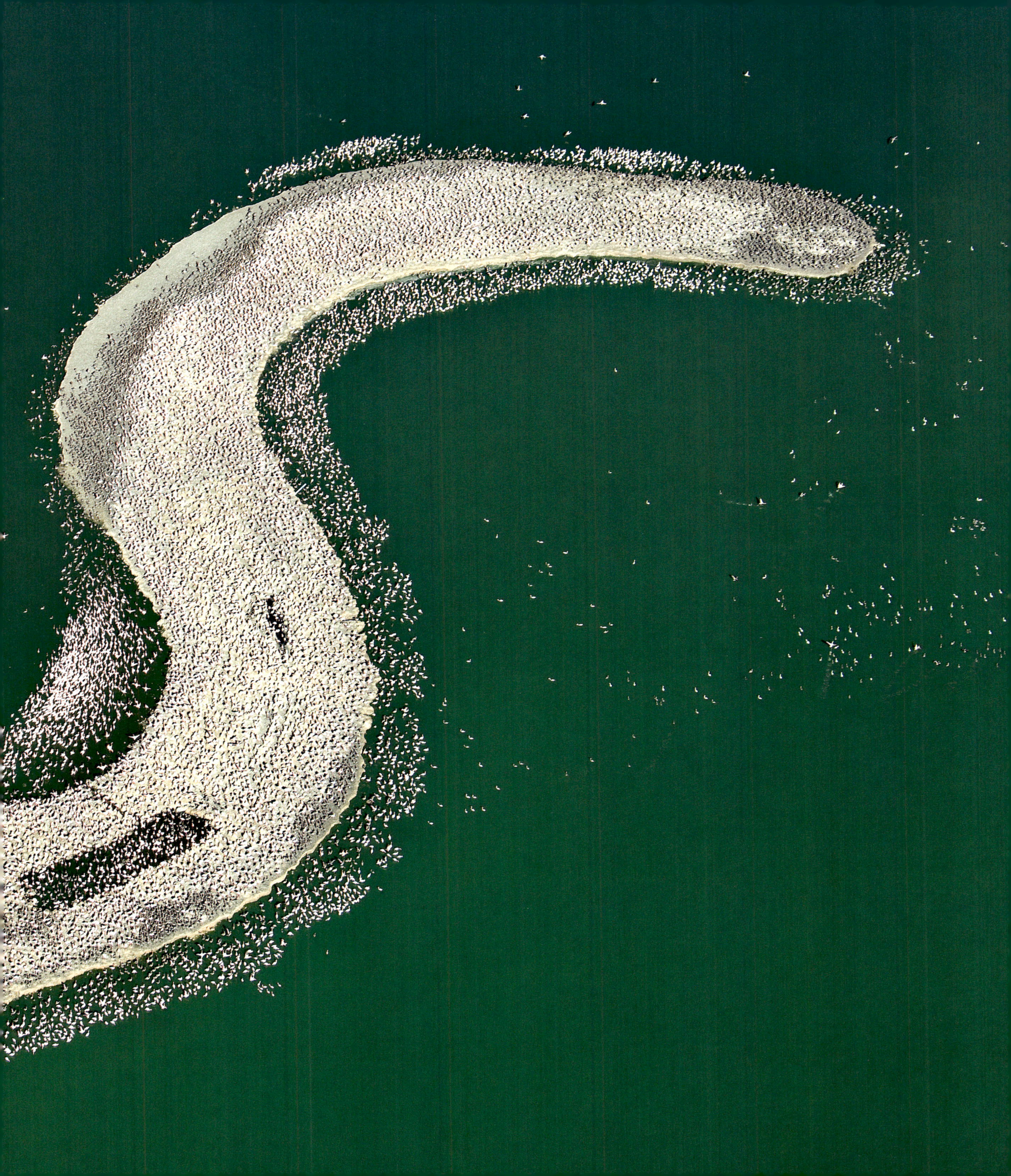

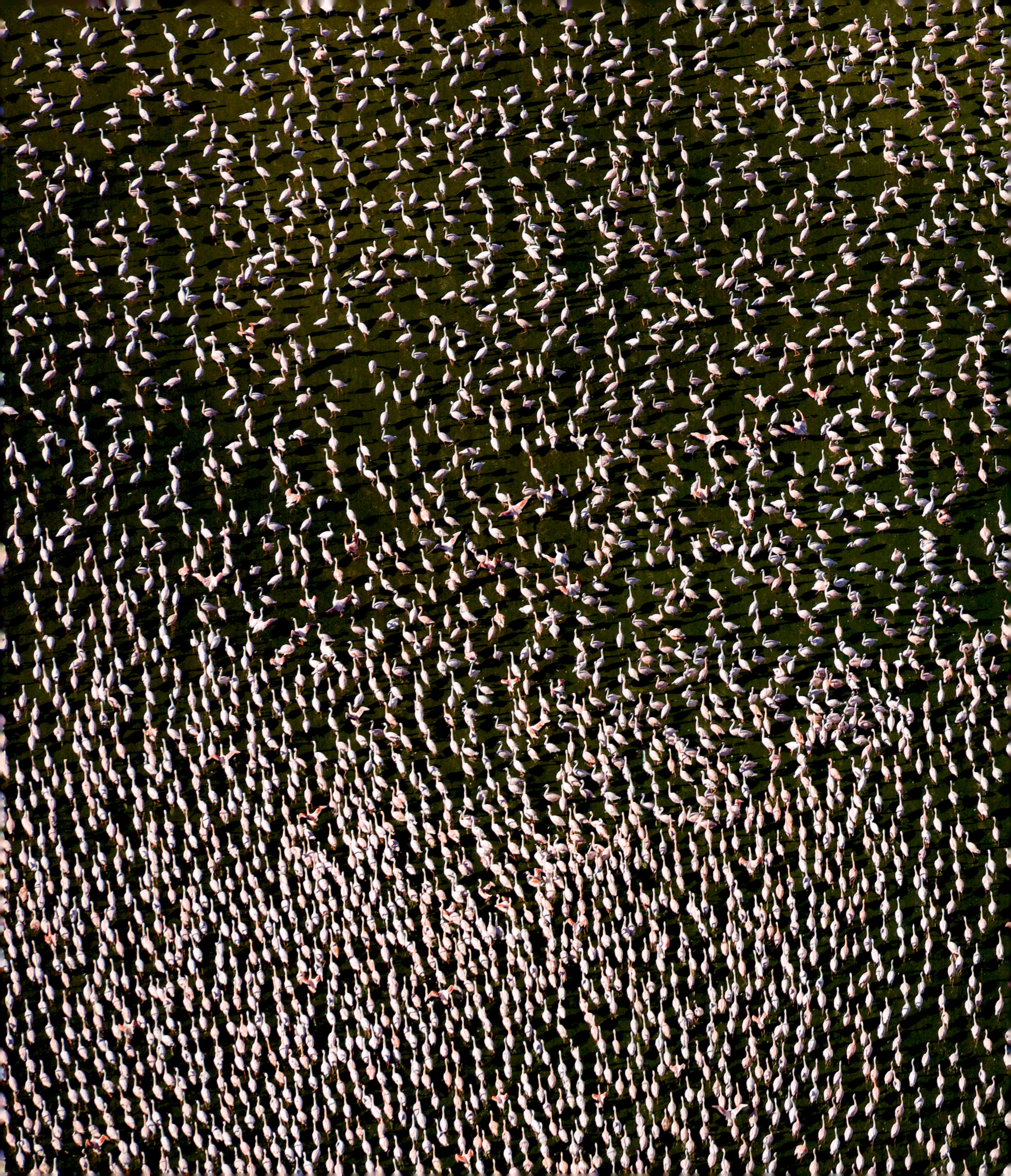

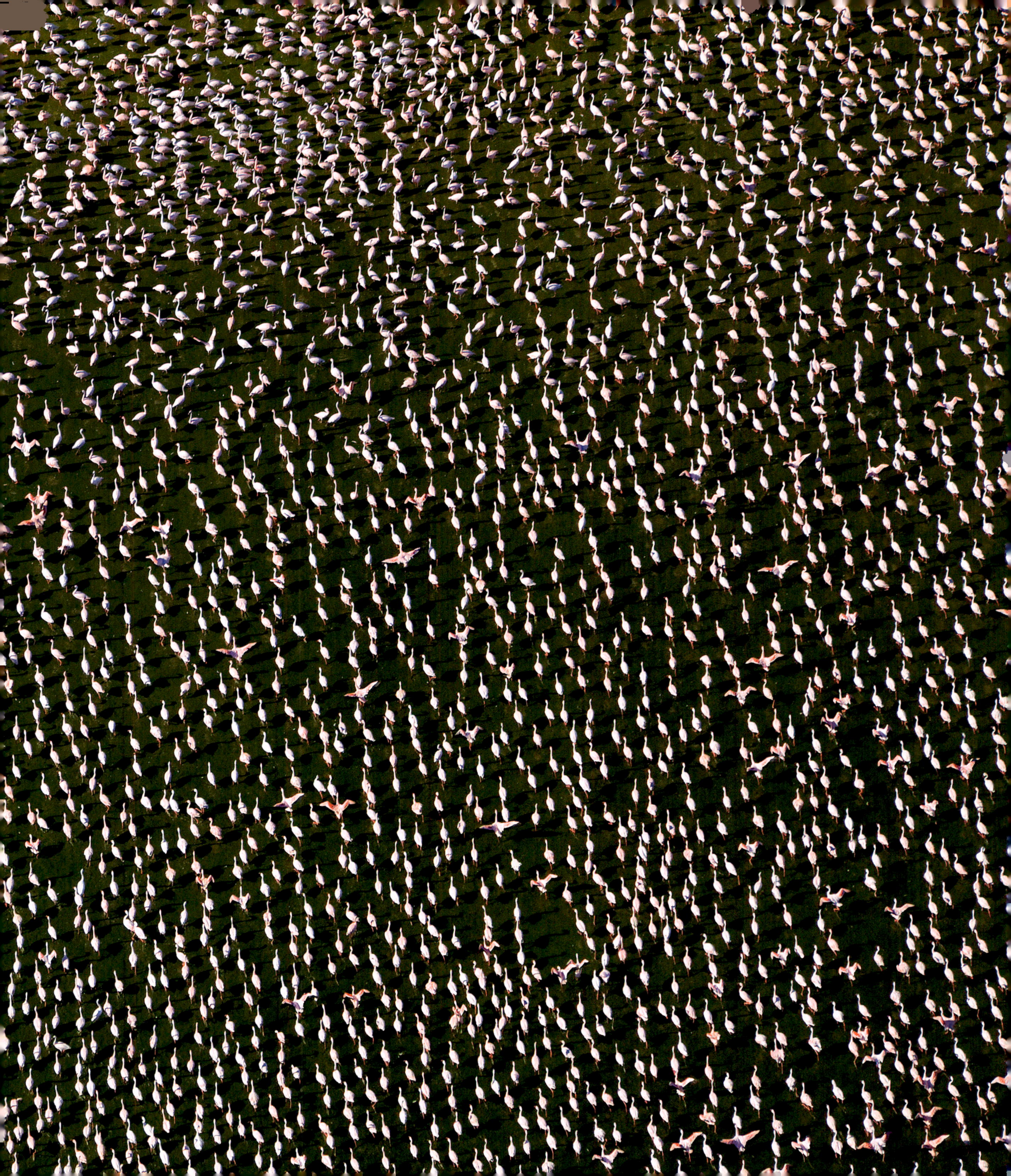

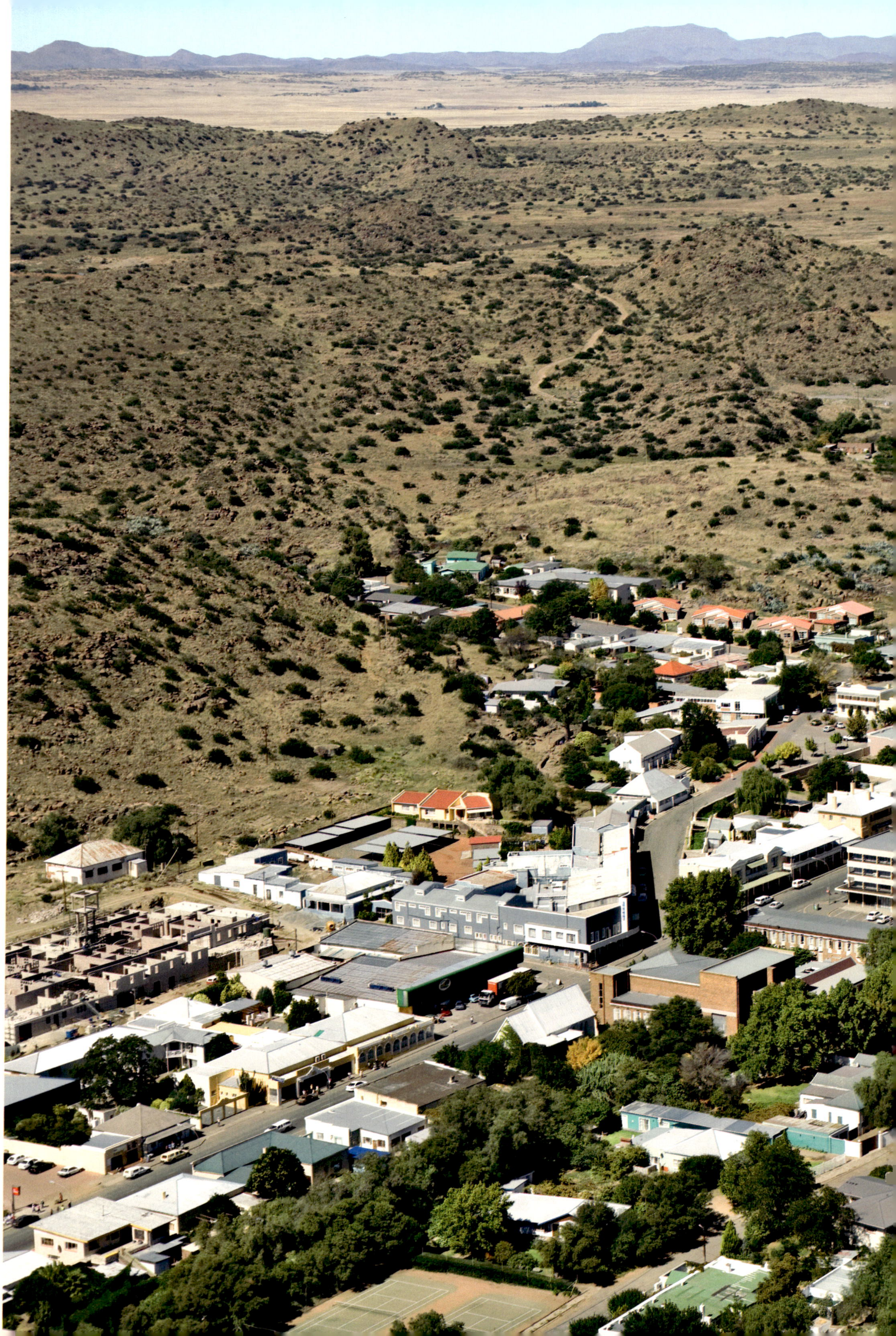

→ Colesberg

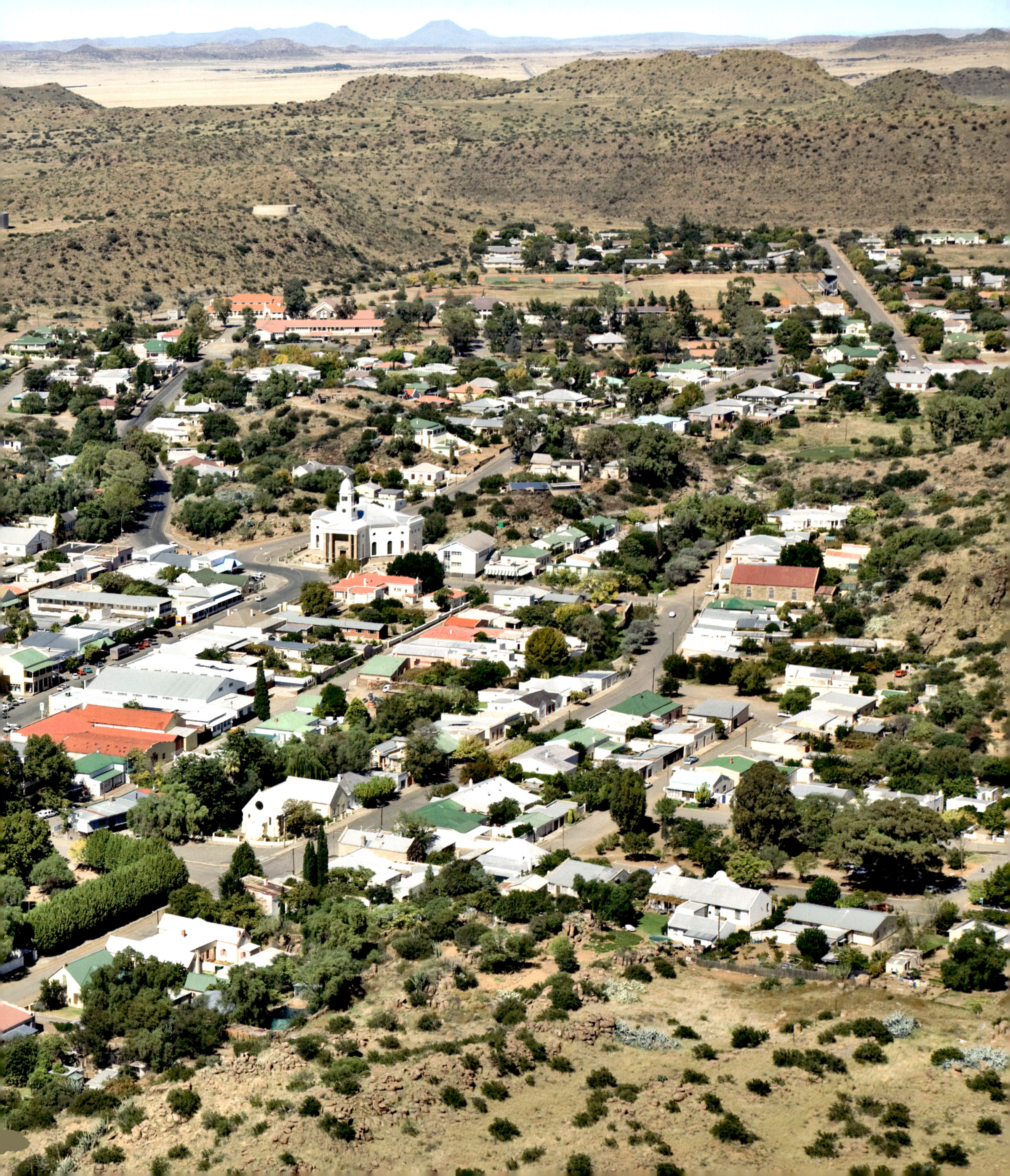

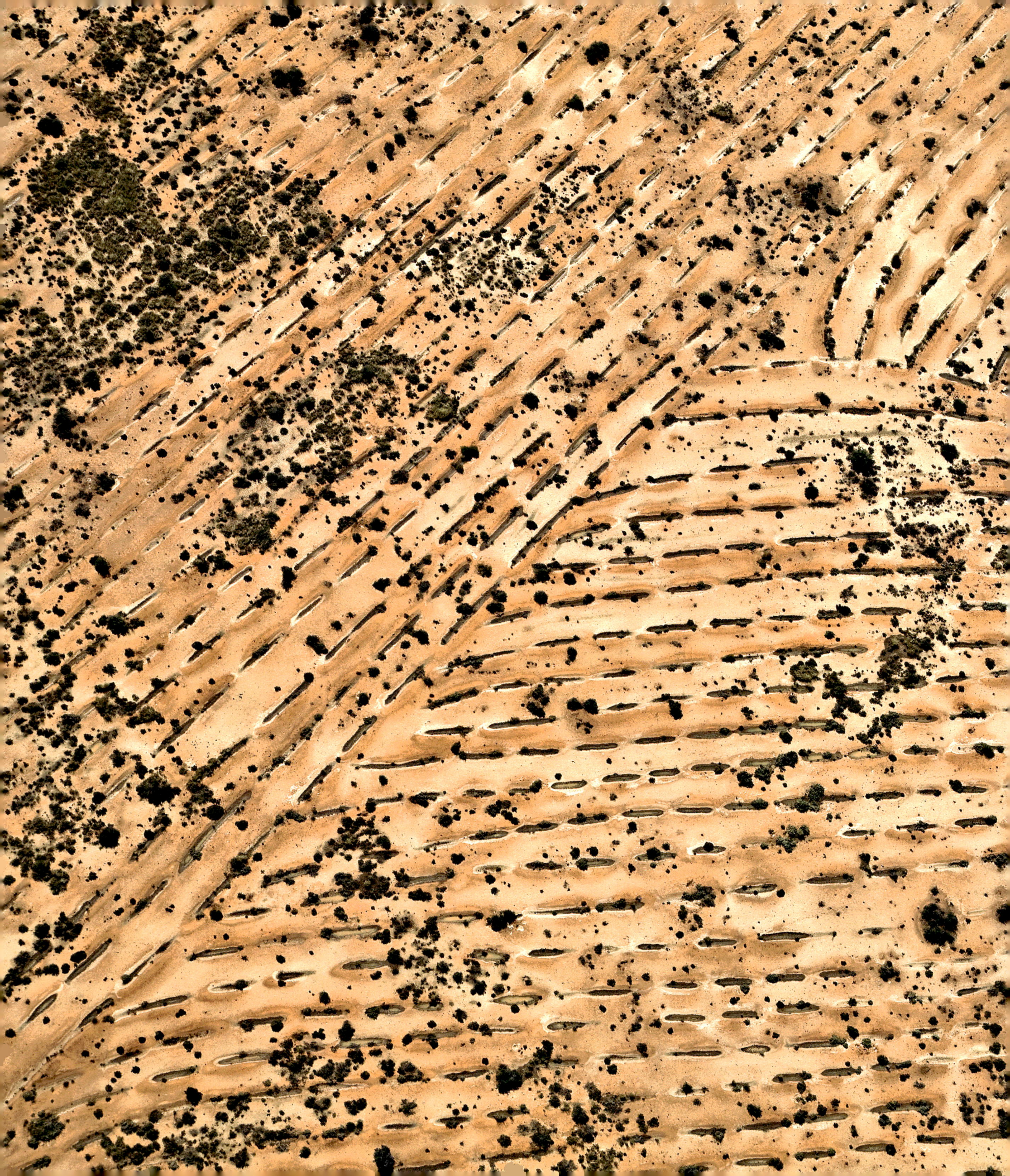

← Brinkspan, artwork created by nature

→ Algae in dam, Victoria West

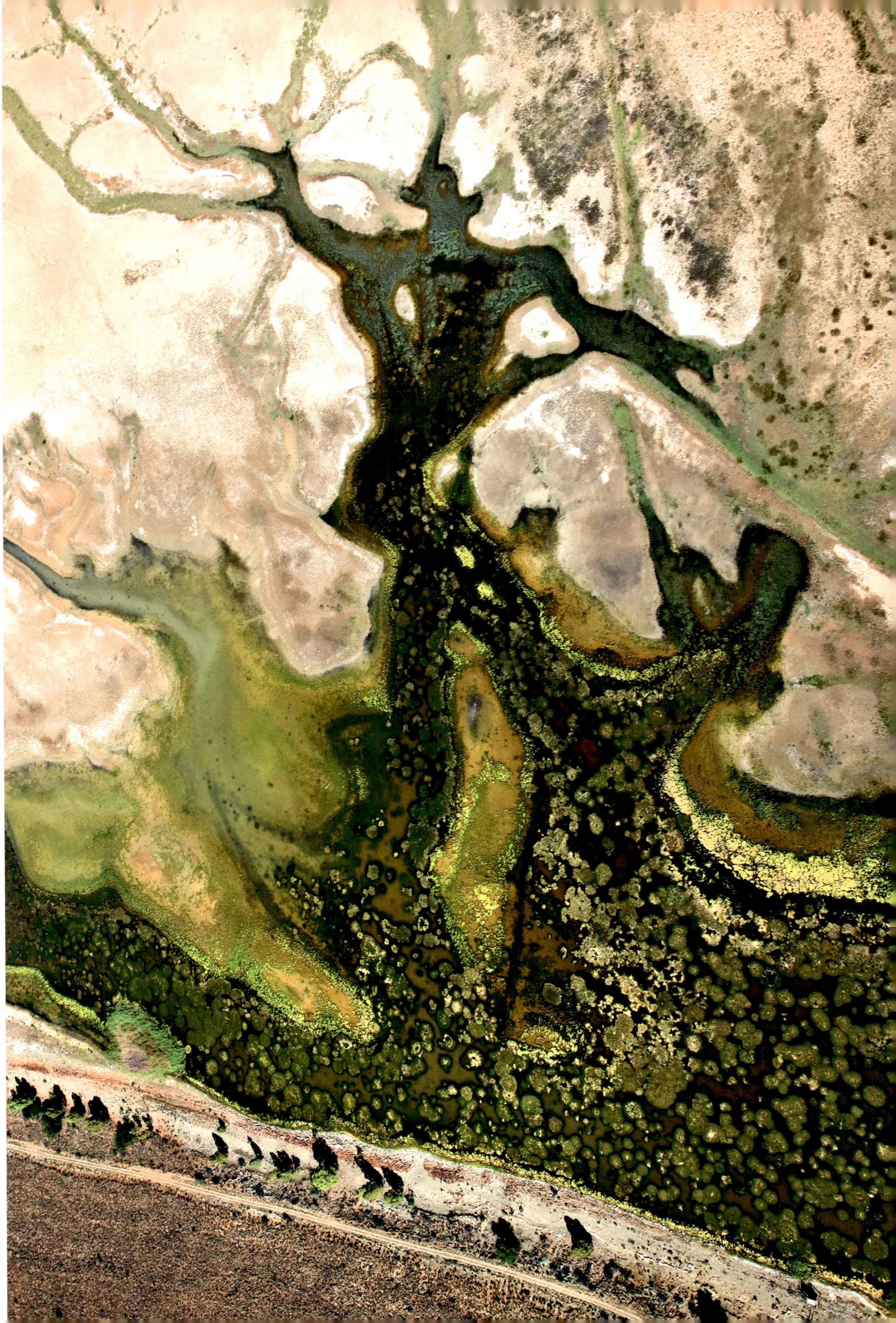

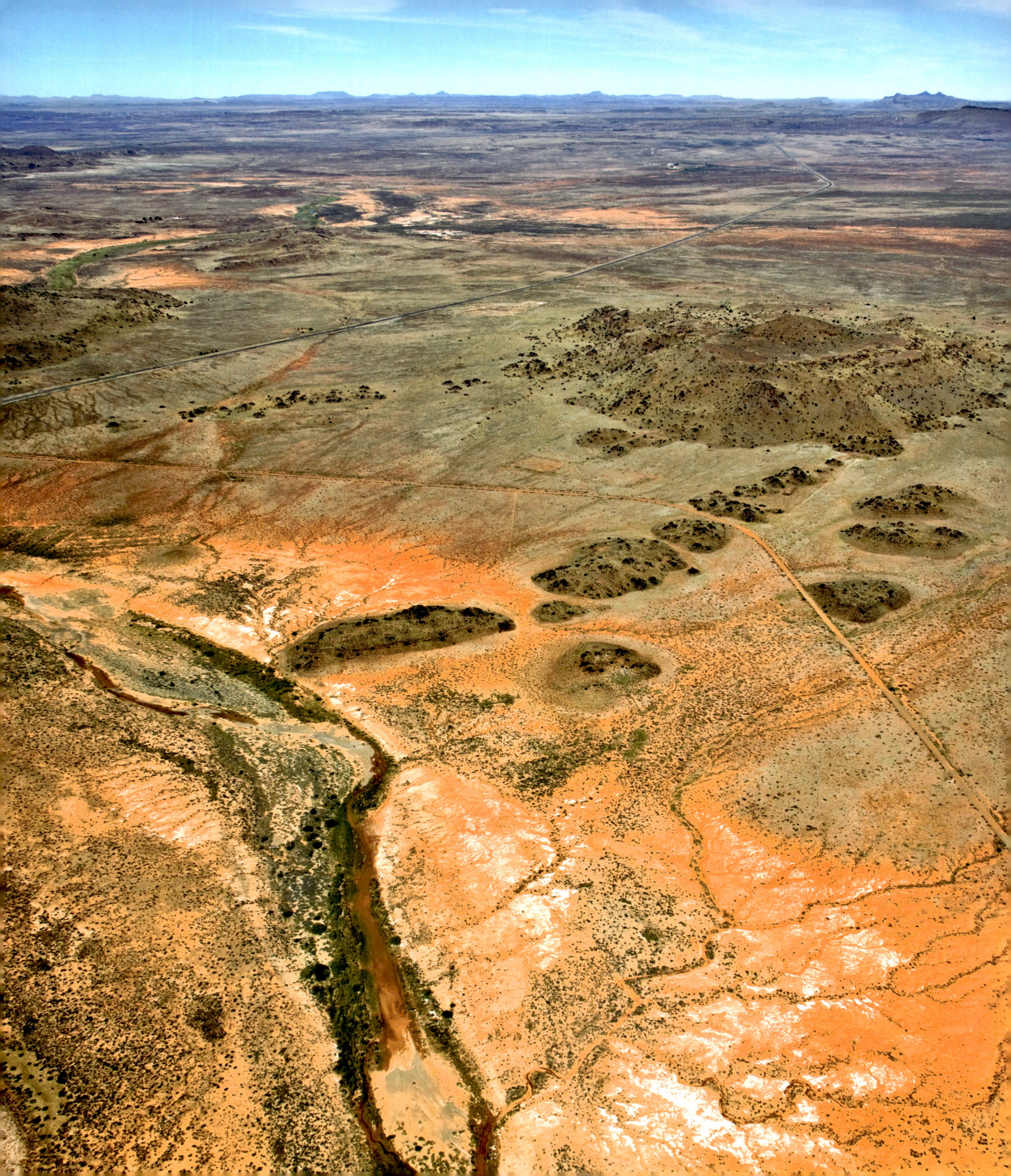

← Great Karoo, between Britstown and Victoria West
↓ Victoria West
→→ Three Sisters, Great Karoo, border area Northern and Western Cape

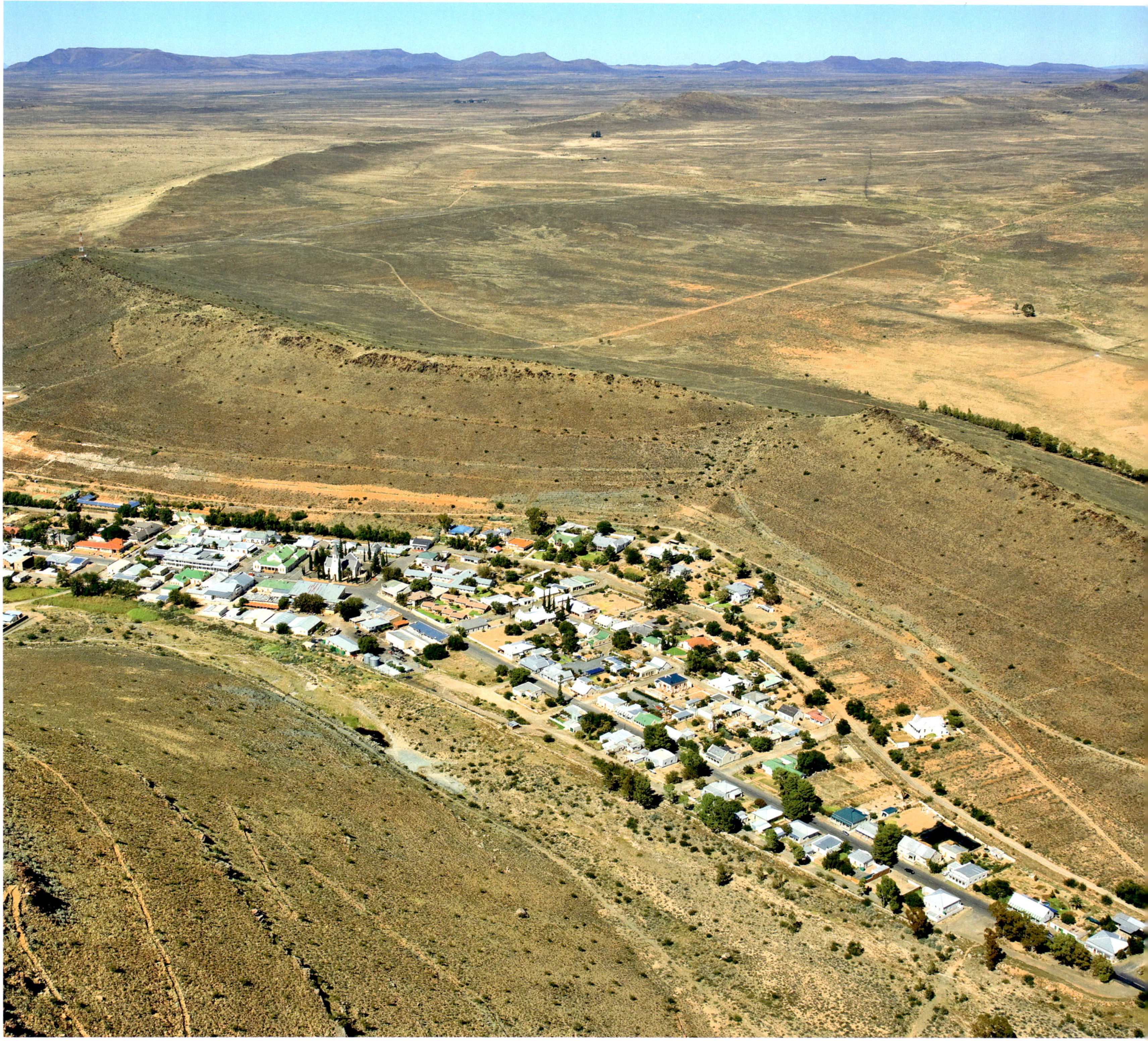

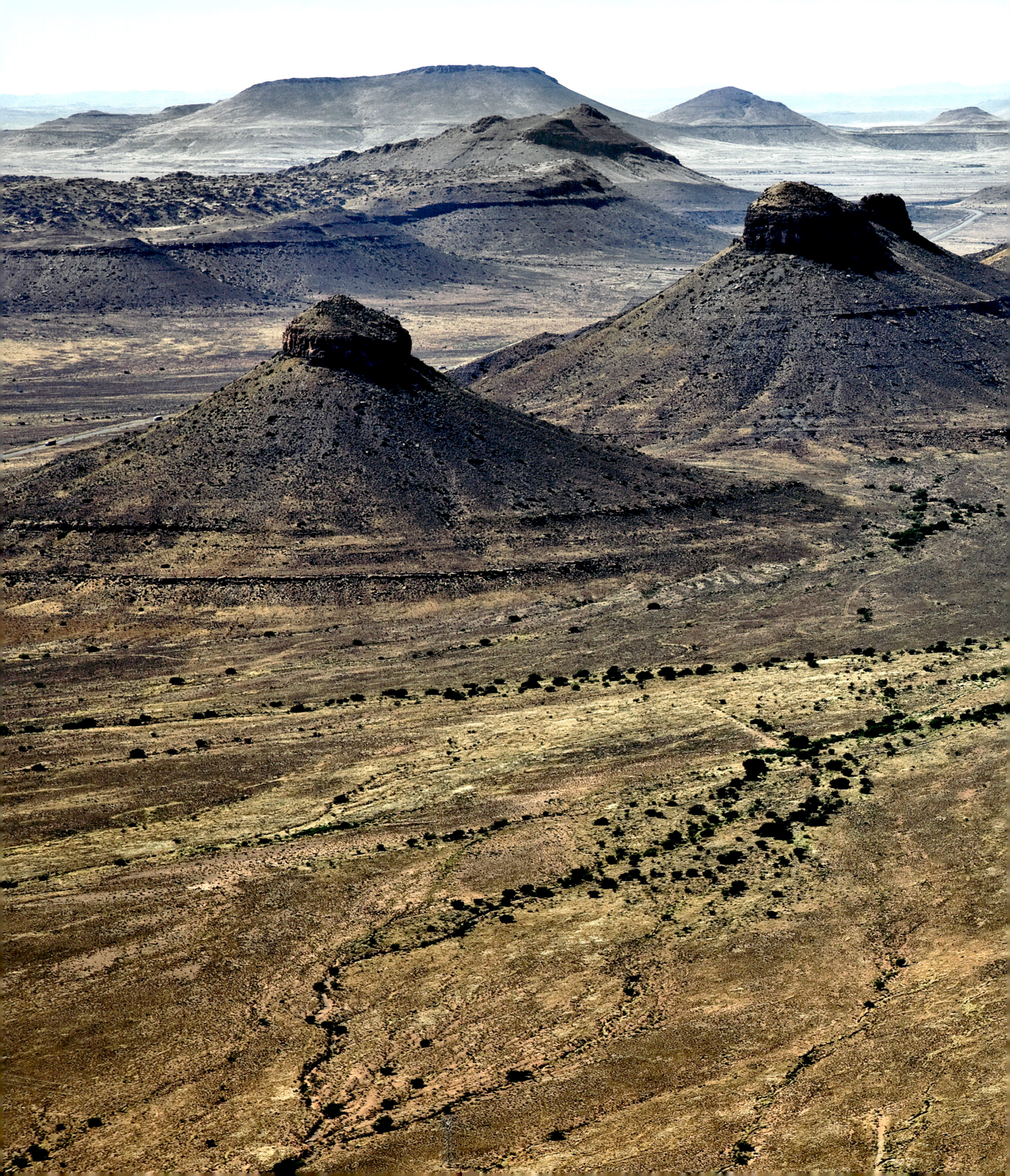

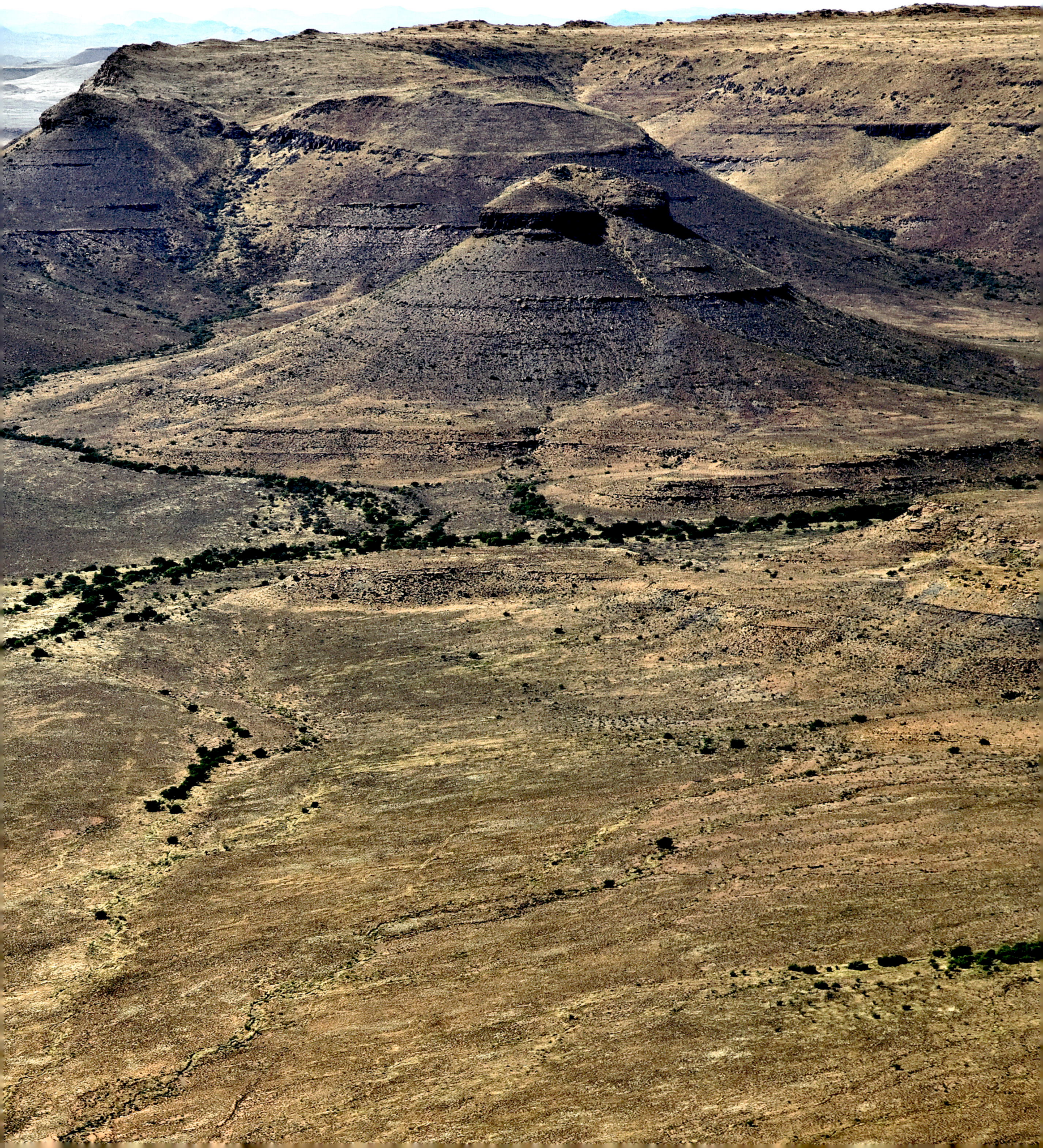

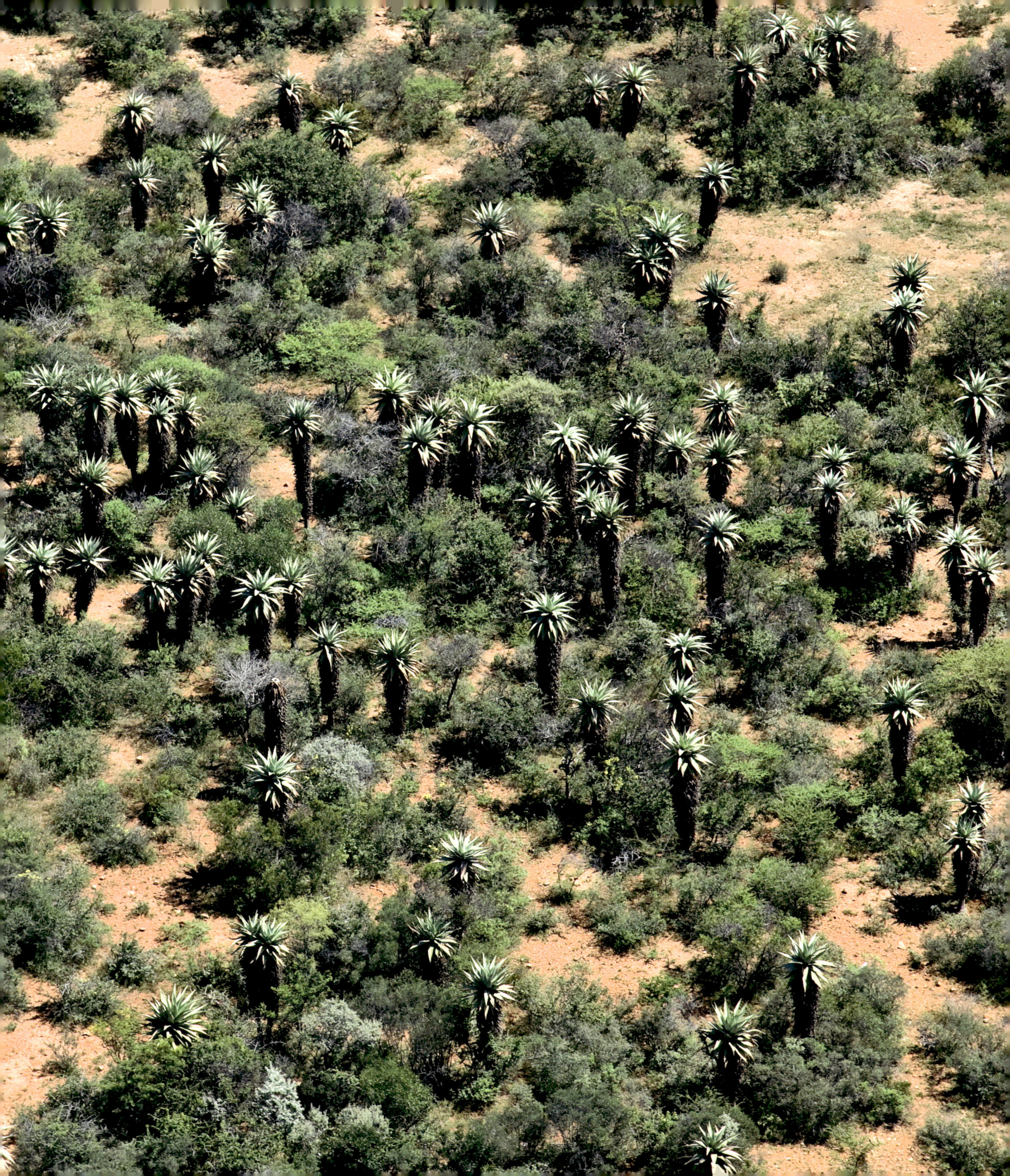

NORTH WEST

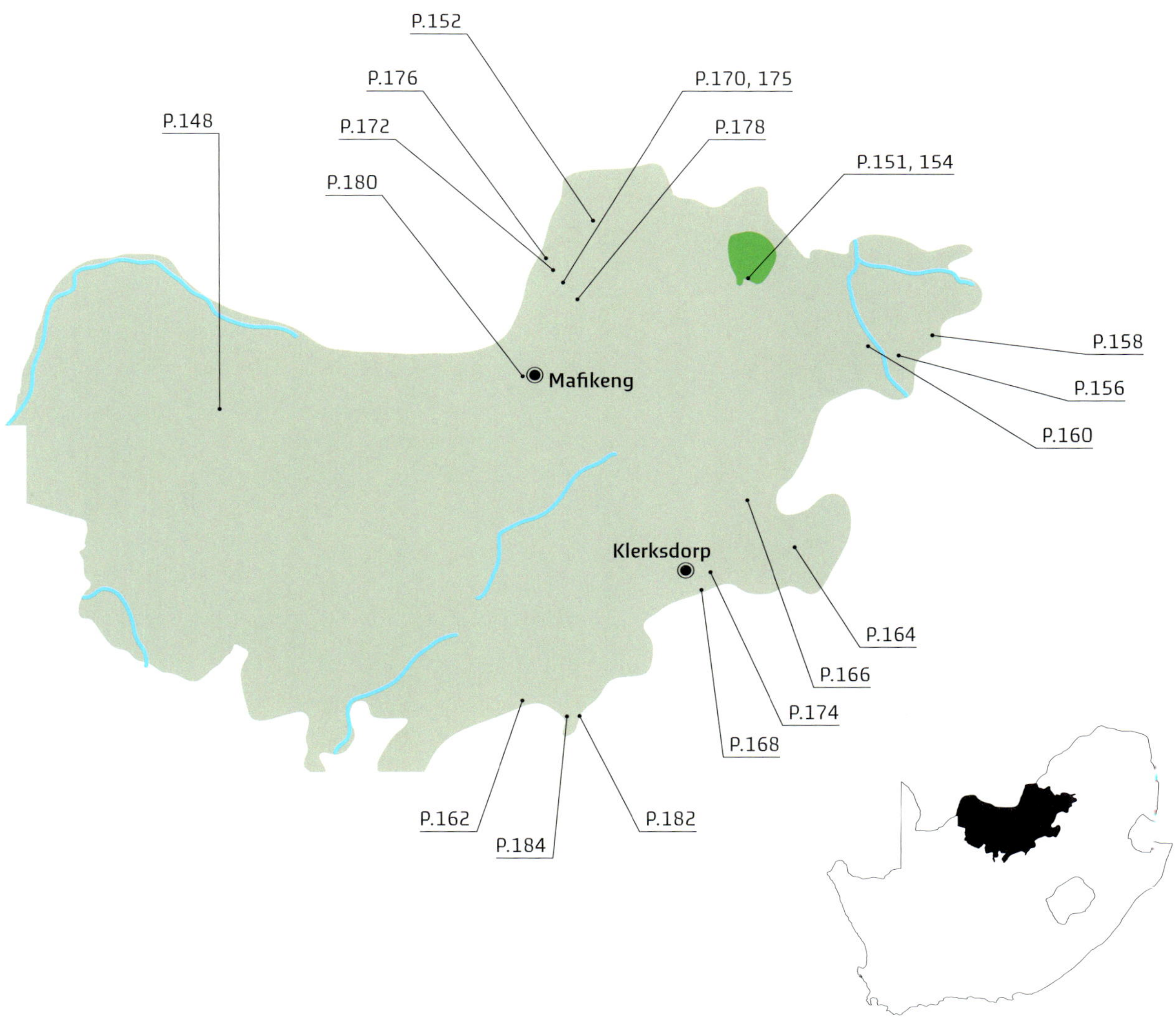
P.152
P.176
P.170, 175
P.148
P.172
P.178
P.151, 154
P.180
Mafikeng
P.158
P.156
P.160
Klerksdorp
P.164
P.166
P.174
P.168
P.162
P.184
P.182

North West. The largest platinum producer in South Africa. Despite its prosaic name, North West is one of South Africa's most interesting provinces. Many only know it because of Sun City, the largest entertainment centre in Africa, boasting many world-class hotels, a casino, theatres and concert halls. But there is much more besides Sun City to discover in North West, the world of hellraiser Herman Charles Bosman.

Cattle, game and mampoer

North West was originally inhabited by the Hurutshe, a Tswana-speaking people who had a flourishing civilisation in the early 19th century. Later, white colonists took over this region with its endless pastures and divided the land up into livestock farms. They started hunting intensively and soon most wildlife was wiped out. Around 1890, the region had been fully transformed into cattle country. It remained that way until the 1980s, when the government decided to actively stimulate tourism and came up with an ambitious plan: Operation Phoenix.

Under Operation Phoenix, 750,000 hectares of land bordering on Botswana were purchased and restocked with wildlife that had originally lived there. It was a mega – some called it megalomaniac – project, but it achieved its aim: today, the malaria-free Madikwe Game Reserve boasts, in addition to the Big Five, around 150 species of mammal. Madikwe is owned by the state and is run by the North West Parks Board, which is emphatic in seeing environmental management as an instrument for socio-economic development. The Board's aim is 'to conserve wild animals, plants and landscapes for the benefit of people'.

To the east, Madikwe borders on the Morico District, the land of home-distilled mampoer. Drinking mampoer is an unforgettable experience. And there are few people who dare to try it a second time. It is distilled from every fruit imaginable and, according to connoisseurs, should have an alcohol percentage of at least 64%. Mampoer is an acquired taste – not everyone can stomach it. Some time ago, a foreign journalist described the drink as a mixture of tequila and kerosene, which can cause 'excessive brain damage'.

One man who did love mampoer was the writer, teacher and journalist Herman Charles Bosman. Bosman was a hellraiser who was jailed for years for the murder of his step-brother. But he was also the master storyteller of Marico and arguably the best writer of short-stories who has ever lived in South Africa. One of Bosman's best-known stories takes place in a bar where a couple of friends are enjoying a drink. With each glass, they become increasingly fascinated by the waitress – or more specifically, by the scar on her chin. Is it true that she got the scar when a demon kissed her? No, they soon discover. That would be too good to be true. It turns out the waitress got the scar when a bottle of mampoer exploded in her face...

Today, many hotels and safari lodges in North West place books by the master storyteller of Marico in their guest rooms. And the guests seem to enjoy them. At least, many of them seem to take the books home with them in their suitcases.

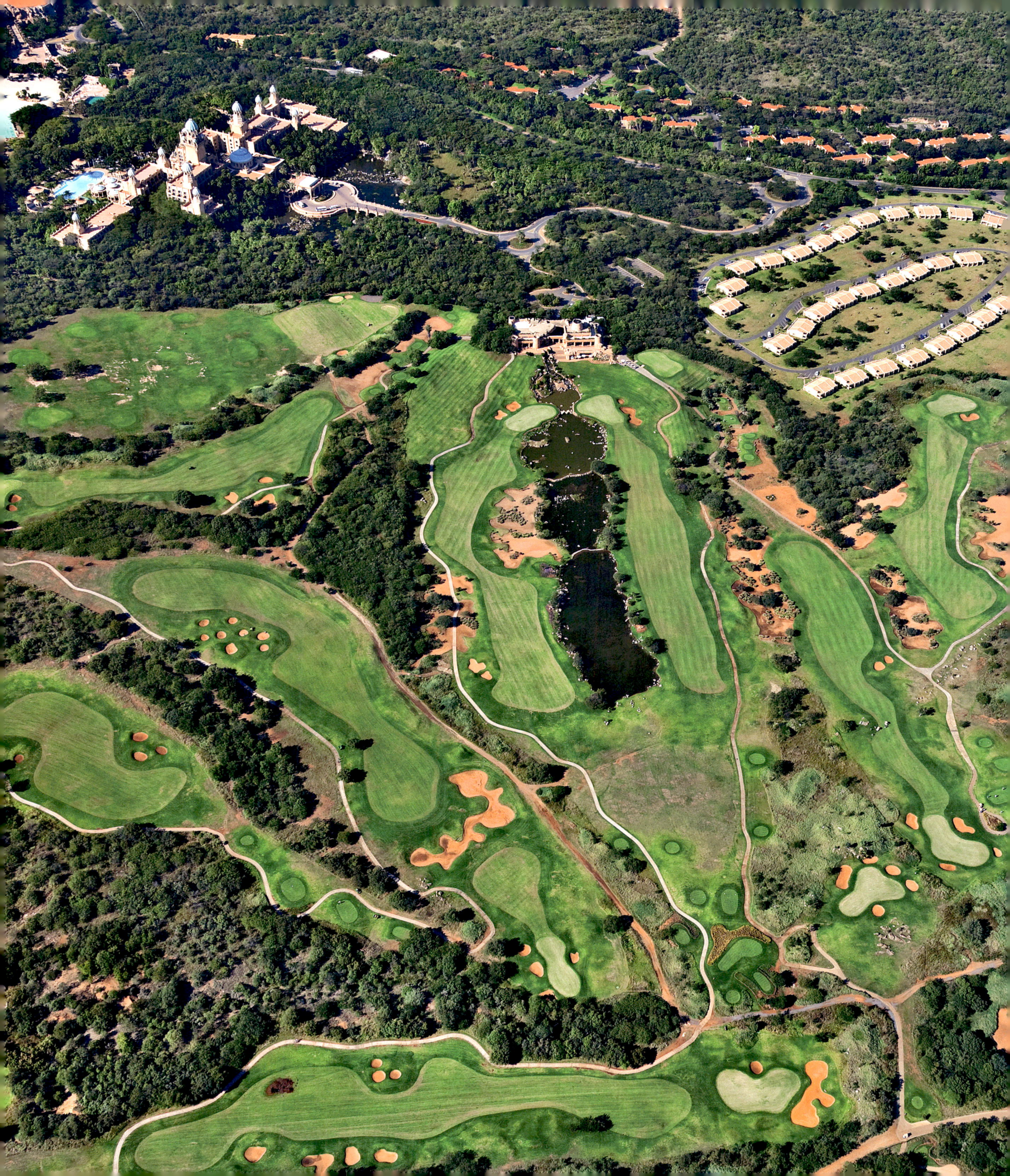

↓ Borakalalo Game Reserve, bird tree
→ Giraffes in Borakalalo Game Reserve

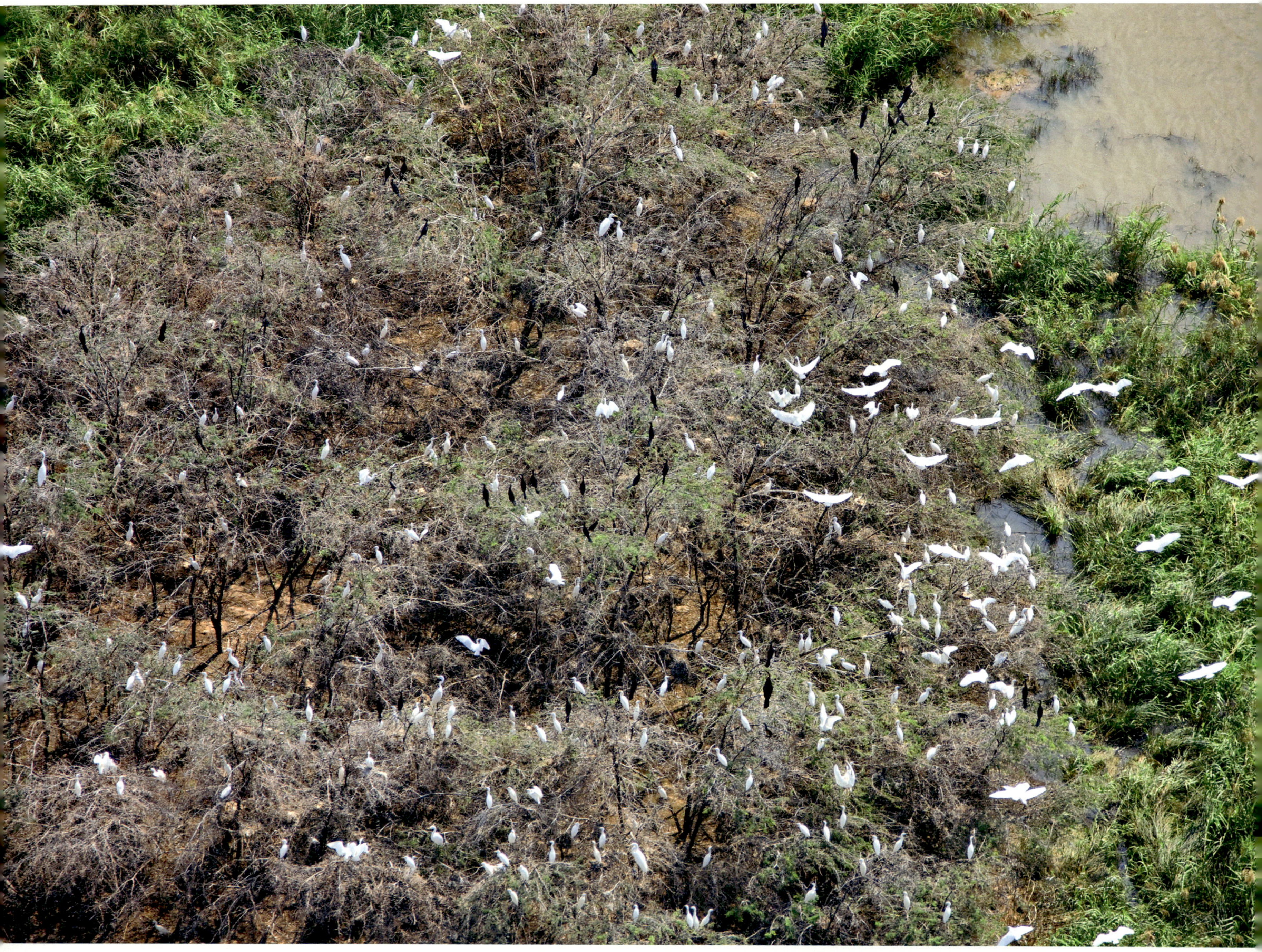

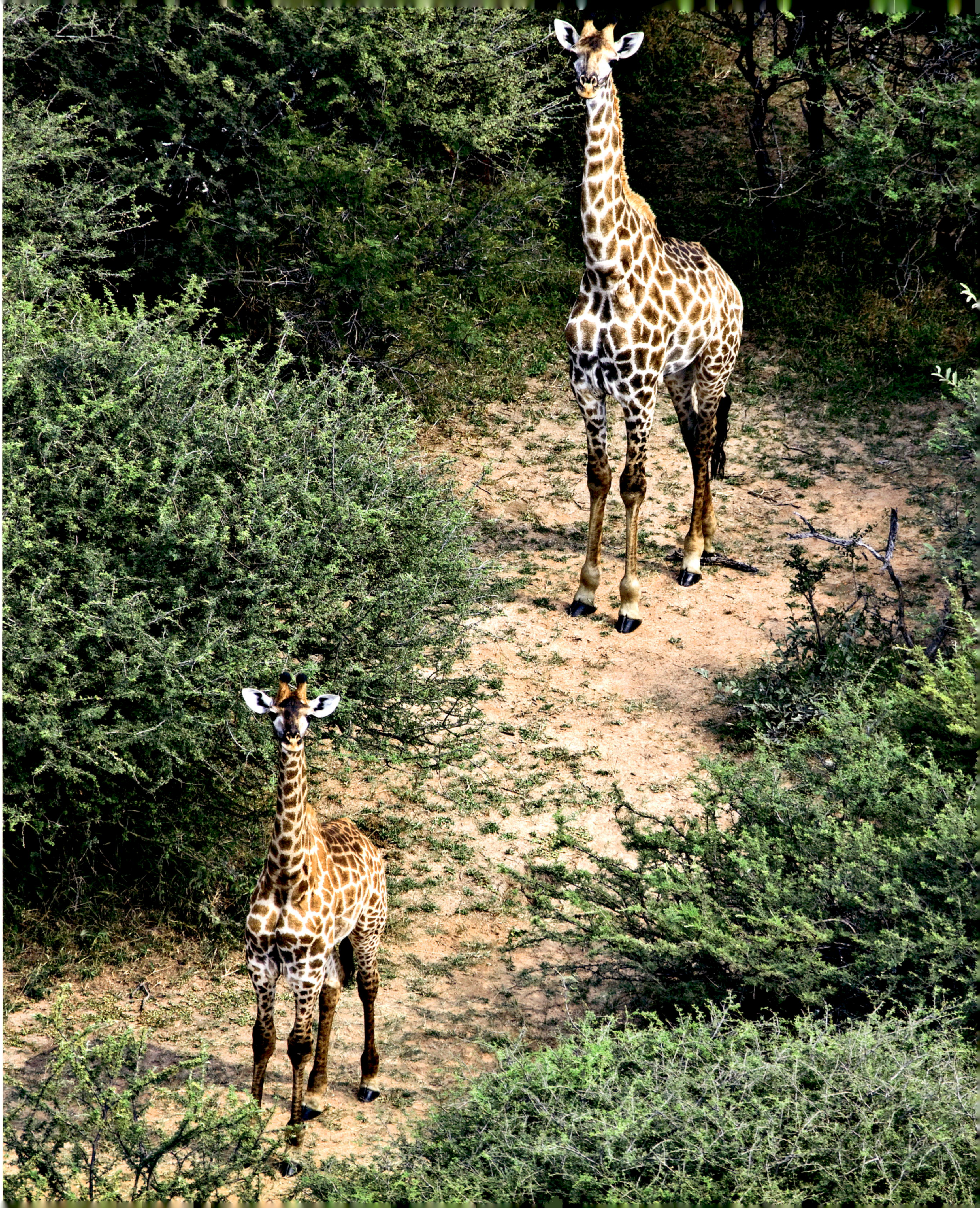

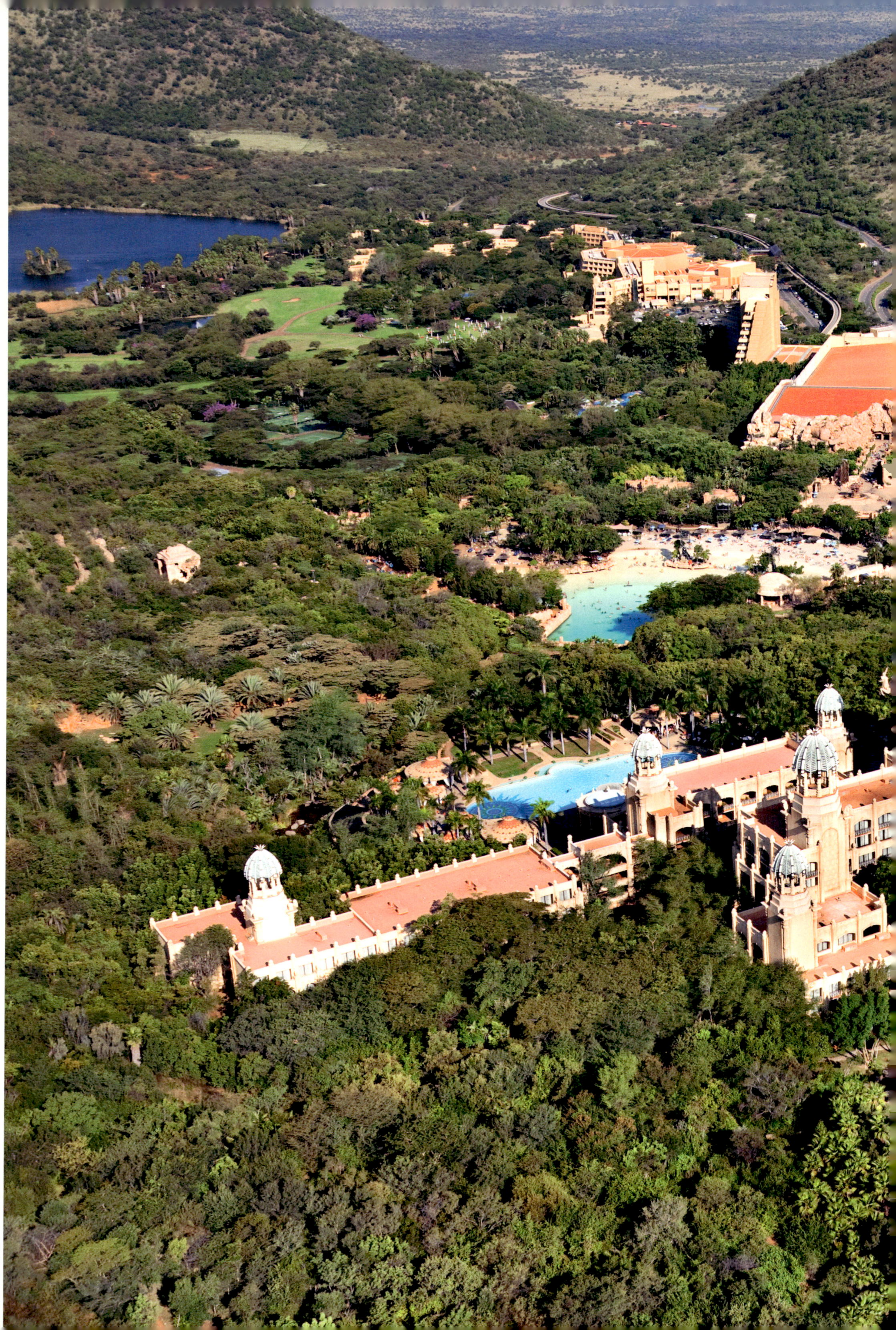

→ The Palace of the Lost City, Sun City

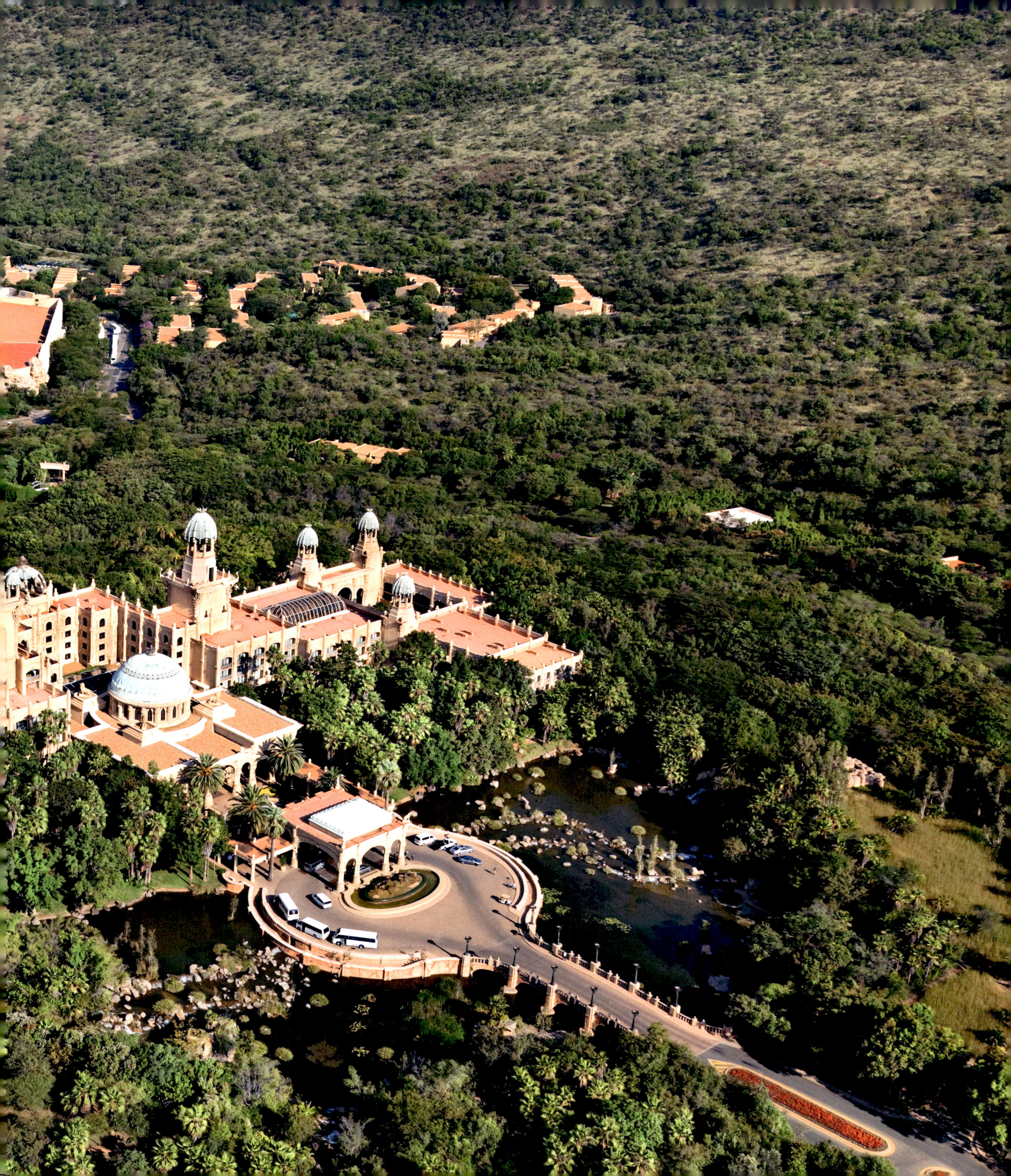

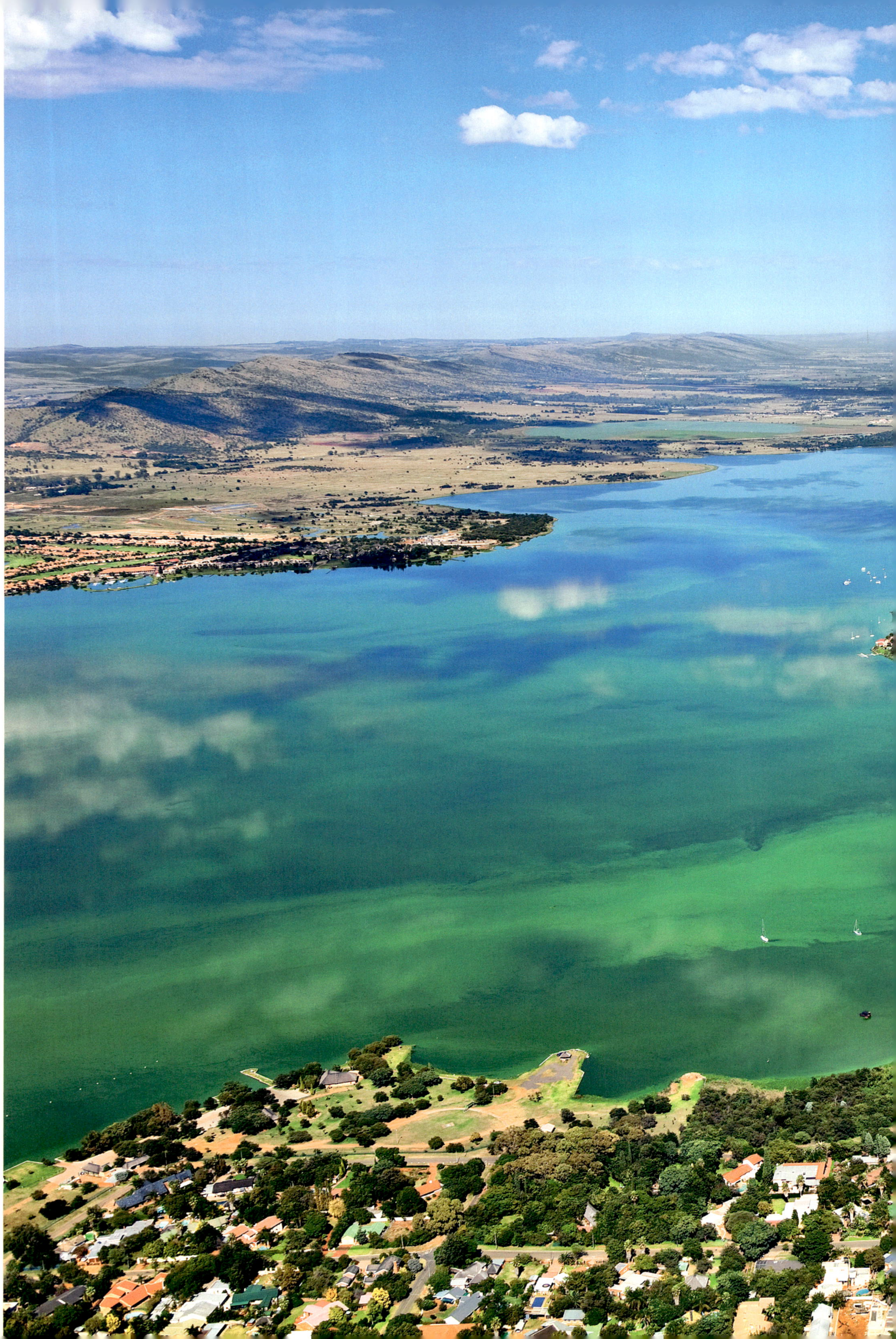

→ Hartbeespoort Dam

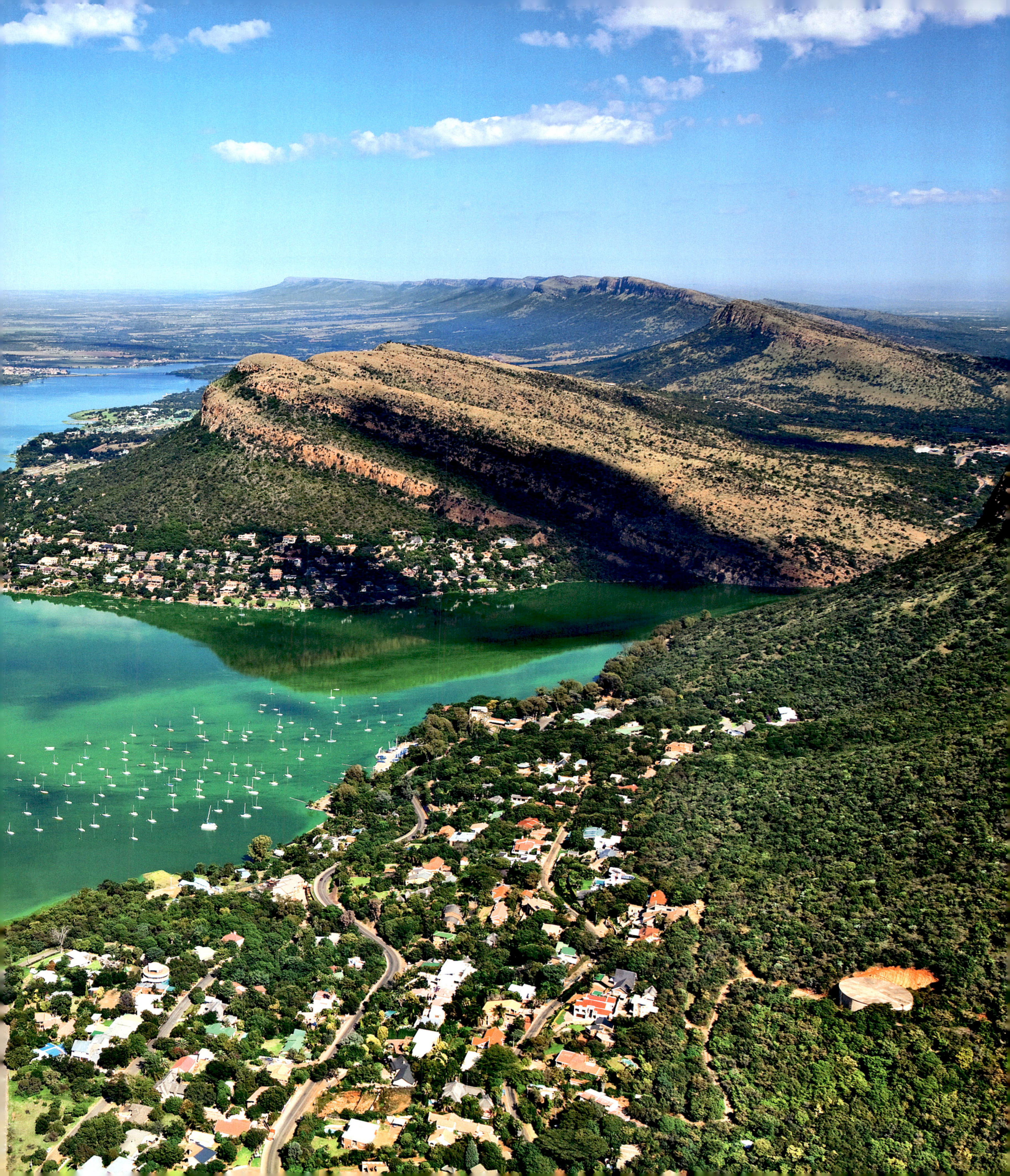

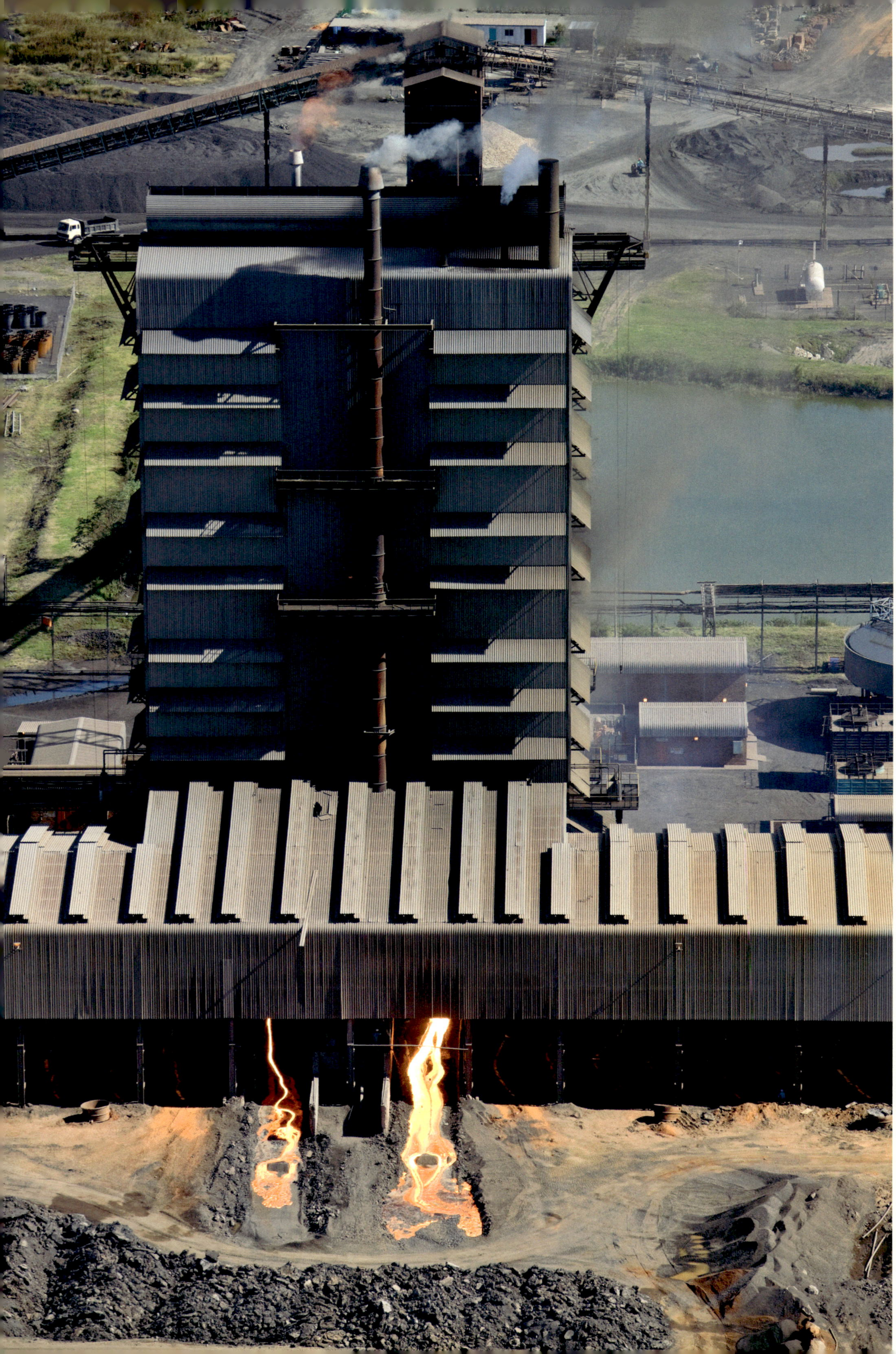

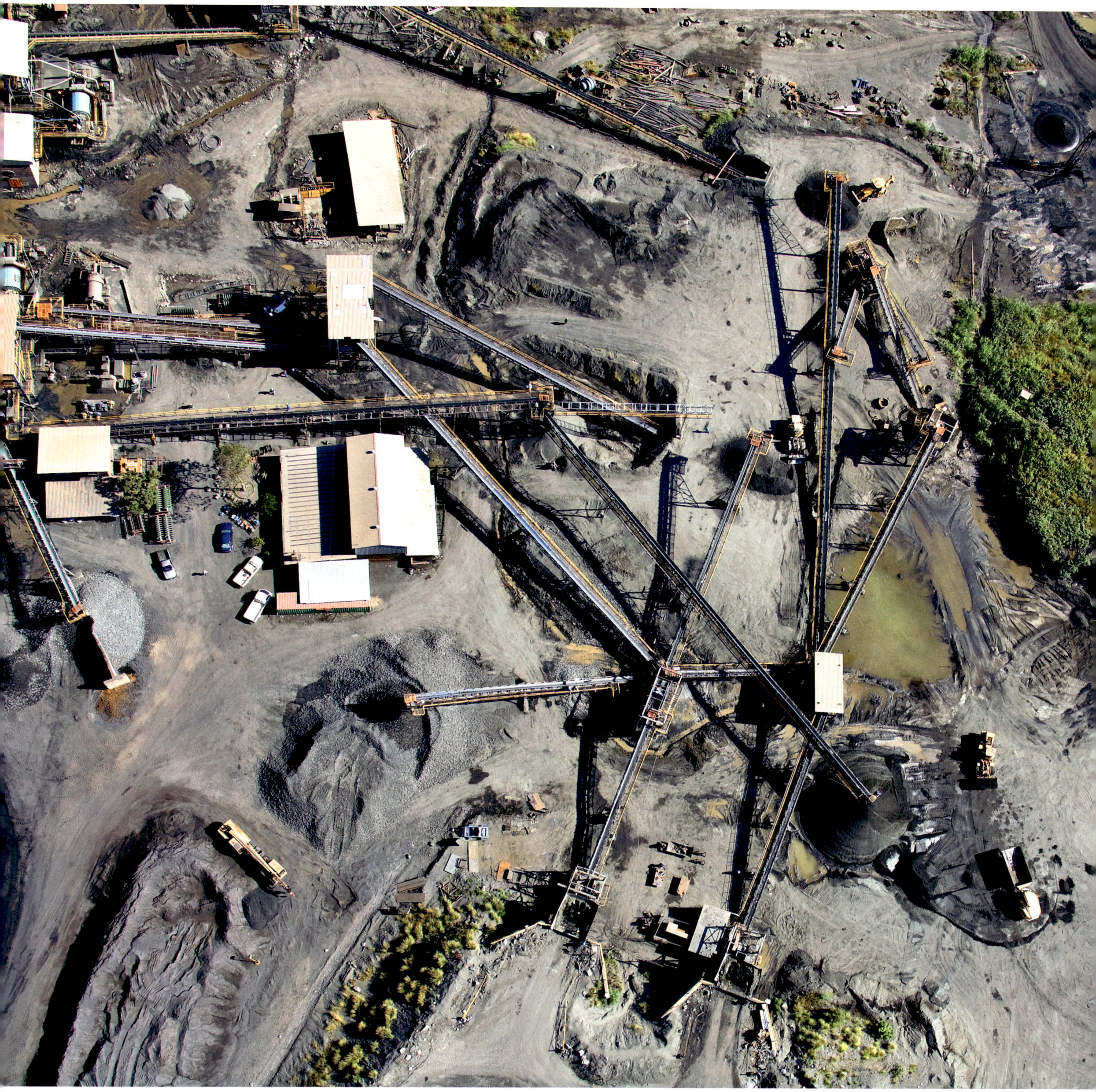

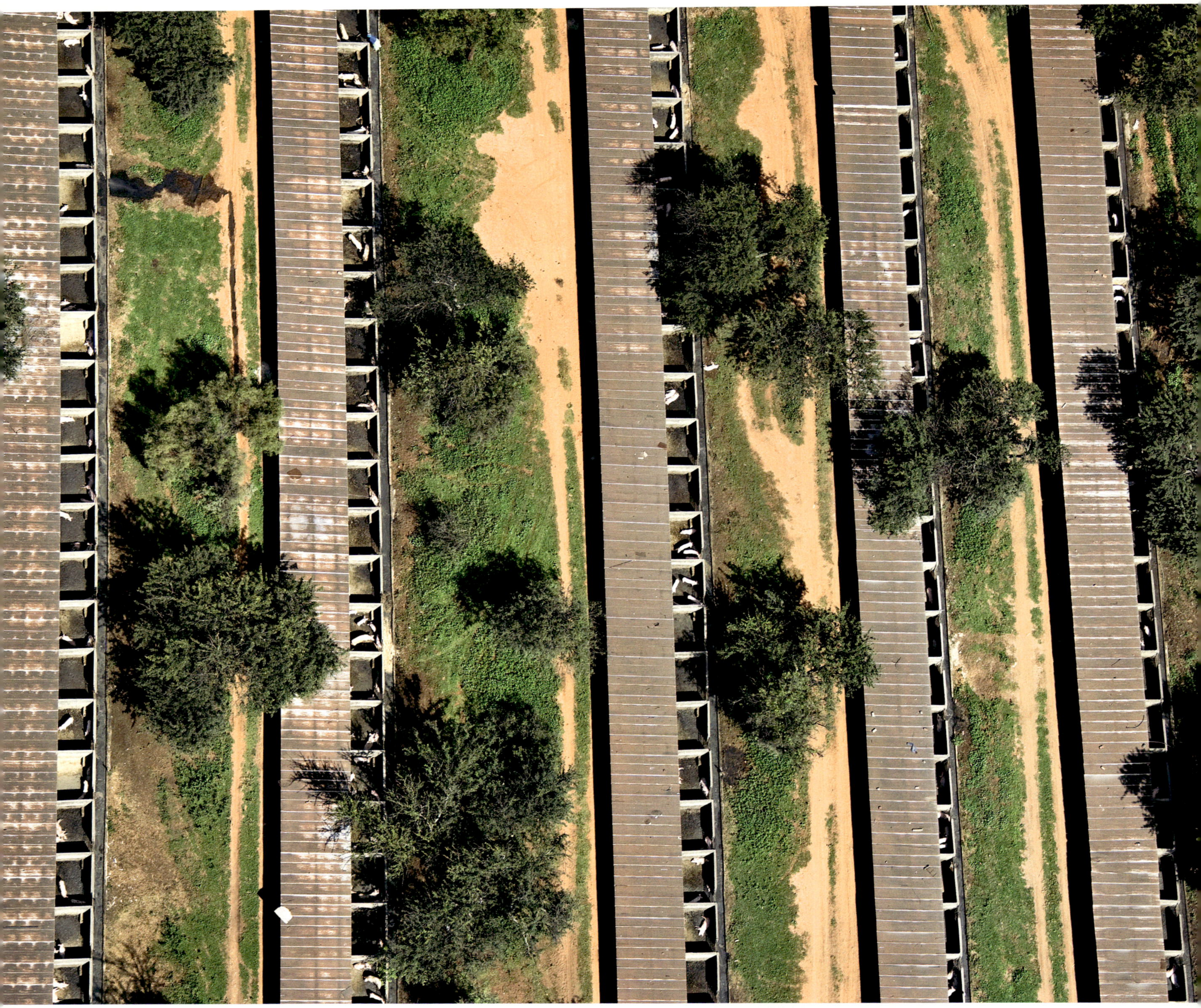

←↓ Free range pig farm and slaughterhouse near Hartbeespoort

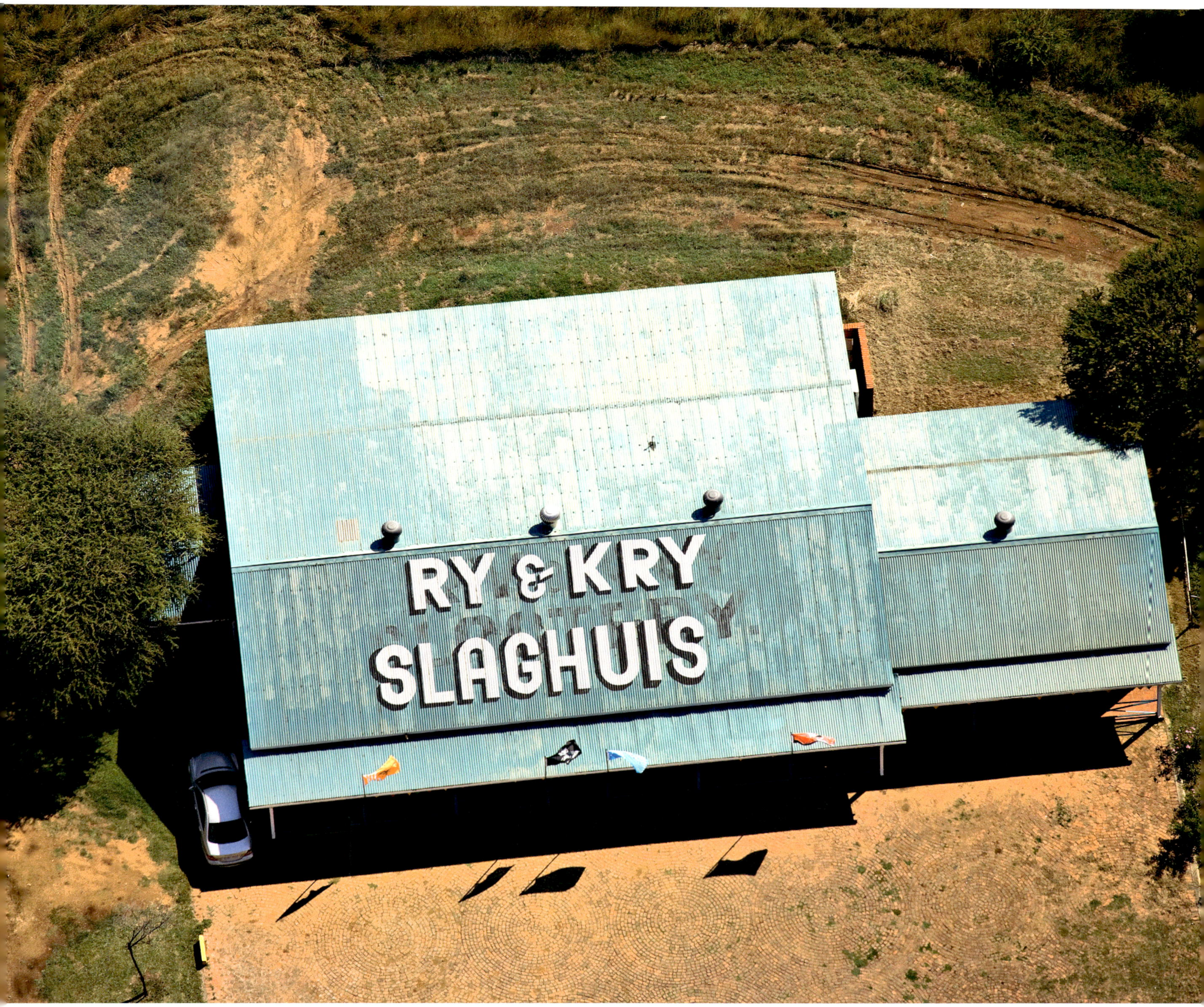

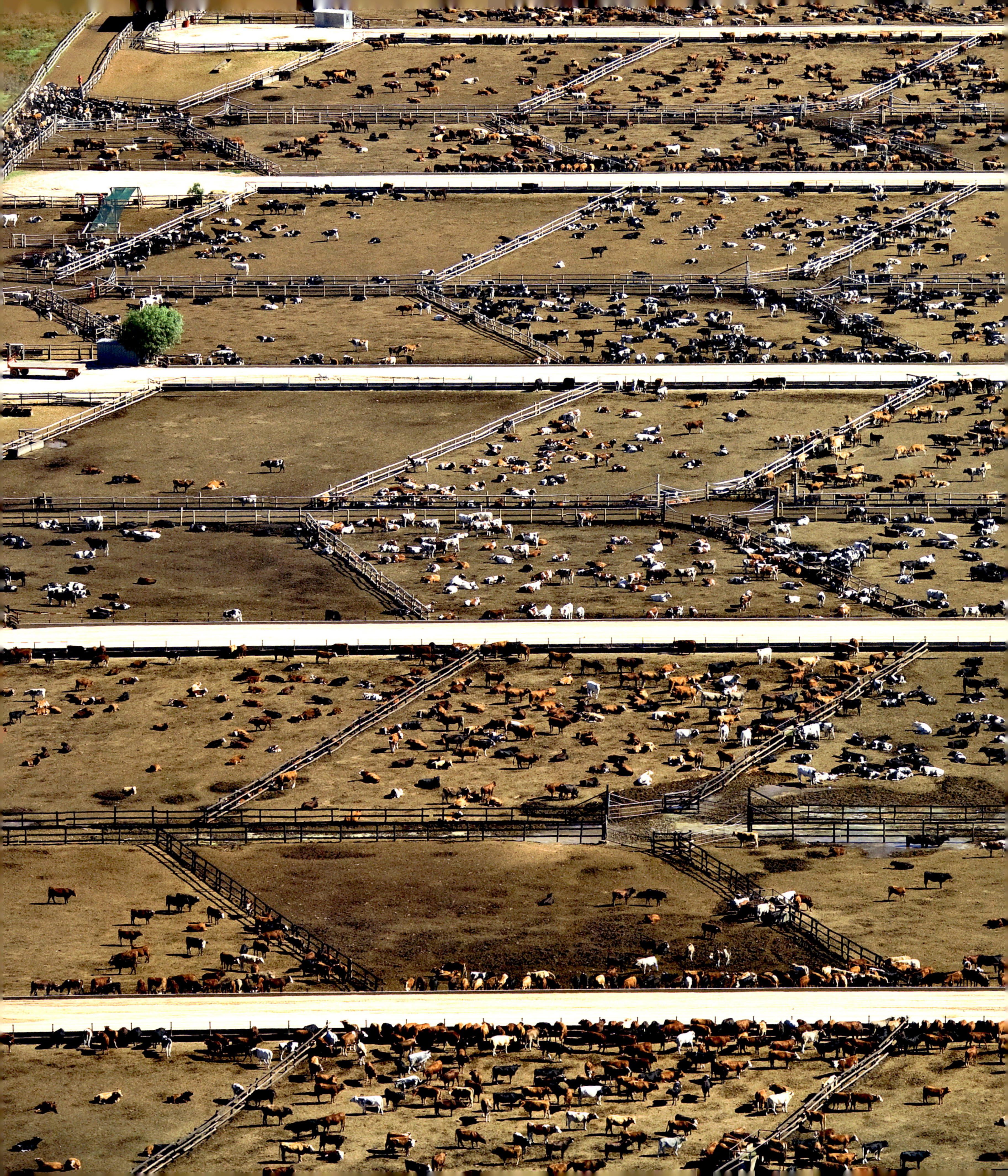

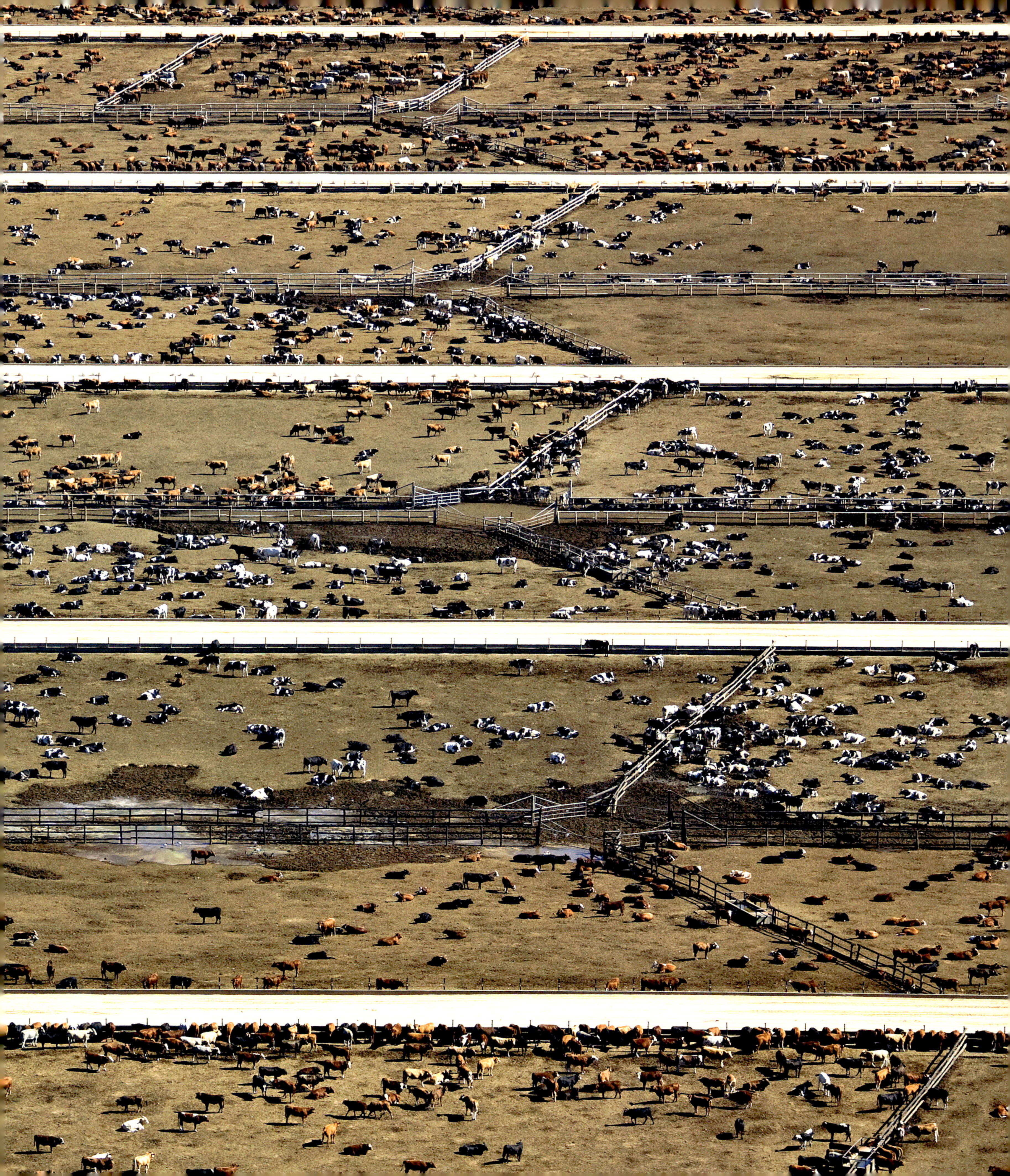

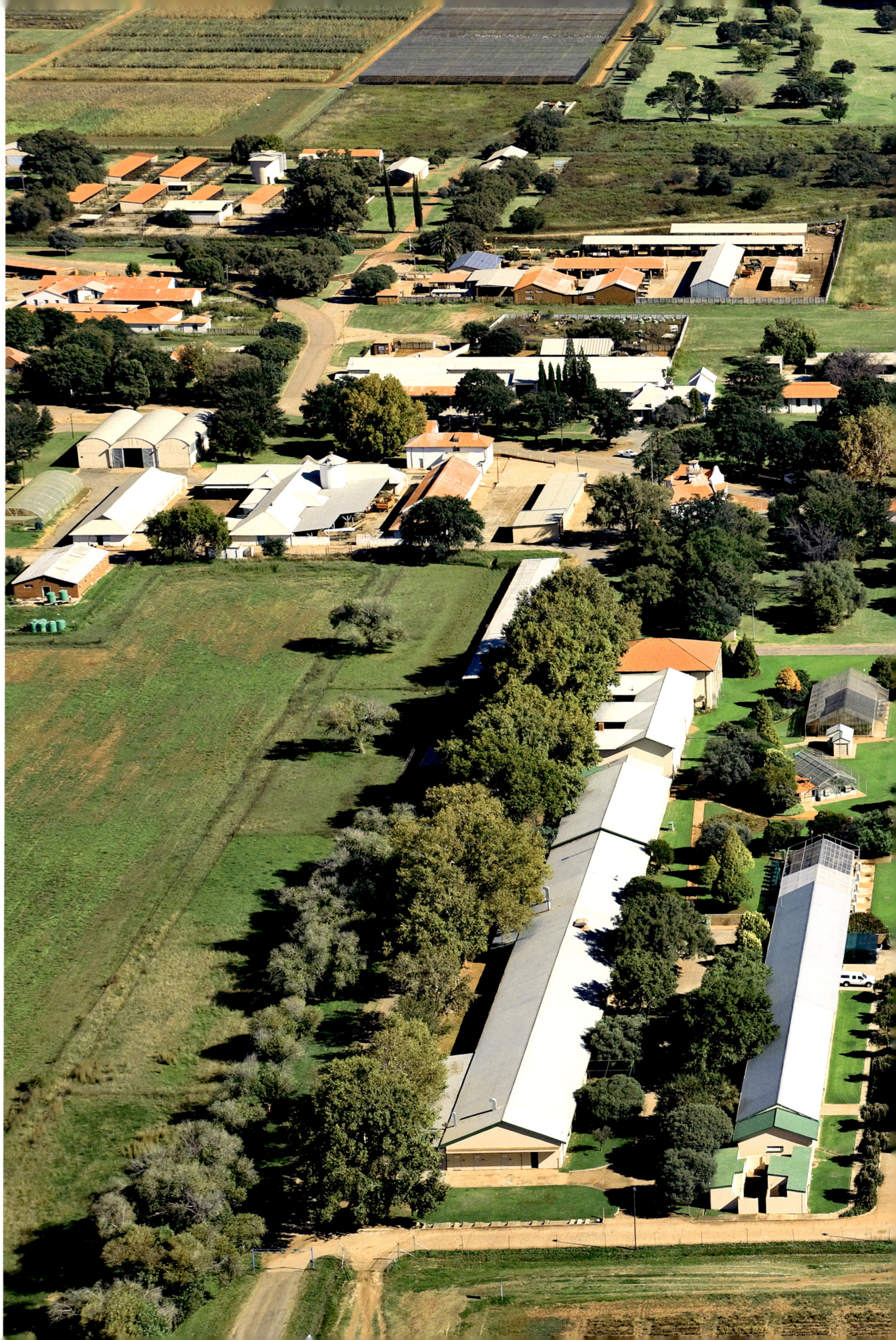

← Large farm with beef cattle
→ College of Agriculture, Potchefstroom

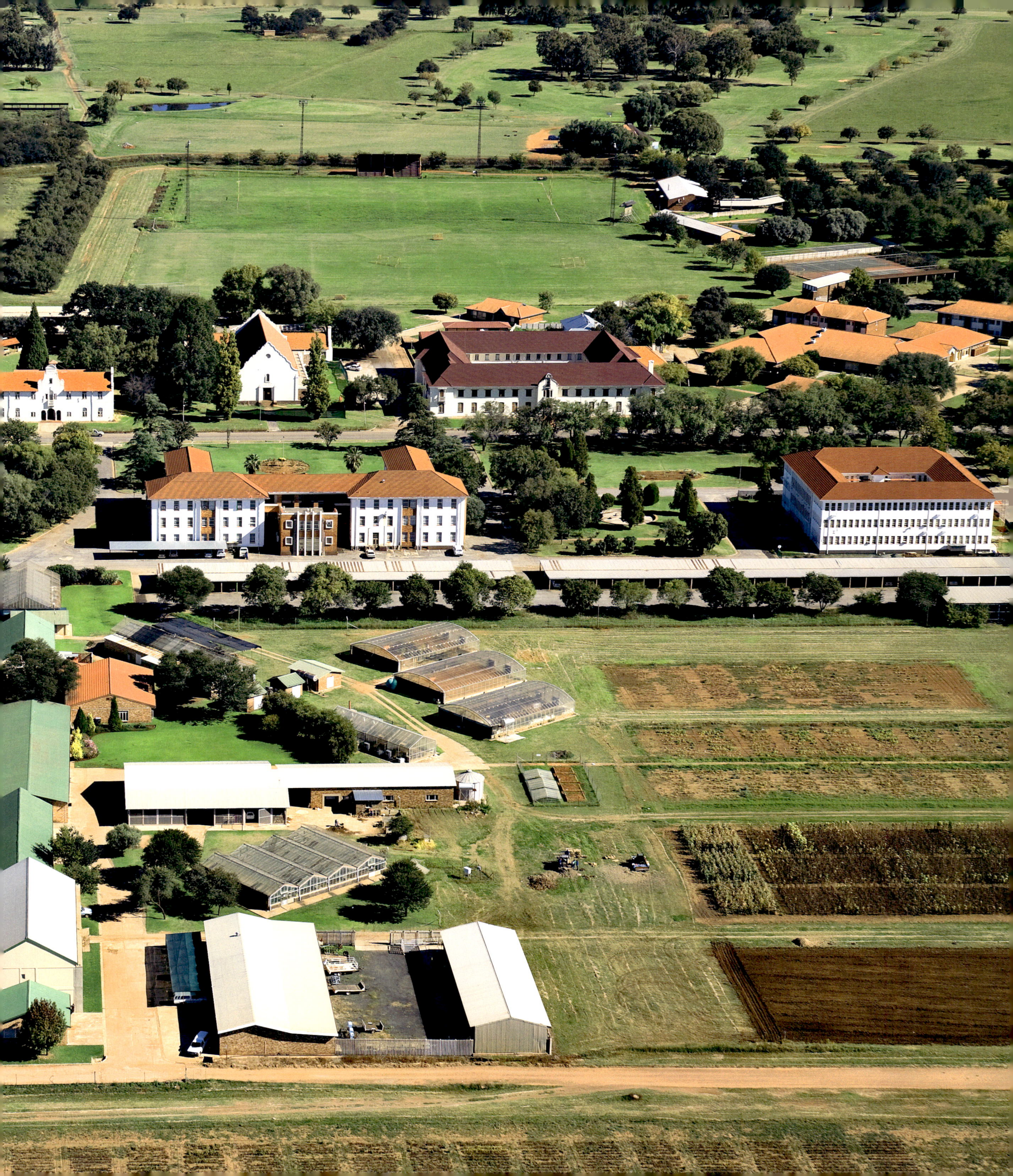

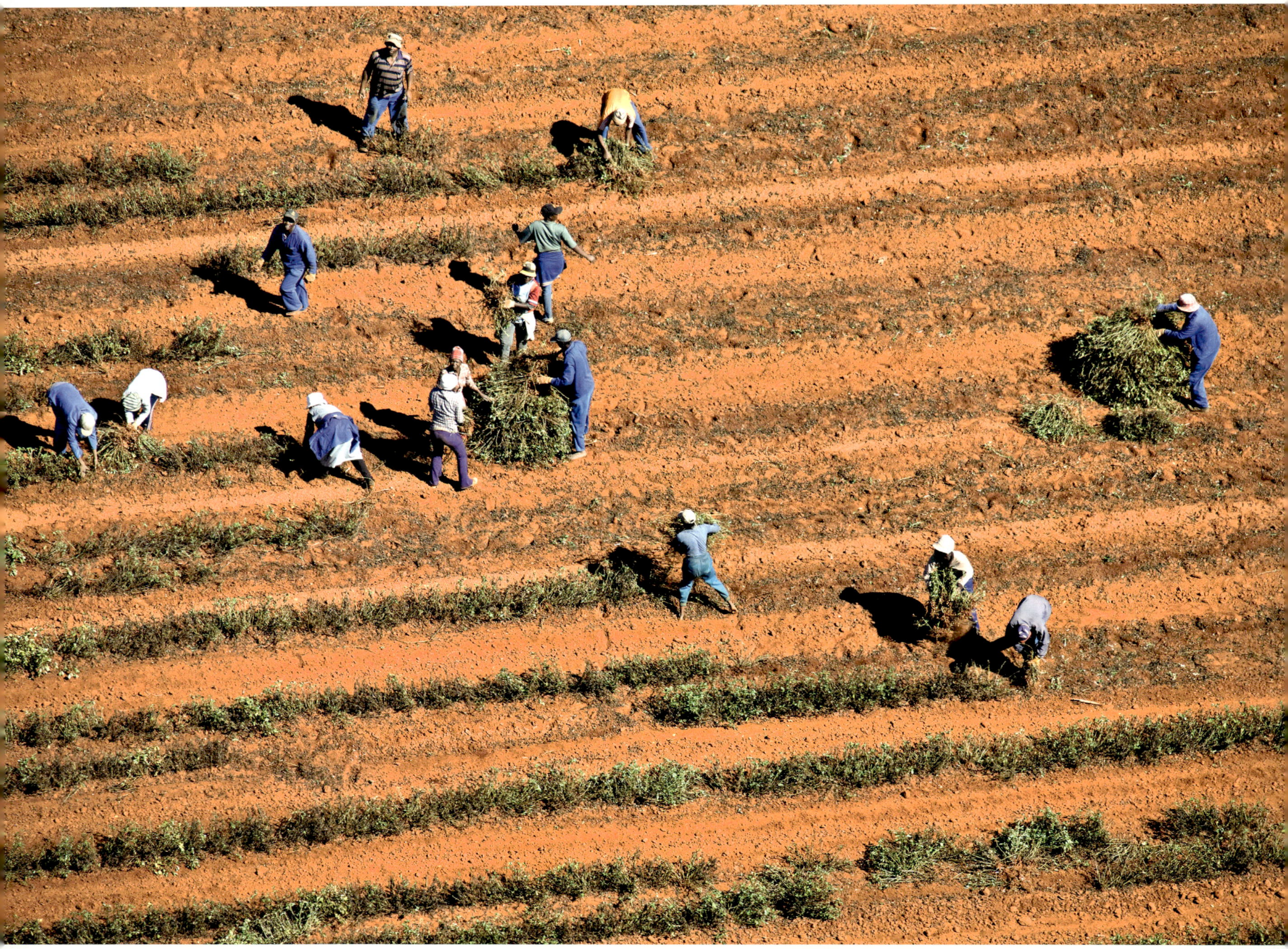

← Working on the land

↓ Harvesting sunflower seeds

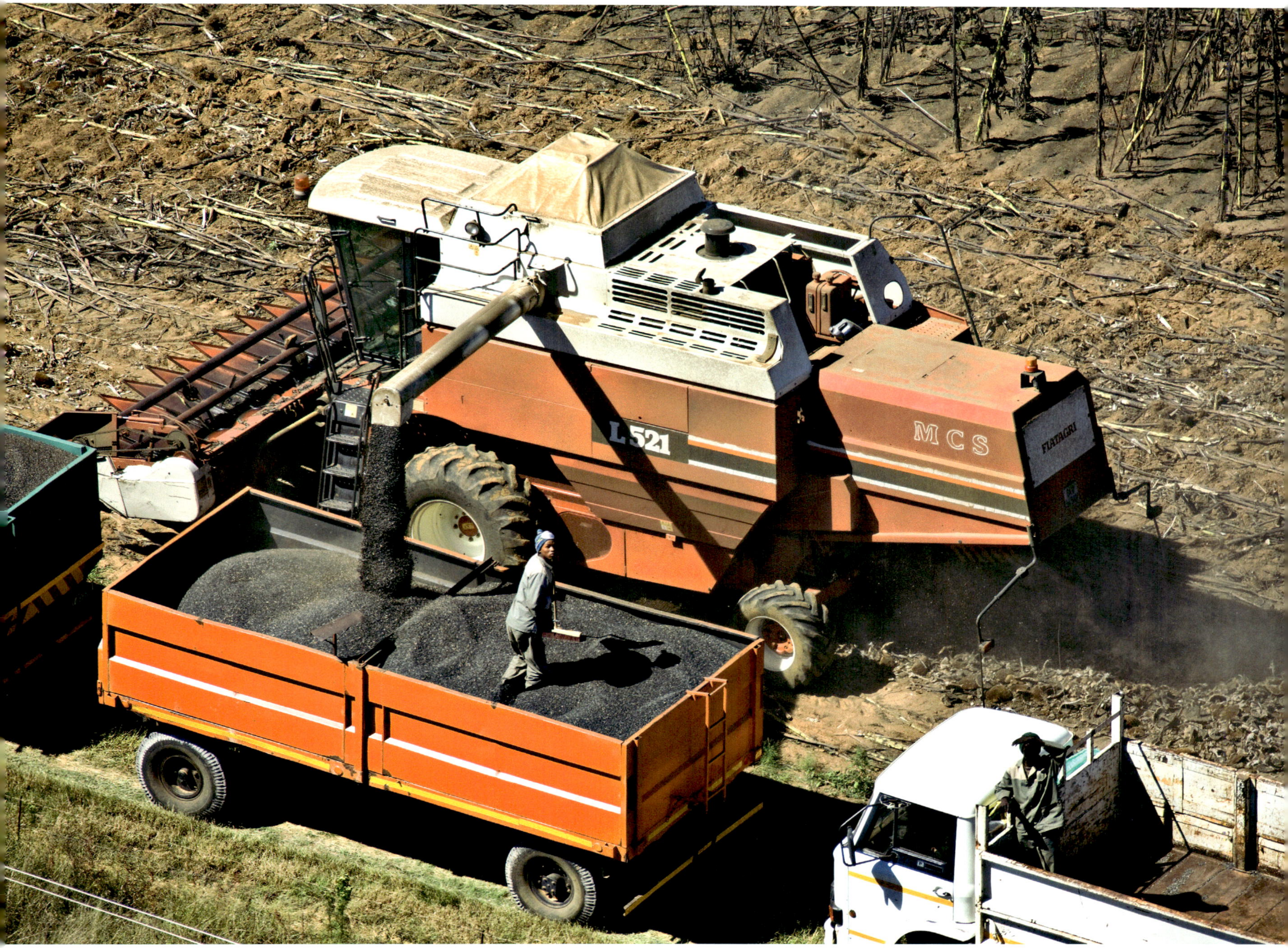

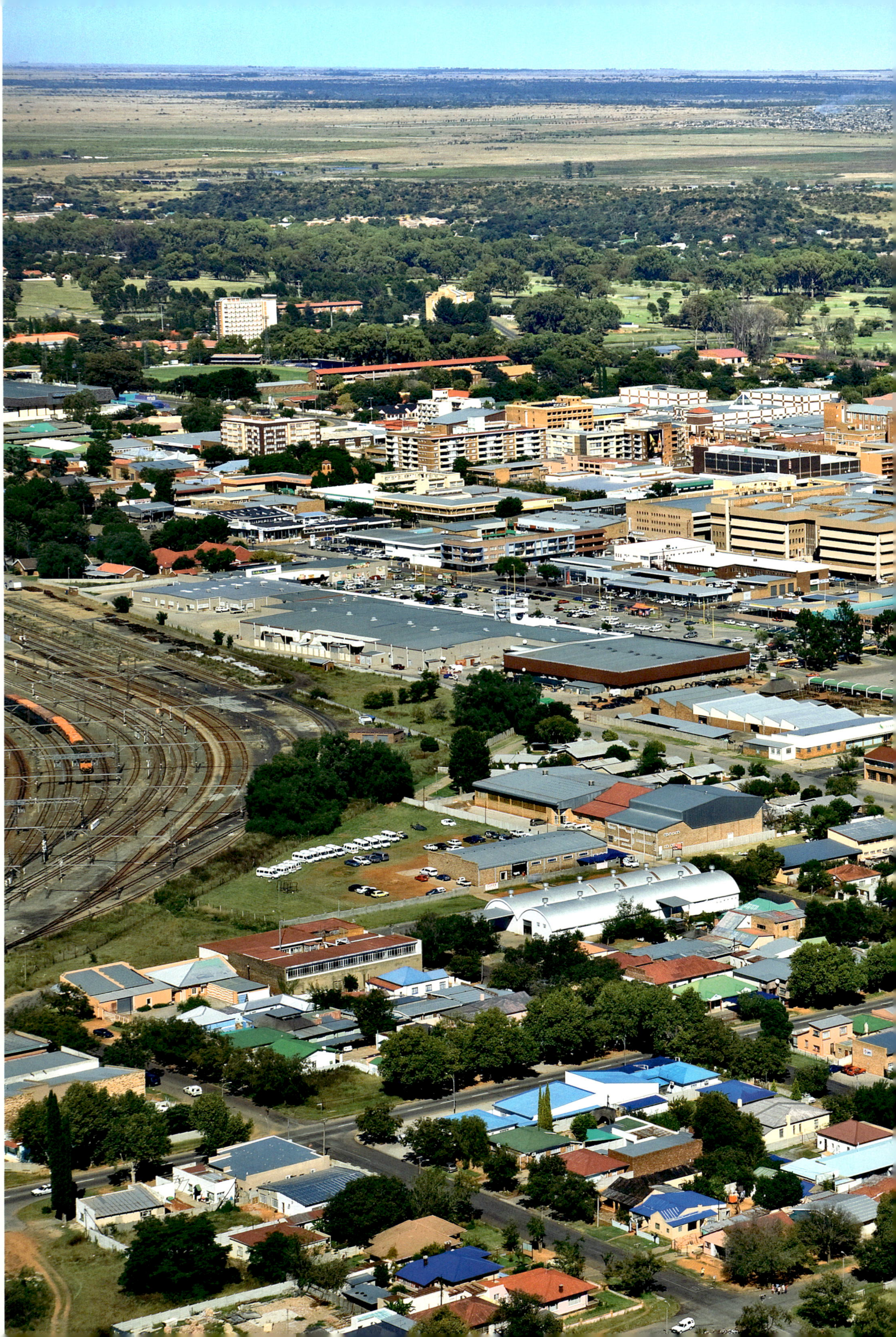

→ Klerksdorp

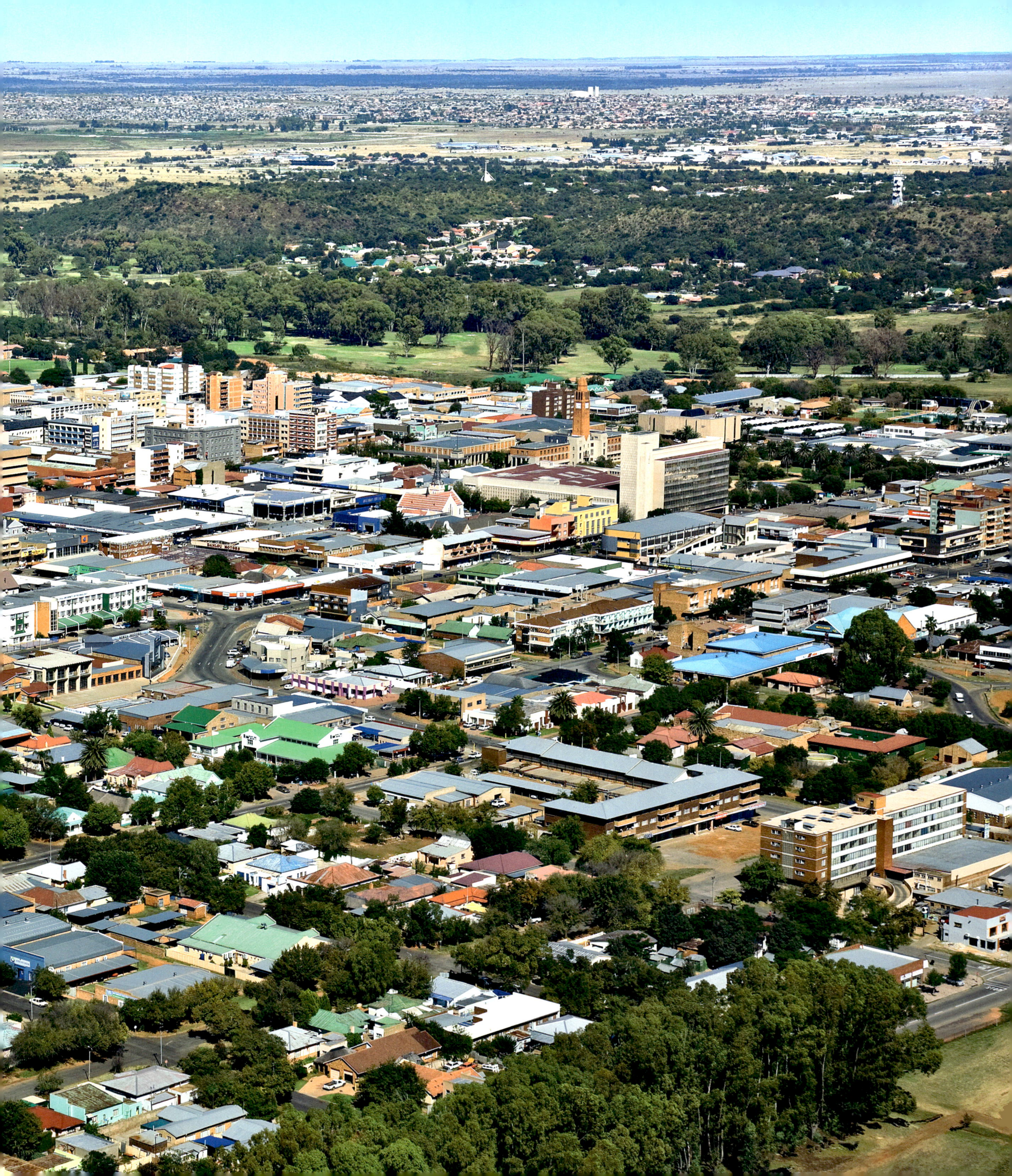

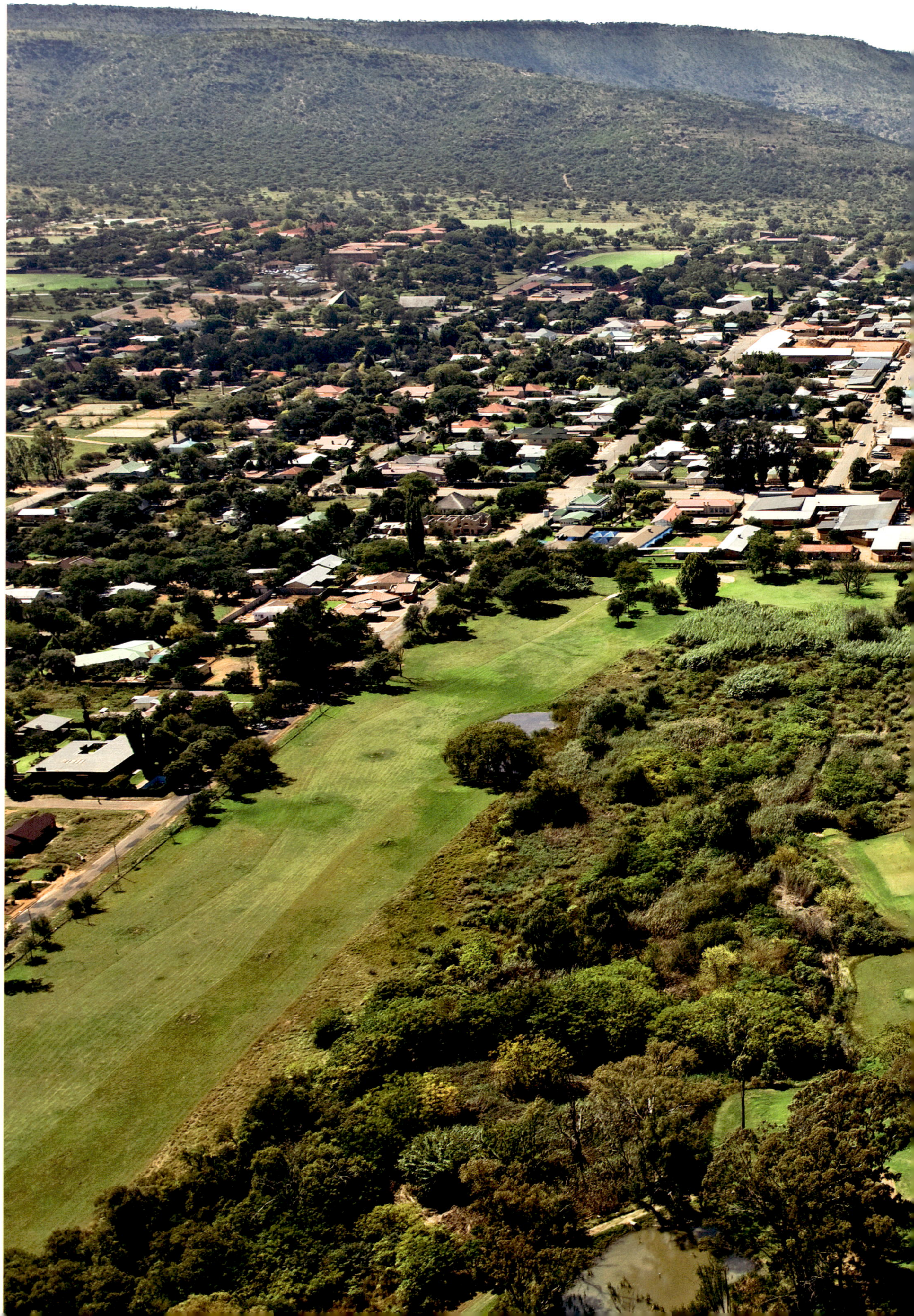

→ Zeerust

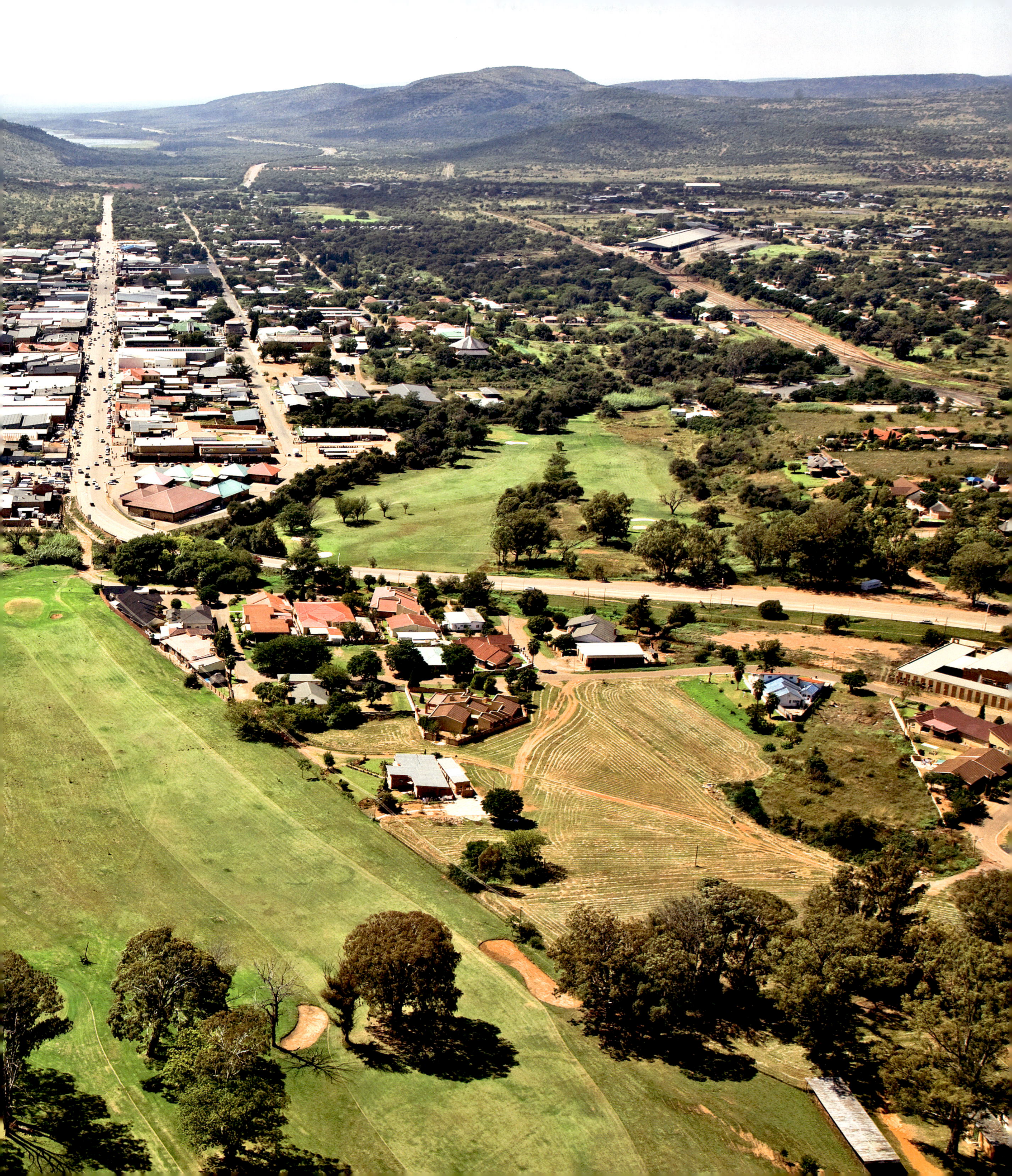

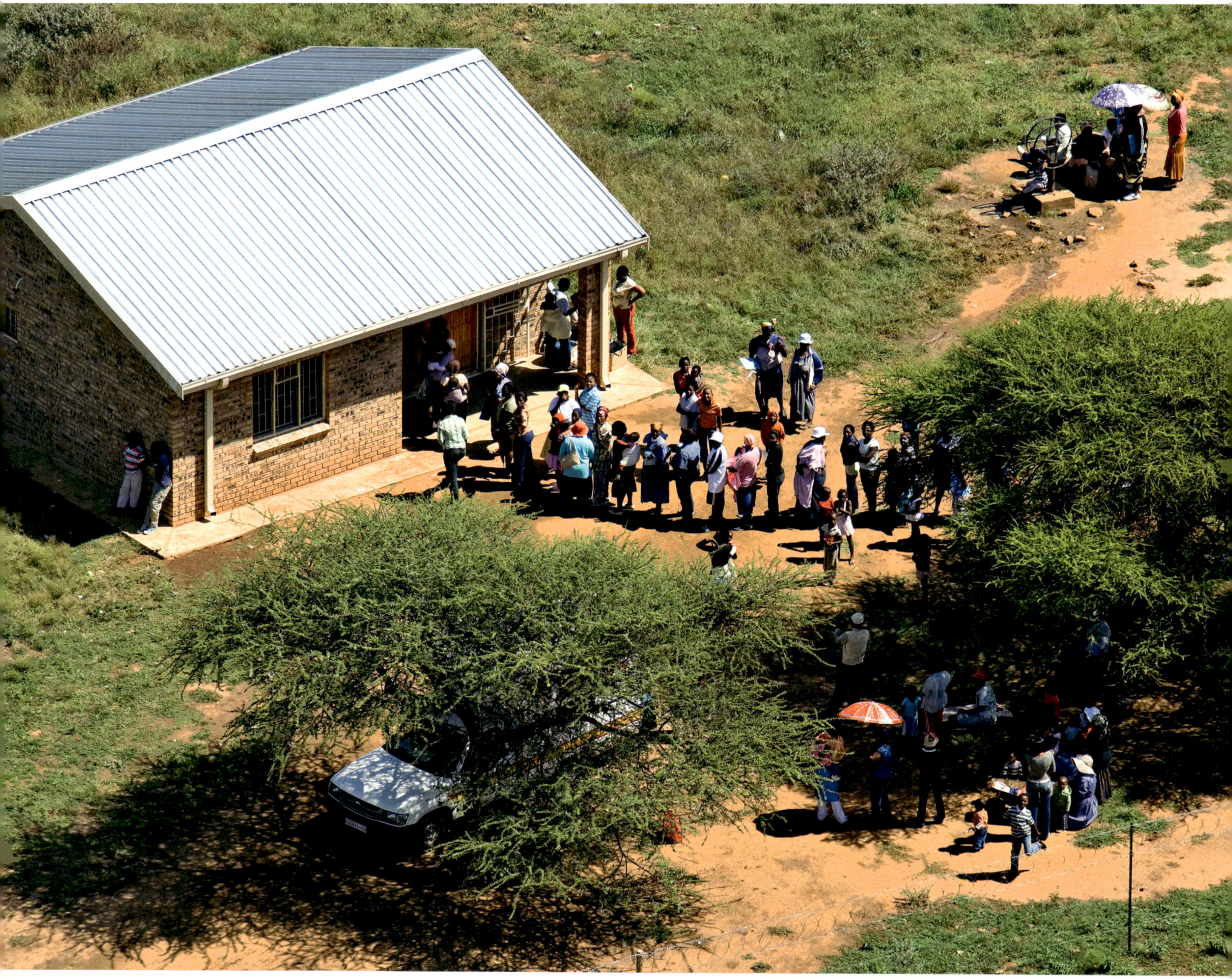

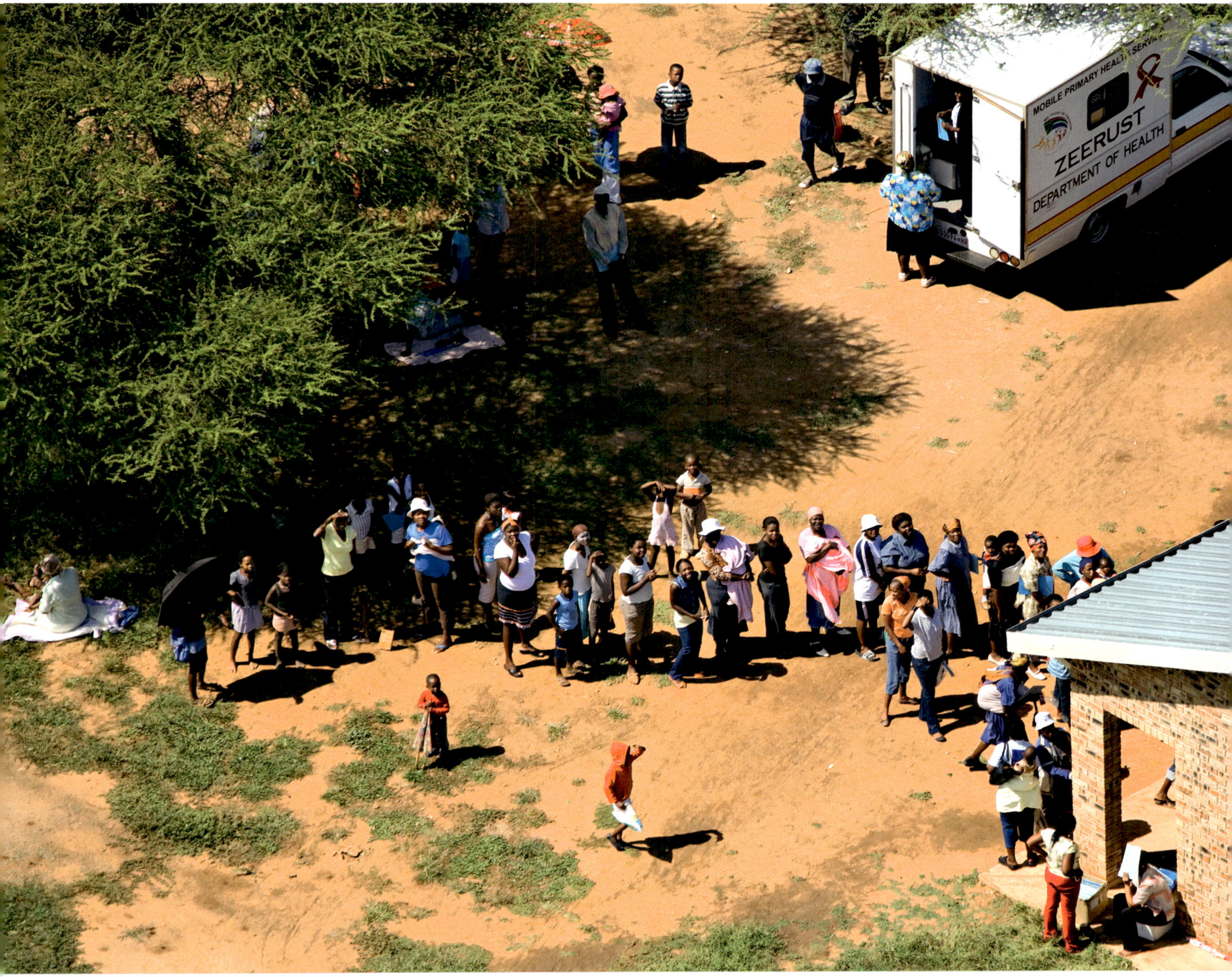
MOBILE PRIMARY HEALTH SERVICES
ZEERUST
DEPARTMENT OF HEALTH

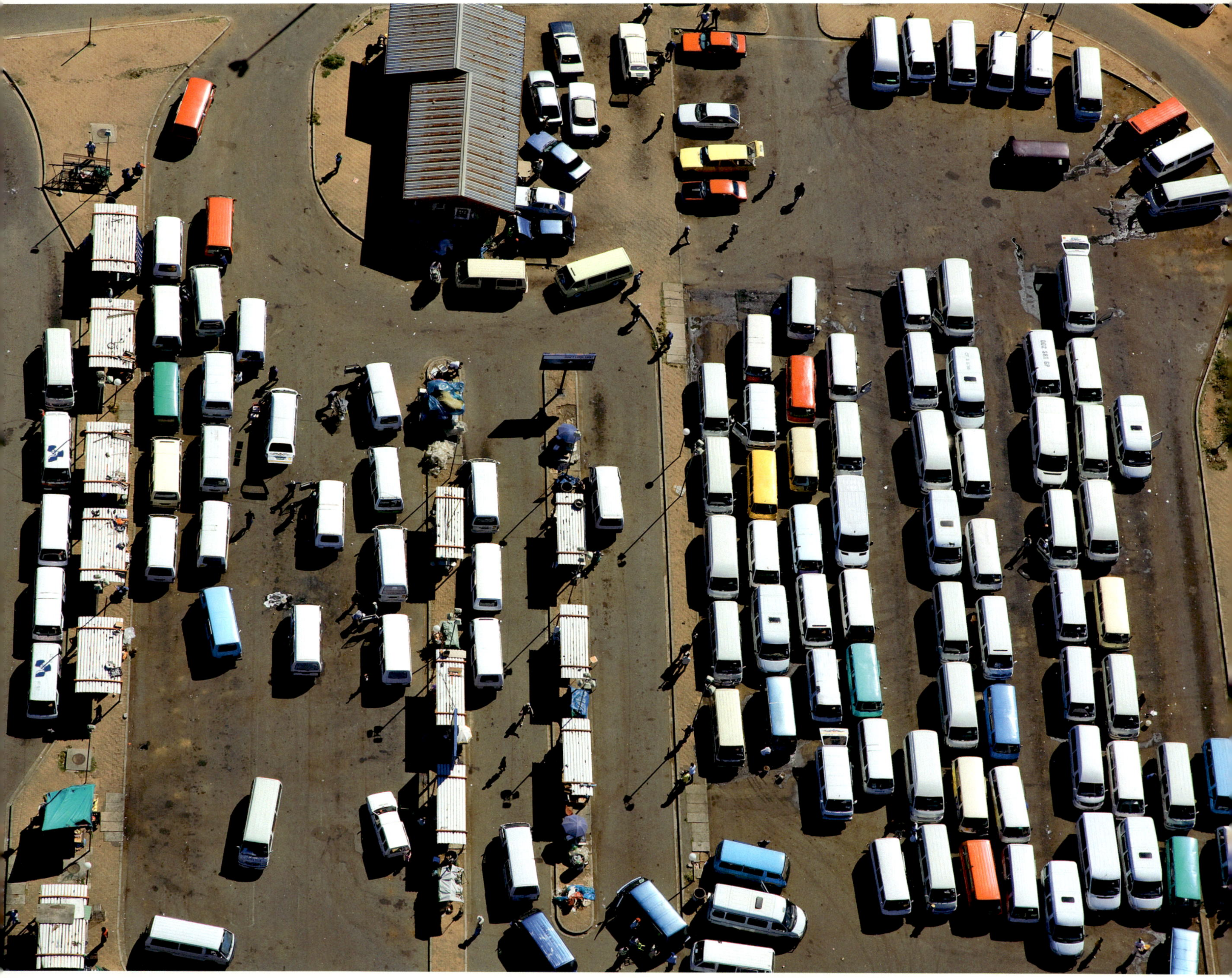

← Parking lot for taxi vans, Klerksdorp
↓ Special architecture, Zeerust

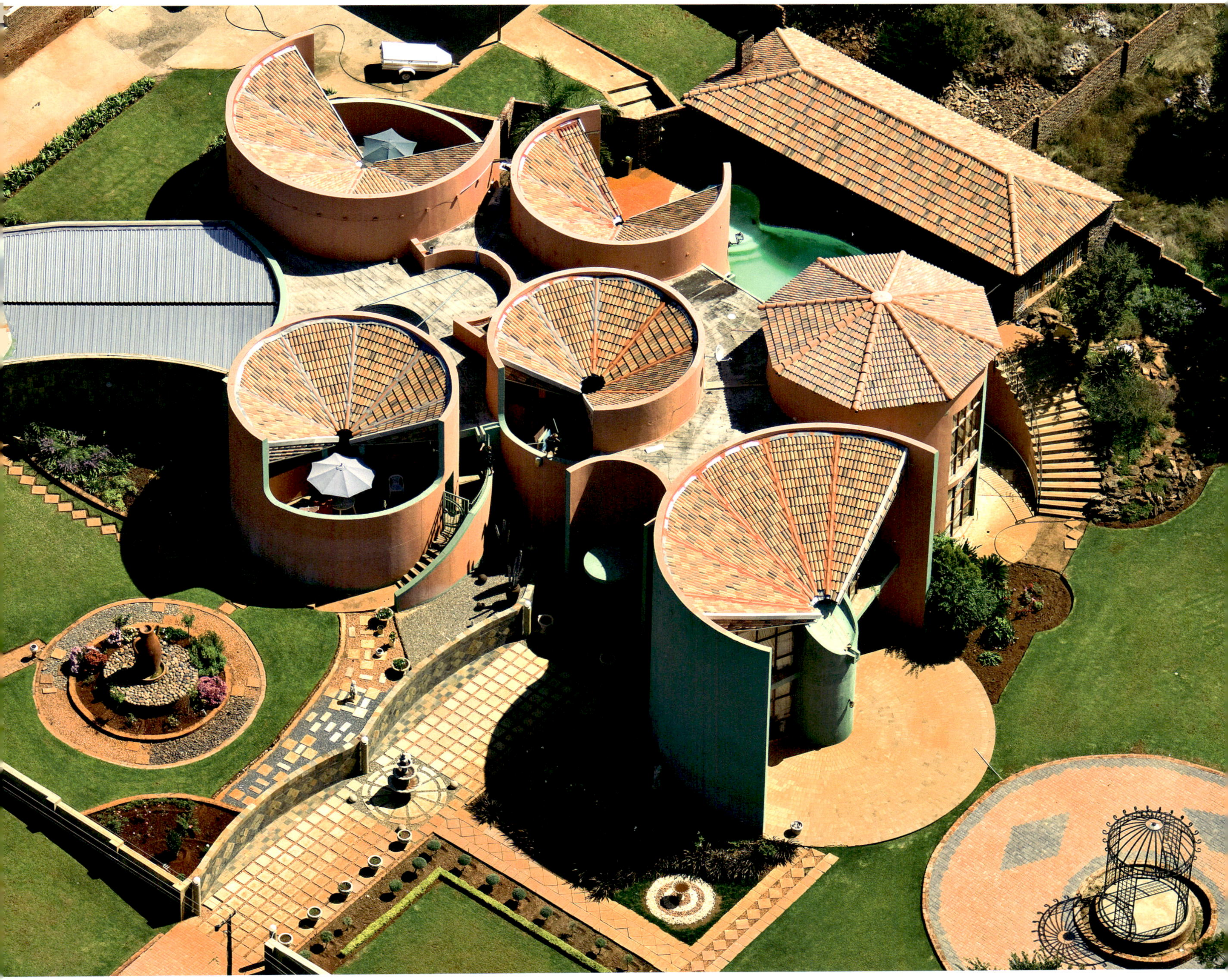

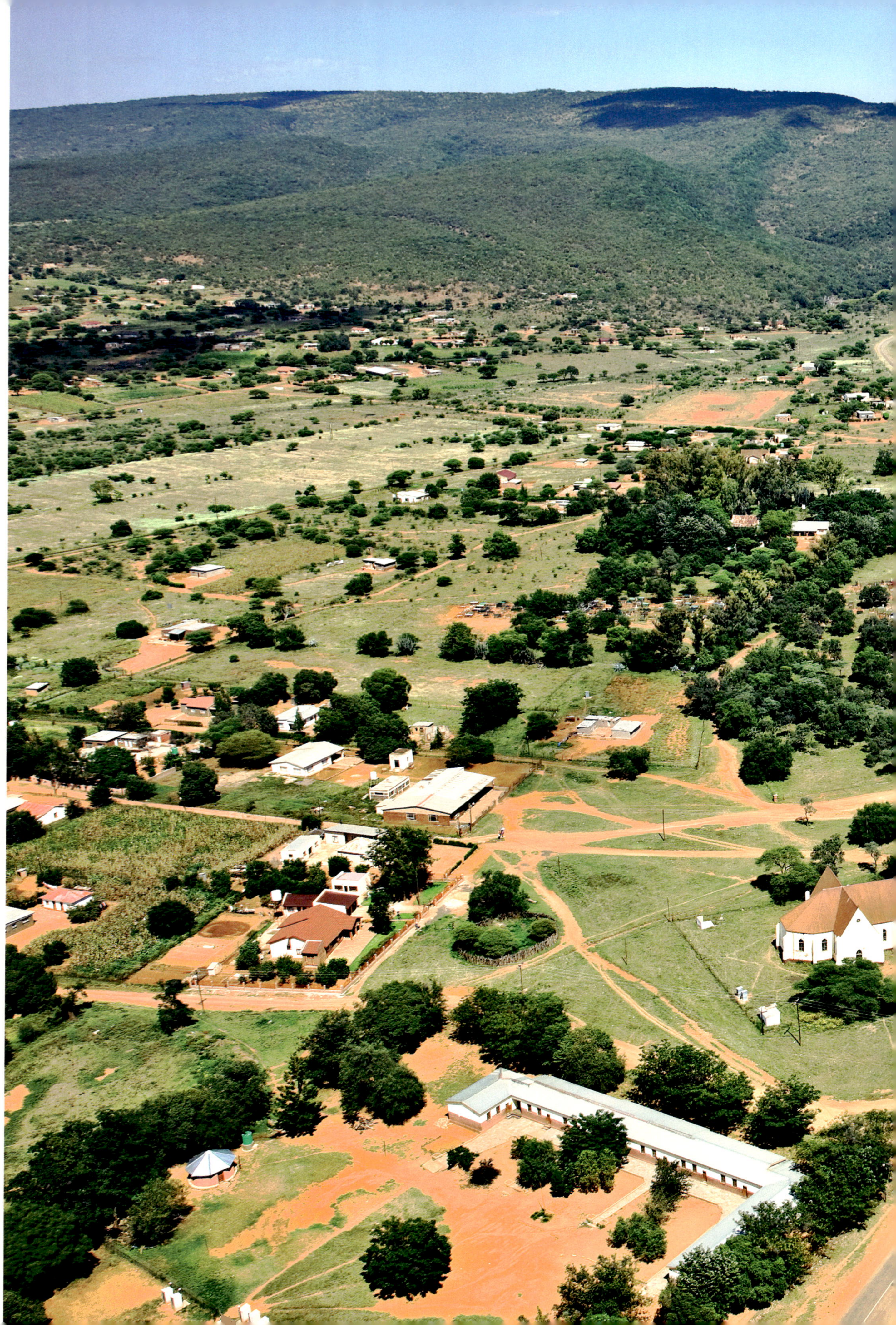

→ Border between South Africa and Botswana, Gopane

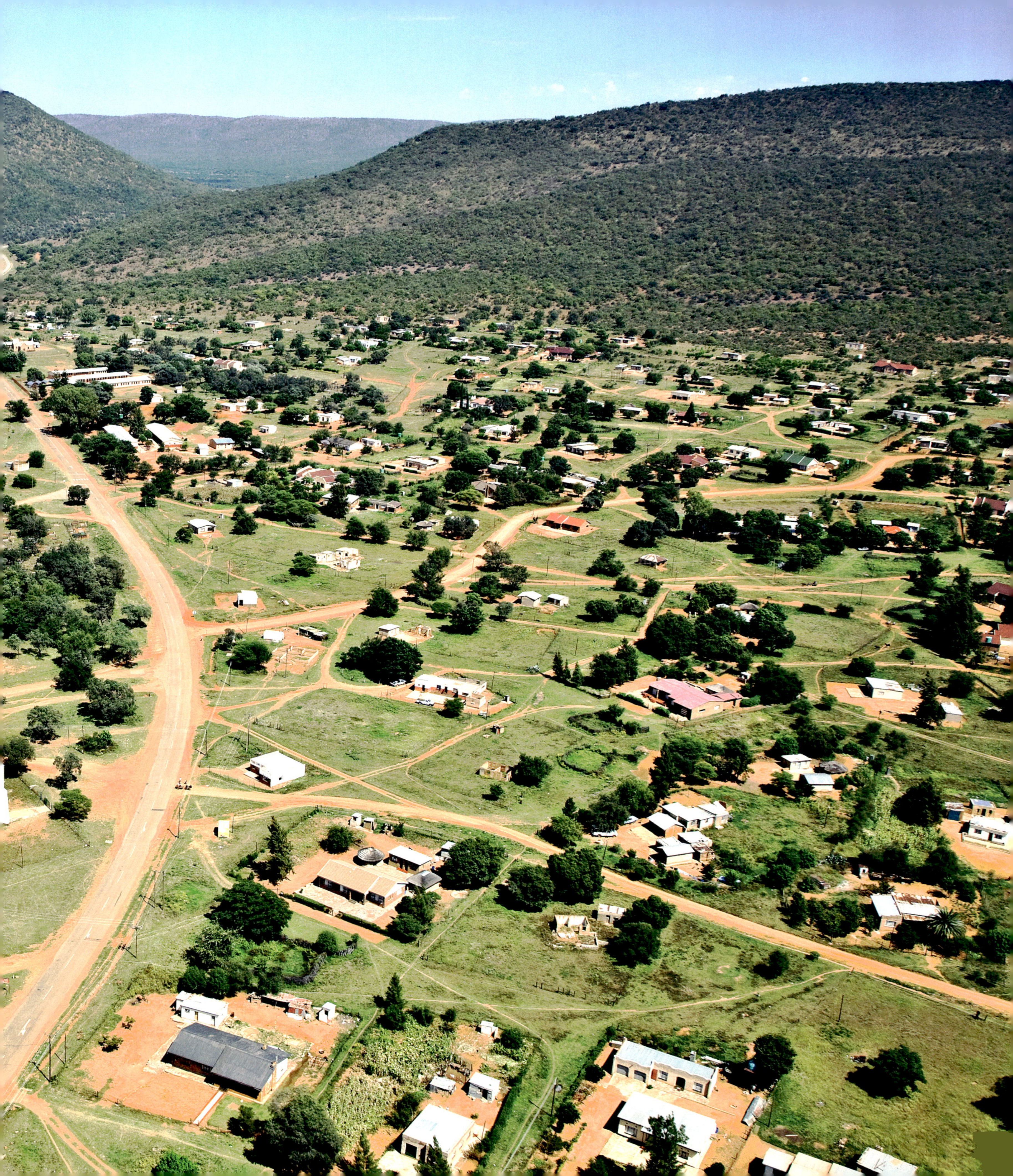

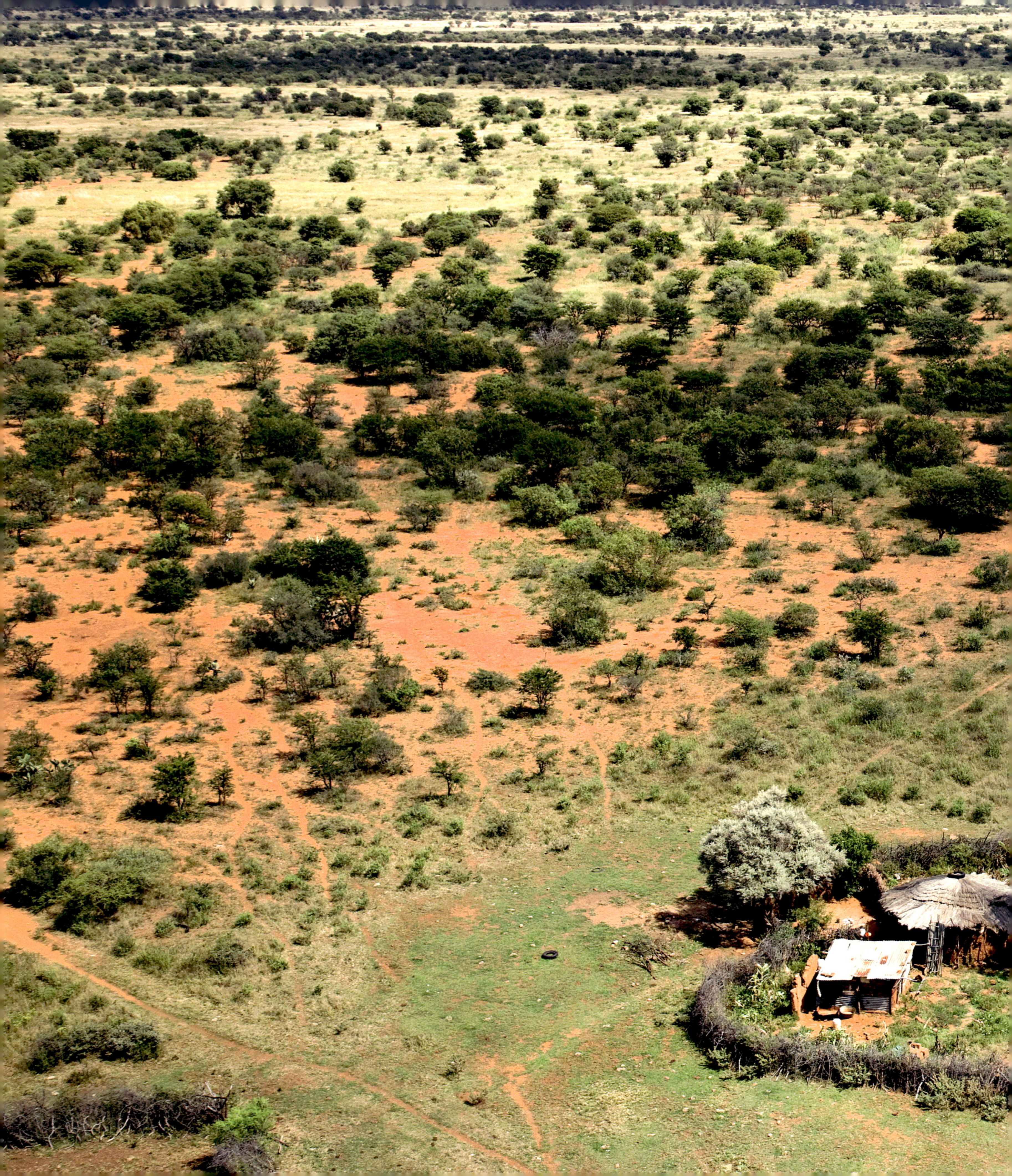

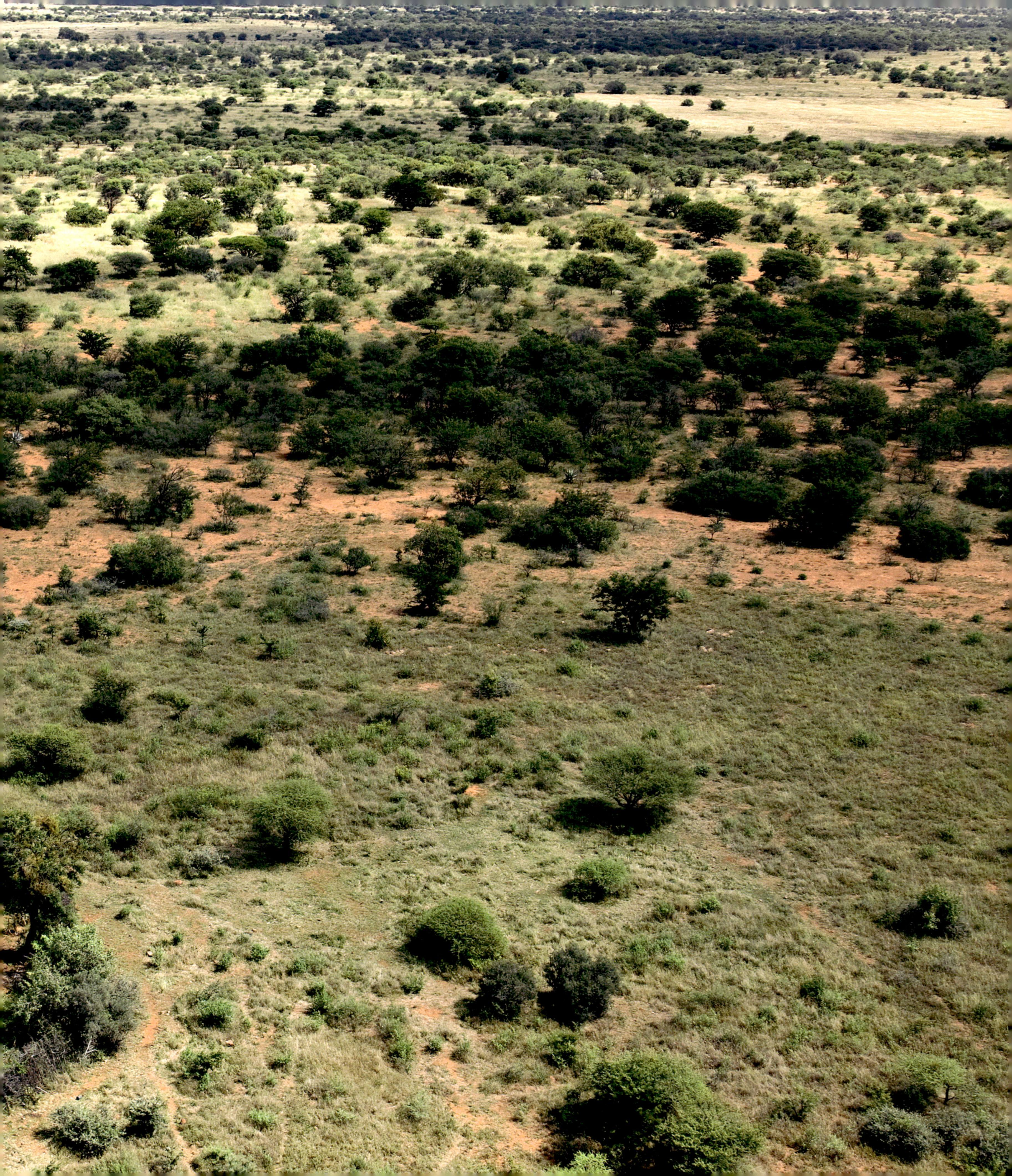

← Lonely hut
↓→ Mafikeng, city of architecture

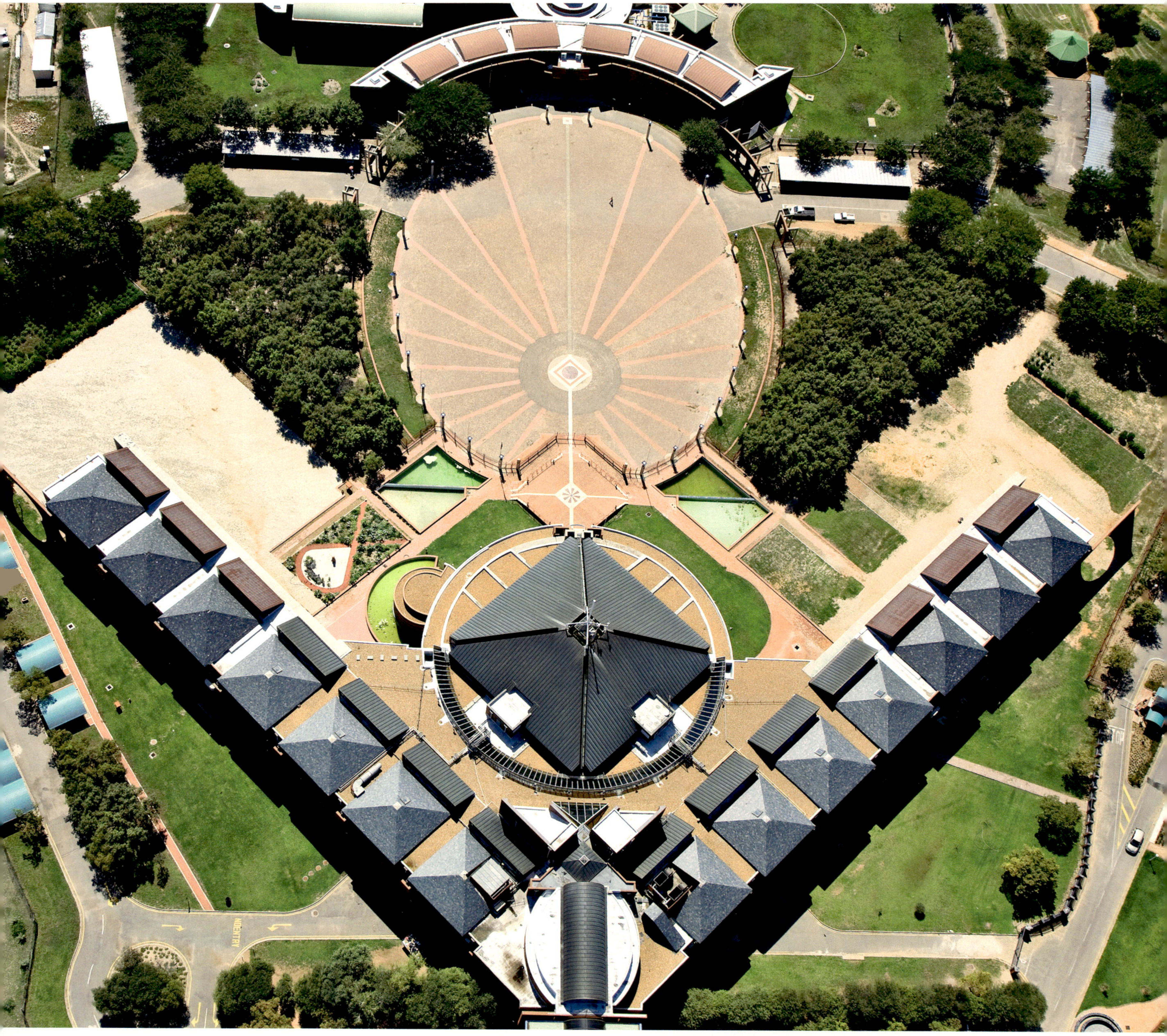

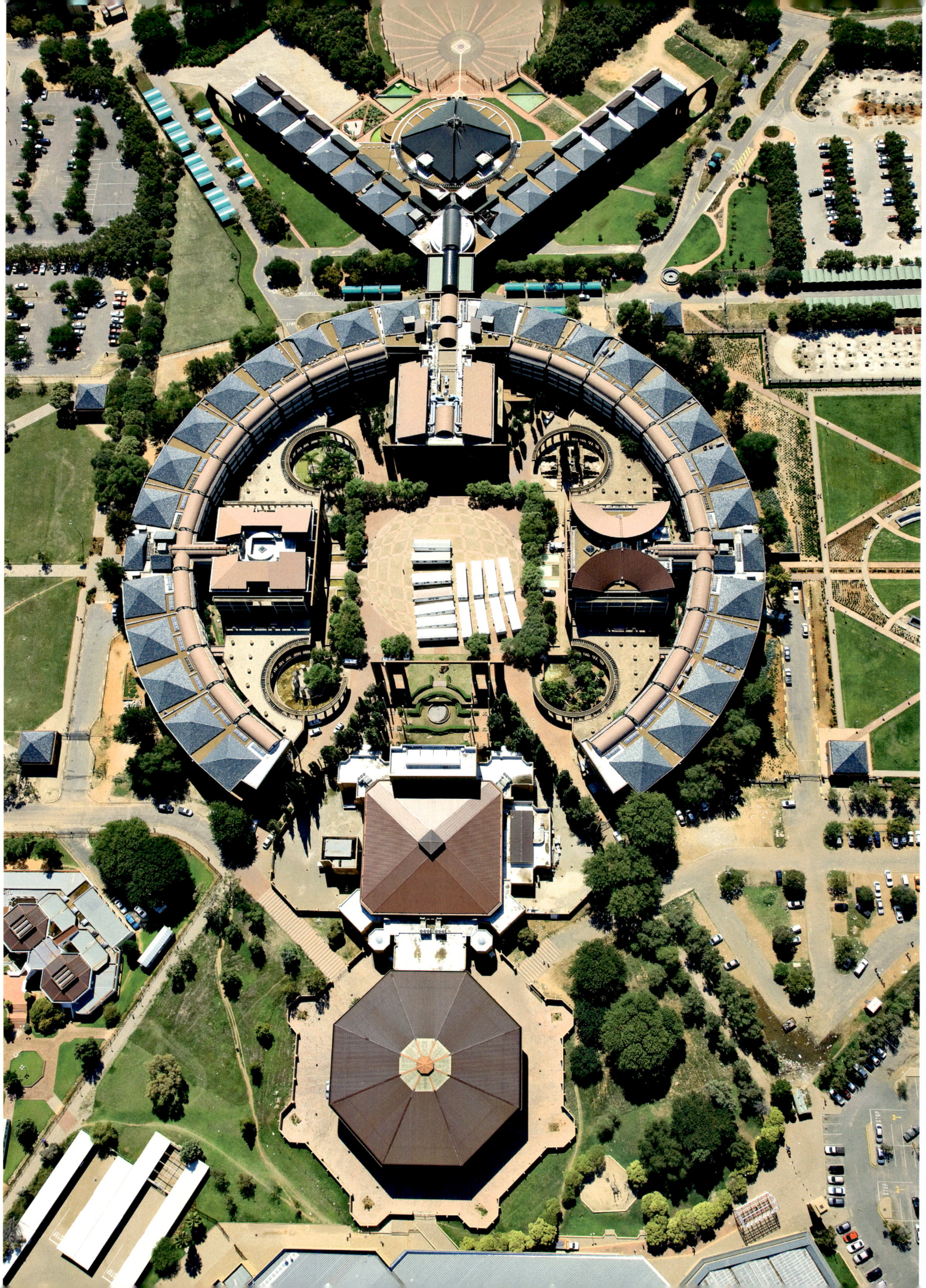

↓→→ Bloemhof Dam Nature Reserve
→ Sandveld Nature Reserve

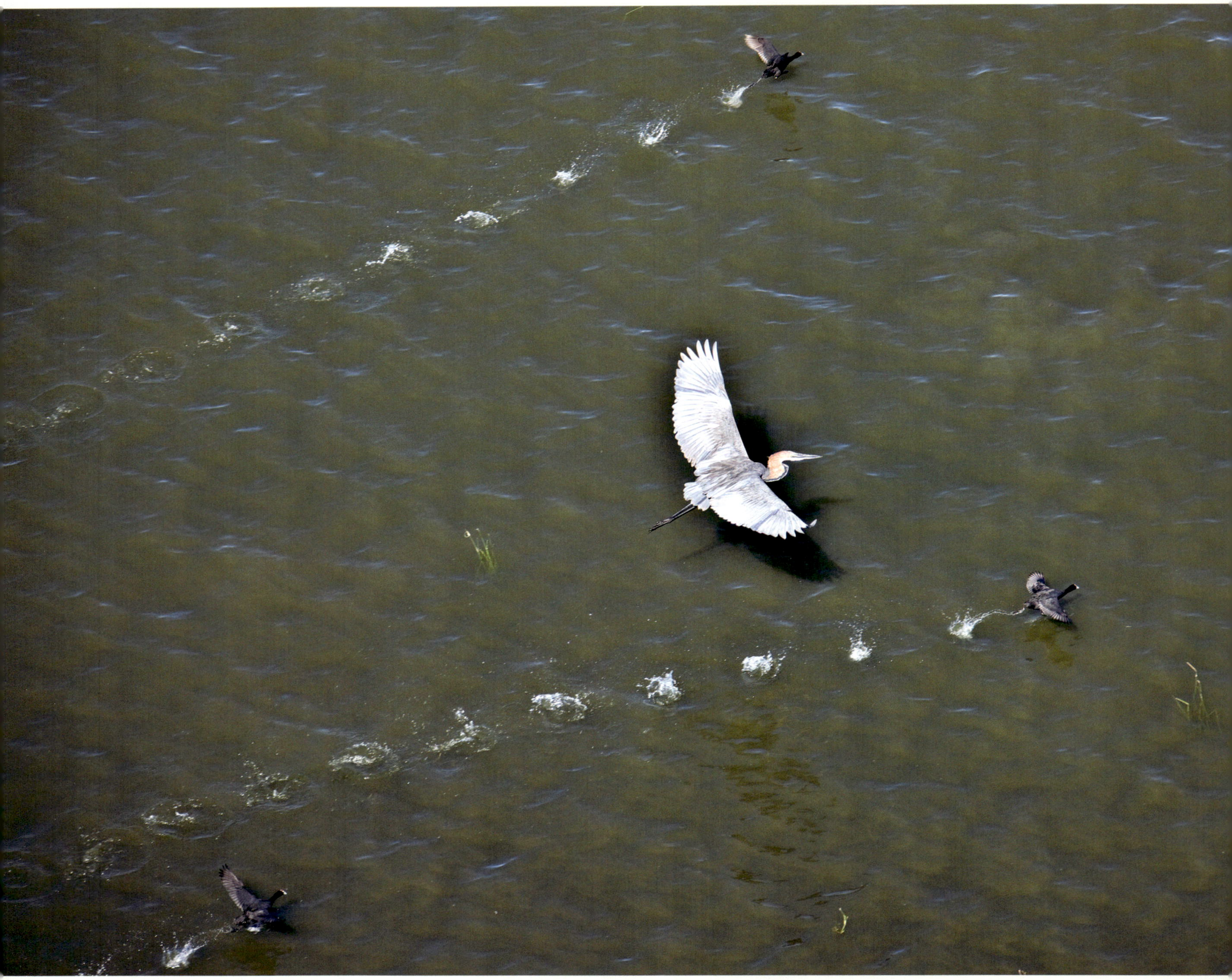

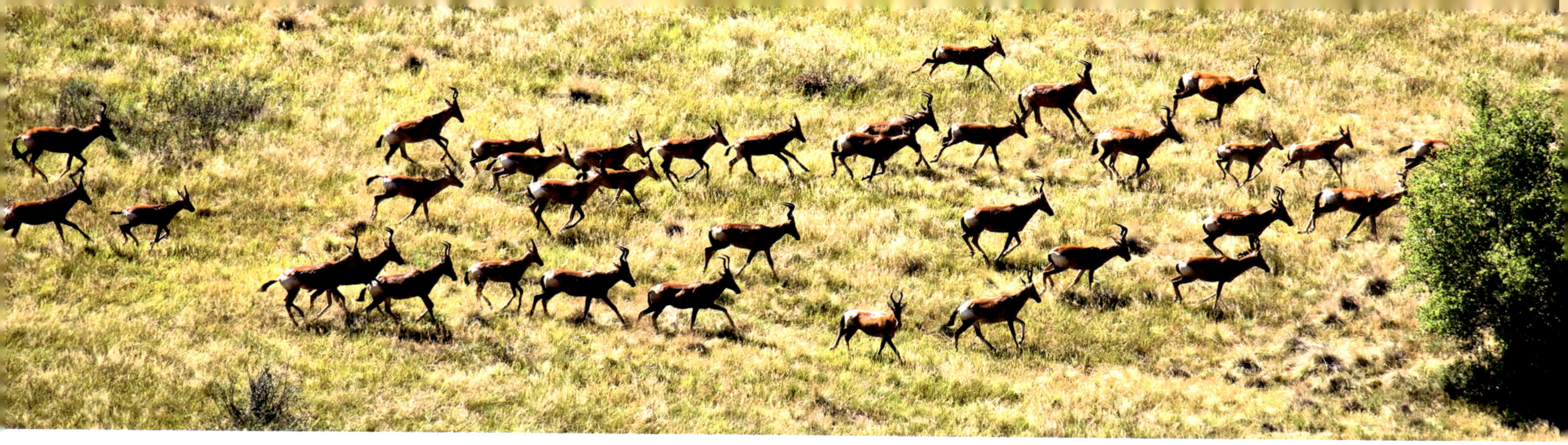

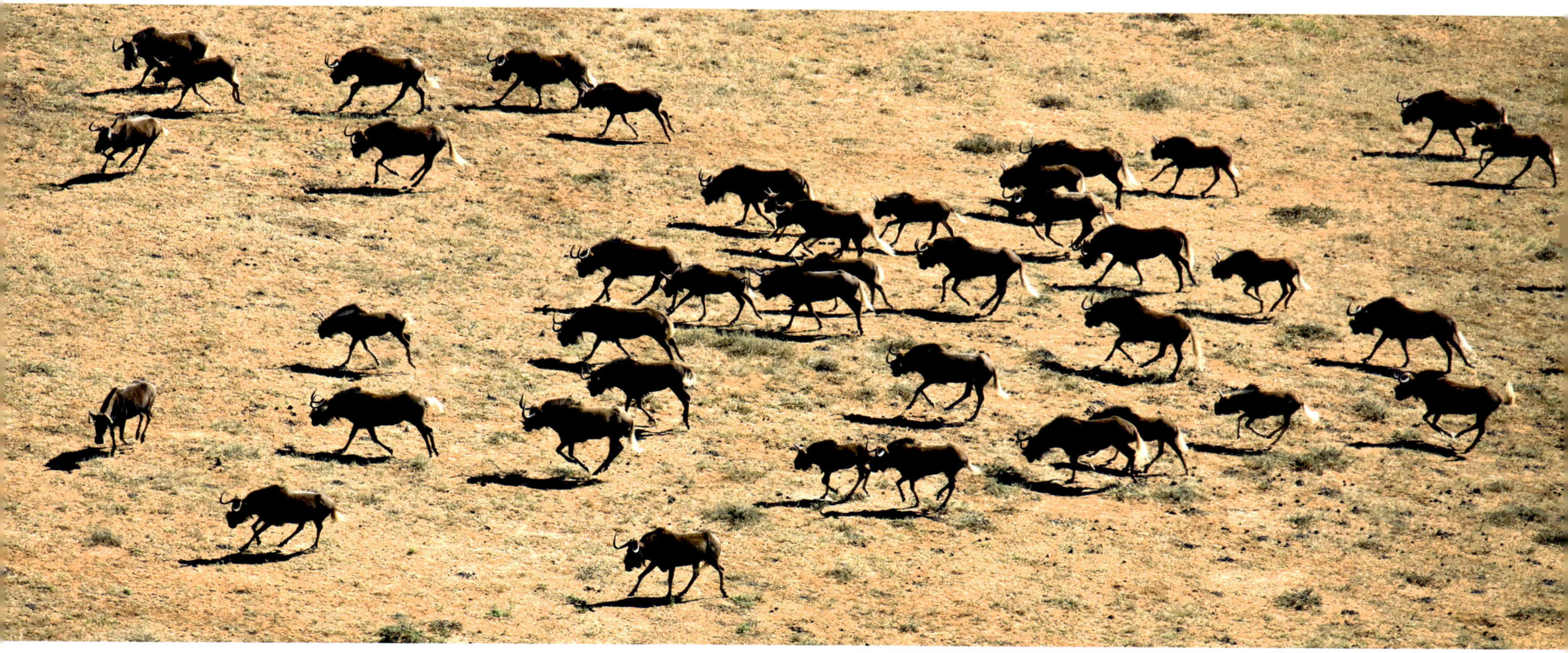

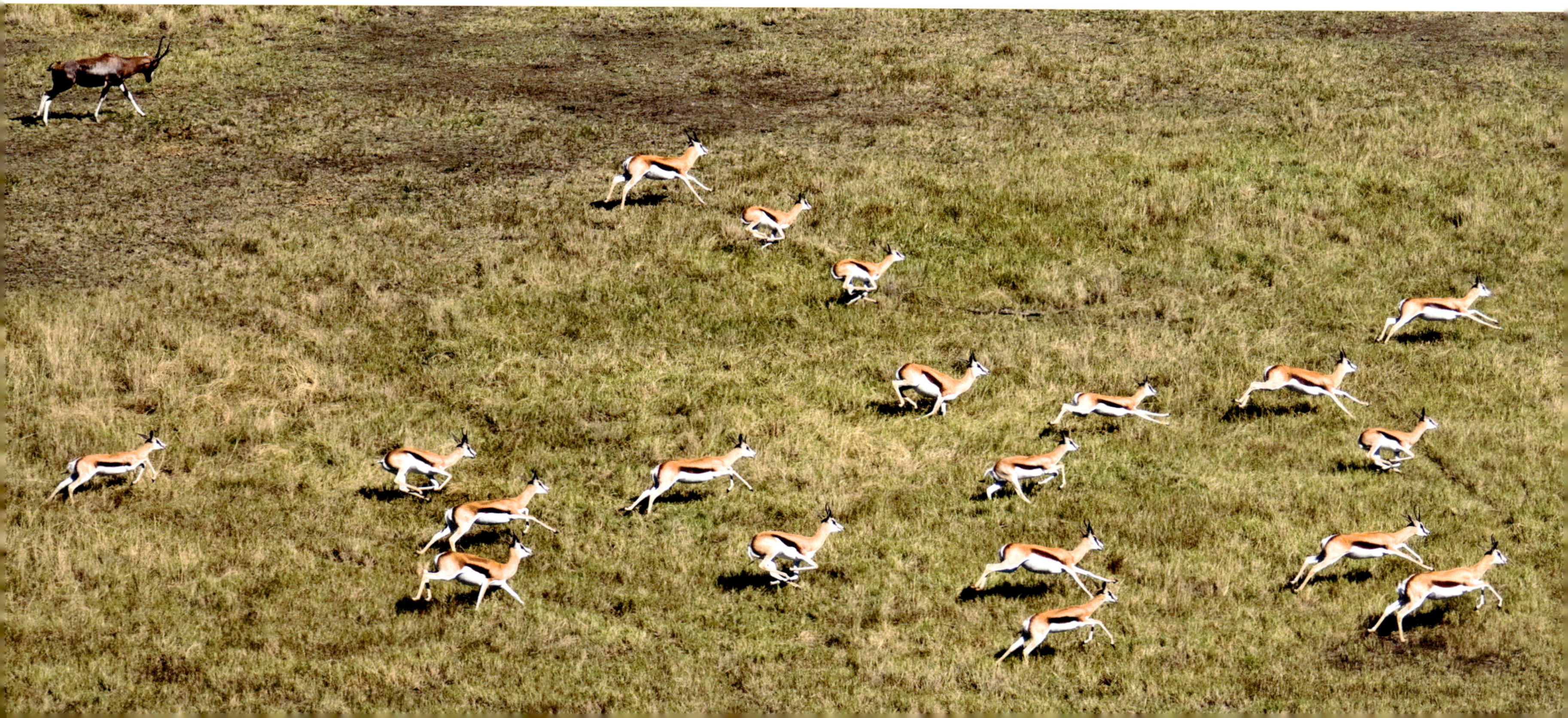

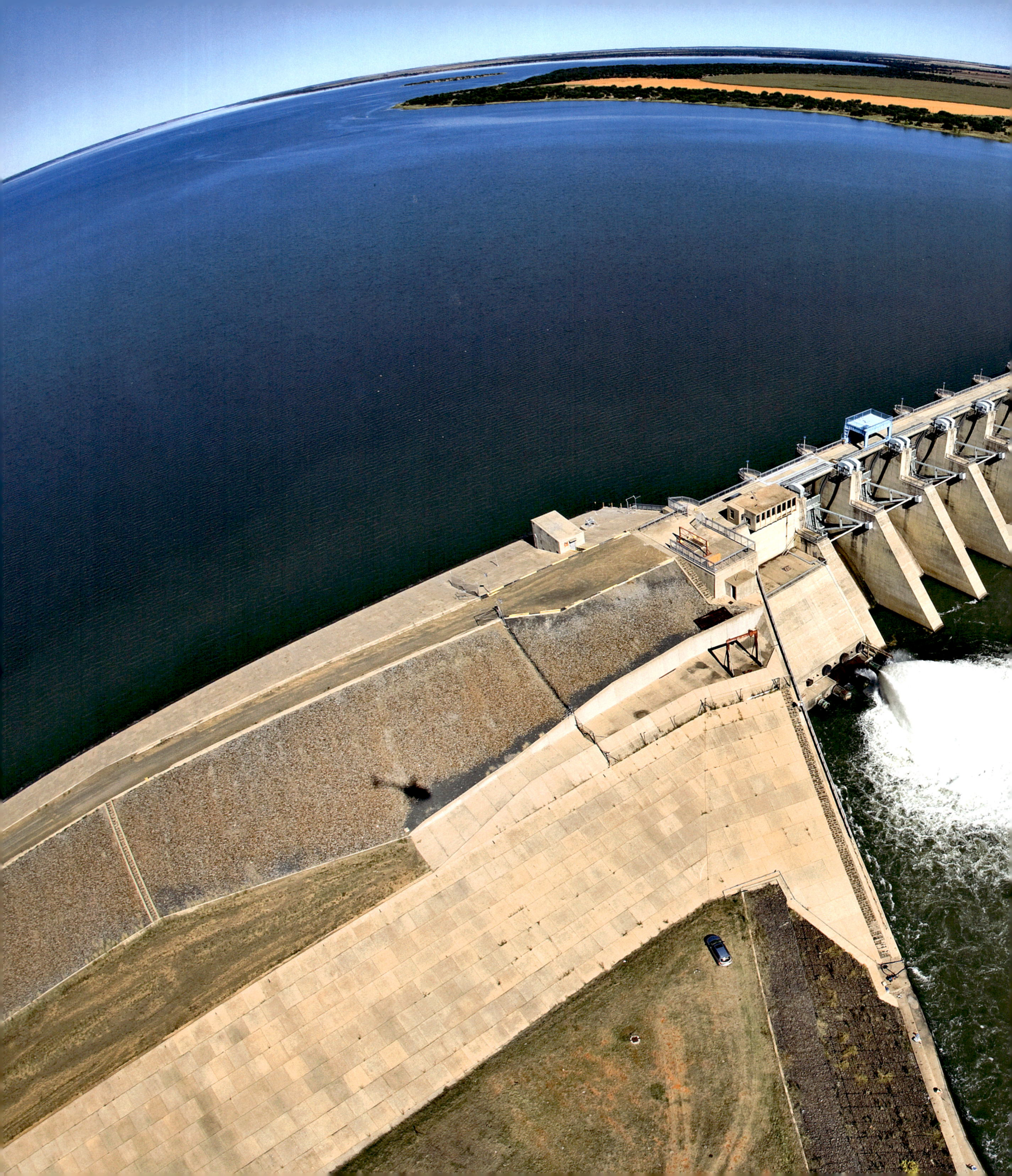

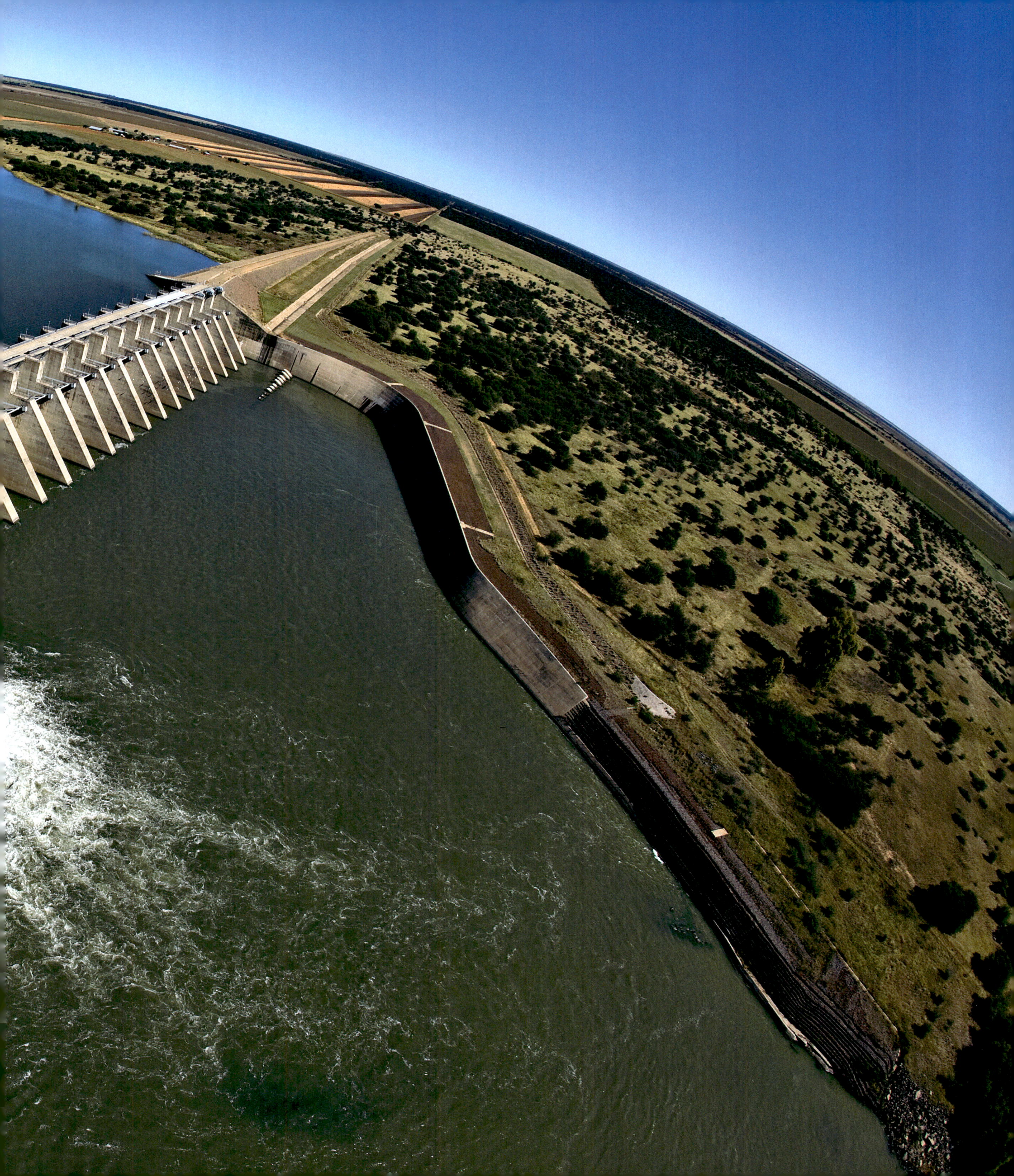

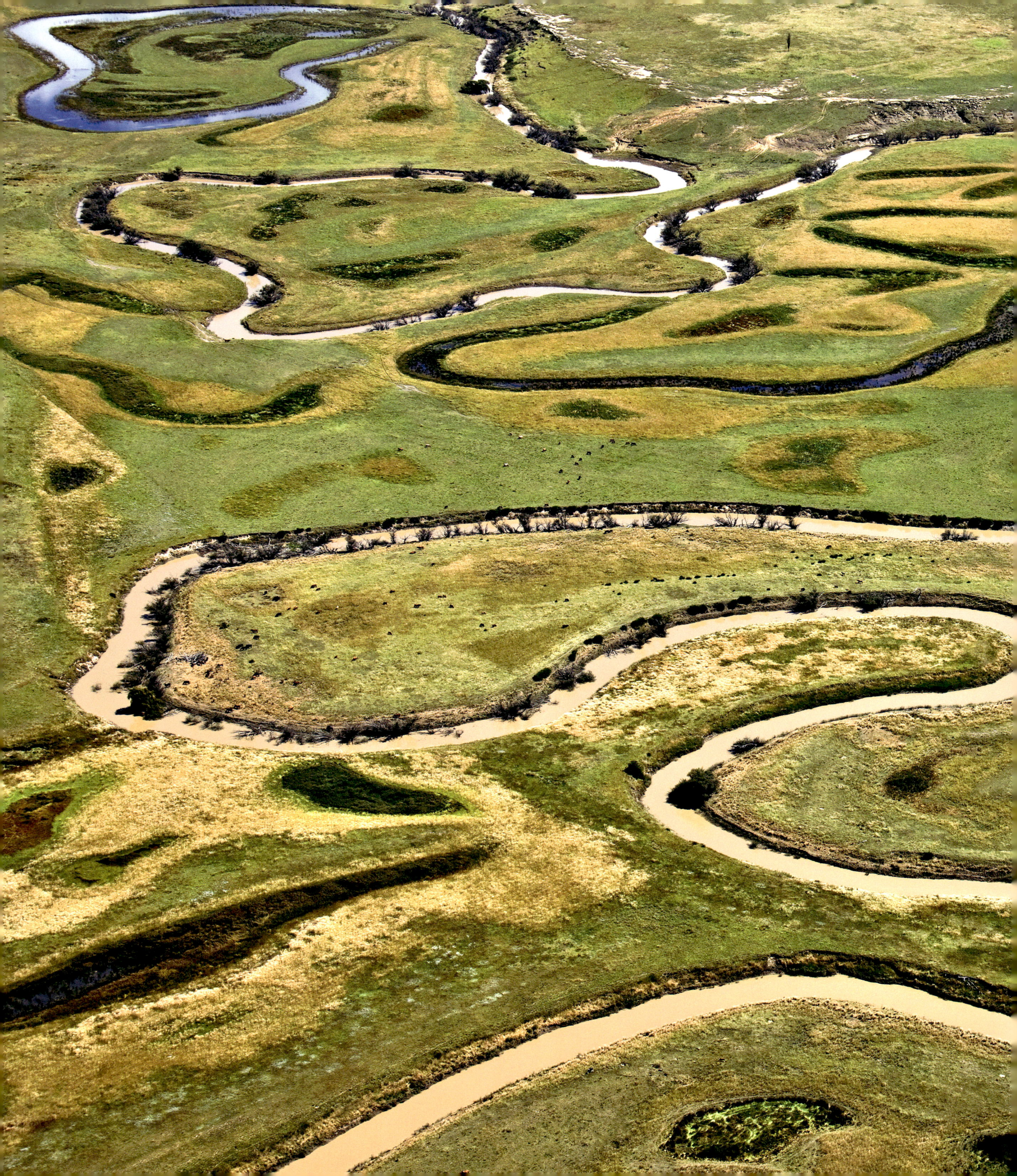

FREE STATE

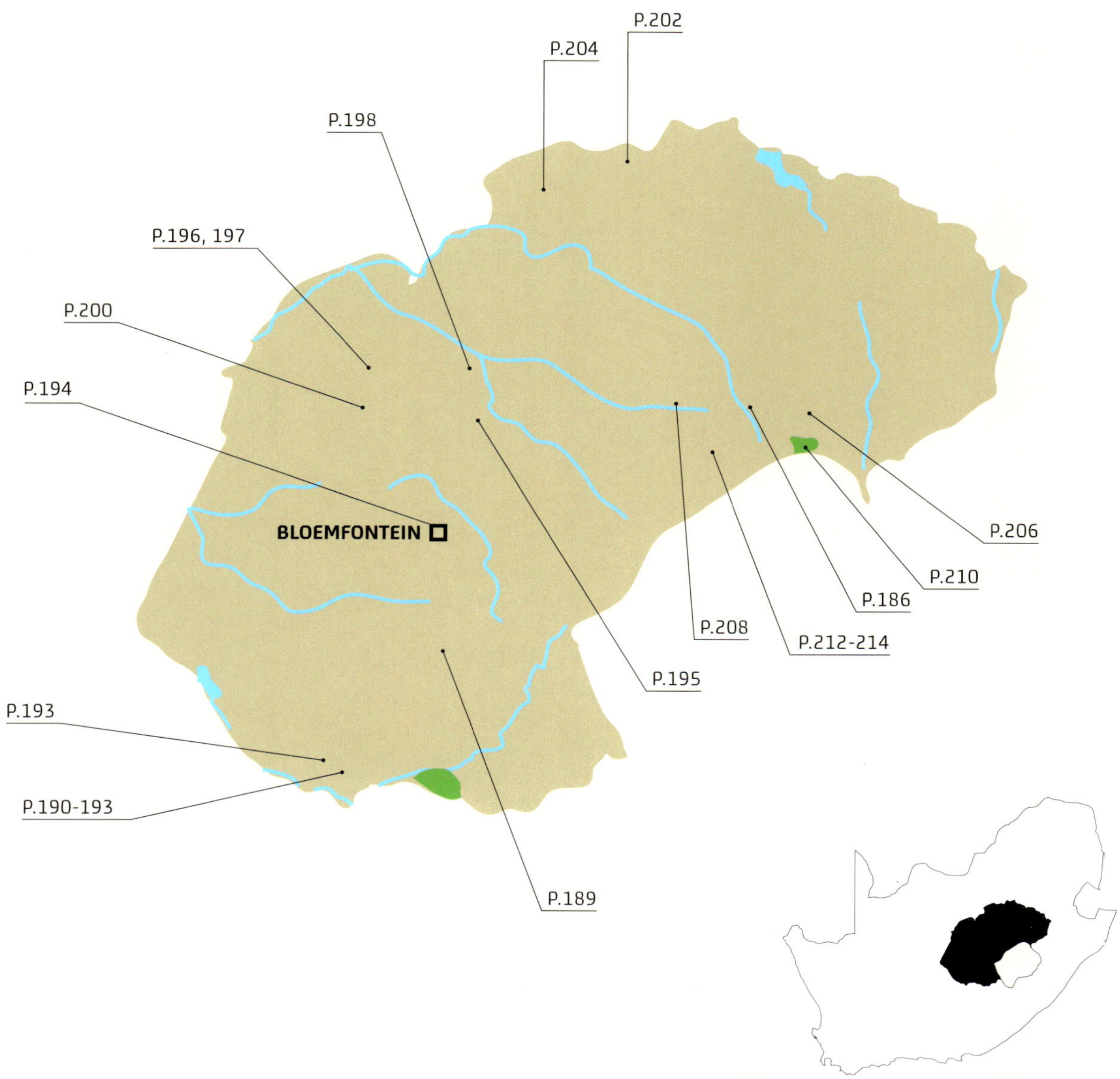
P.202
P.204
P.198
P.196, 197
P.200
P.194
BLOEMFONTEIN
P.206
P.210
P.186
P.208
P.212-214
P.195
P.193
P.190-193
P.189

The story goes that the white Voortrekkers who left what was then the British Cape Colony around 1840 came upon a traffic sign somewhere just above the Orange River. One arm pointed south, to the Cape. The second pointed north, to the Vaal River. Those who were homesick turned round and returned to the Cape Colony. Others thought they were not yet far enough away from British territory and ventured farther into the interior. A third group of Voortrekkers couldn't read and didn't know what was written on the sign. They stopped here and founded a Boer Republic: the Orange Free State.

From granary to Big Sky Country

Today, the Free State is at the geographic heart of South Africa and is known as the country's granary. The traditional image of Vrystaters as very hospitable but somewhat backward country bumpkins, however, belongs entirely to the past. As too does the cliché image of the province as a cultural wasteland. That is particularly noticeable in the historic capital Bloemfontein, where two of South Africa's largest art festivals – the Volksblad Kunstefees and the Mangaung African Cultural Festival – attract many thousands of visitors every year.

Grain silos and colourful fields filled with wheat, corn and sunflowers, which seem to stretch out into infinity. Farms that cover thousands of hectares. That is the essence of the Free State. A large number of reservoirs have been created throughout the province to turn even the driest areas into fertile agricultural land. The most famous of these is the Gariepdam which, with a surface area of more than 350 km2, is the largest freshwater reservoir in South Africa. The dam lies in the south, in the semi-desert of the Great Karoo (Khoisan for 'hard' or 'dry'), where it is not unusual for summer temperatures to climb far above 40°.

It is much cooler in the Drakens or Maluti Mountains, in the east of the Free State, where the beautiful Golden Gate Highlands National Park attracts visitors all year round. According to legend, it was in the most inaccessible parts of the Malutis that witchdoctors used to train their tokeloshes, kidnapped children or captured baboons who were gradually transformed over a number of years into evil, repulsive creatures who were doomed to spend the rest of their lives as slaves of their captors.

Just a story? Undoubtedly. But anyone who has heard the shrill cry of the martial eagle and the challenging screams of the baboon in the Malutis, or seen the ancient, mystical rock paintings of the San, knows that this is a world where dreams and nightmares all too easily take root.

Much has changed since the days of the Boer Republic. Now, large gold mines are operated in and around Welkom, while Sasolburg, which was built in record time in 1952, is an important centre of the South African petrochemical industry. Bloemfontein has become part of the municipality of Mangaung – the place of the cheetah – and the province no longer presents itself as the granary of South Africa but as Big Sky Country. What has remained is the hospitality of the Vrystaters.

A hospitality which is typical of a province where distances between villages and cities are often very large and the number of people is limited; it is typical of what is still, in essence, a rural community.

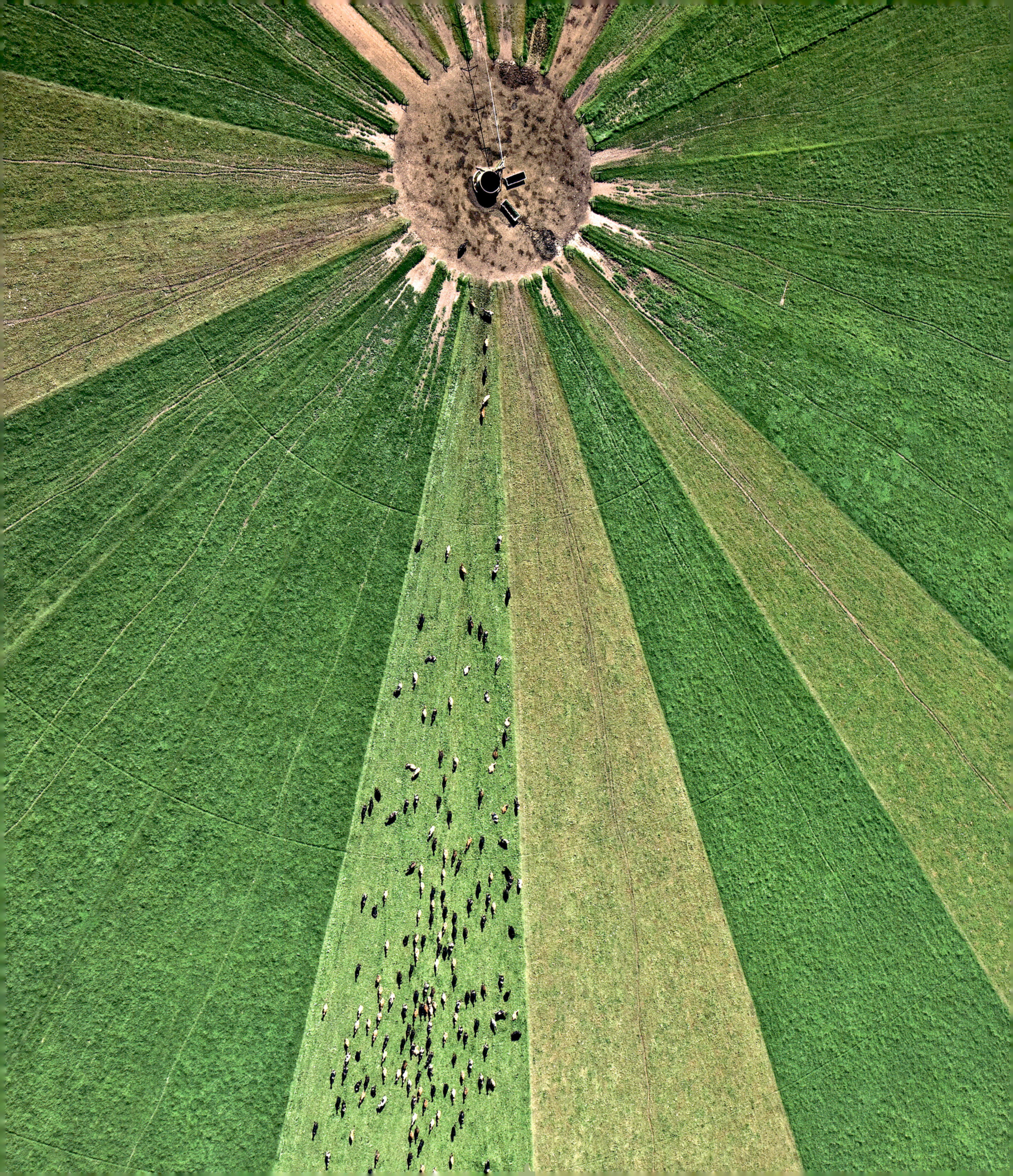

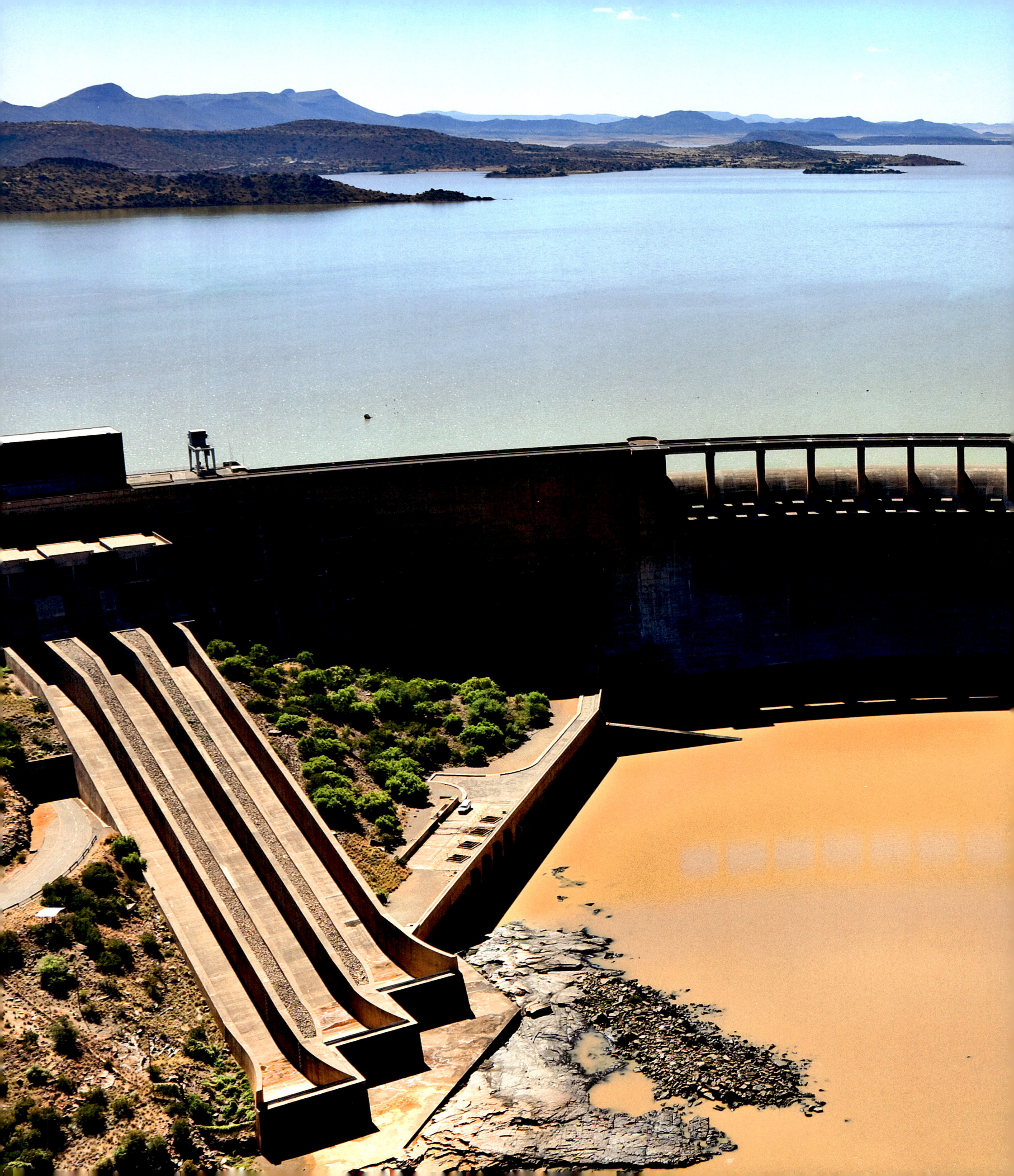

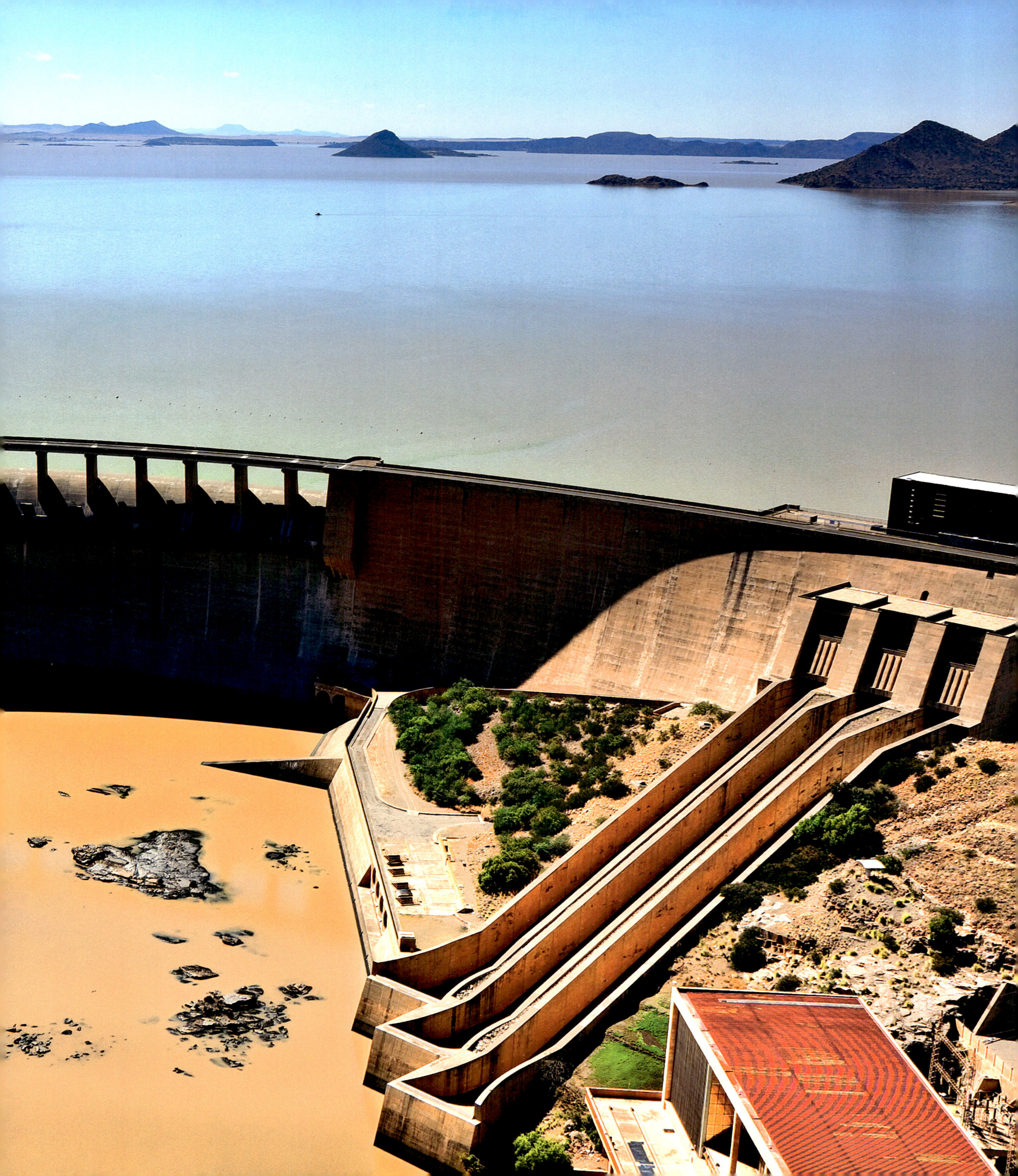

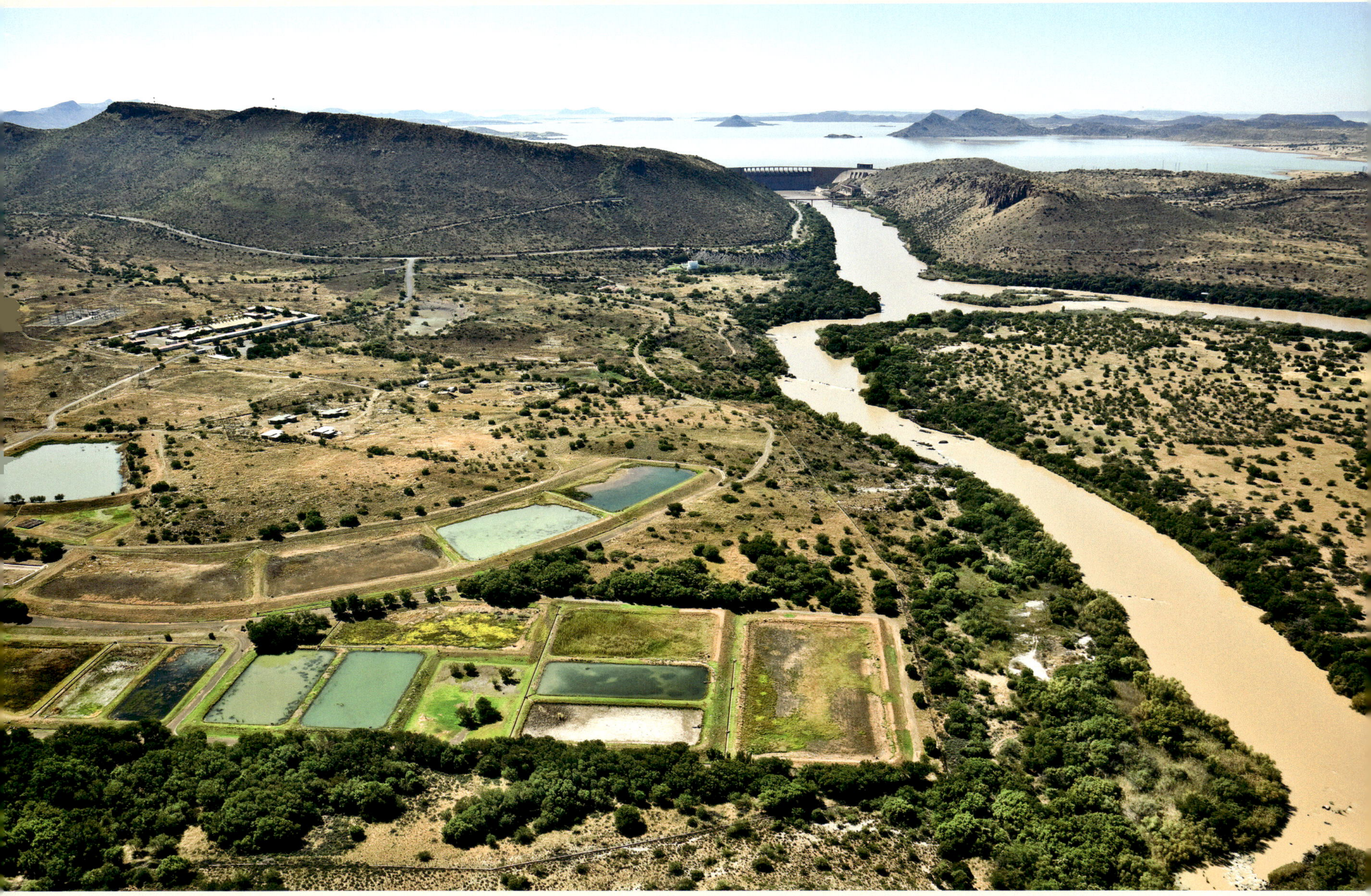

←← Gariep Dam
← Orange River, Gariep Dam
↓ Gariep Dam, border of Free State and Eastern Cape

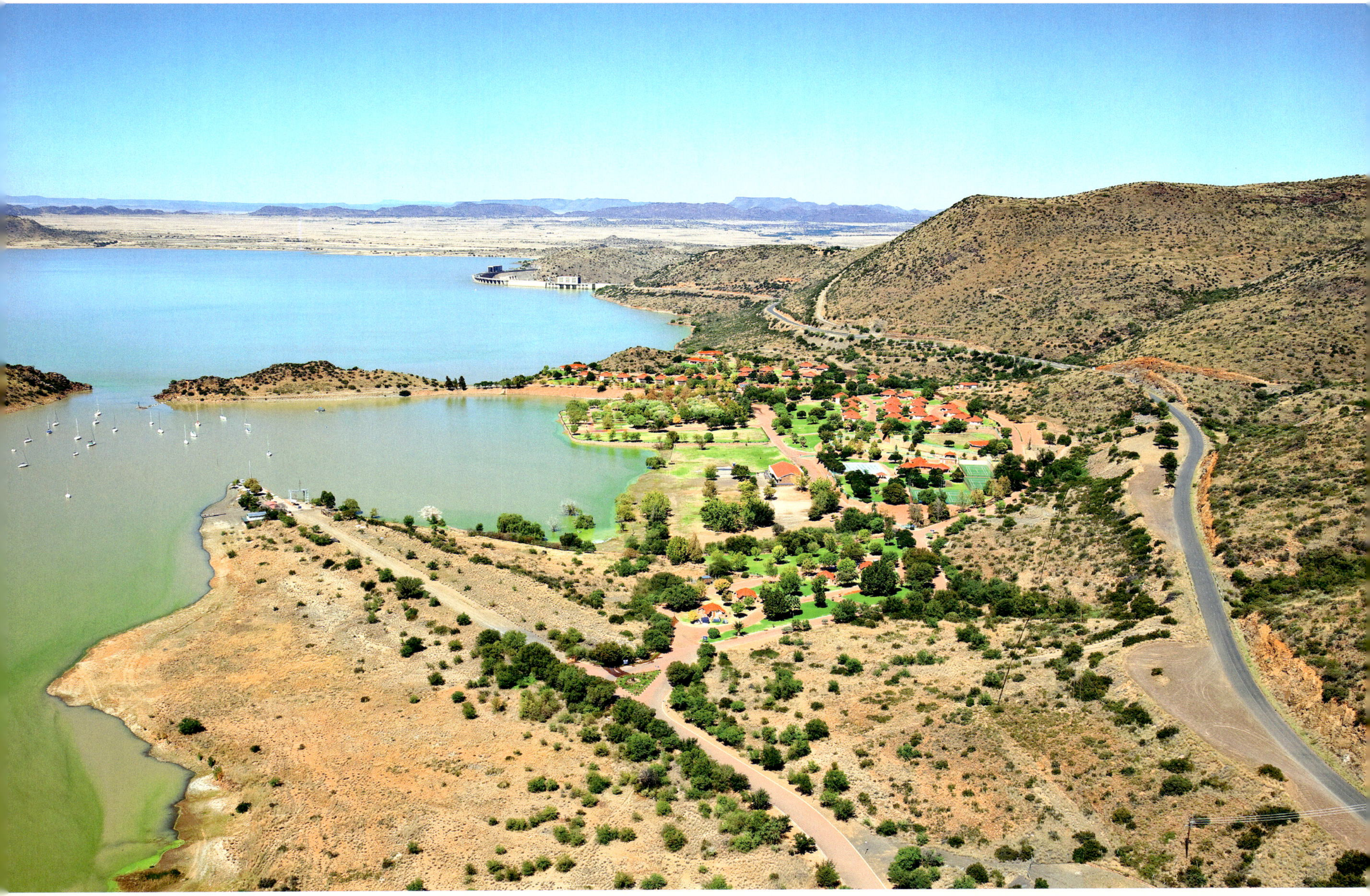

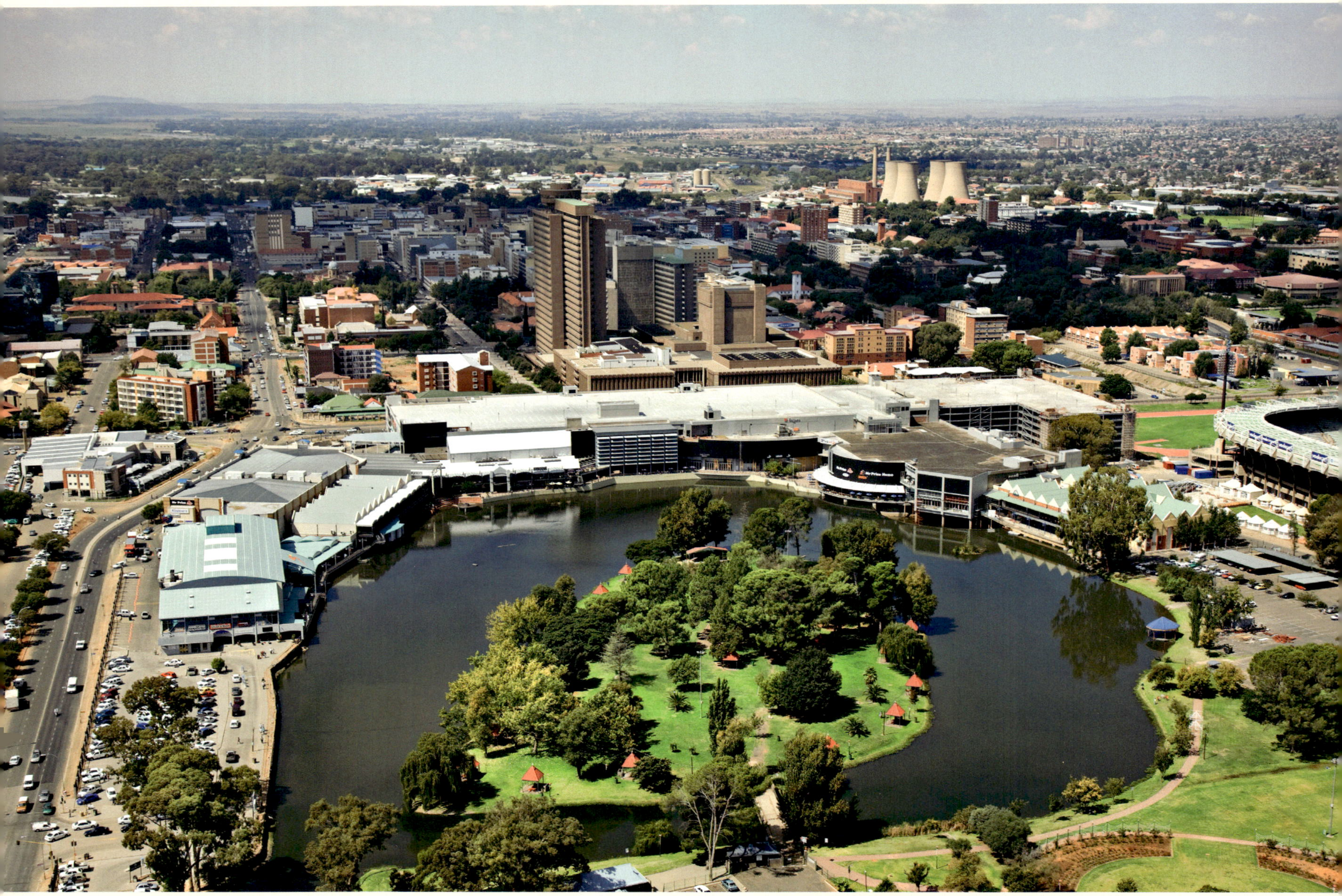

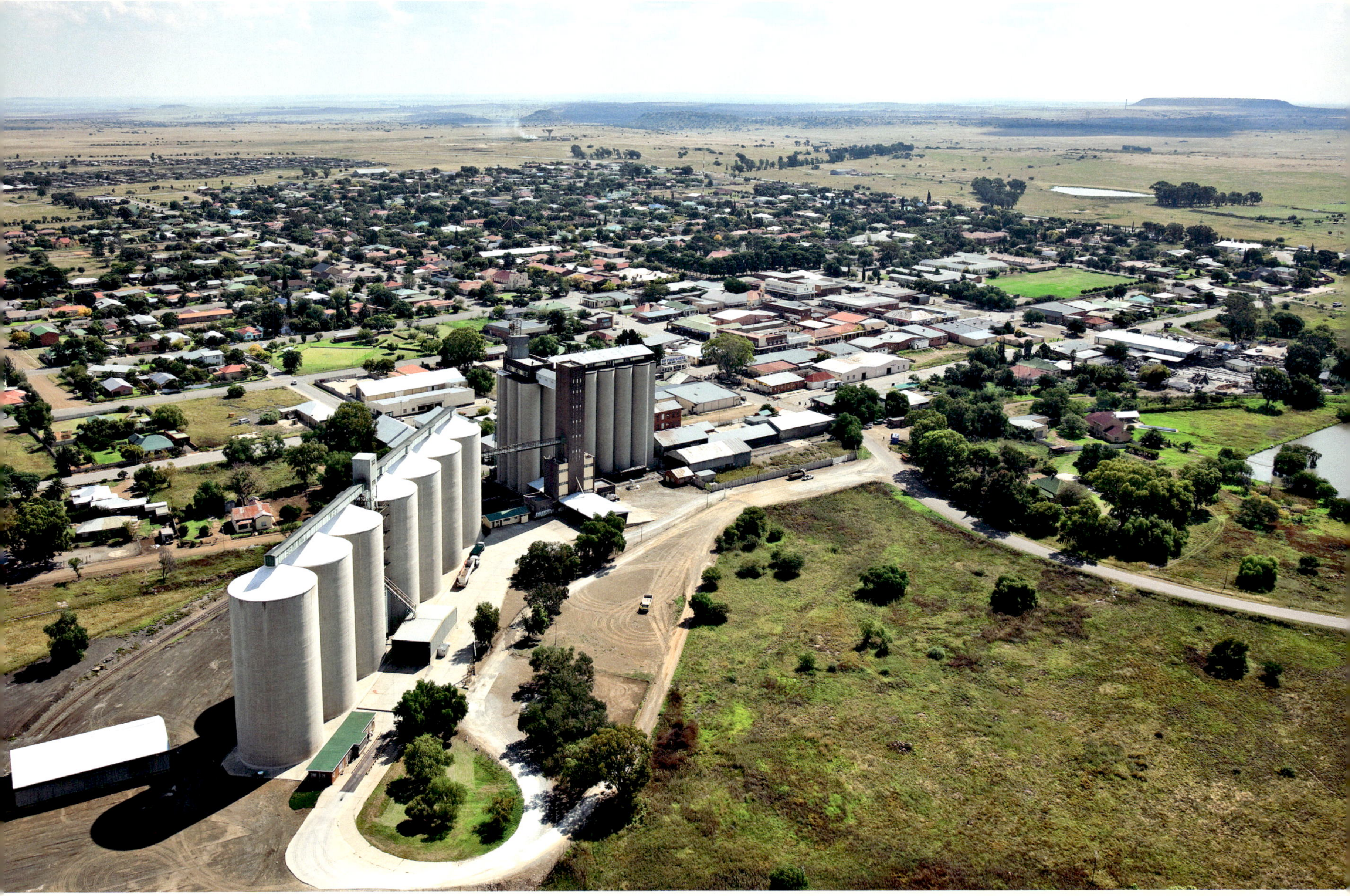

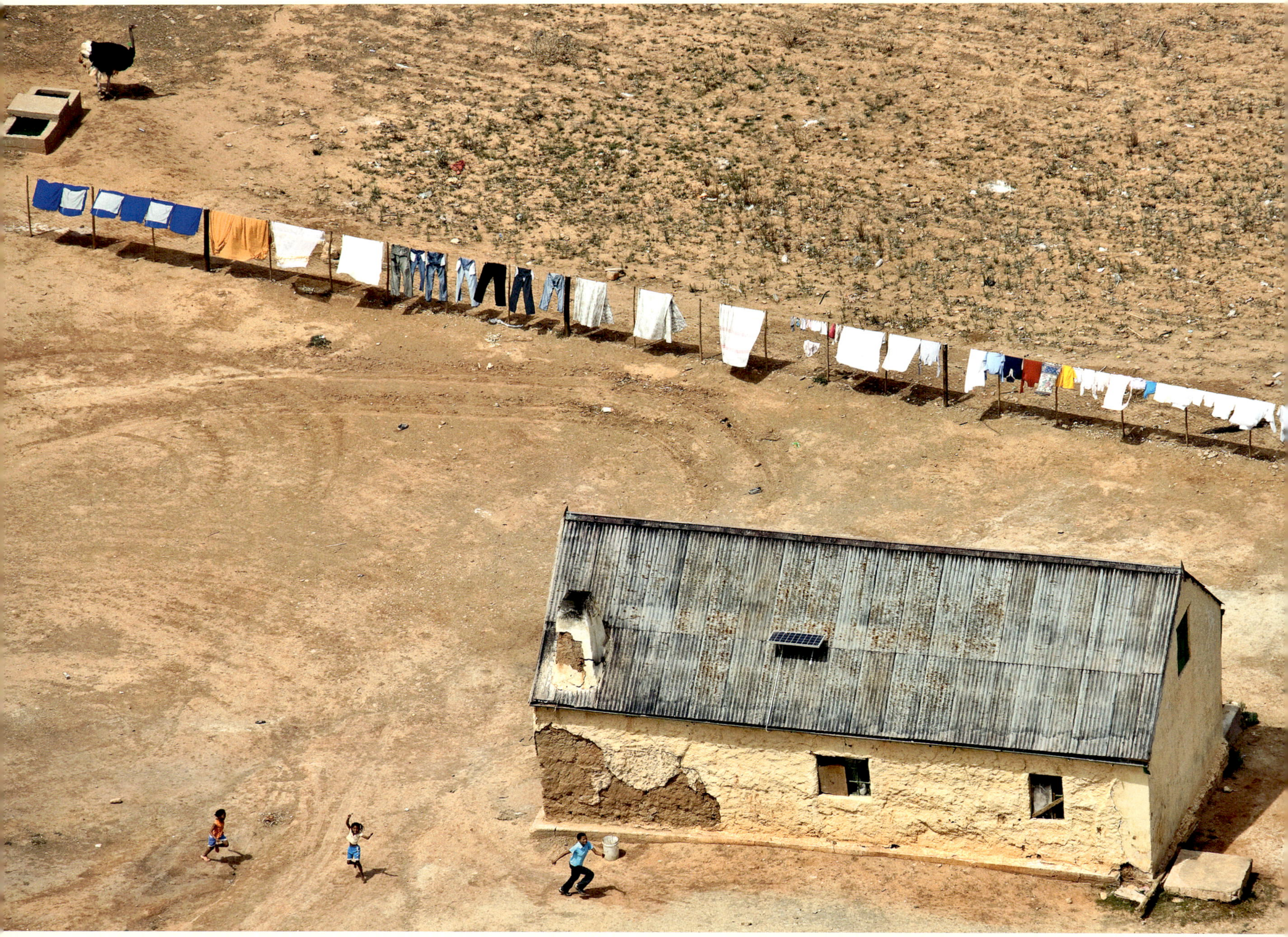

← A sunny washing day
↓ Give way to cattle

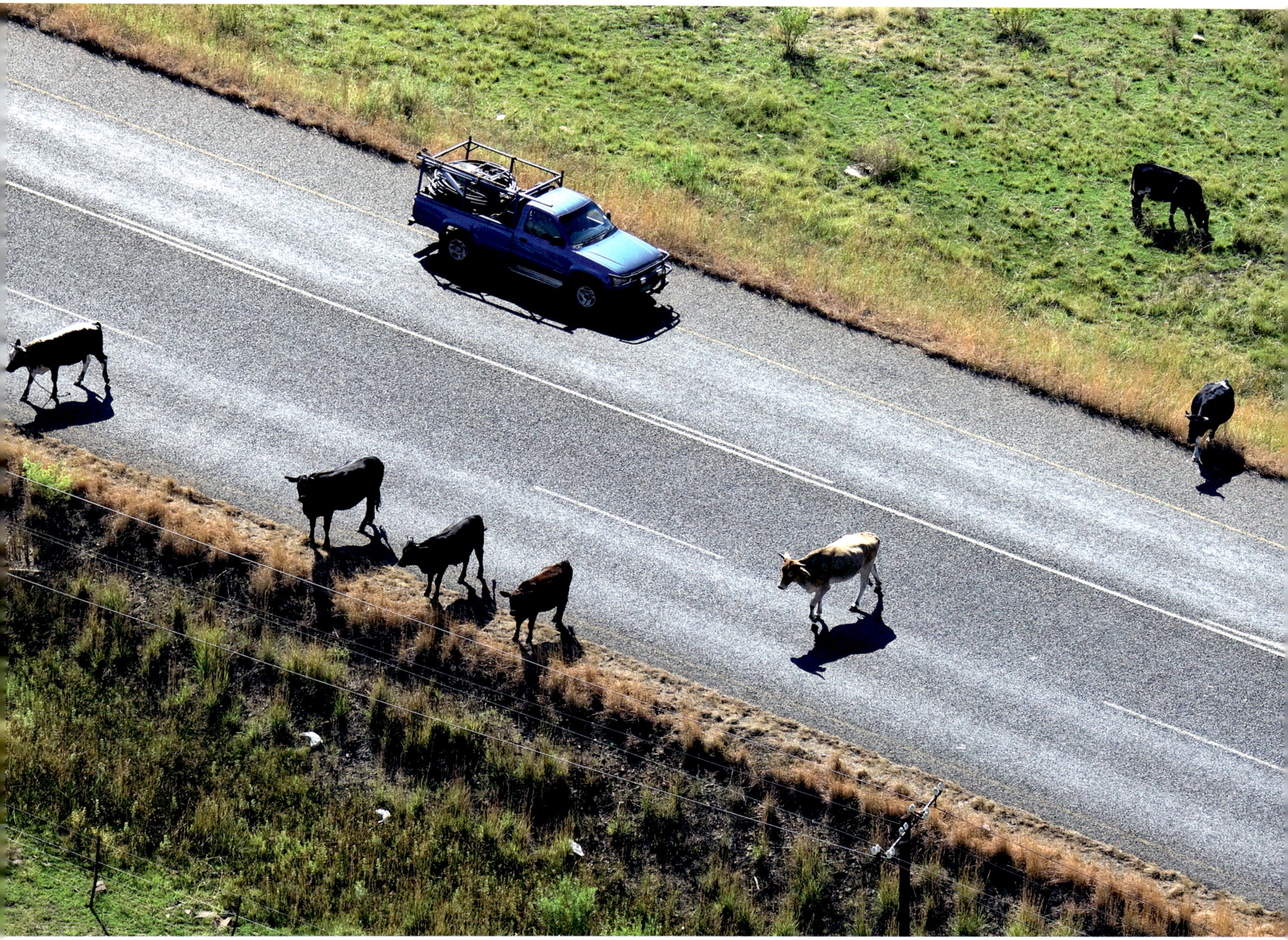

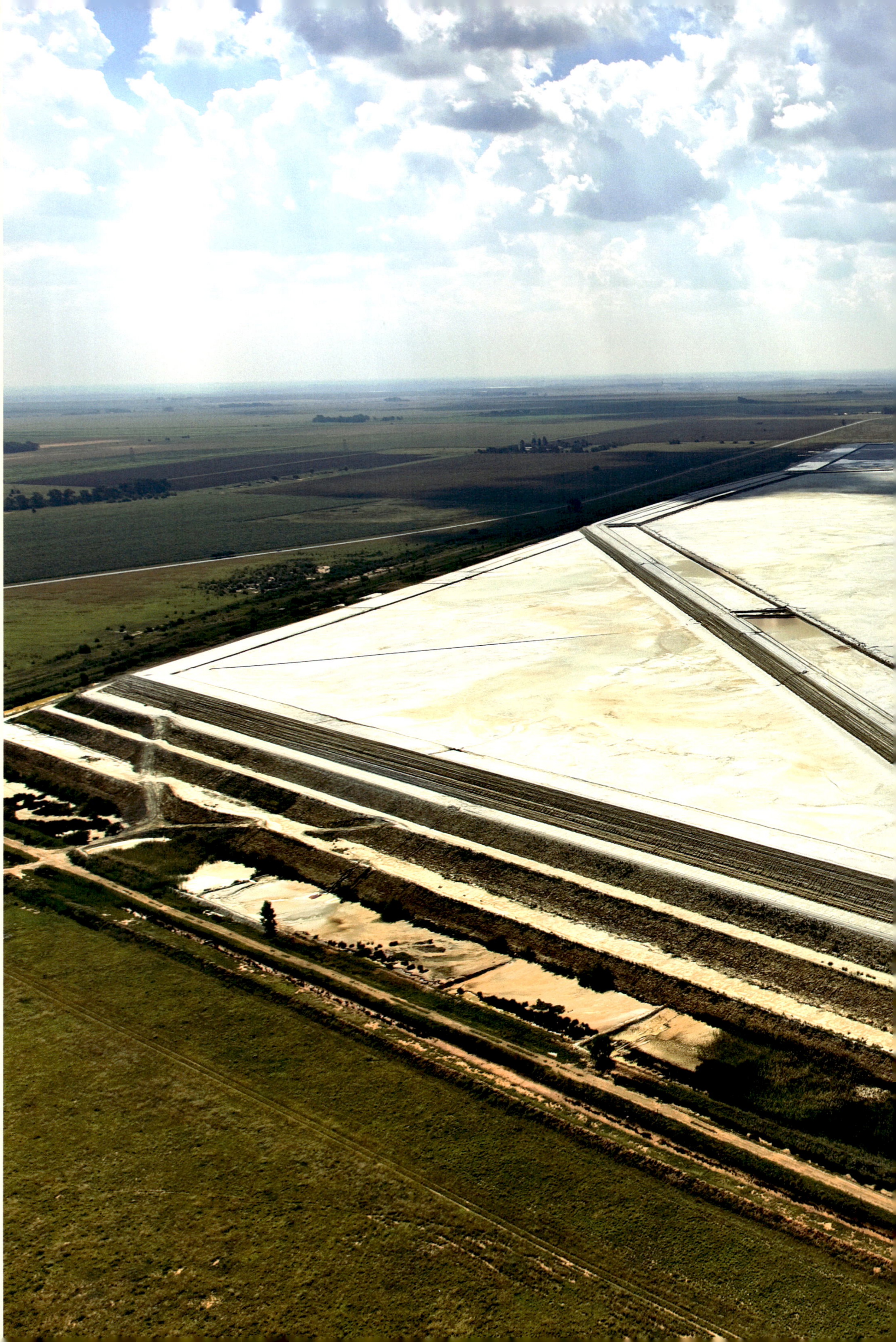

→ Gold mine dump, 20 km north of Theunissen

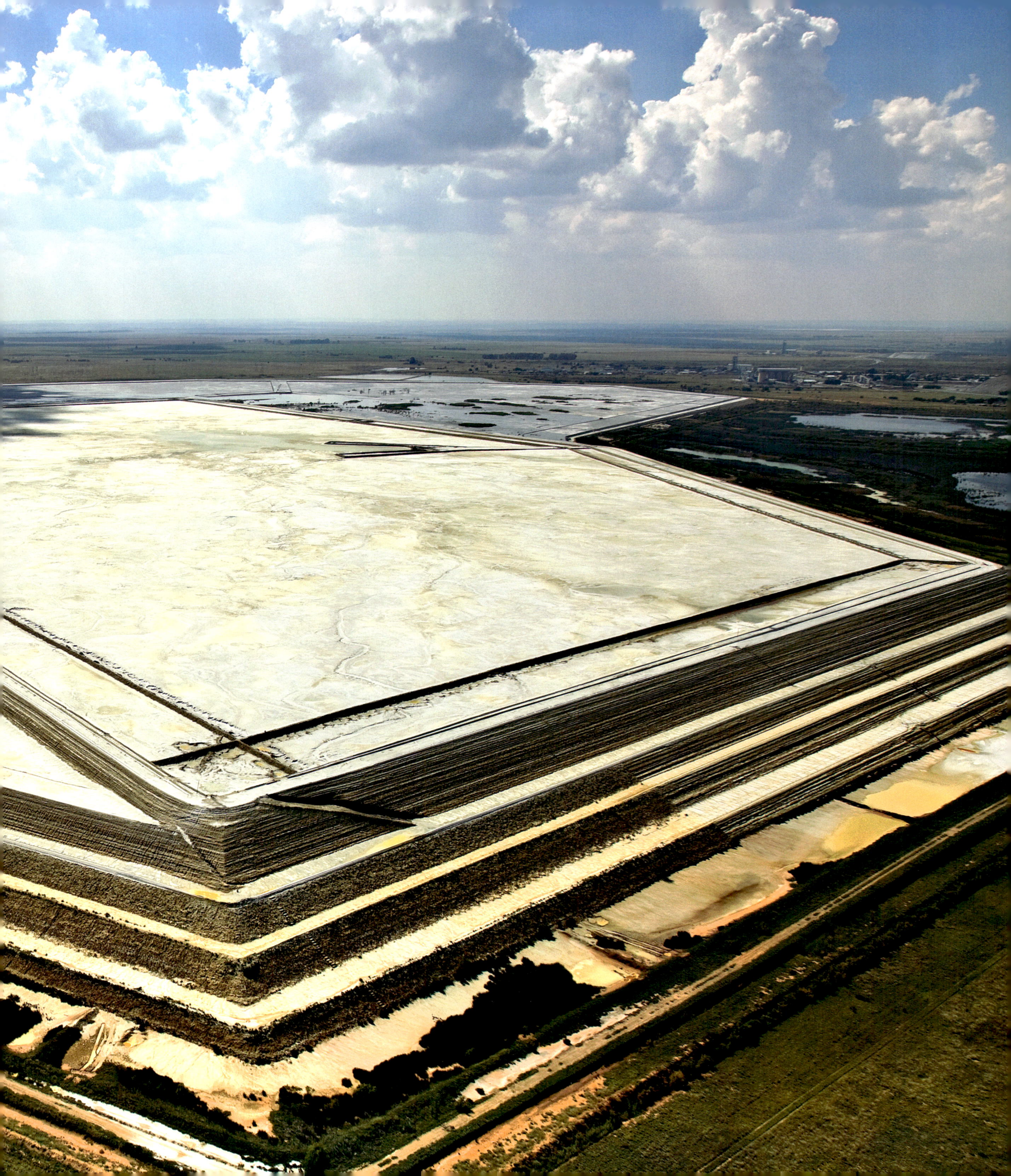

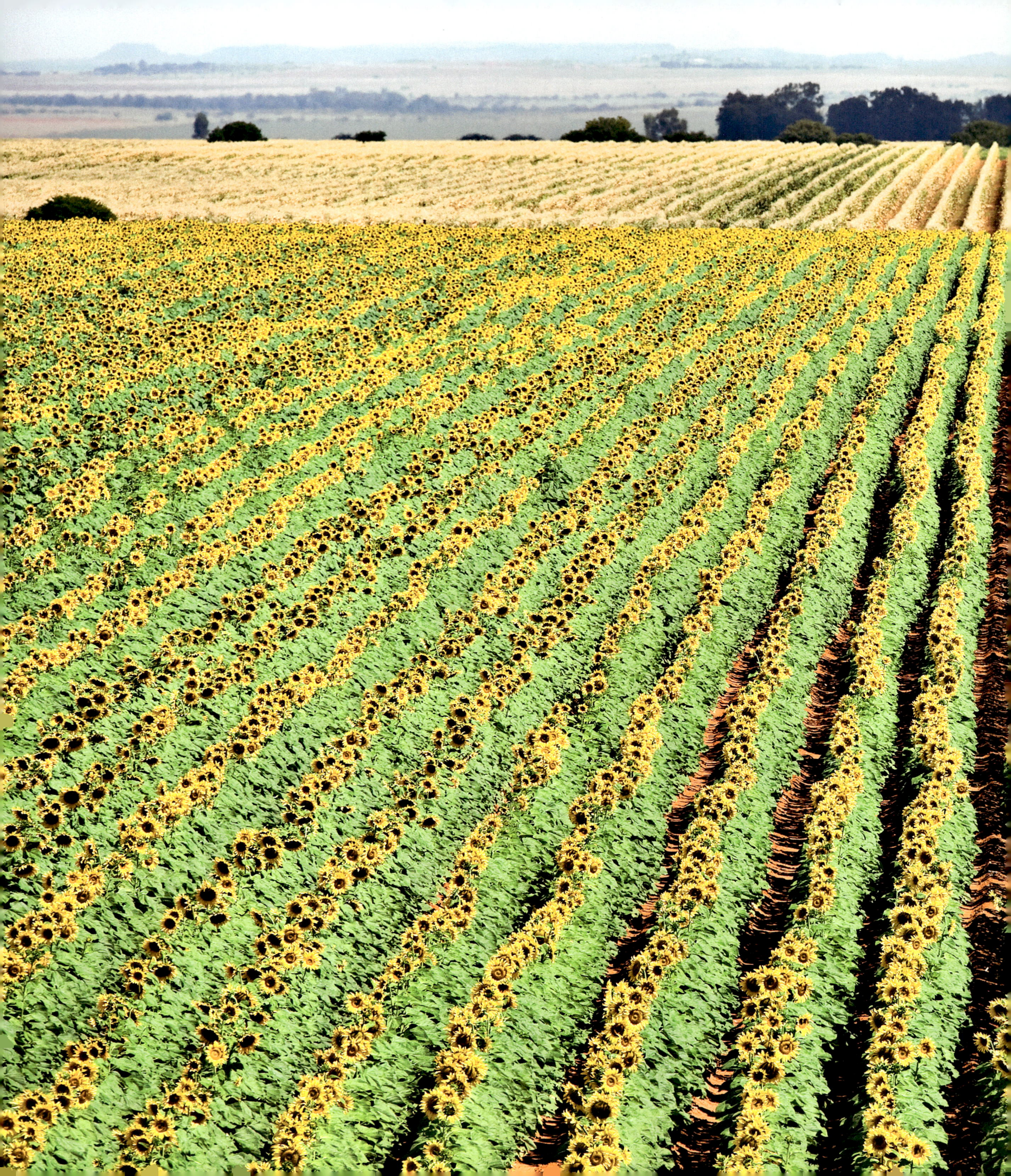

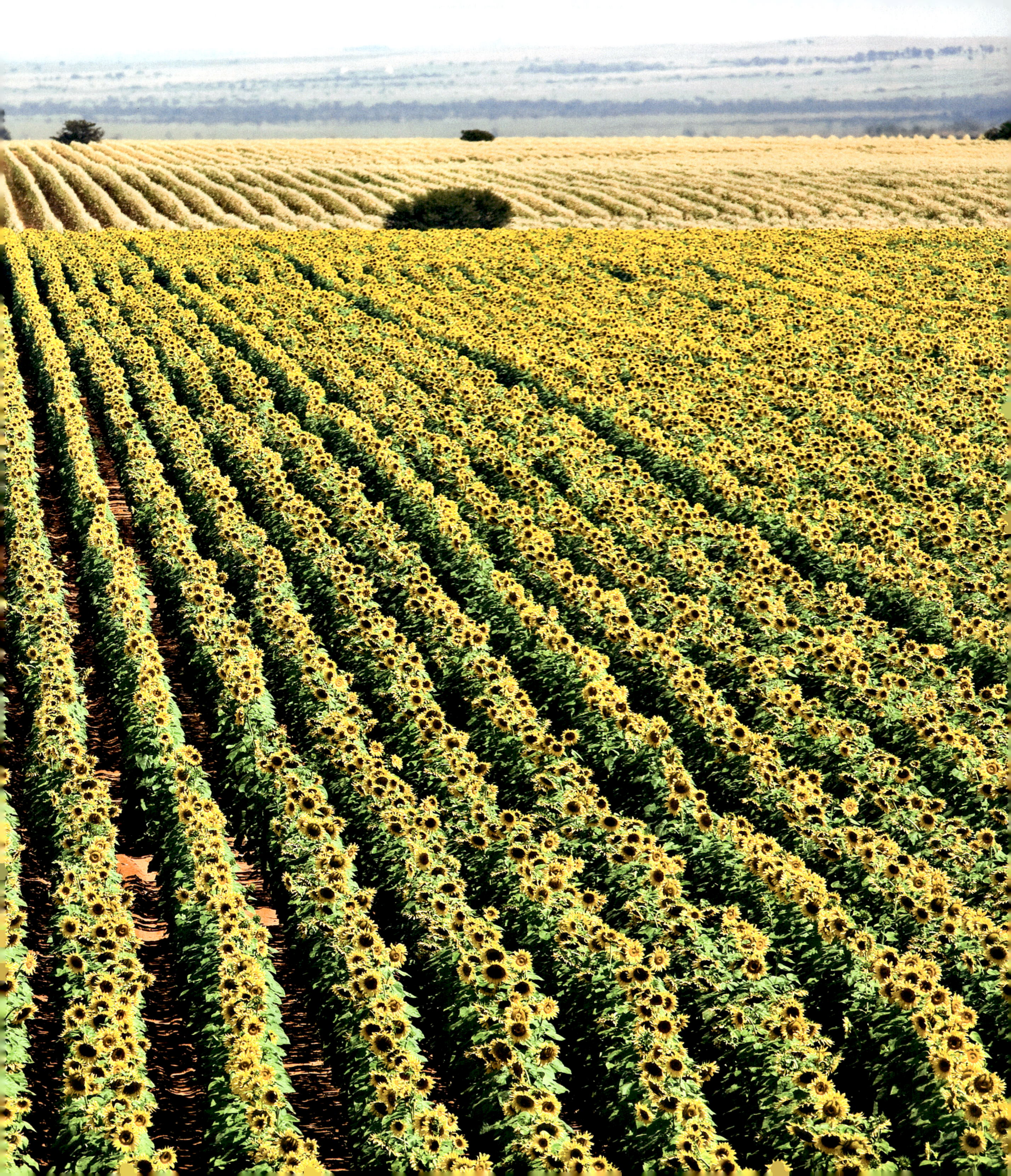

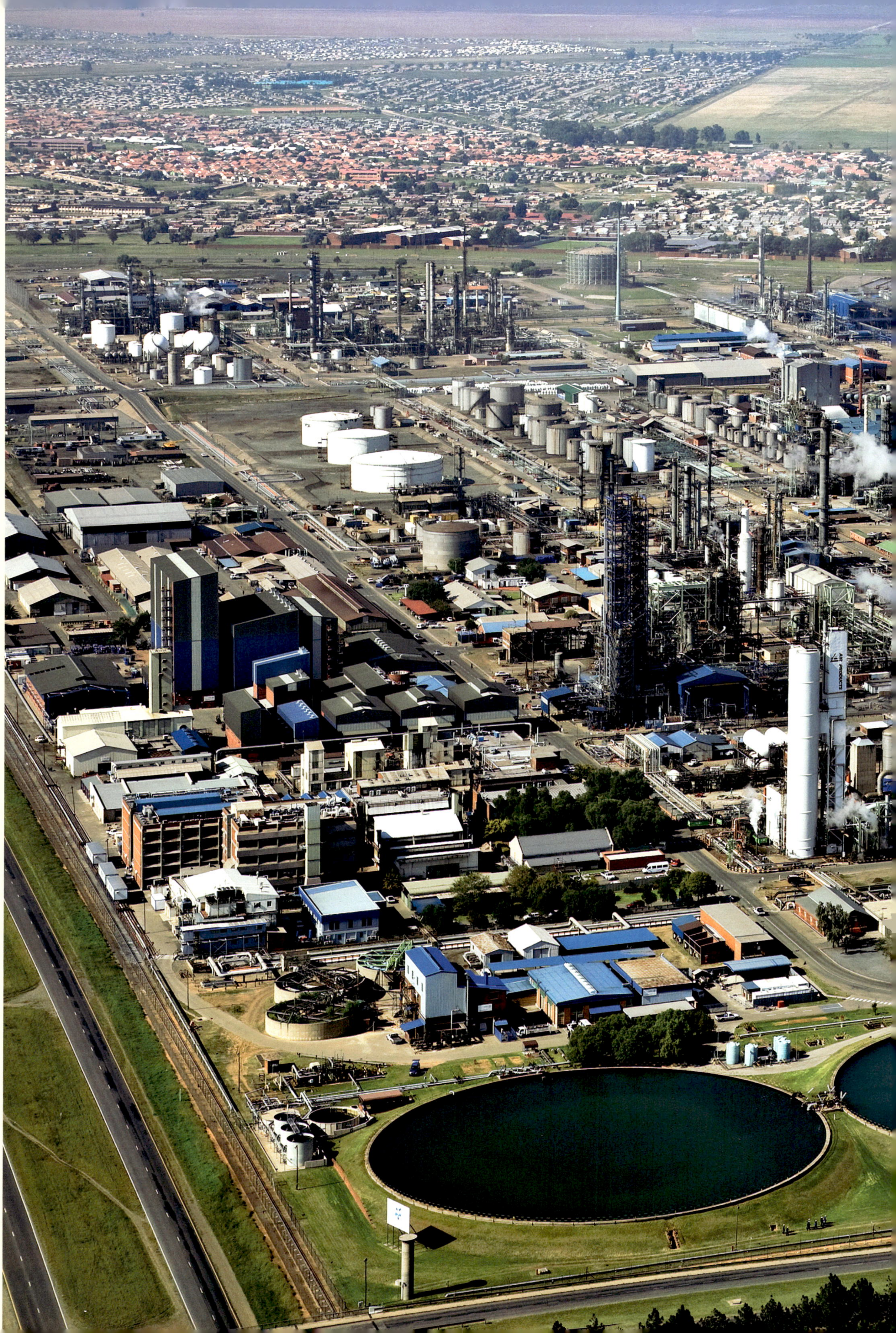

← Sunflower fields, the beauty of the Free State
→ Petrochemical plant, Sasolburg

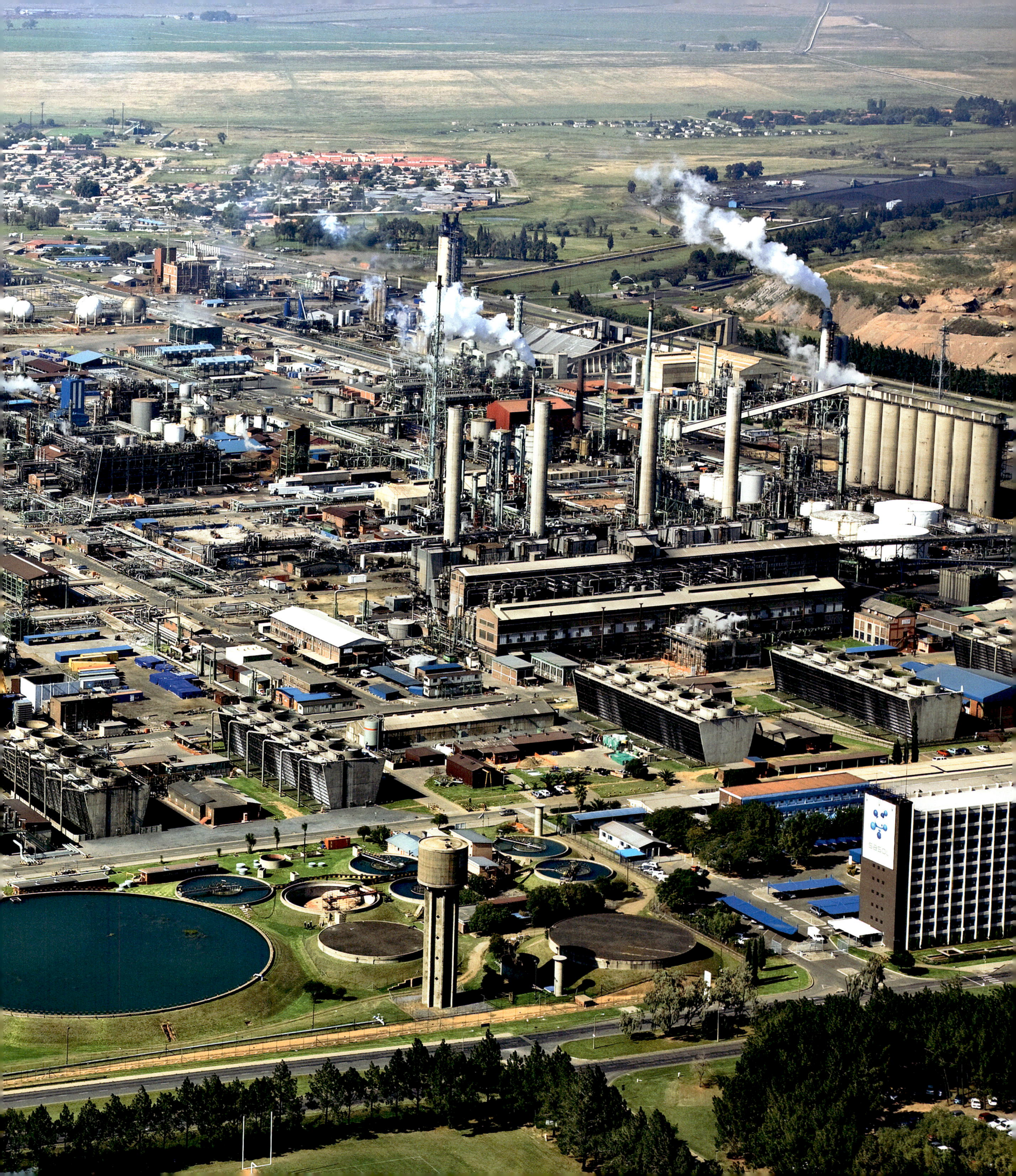

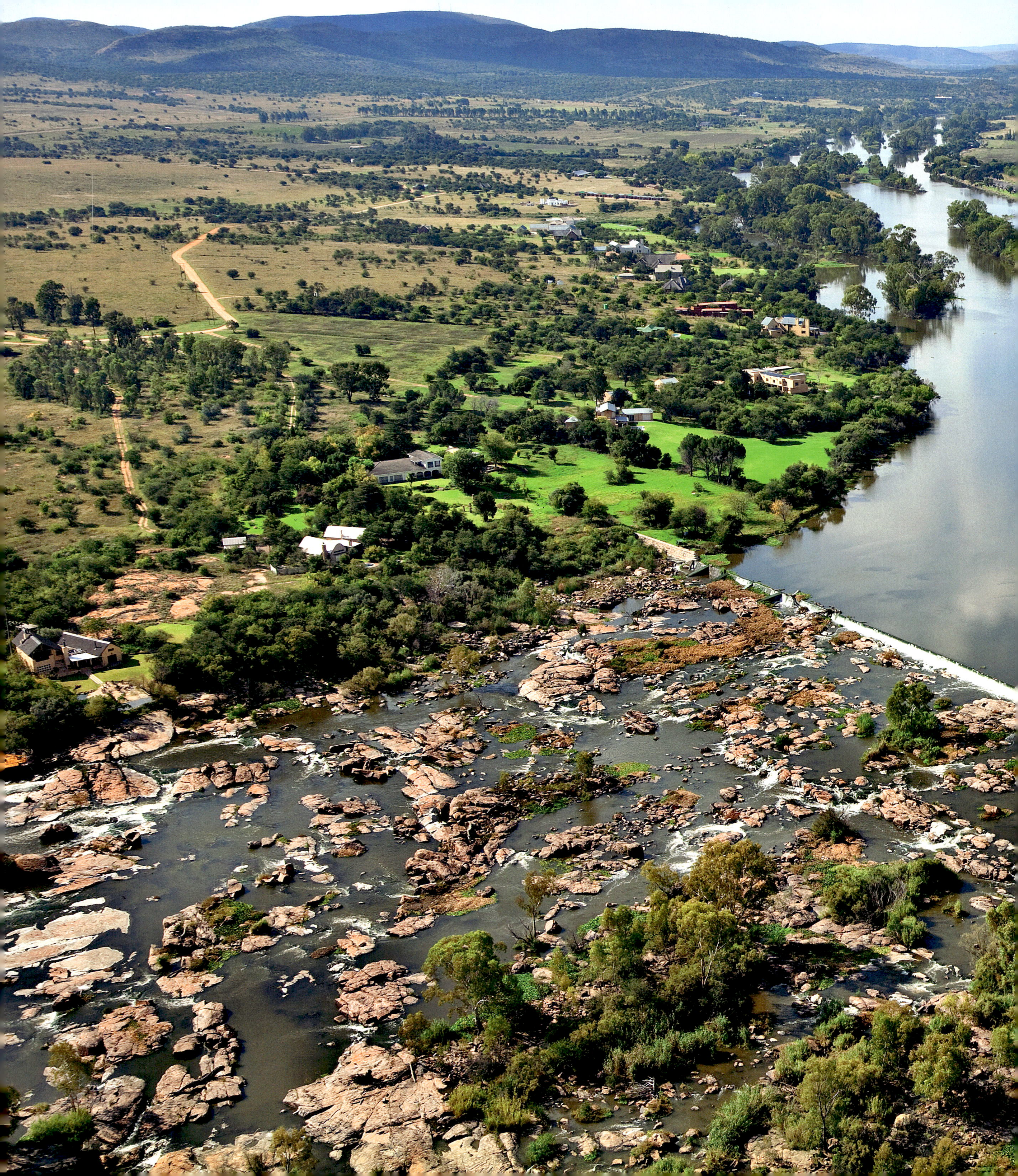

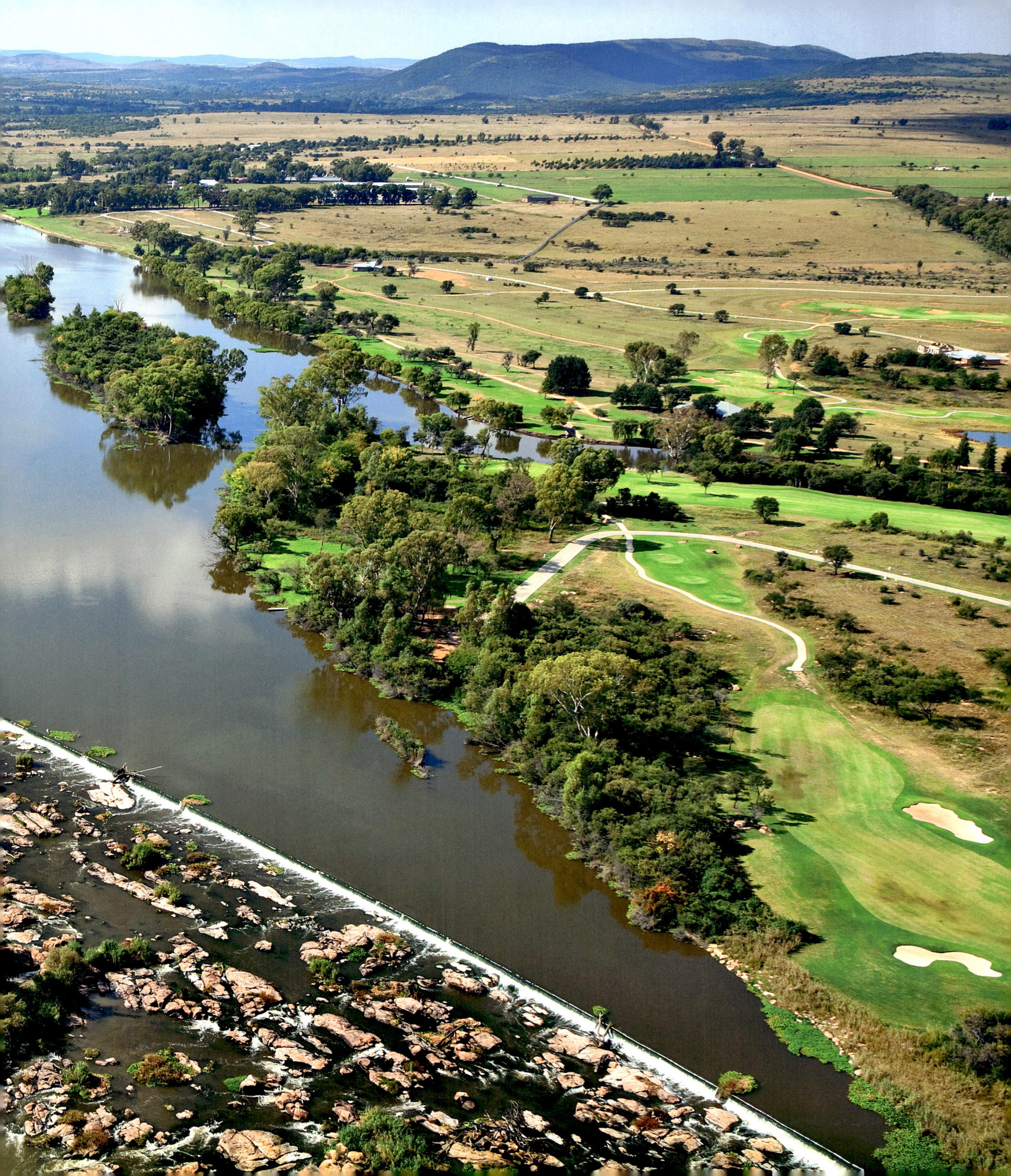

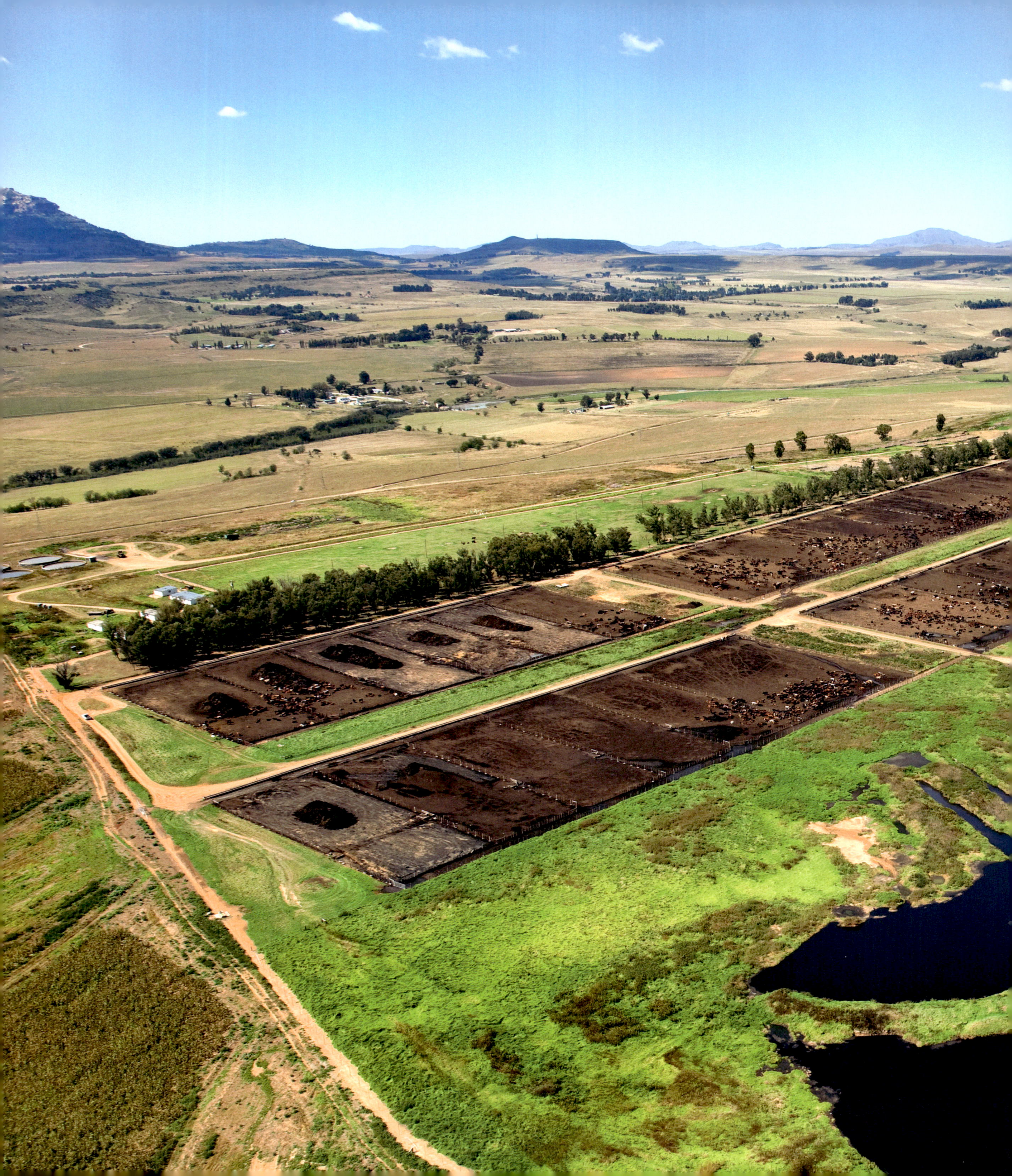

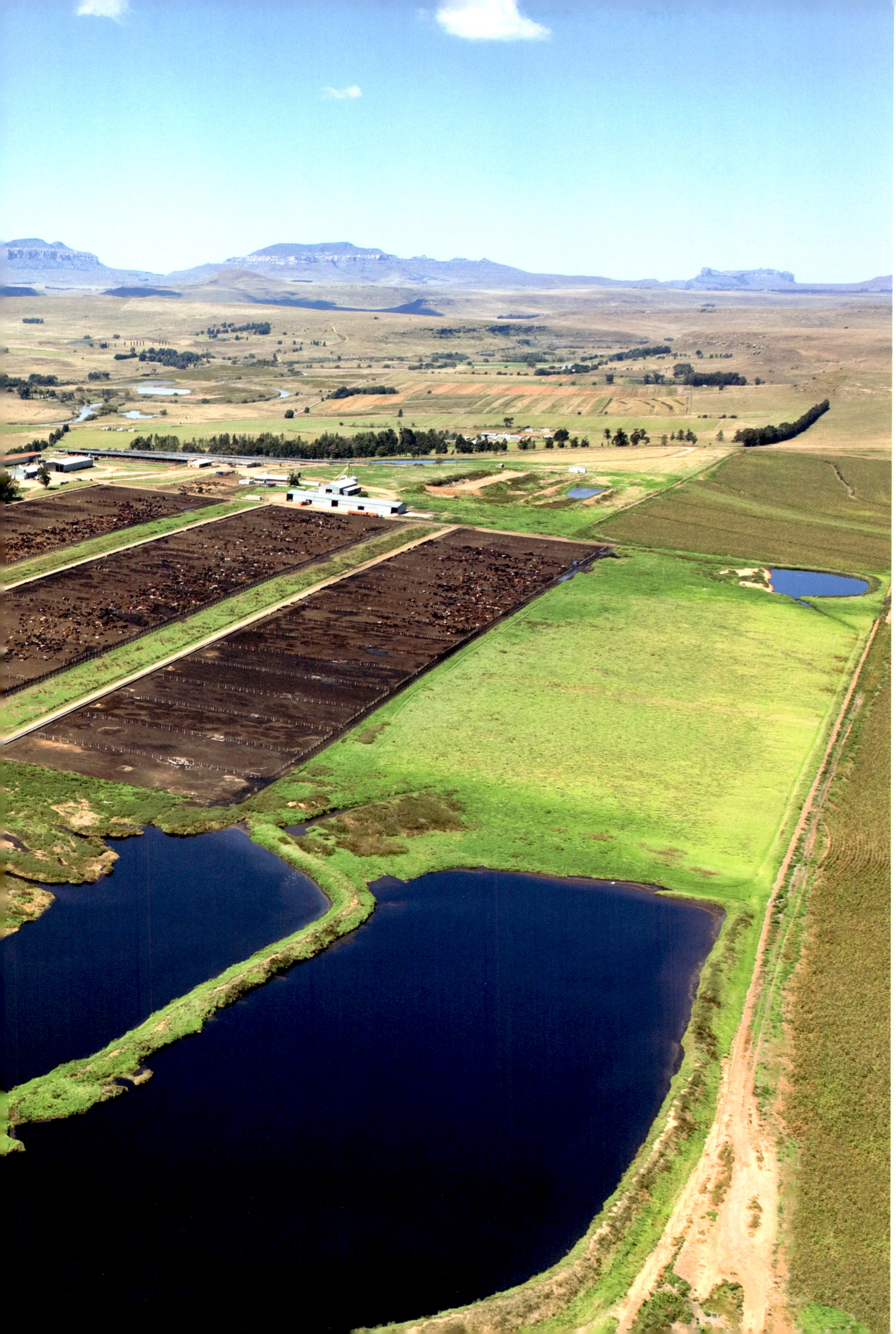

←← Vaal River, Parys
← Cattle ranch, Harrismith

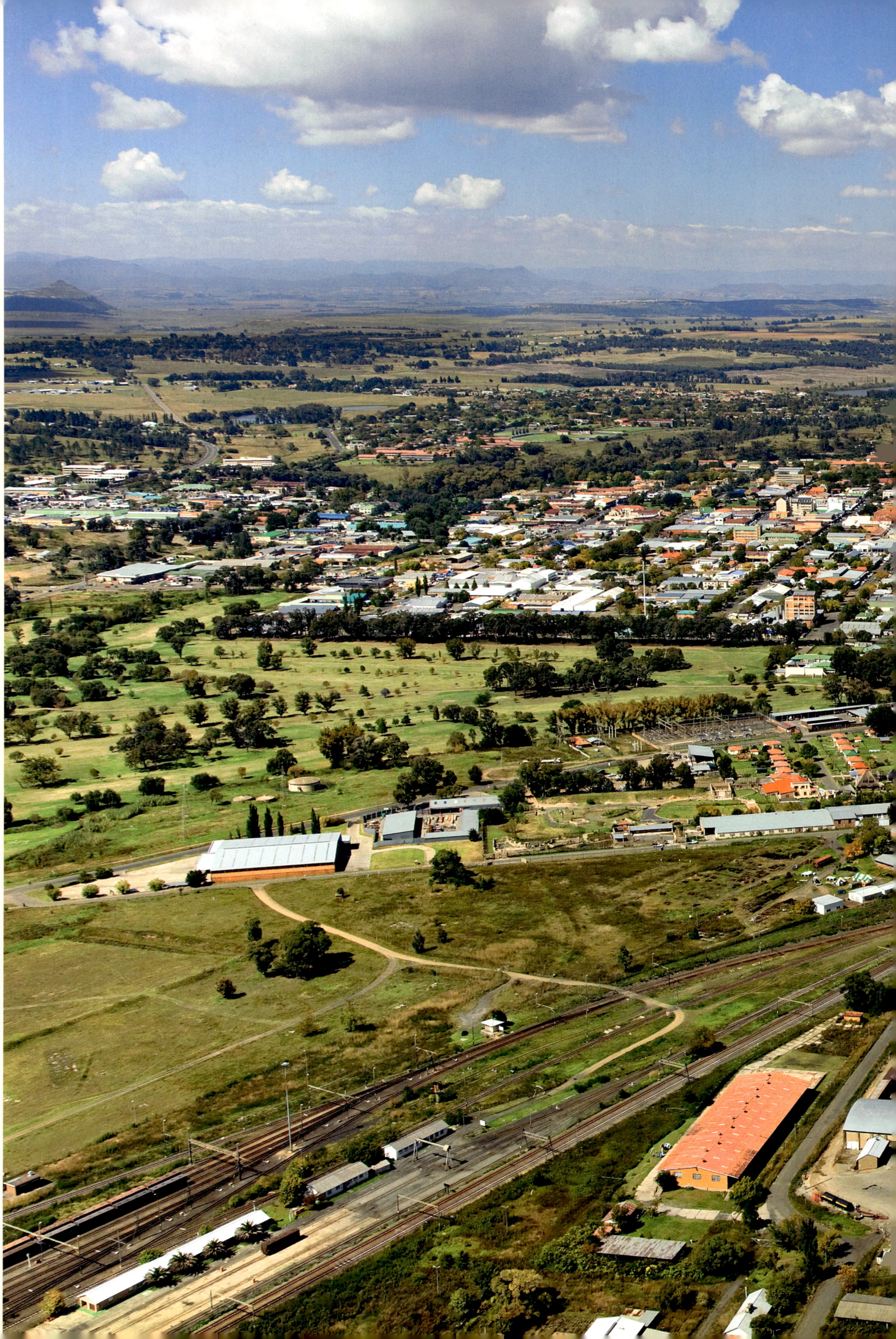

→ Bethlehem

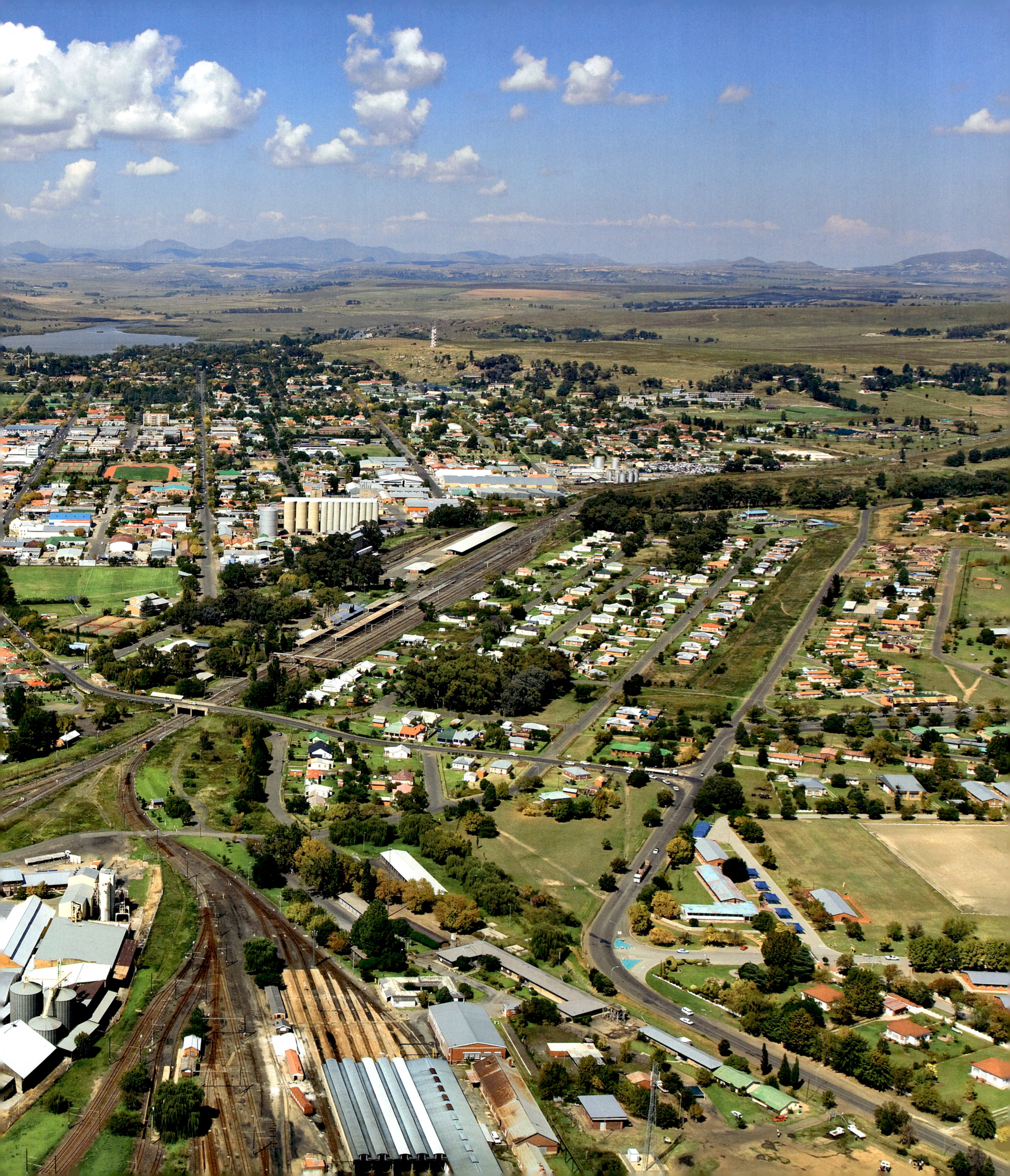

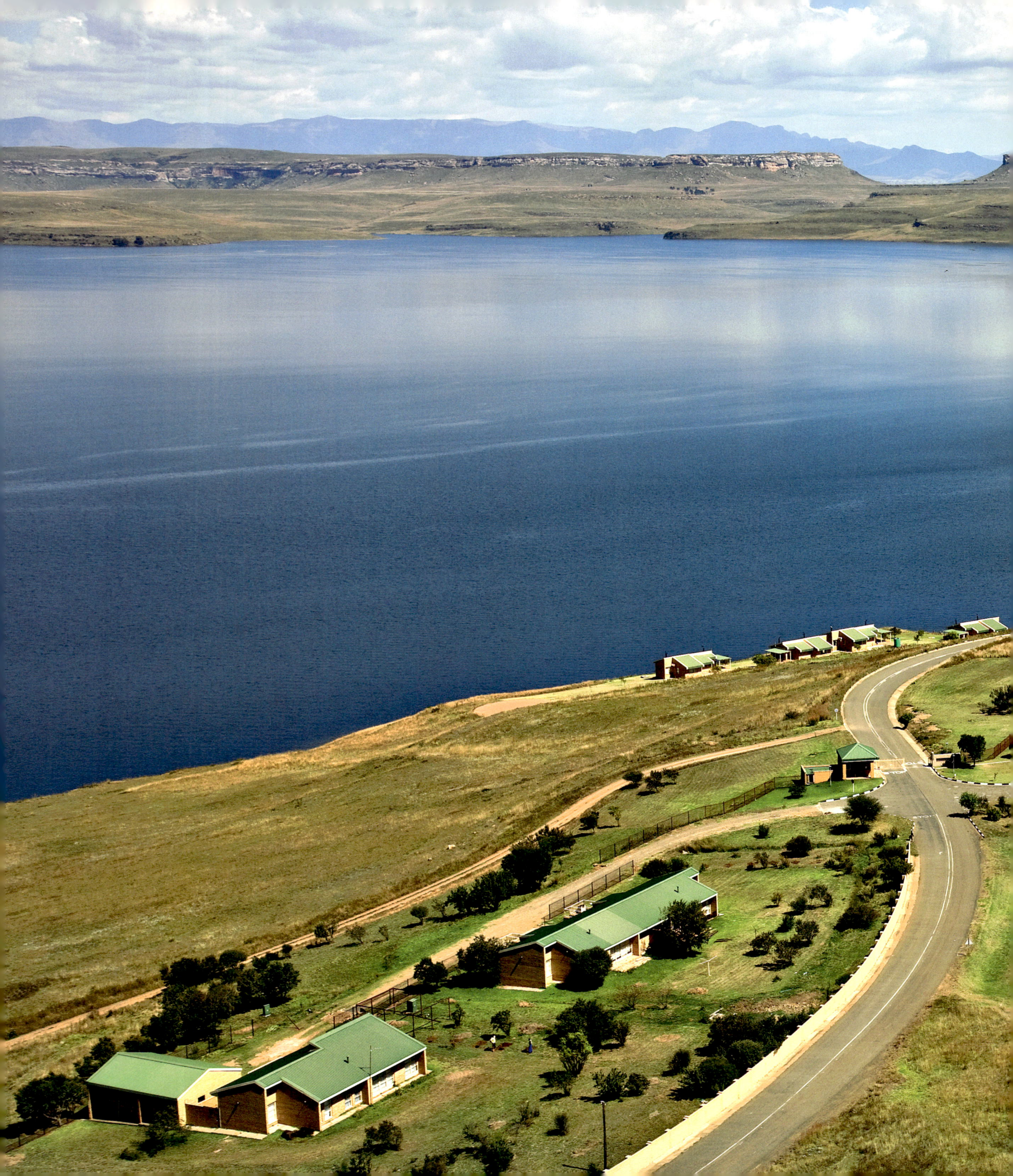

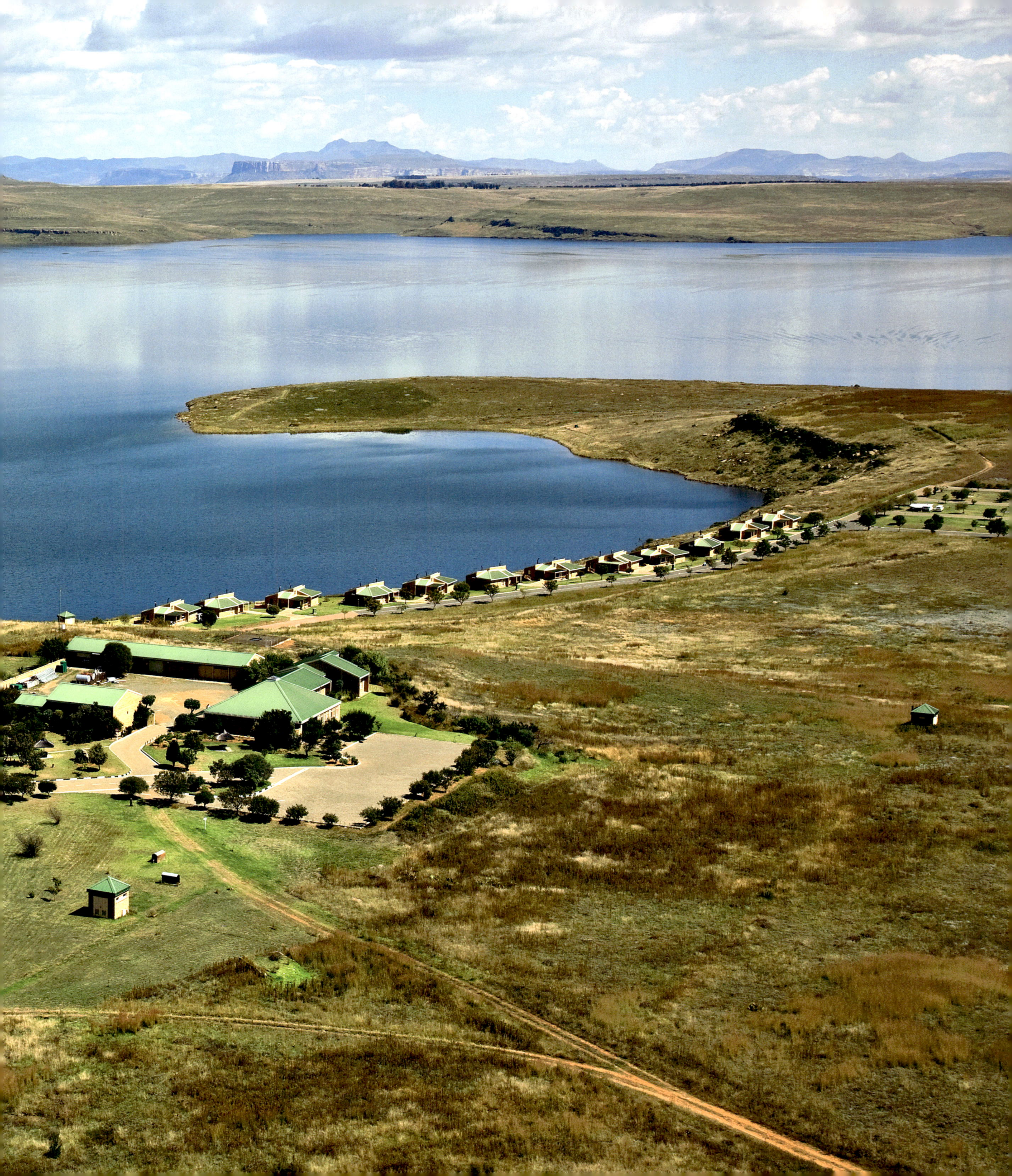

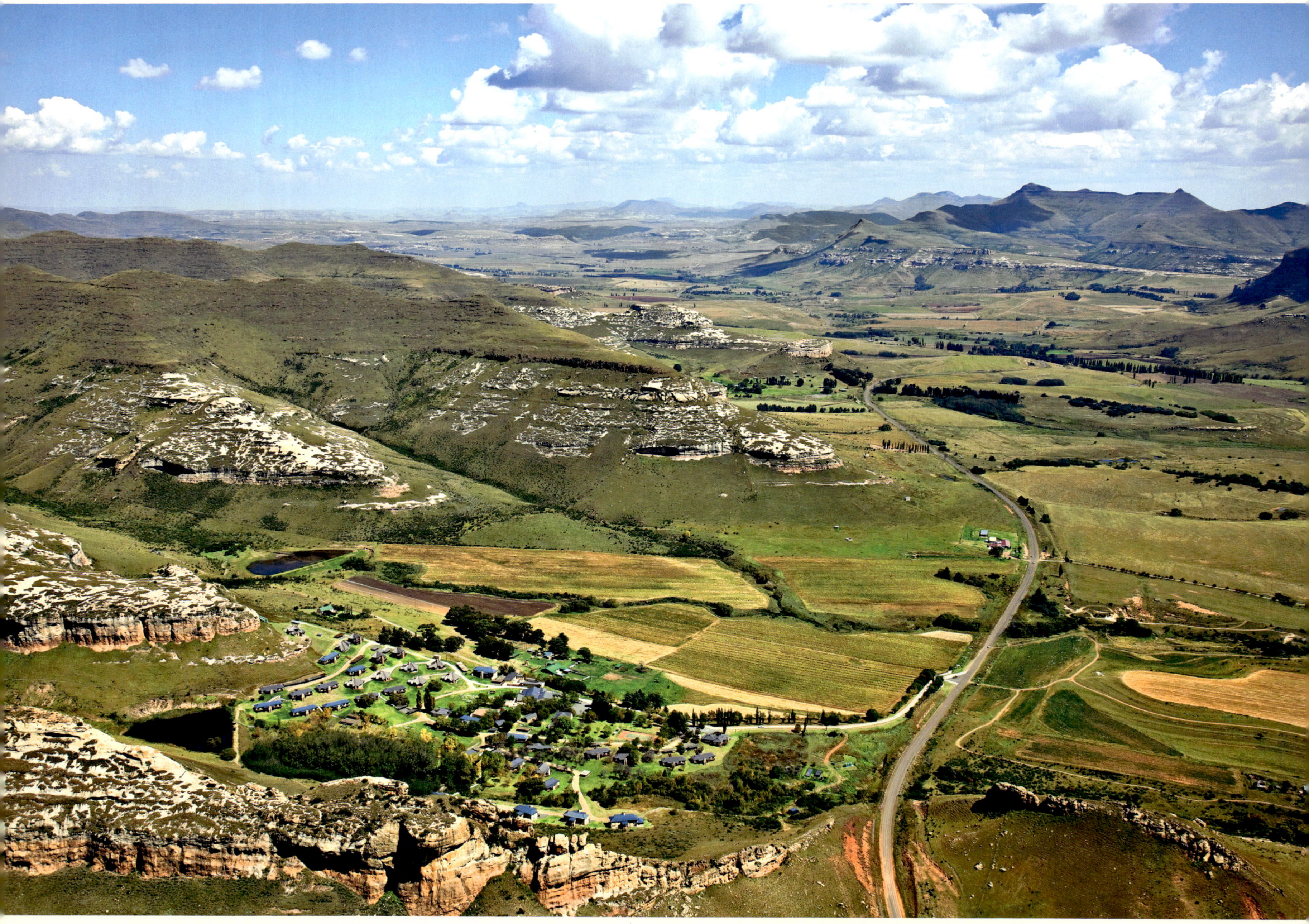

←← Sterkfontein Dam

←↓→ Golden Gate Highlands National Park

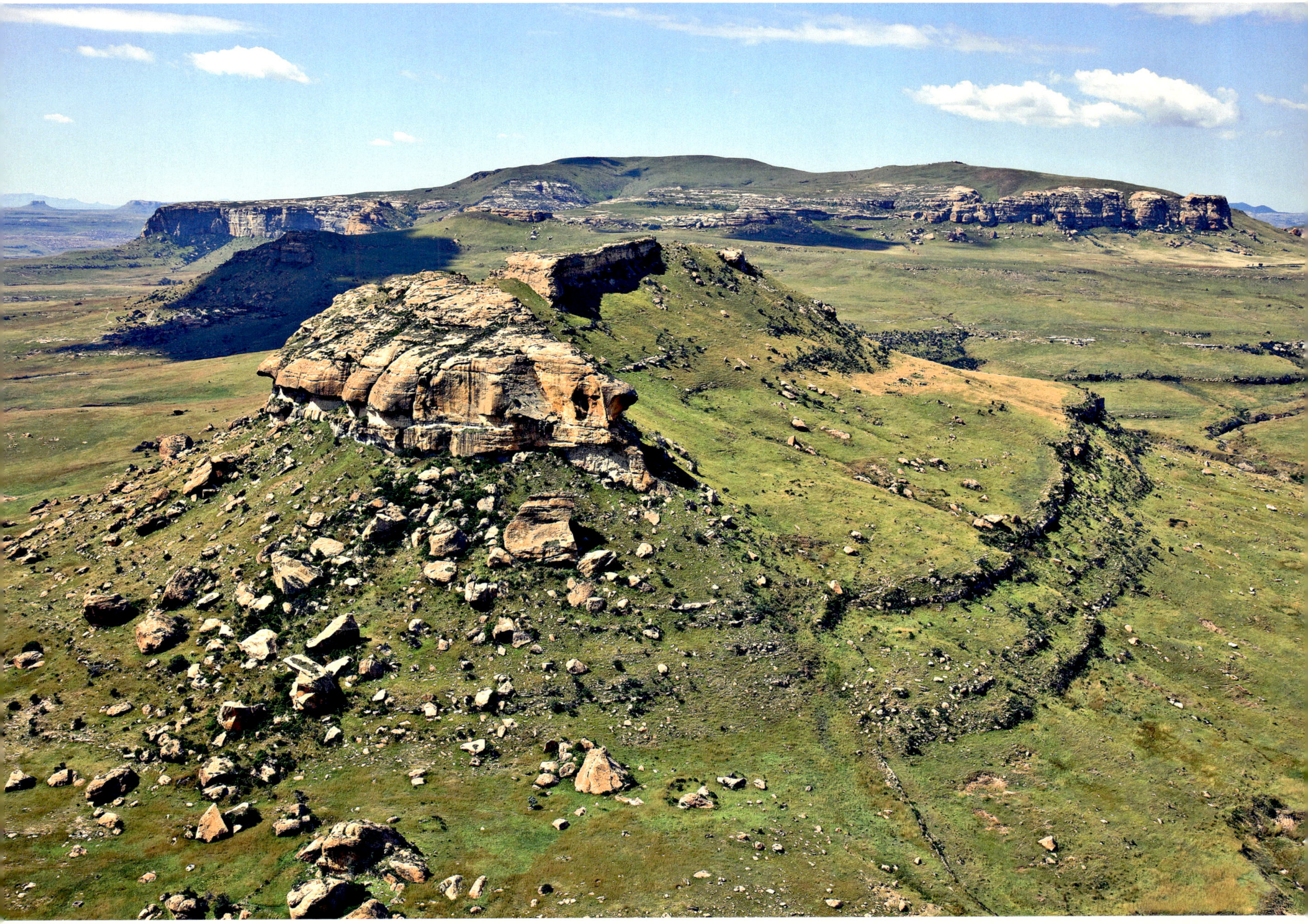

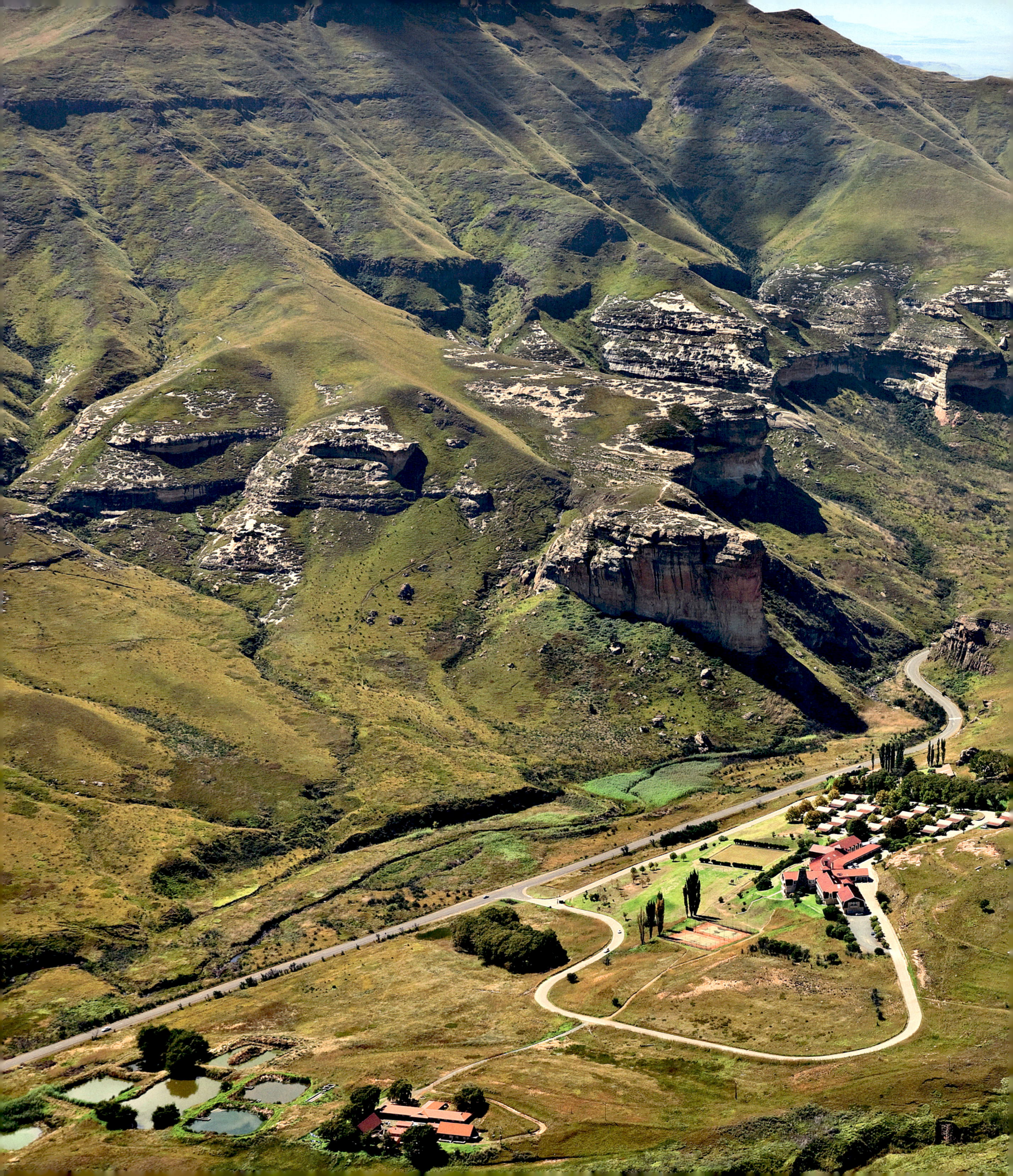

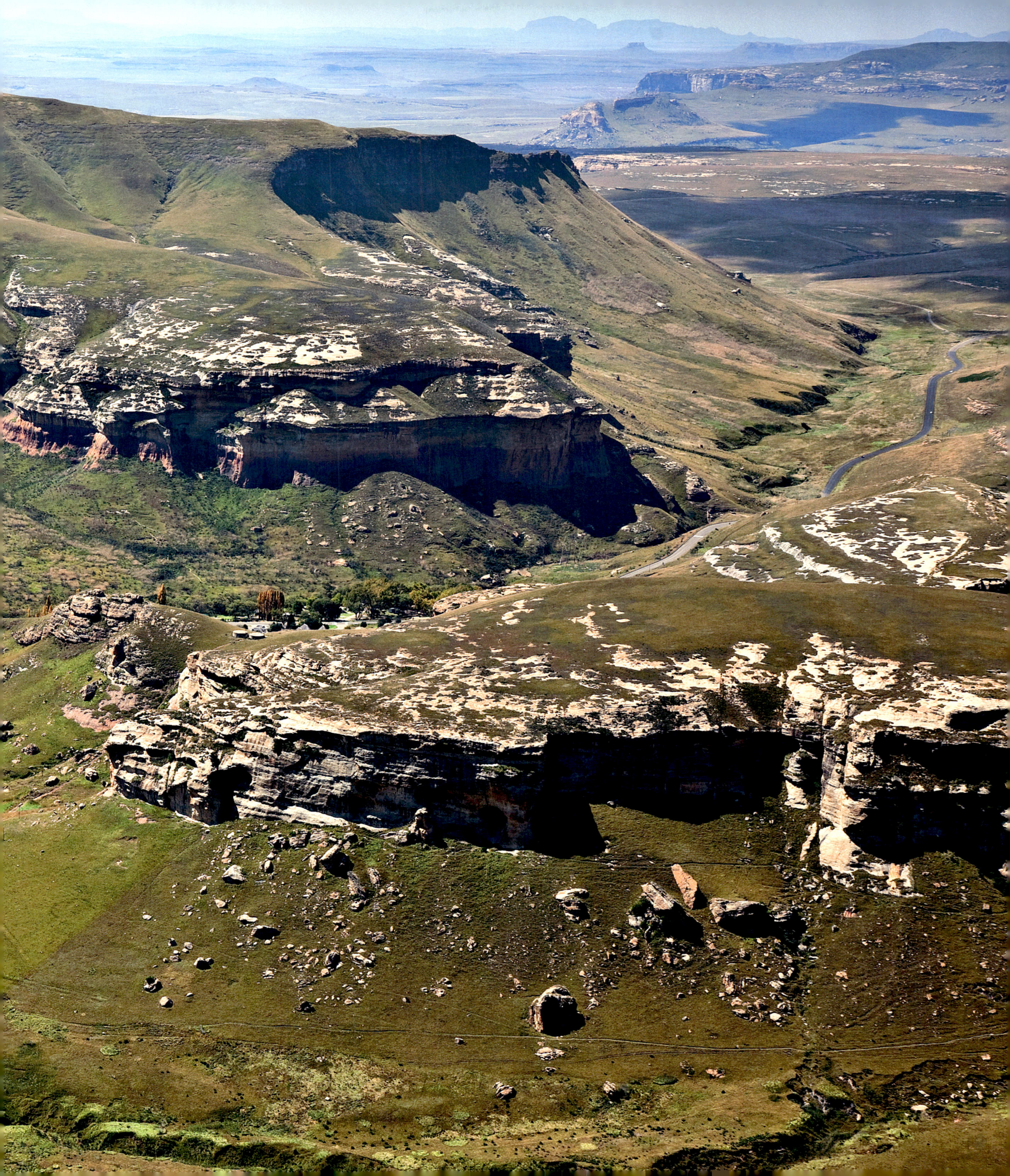

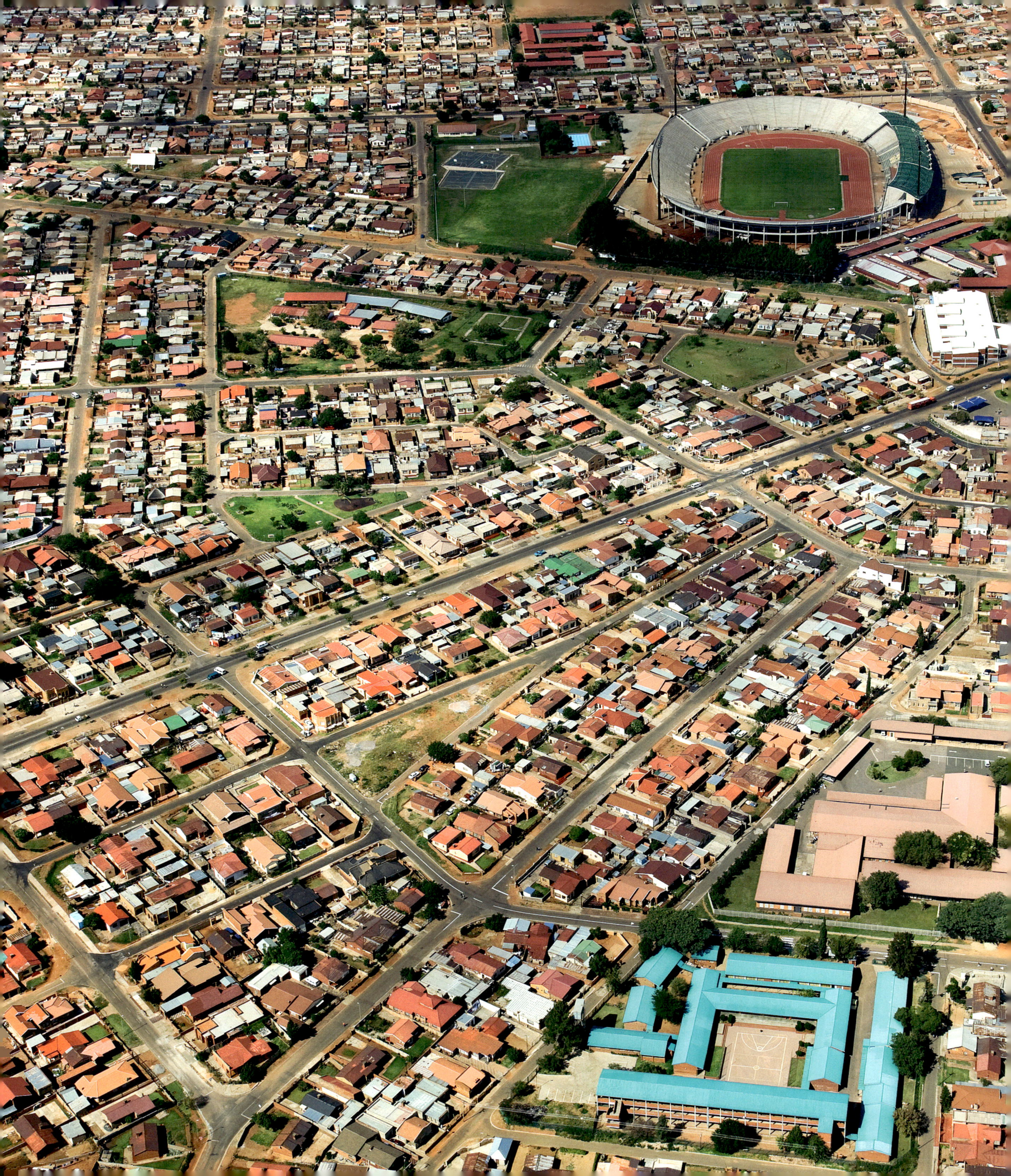

GAUTENG

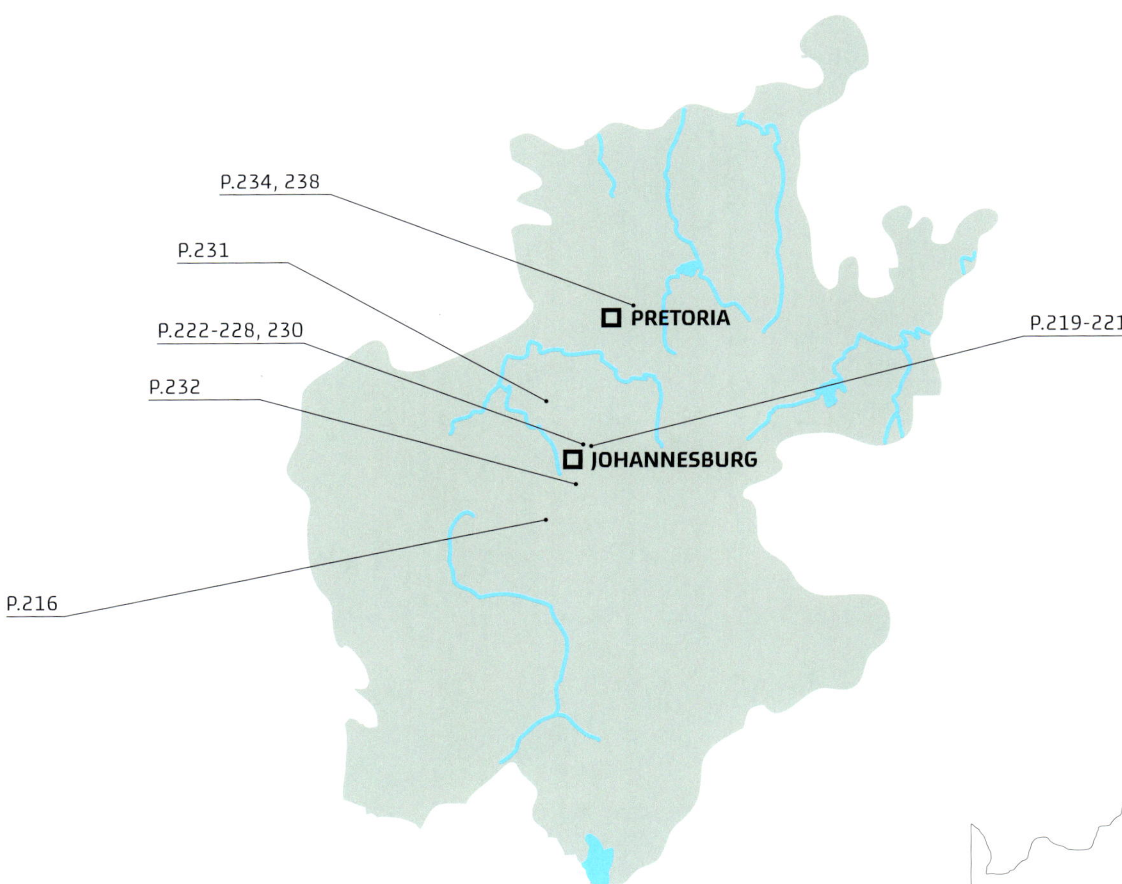
P.234, 238
P.231
P.222-228, 230
P.232
P.216
PRETORIA
P.219-221
JOHANNESBURG

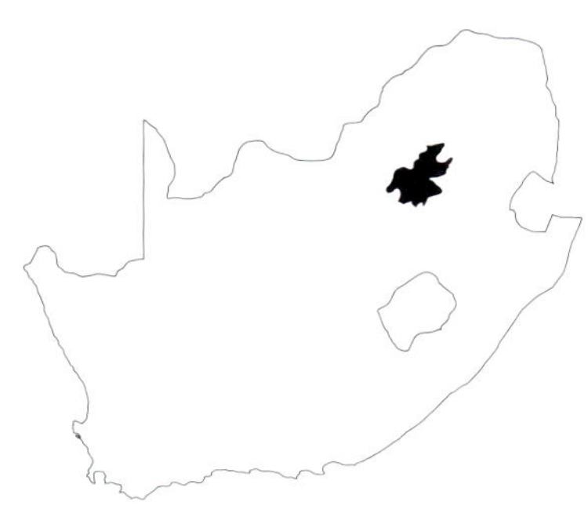

O.R. Tambo International Airport, Johannesburg. The steel blue skies promise a clear day. Many foreign visitors are picked up by hotel buses, mini buses and coaches. Others rent a car and immediately set off on their trip through South Africa. Most leave Gauteng, the smallest and most prosperous province in the country, as quickly as possible. And that is a pity. Because the 'place of gold' is much more than an arrival and departure point.

The place of gold

Anybody who thinks of the province as South Africa's economic powerhouse is correct. But not entirely. For Gauteng is not just gold country. It is also an old country. Three million years ago, it was the cradle of humanity. To the north west of Johannesburg lies the Cradle of Humankind, a gigantic open-air museum, where visitors can learn about three million years of history. It boasts one of the oldest human skulls ever found: that of an Australopithecus africanus. The skull is called 'Mrs. Ples', because the discoverer initially thought it belonged to an unknown human sub-group (Plesianthropus transvaalensis).

From prehistoric times until late in the 19th century, the area that is now Gauteng was a region where livestock farmers tended their herds. That changed abruptly in 1886, when a certain George Harrison, who worked as a carpenter on the Langlaagte farm, accidentally stumbled across a gold-bearing rock formation during a Sunday stroll. That was the start of a gold rush that, within a year, resulted in the foundation of a flourishing mining city that was dubbed Johannesburg – after the surveyors Johannes Rissik and Johannes Meyer.

Today, Johannesburg is not only the financial heart of South Africa, it is also a city where the memories of a tumultuous past are kept alive by the impressive apartheid museum. In addition, it is a cultural hotspot: the city of jazz legends Miriam Makeba and Hugh Masekela; the birth place of the typically South African kwaito music and the home-base of internationally renowned graffiti artists like Breeze, Hac 1 and Rasty.

Although it is only an hour's drive from Johannesburg to Pretoria – which is now part of the municipality of Tshwane – the two cities feel much farther apart. With its purple blossoming jacaranda trees and stately, late Victorian buildings, Pretoria exudes a quieter, more restrained atmosphere. Pretoria, the administrative capital of the rainbow nation, is a city of statues erected in memory of former government leaders like 'uncle' Paul Kruger and General Louis Botha. It is also home to the colossal Voortrekker Monument and countless other museums.

And what about the similarities between the two cities? Like the rest of Gauteng, they are cultural melting pots. The mining industry that turned the province into the turbocharger of the national economy has also ensured that virtually every group in the multiethnic South African population has encountered and worked with each other here. That can still be heard in fanagalo, the lingua franca spoken in the mines. And experienced in the many cultural villages where the traditional way of life of the Sotho, the Xhosa, the Zulus and the Venda is brought to life.

Gauteng offers three million years of history and more cultural diversity than any other South African province. The 'place of gold' deserves to be much more than just an arrival and departure point.

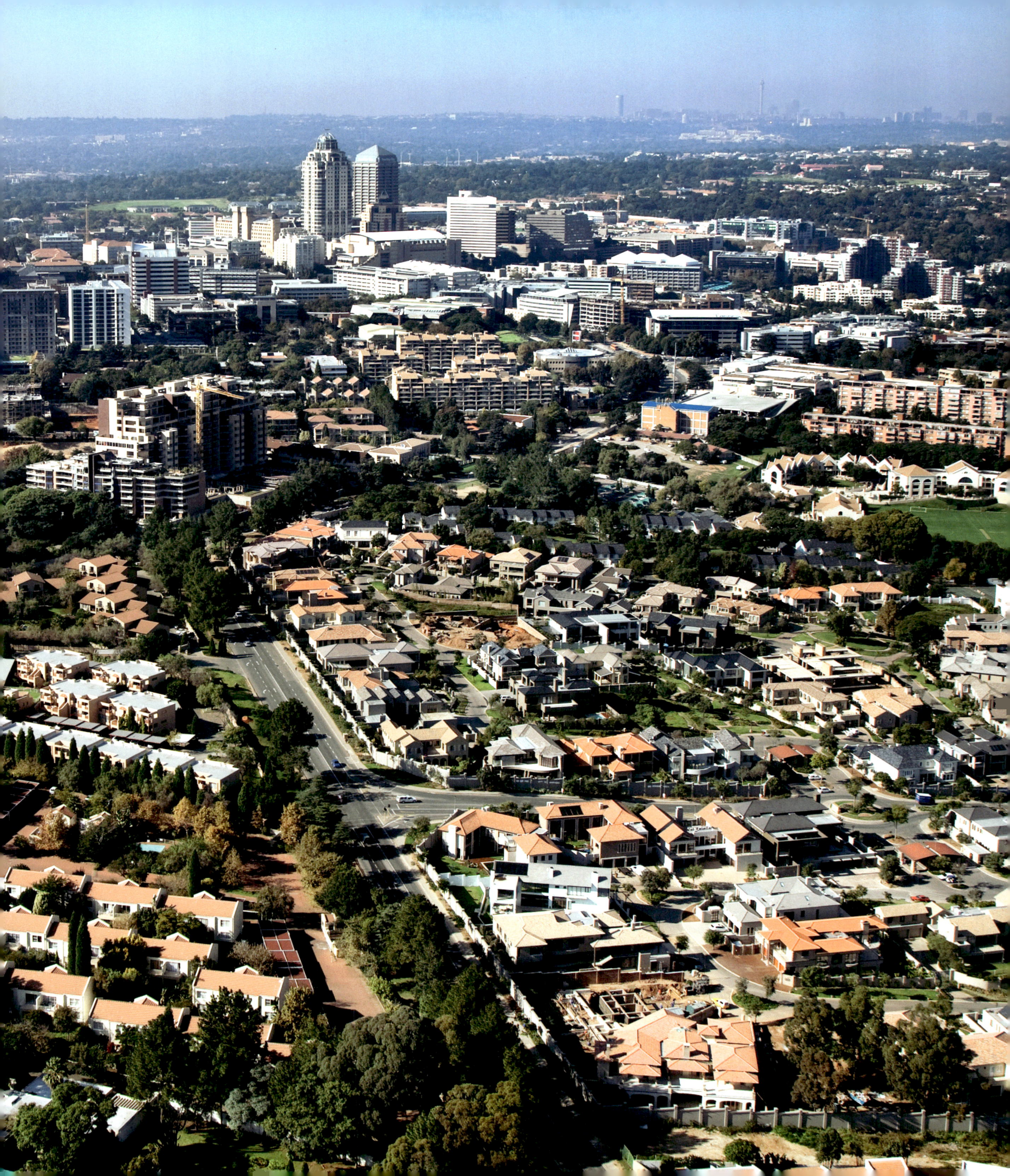

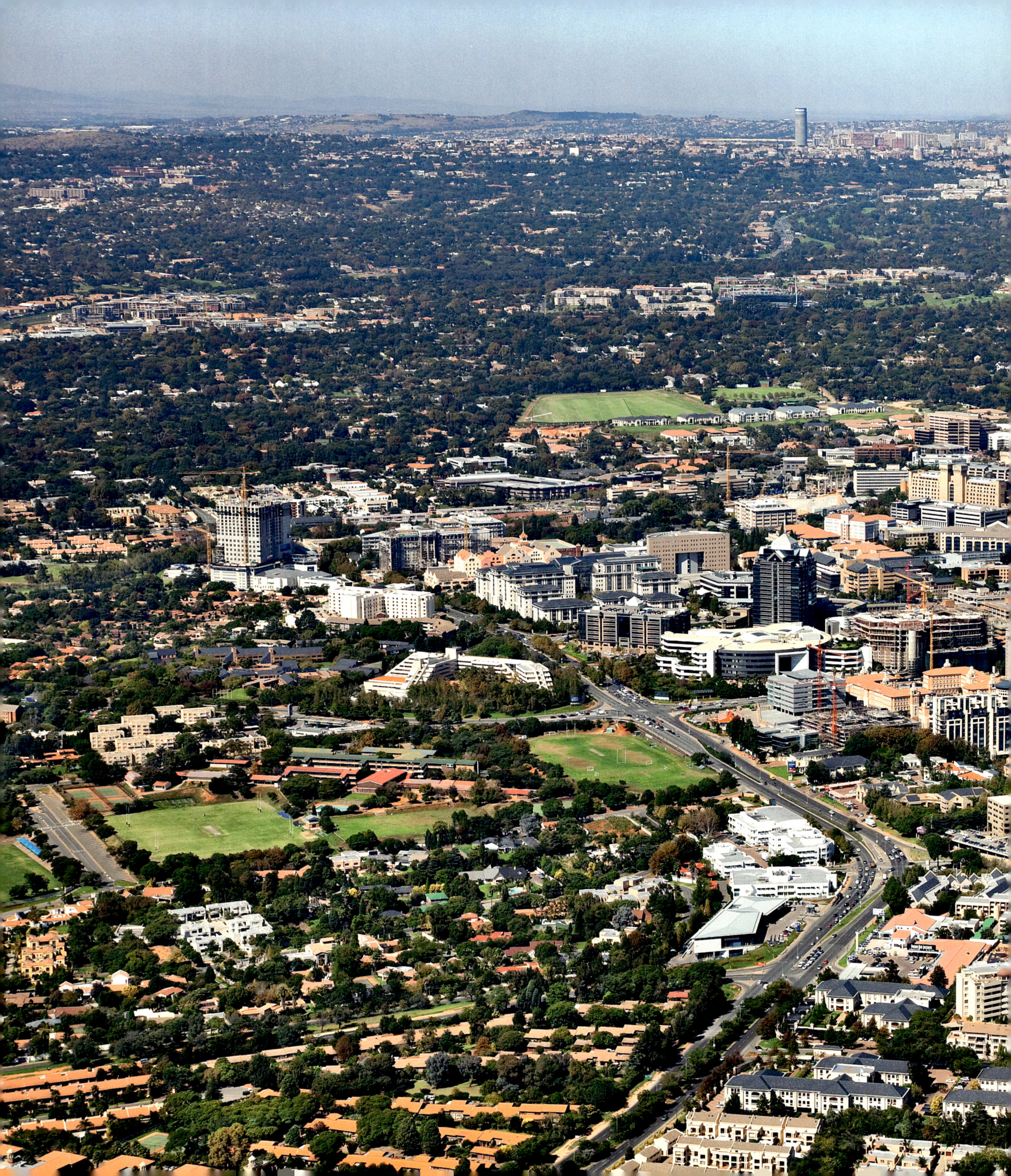

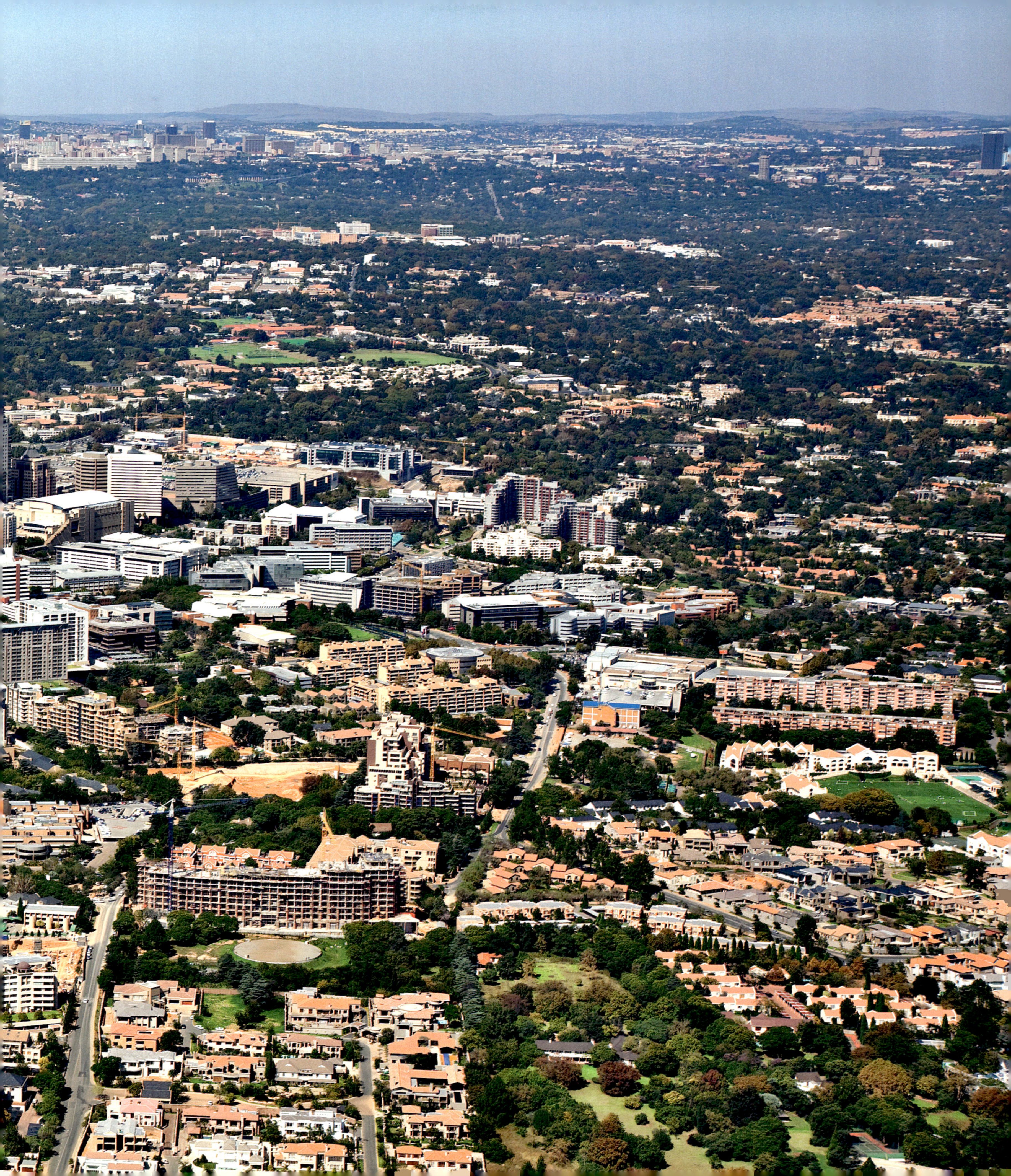

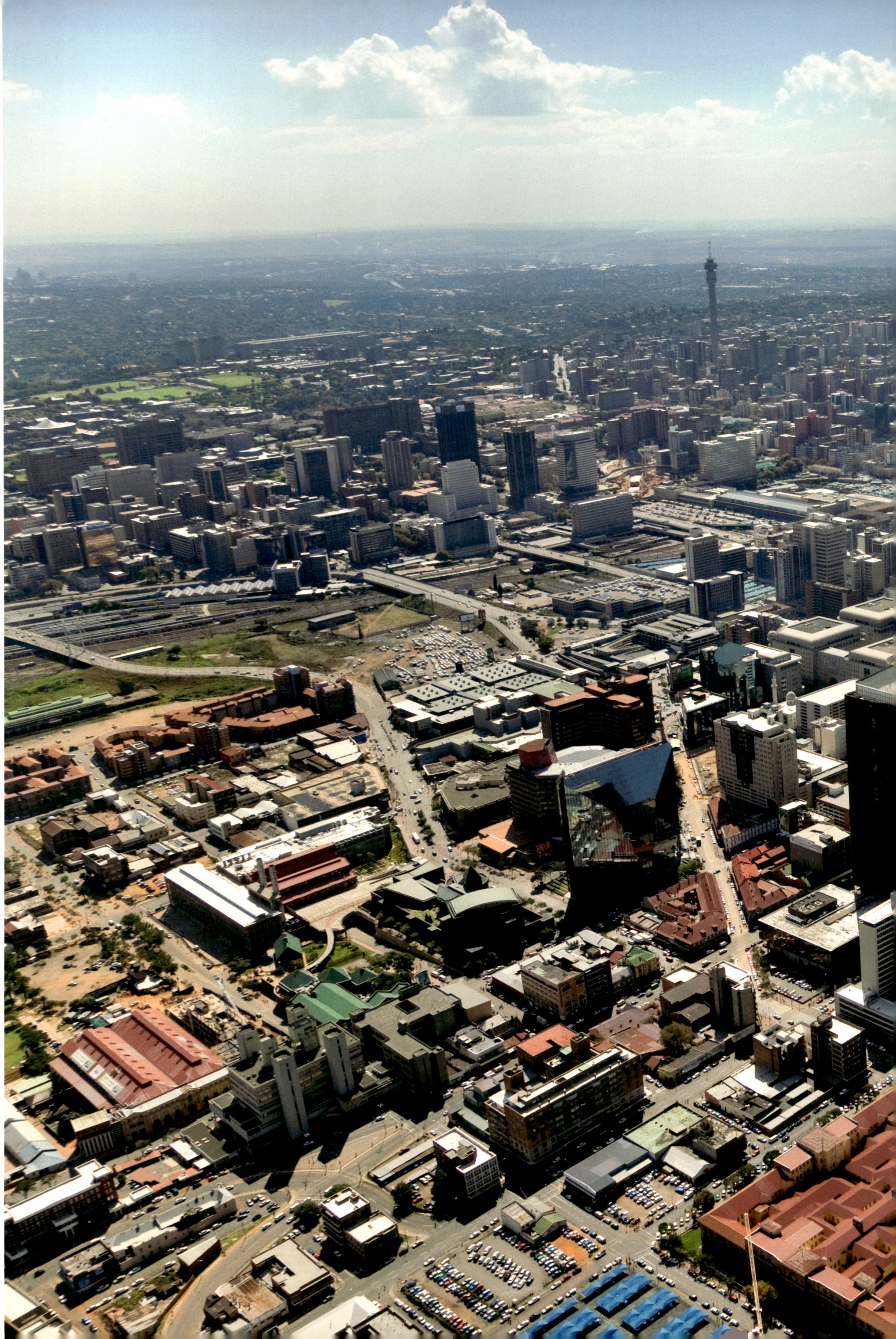

← Sandton
→ Johannesburg

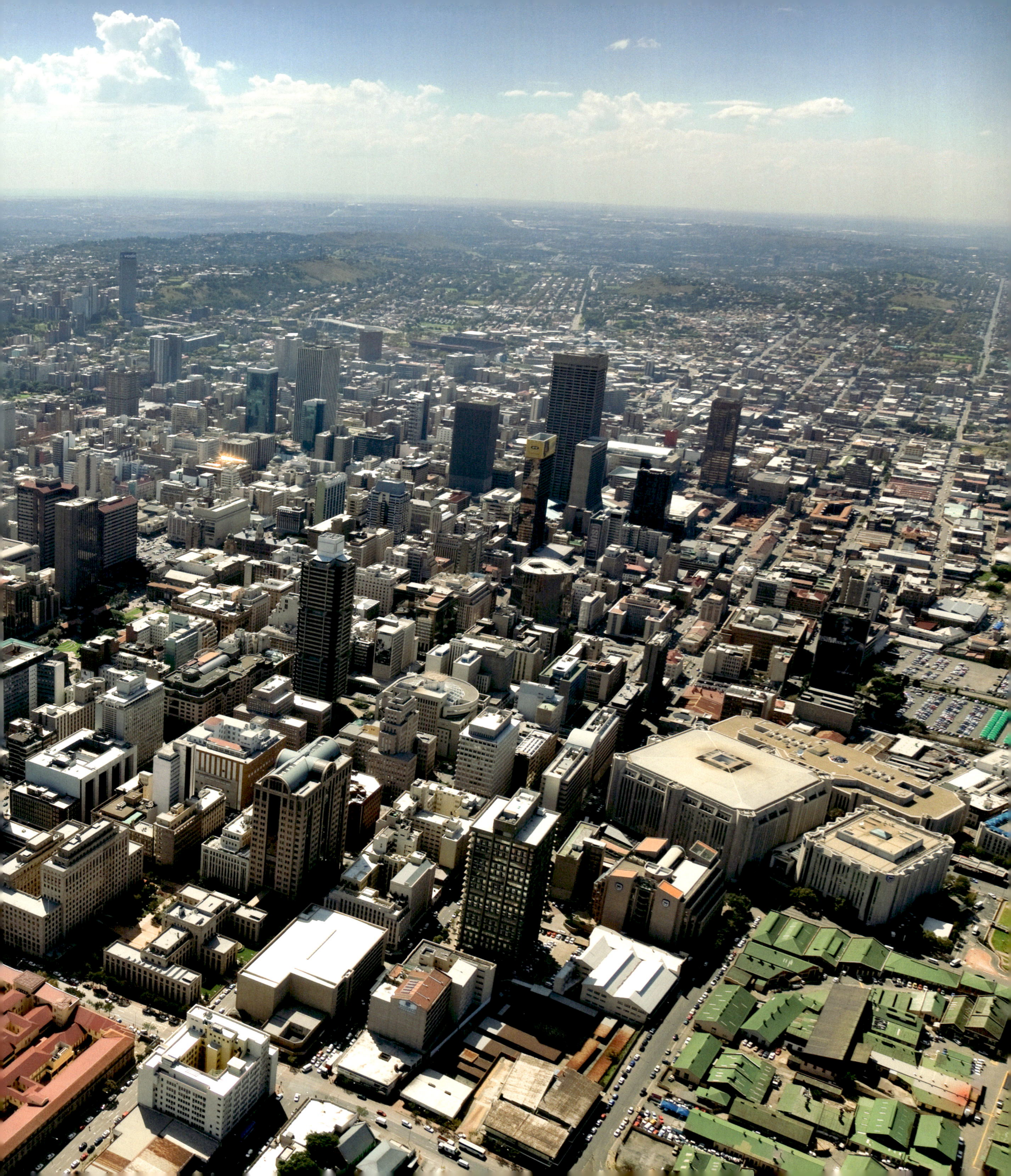

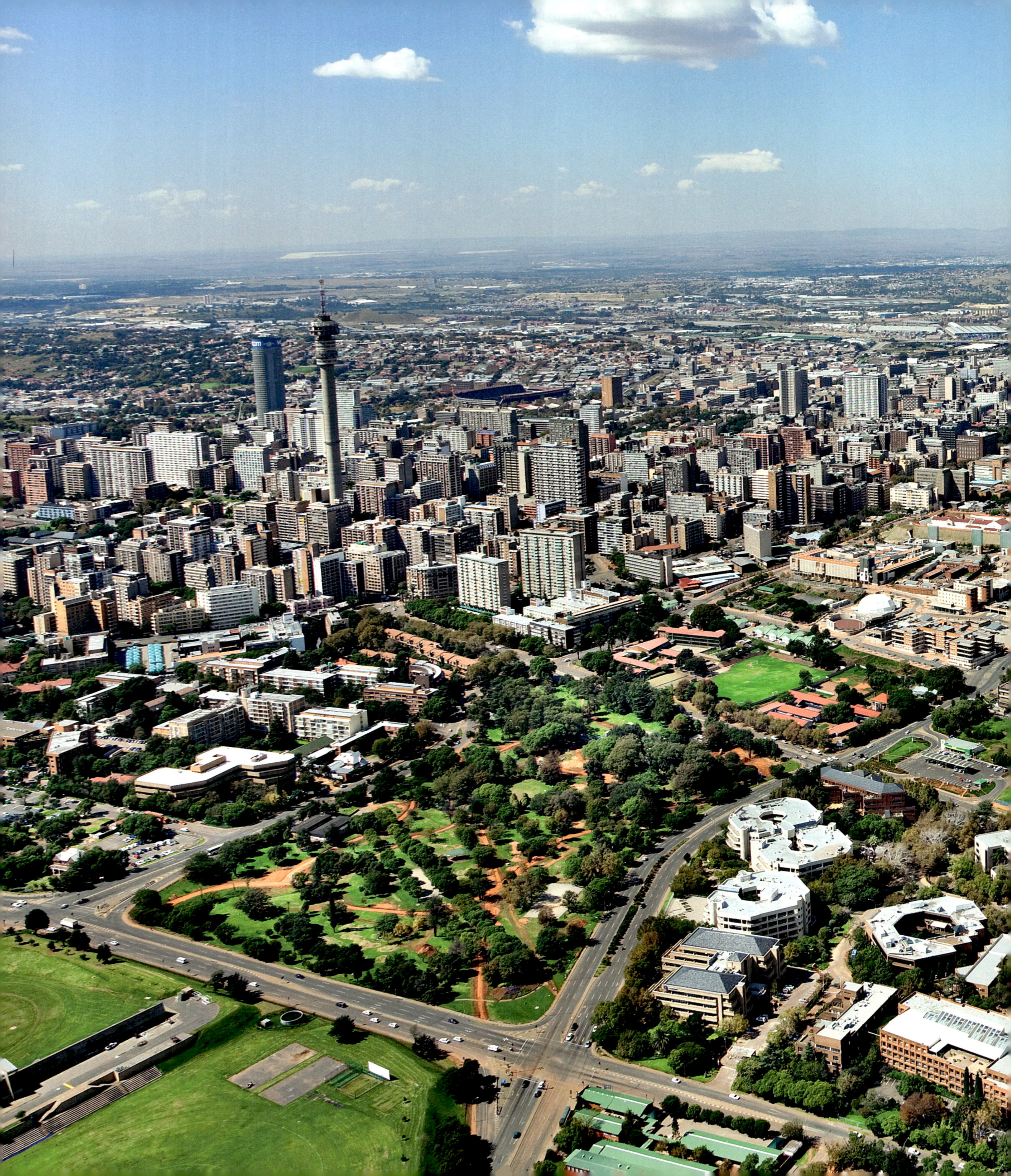

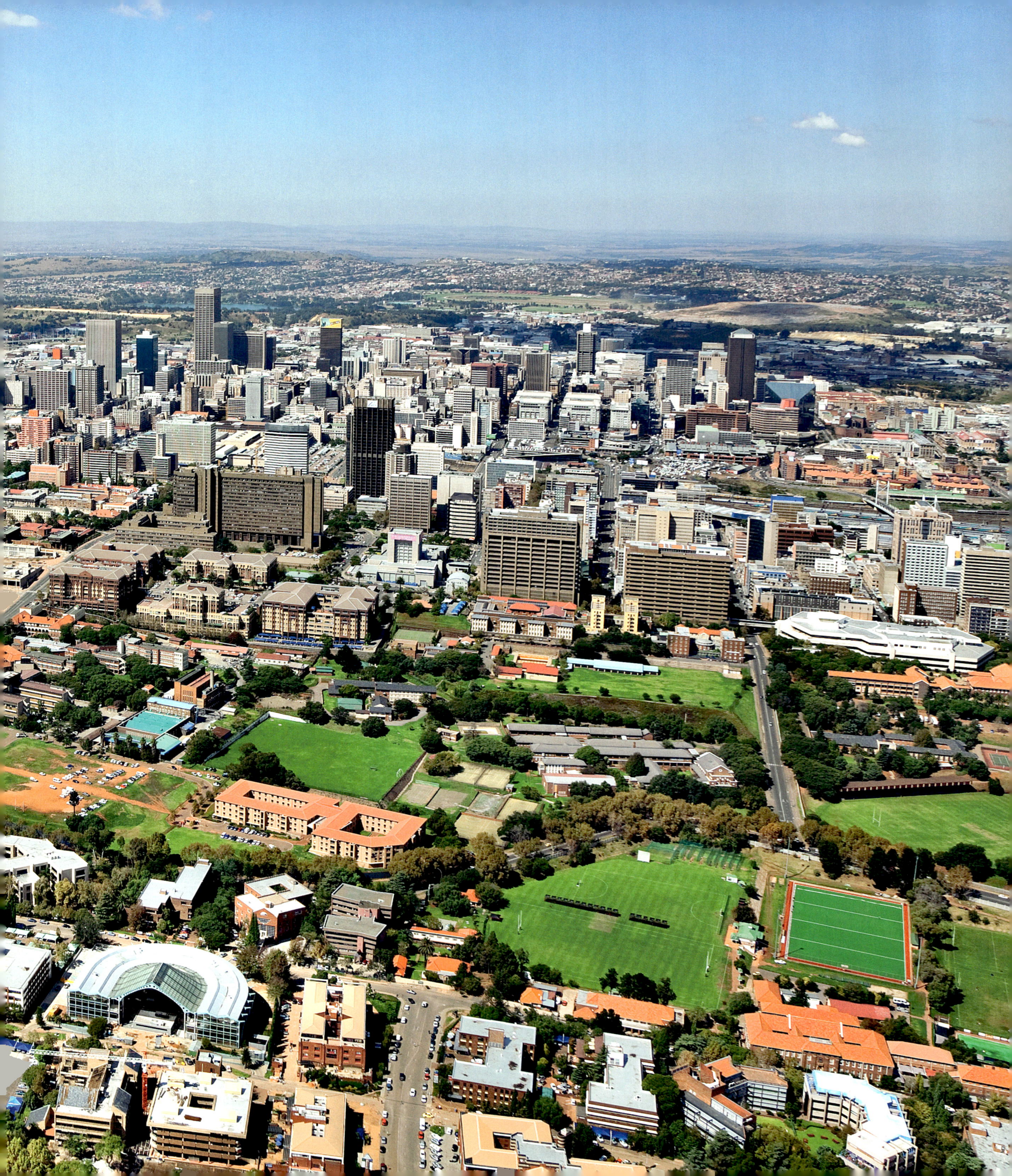

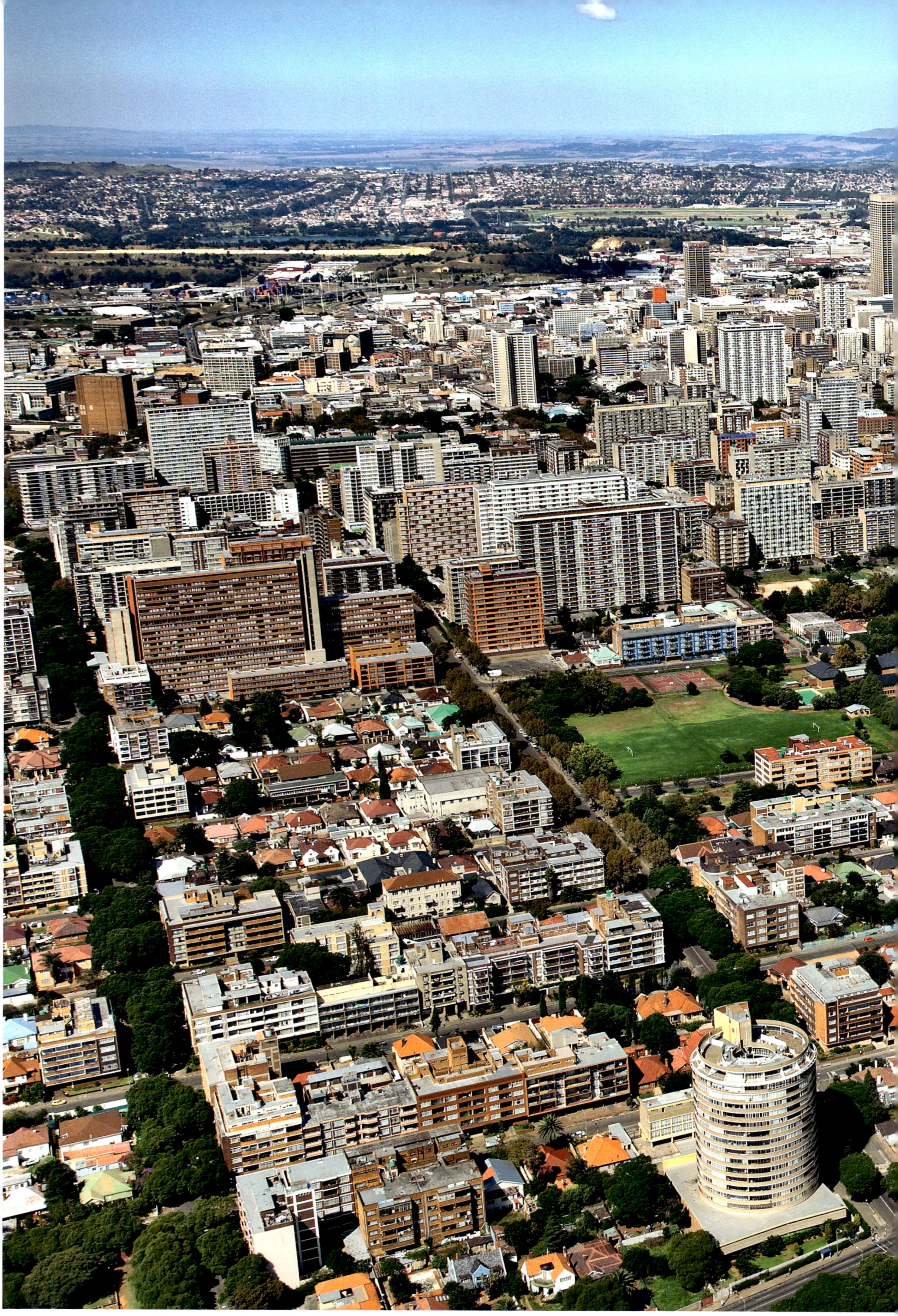

←→ Johannesburg

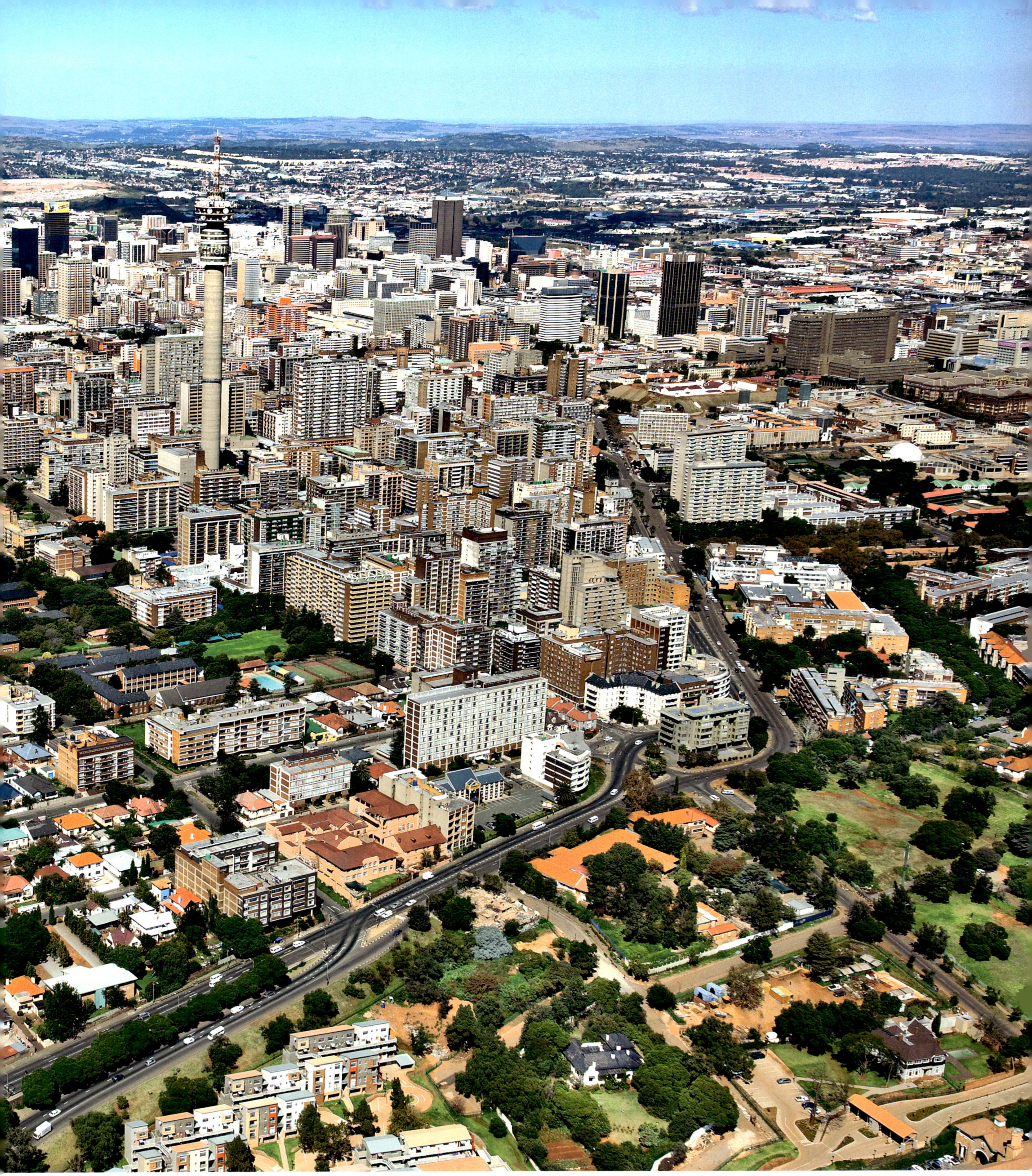

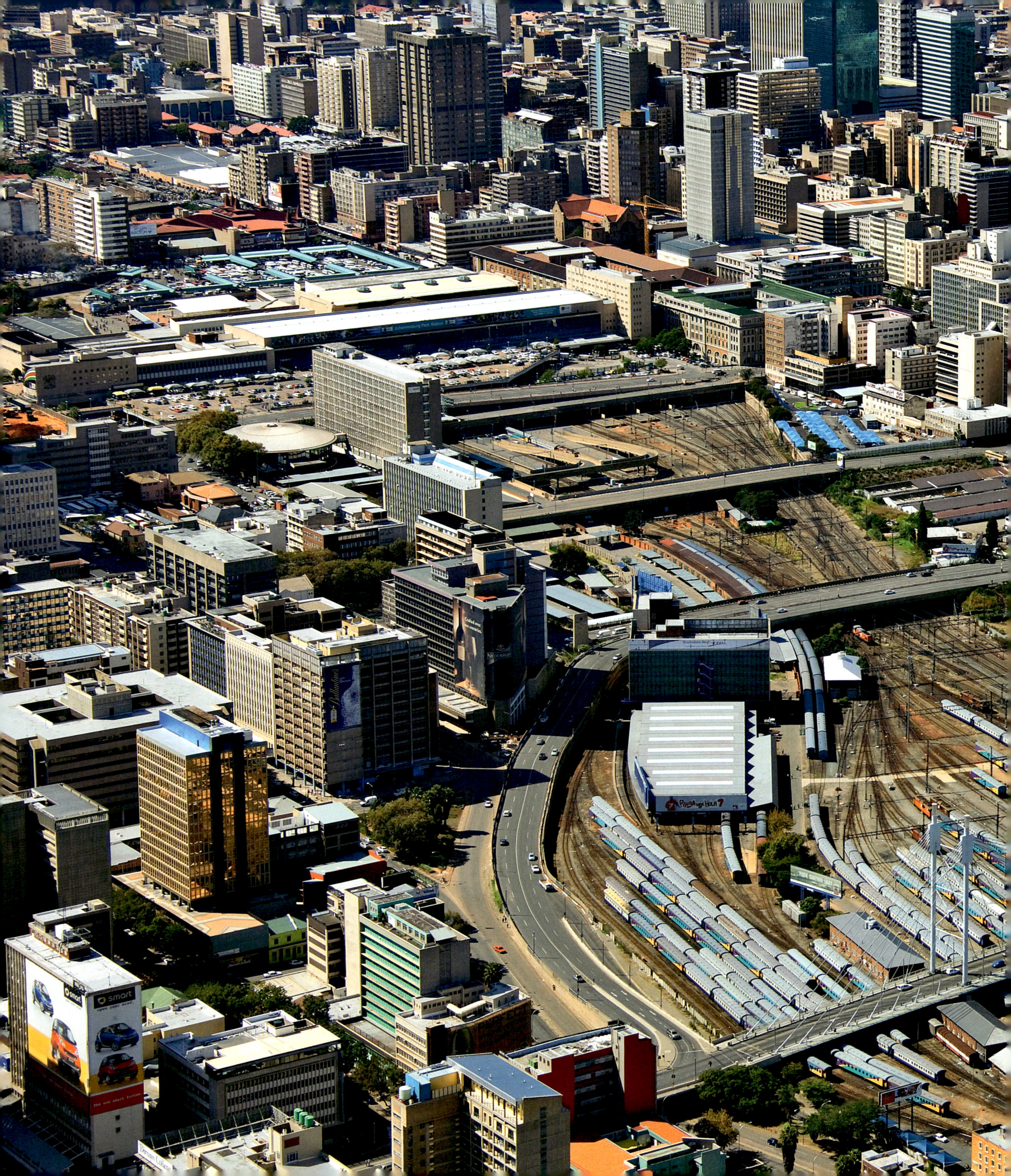
smart

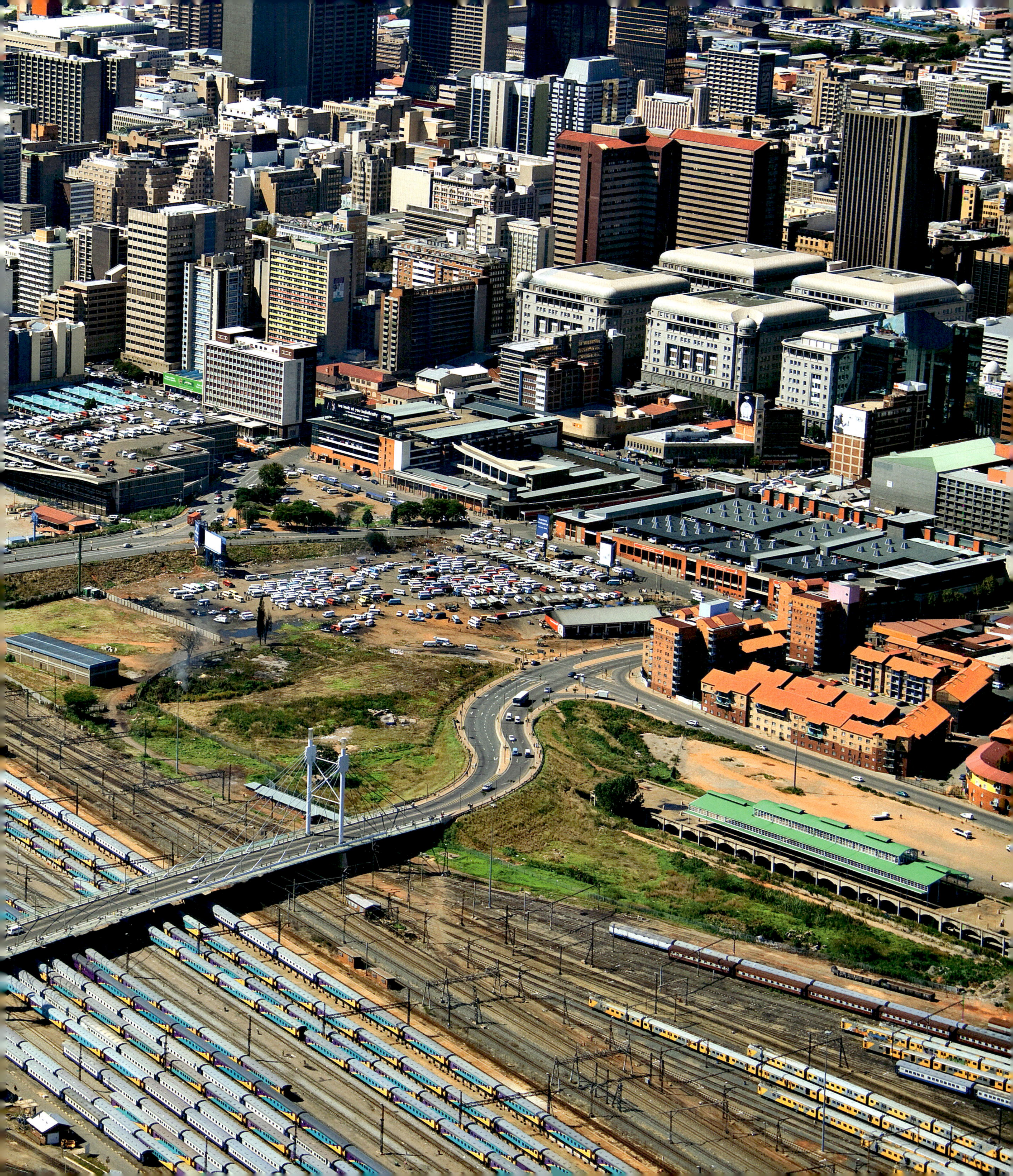

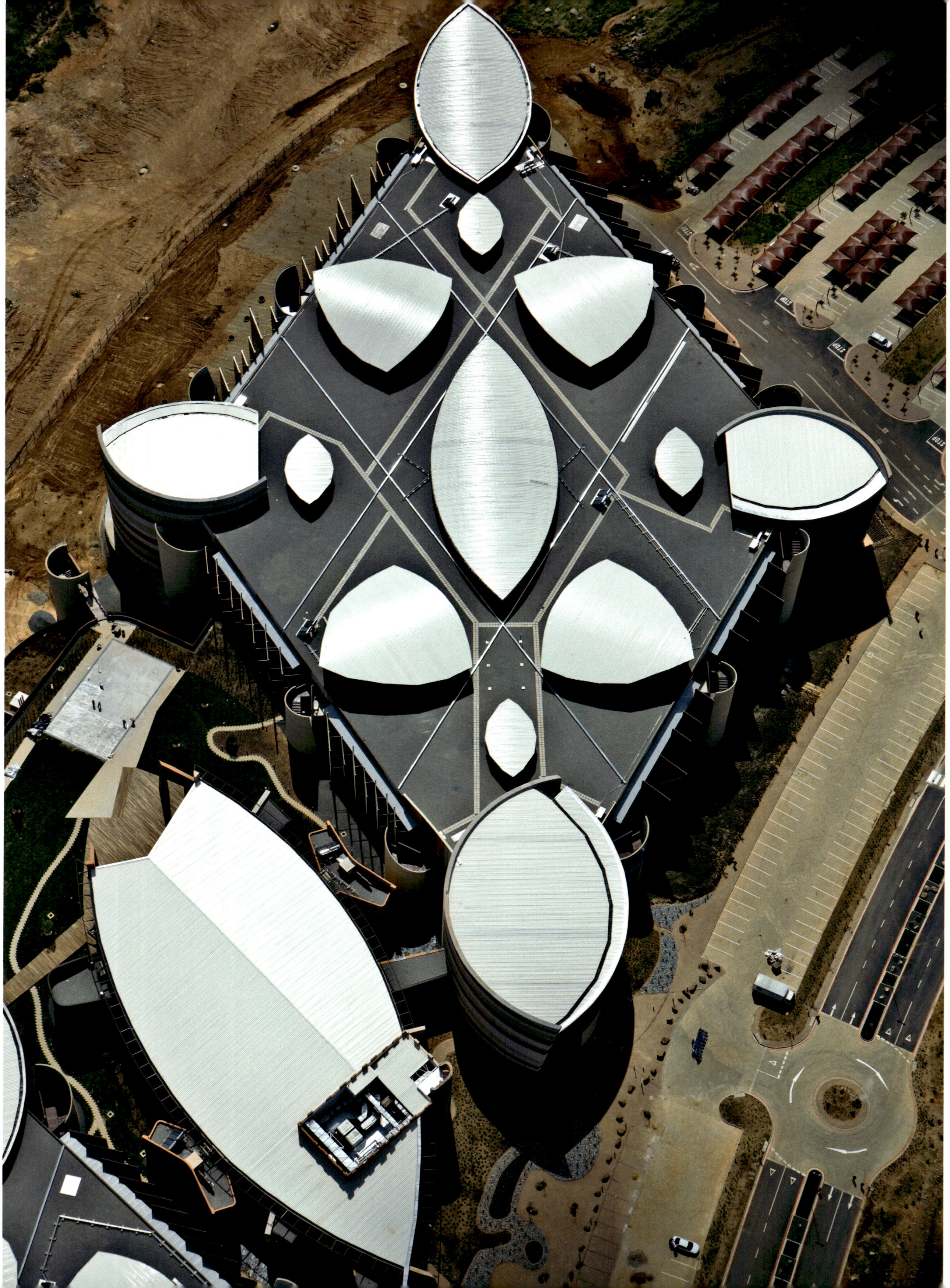

←← Johannesburg
← Roof of the Wesbank, Randburg, Johannesburg
↓ The Dome, between Lanseria and Randburg

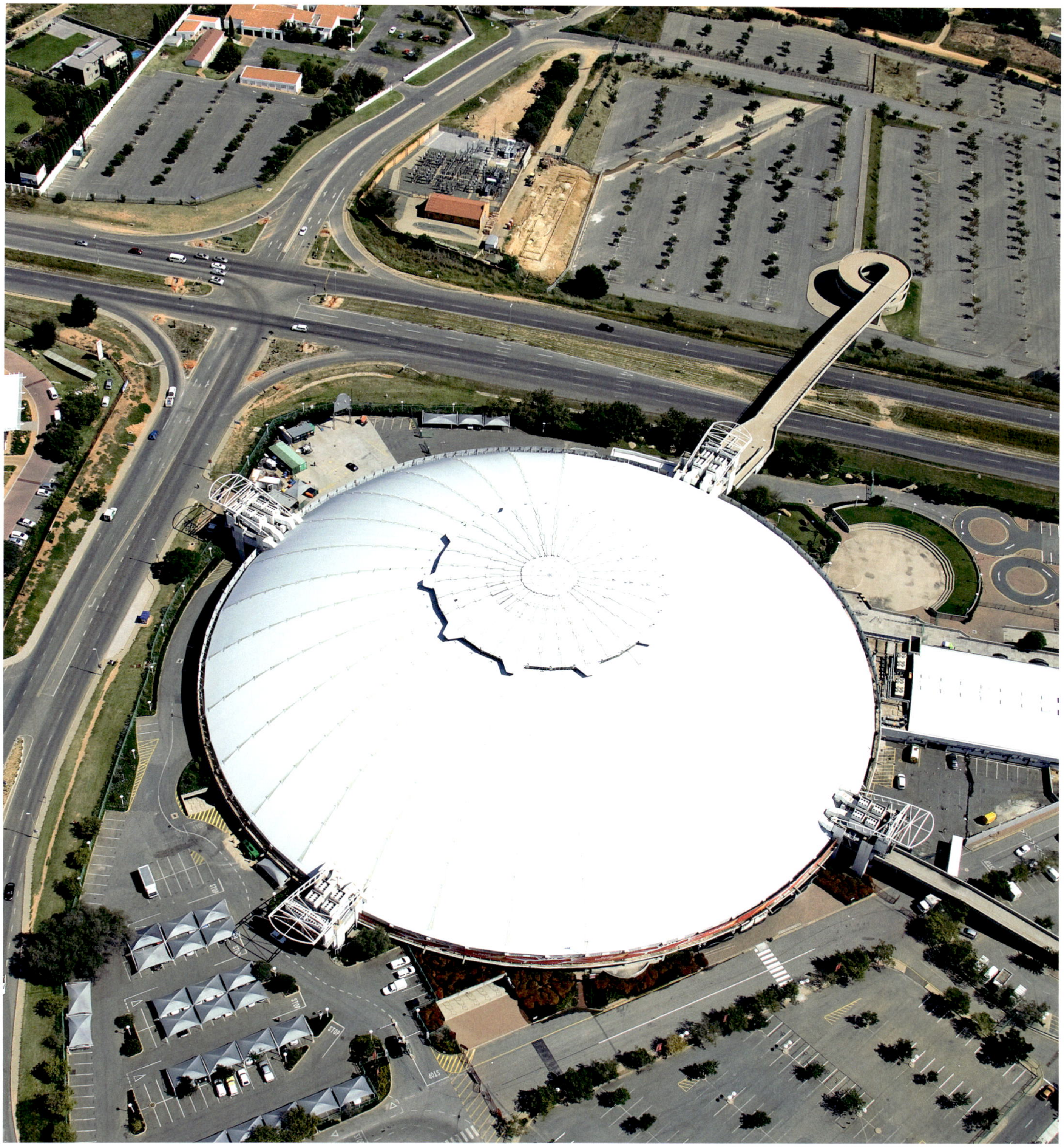

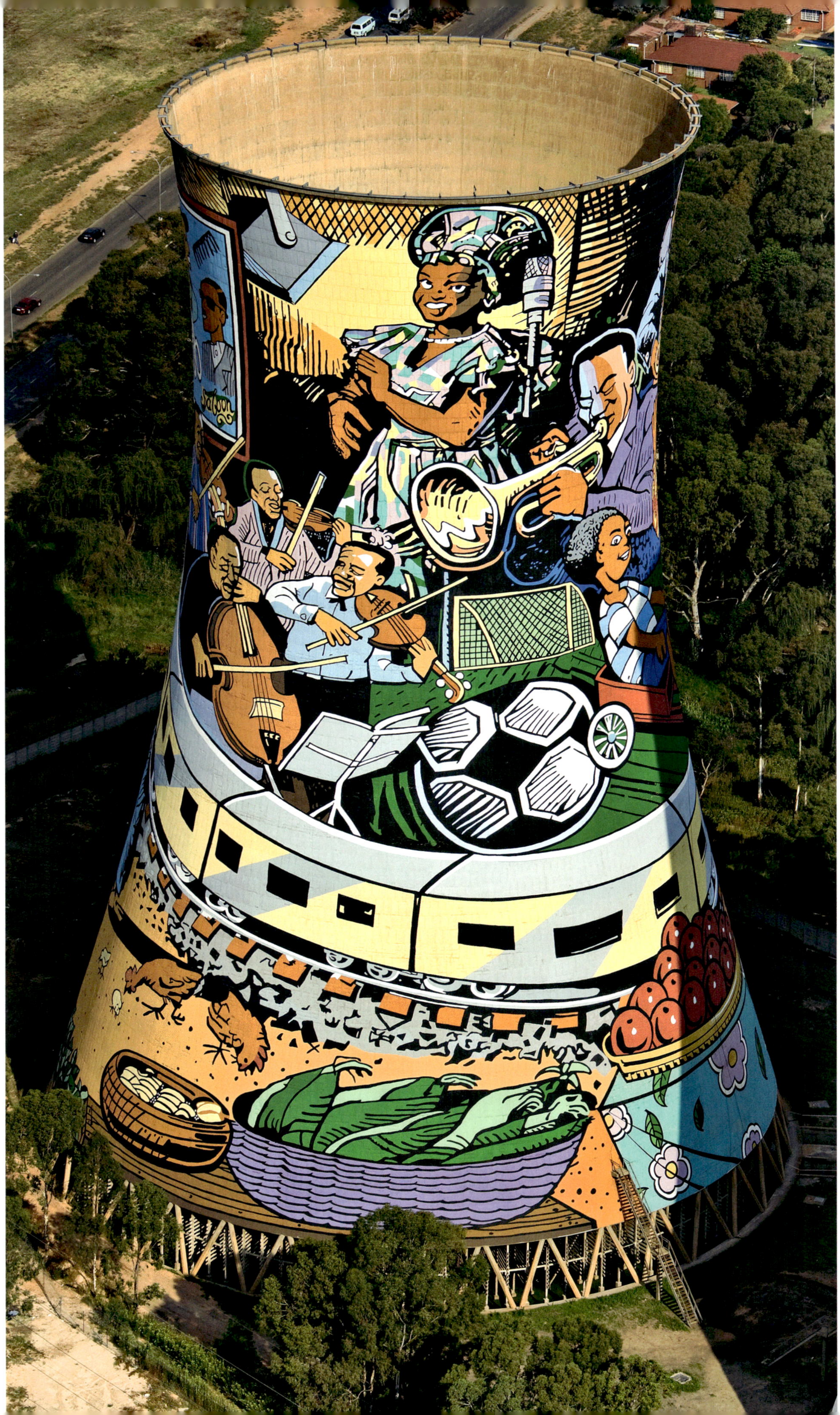

←→ Artwork on the cooling tower, Orlando Power Plant, Soweto

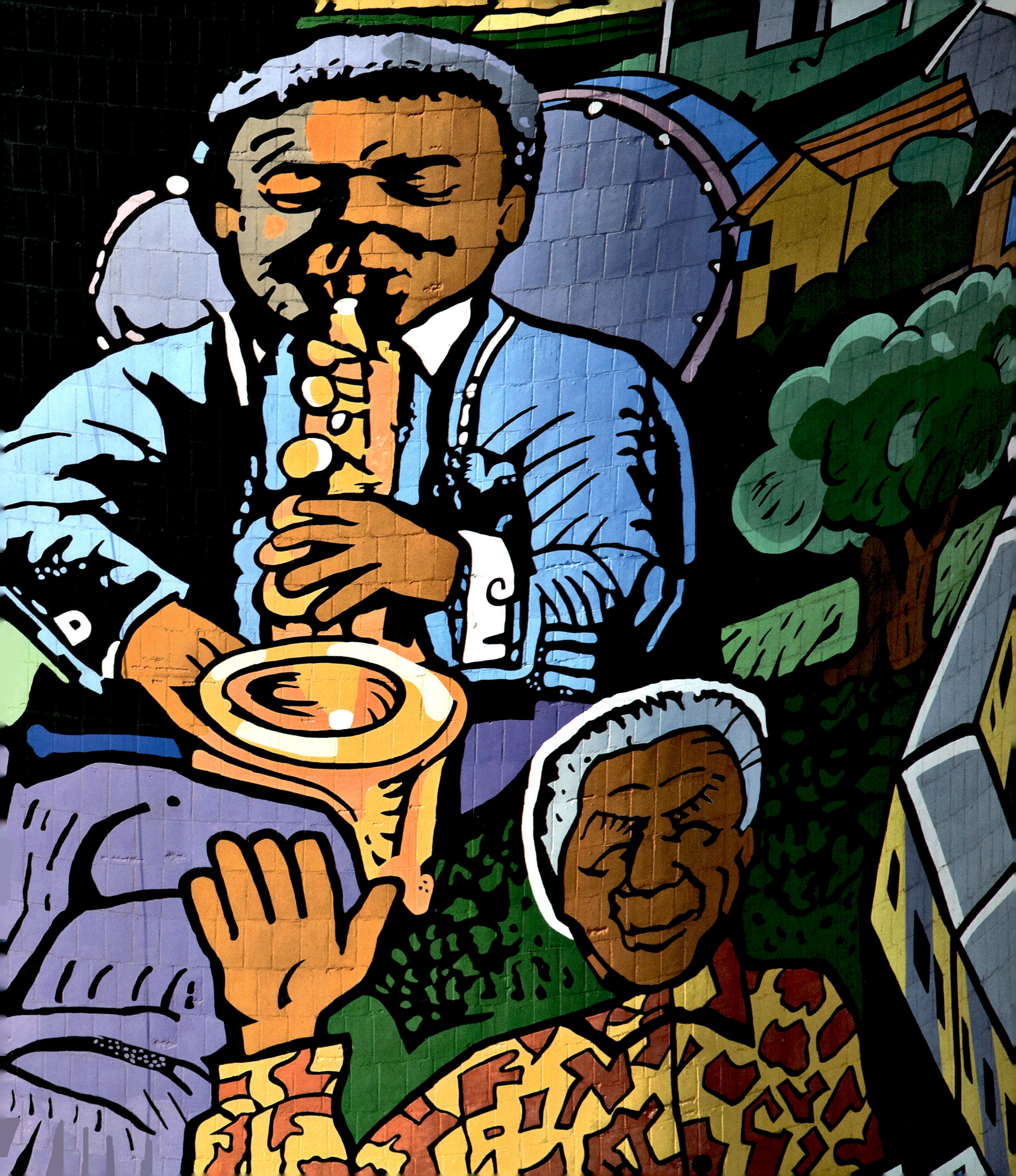

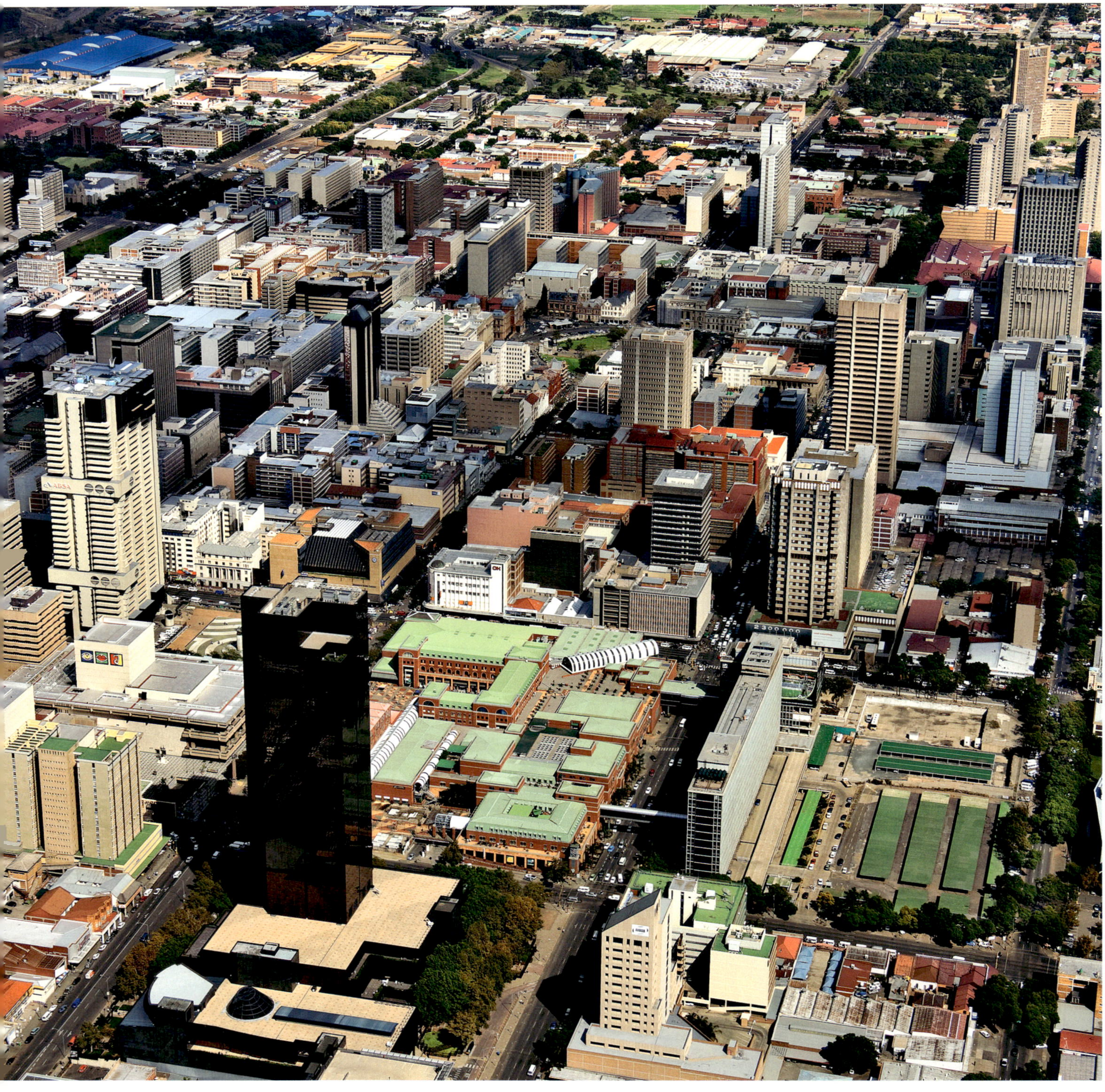

← Pretoria
↓ Church Square, Pretoria

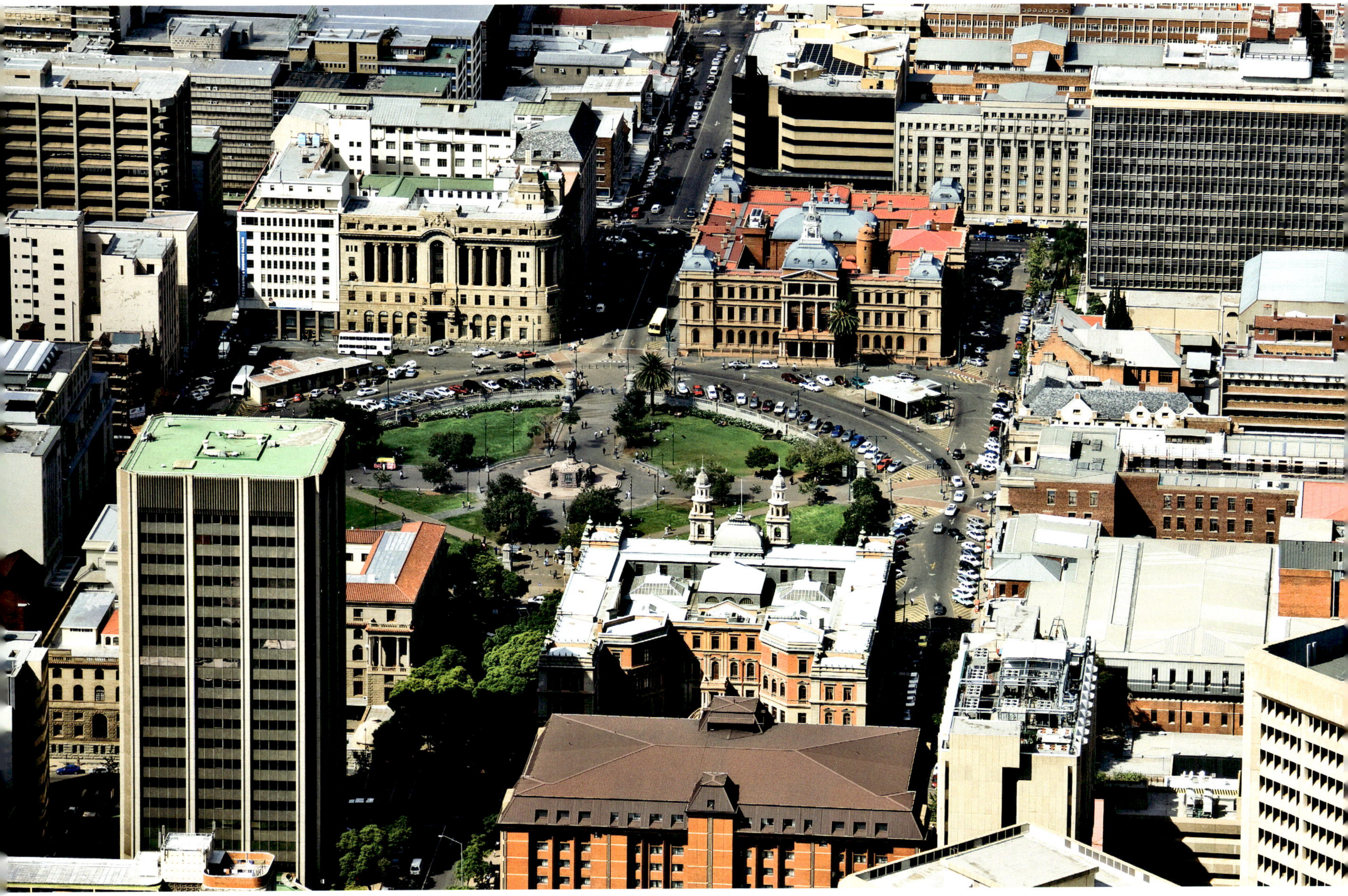

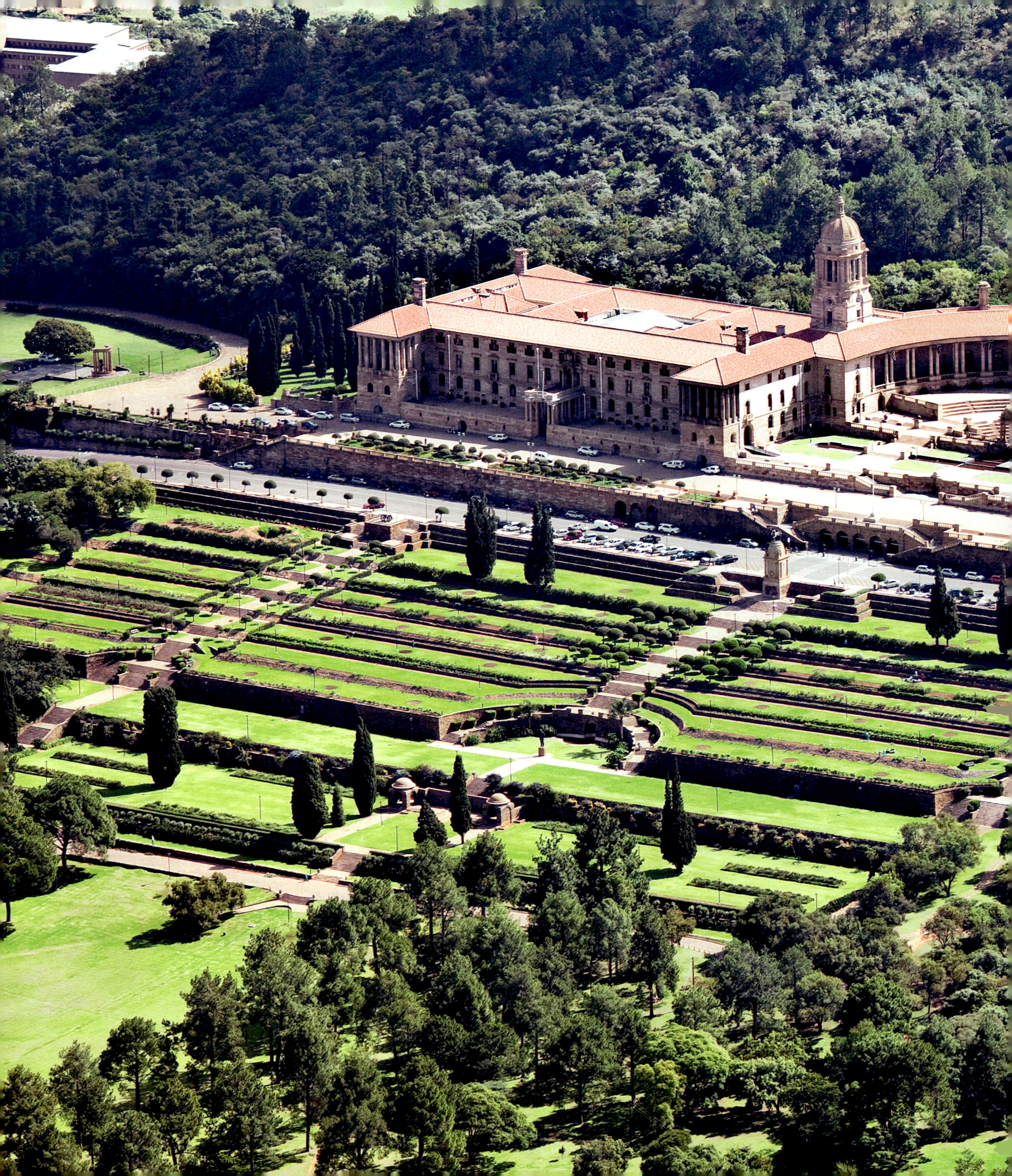

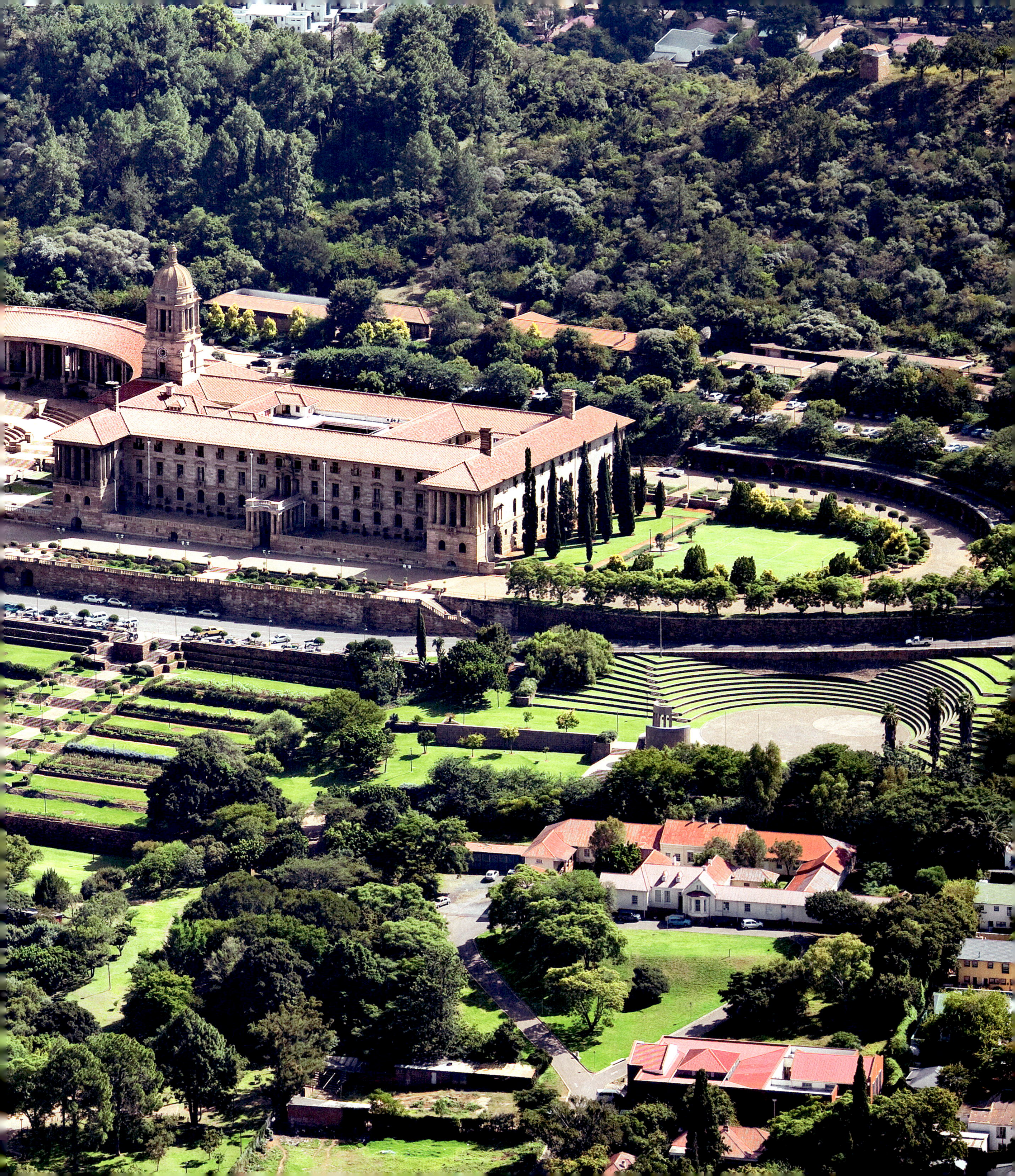

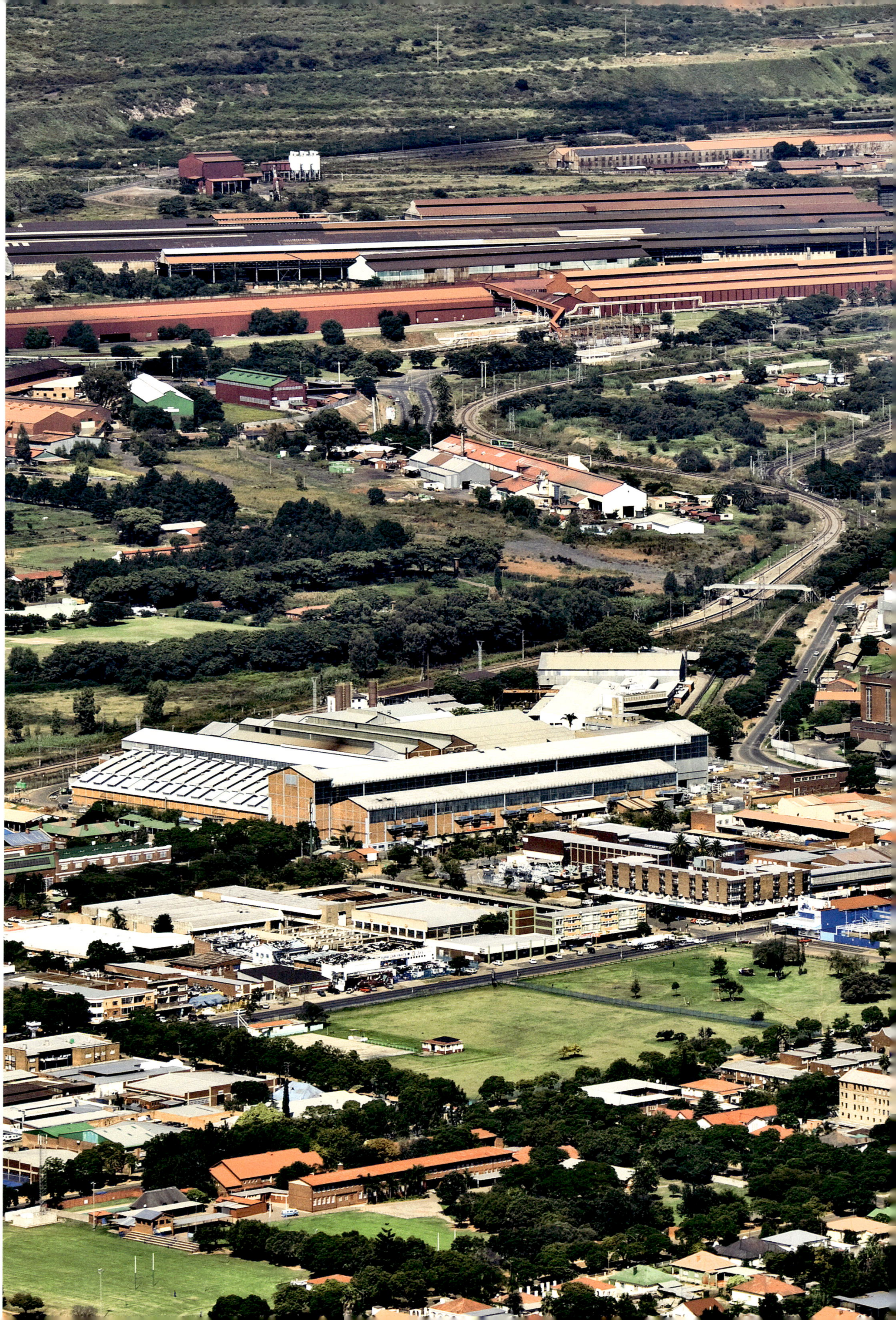

← Pretoria, the Union Buildings on Meintjes Kop
→ Industrial area, Pretoria

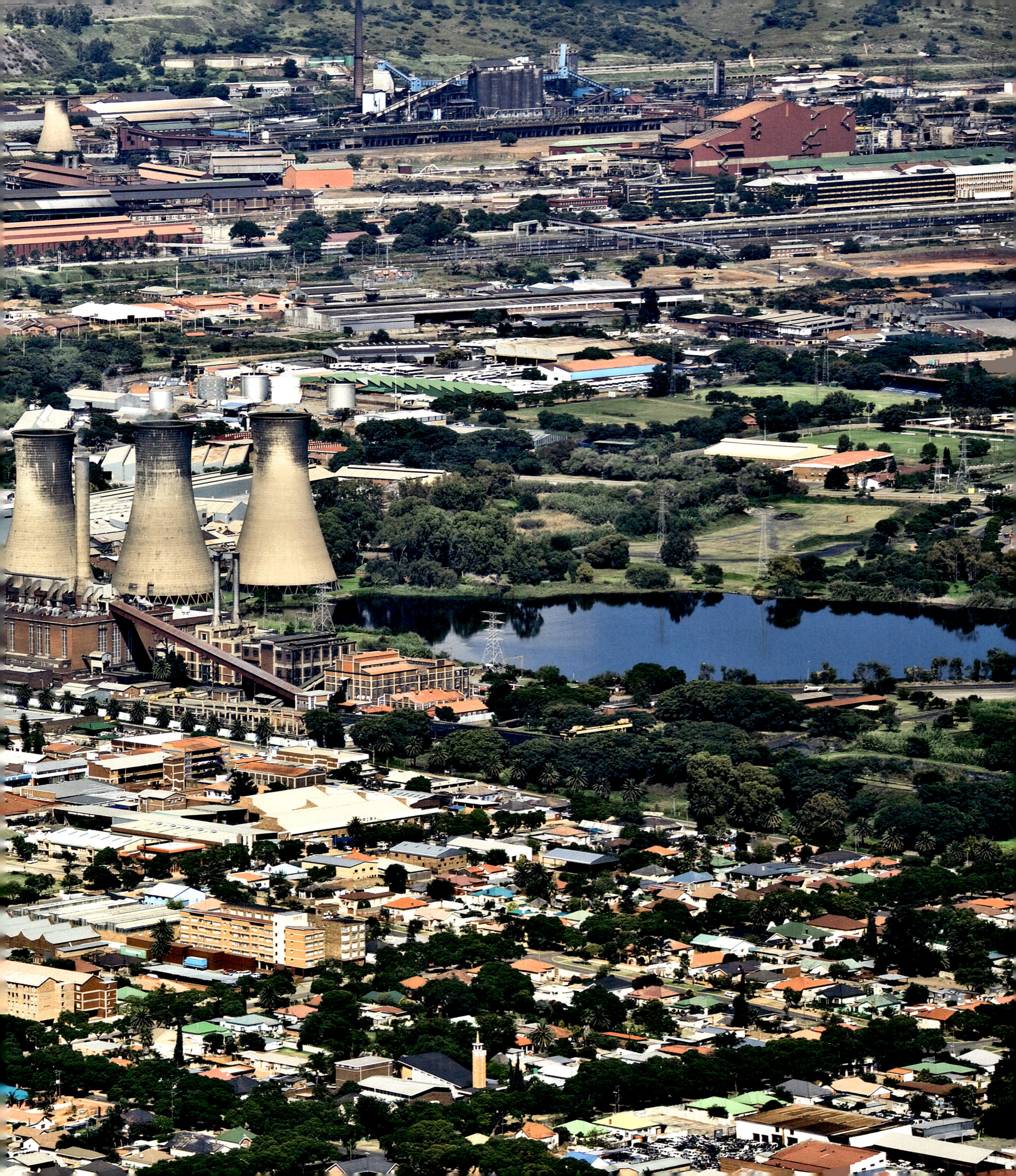

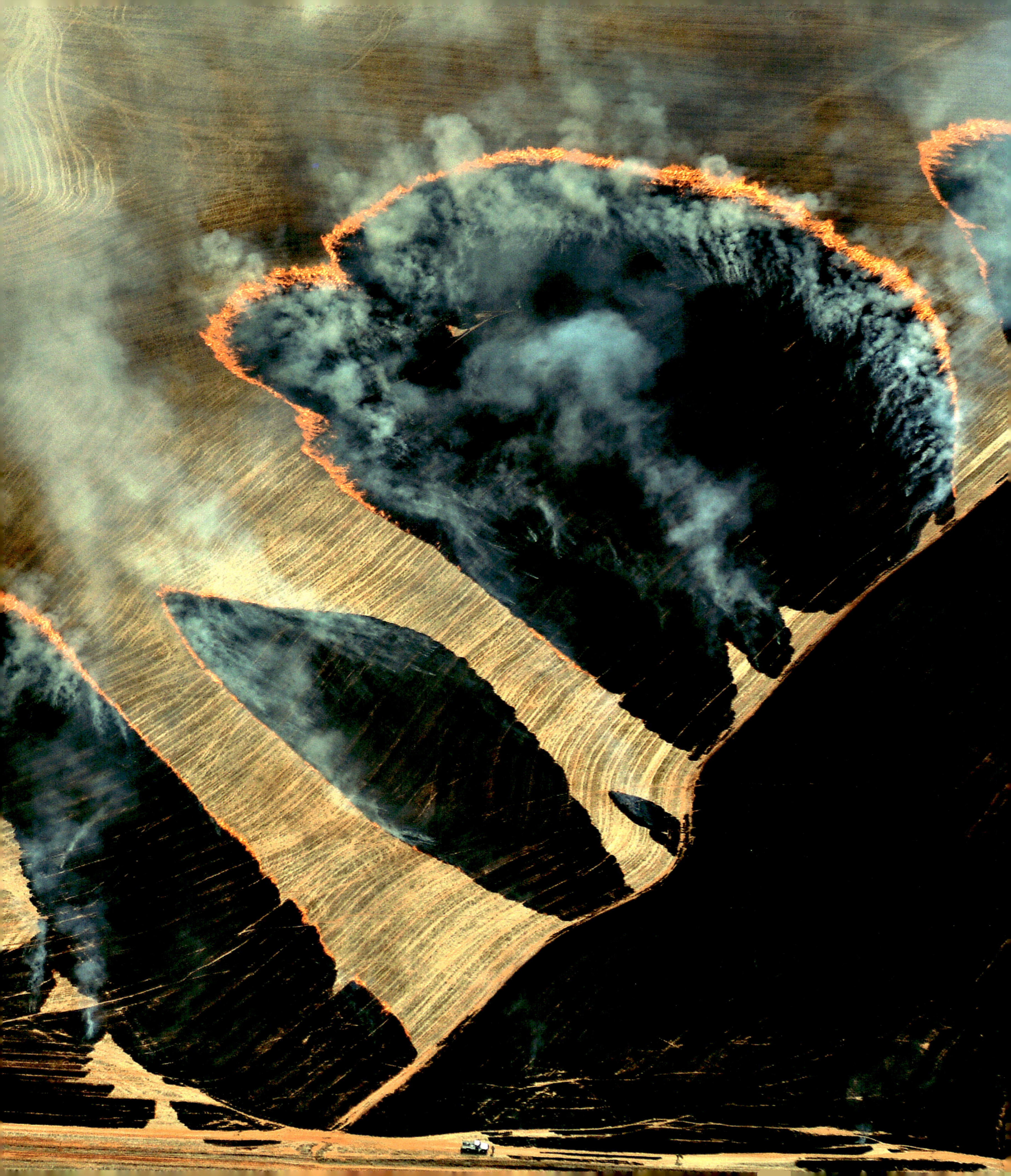

LIMPOPO

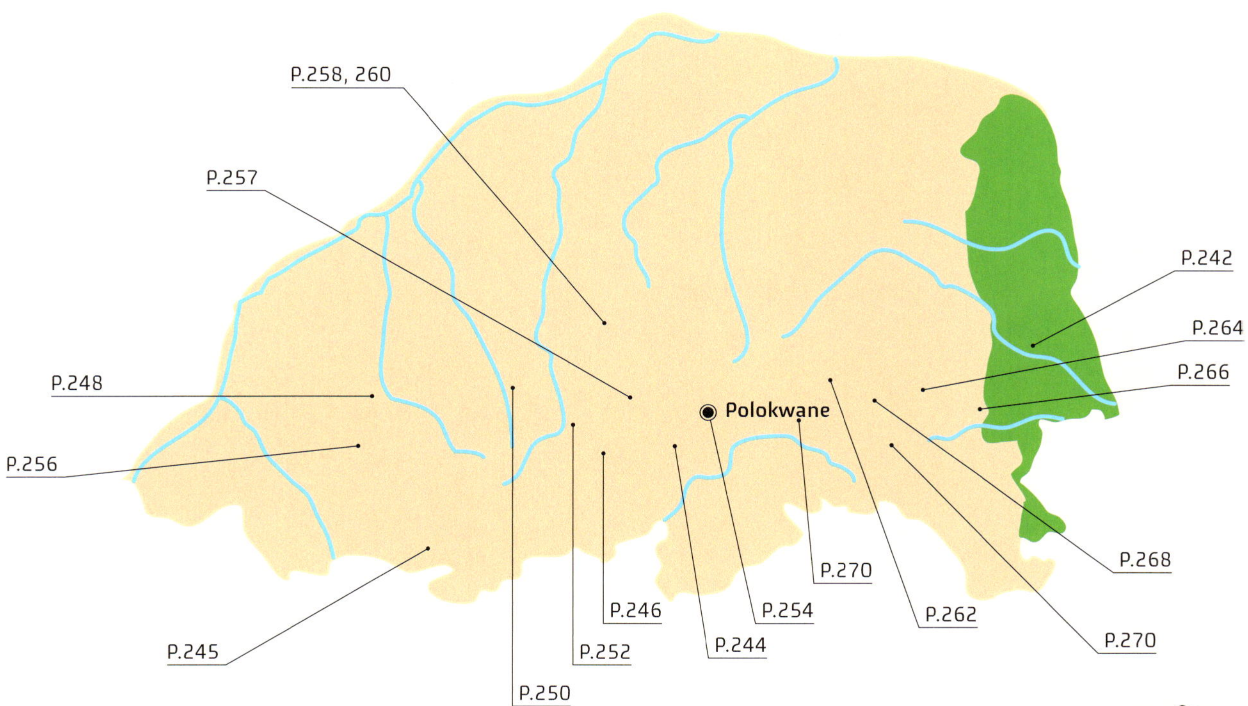
P.258, 260
P.257
P.242
P.264
P.266
P.248
Polokwane
P.256
P.268
P.270
P.246
P.254
P.262
P.270
P.245
P.252
P.244
P.250

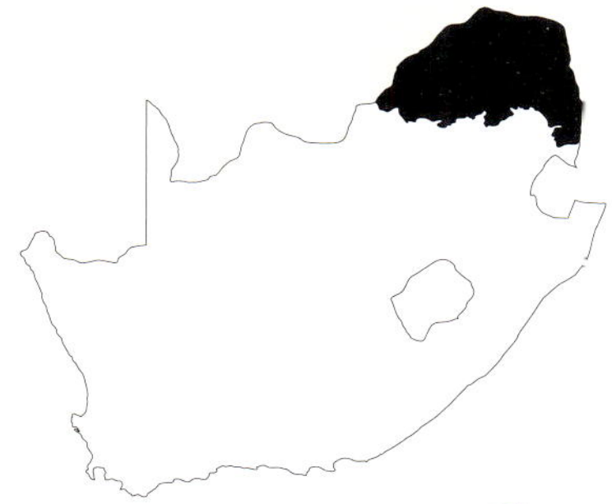

Limpopo is a country full of contrasts. The most northerly province of South Africa has steep mountain ranges, and gently rolling bushveld. Areas where enormous boulders seem to have been strewn about at random, and coffee and tea plantations laid out with geometric precision. Open mining, game and crocodile farms, and unspoilt nature.

The gateway to Africa

Limpopo borders on Zimbabwe to the north, Botswana in the west and Mozambique in the east; this has earned it the name of South Africa's Gateway to Africa. And that is what it is, certainly in atmosphere. Nowhere else are so many bush stories told with so much enthusiasm. Stories about how the baboon and the leopard went from being each other's closest friends to arch enemies; about the girl that was given in marriage to a snake; and about the murderous hares that targeted little old ladies.

Archaeological research has shown that Limpopo had an advanced civilisation more than 1,000 years ago, complete with mining and metal processing. At that time, beer was brewed from the fruits of the marula tree. The marula is sometimes called the elephant tree, because in autumn elephants like to feast on the dark yellow and vitamin-rich fruits. It is, by the way, a fable that elephants can get drunk from drinking fermented marula fruits; for that to happen, they would have to consume unbelievably large quantities of the fruit.

But be that as it may, the marula – the bark and leaves of which have medicinal properties – is, according to local tradition, a sacred tree, which symbolises fertility and loyalty. Tradition also teaches that the baboons of Lwamondo Hill, in the Soutpans Mountain Range, are sacred animals and that the beautiful Lake Funduzi is dedicated to the python god who protects his followers and blesses them with rain – as long as they sacrifice a young girl to him every year. The 19th century Voortrekkers also had their stories and their dreams. Around 1860, a group of orthodox-Calvinist white farmers set off to the north in search of the Holy Land. When they reached the Mogalakwena River, it reminded them of the Nile and they founded a settlement which they called Nylstroom. The name has since been changed to Modimolle, 'the place of the spirits', and the village is now an important centre for eco-tourism.

Everything suggests that spirituality has always played an important role in Limpopo. It is therefore hardly surprising that it was here that the Zion Christian Church was founded at the start of the 20th century. The church combines African and Christian beliefs and currently has an estimated four million members in South Africa. The headquarters of the church is in the town of Moria, about 35 kilometres from the provincial capital Polokwane, 'the place of safety'. Annually, up to a million believers travel to Moria to hold mass religious celebrations.

Outside these peak periods, it is generally quiet in Limpopo. Too quiet, according to the government, which is trying to market the province variously as the garden of South Africa, a paradise for trophy hunters, and South Africa's best kept secret.

The latter is certainly true. But that is exactly what makes Limpopo so special.

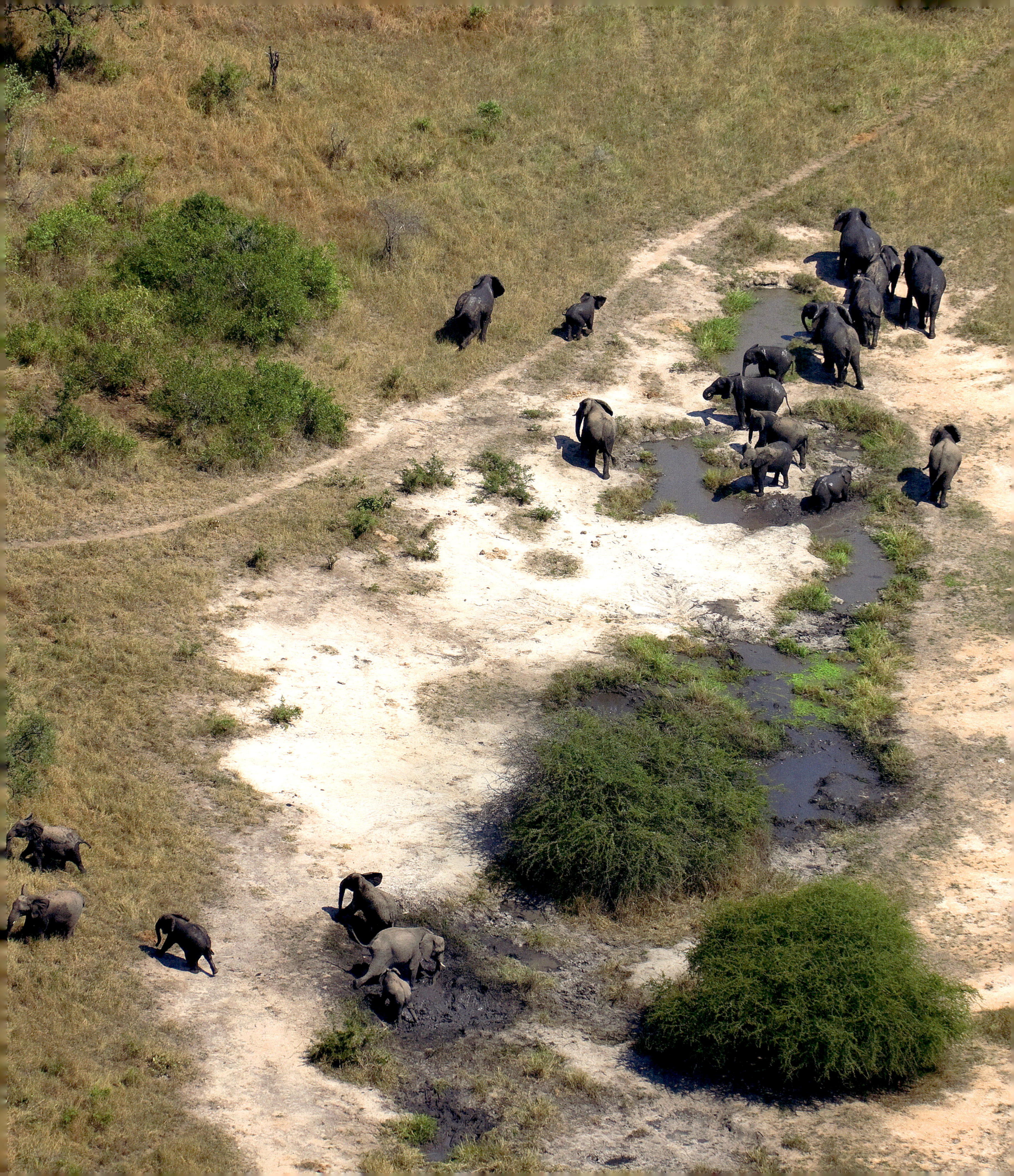

↓ Farmer's 'monument', between Polokwane and Mokopane

→ Blood basin of chicken slaughterhouse, Bela Bela

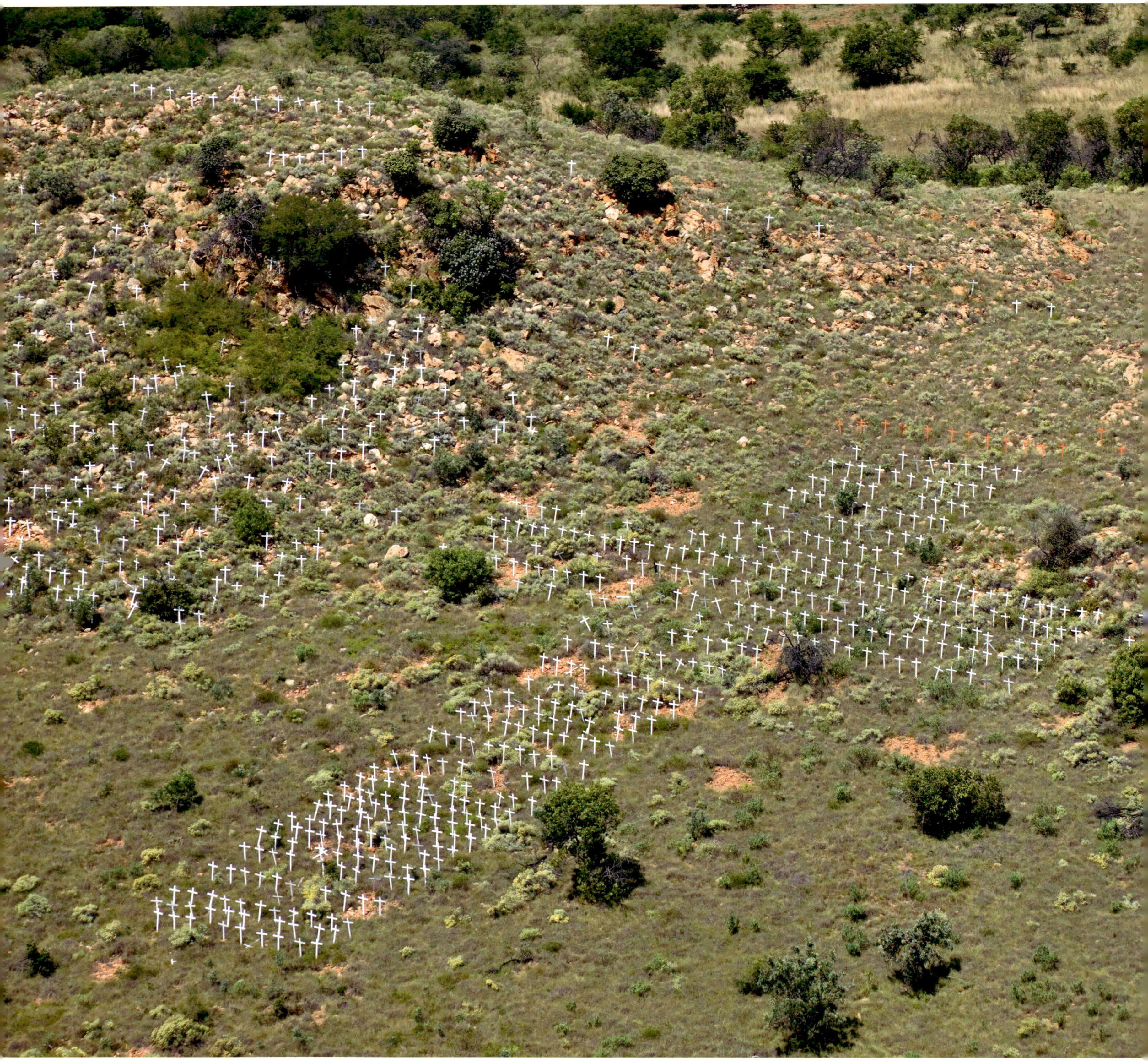

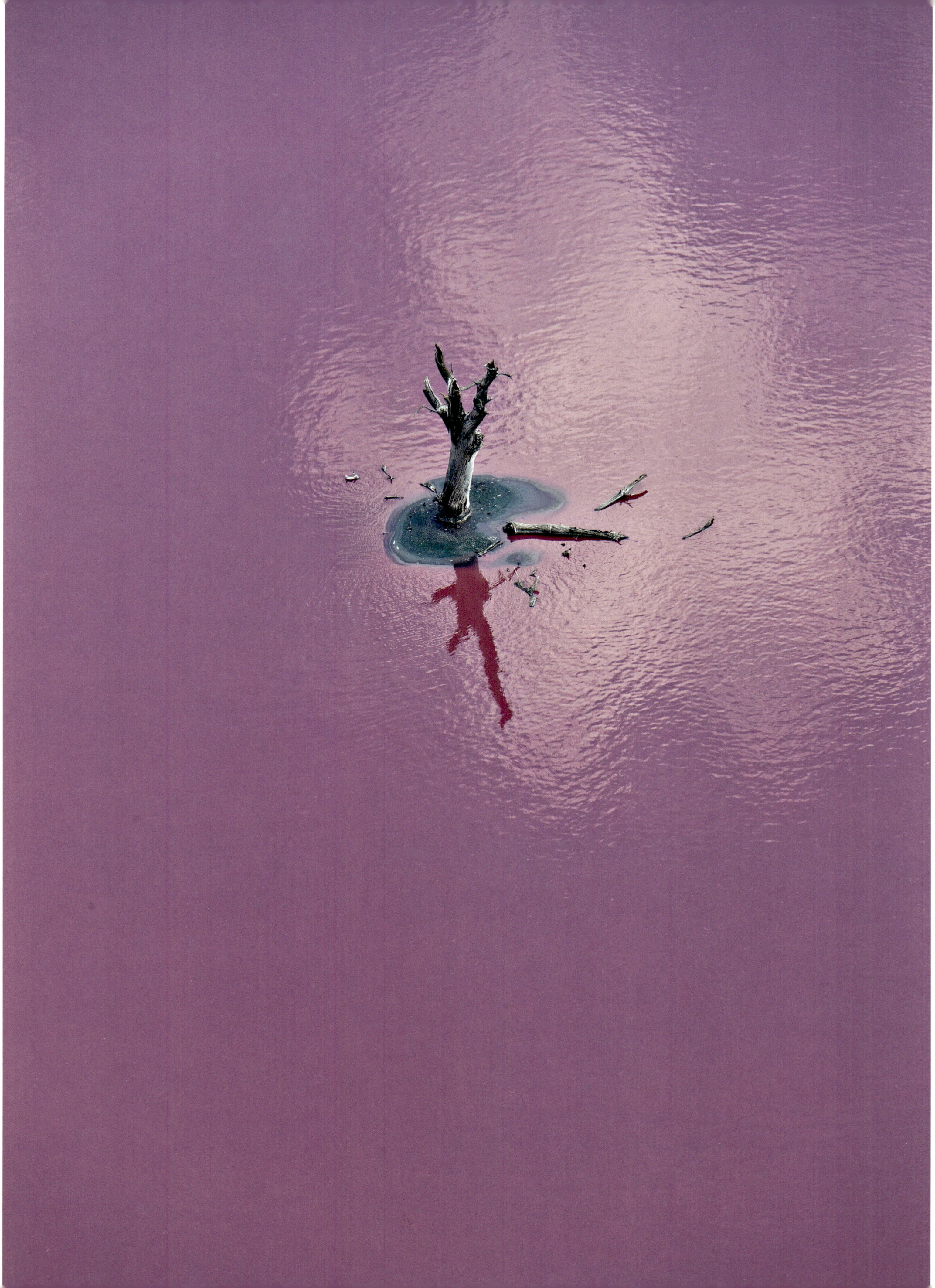

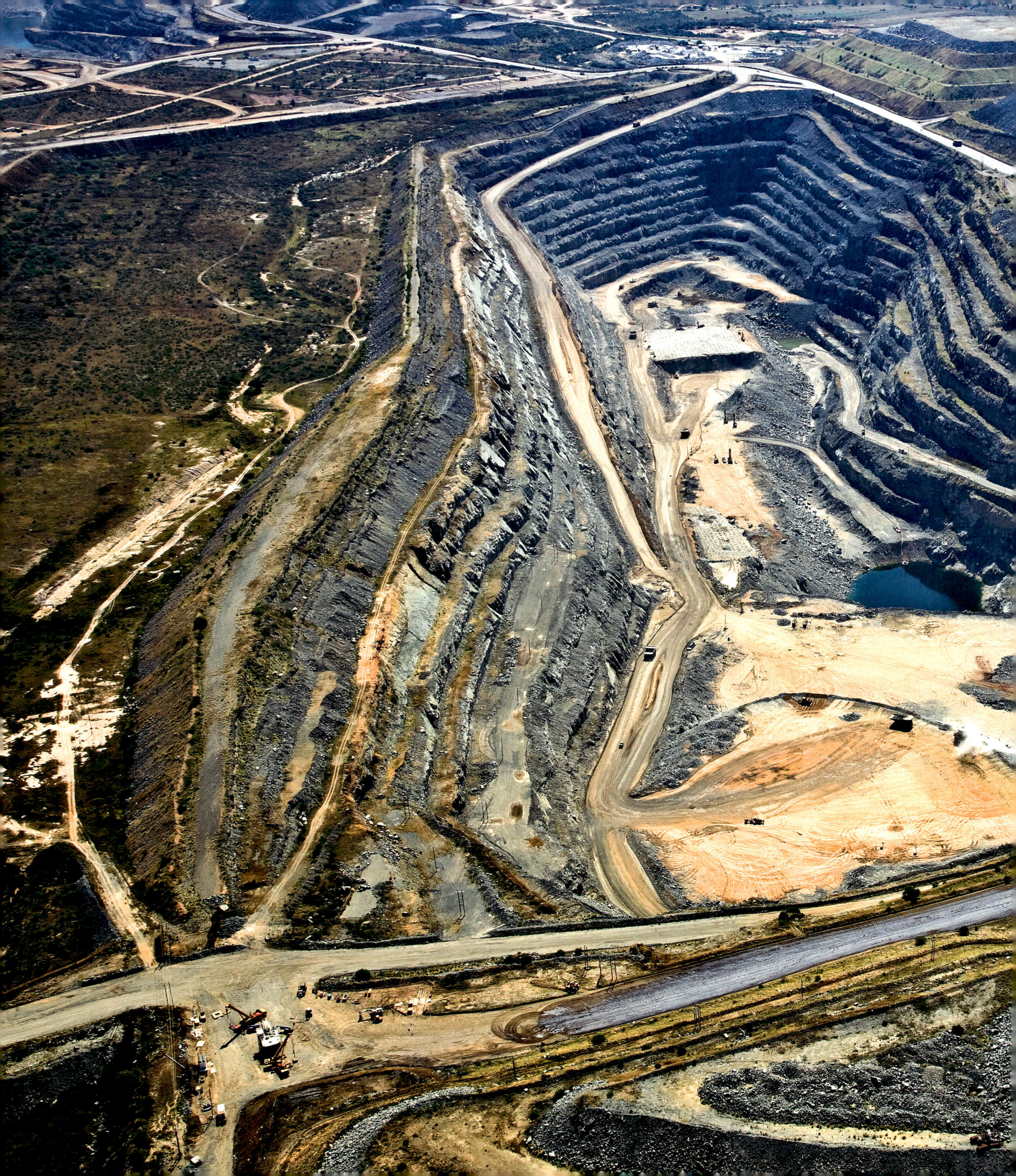

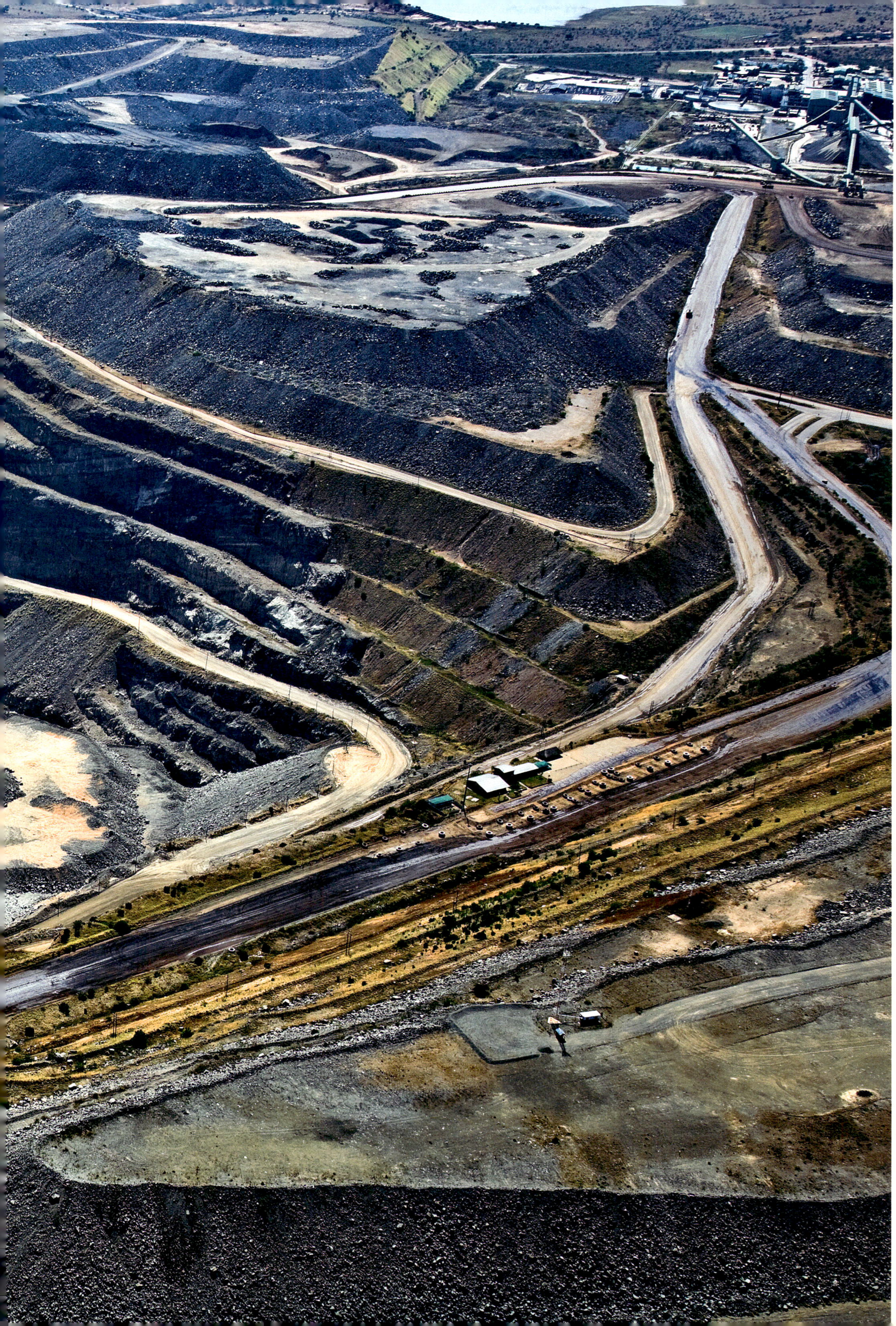

← Tin mine, 20 km northwest of Mokopane

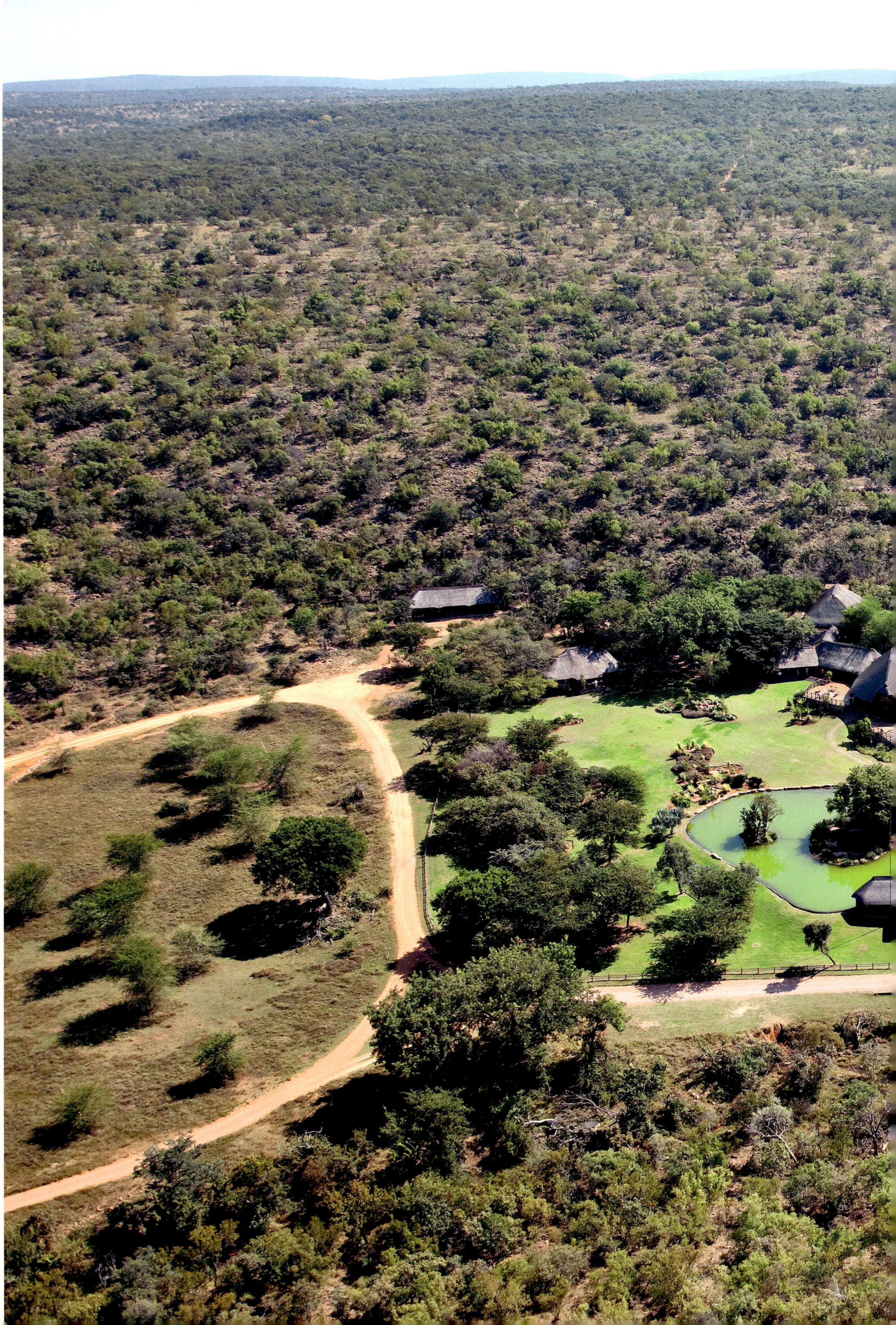

→ Ka'Ingo Private Game Reserve, Mokolo

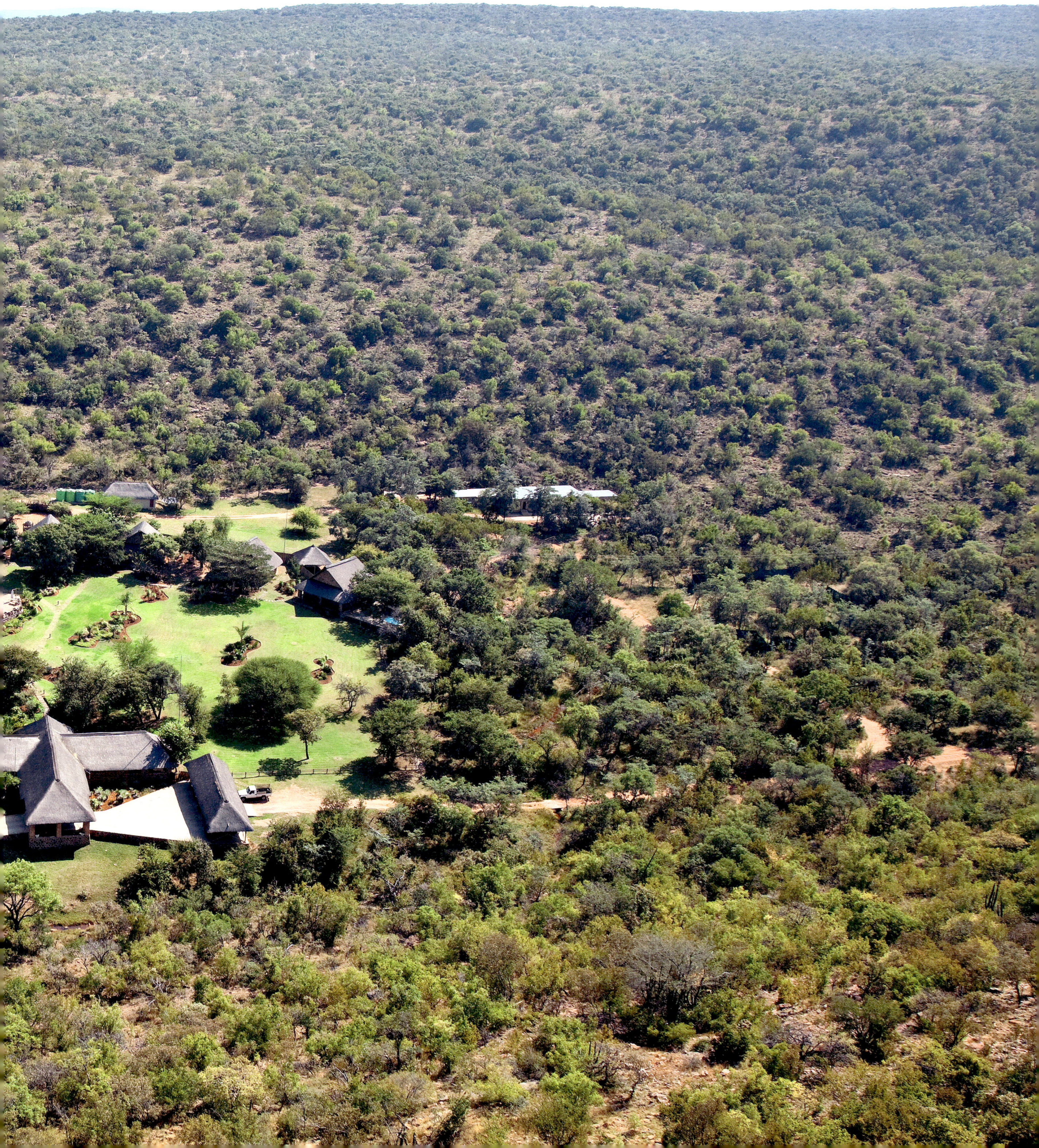

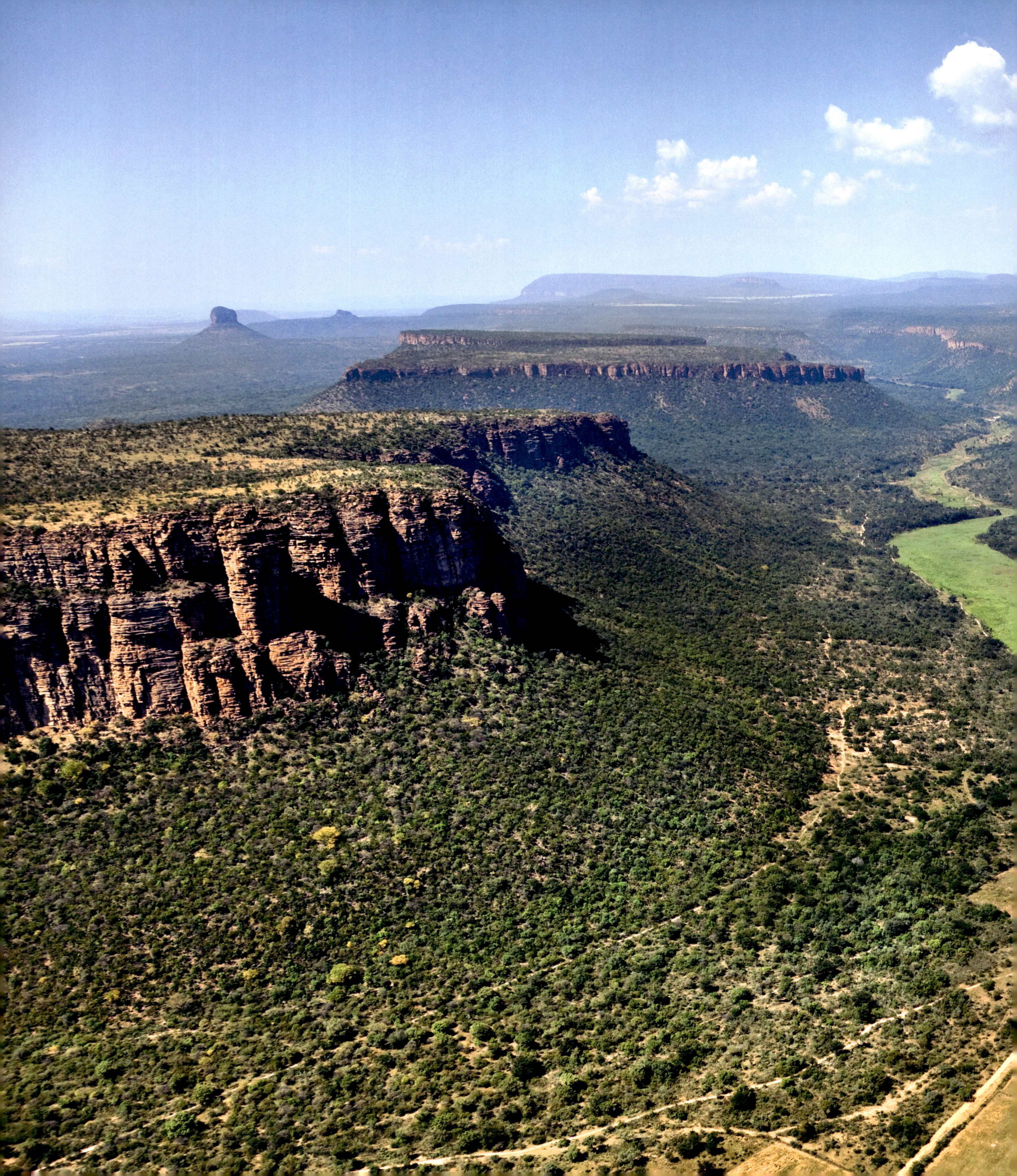

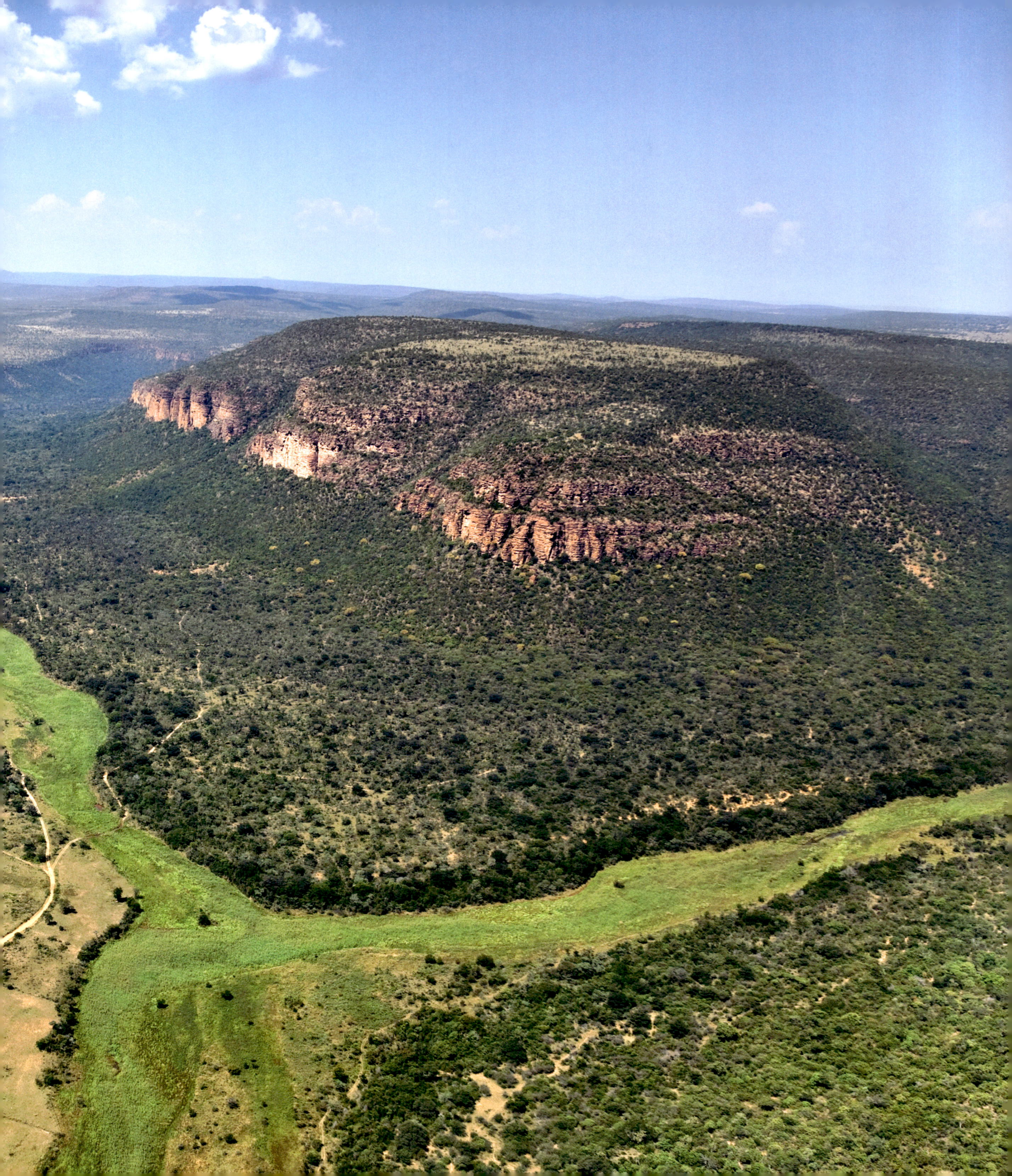

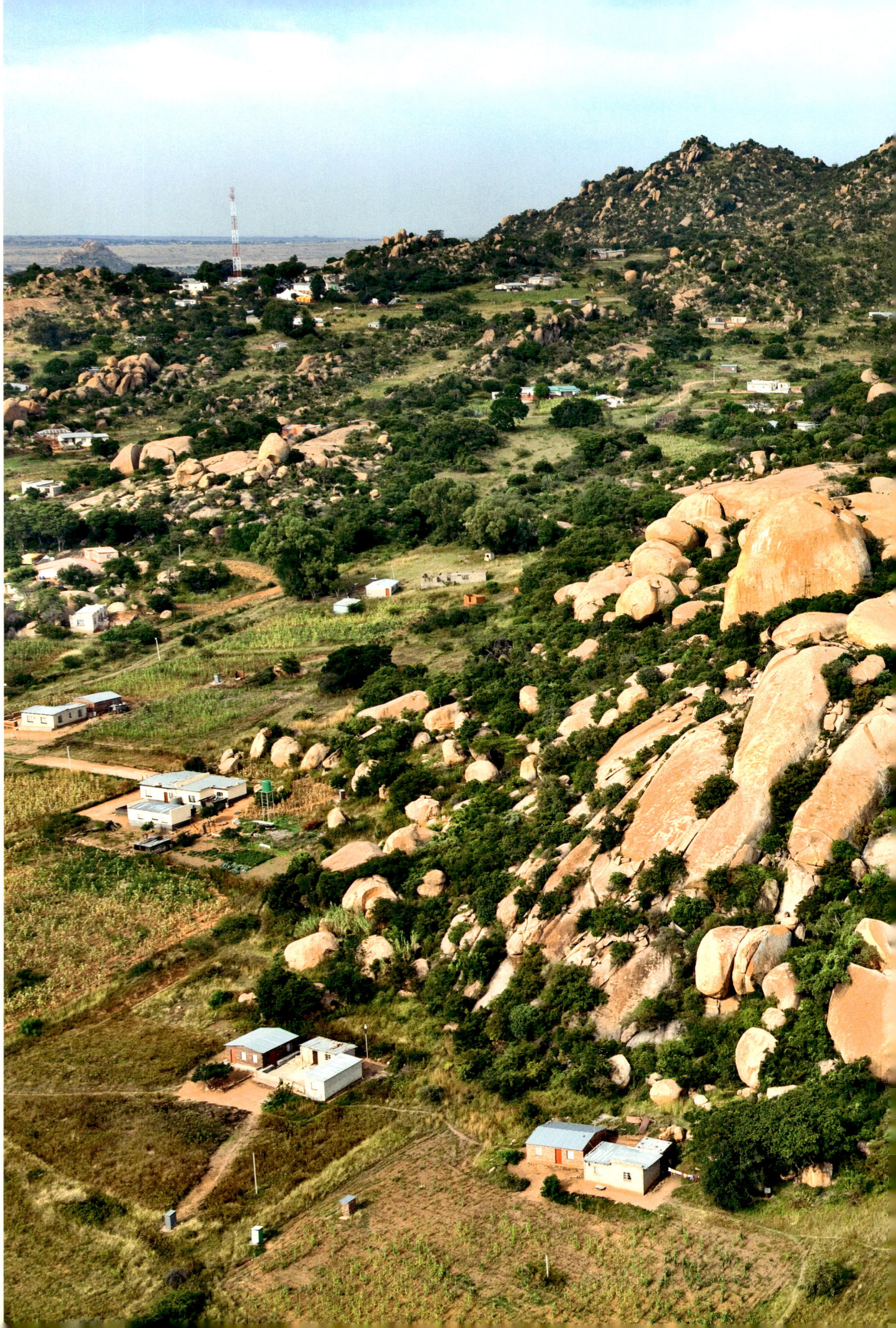

← Bakenberg
→ gaMashashane

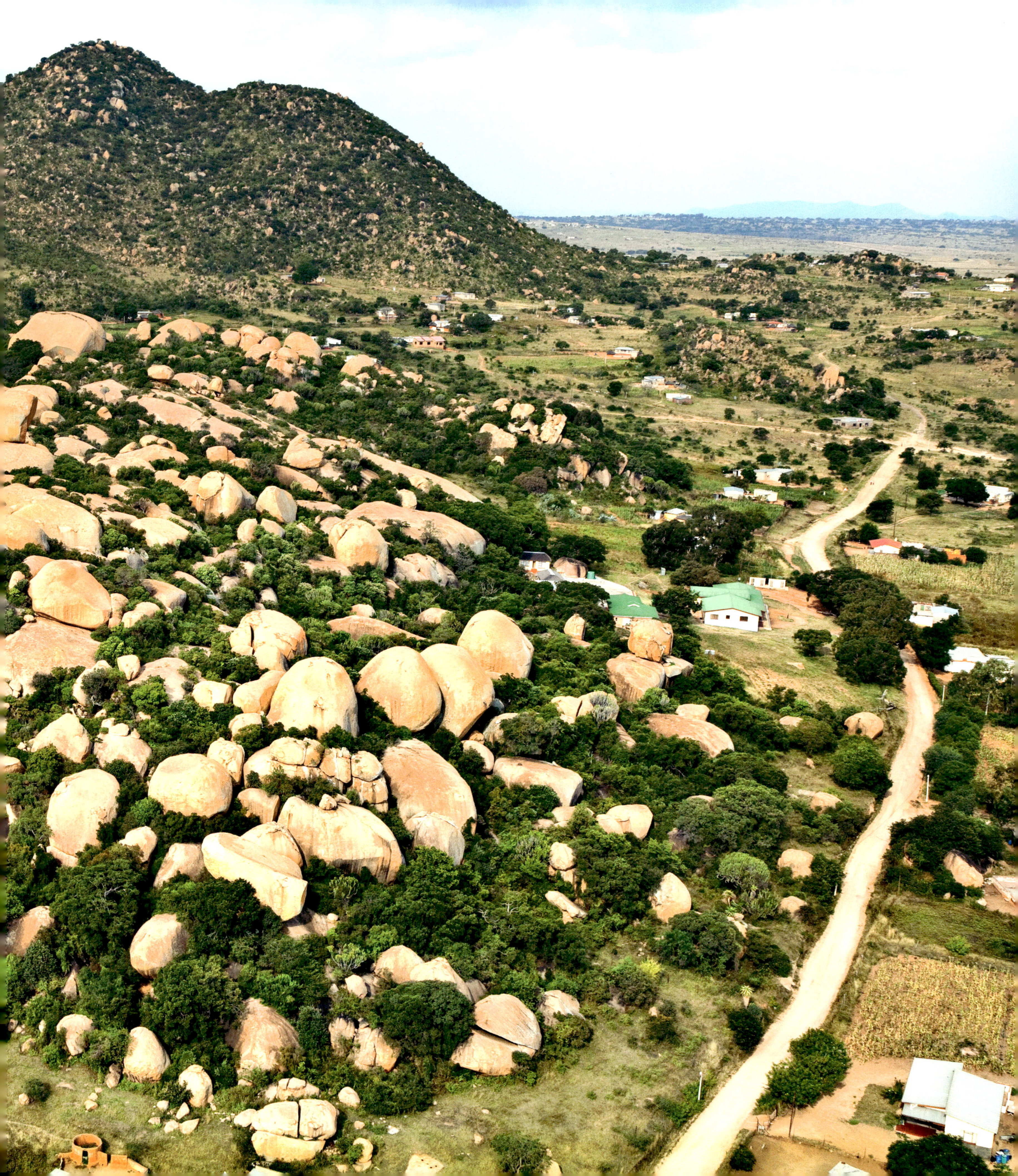

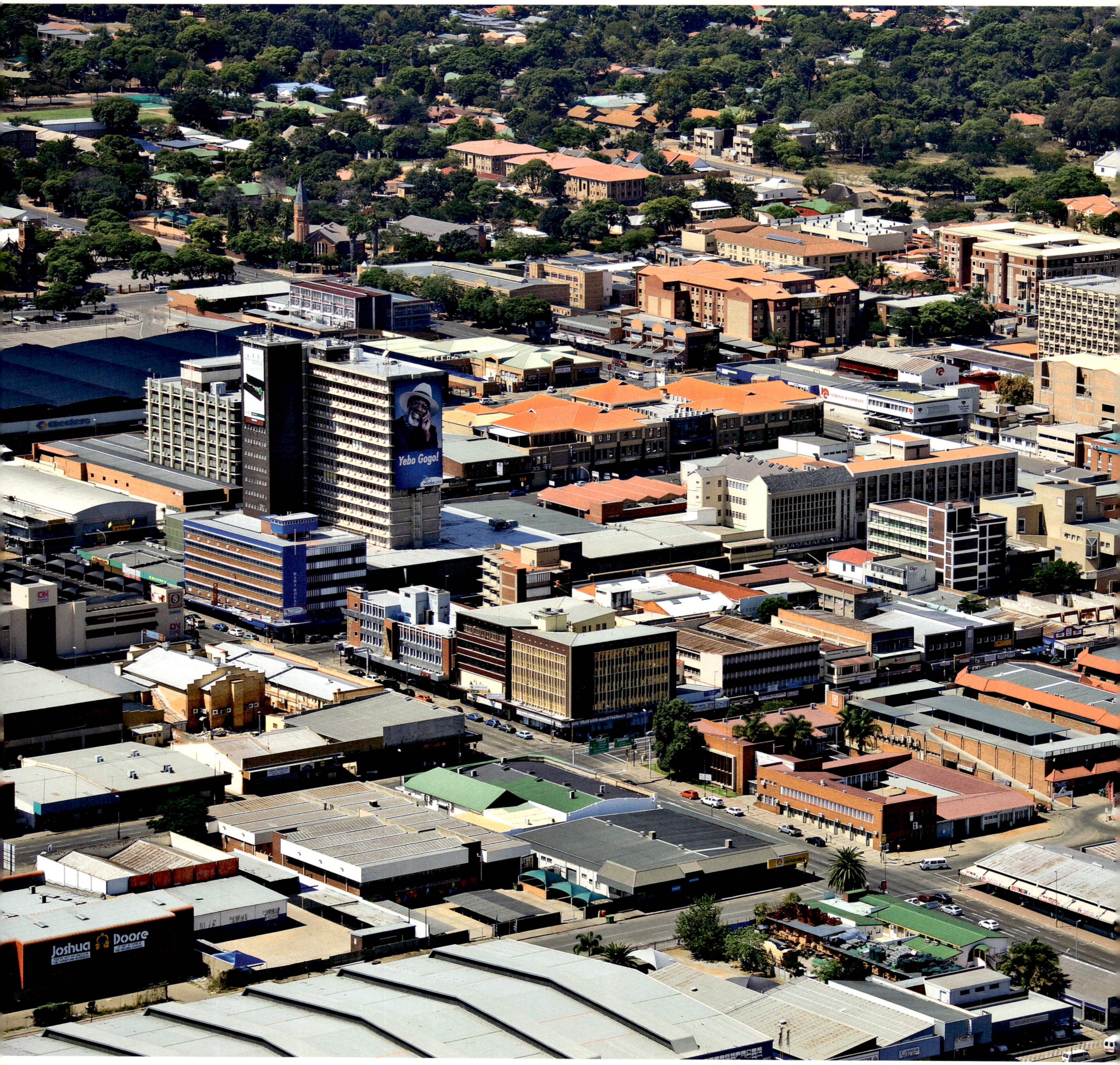
Yebo Gogo!
Joshua
Doore

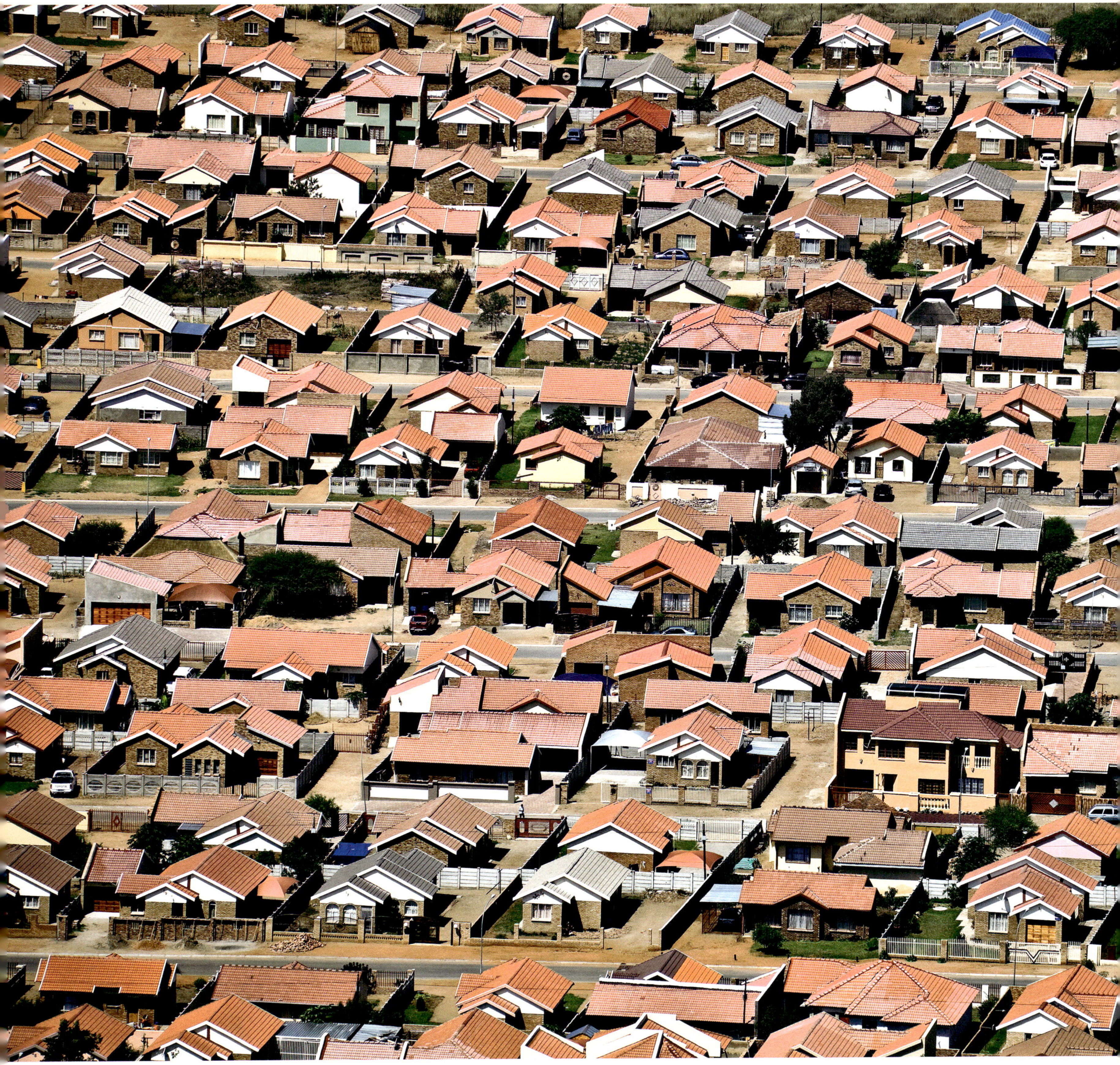

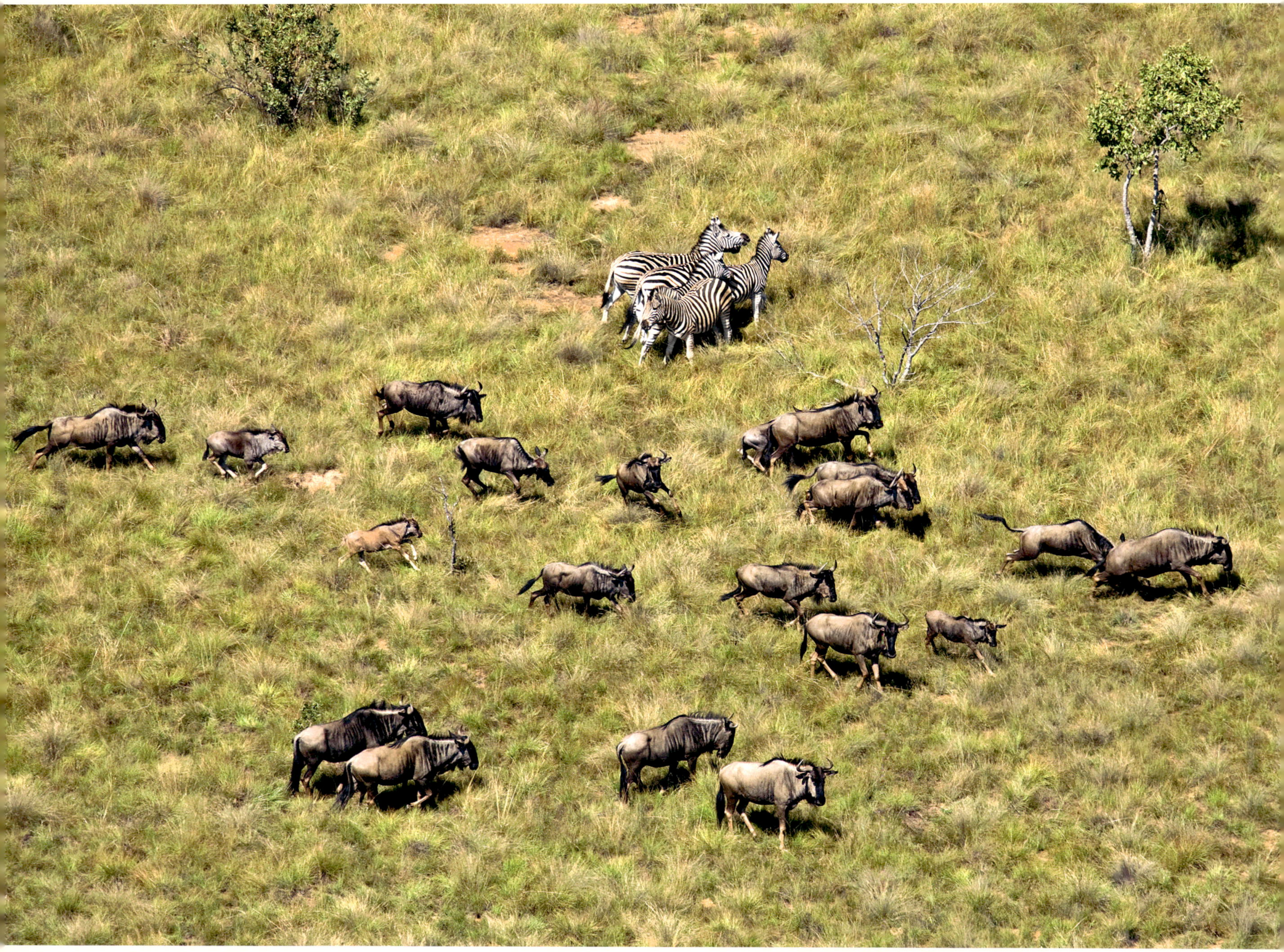

← Marakele National Park, Waterberge
↓ Bakenberg

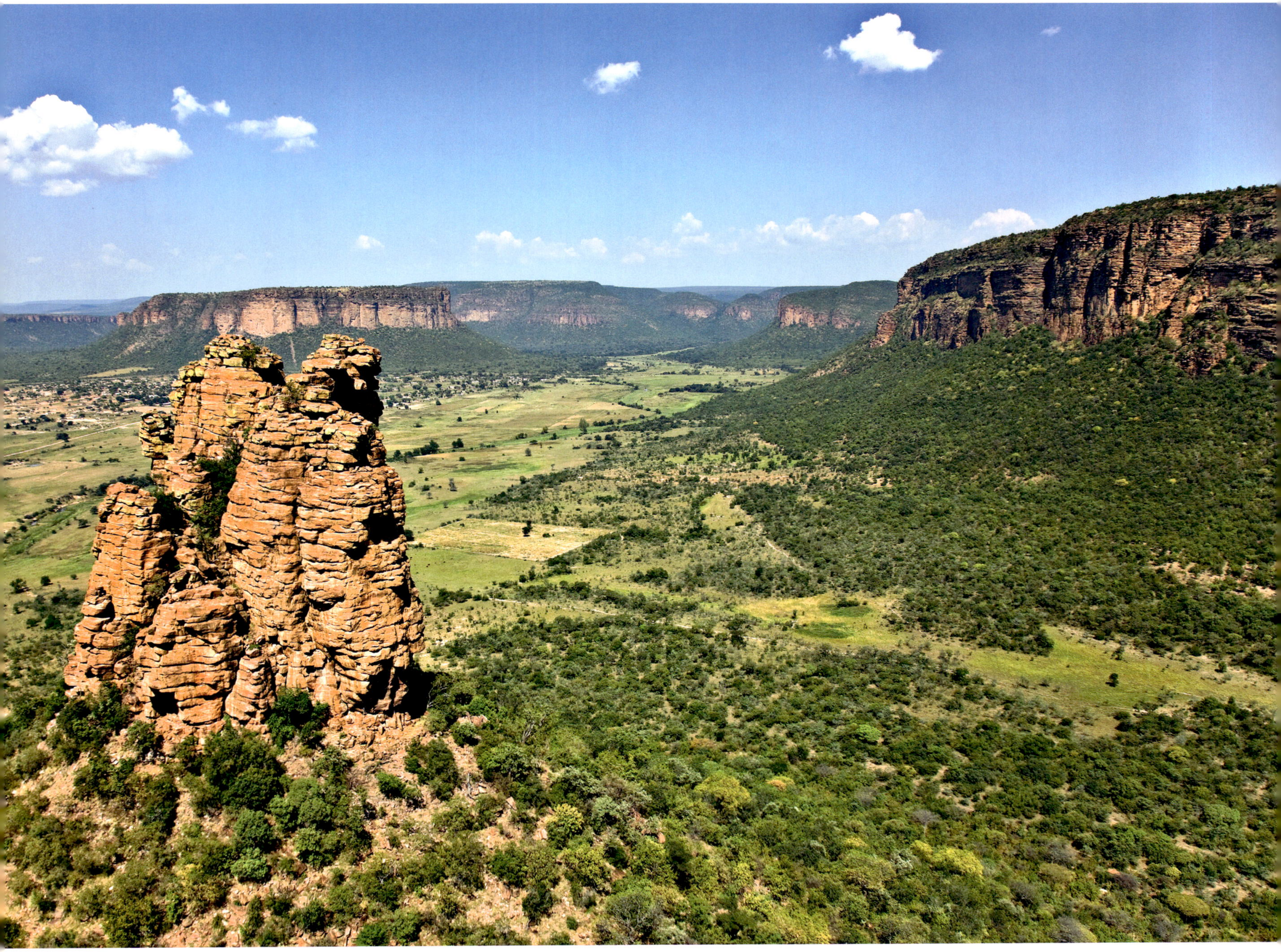

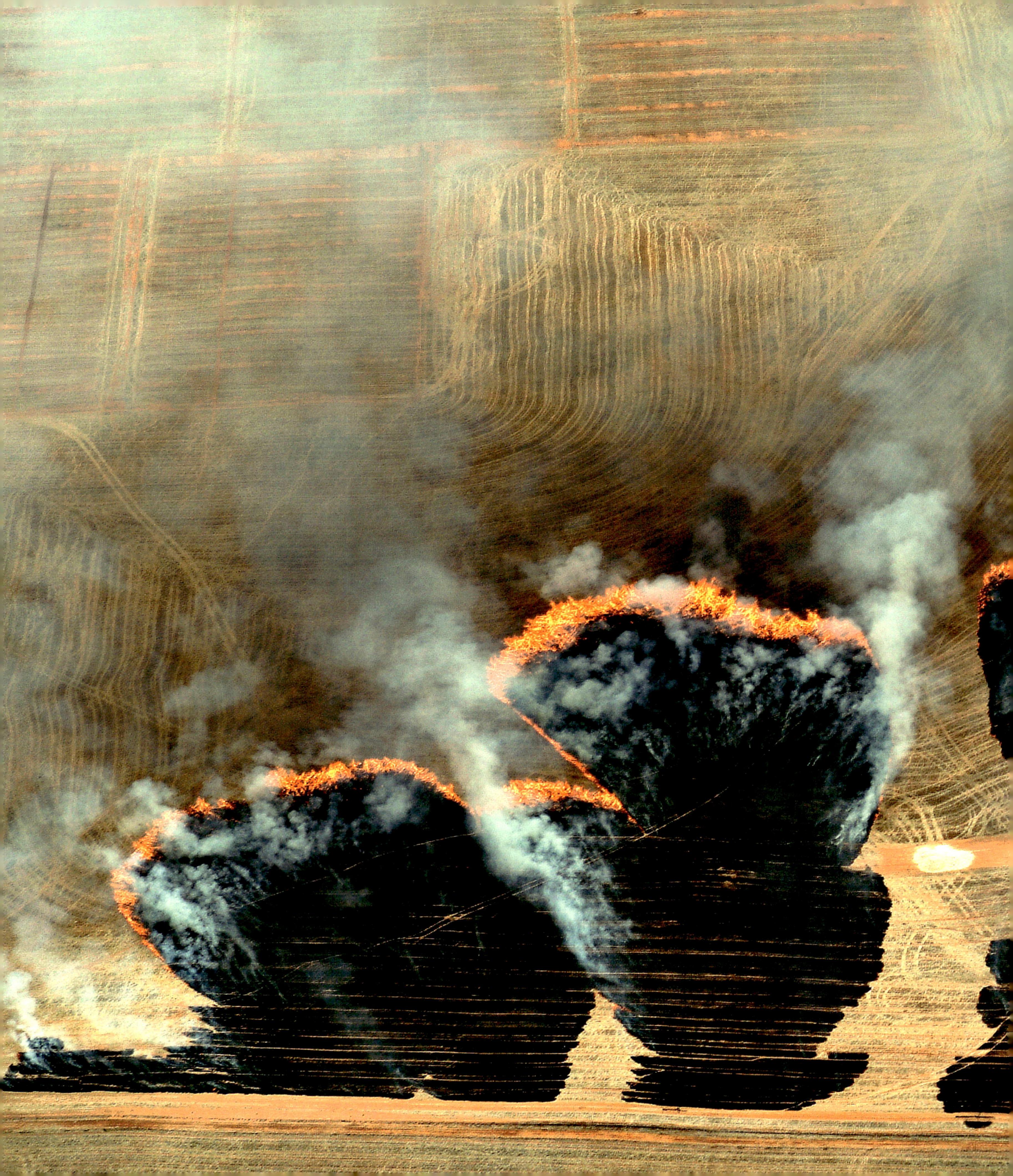

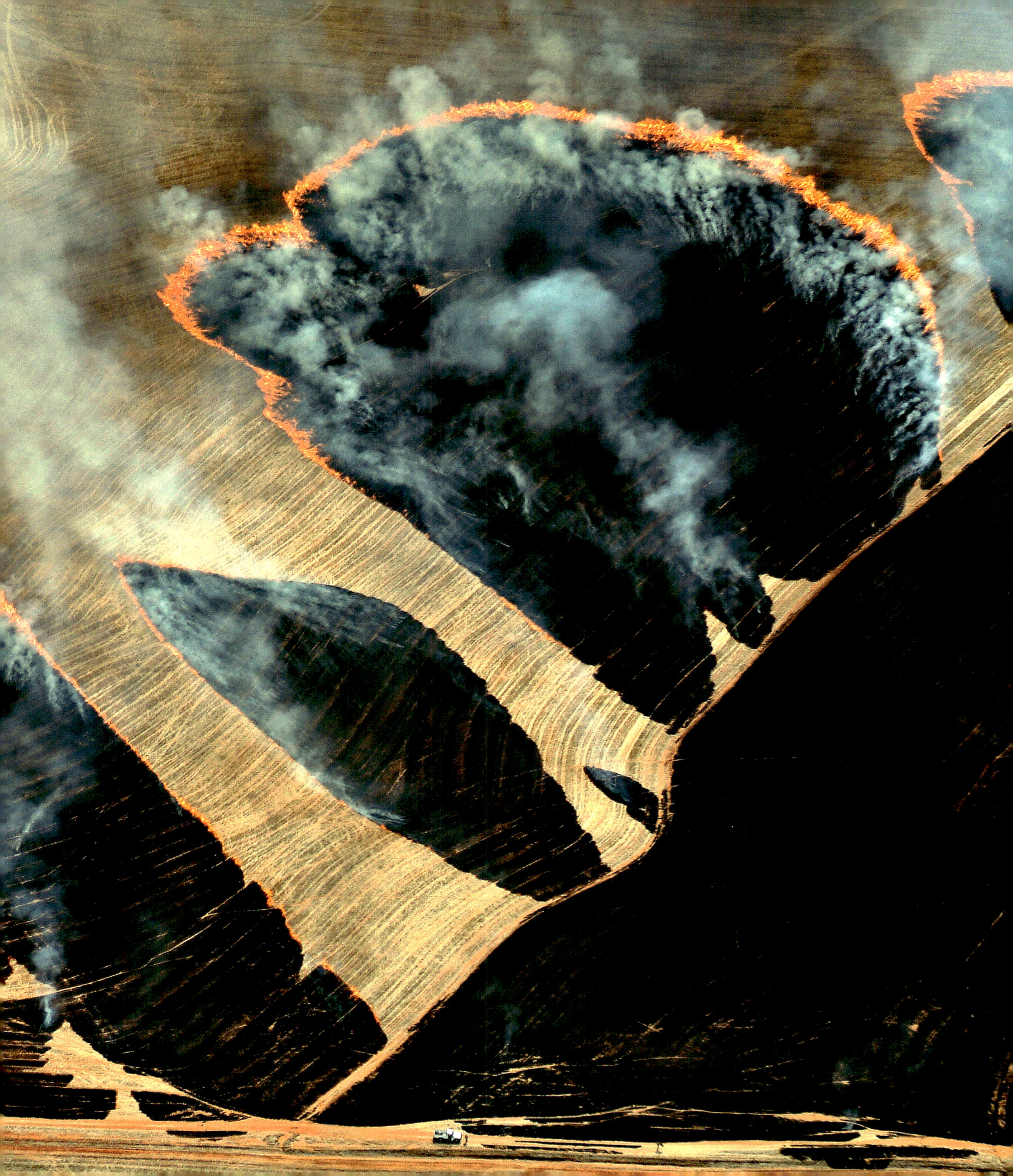

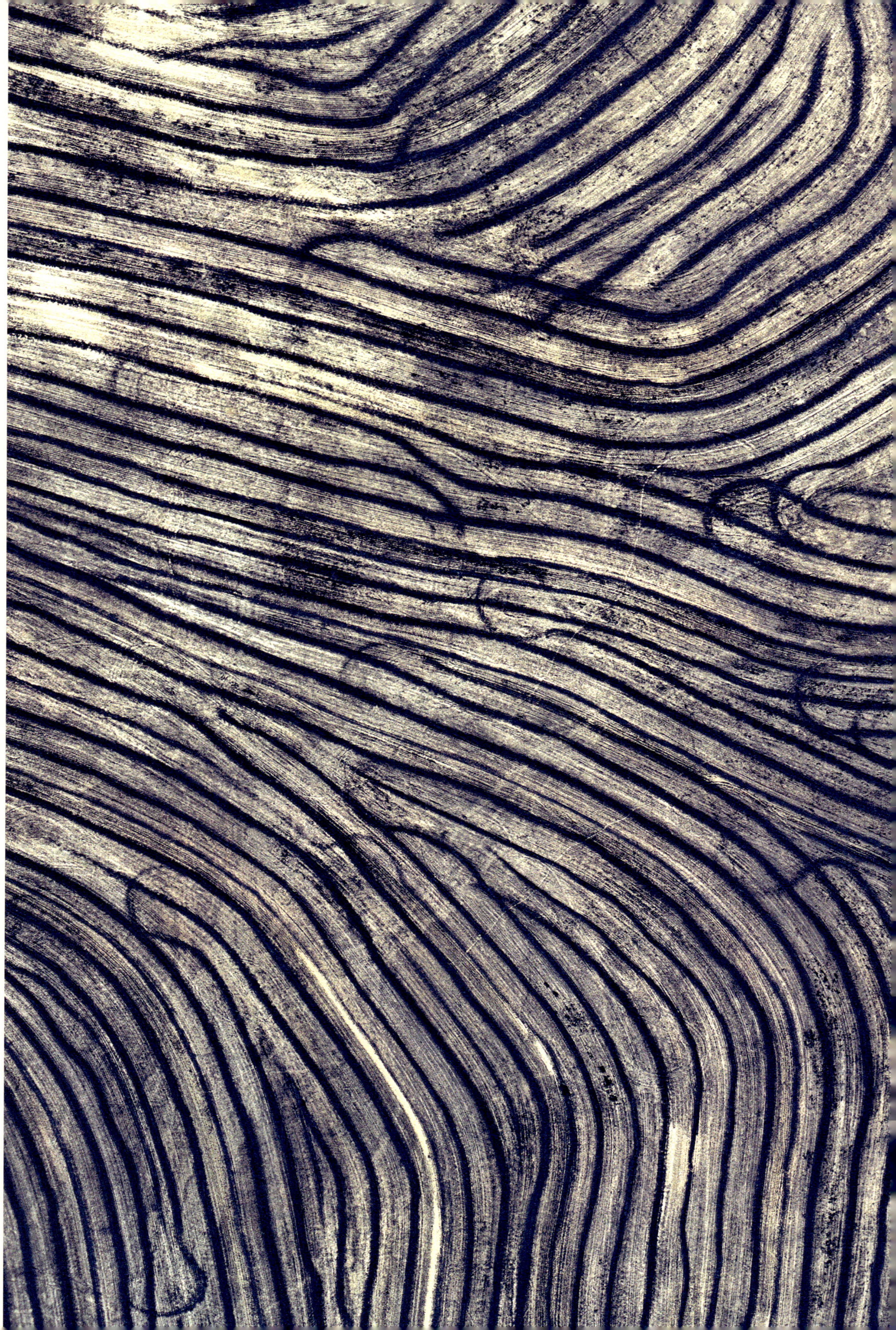

← The art of burning
→ Burned land

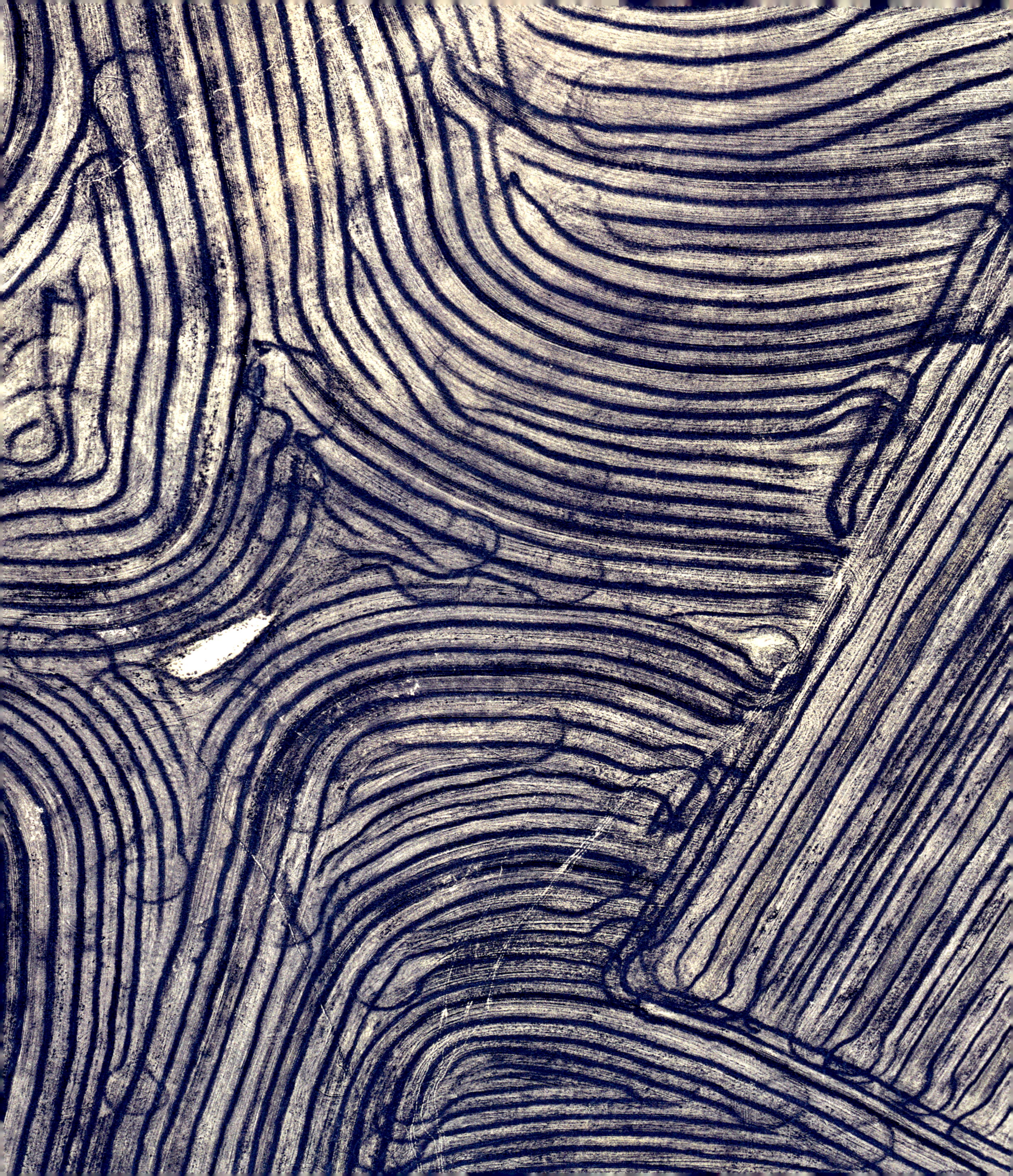

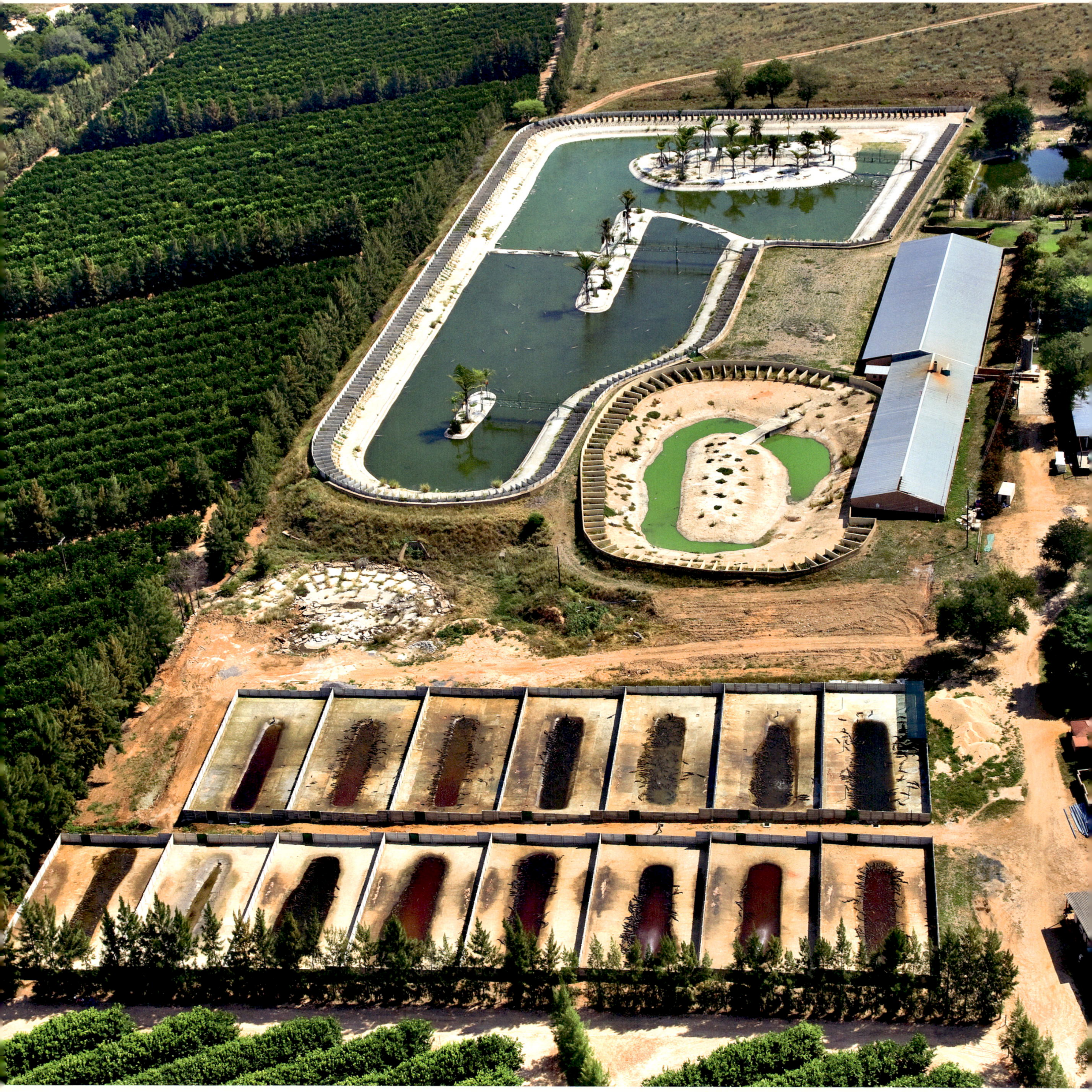

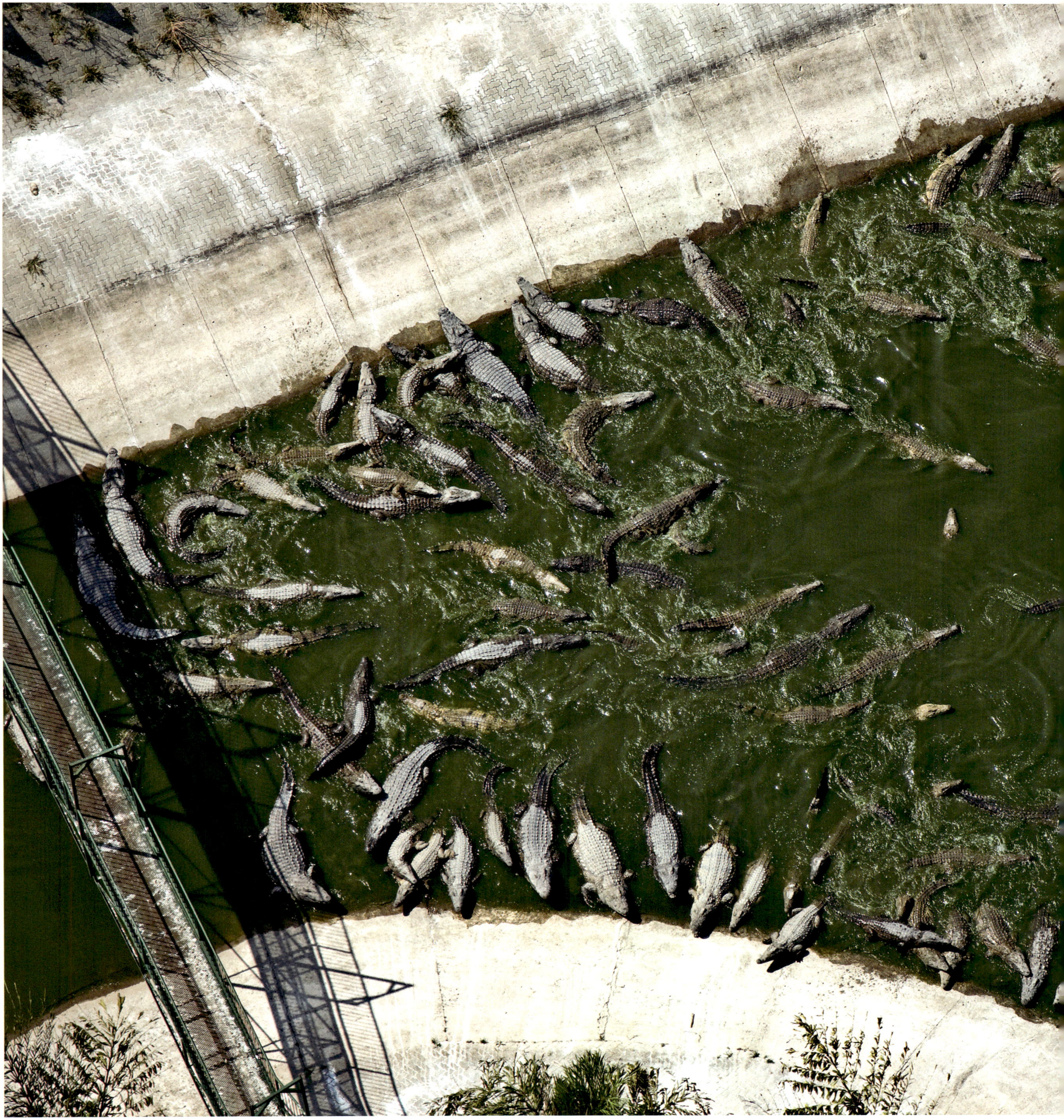

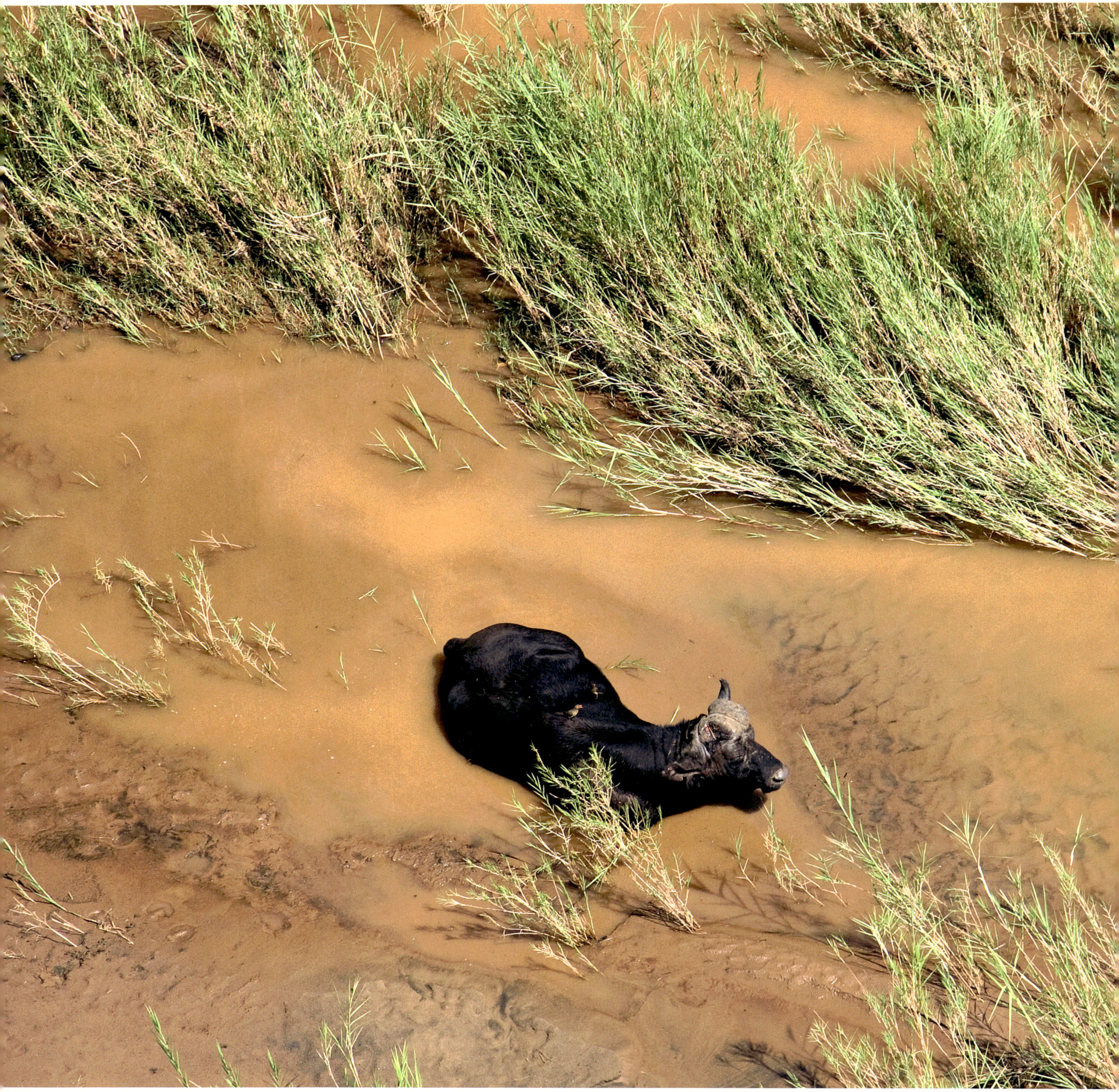

←↓ Elephants River, west side Kruger Park

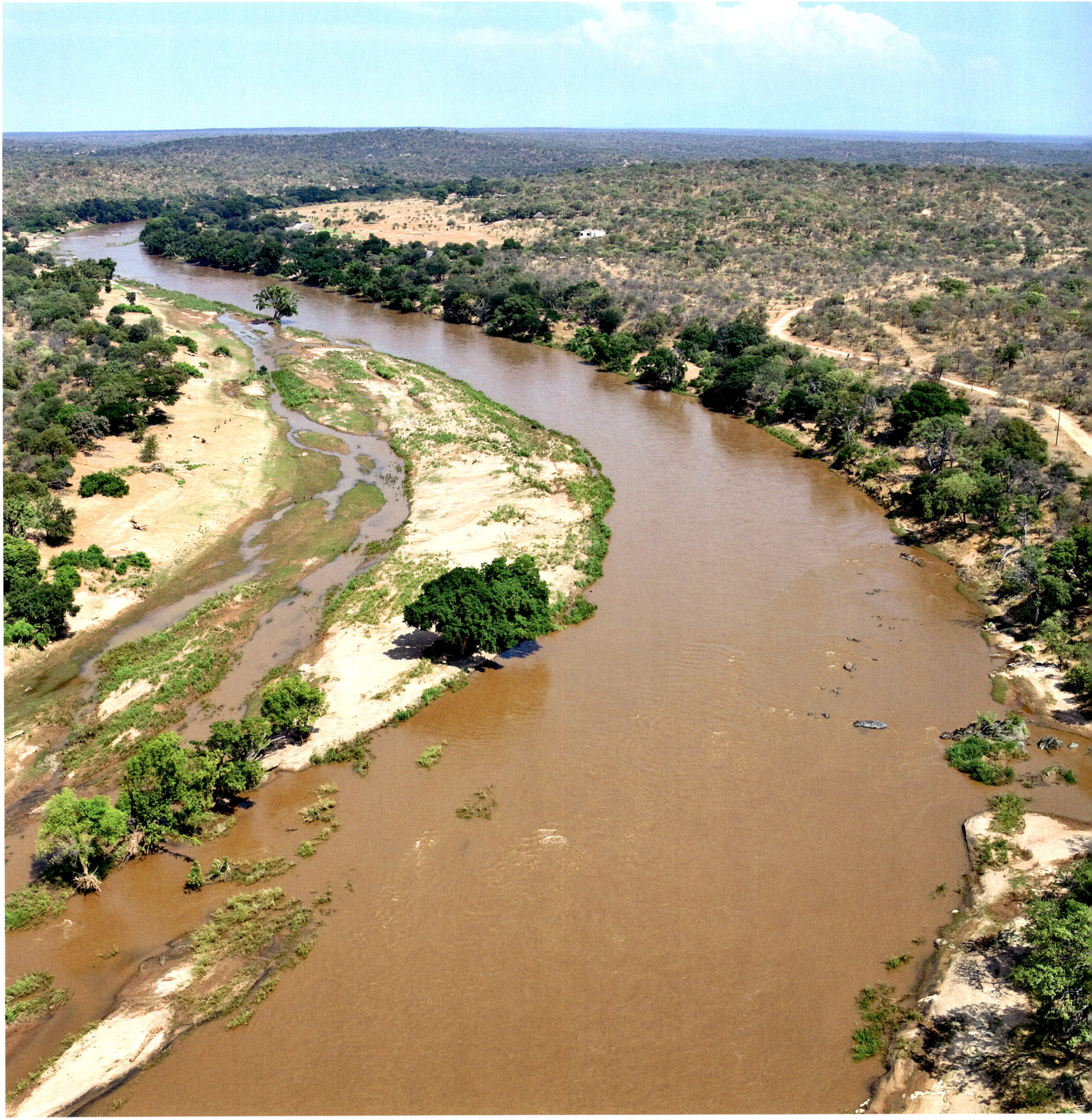

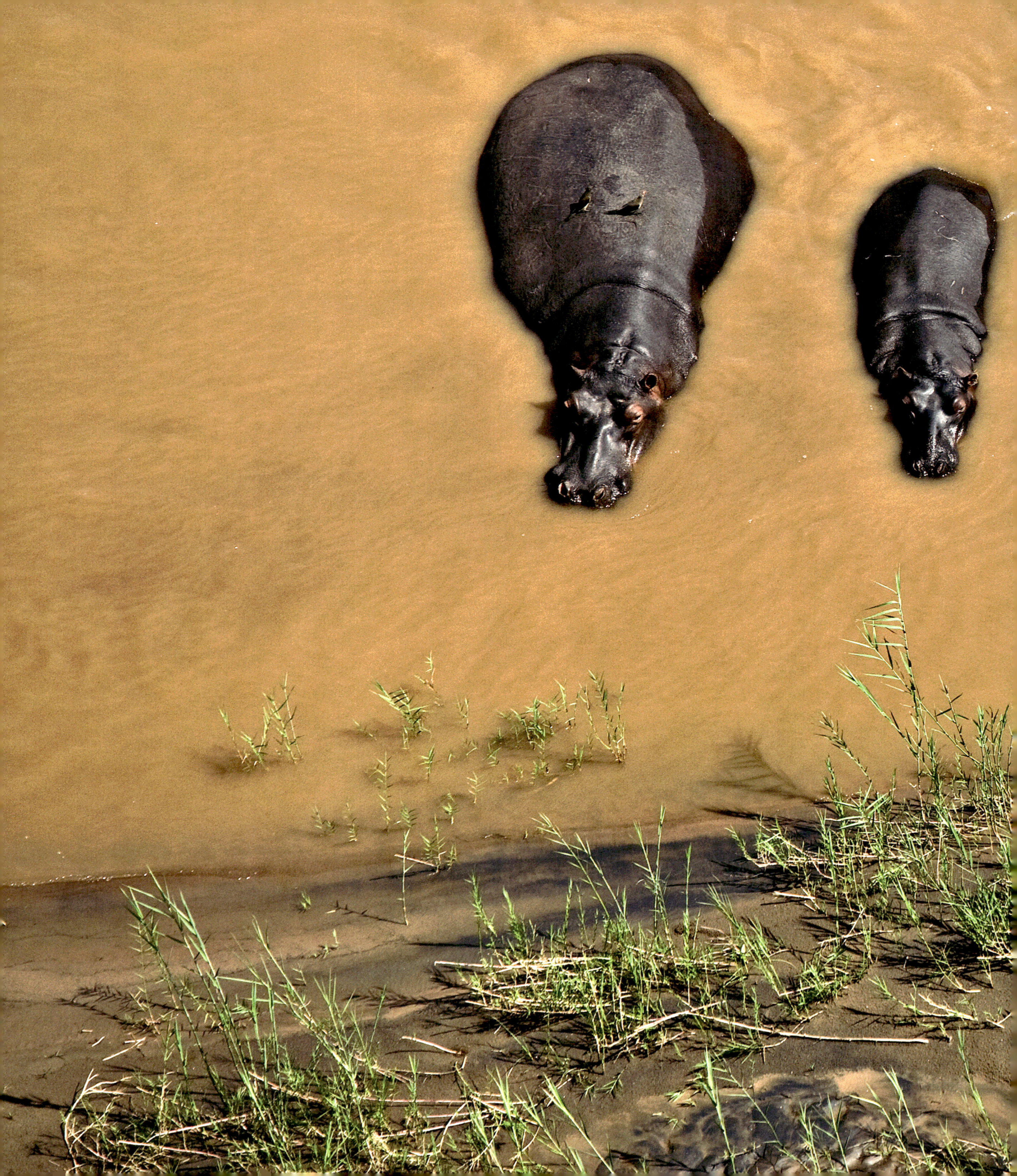

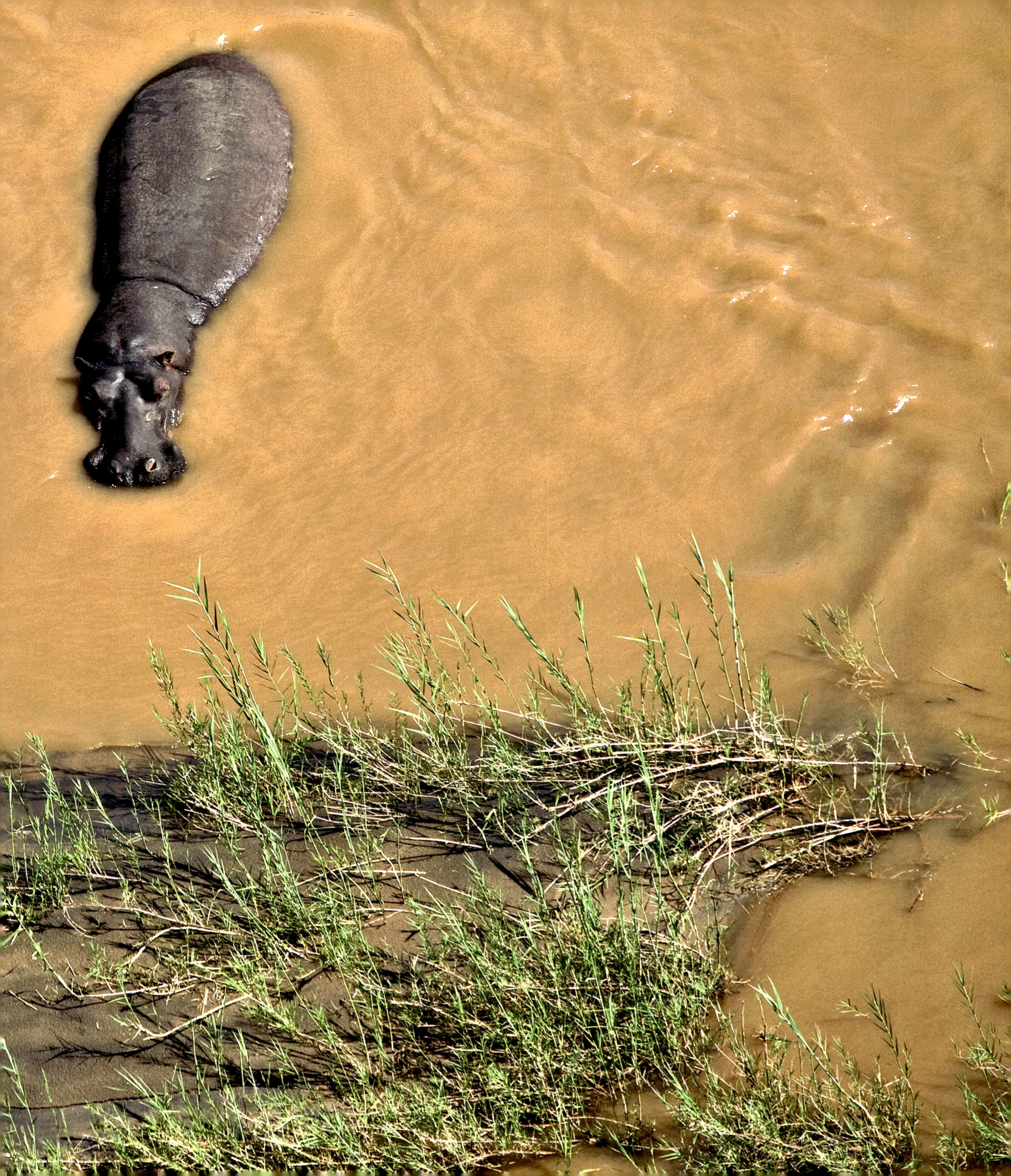

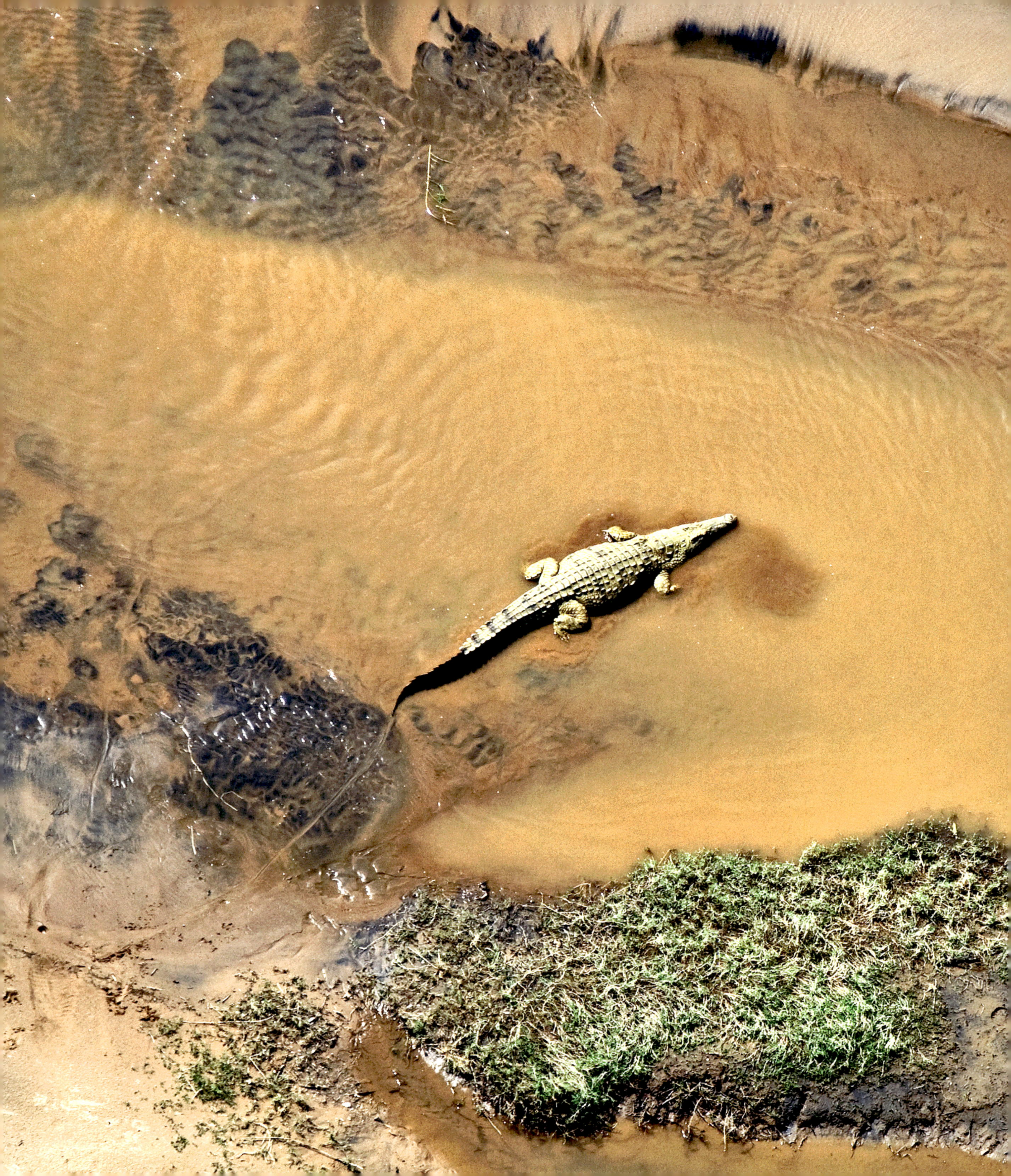

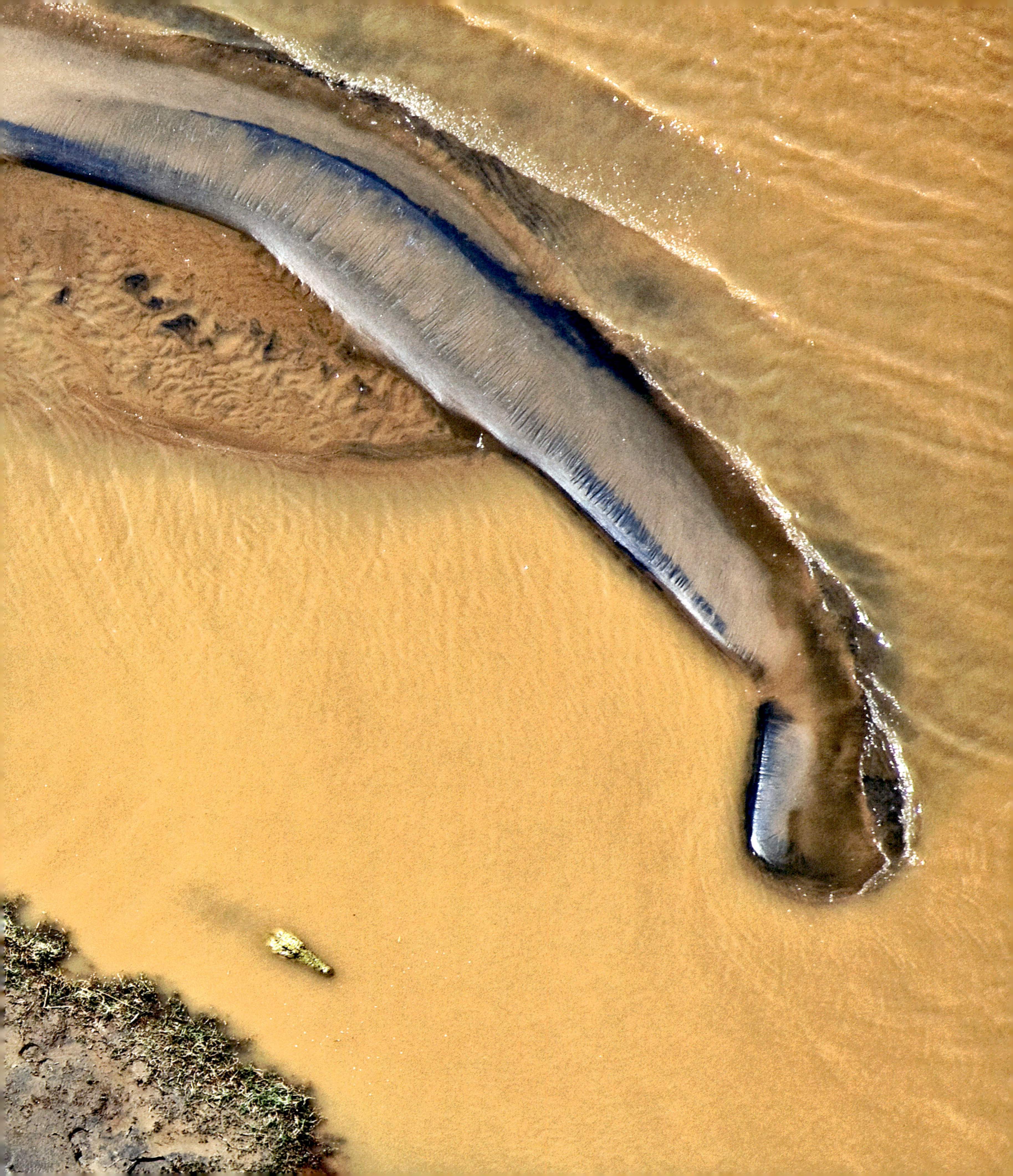

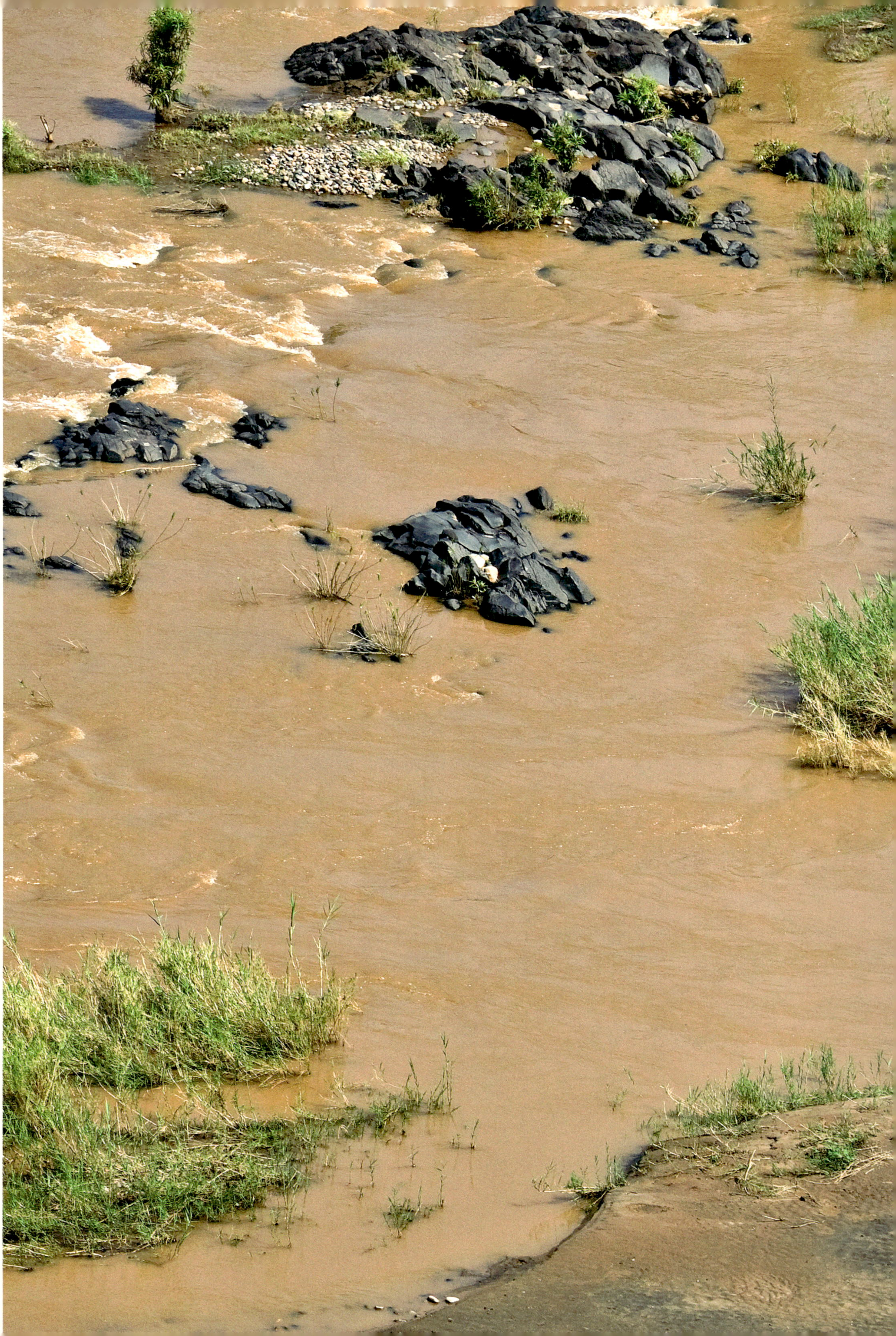

Elephants River:
←← Hippopotamuses
← Crocodile
→ Elephant

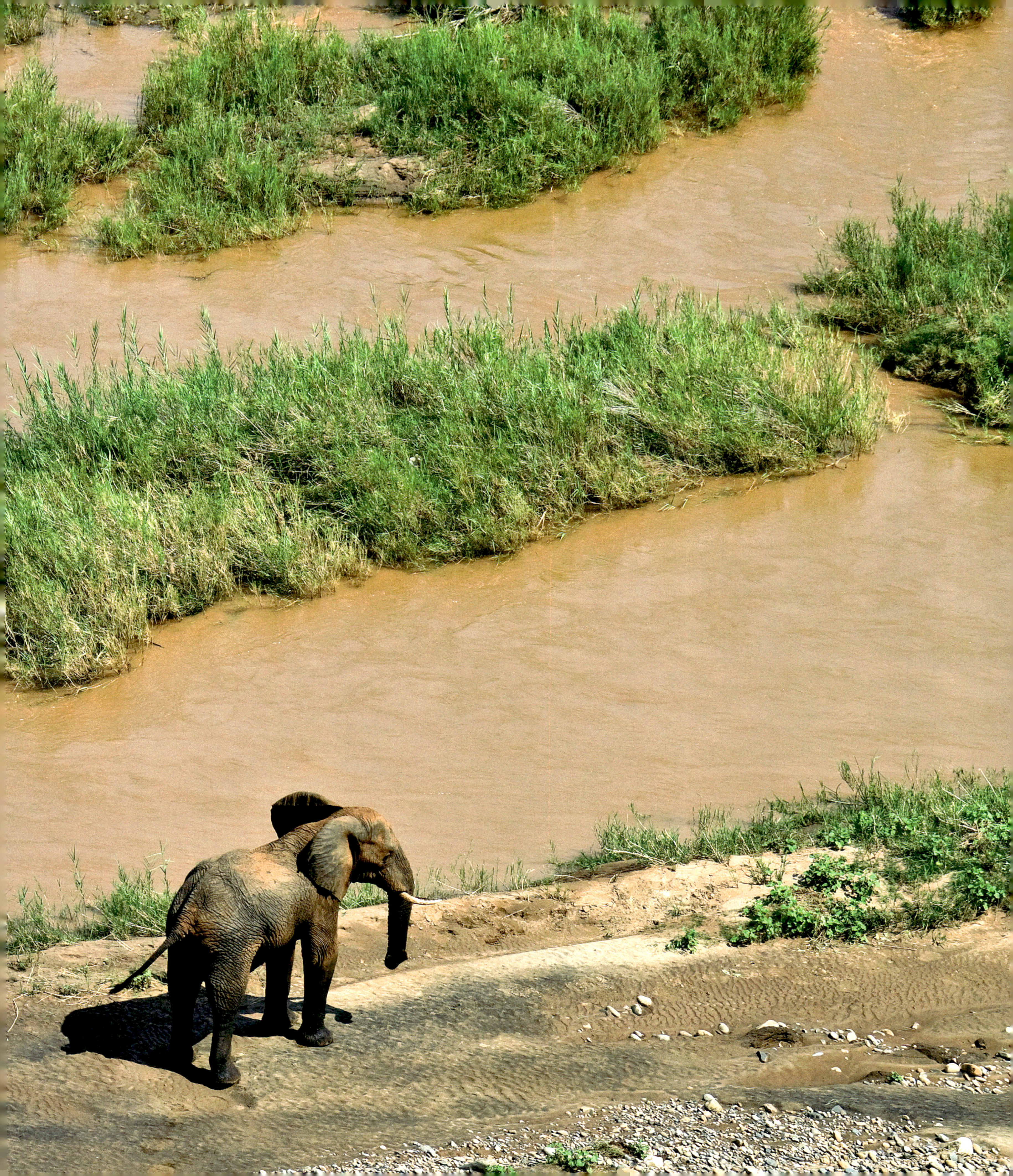

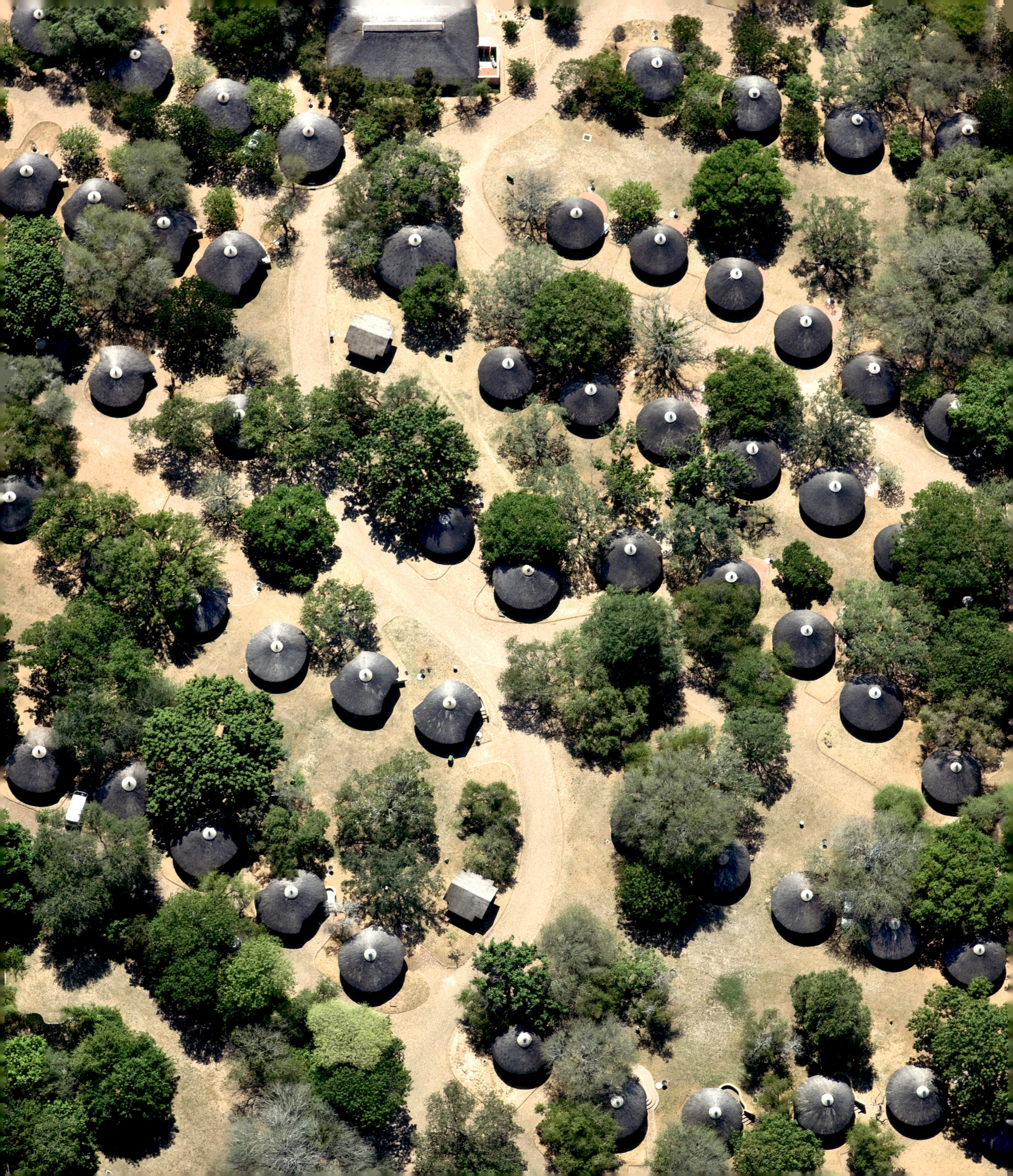

MPUMALANGA

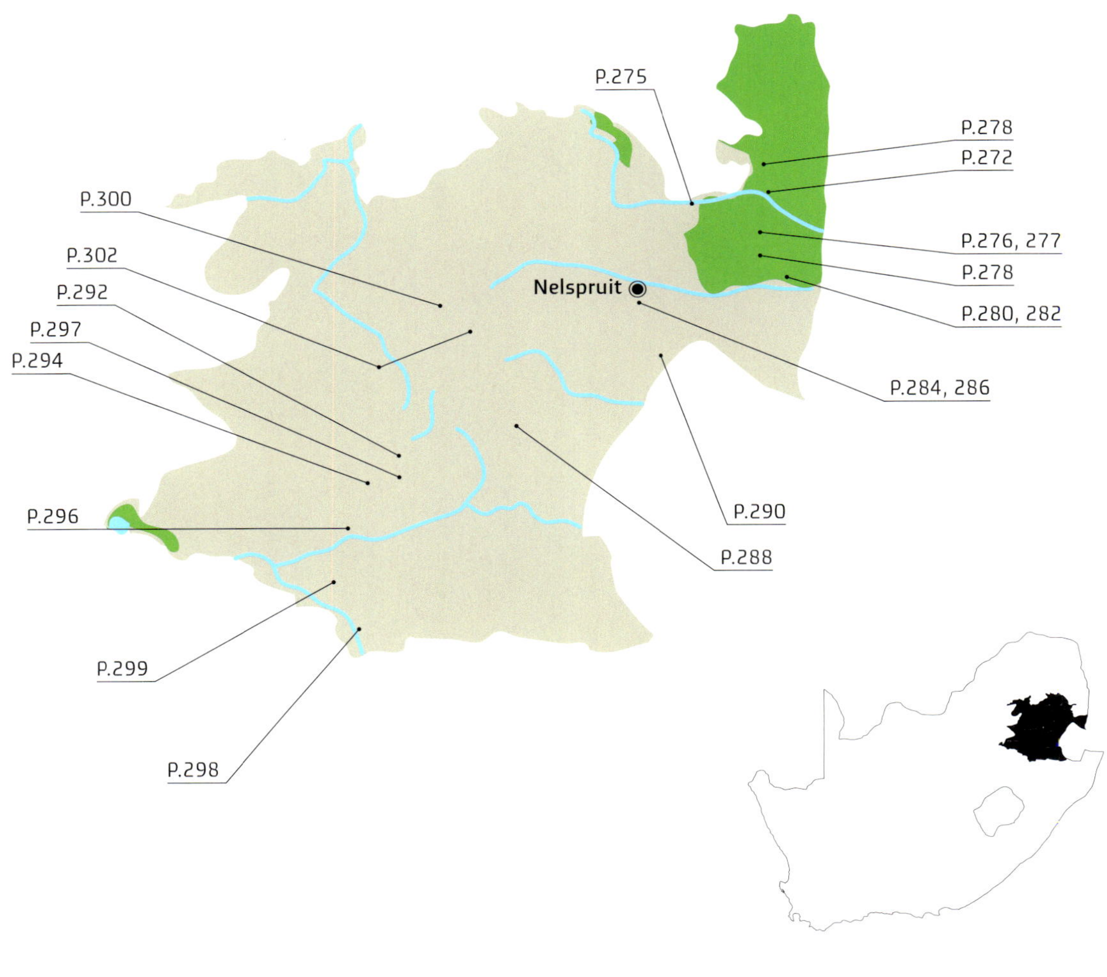
P.275
P.278
P.272
P.300
P.302
P.276, 277
P.278
Nelspruit
P.280, 282
P.292
P.297
P.294
P.284, 286
P.290
P.296
P.288
P.299
P.298

There is an old South African saying: 'Where elephants fight, no grass will grow'. But even if they are not fighting, they can still often cause problems. A herd of elephants eats so much grass, leaves and bark every day that virtually nothing is left for other grazers. No wonder then that elephant management is an important business in South Africa's nature reserves. And that applies more to Mpumalanga than anywhere else, for more than three quarters of the South African elephant population lives within the boundaries of Kruger National Park. The park has experimented with contraceptives, without any great success, and has been an important exporter of elephants for years. That, too, has so far had little effect. Elephants shipped over the border into Mozambique promptly did an about-turn and were back in the park in no time. In short, if you want to see elephants, you'll be in your element in Kruger Park: there are an estimated 12,000 of these magnificent beasts roaming around.

The place where the sun rises

Mpumalanga, a Zulu word that means 'the place where the sun rises', is a province with enormous variations in landscape. The western part is highveld, pastures 1500 metres above sea-level with temperate summers and cold winters. The east is made up of sub-tropical savannah-like lowveld, which extends to the border with Mozambique.

The province is rich in minerals, although not as rich as people thought and hoped in the past. At the start of the 18th century, the Dutch United East India Company searched here for the legendary kingdom of Monomotapa, and when that proved elusive, new rumours emerged that King Solomon's mines could be found here. Gold deposits were eventually discovered in Mpumalanga, but they proved smaller and less abundant than the gold fields around Johannesburg. And although gold is still mined, mainly in the surroundings of Barberton, coal is now by far the most important mineral in Mpumalanga.

Until the late 19th century, the lowveld formed a natural barrier for Afrikaner Boers who were moving north, and many succumbed to malaria. Nevertheless, the hunger for land drove the Boers ever farther northwards. Names such as Lydenburg ('town of suffering') and Treurrivier ('river of mourning') are reminders of the deprivations to which the Boers exposed themselves.

The search for Monomotapa and King Solomon's mines... Mpumalanga has always been shrouded in a cloak of mystery. And it still is. Is this where a seafaring Hindu nation built an advanced civilisation thousands of years ago? And who were the mysterious strangers dressed in white who, long ago, traded with the inhabitants of the Echo Caves?

Mpumalanga has not yet given up all its secrets.

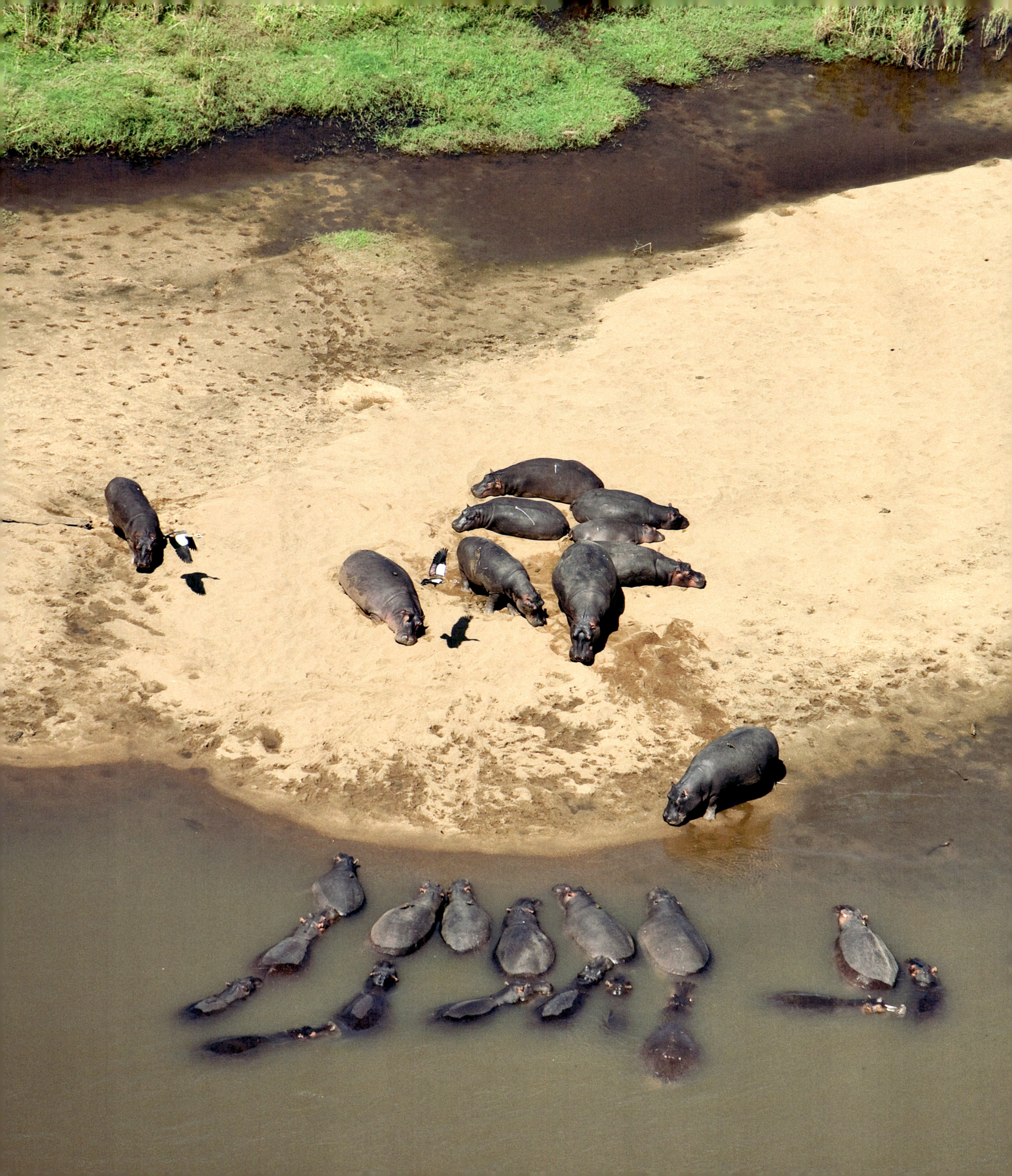

↓ Rhinos, Kruger National Park
→ Elephants during a hot dry day, Kruger National Park

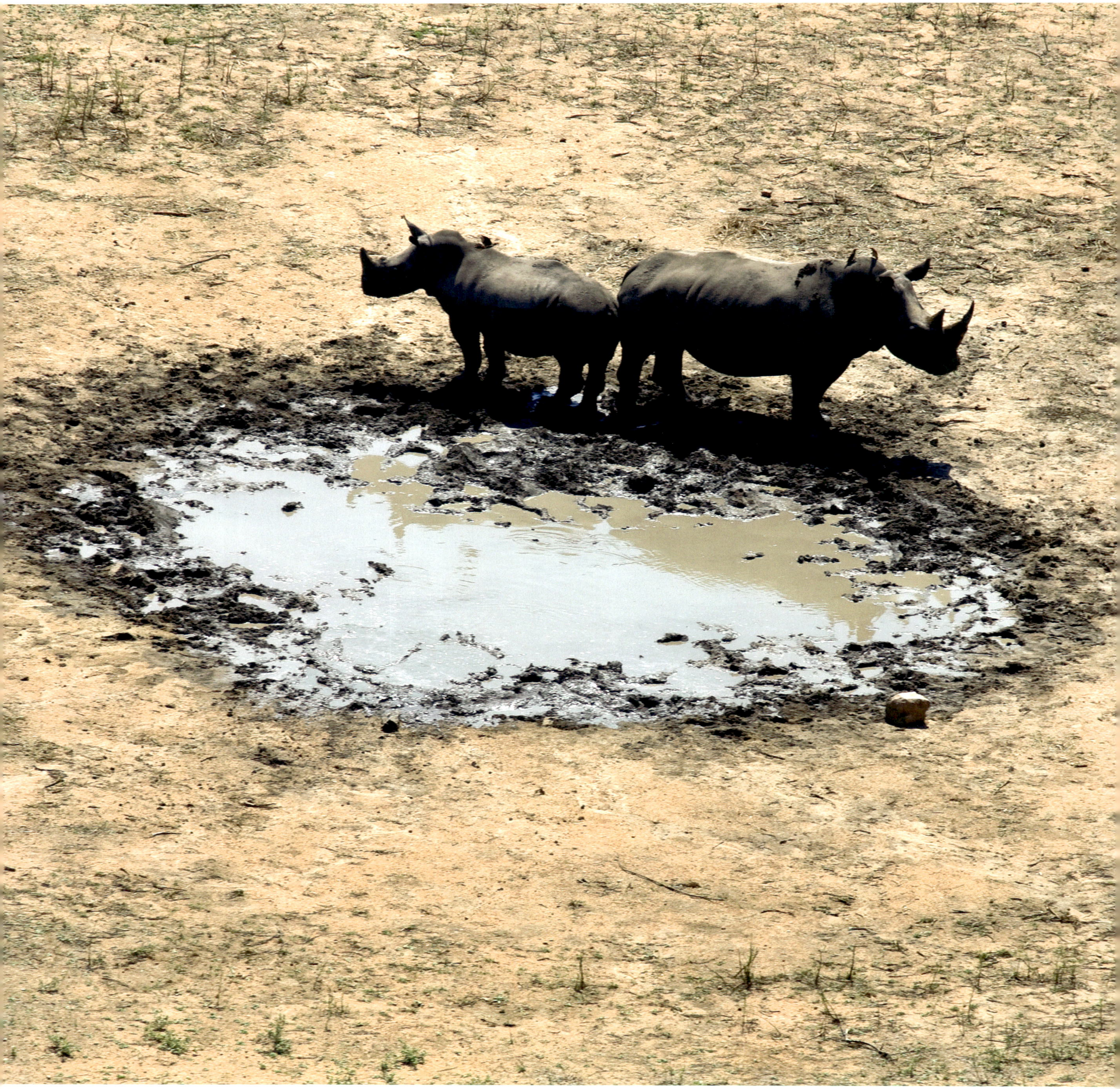

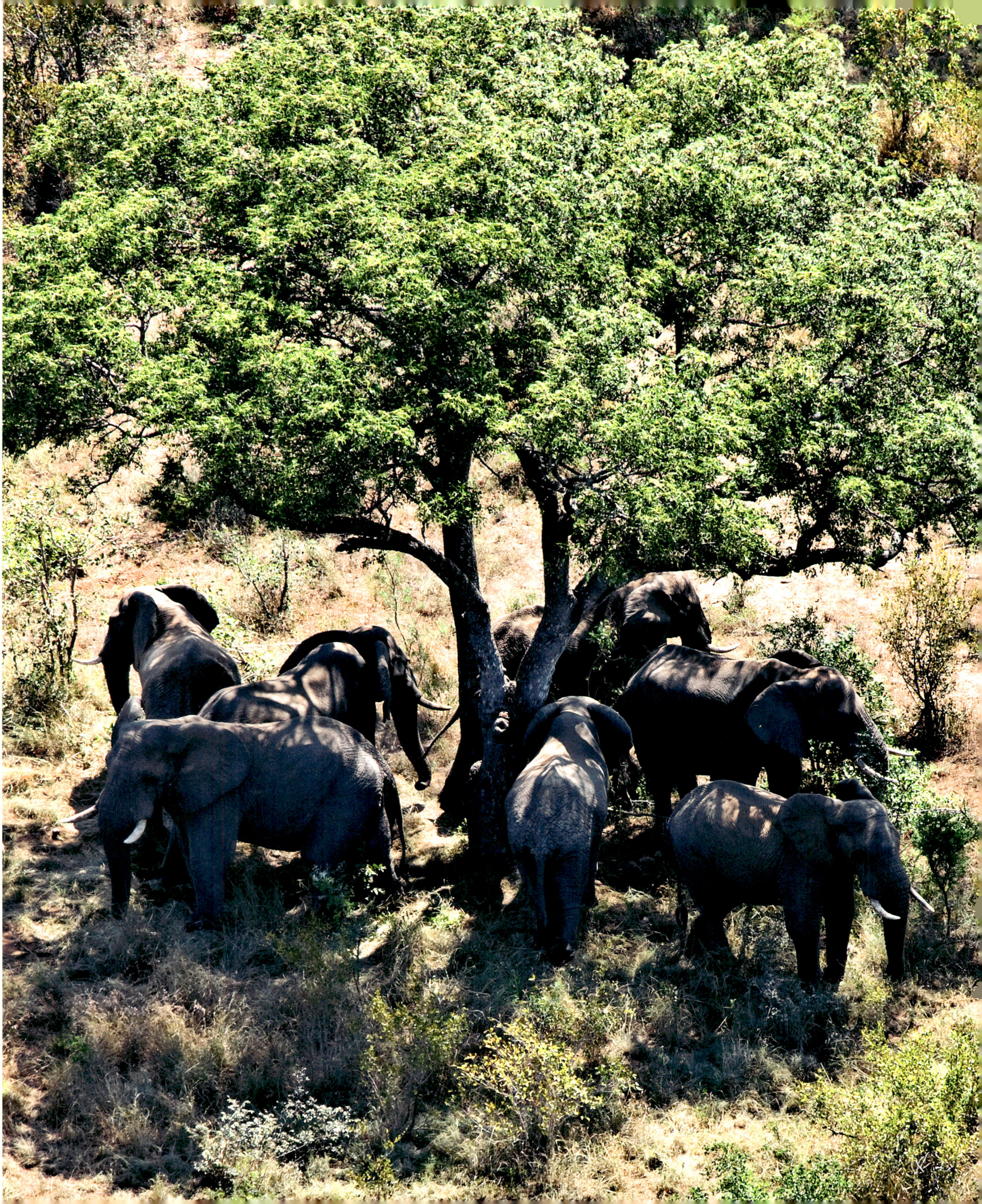

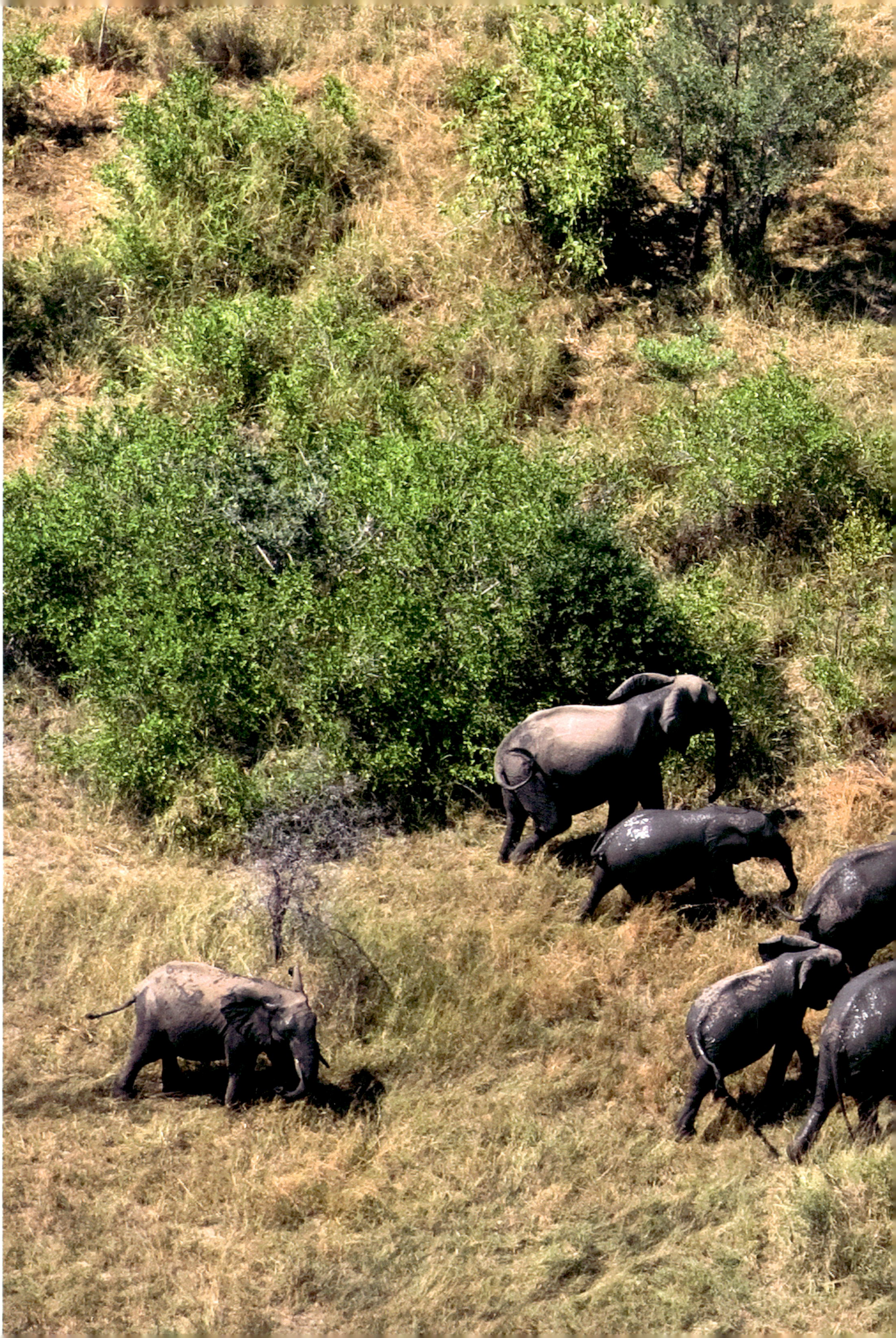

→ Elephants after a bath,
Kruger National Park

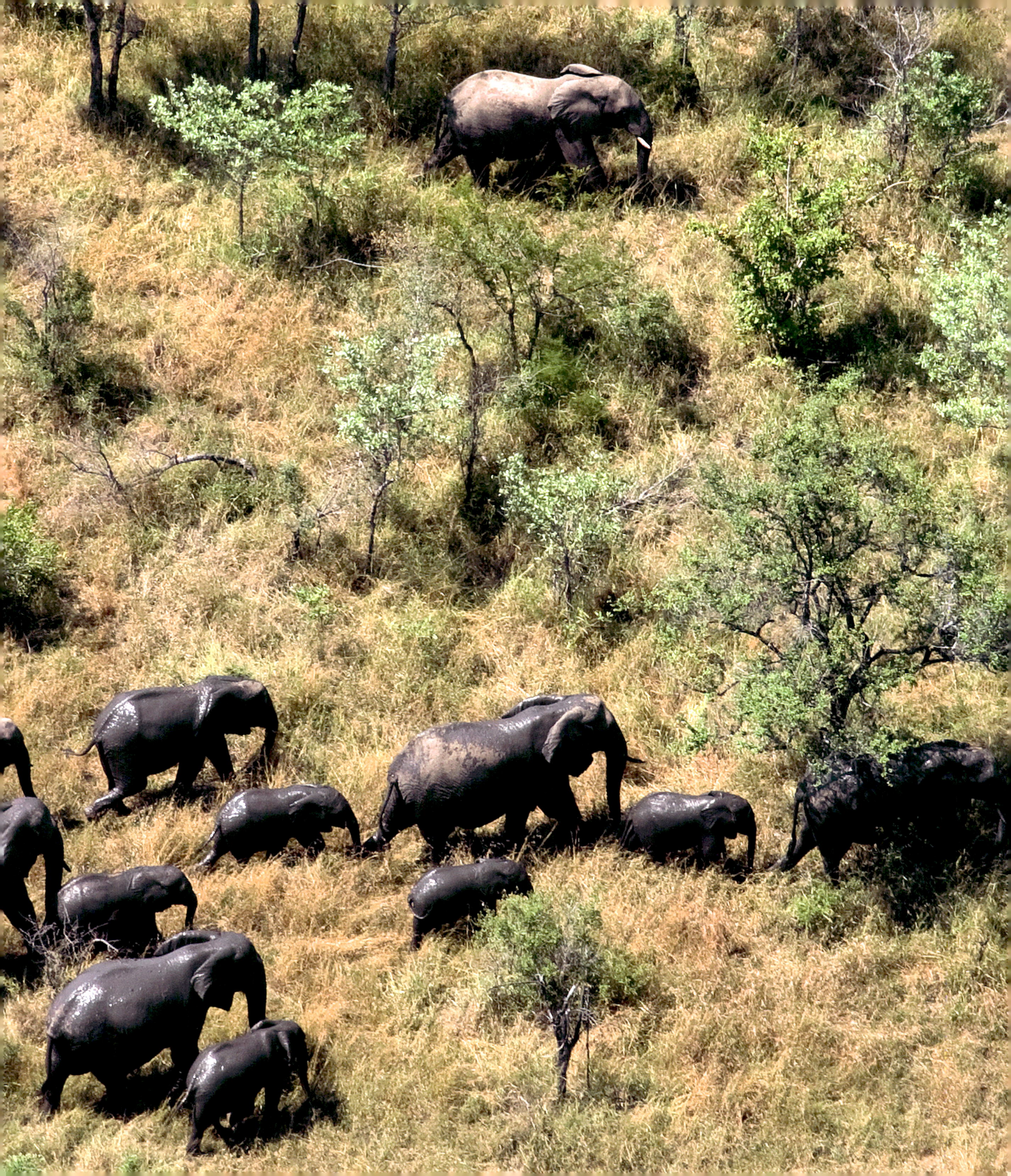

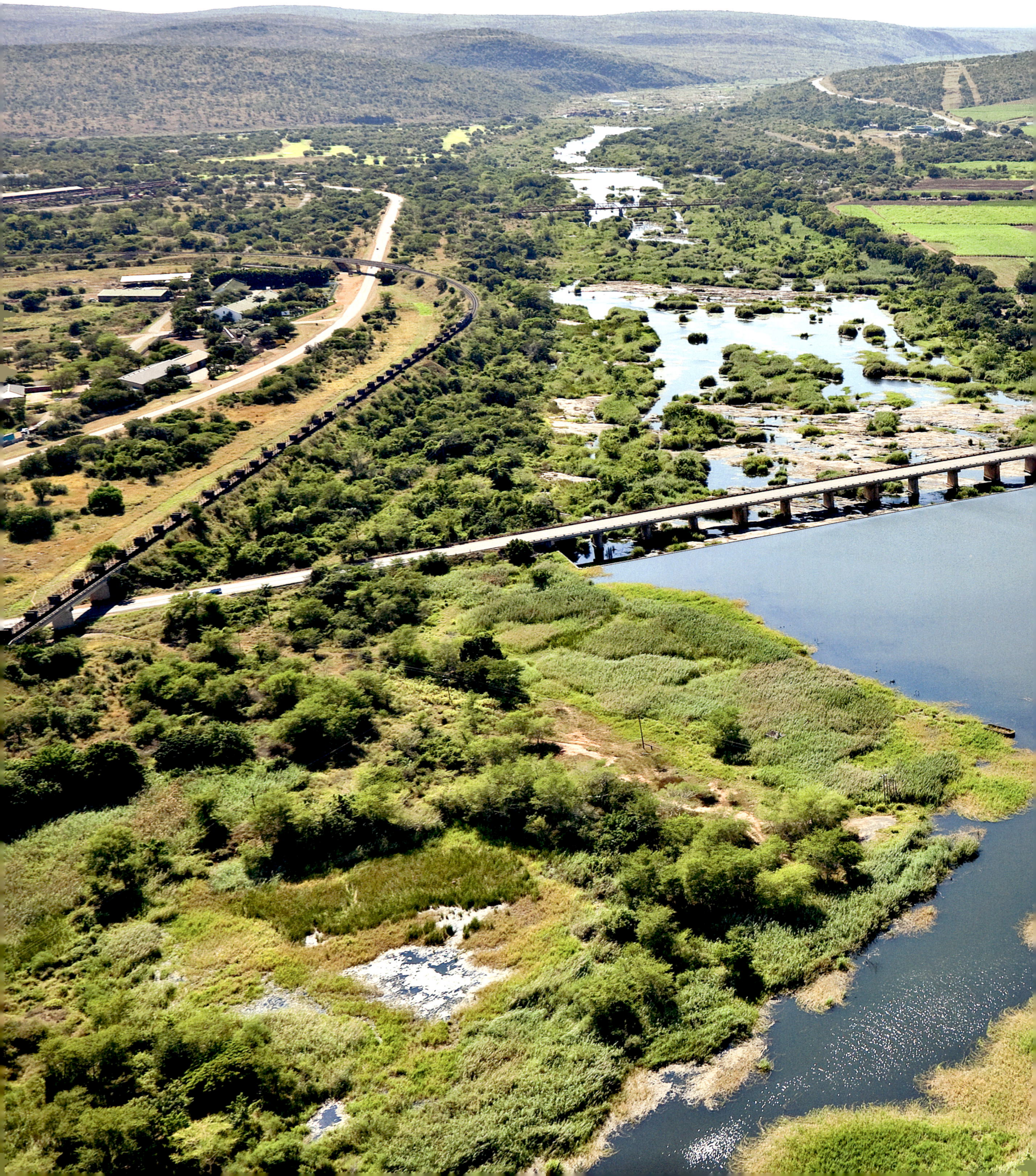

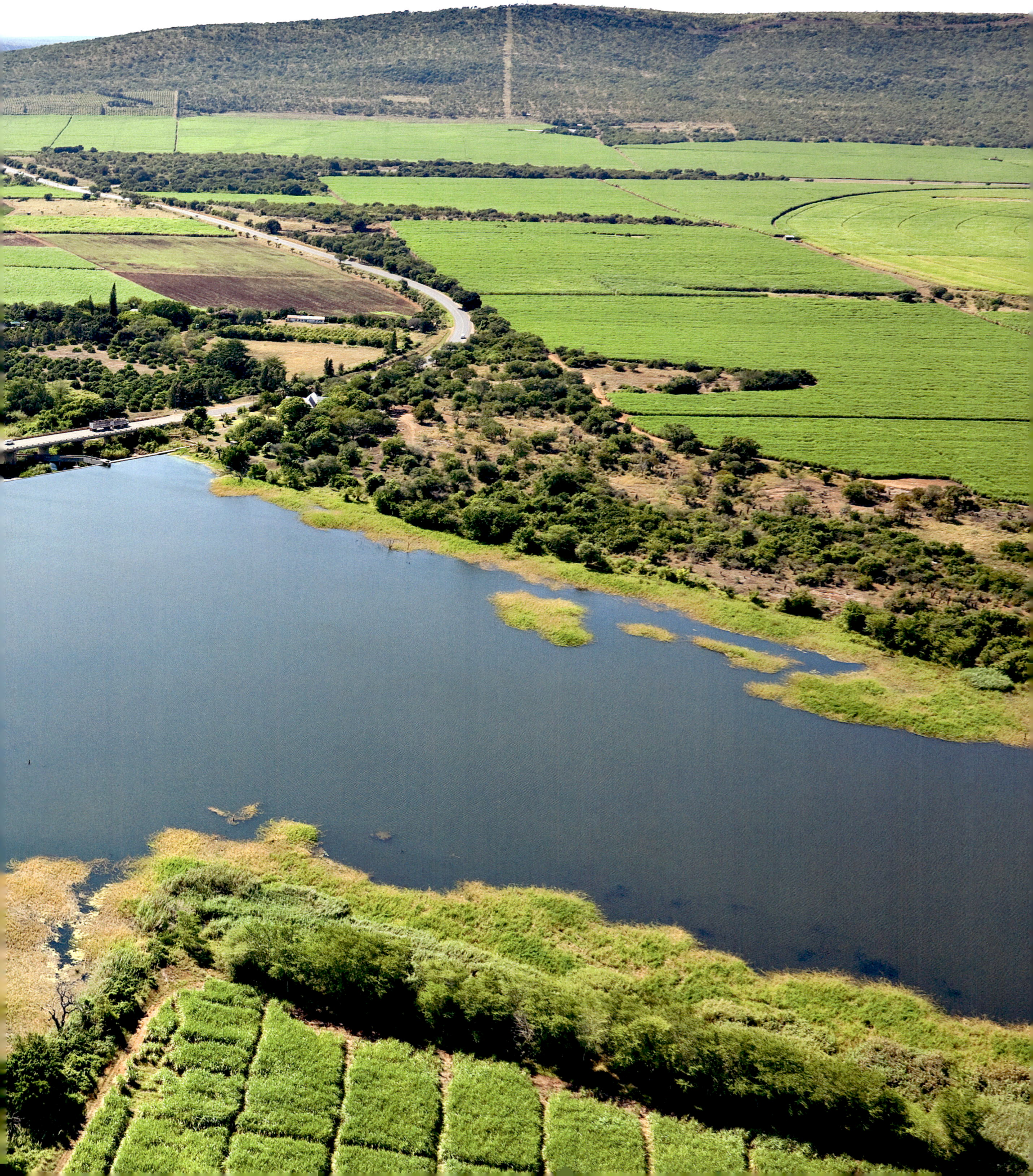

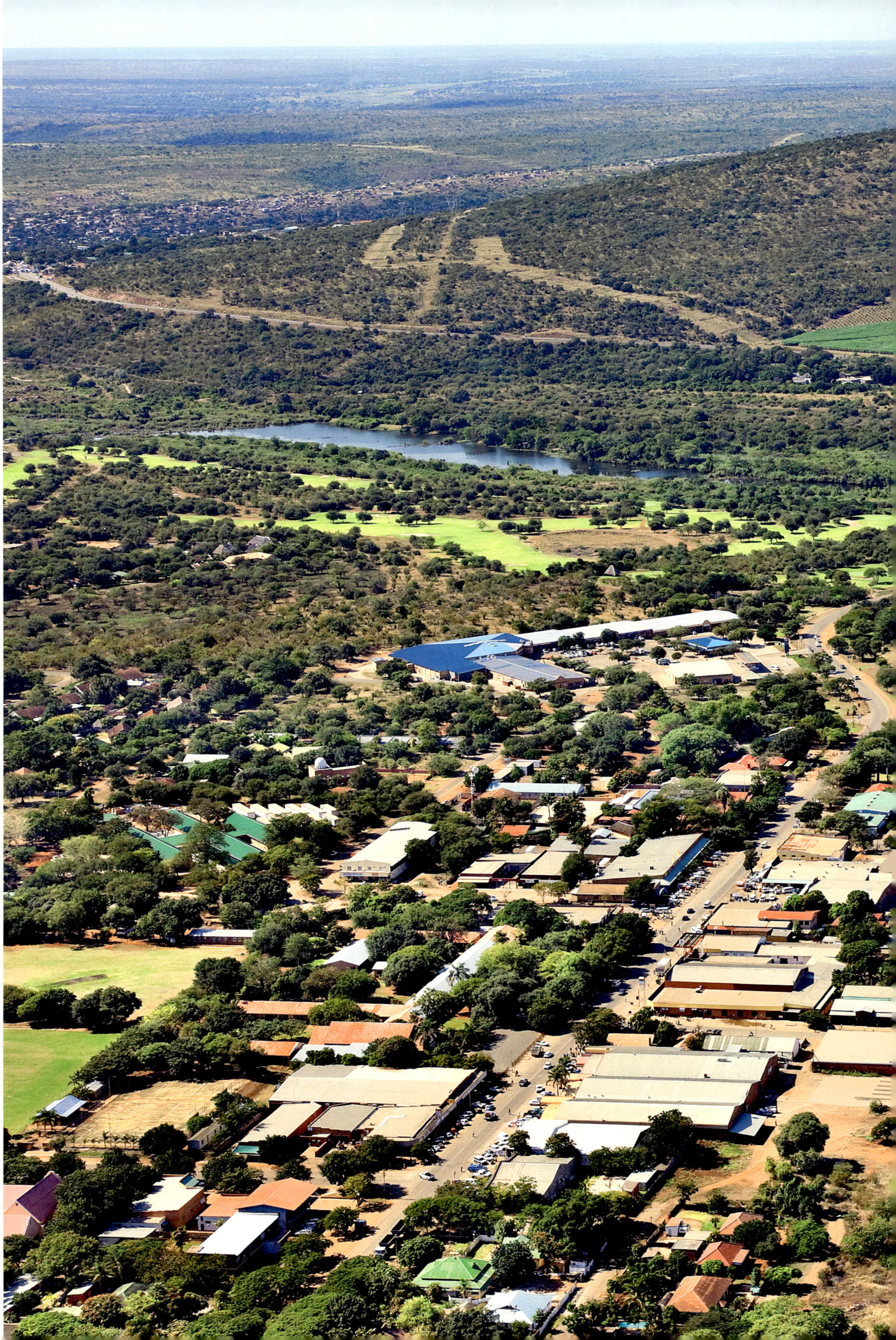

←→ Border between Mozambique and South Africa, Komatipoort

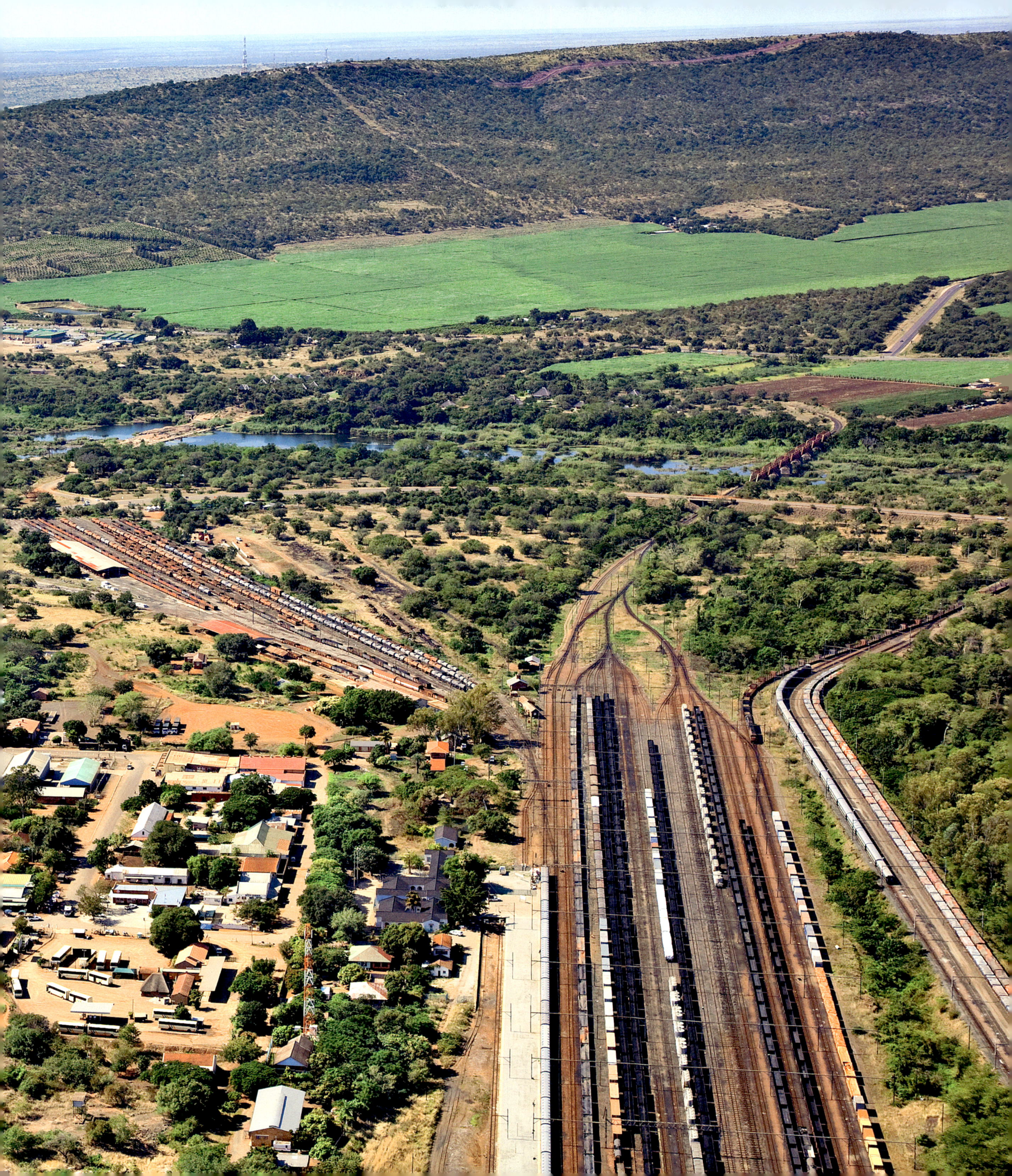

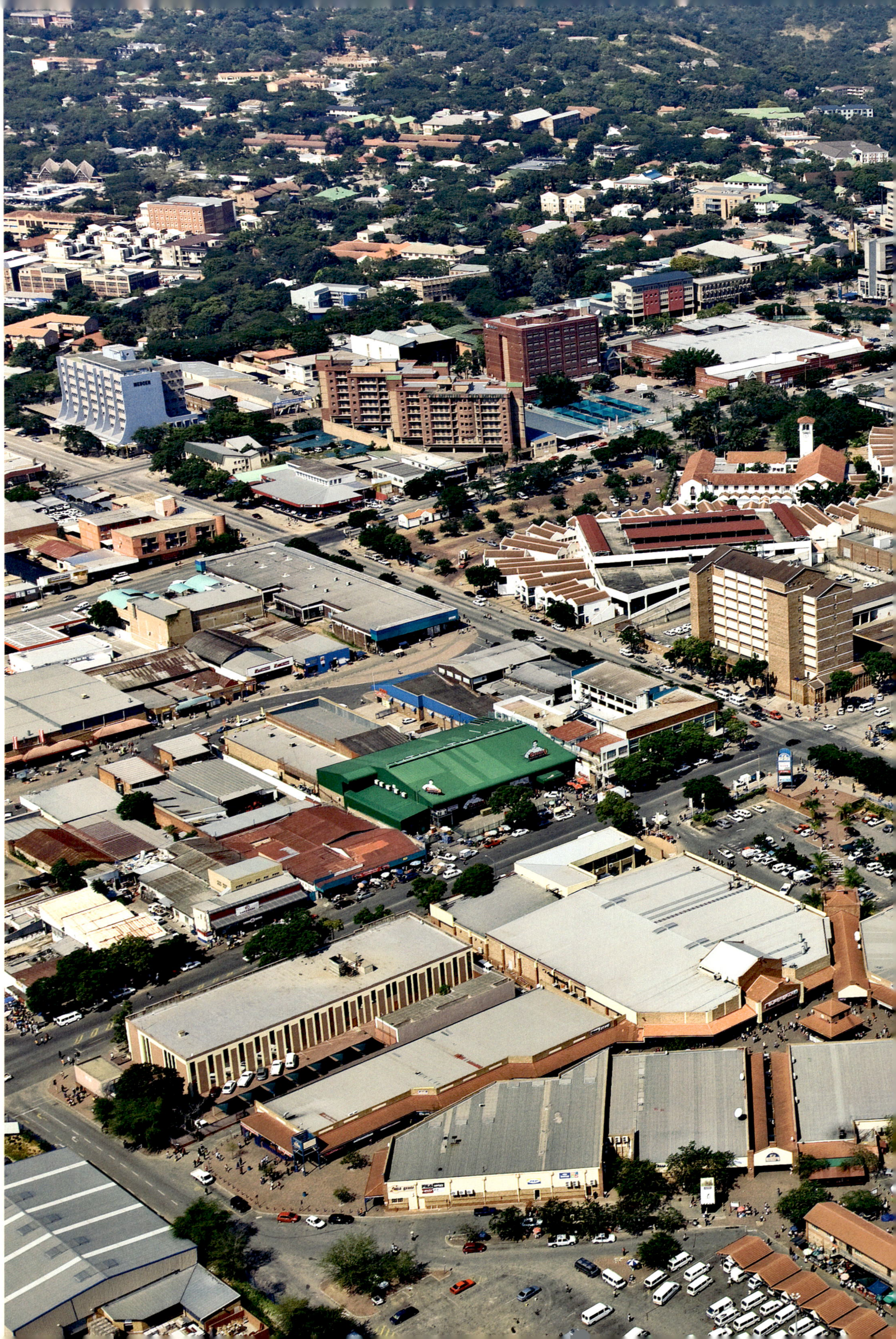

→ Nelspruit

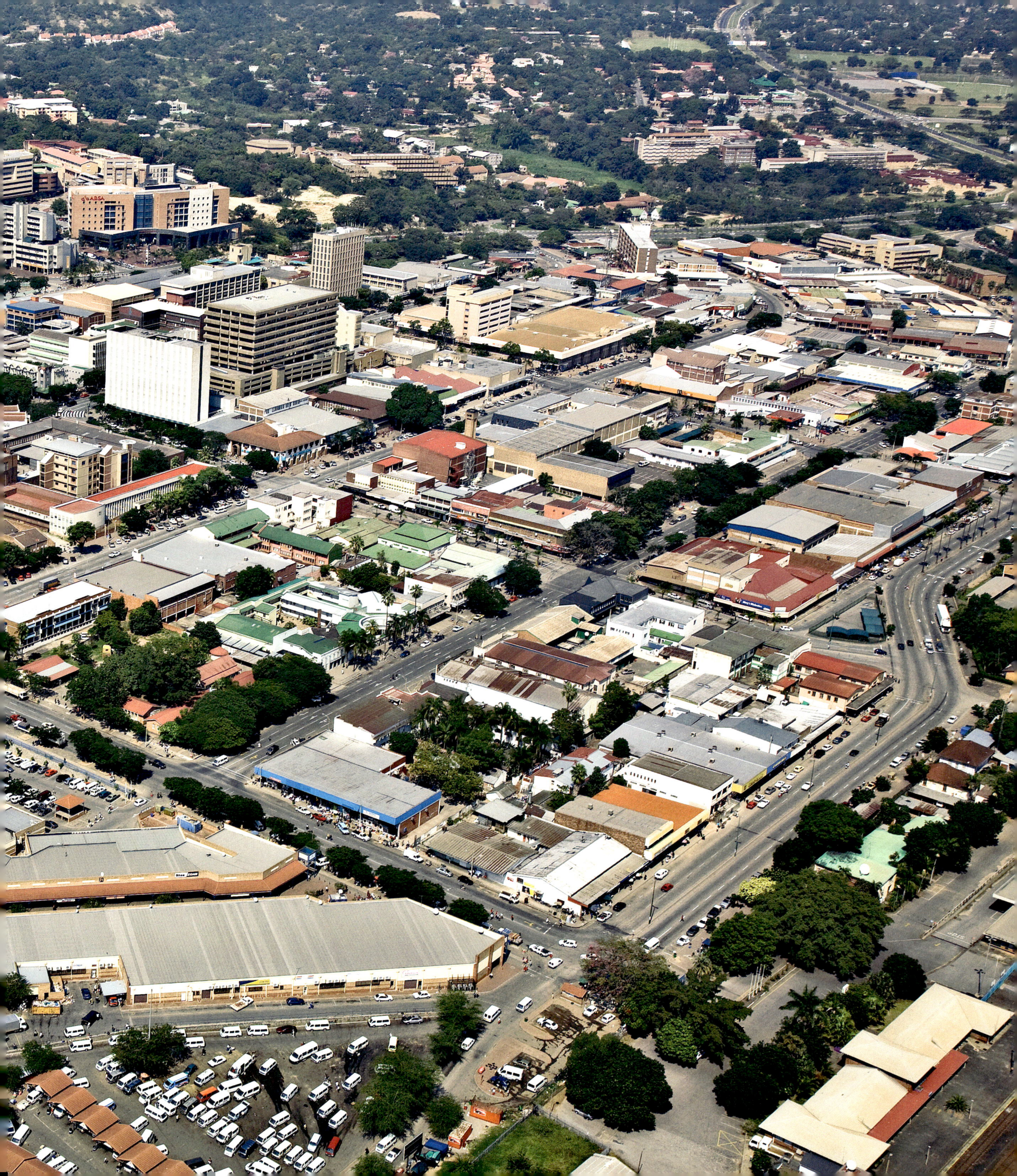

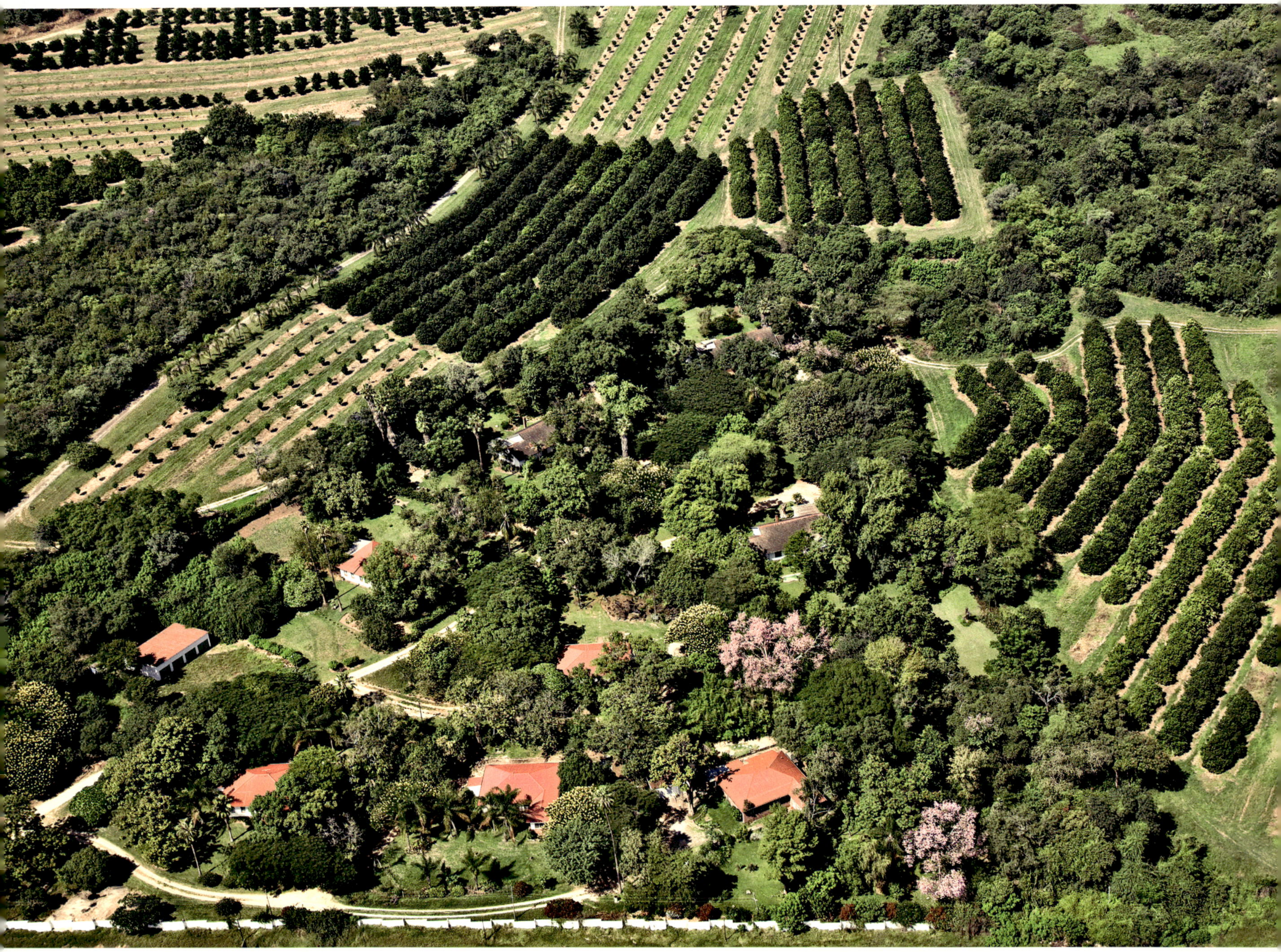

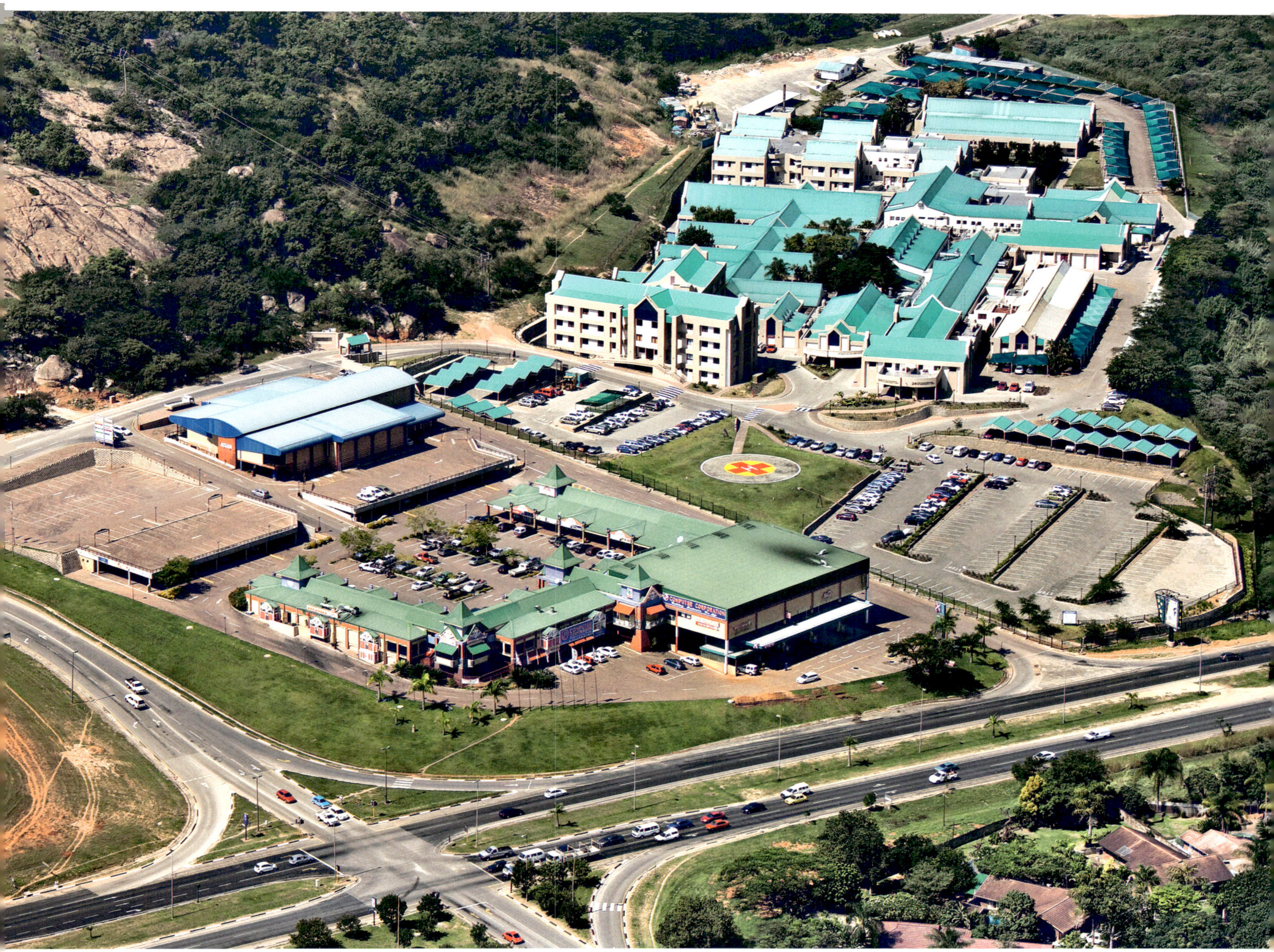

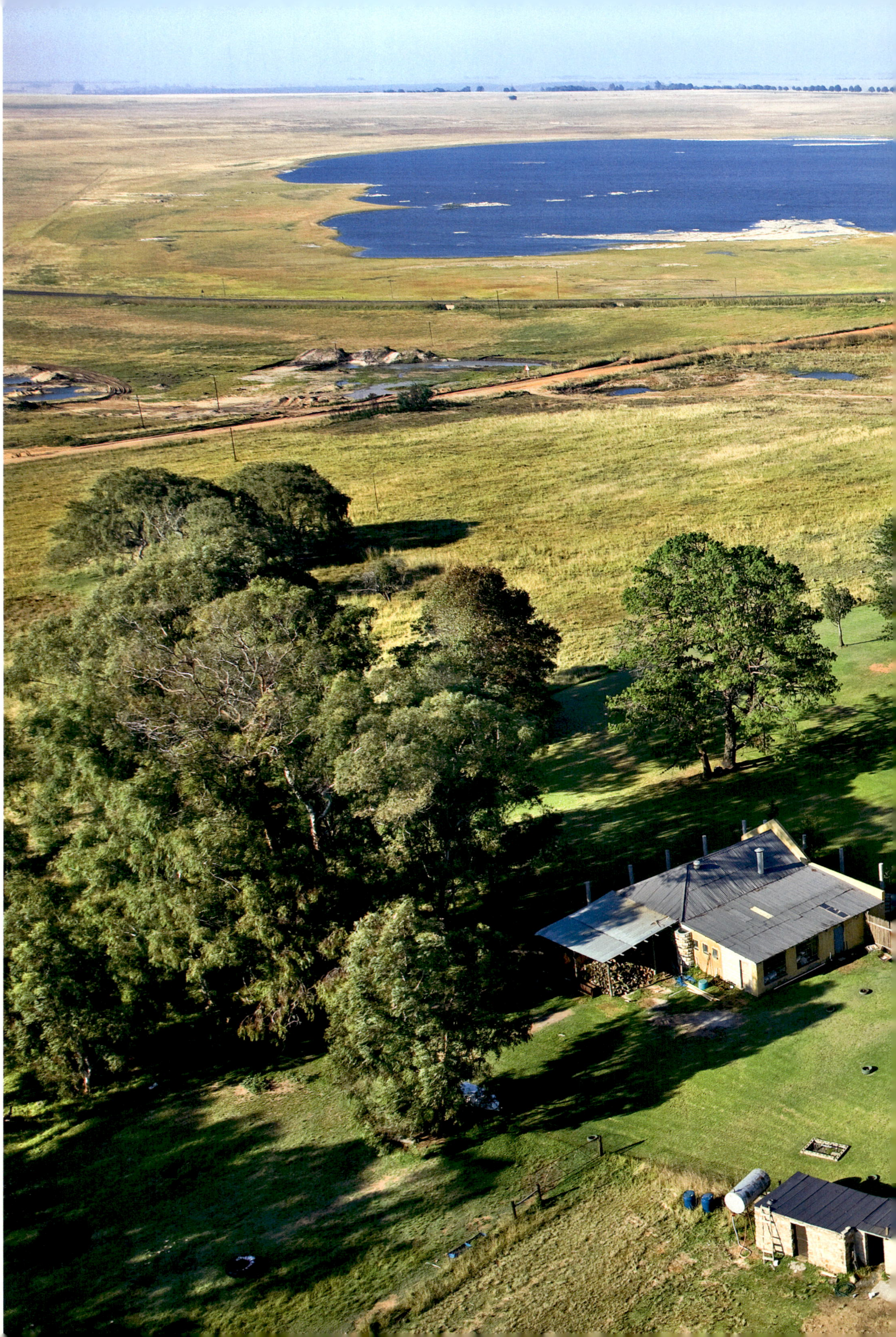

→ Florence Guest Farm
with Lake Chrissiesmeer

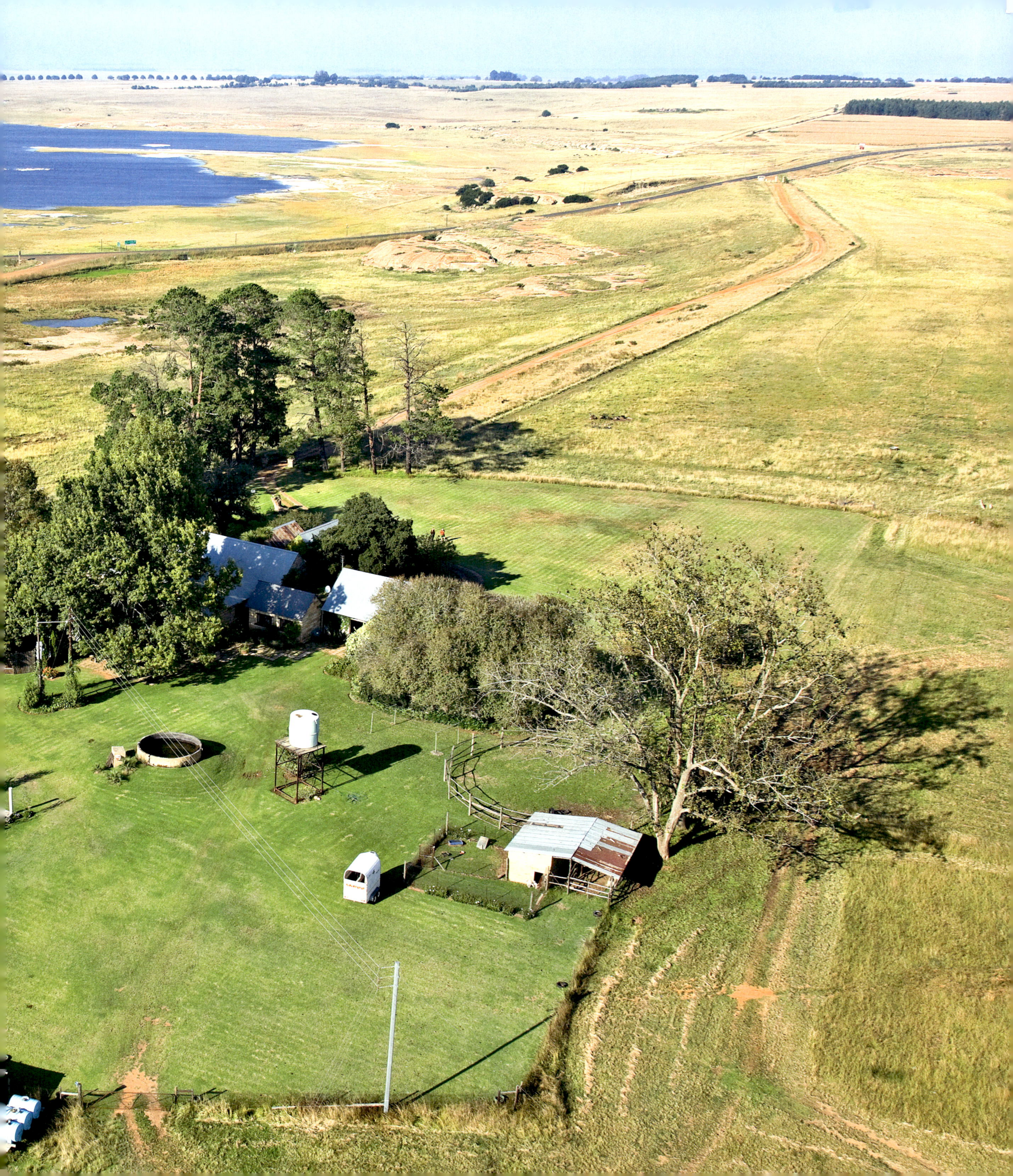

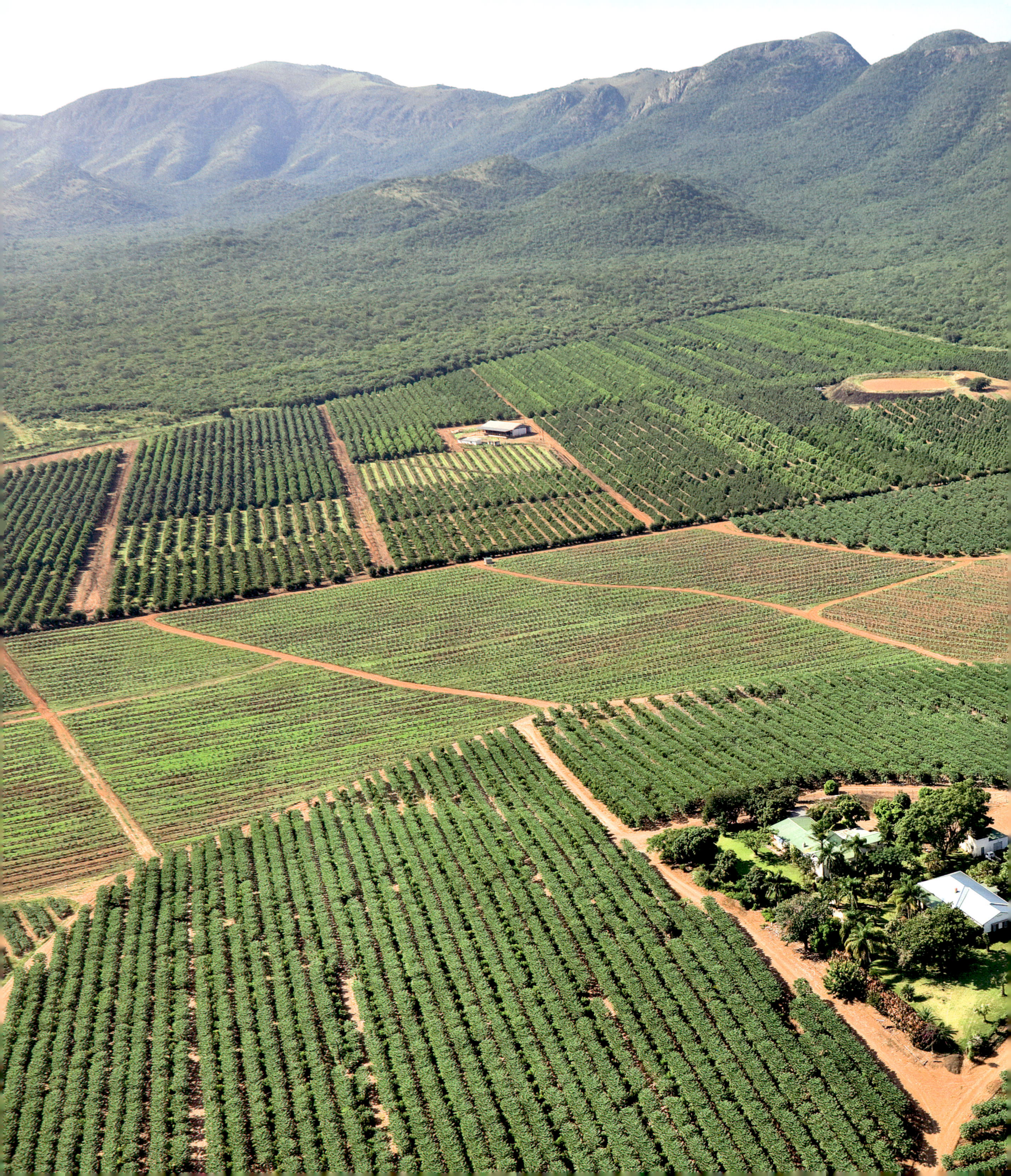

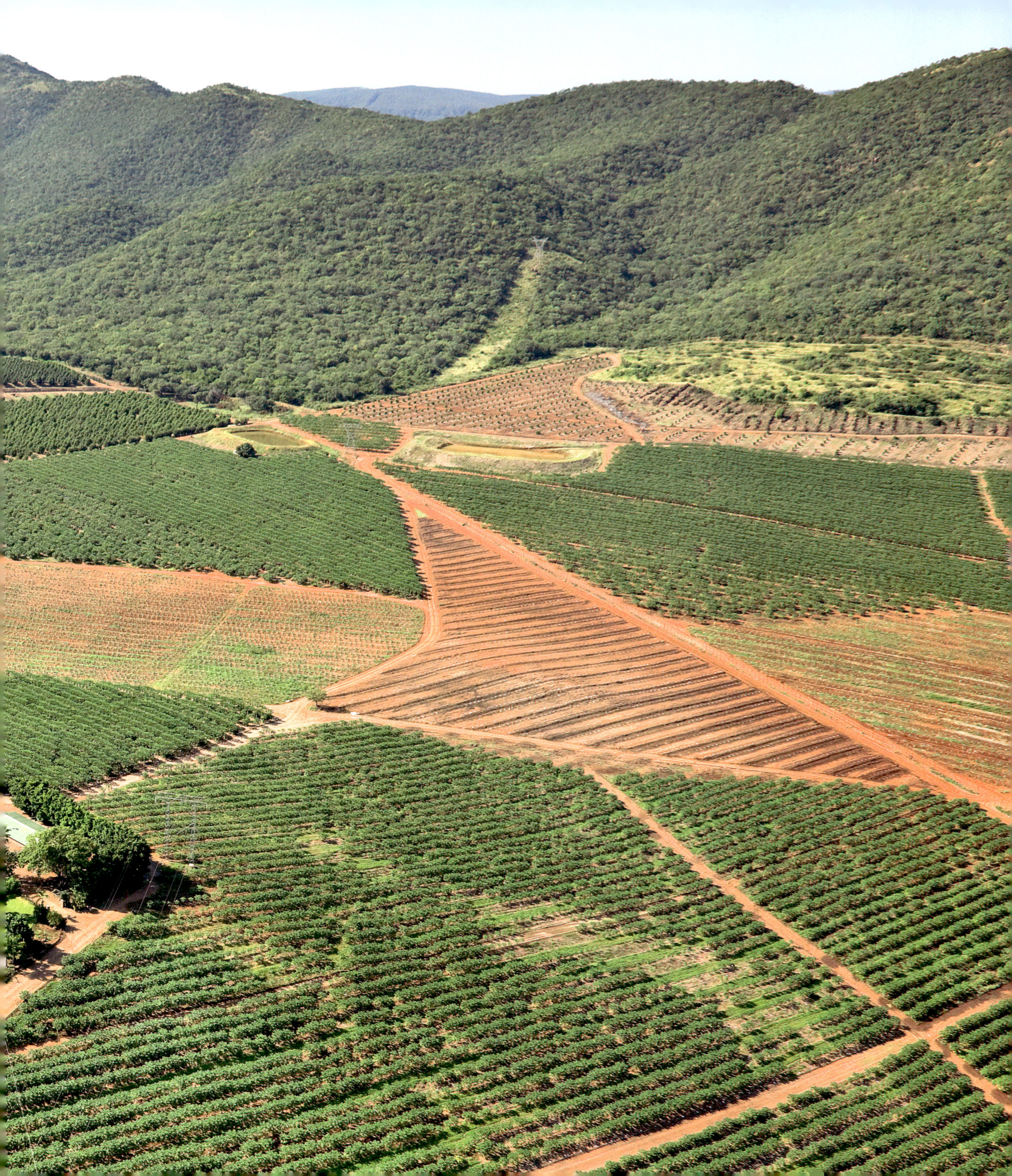

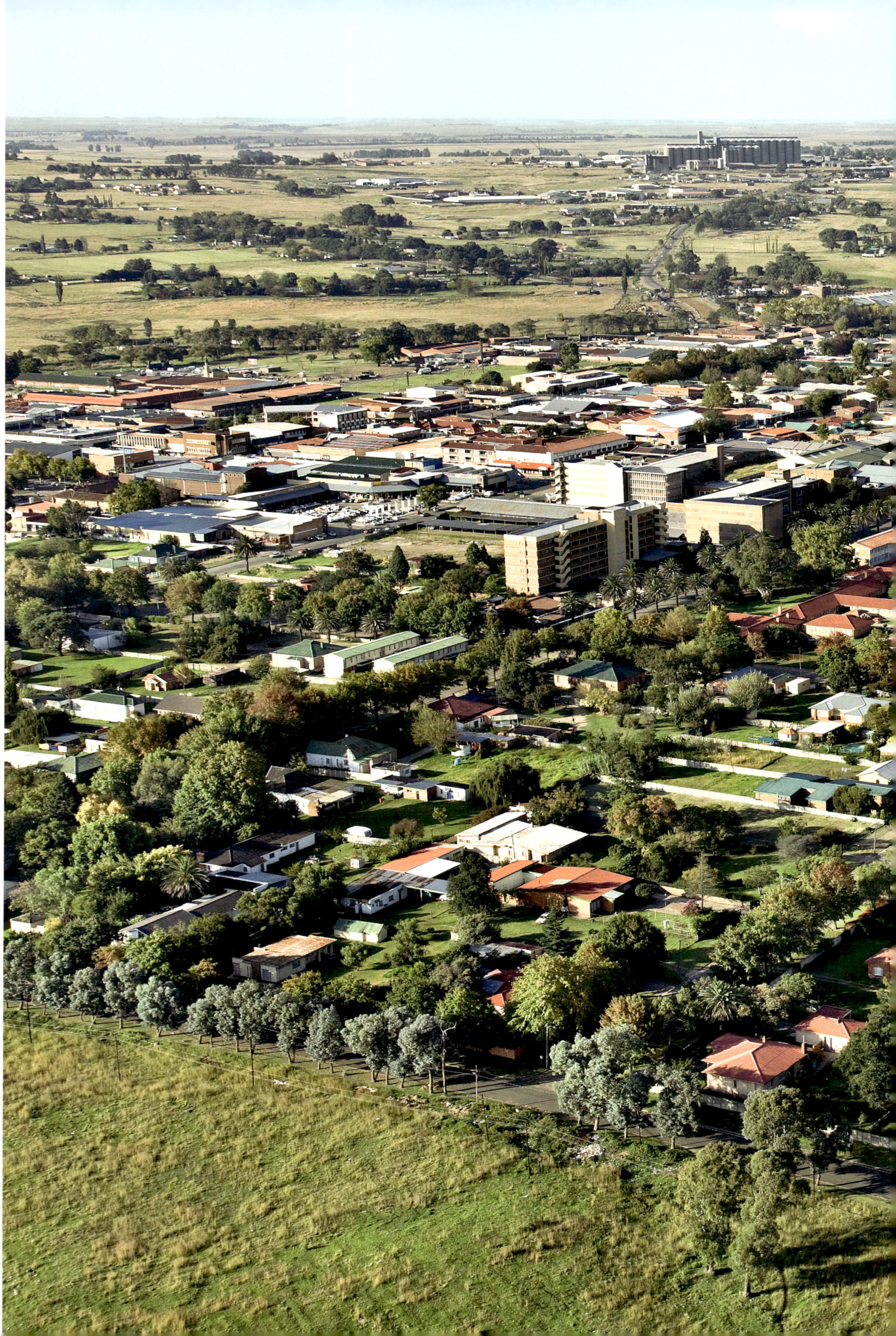

← Agriculture, Driekoppies area
→ Bethal

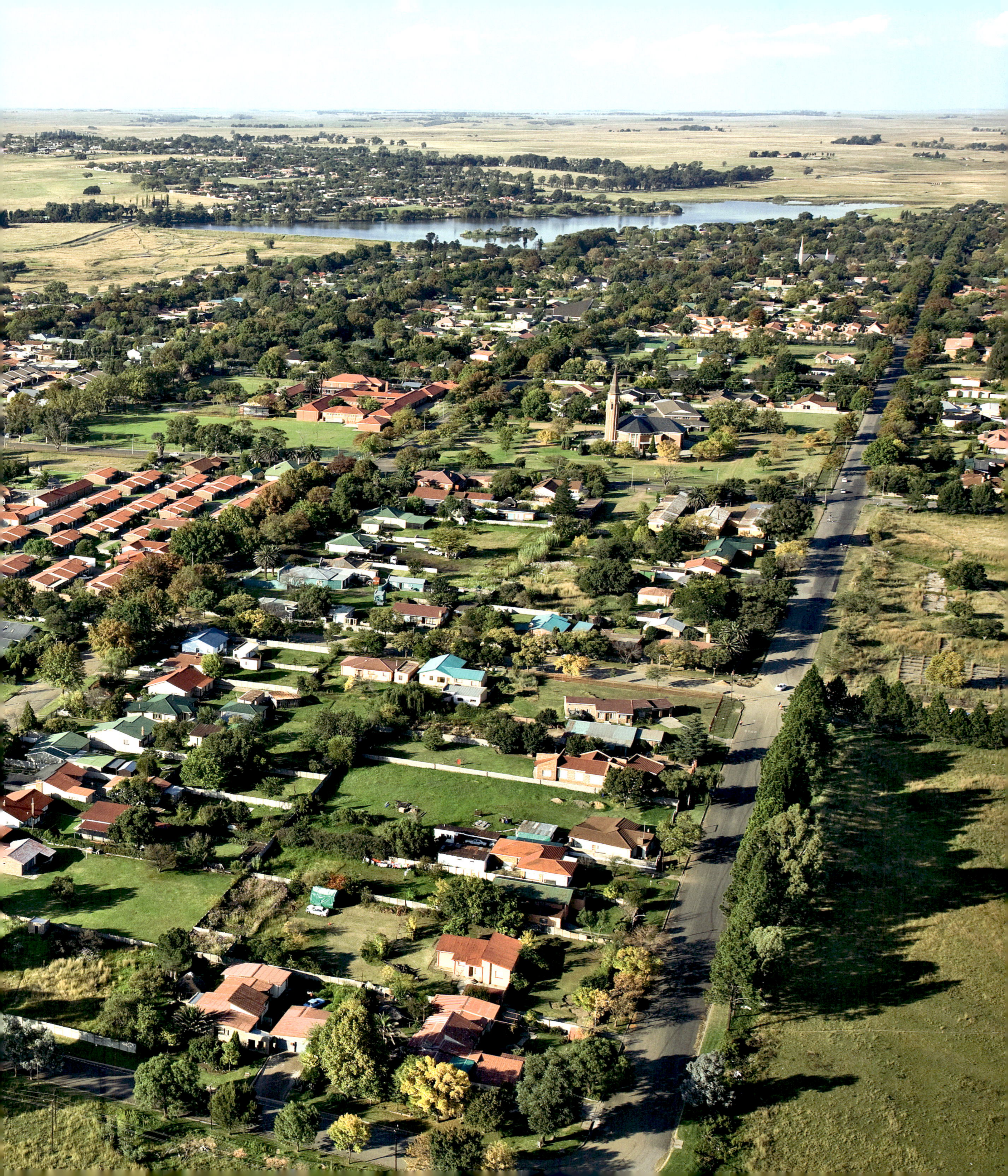

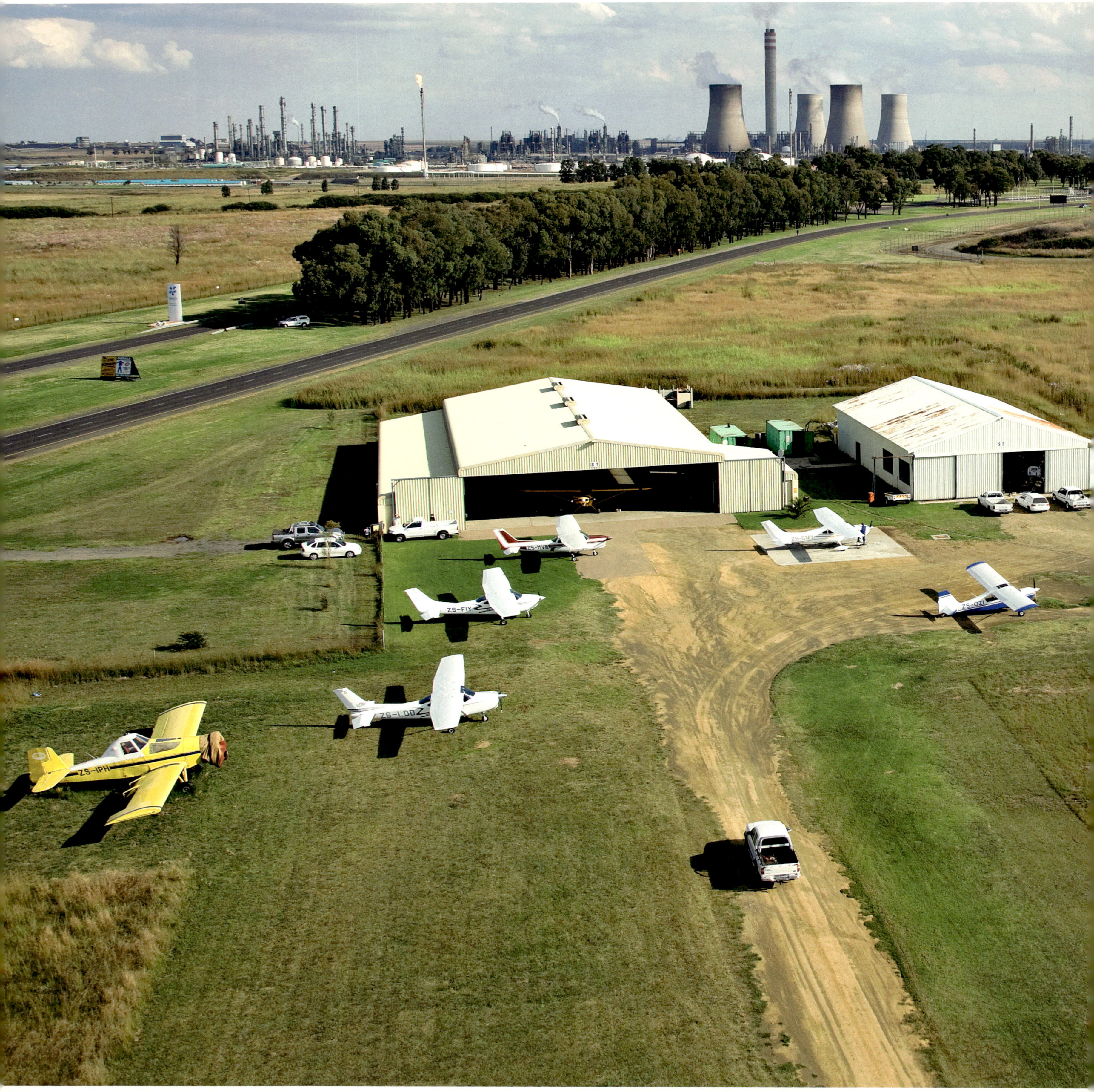

← Secunda Airport
↓ Graceland Hotel and Casino, Secunda

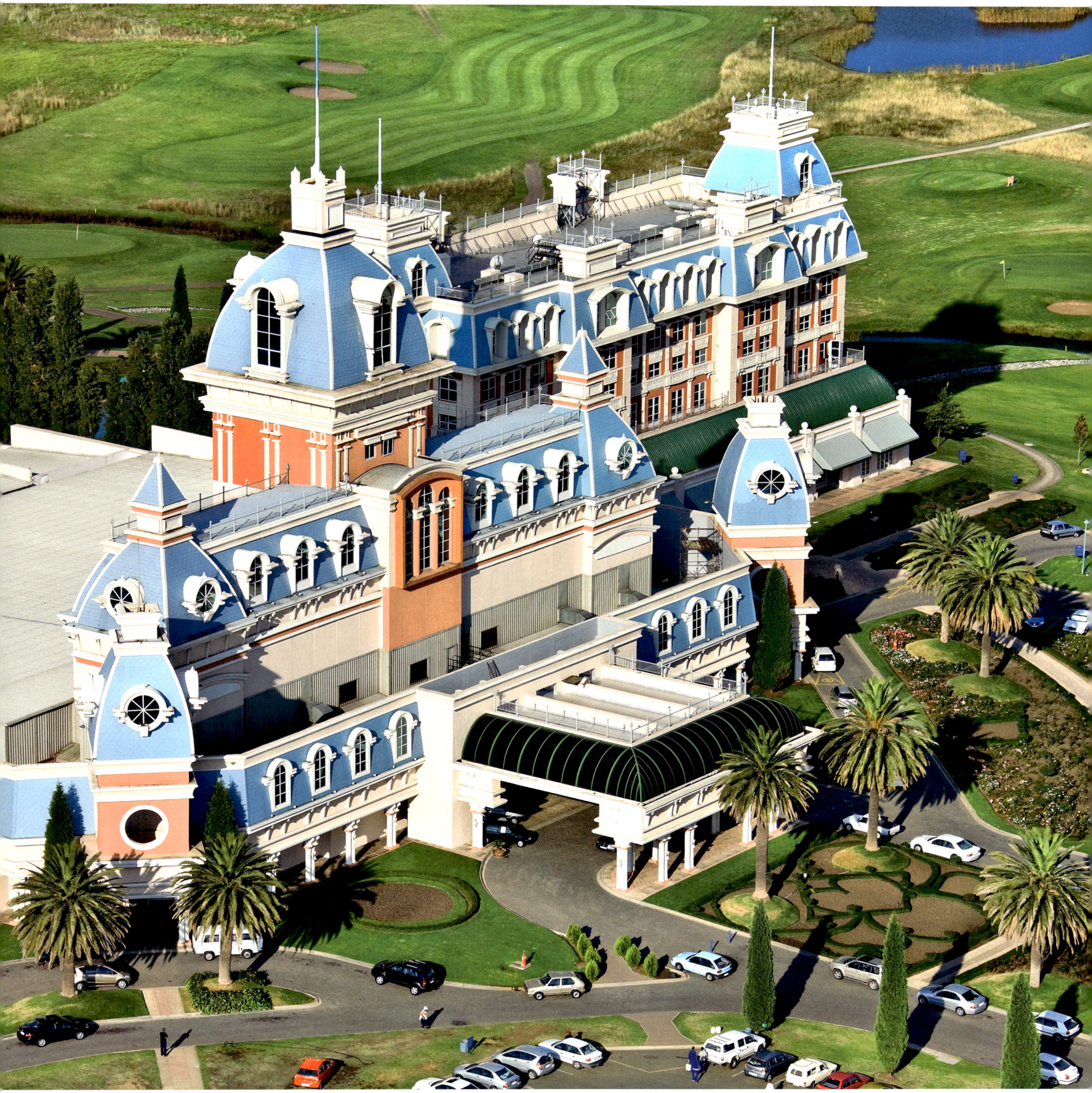

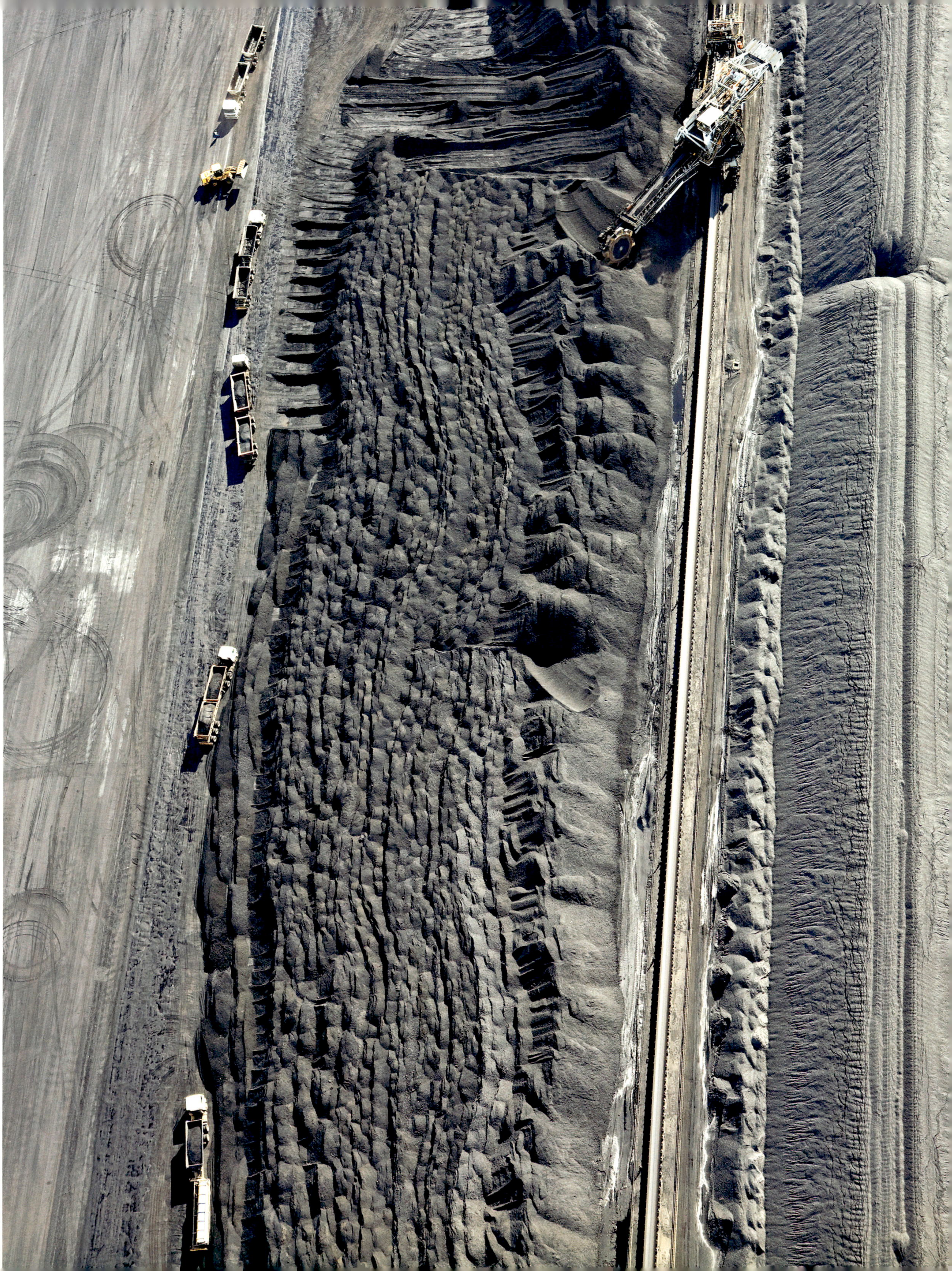

←↓ Power plant between Sanderton and Secunda
↓↓ Sasol Refinery, Secunda

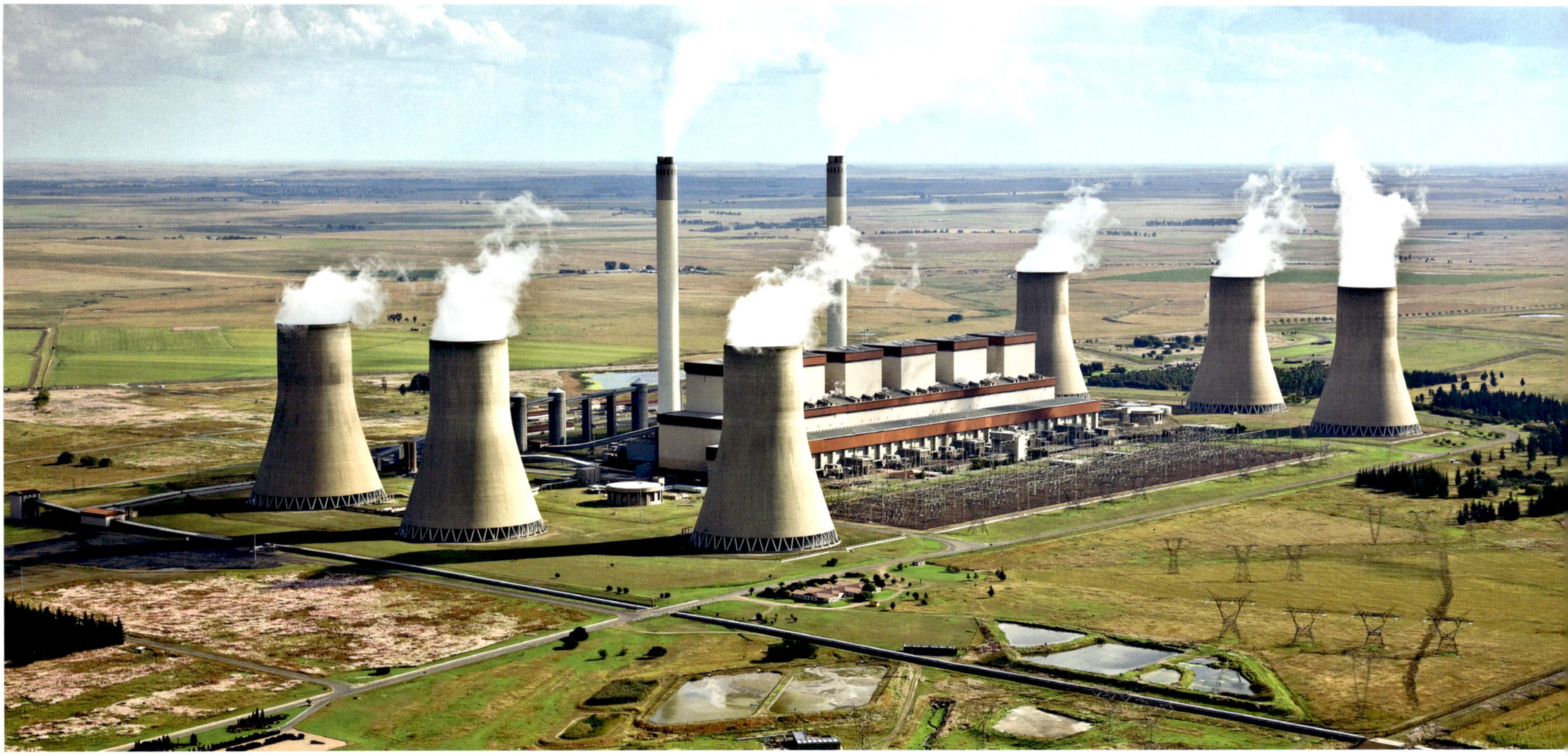

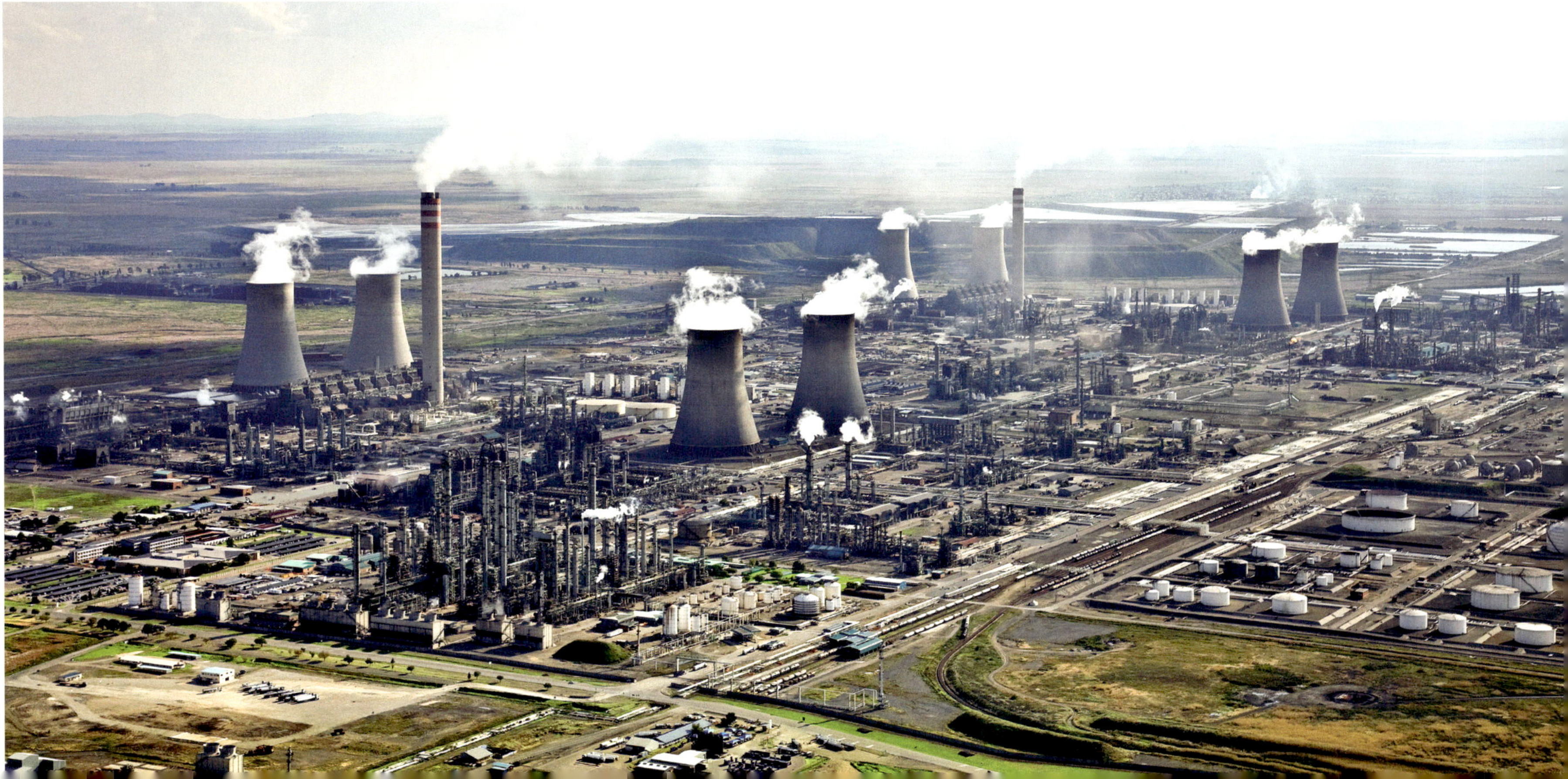

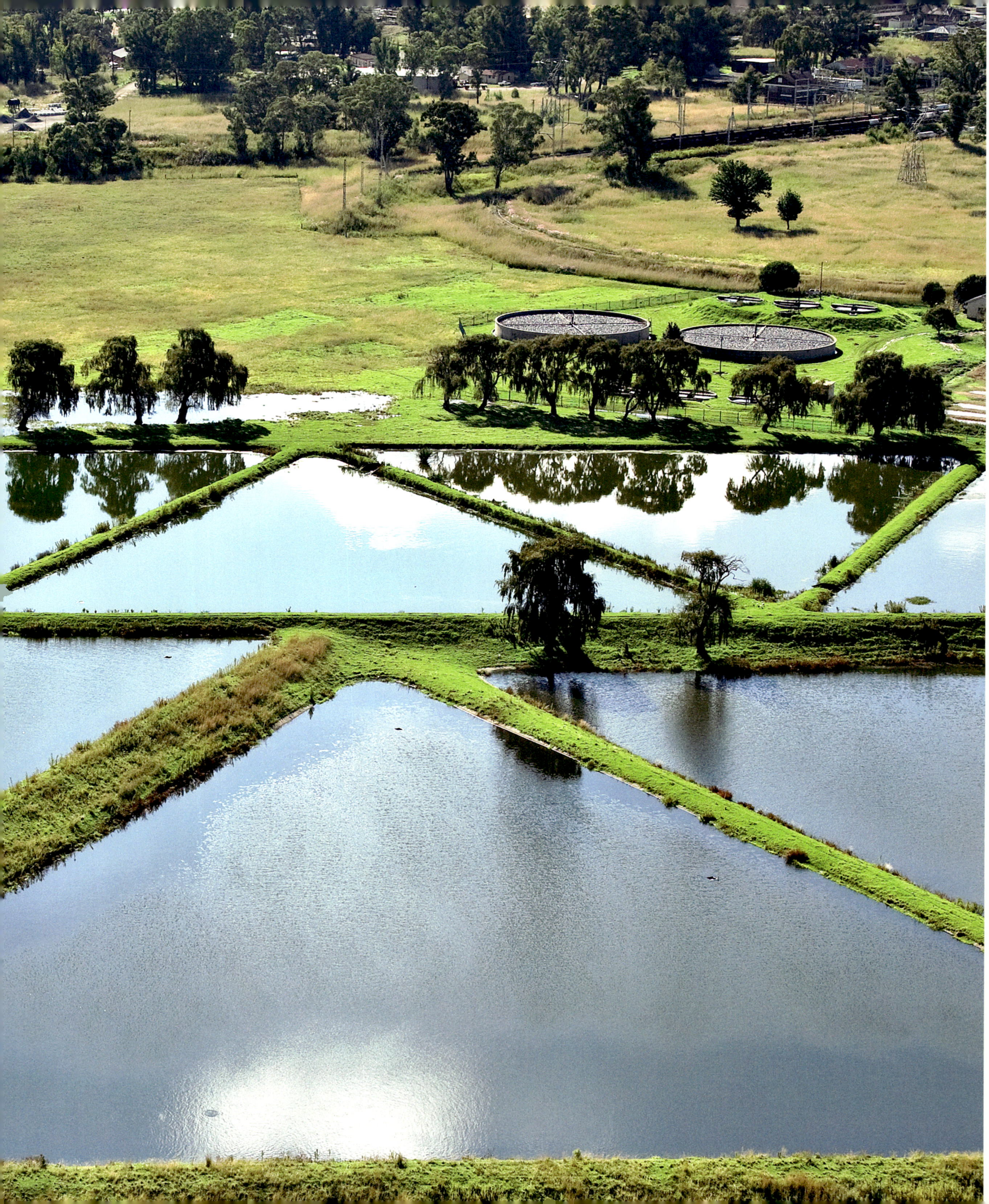

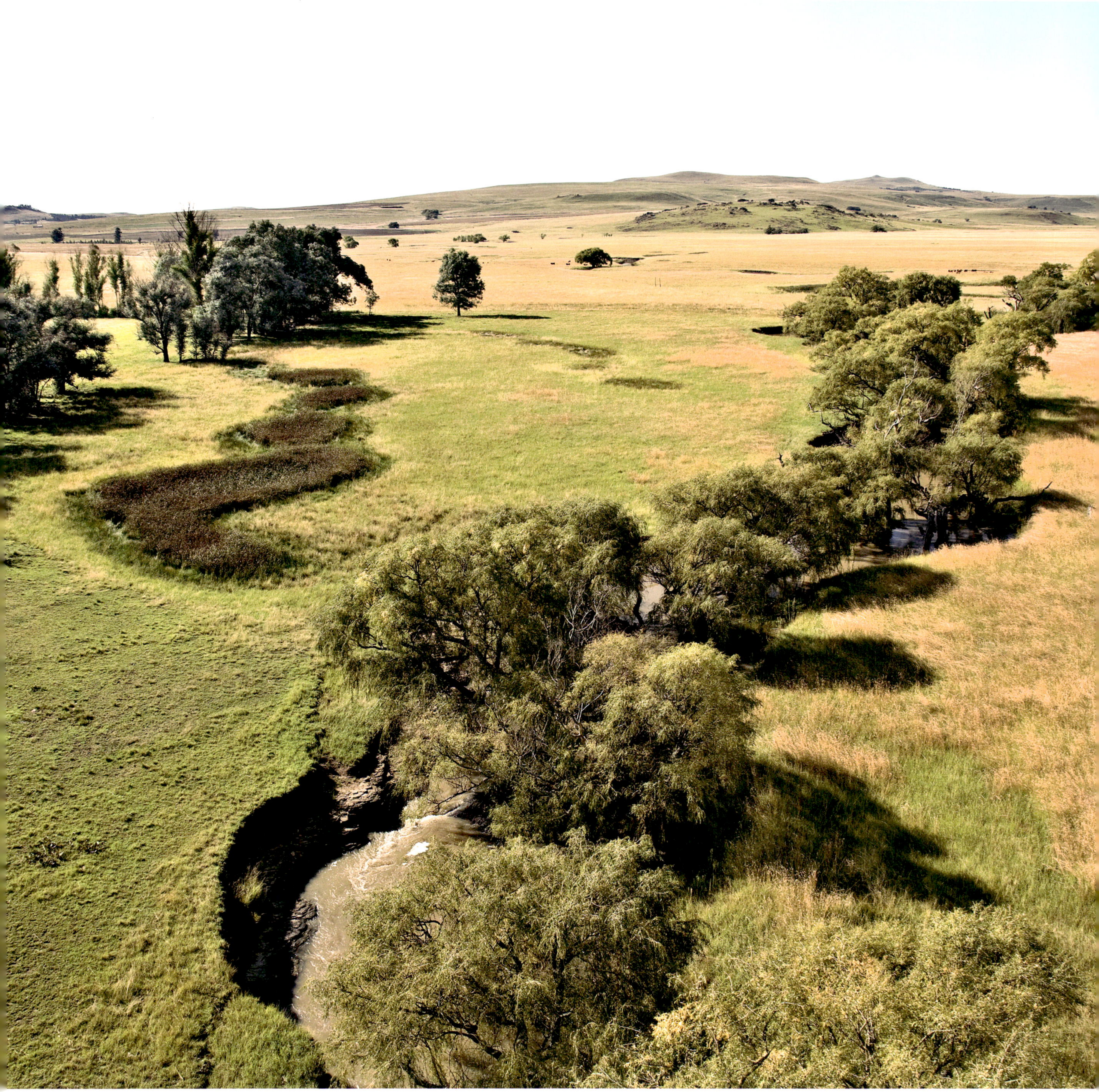

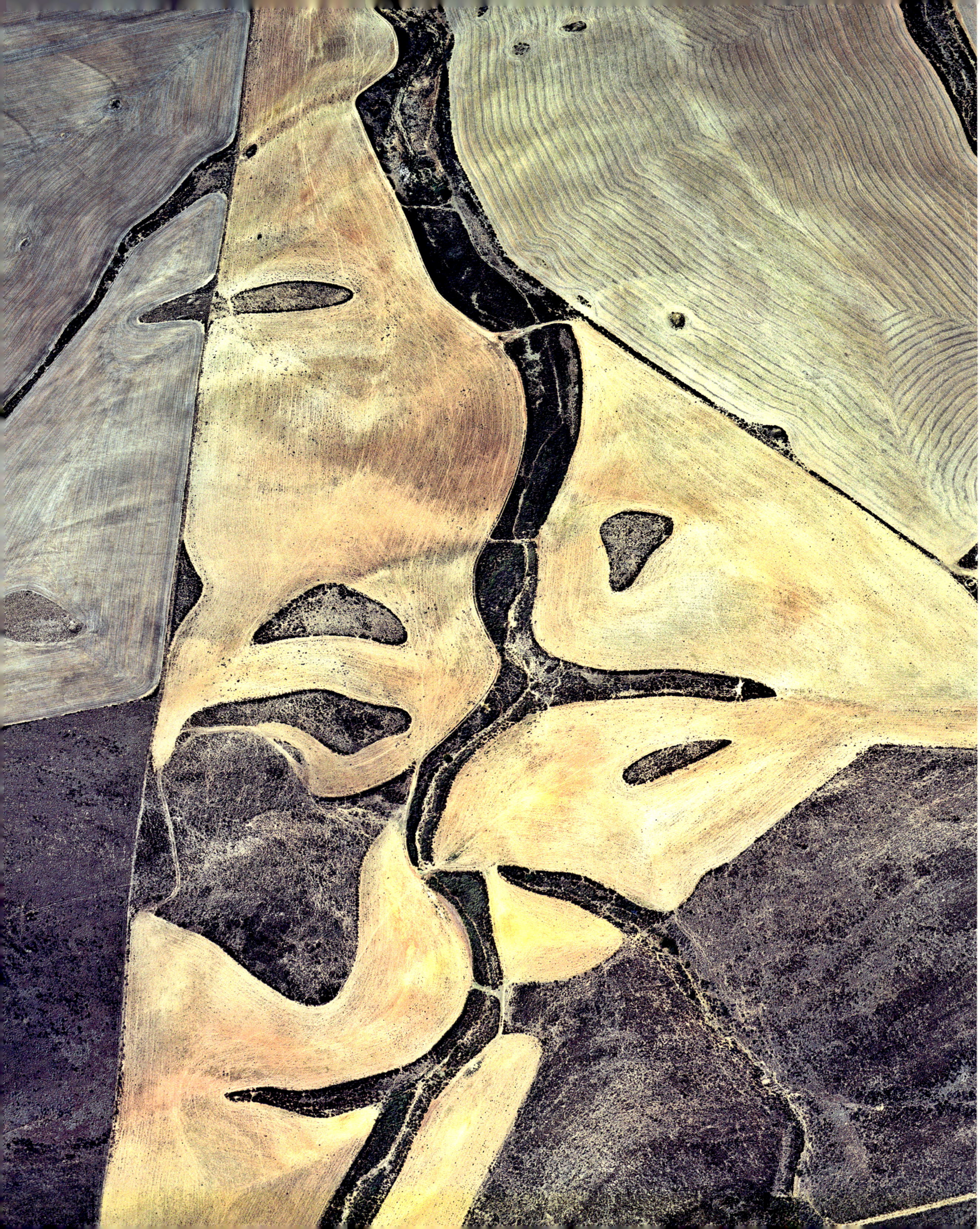

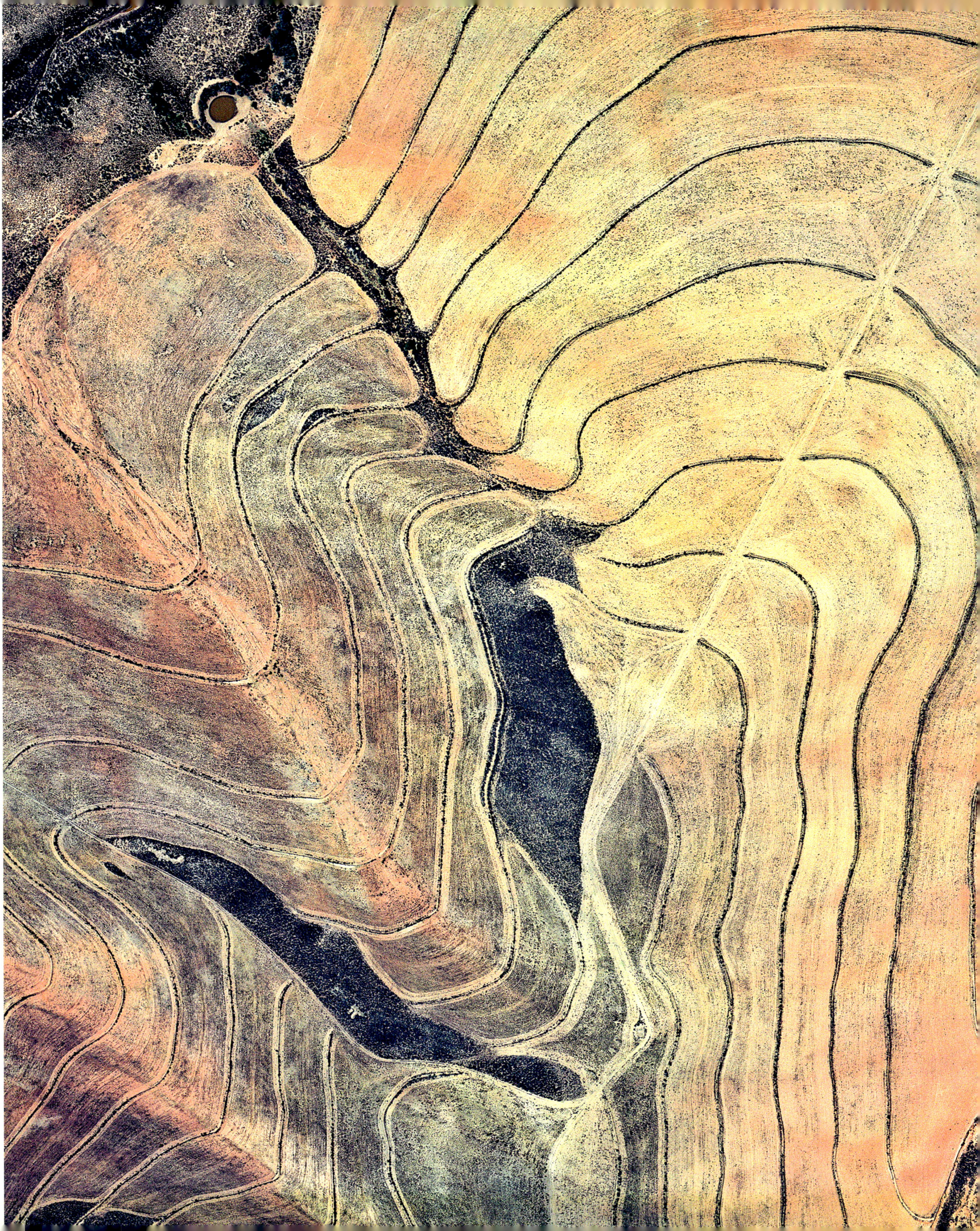

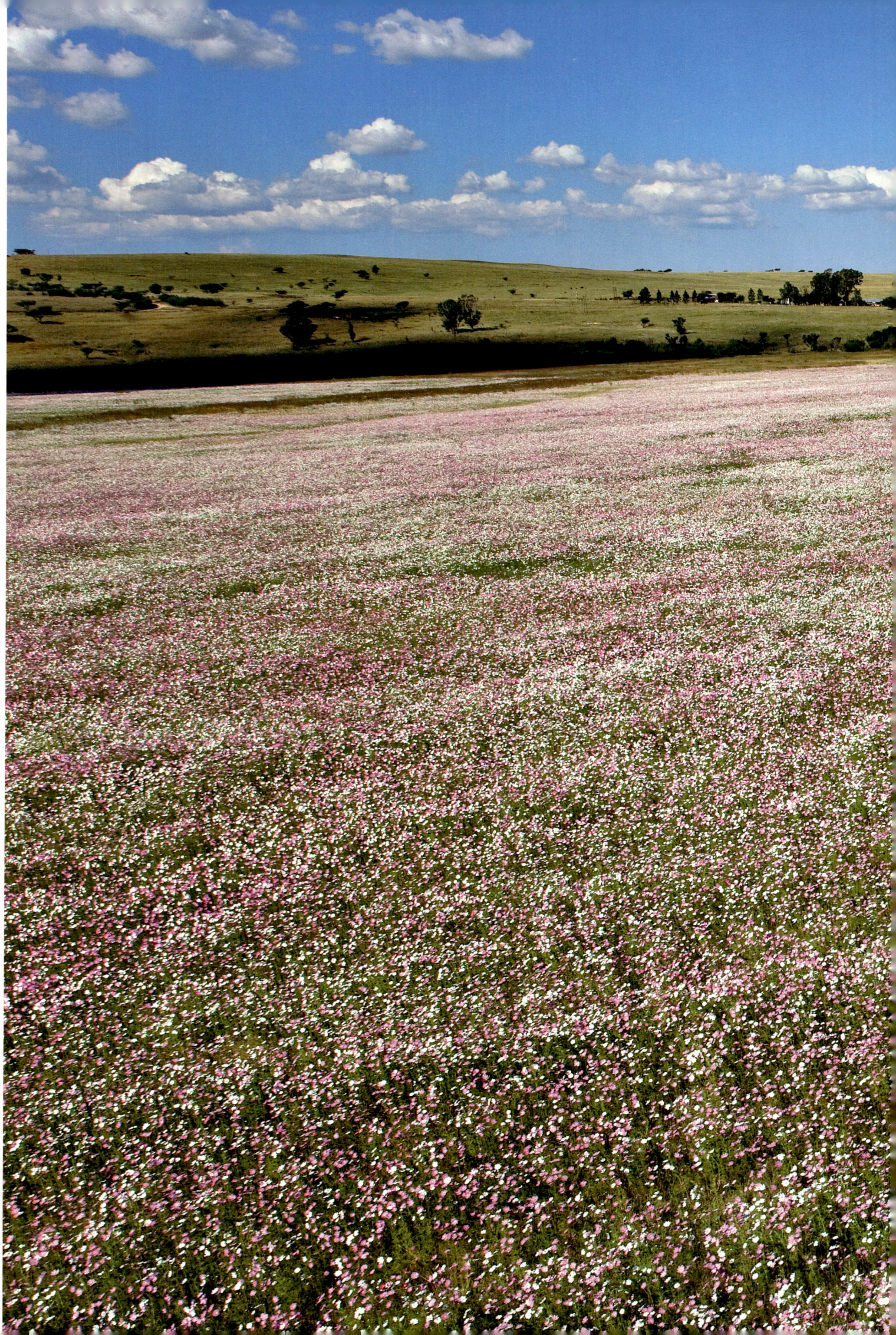

← Agricultural land
→ Cornflowers

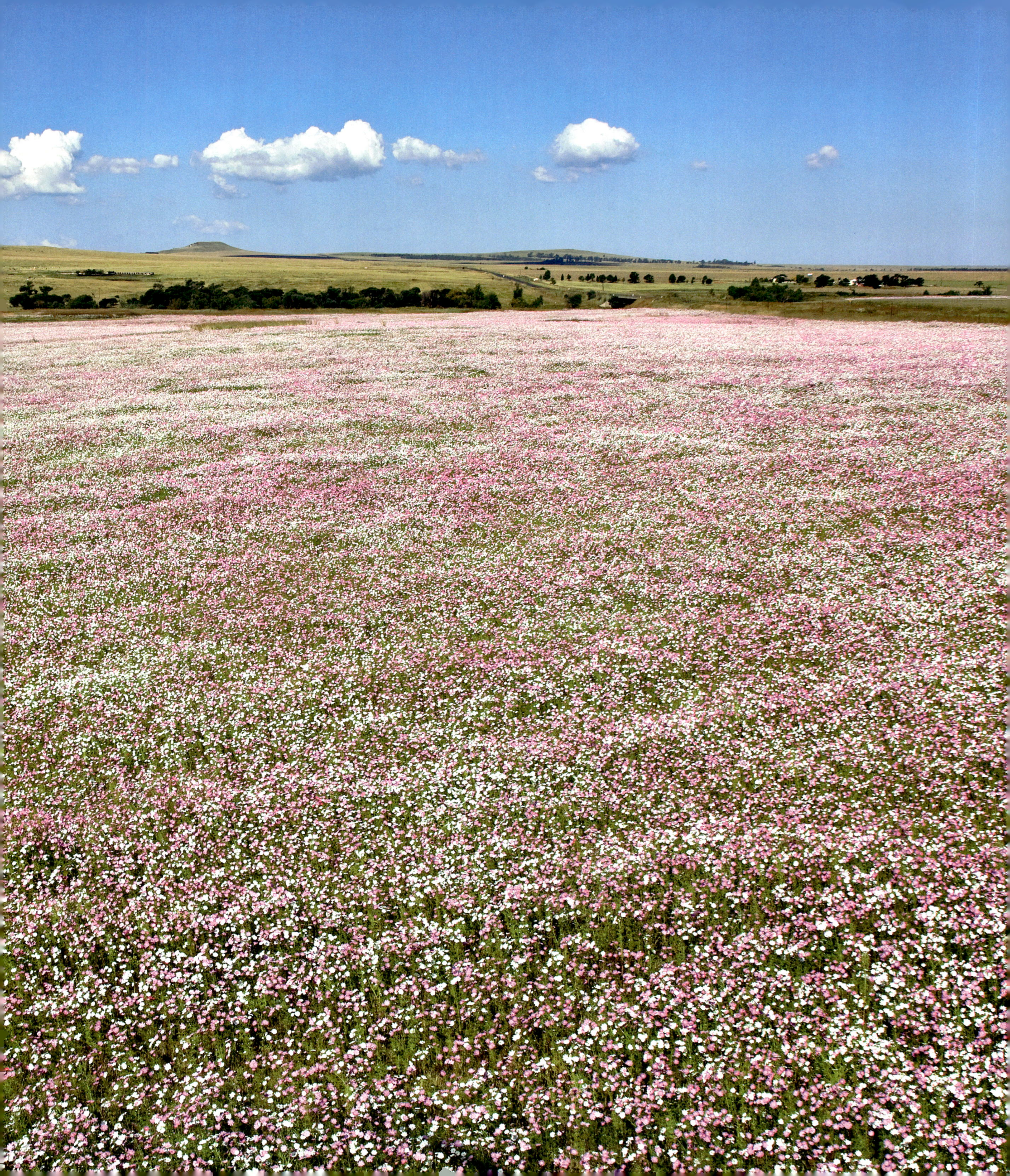

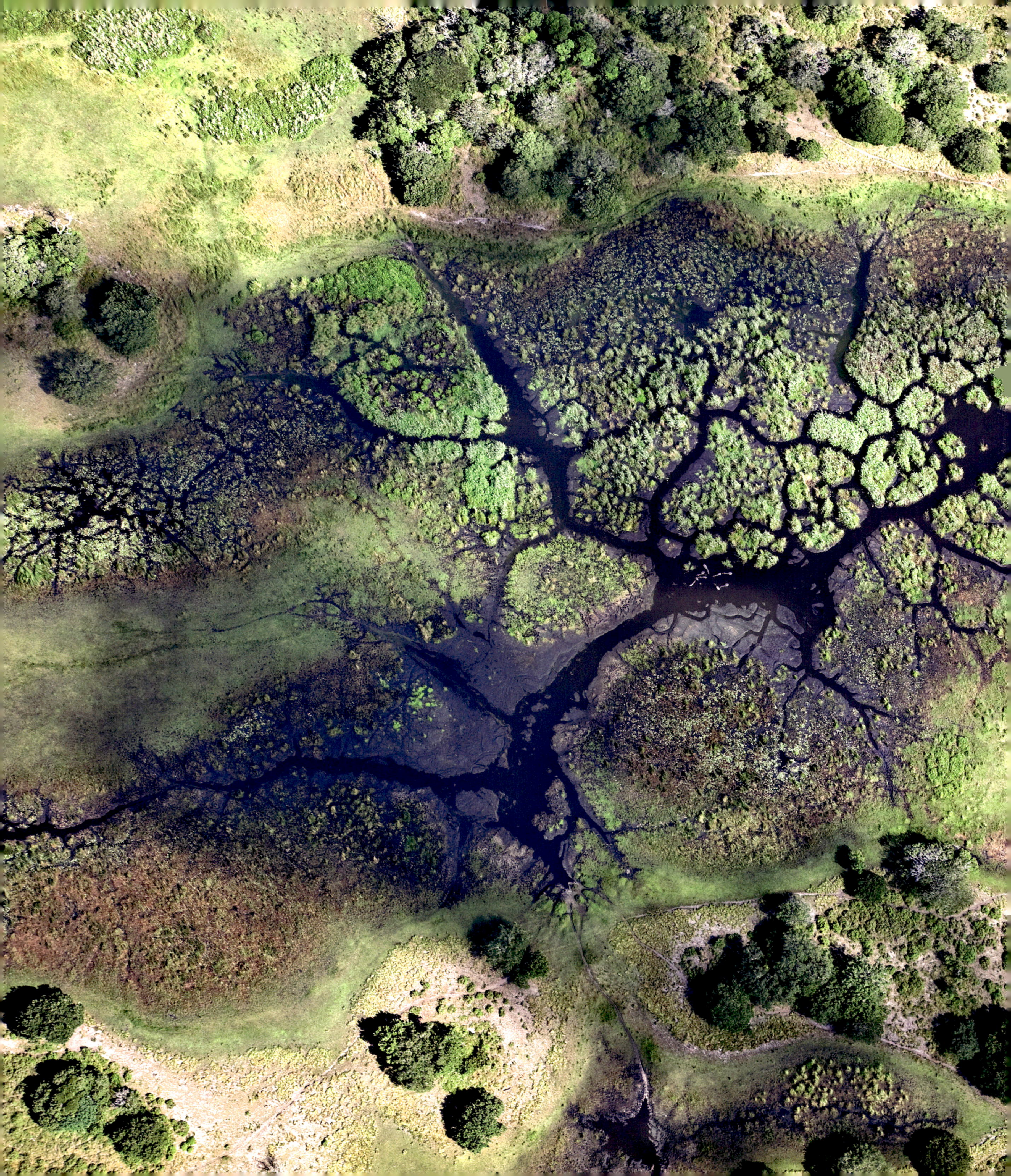

KWAZULU-NATAL

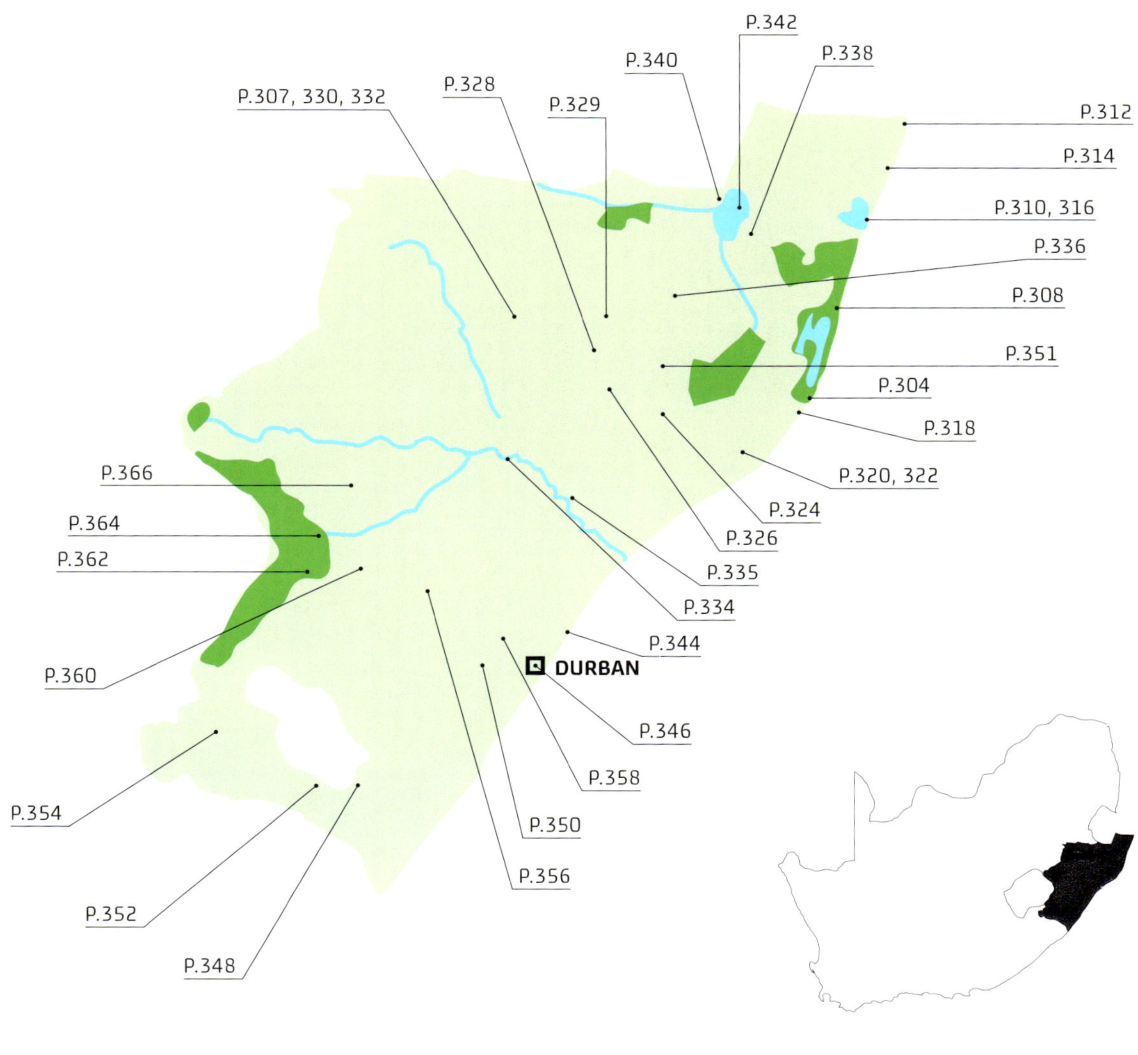

15 December 1838. On the banks of the Ncome River, a commando of 470 Afrikaner Boers form a laager, a line of defence consisting of a circle of ox-wagons. The following morning, a 10,000-man strong Zulu army attacks the laager. They attack in three waves, in quick succession. All three are repelled. When evening falls, the river runs red with the blood of thousands of dead Zulu; miraculously, the Boers have suffered only three wounded. 16 December is now Reconciliation Day in South Africa and the battleground has become a museum. On the west bank of the Ncome/Blood River there are bronze replicas of the 64 ox-wagons that made up the Boers' laager; on the east bank, a monument has been erected in memorial of the Zulu who died in battle.

Land of miracles

KwaZulu-Natal: the homeland of the Zulu that Portuguese seafarers named Terra do Natal in 1497. The country of a thousand hills, of sub-tropical beaches and of heroic strife between the Zulus and the Boers, the Boers and the British, and the British and the Zulus. The country with a coast that has been known for centuries as extremely treacherous. No one knows how many ships have been wrecked here in the course of history, but in the second half of the 17th century, so many shipwrecked English sailors lived in the area that is now known as Durban, that Dutch sailors mockingly called it The Englishman's Inn.

The inhabitants of KwaZulu-Natal are proud of their history. That is clear by the way they keep it alive. The museum of Blood River, for example, is only one part of the Battlefield Route, a tourist attraction that also includes museums dedicated to the battles at Rorke's Drift, Spionkop and Isandlwana. In this last battle, on 22 January 1879, British troops suffered a disastrous defeat at the hands of the Zulu army of king Cetshwayo.
KwaZulu-Natal fortunately pays as much attention to its more peaceful traditions, as shown by the many cultural villages depicting everyday life of the Zulu in former times. And by the fact that the Zulu monarchy still exists although, under the current constitution, the sovereign no longer has any direct political power.

If you are more interested in nature, it is worth knowing that KwaZulu-Natal has more nature reserves than any other South African province. The best known is iSimangaliso ('miracle') Wetland Park, a three-hour drive to the north of Durban. The reserve contains eight different eco-systems, where visitors can see elephants and whales, sea turtles, crocodiles and the largest hippopotamus population in South Africa. In 1999, thanks to this unique biodiversity, UNESCO declared iSimangaliso a World Heritage Site. The area near the border with Swaziland, where the rugged Ngotshe Mountains rise into the sky, is another wonder. Legend claims this part of the world was not created by God but by the Devil. When he had finished his work and saw that his creation was far from equal to that of God, the devil threw himself to the ground in a rage and began to thrash around with his arms and legs. And from that demonic act of destruction, the inhospitable Ngotshe Mountains, with their steep crevices, their impenetrable thorn bushes and strange rock formations, were born...

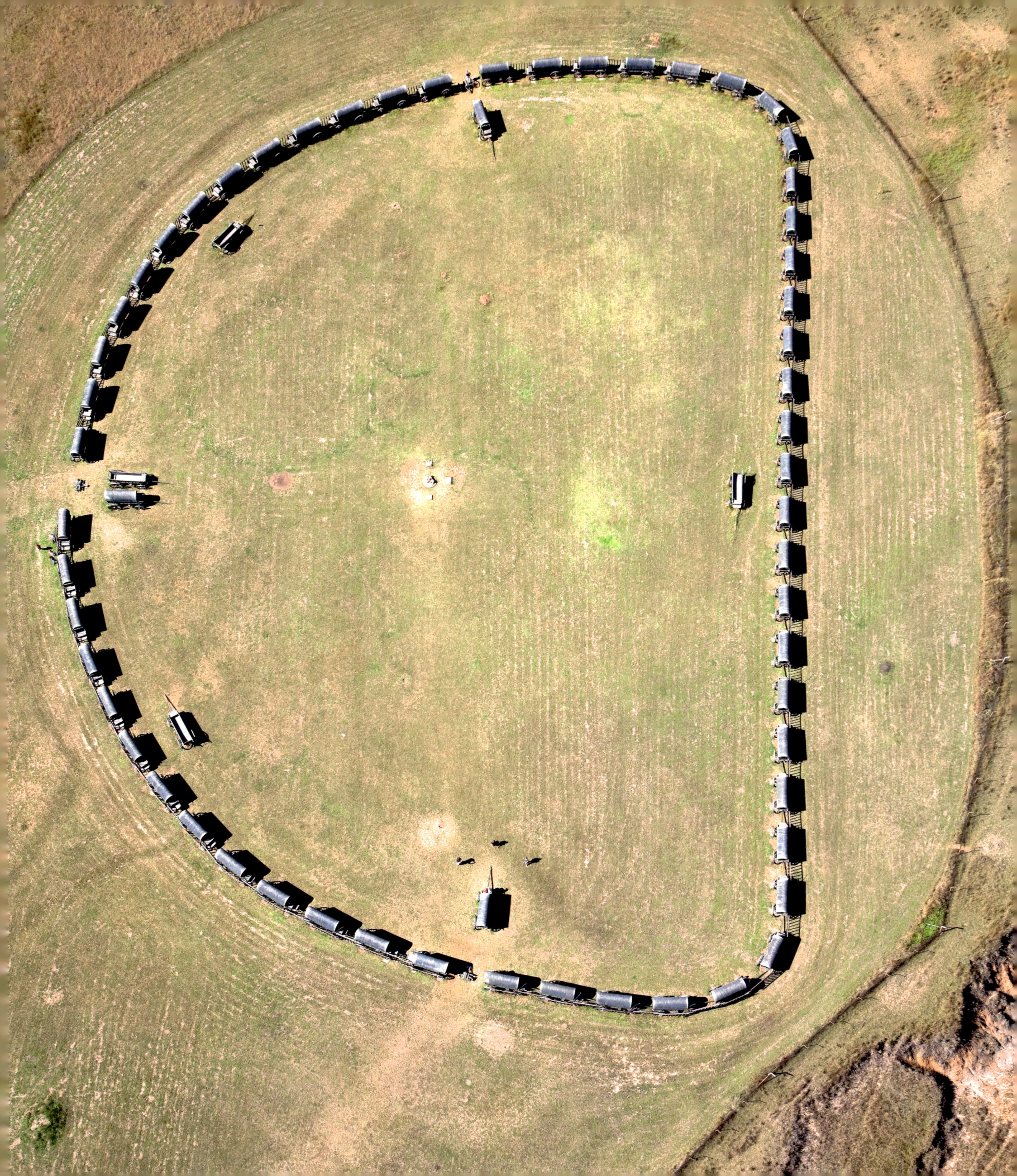

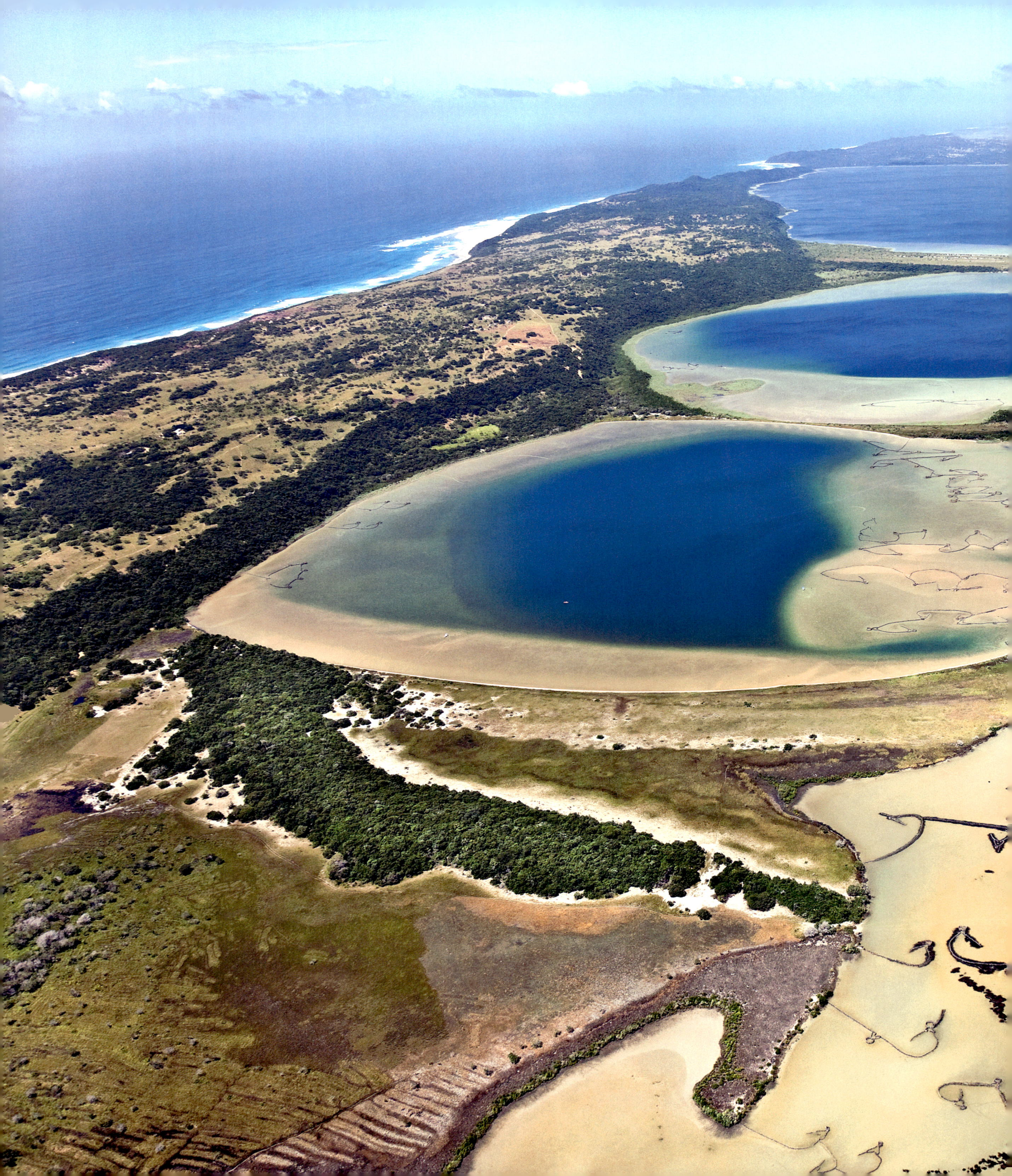

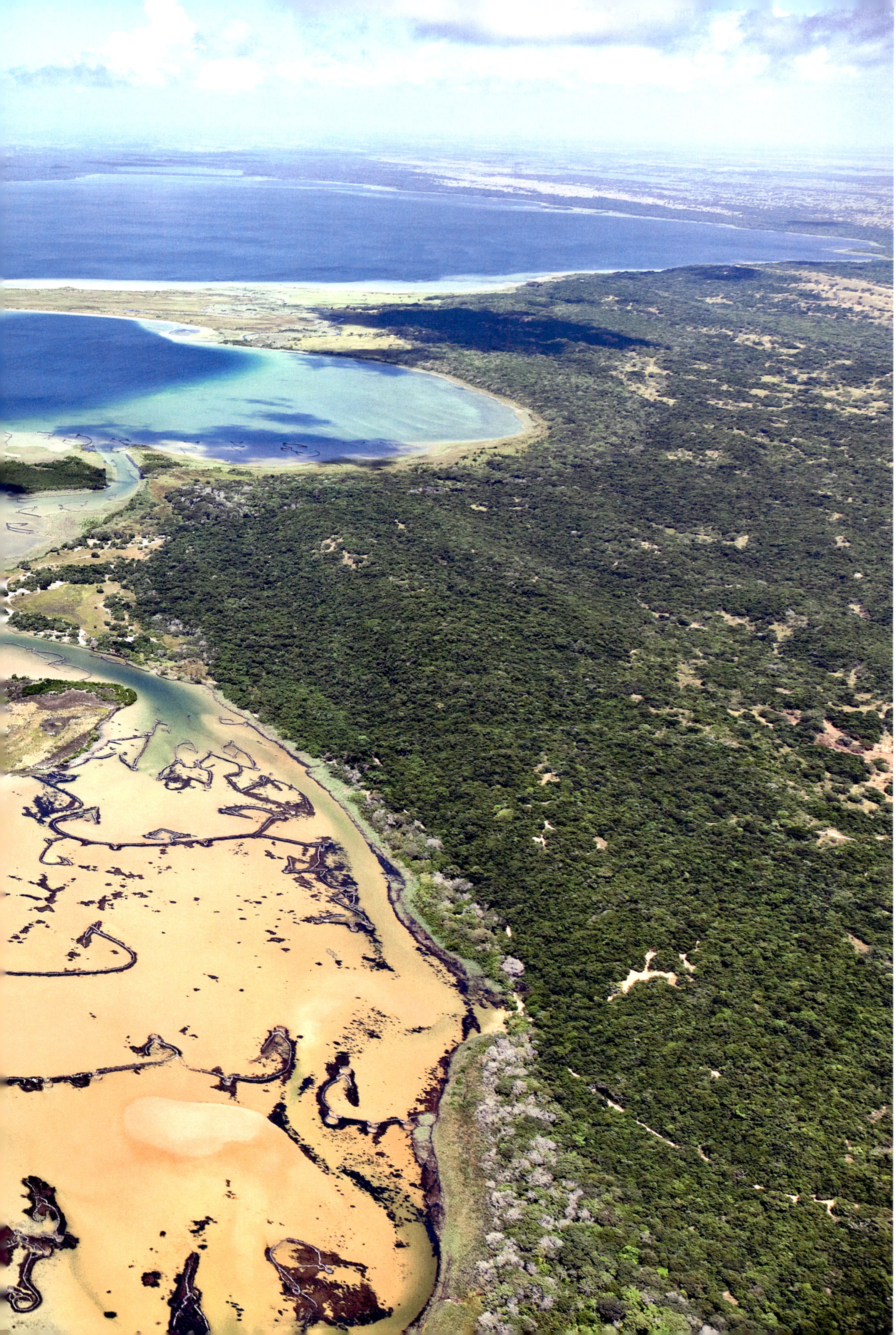

← Kosy Bay with Tsonga fishing traps in the foreground

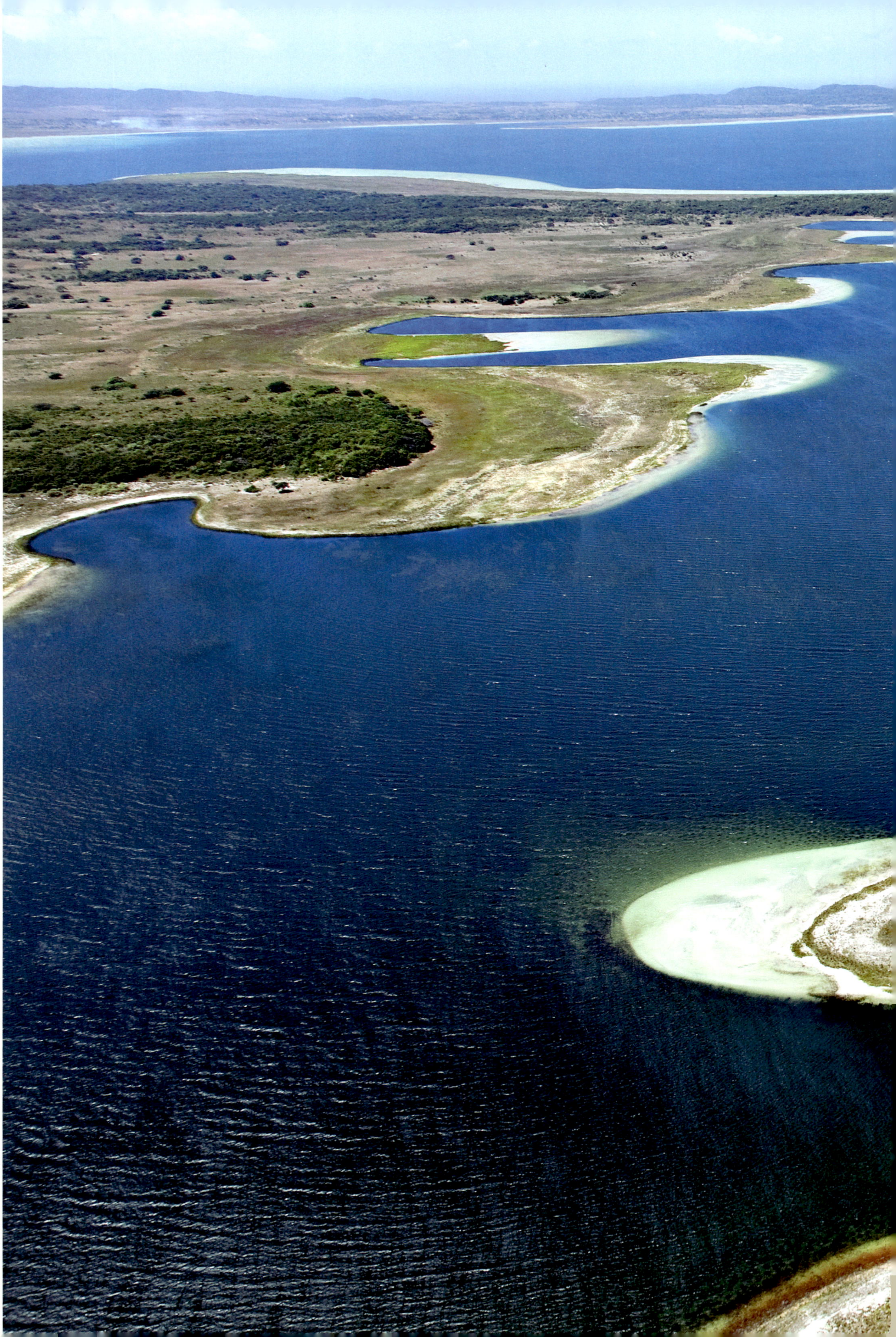

→ Lake Sibaya

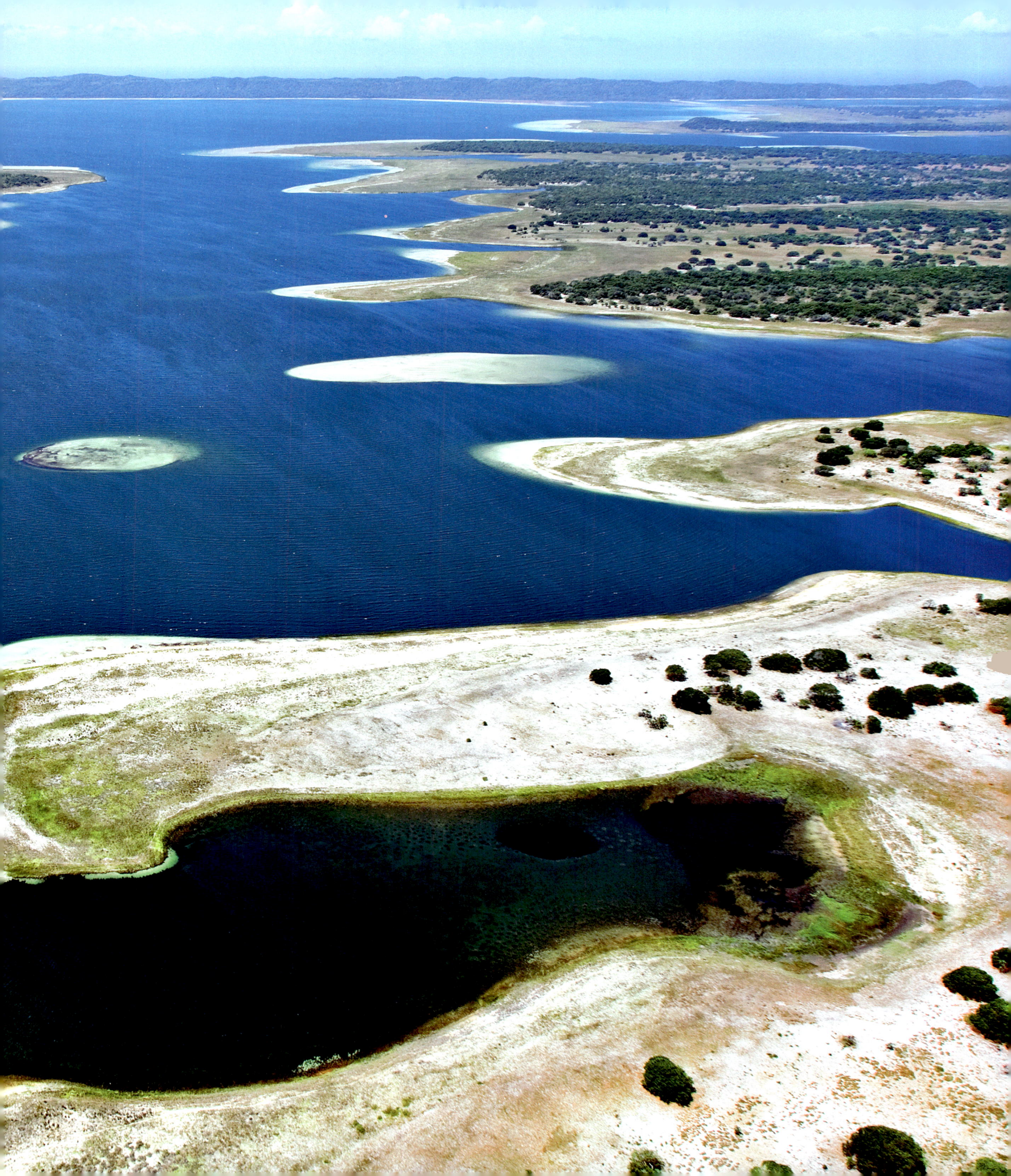

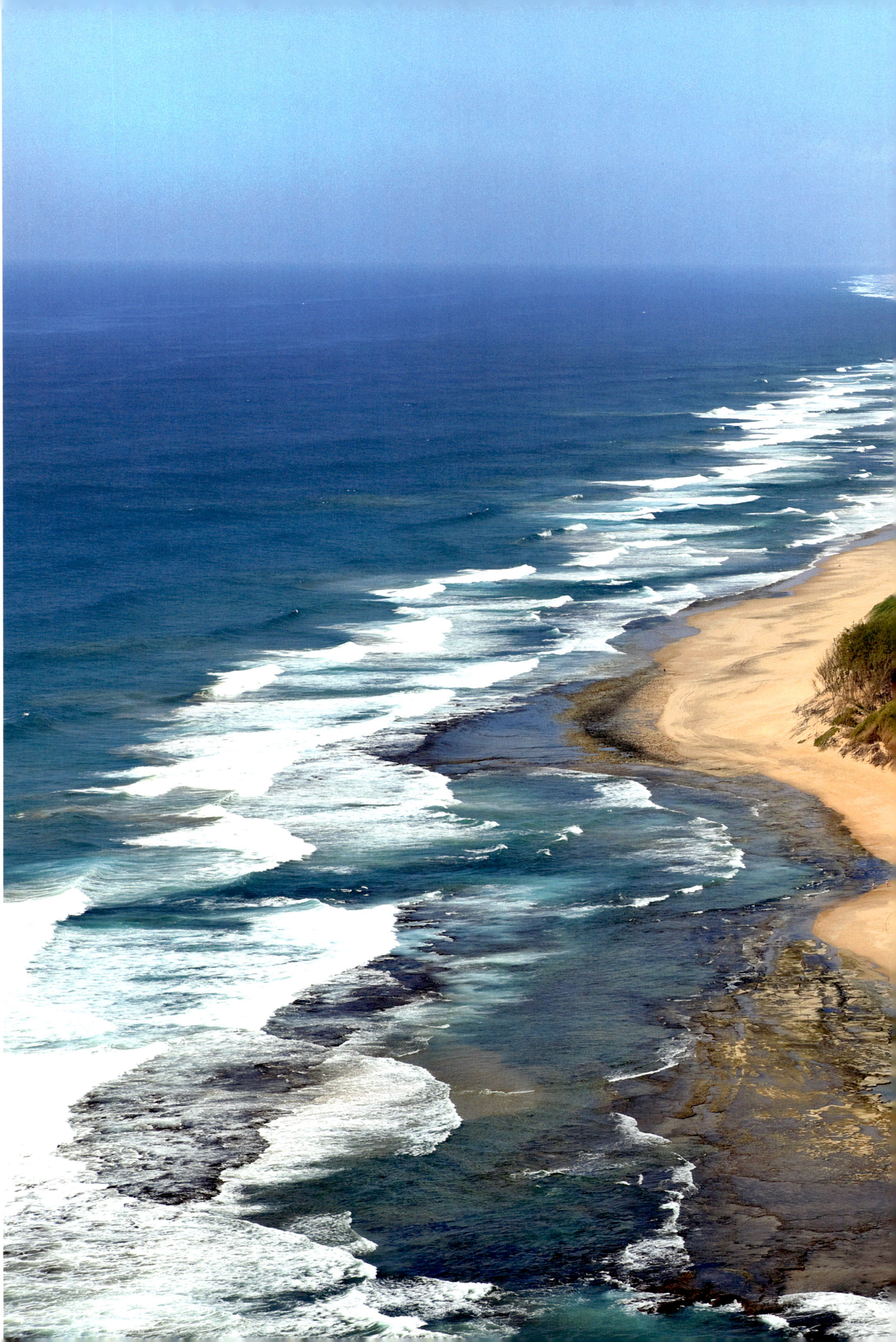

→ Sodwana Bay National Park

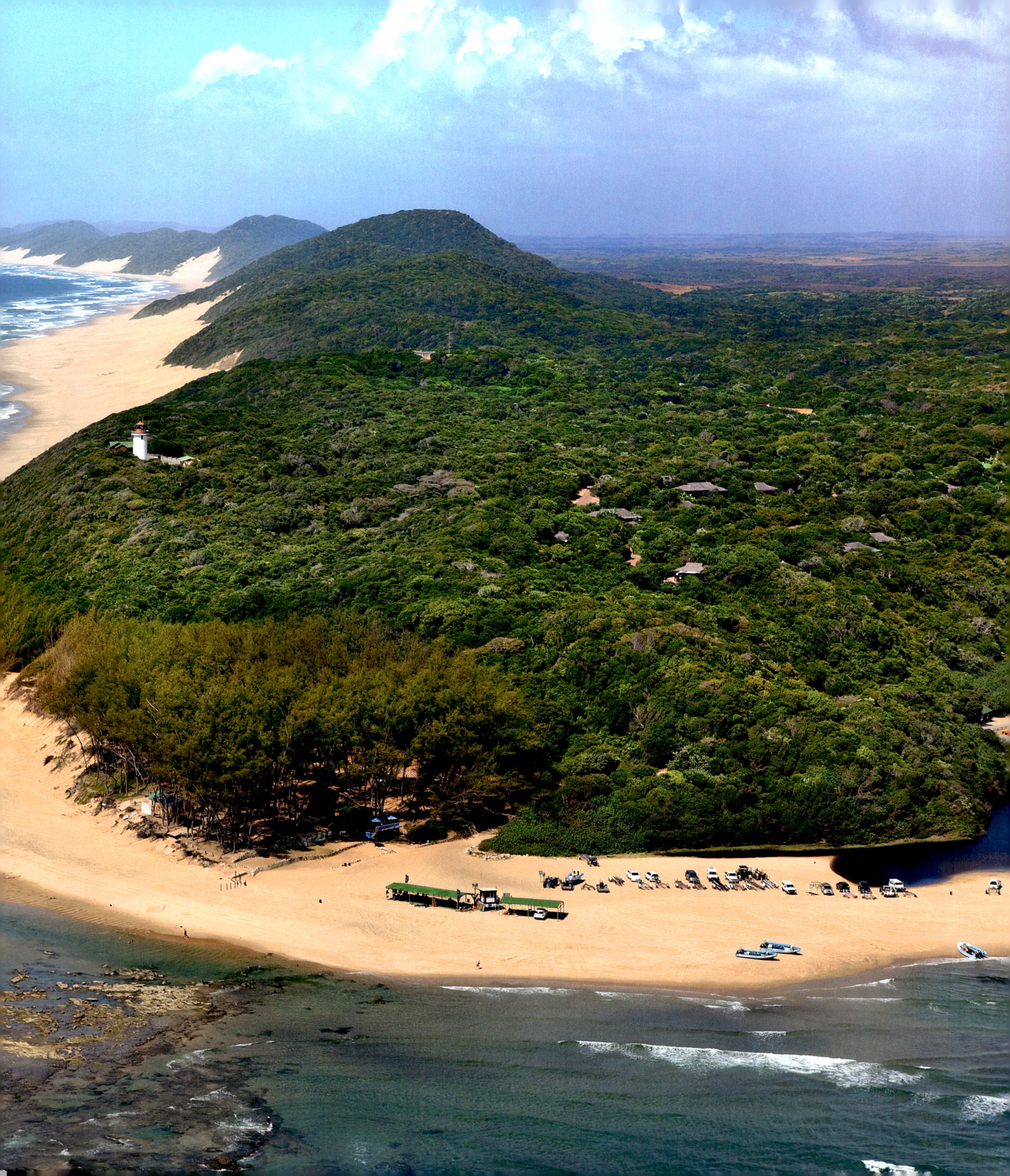

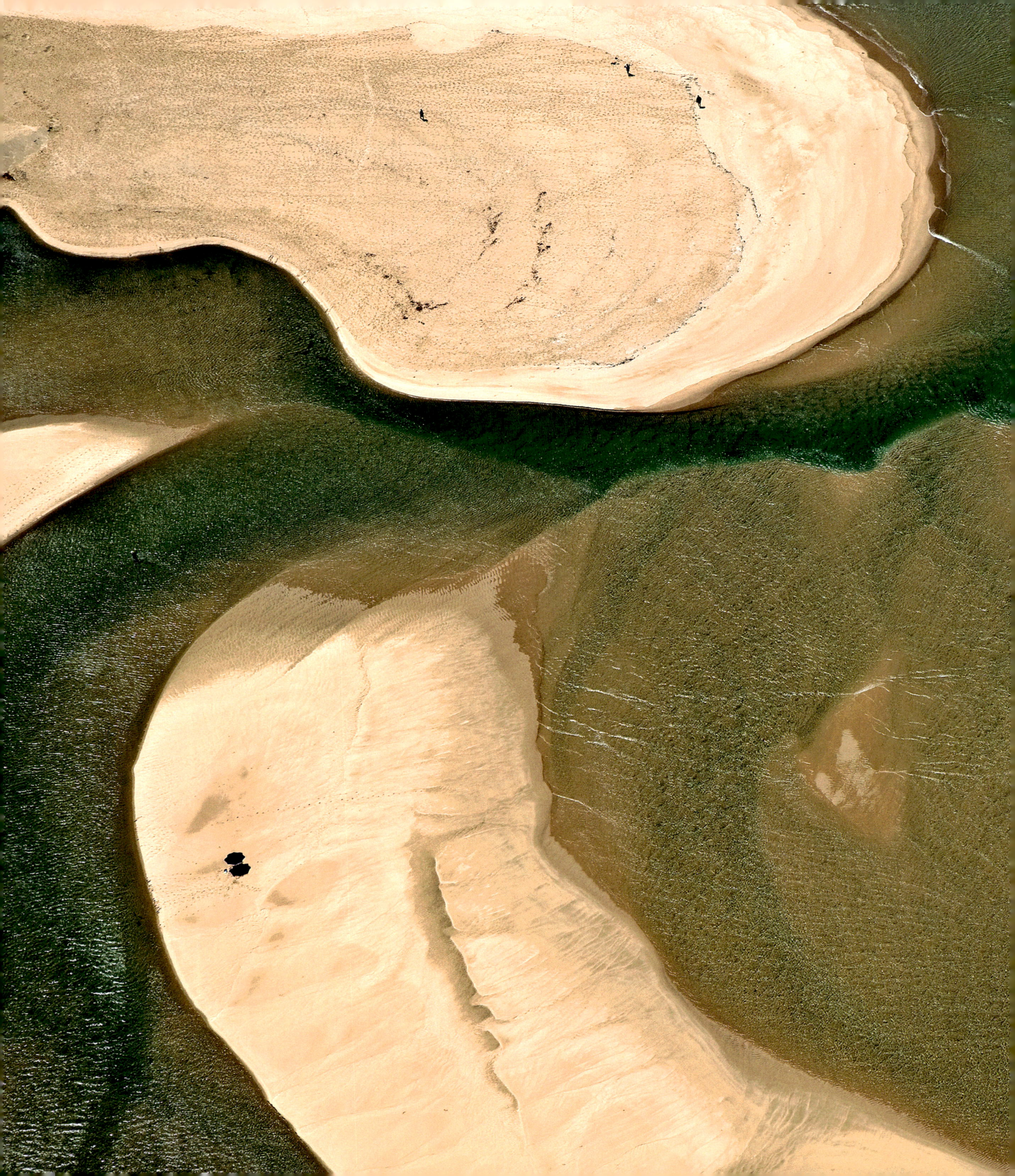

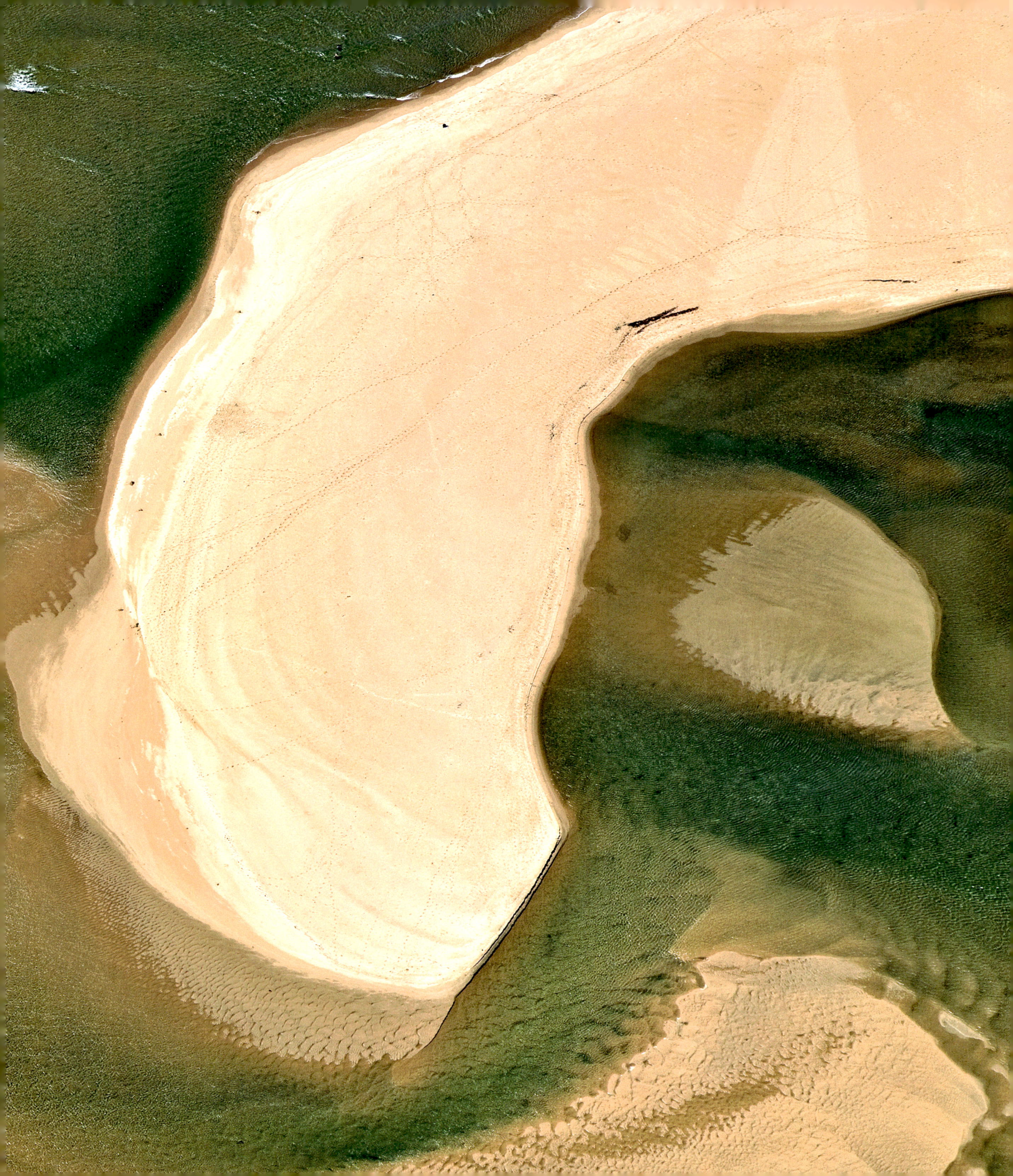

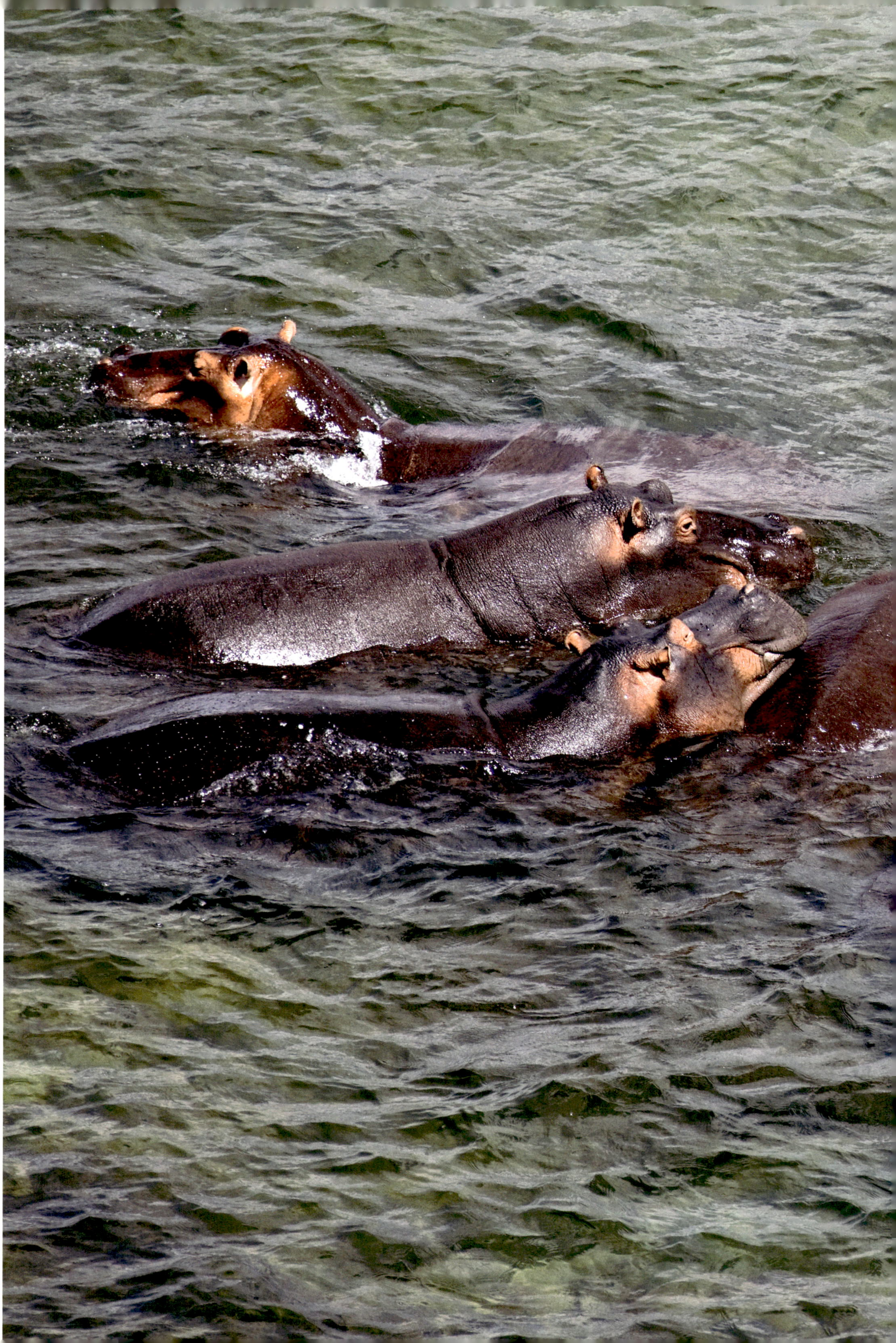

← Kosi Bay Mouth,
→ Hippos in Lake Sibaya

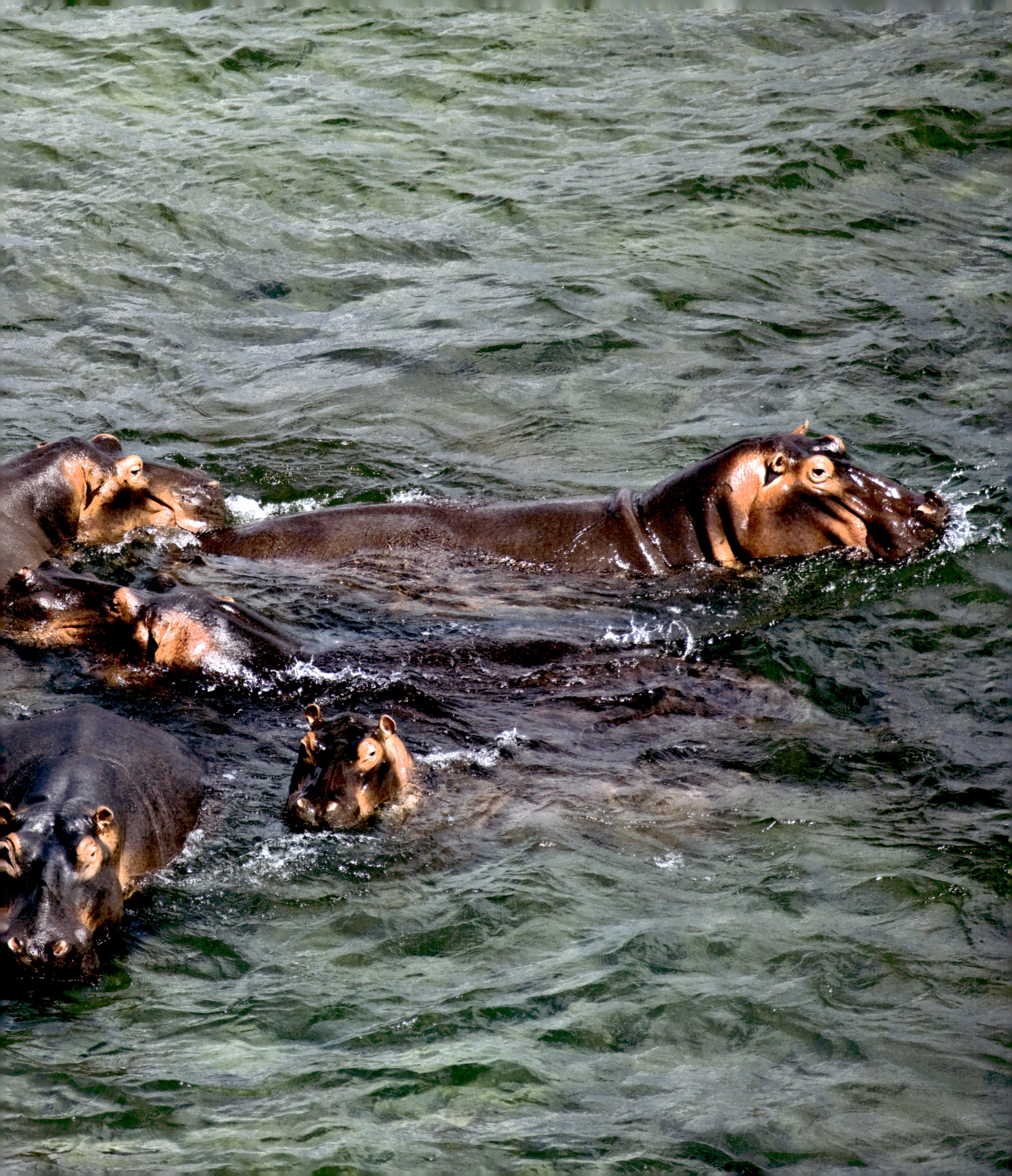

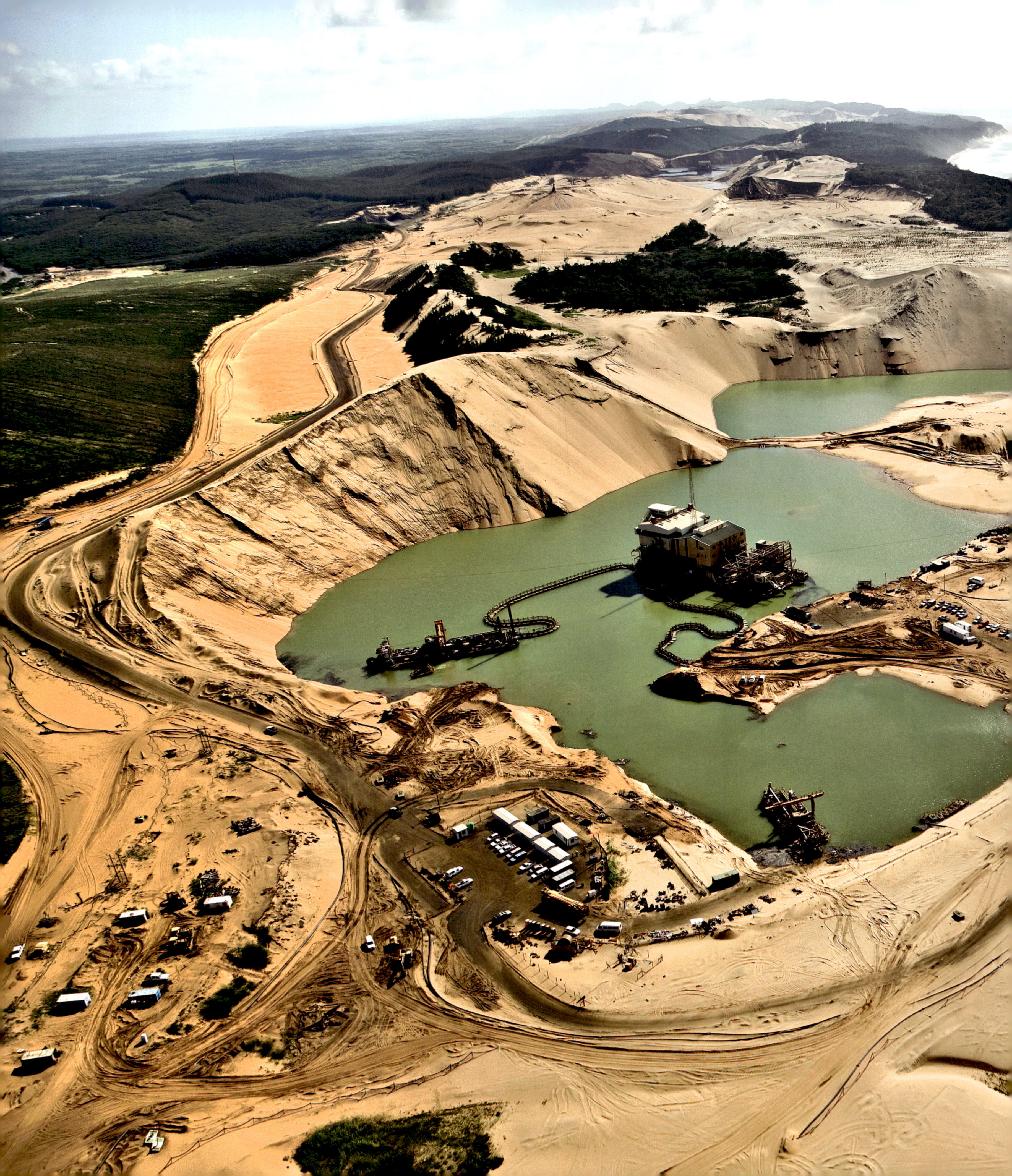

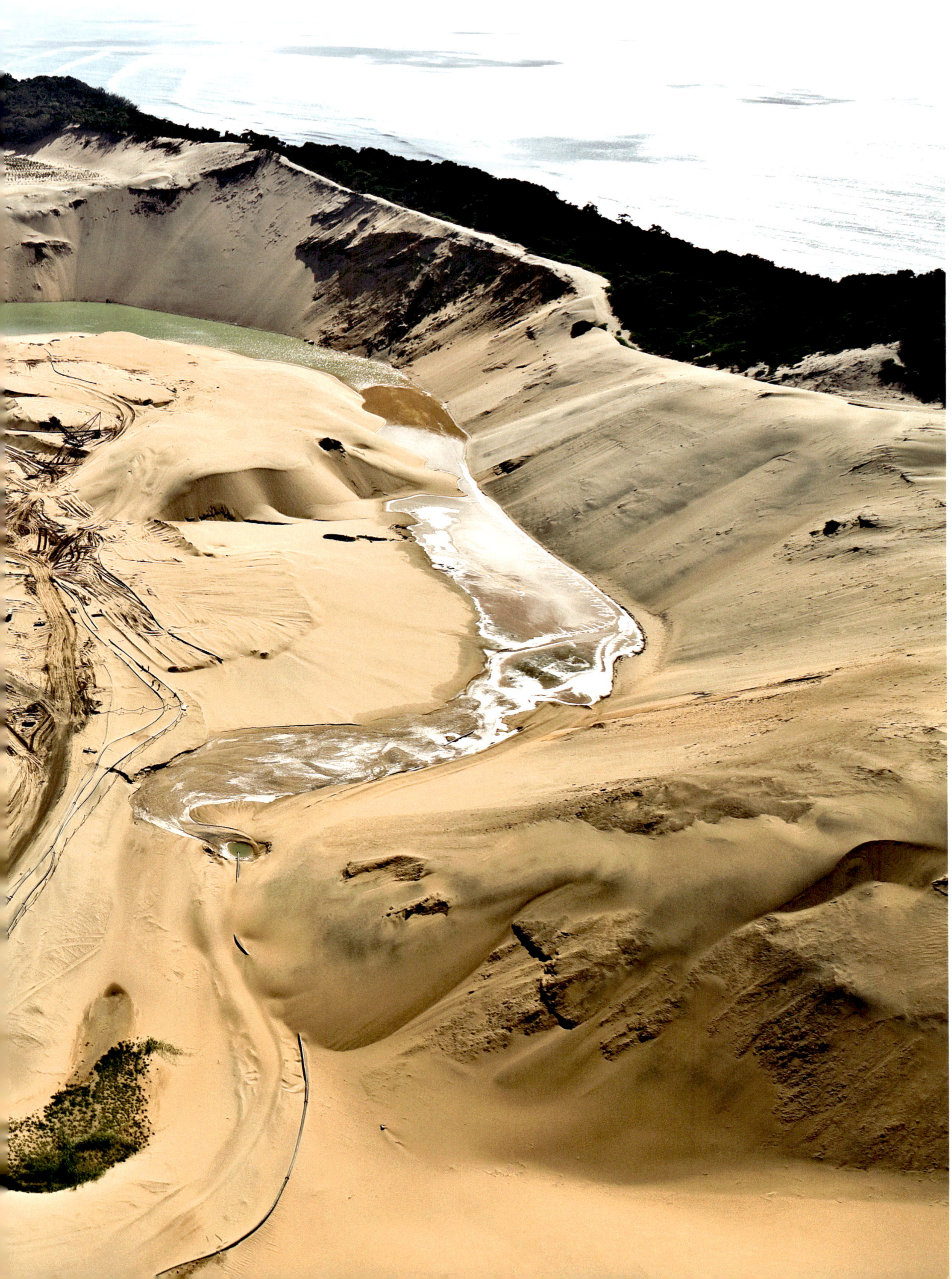

← Titanium mining, Richards Bay

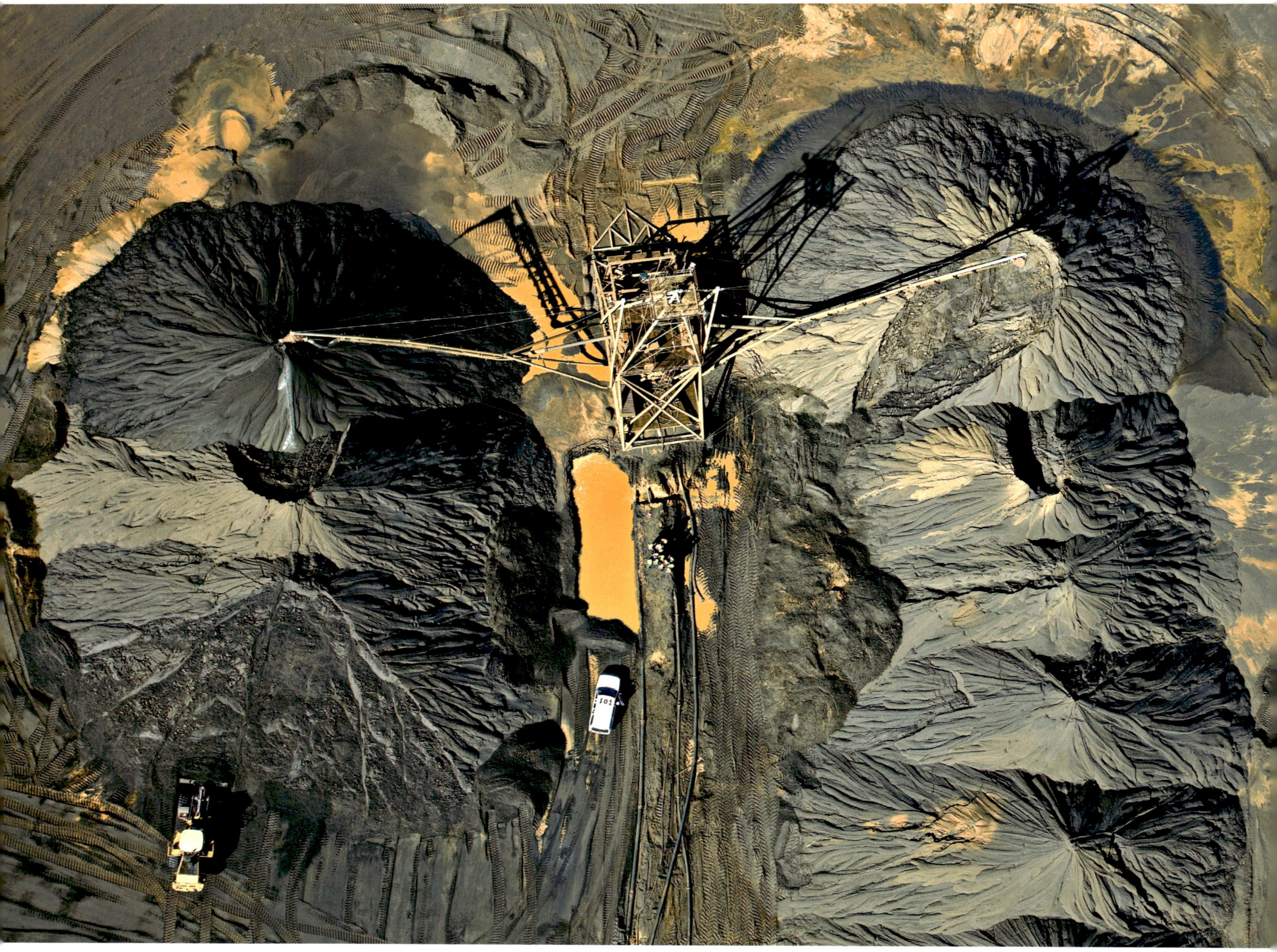

← Titanium mining, Richards Bay
↓ The cooling of molten steel, Richards Bay

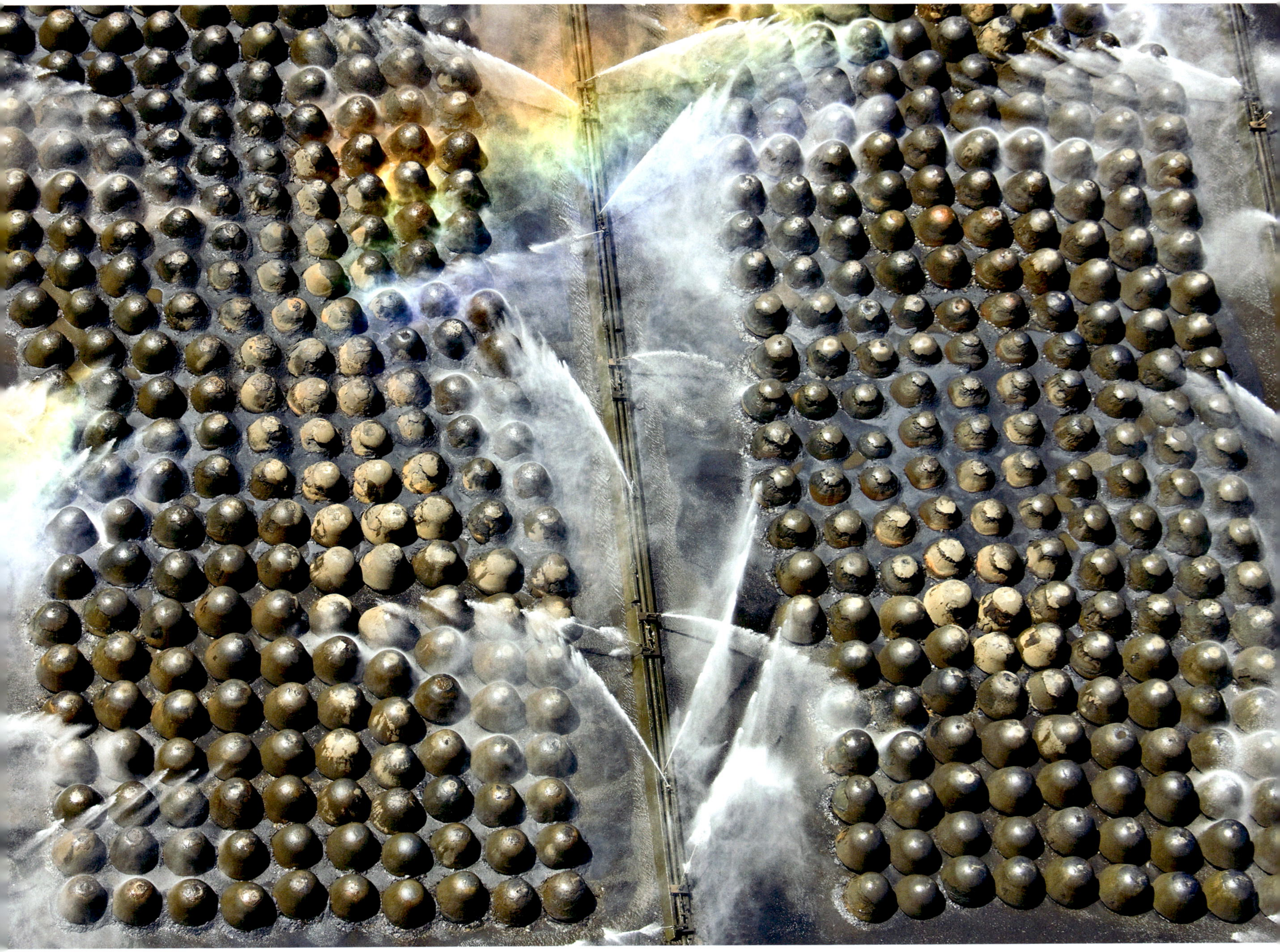

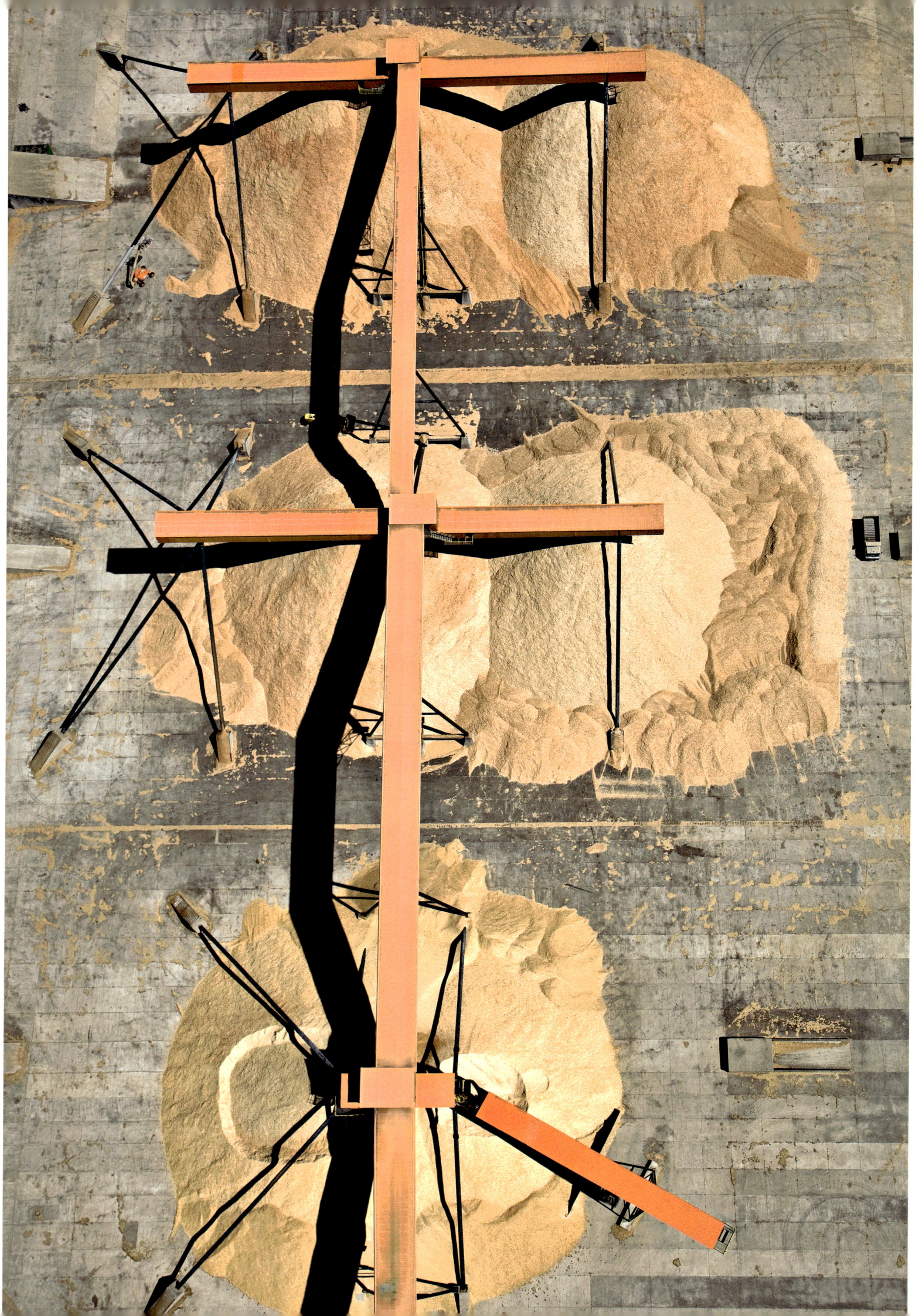

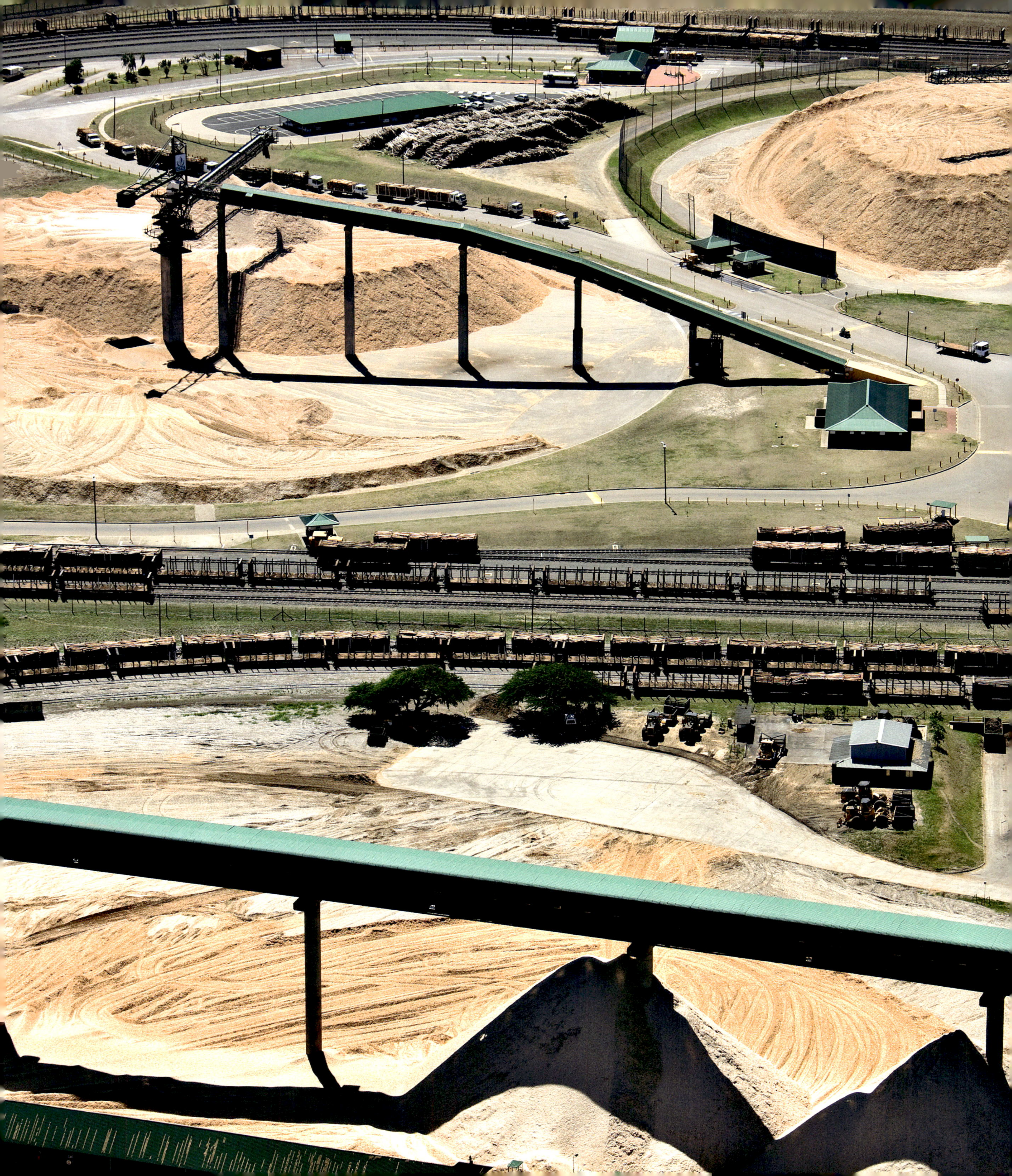

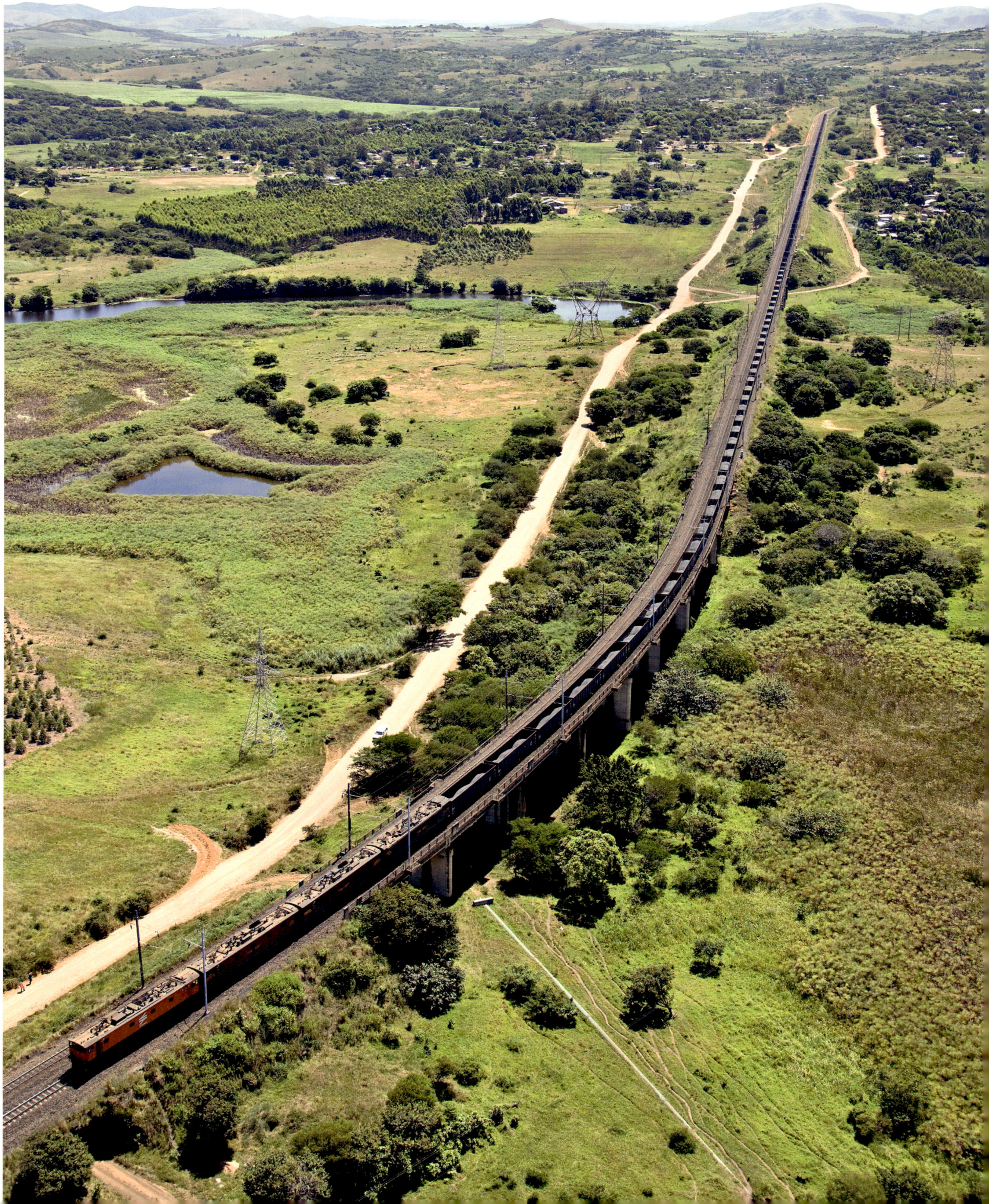

←← Heavy industry, Richards Bay
← Long coal train on its way to Richards Bay
→ Molten aluminium blocks, Richards Bay

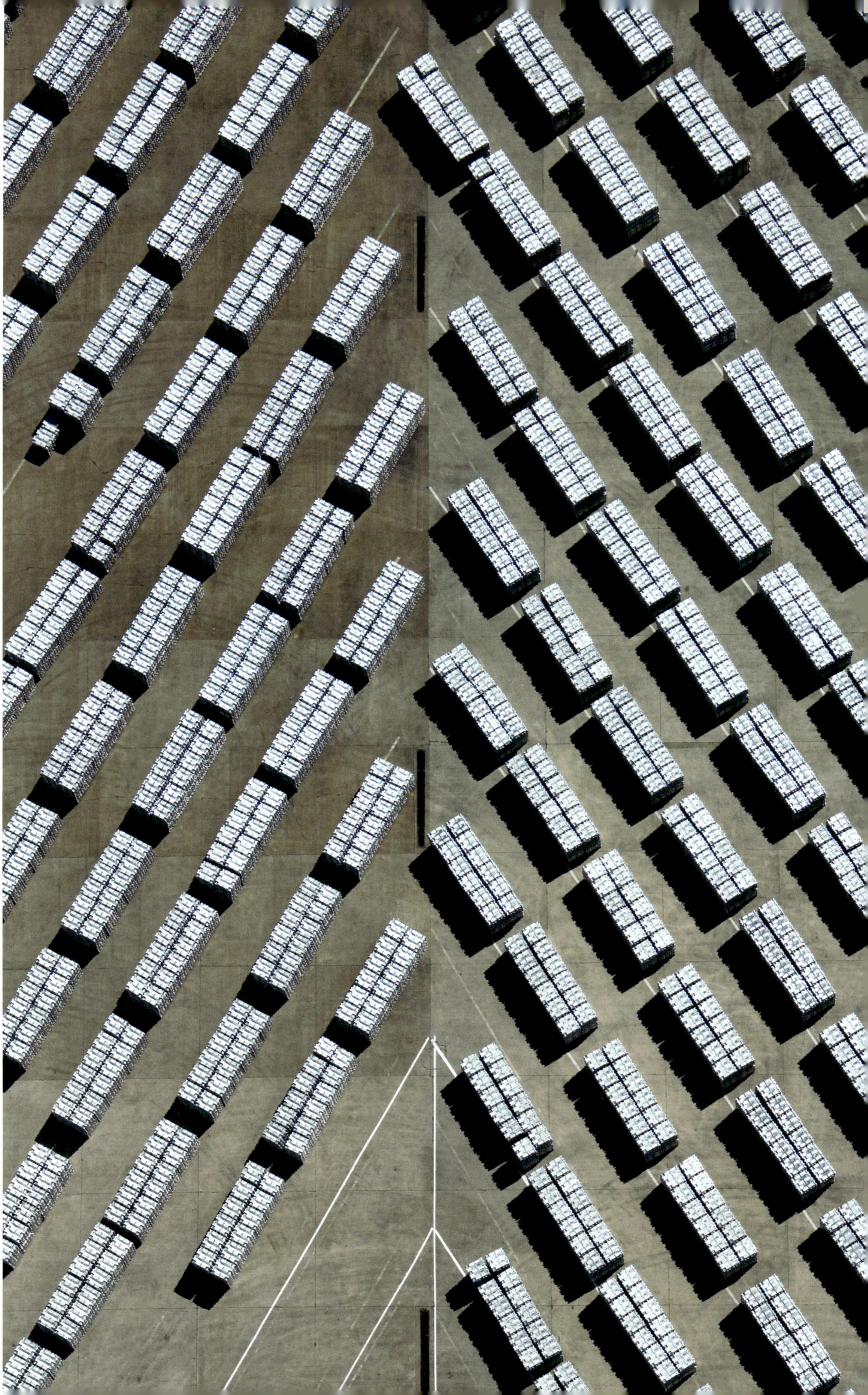

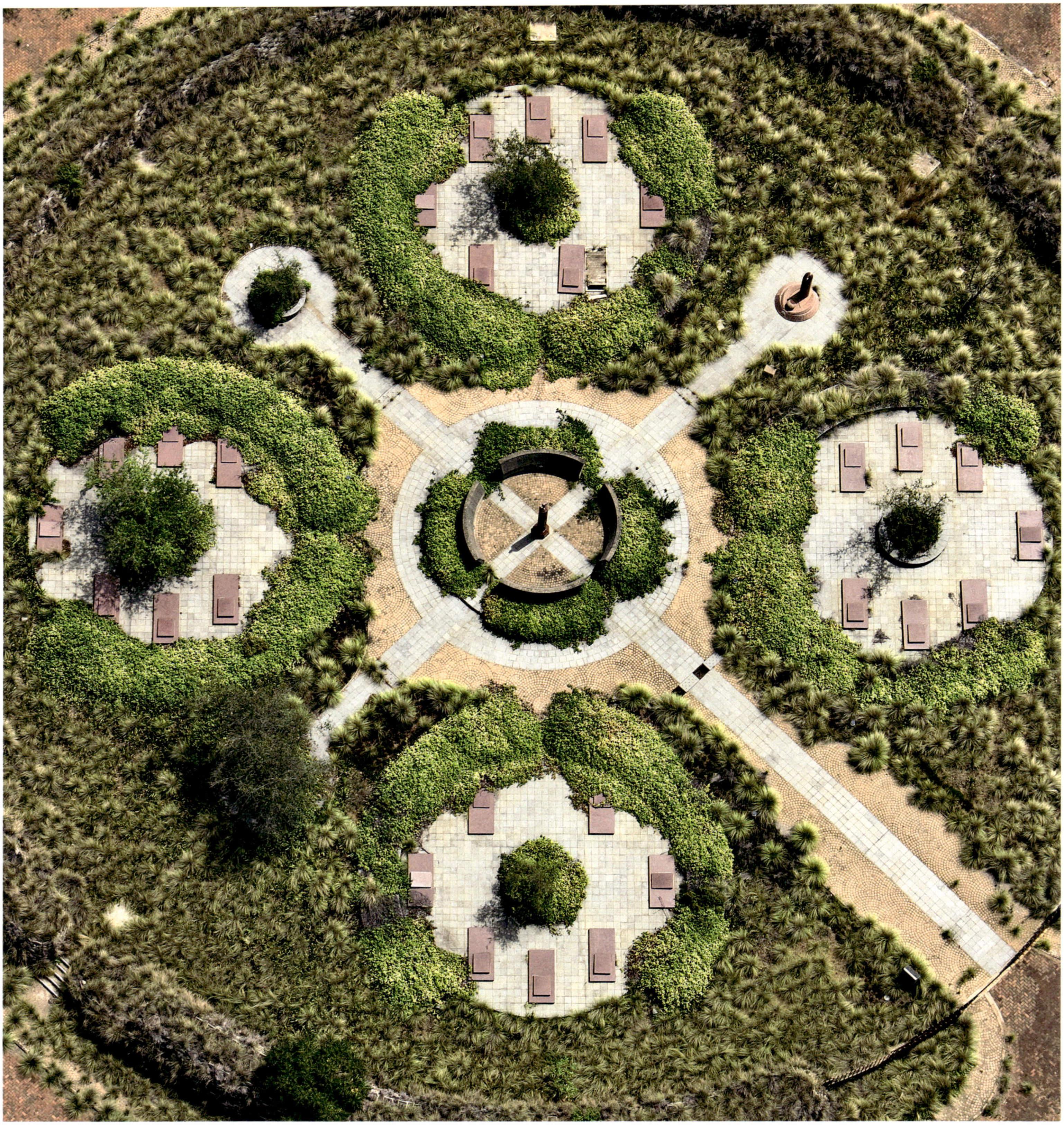

←↓ Zulu Monument in Ulundi, capital of KwaZulu-Natal

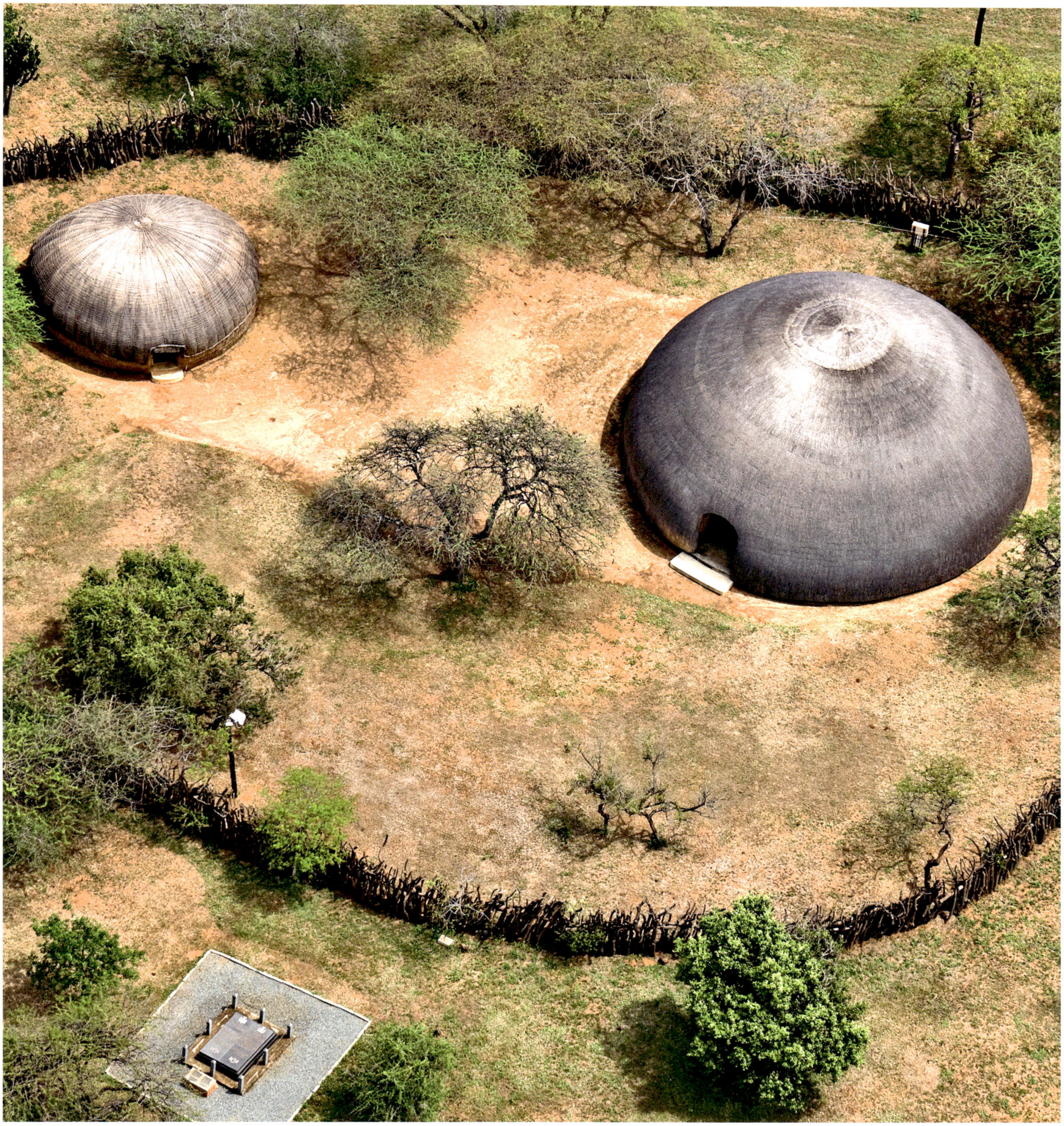

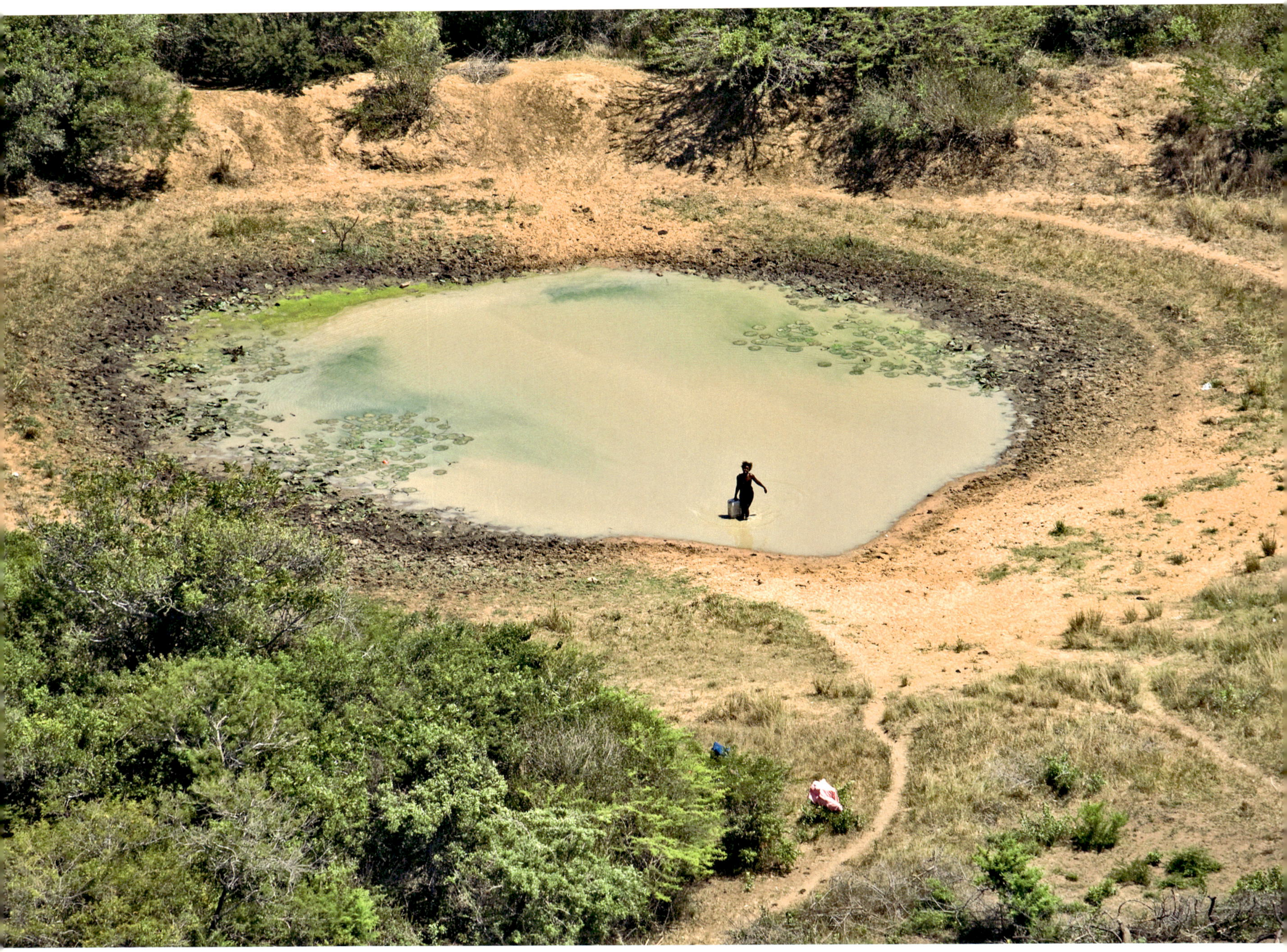

← Water for washing
↓ Cornfield with housing for the workers

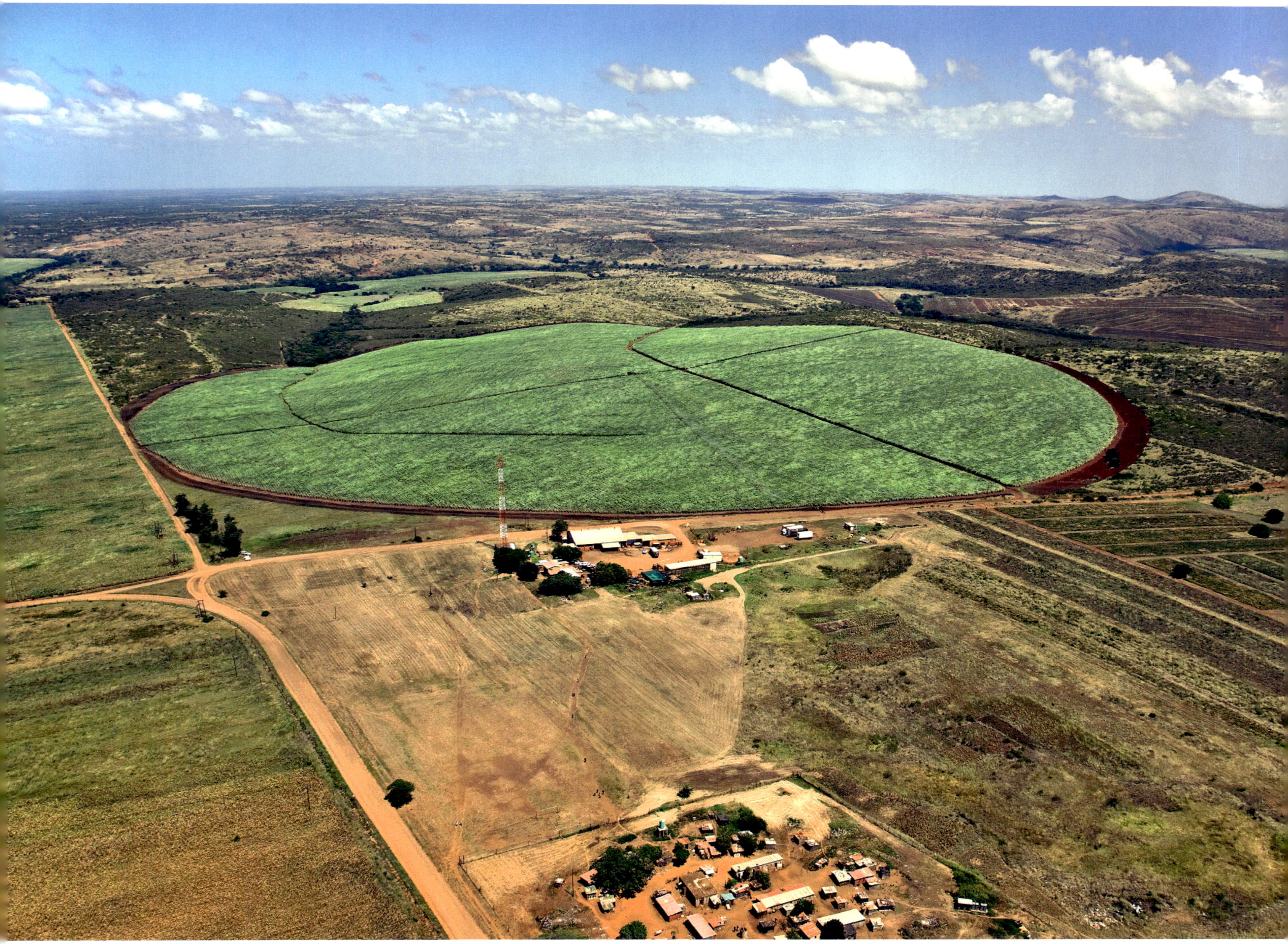

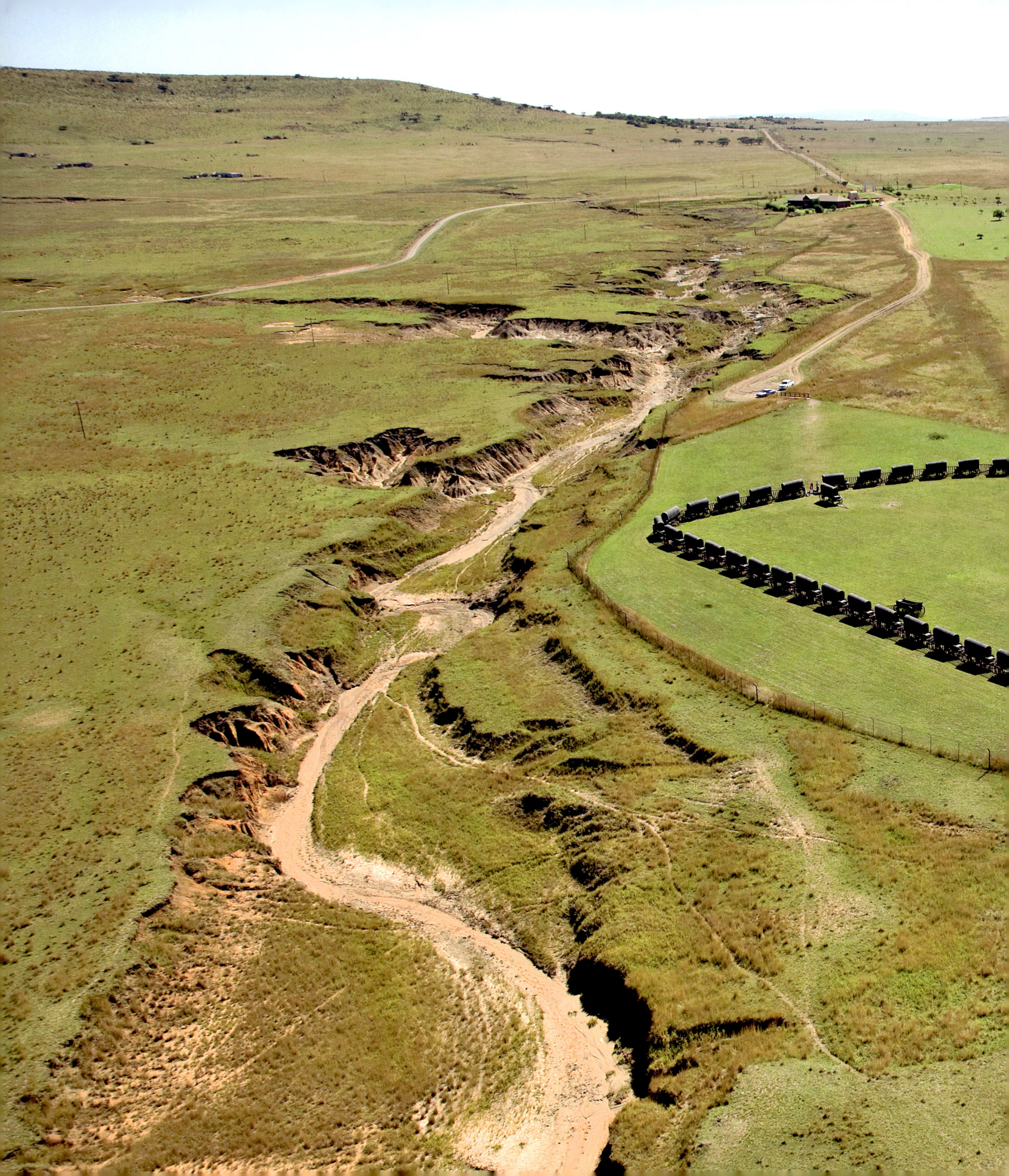

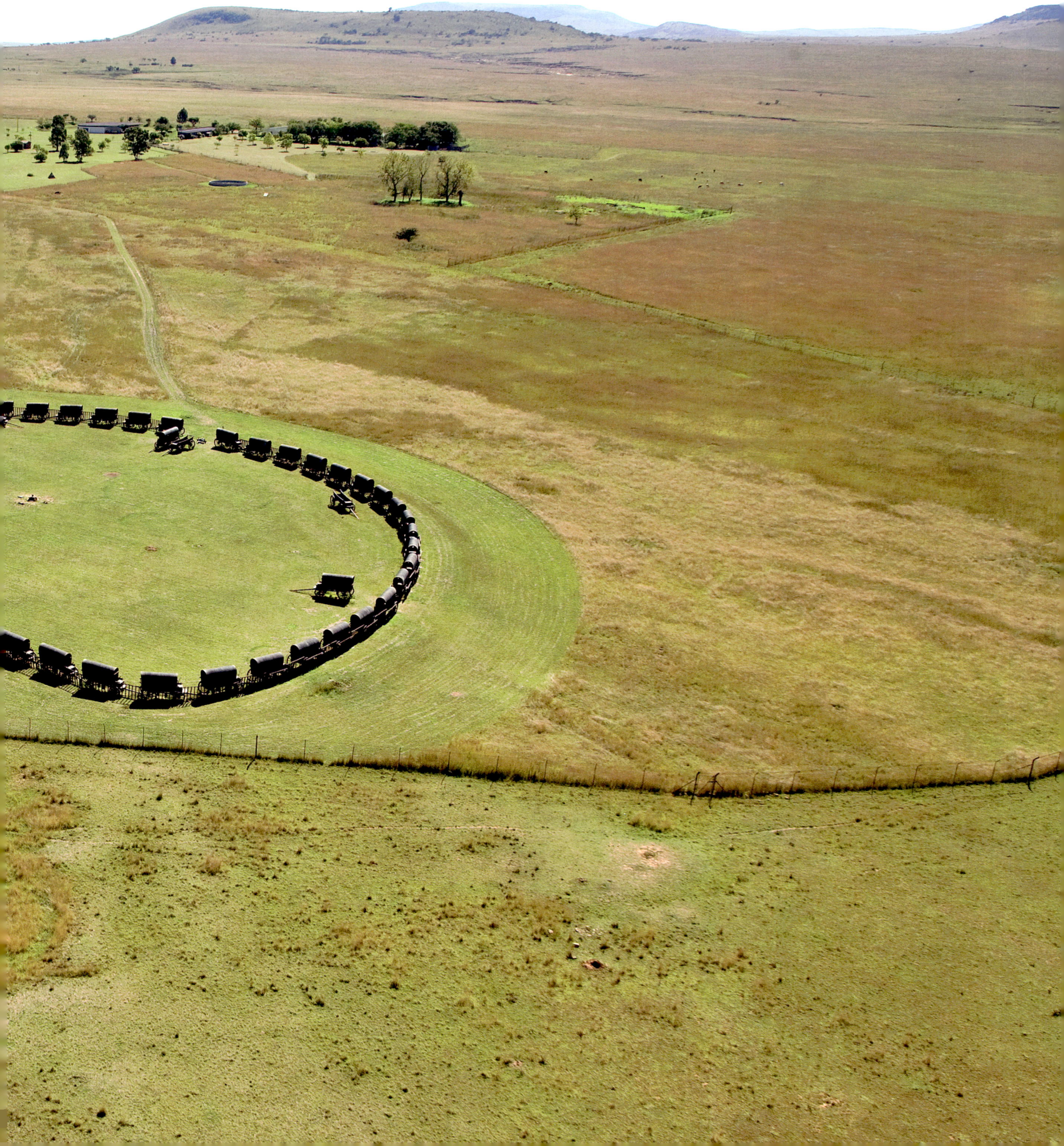

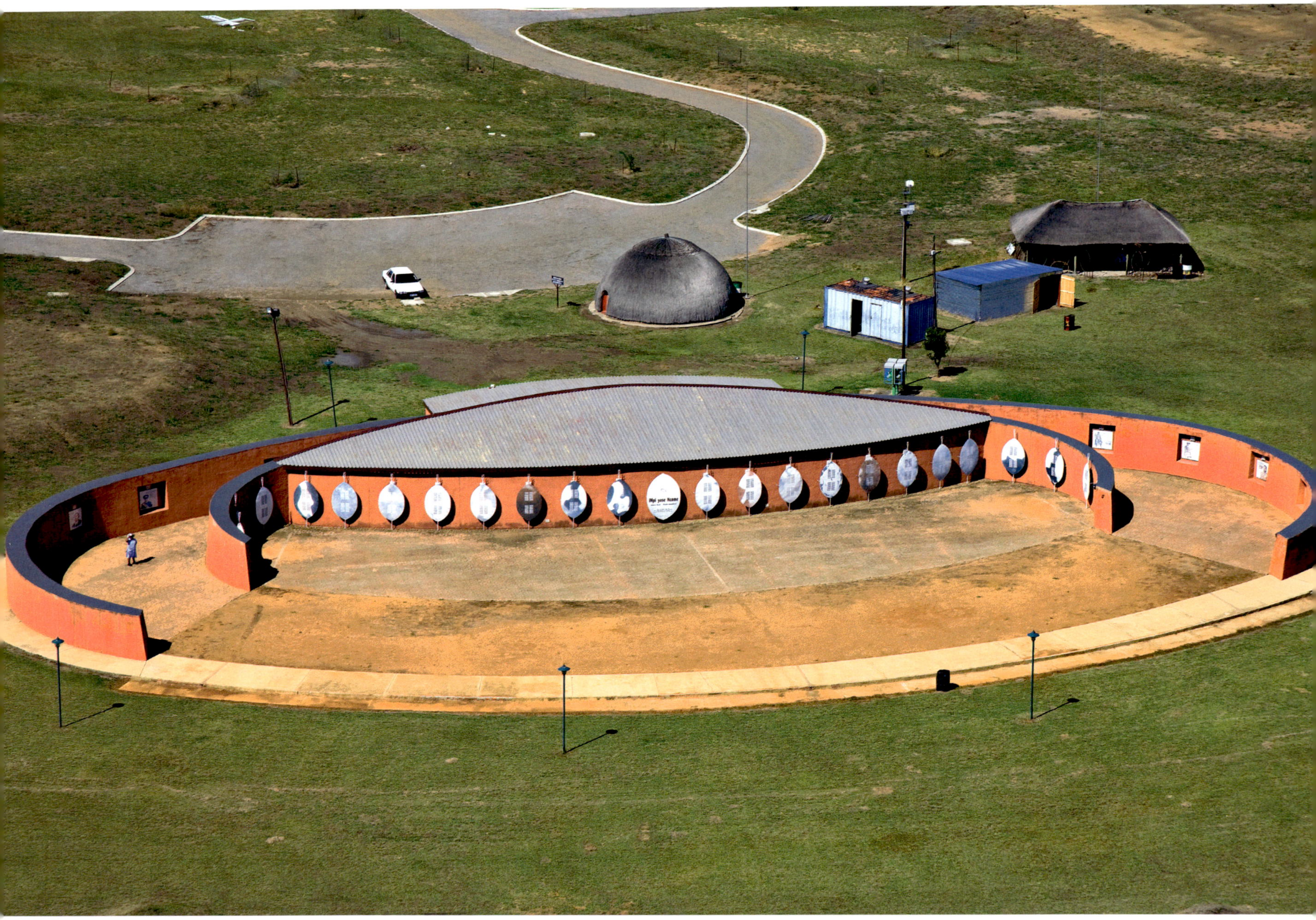

←← Blood River Memorial
← Zulu Memorial, Blood River
↓ Ox-wagon replicas, Blood River

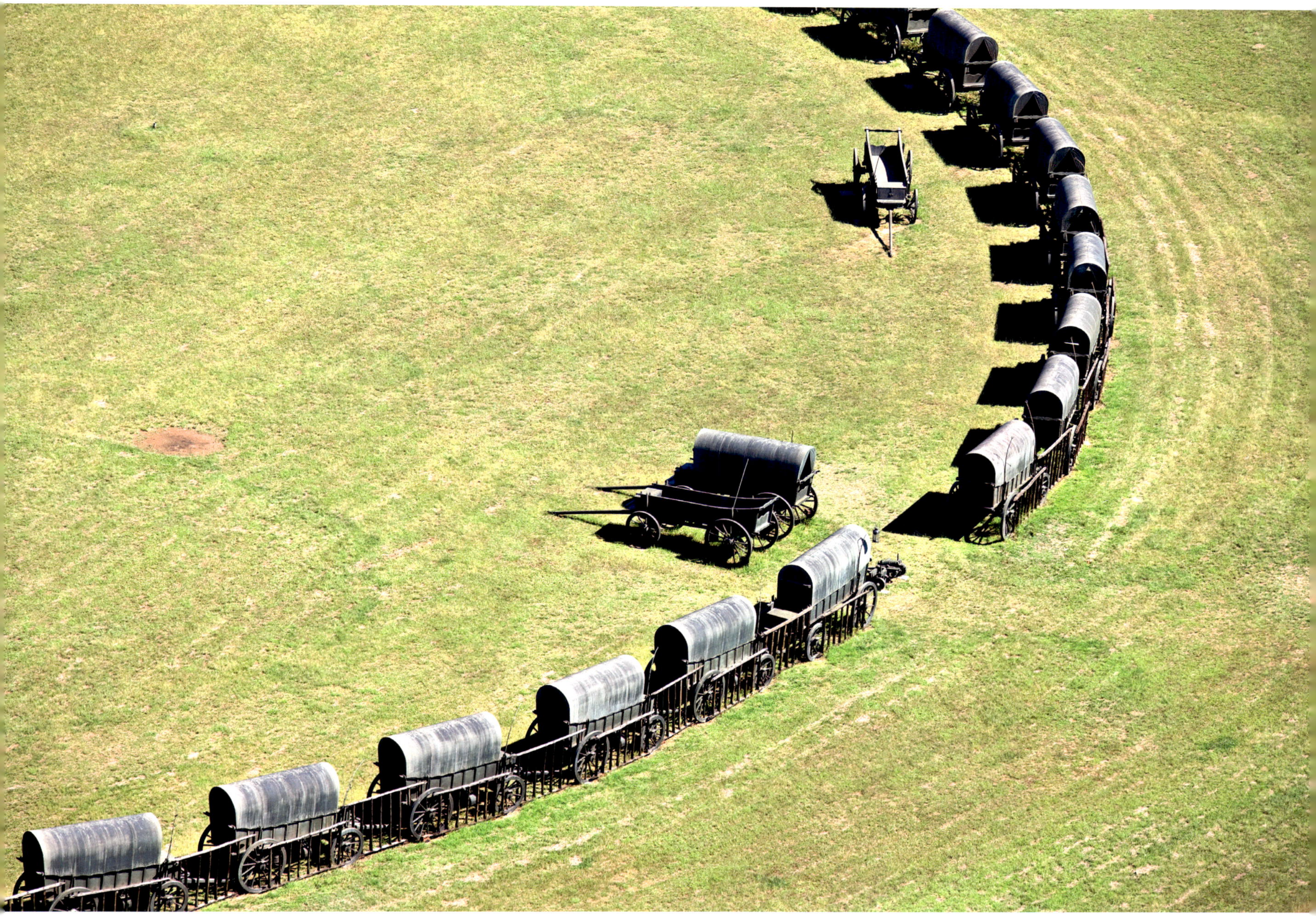

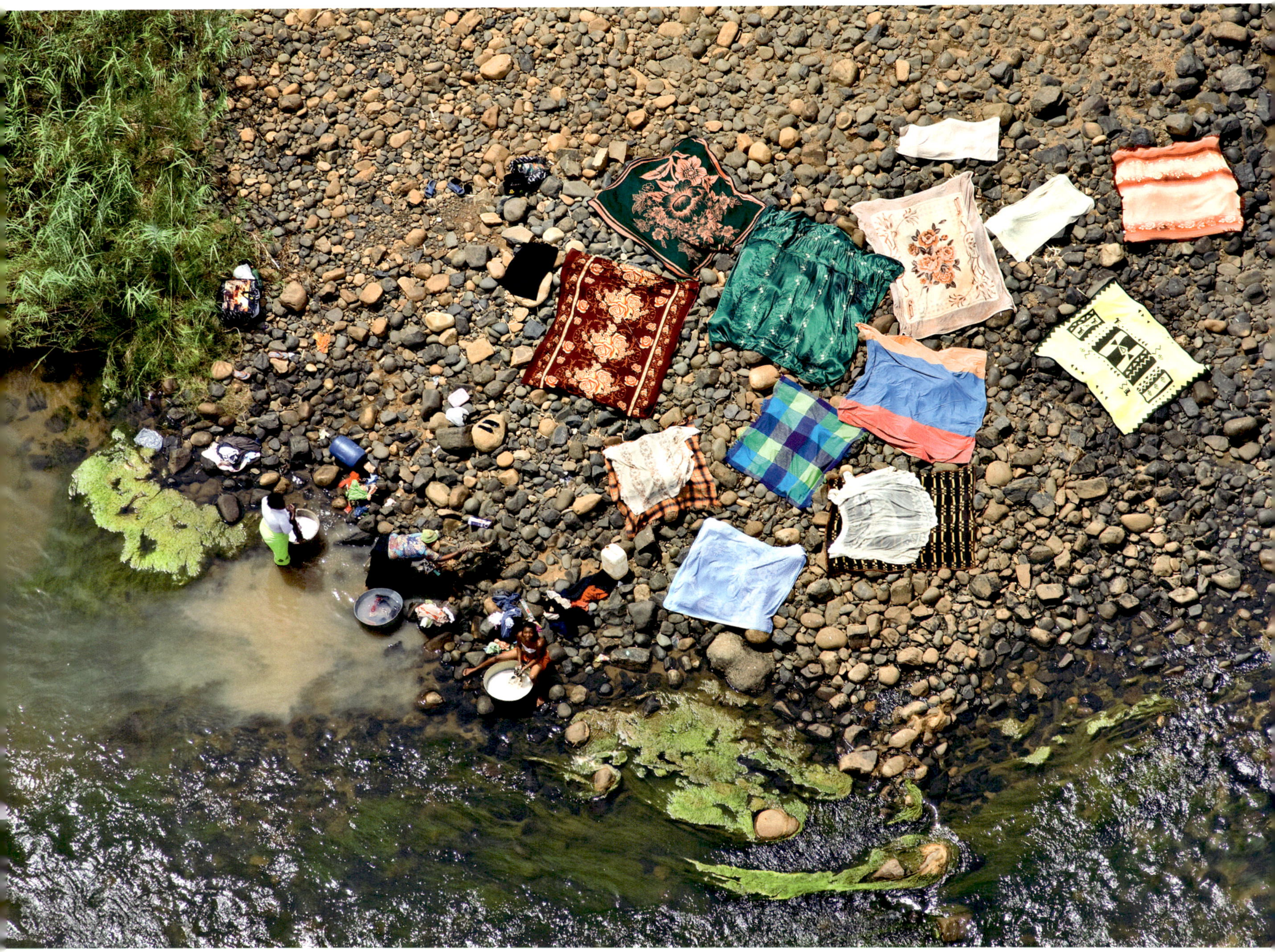

← Washing day at the river mouth
↓ Wild buffalo in the Mkuze River

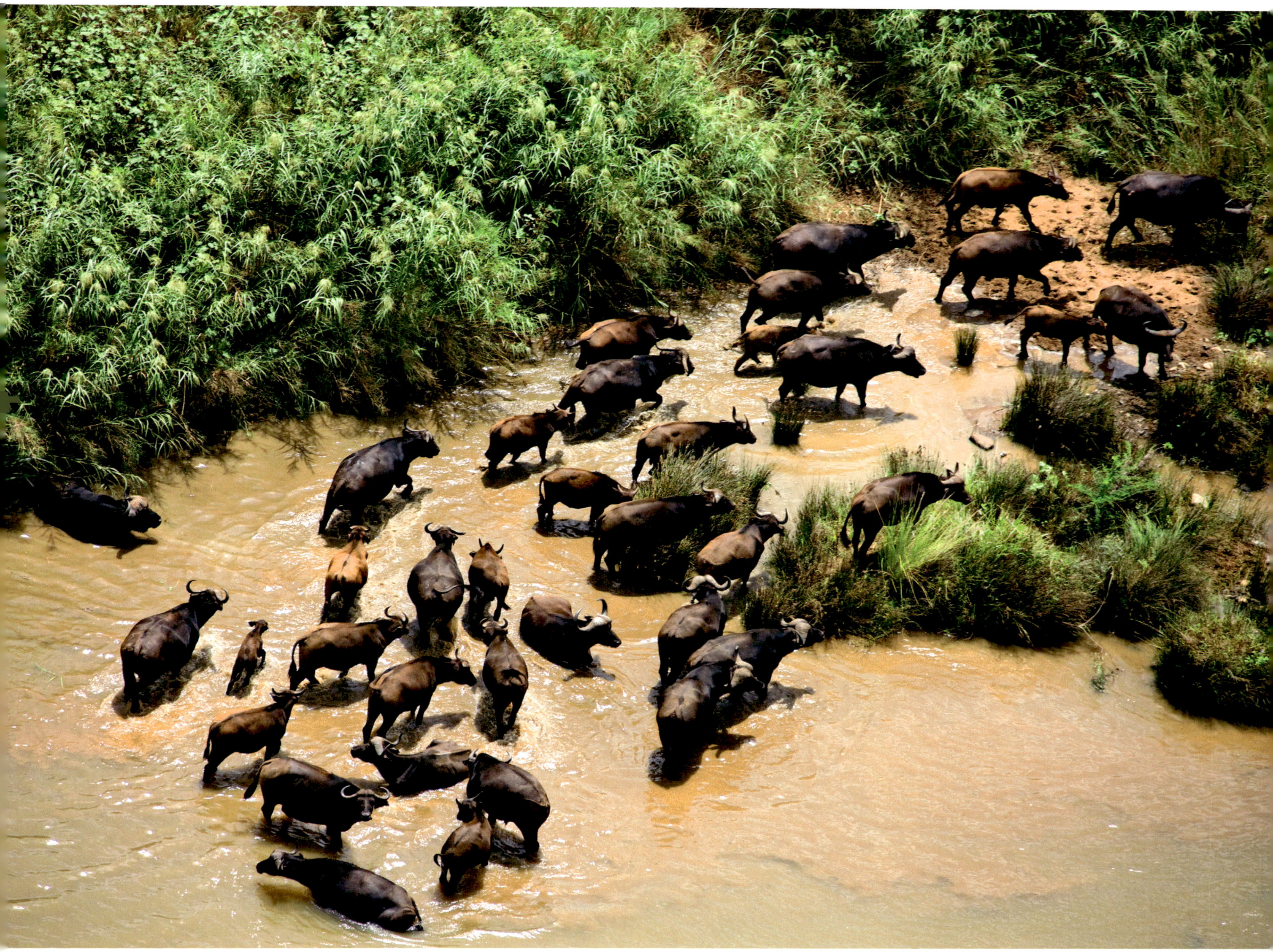

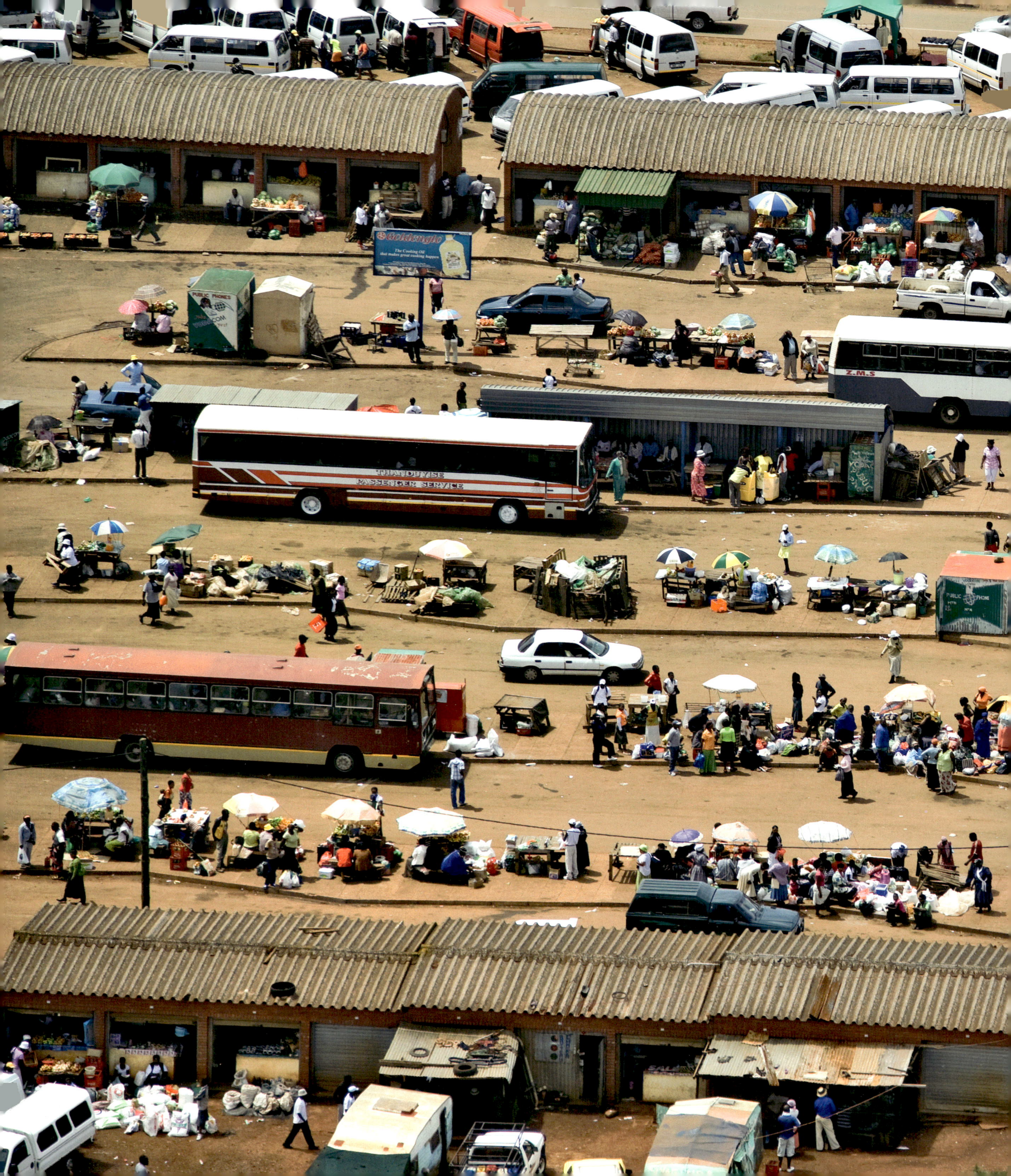
PUBLIC PHONES
THANDUYISE
PASSENGER SERVICE
Z.M.S

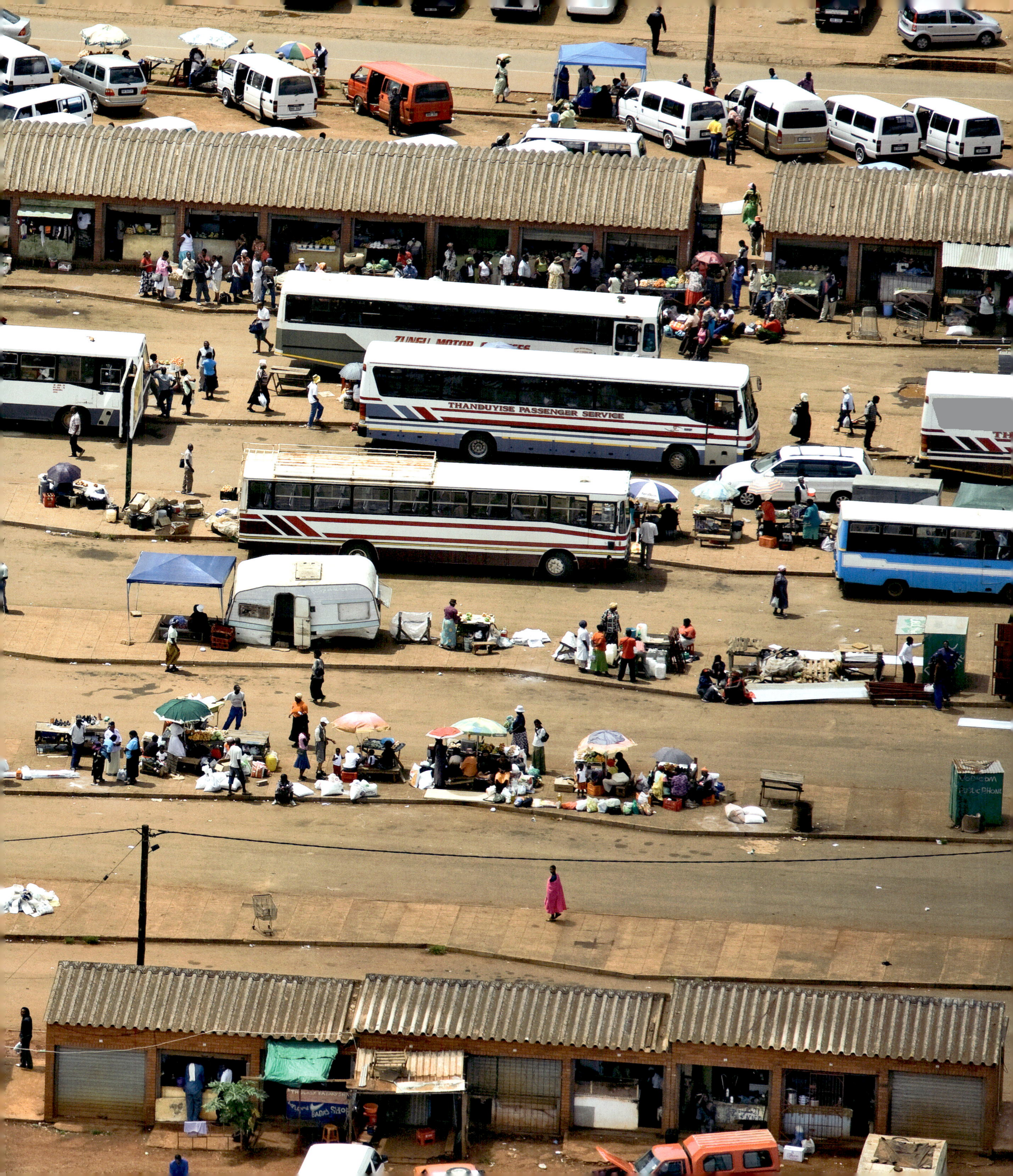
THANDUYISE PASSENGER SERVICE

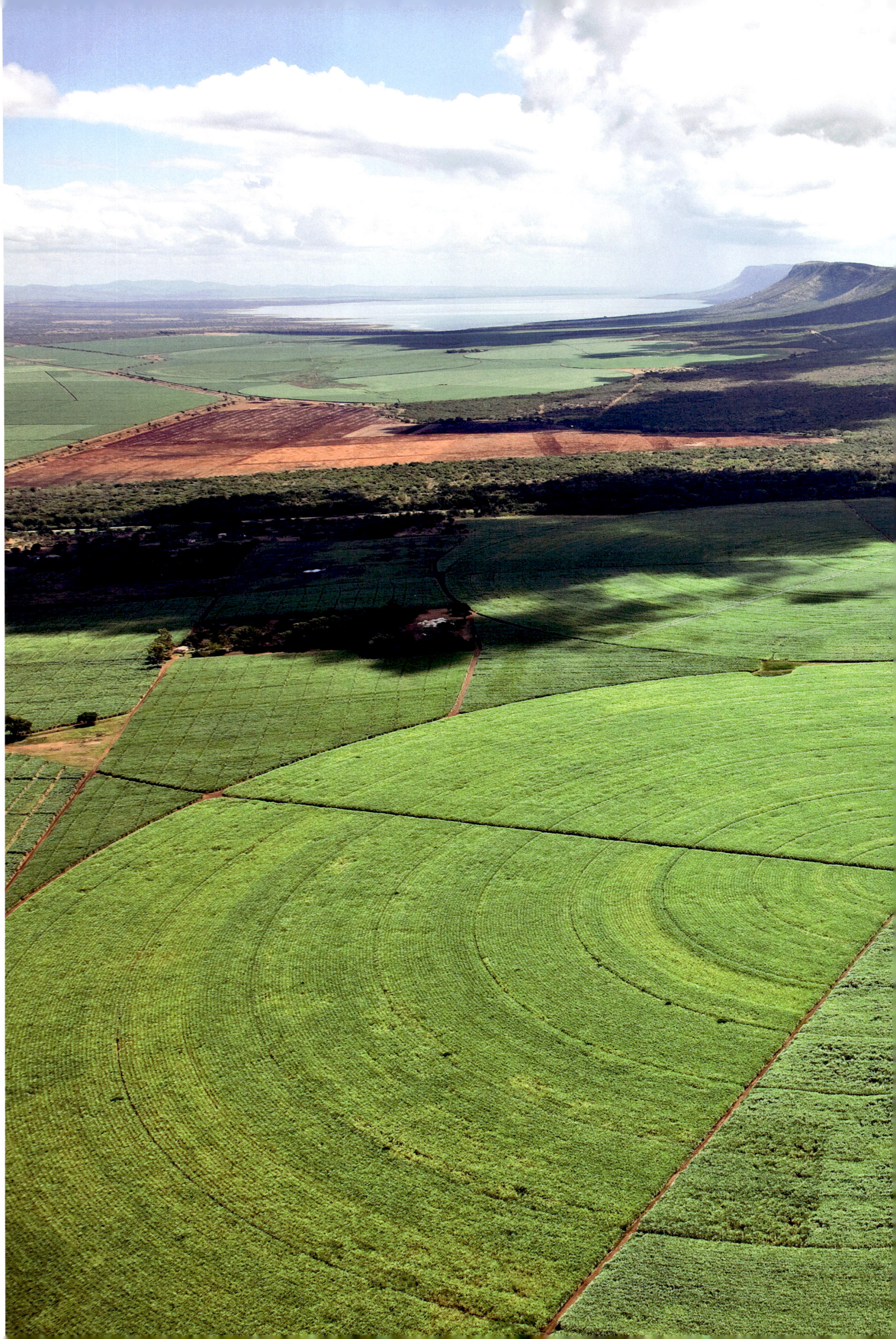

← Nongoma
→ Agriculture along the Phongholo River

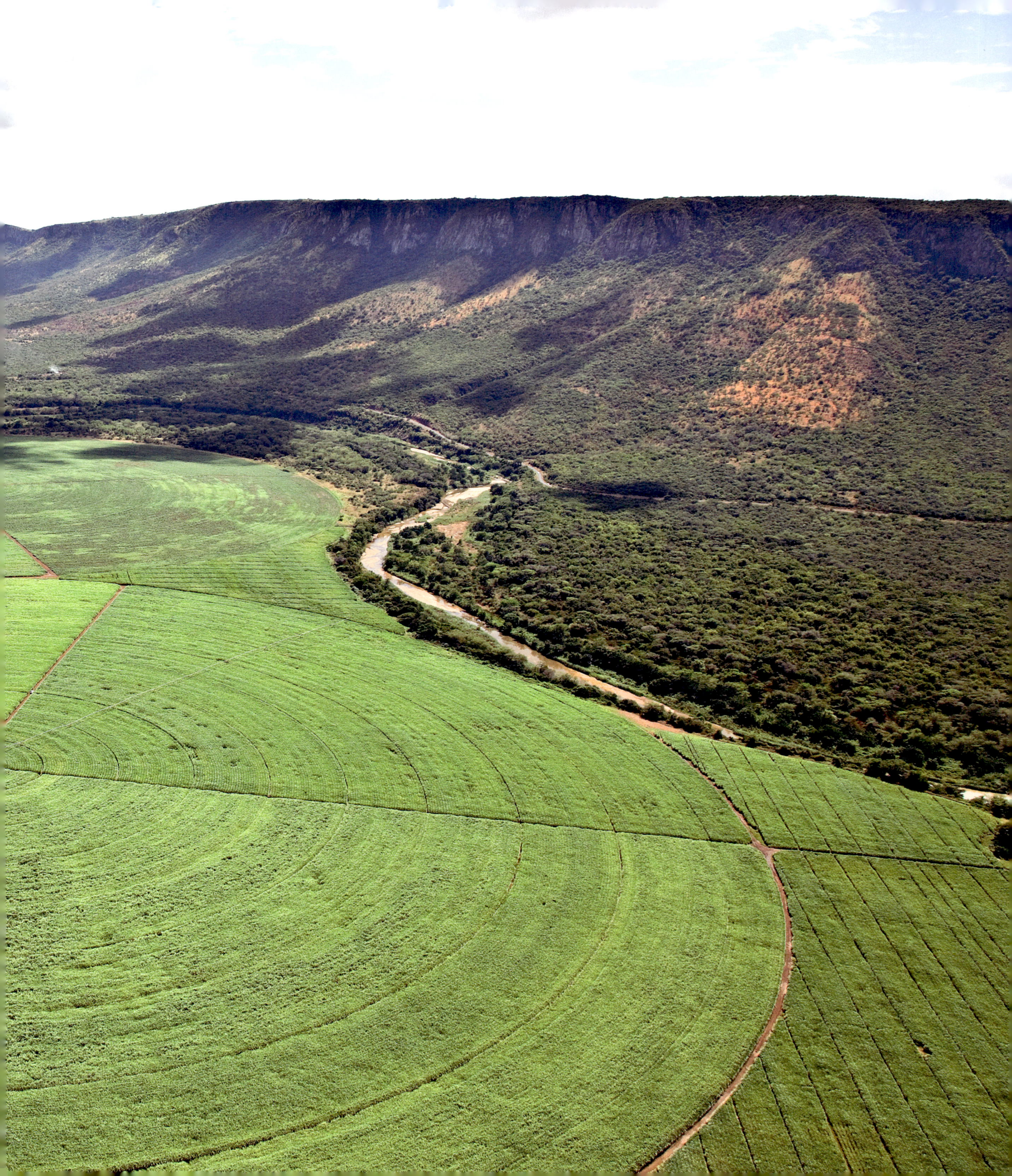

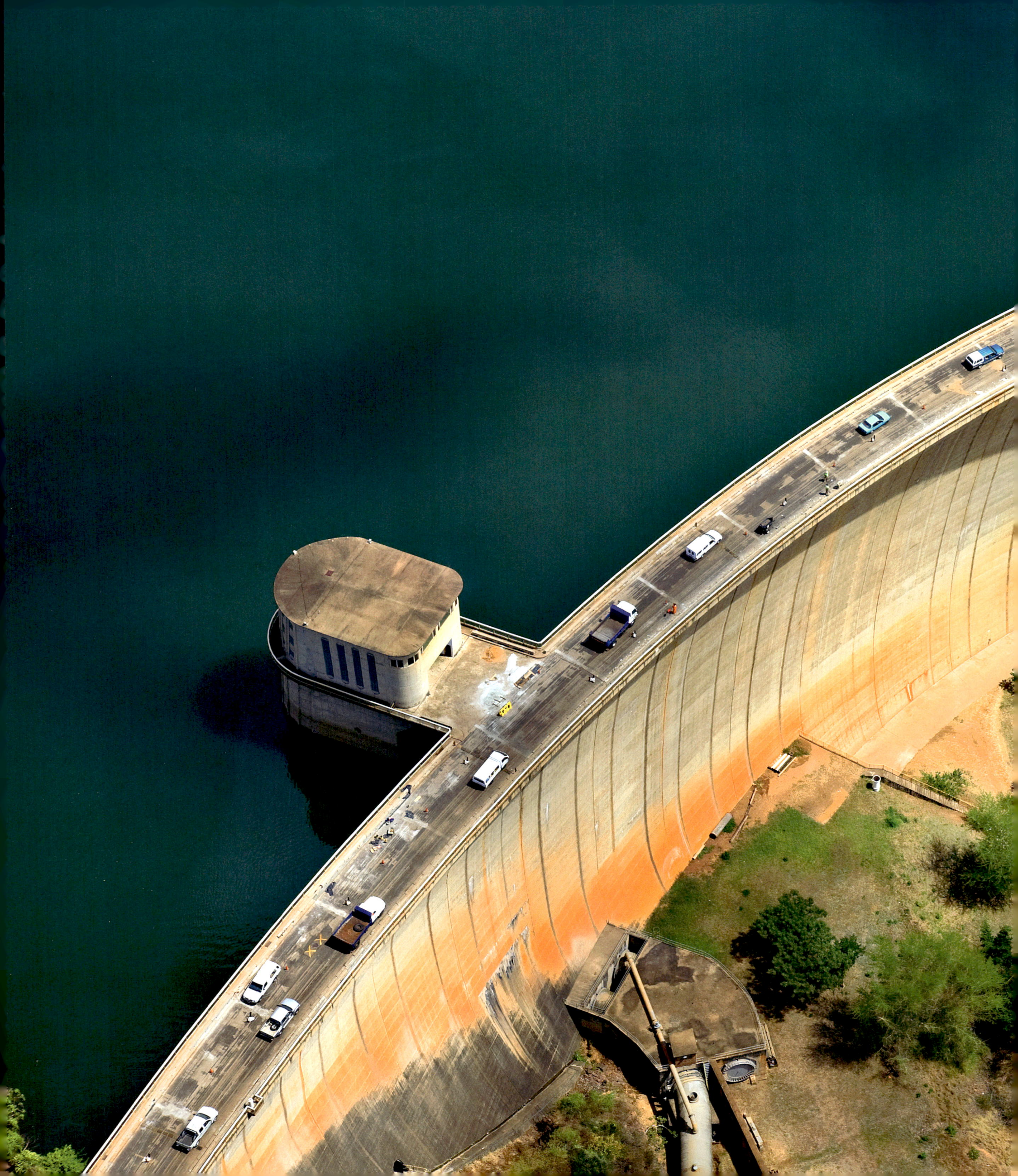

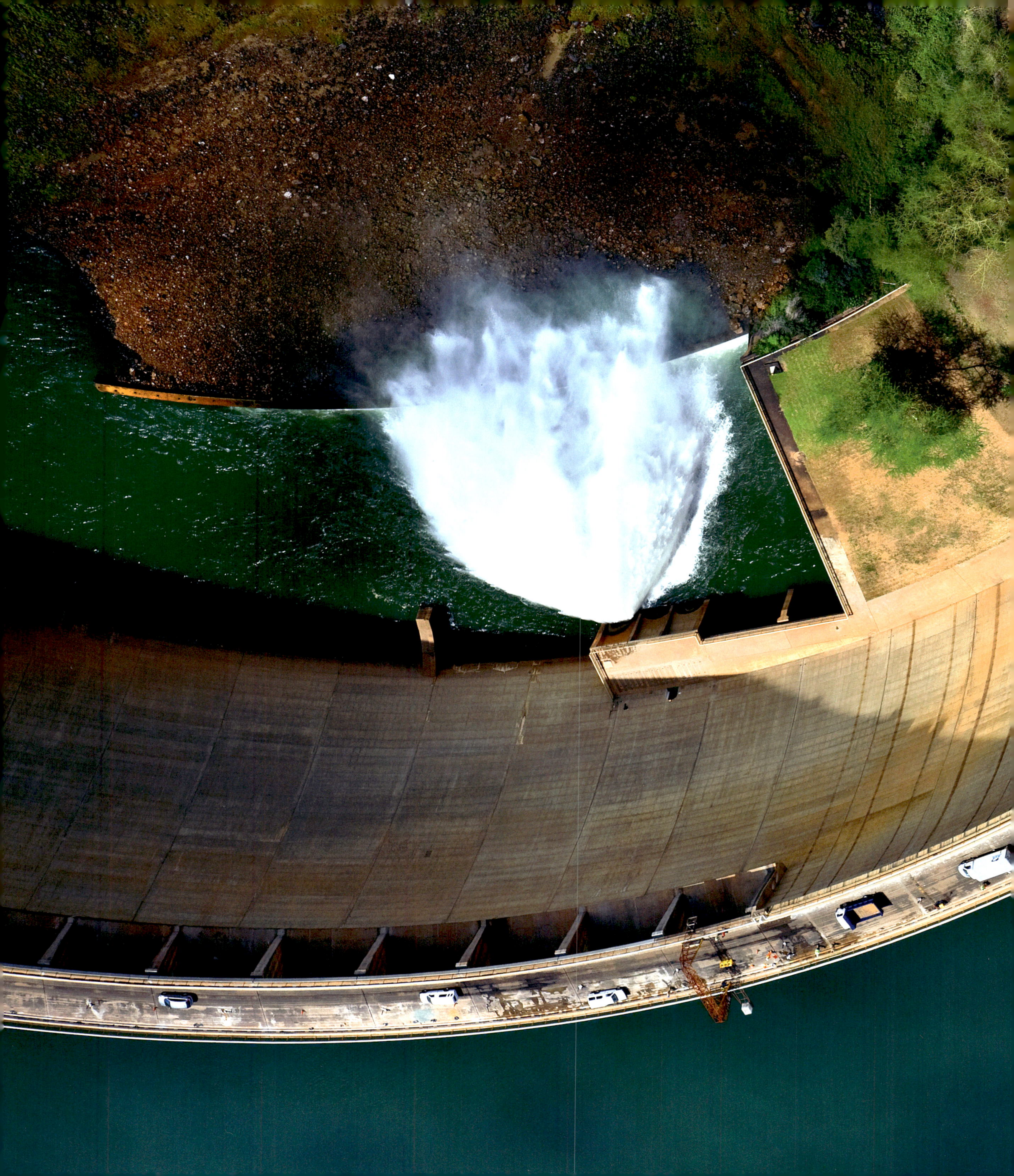

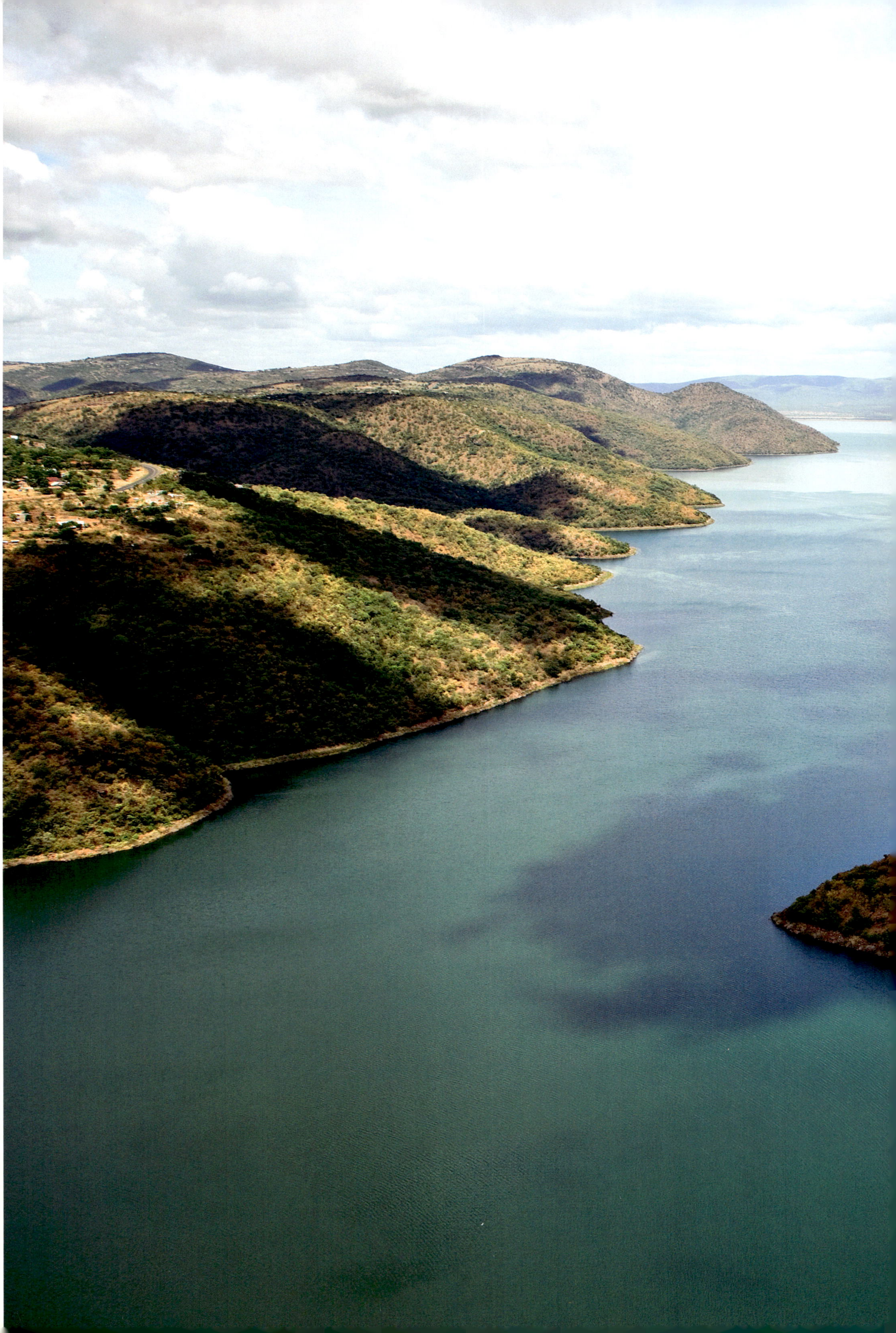

← Pongolapoort Dam
→ Pongolapoort River

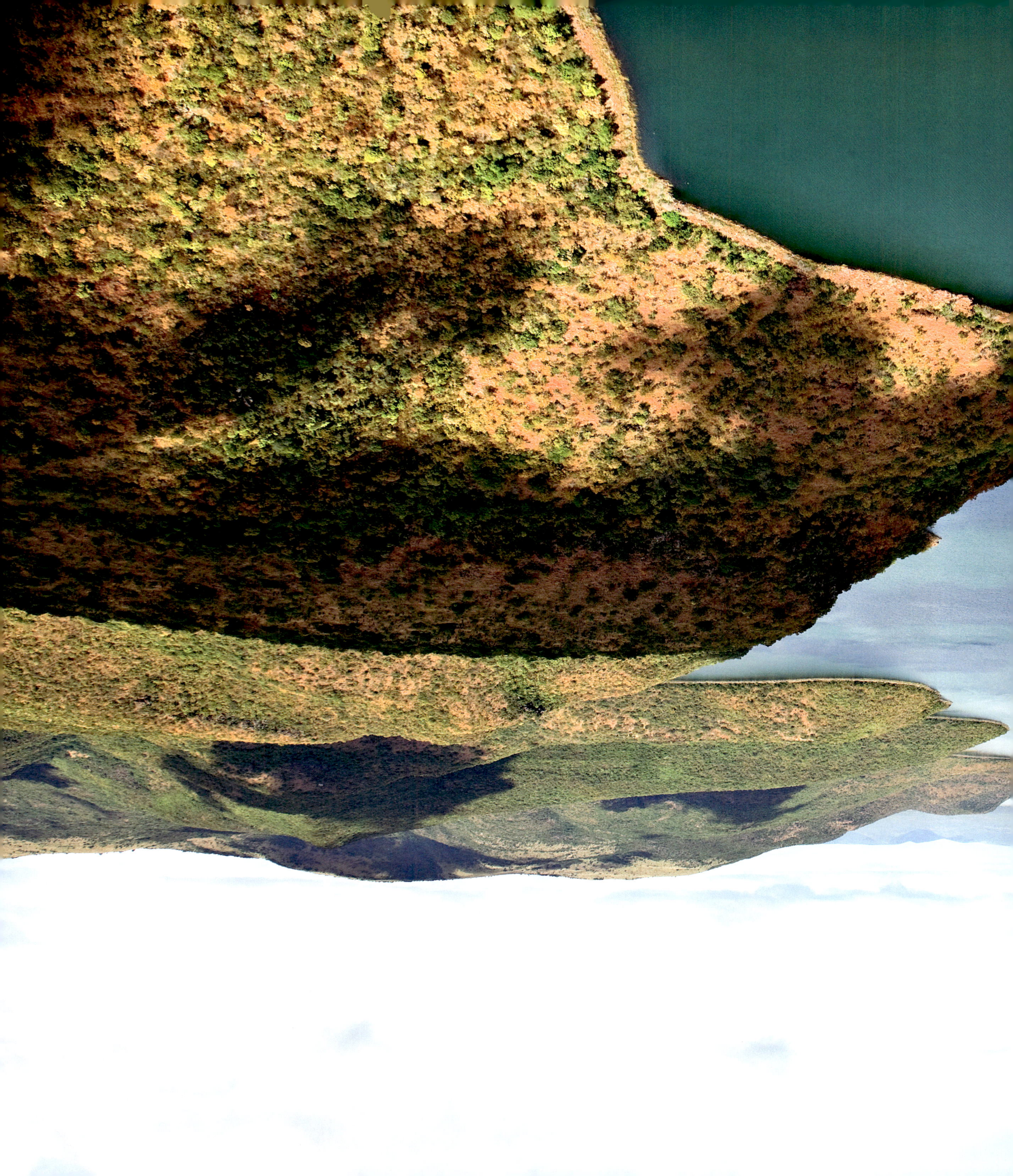

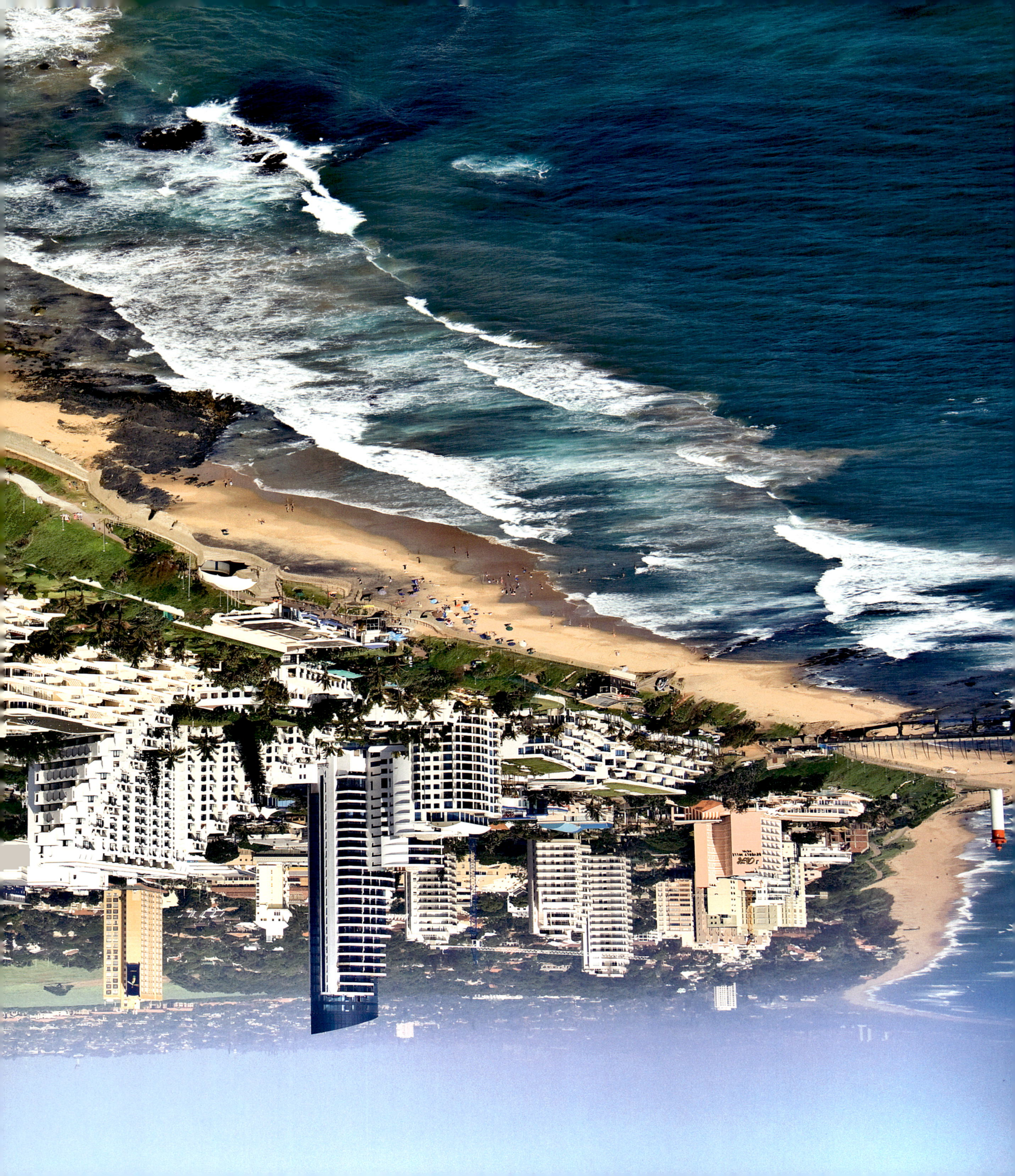

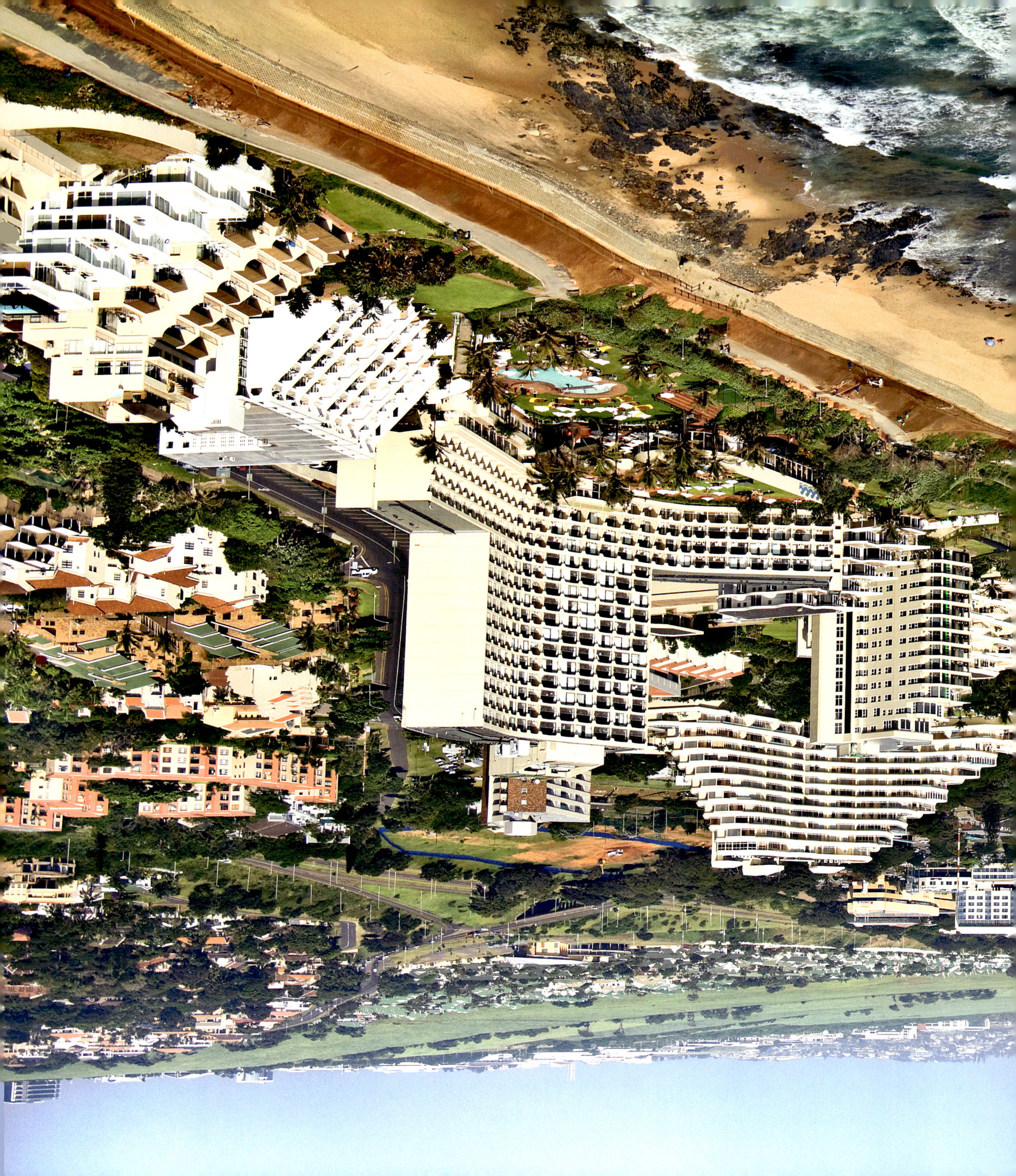

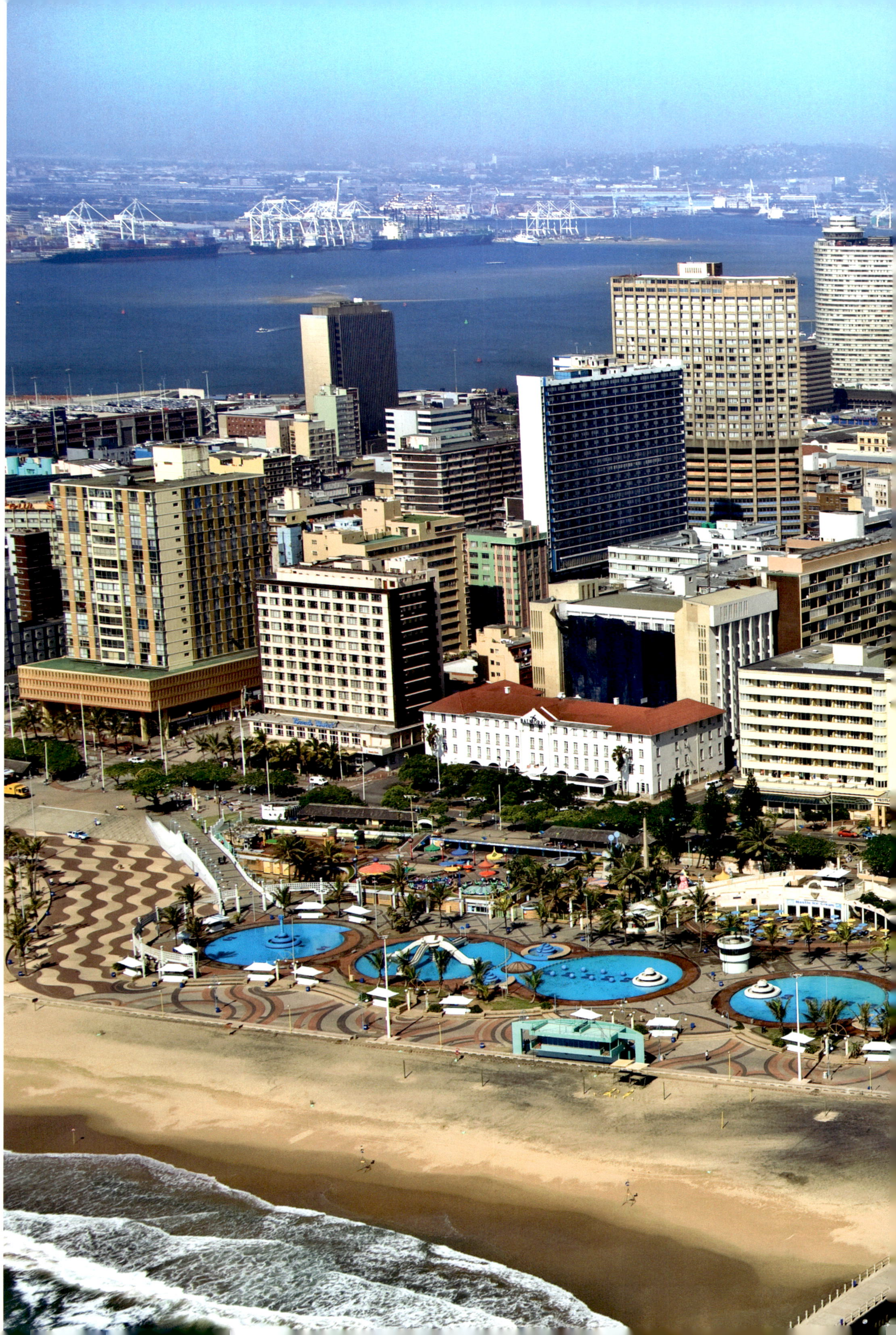

← Umhlanga Rocks
→ Durban

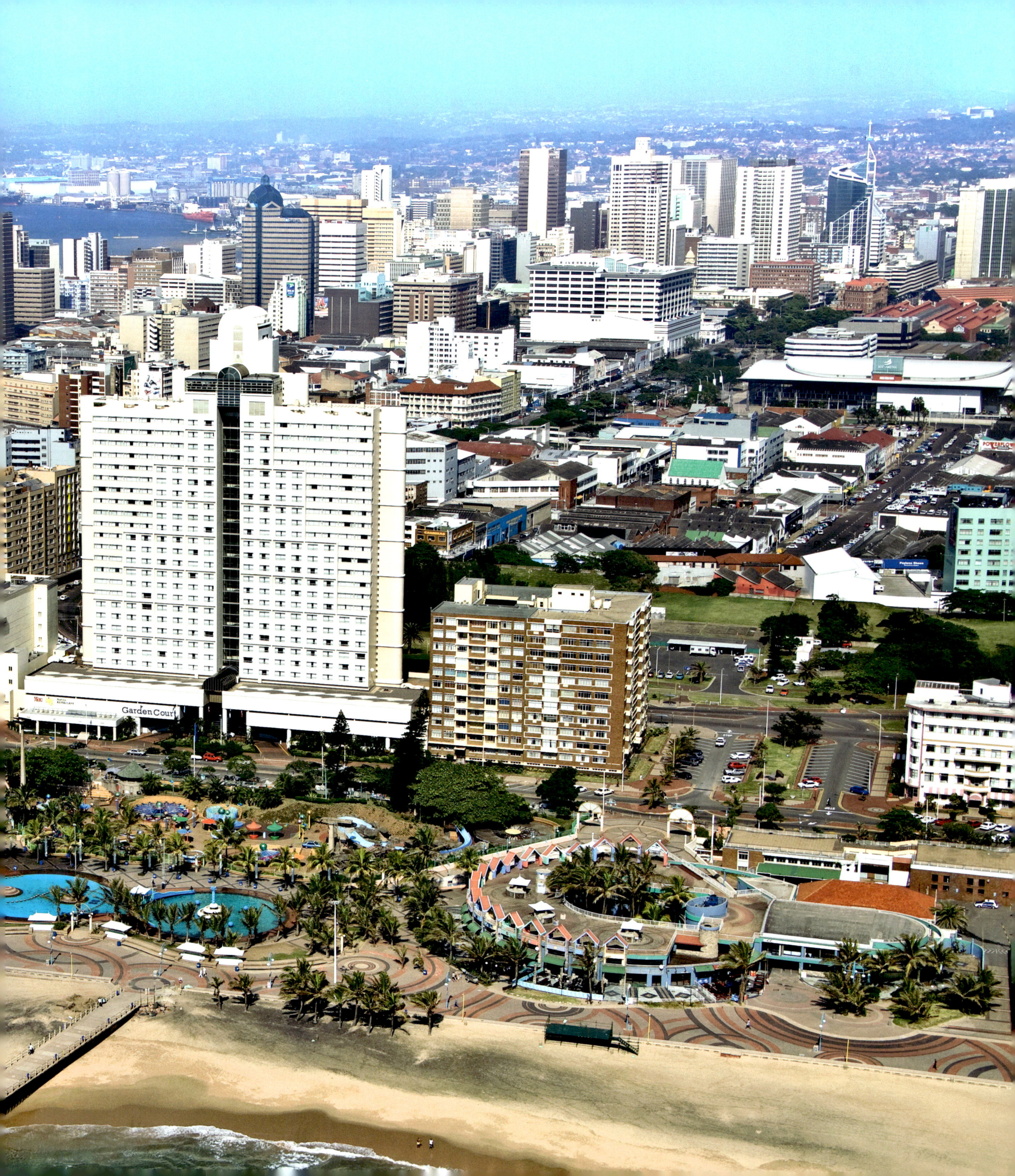
Garden Court

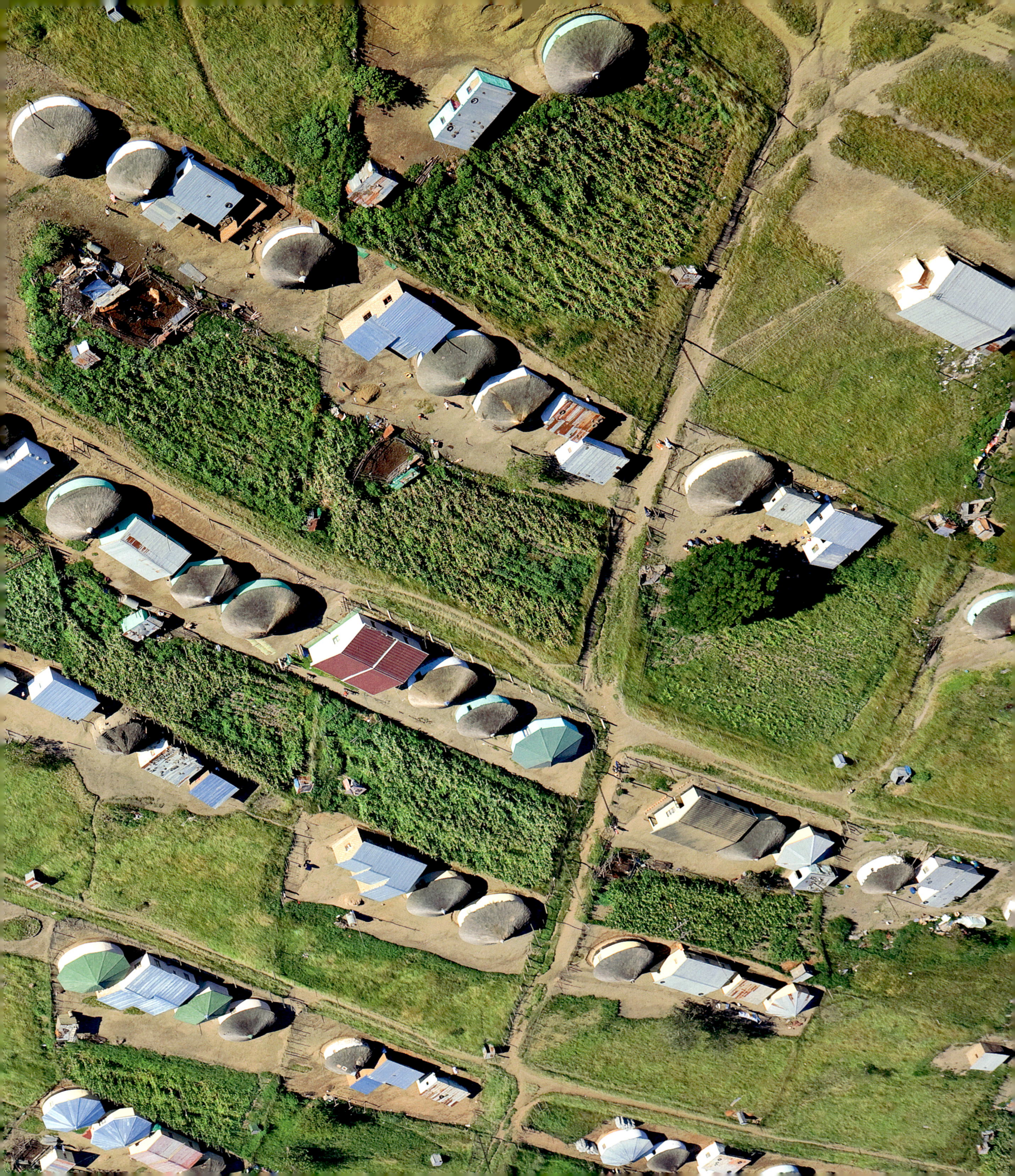

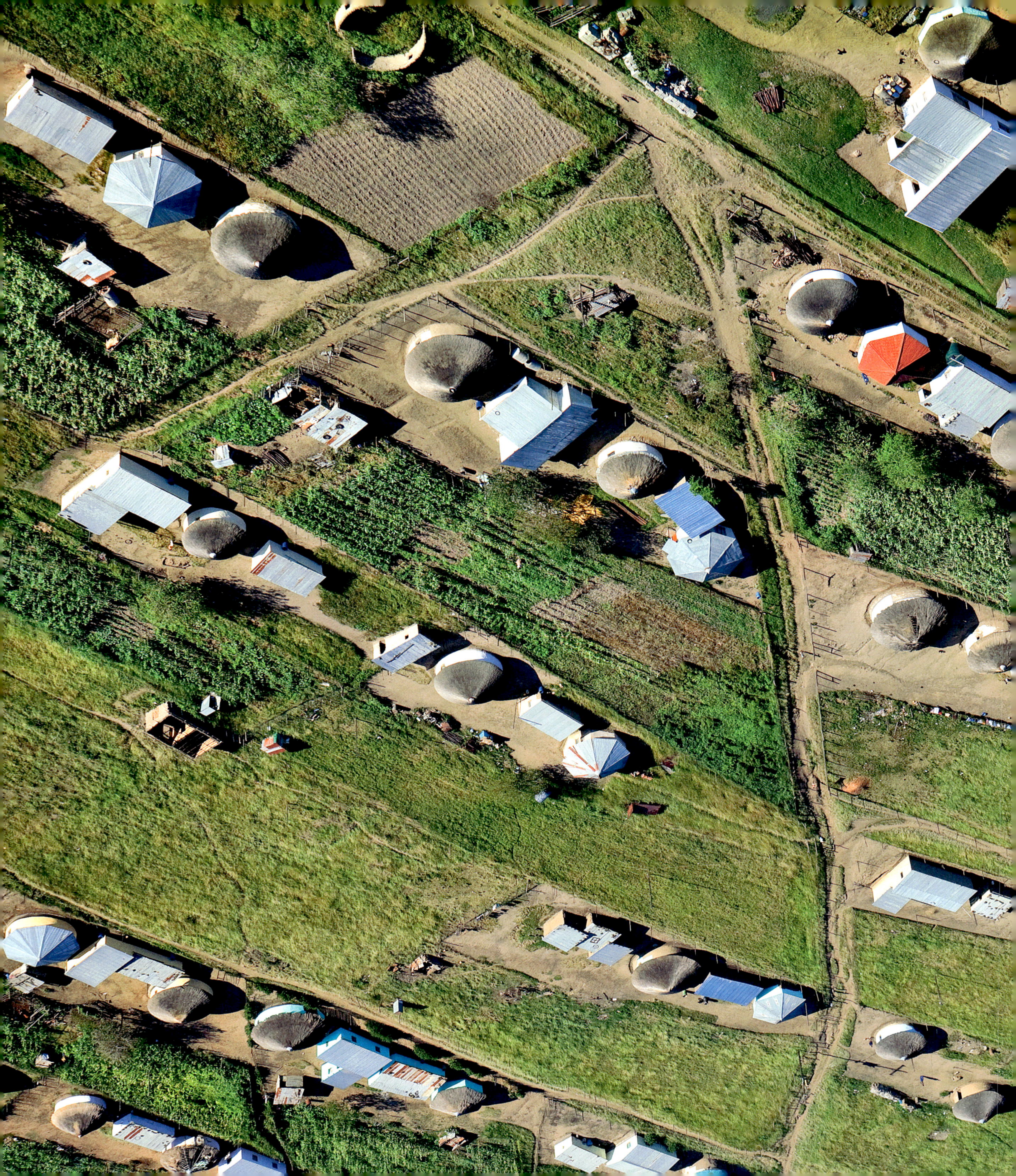

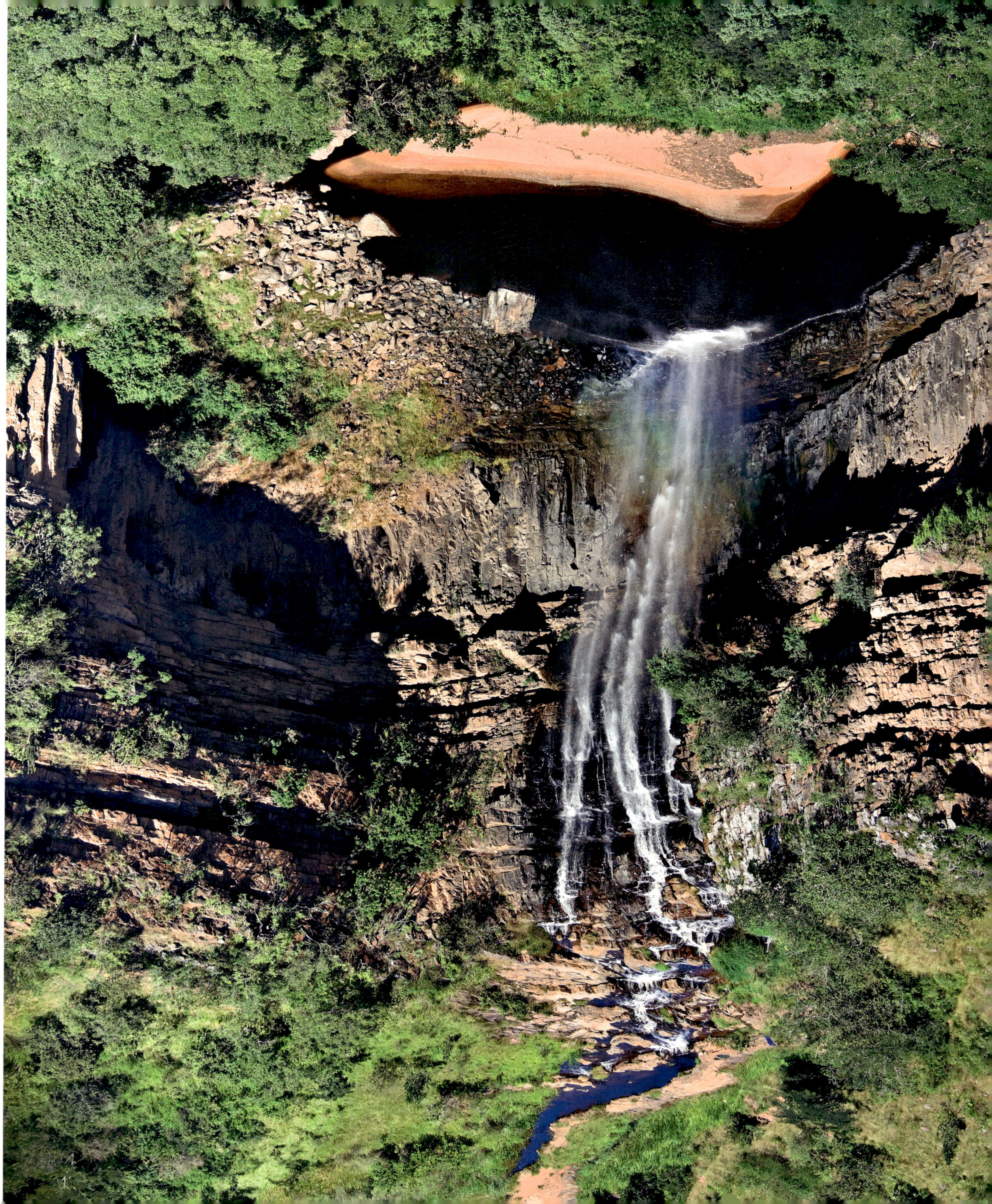

←← Zulu village, Harding
← Waterfall, Hammersdale
↓ Zulu family homes, Ulundi

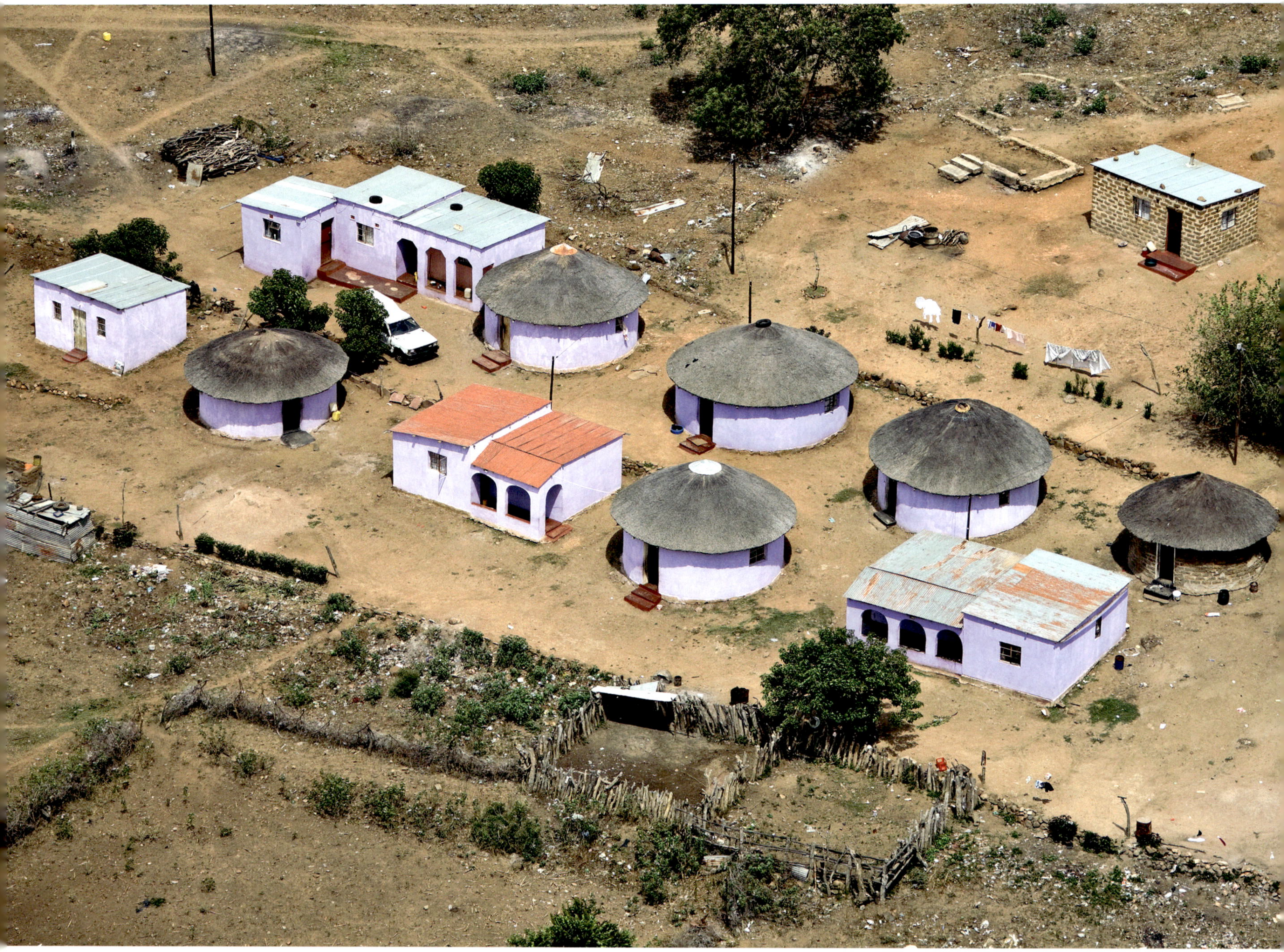

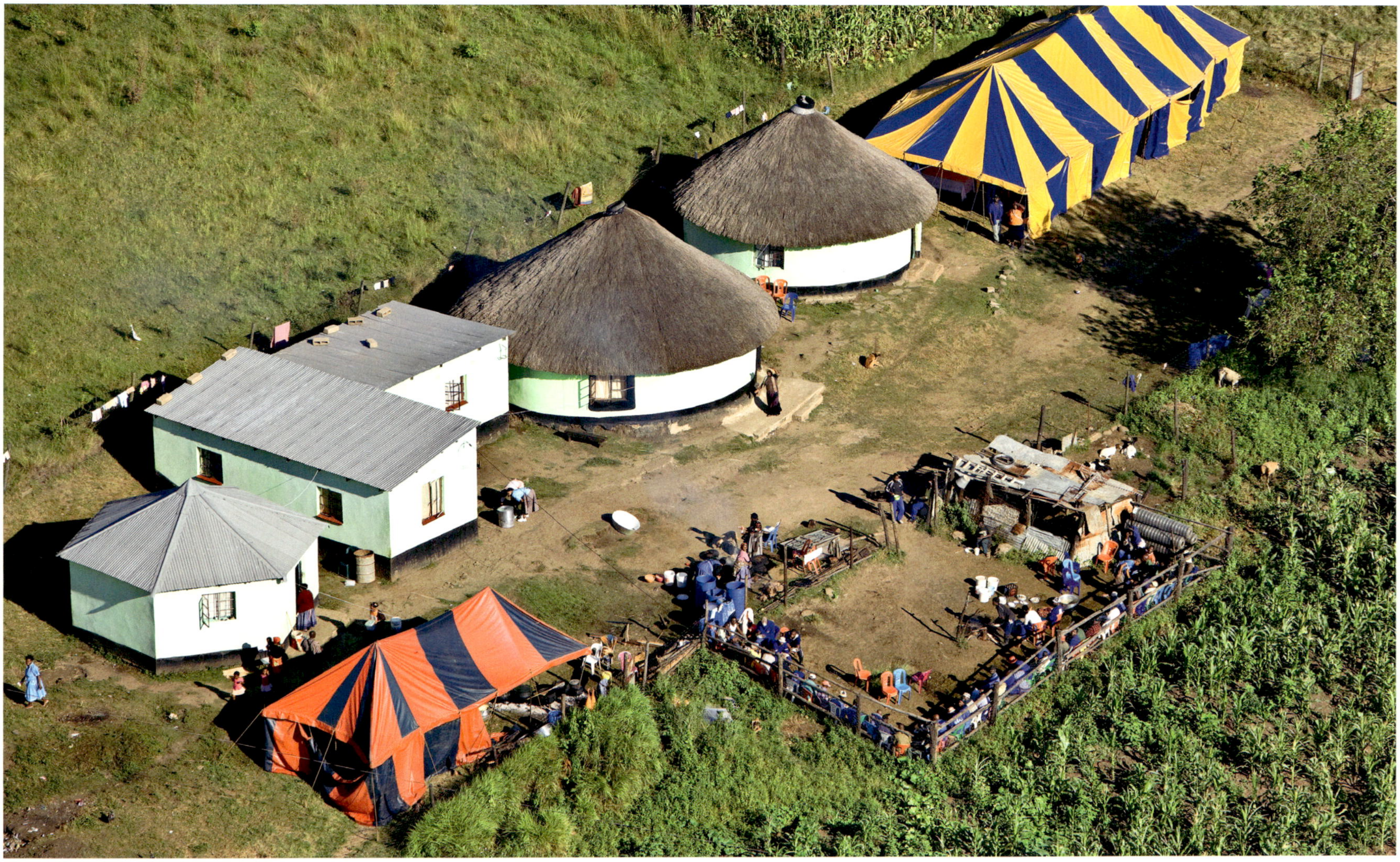

←↓ Together after a funeral, Kok's Hill

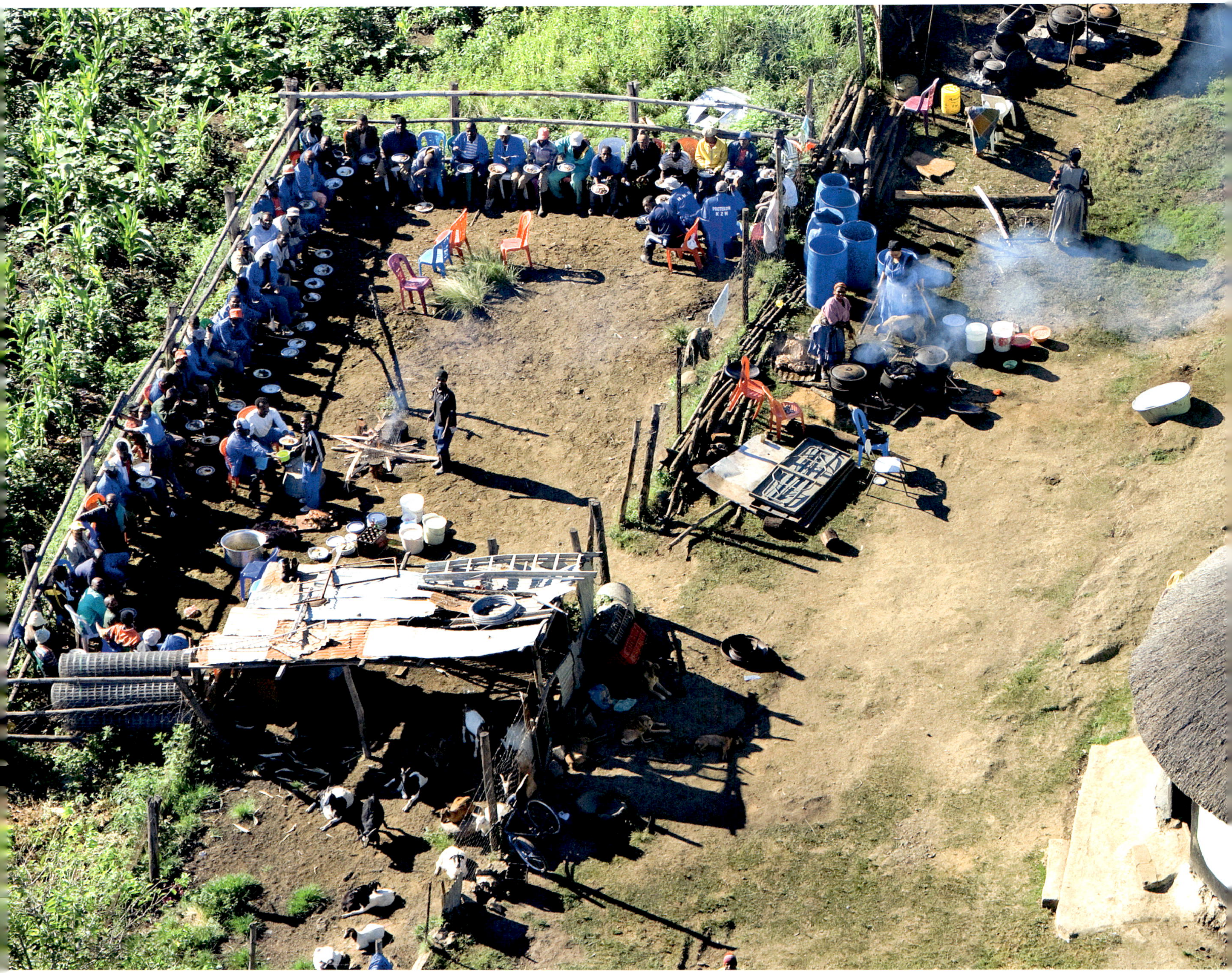

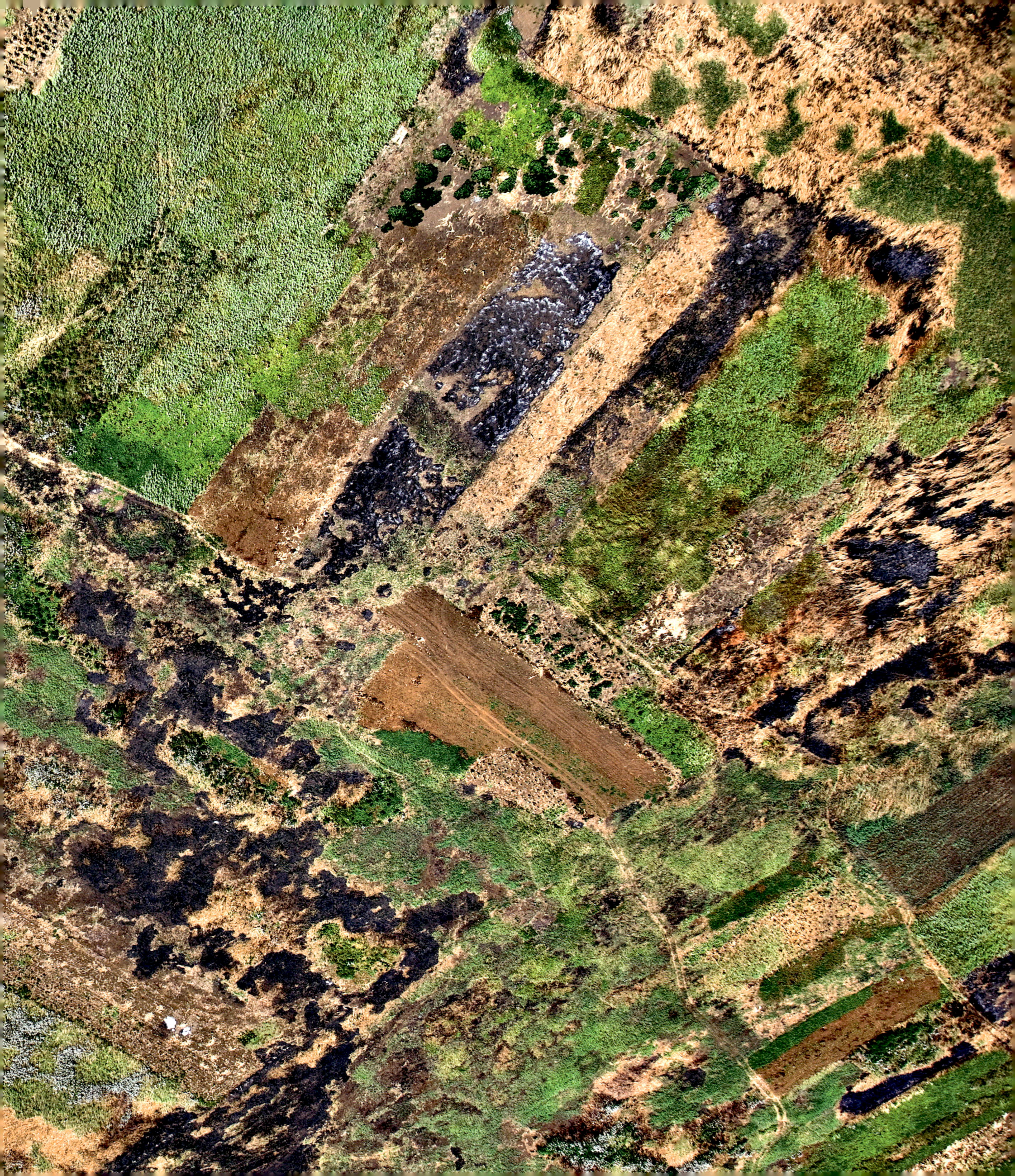

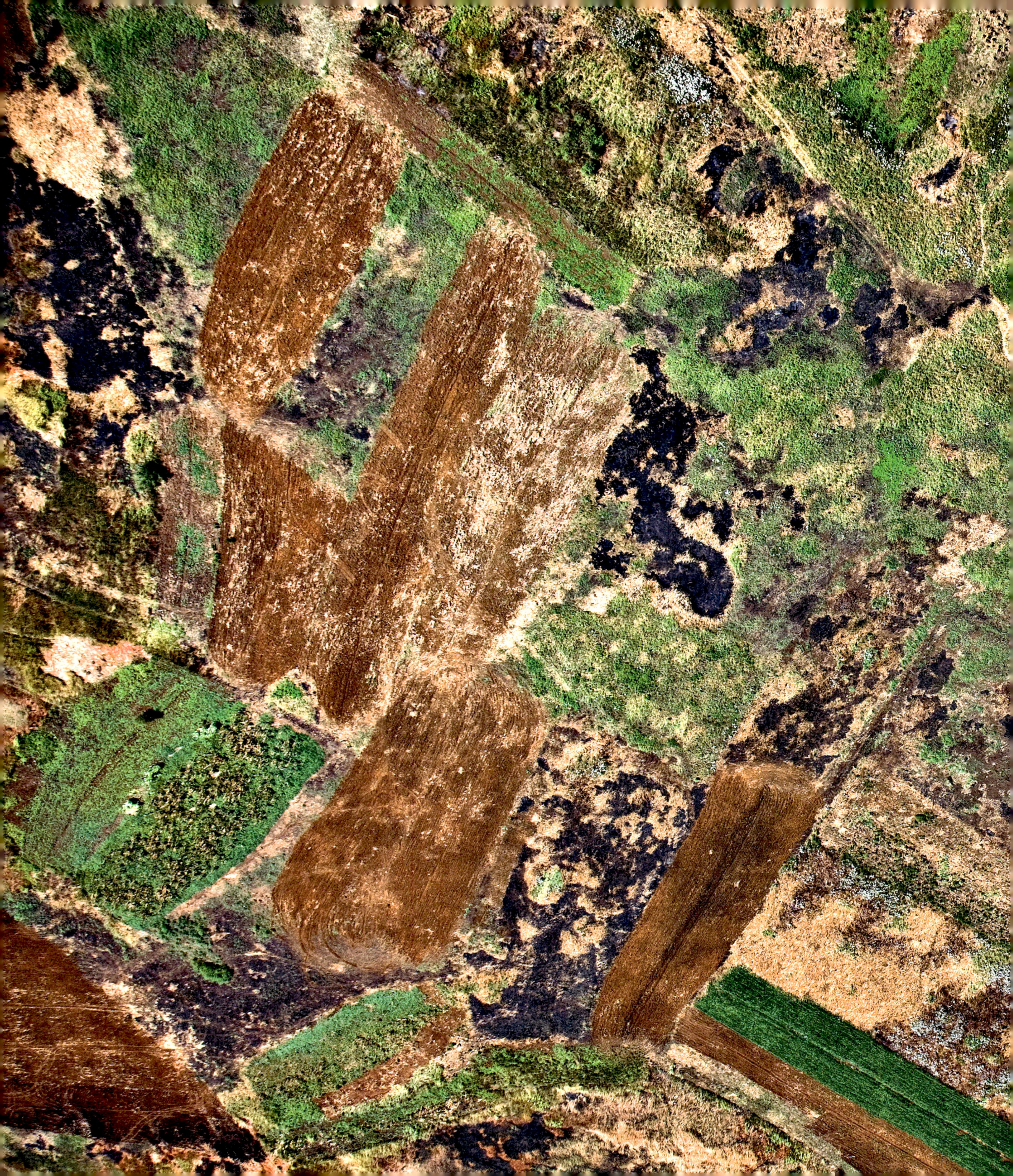

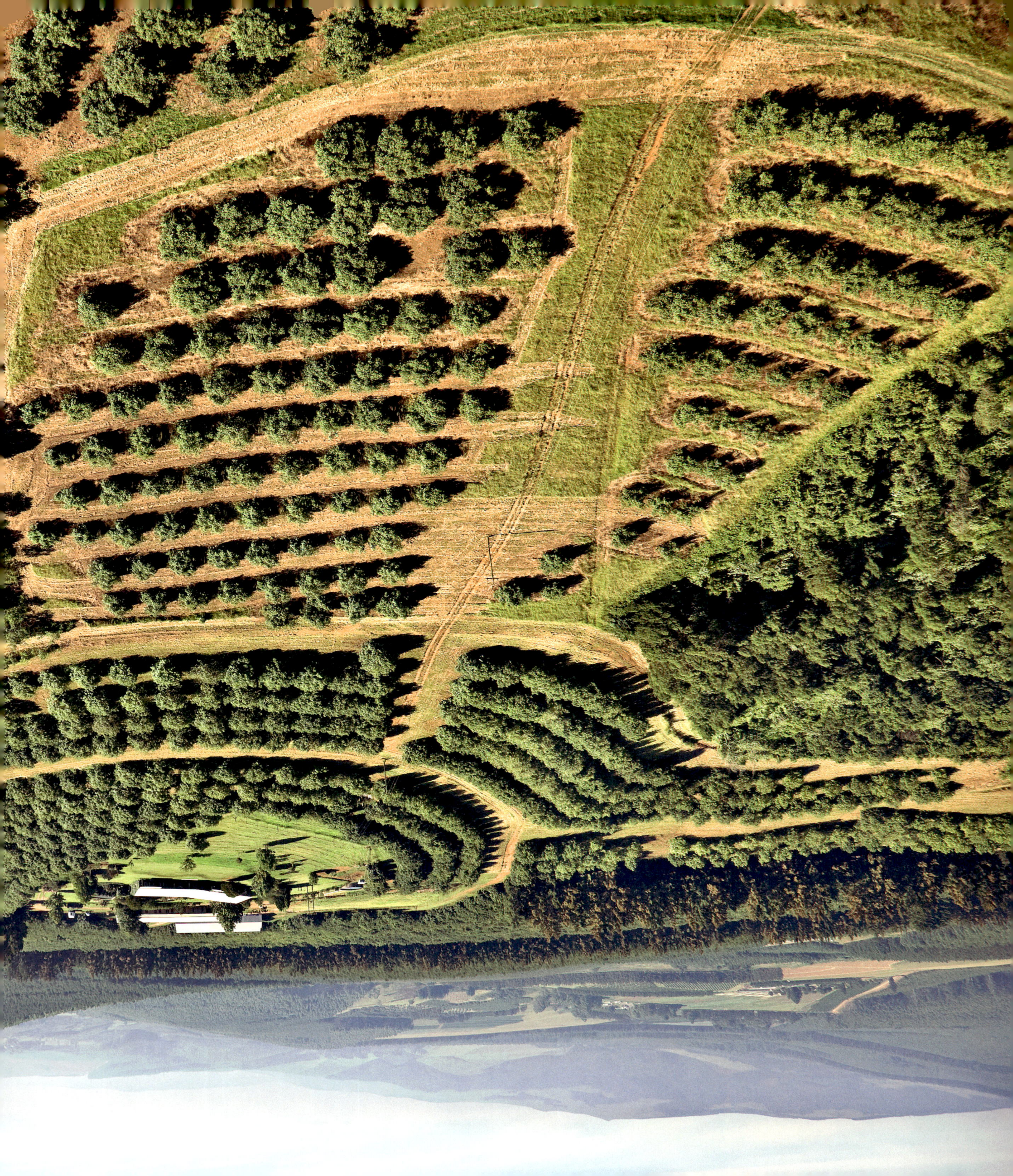

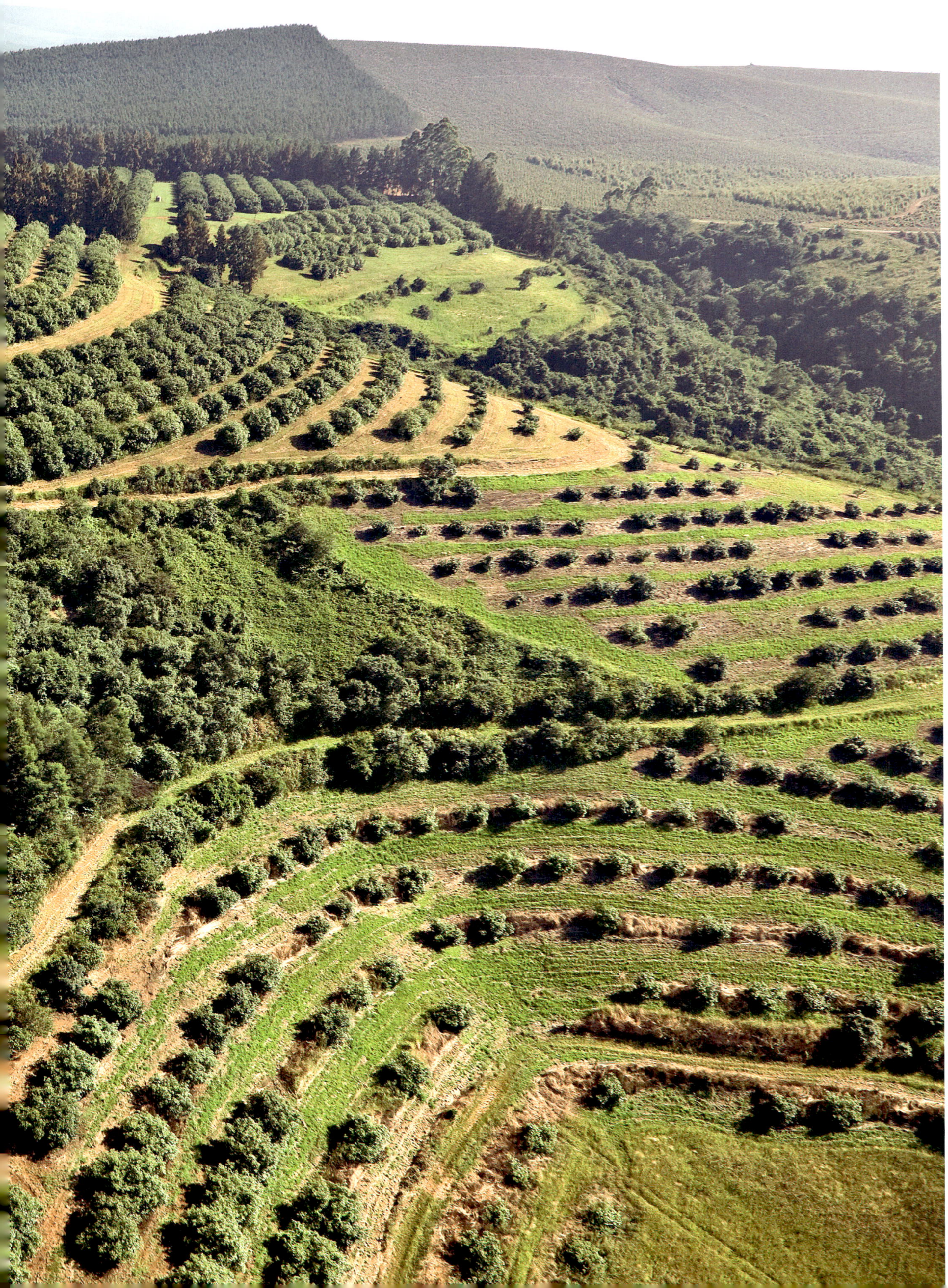

←← Zulu agricultural plots
← Mango farm, Richmond

↓→ Pietermaritzburg

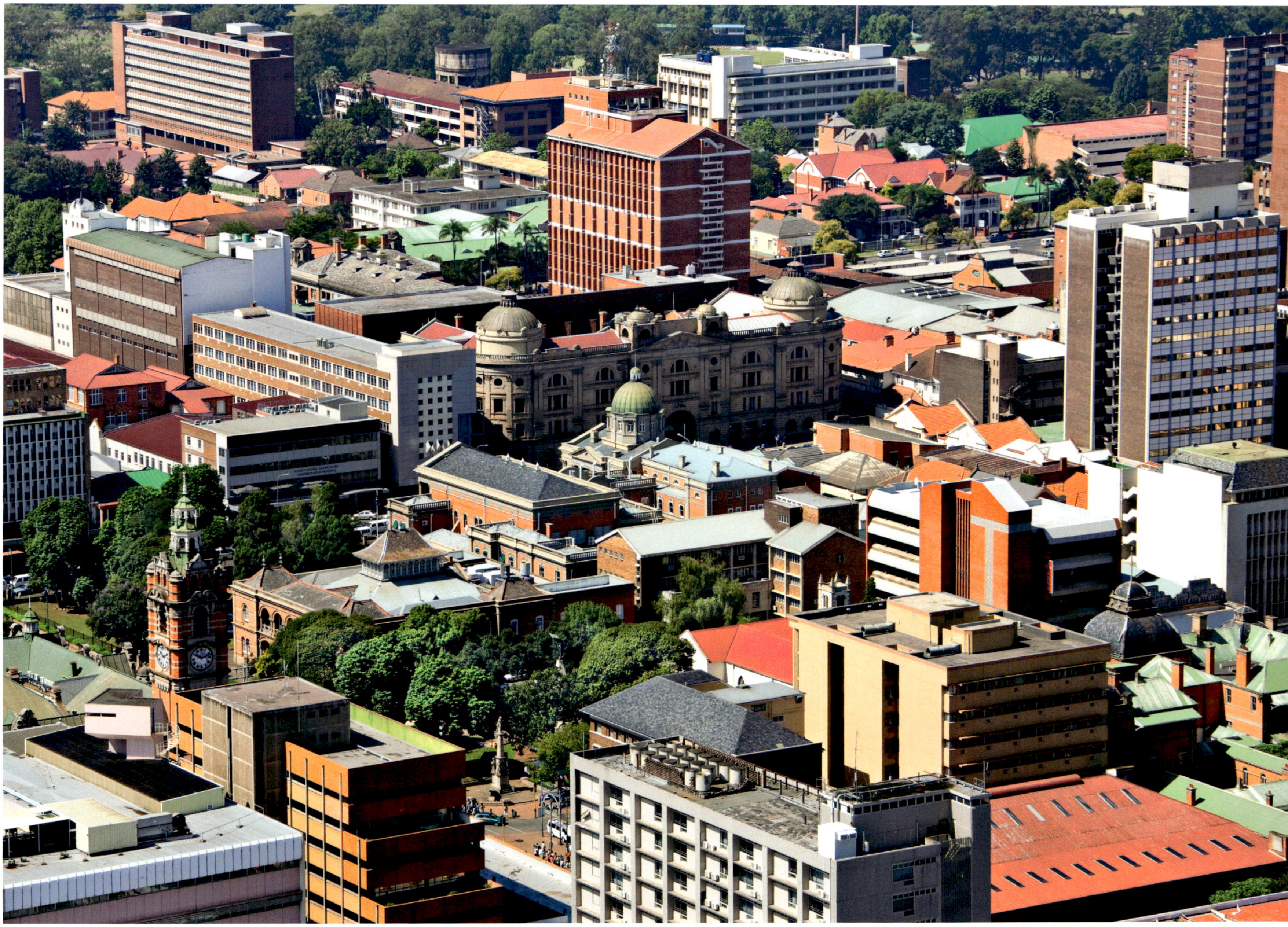

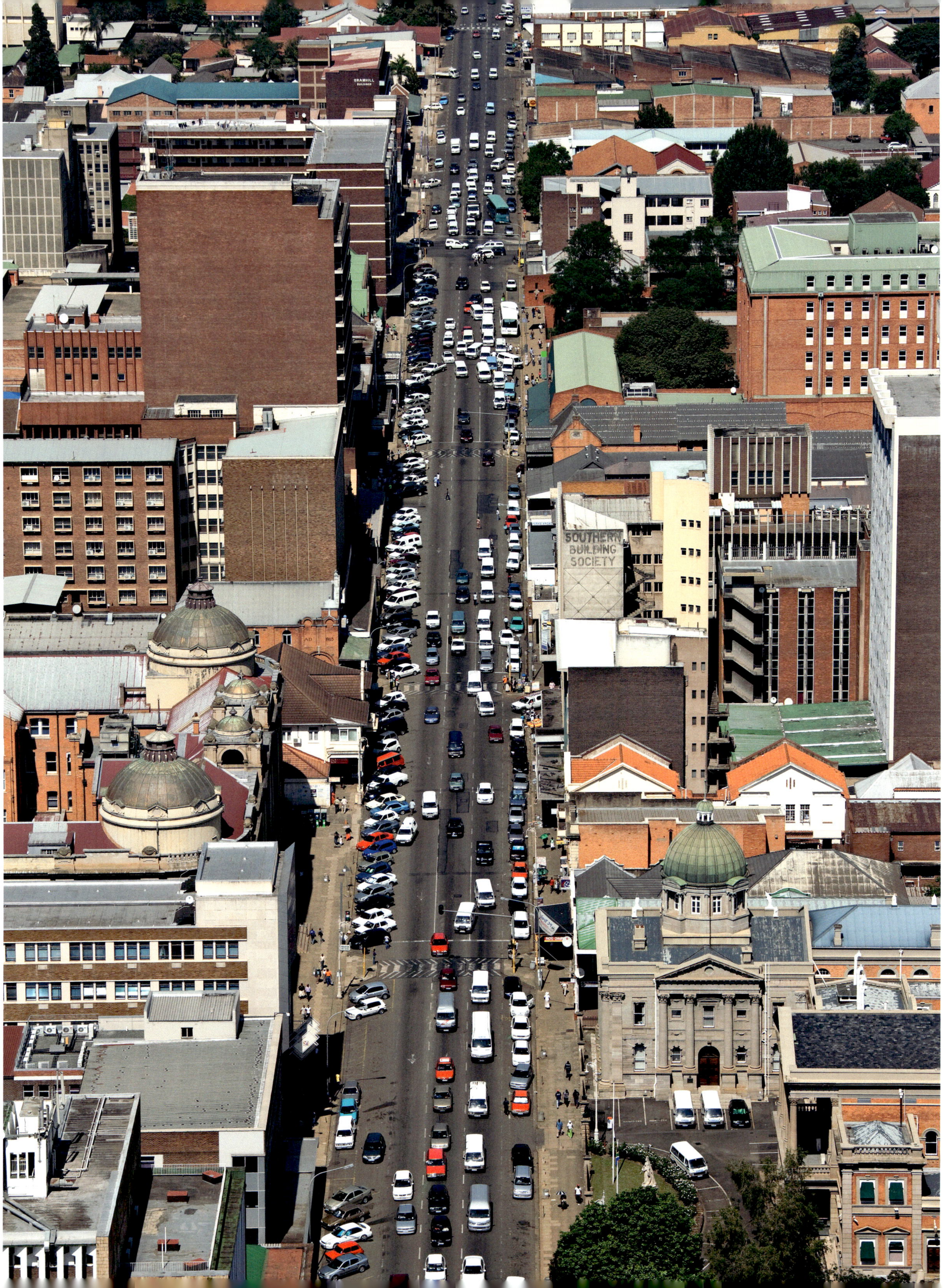
SOUTHERN
BUILDING
SOCIETY

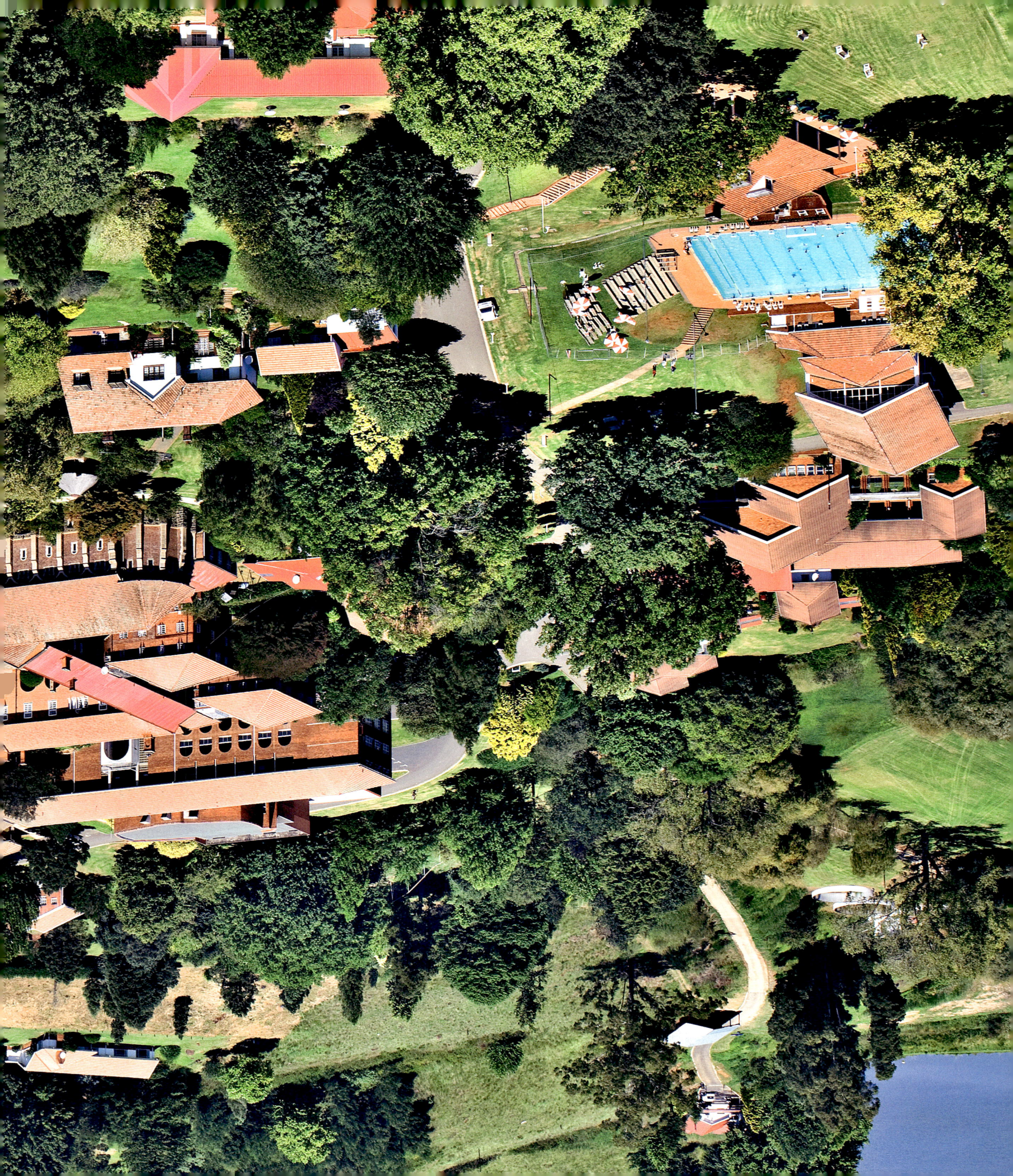

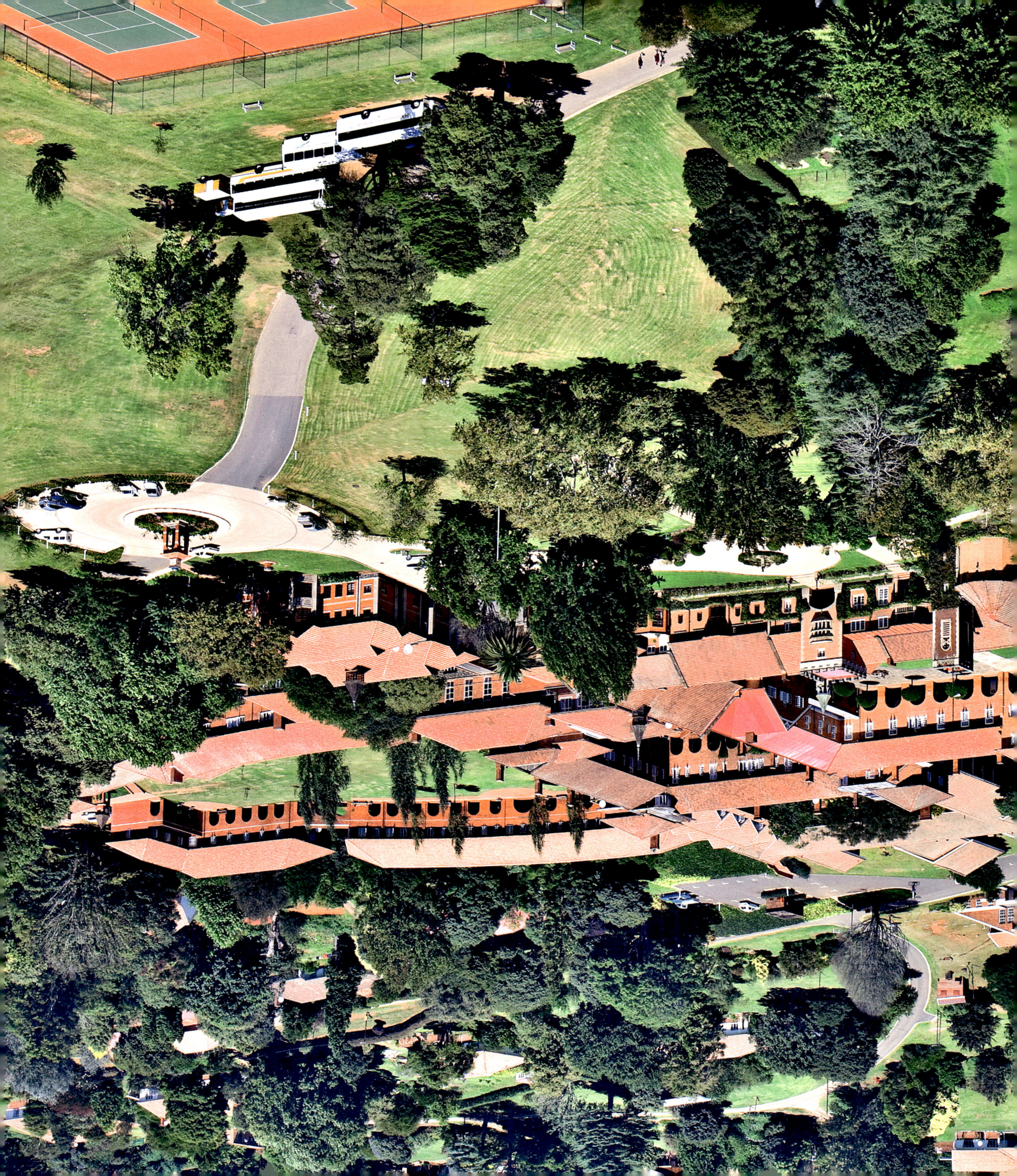

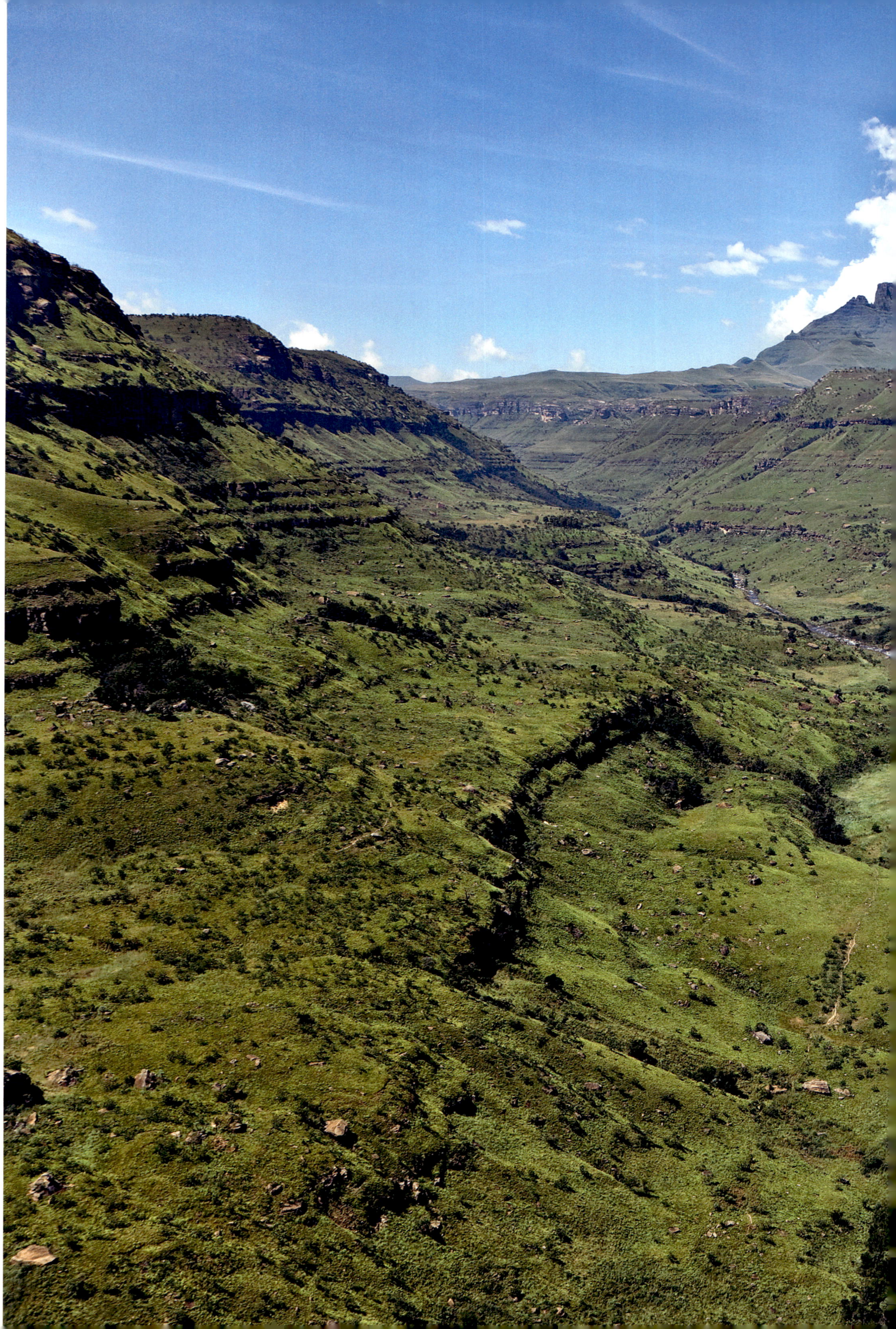

← College buildings in the village of Nottingham Road
→ Drakensberg

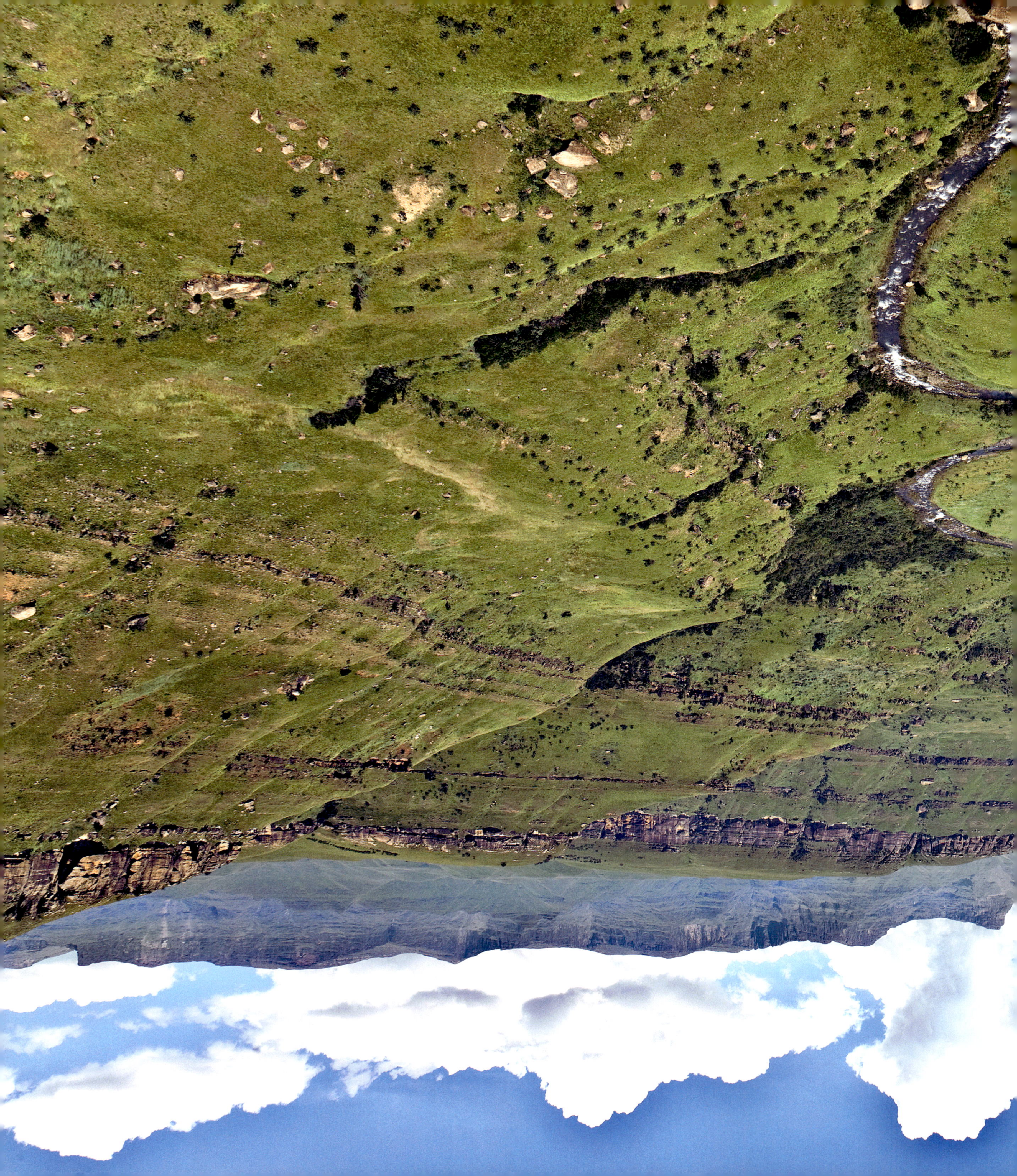

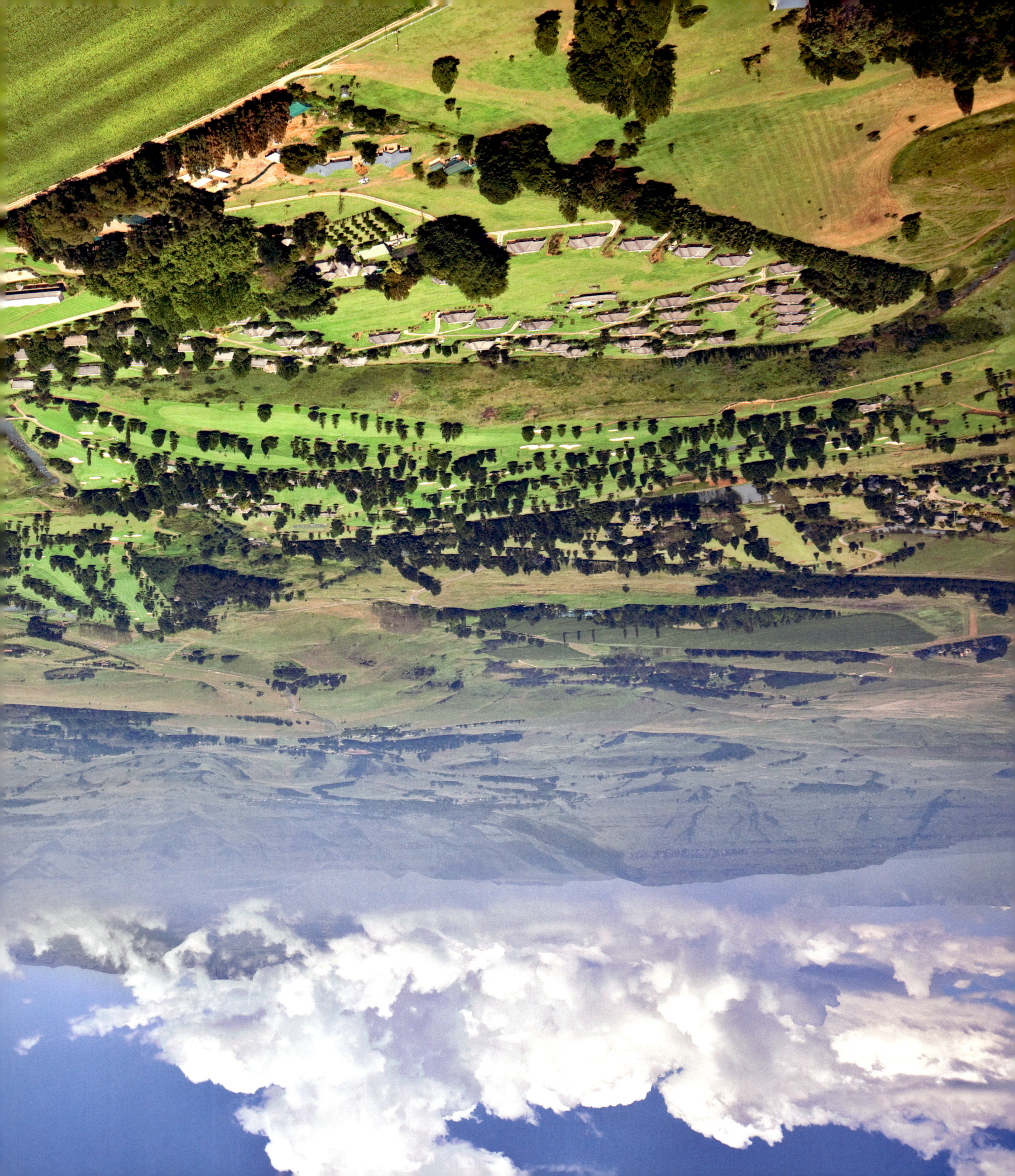

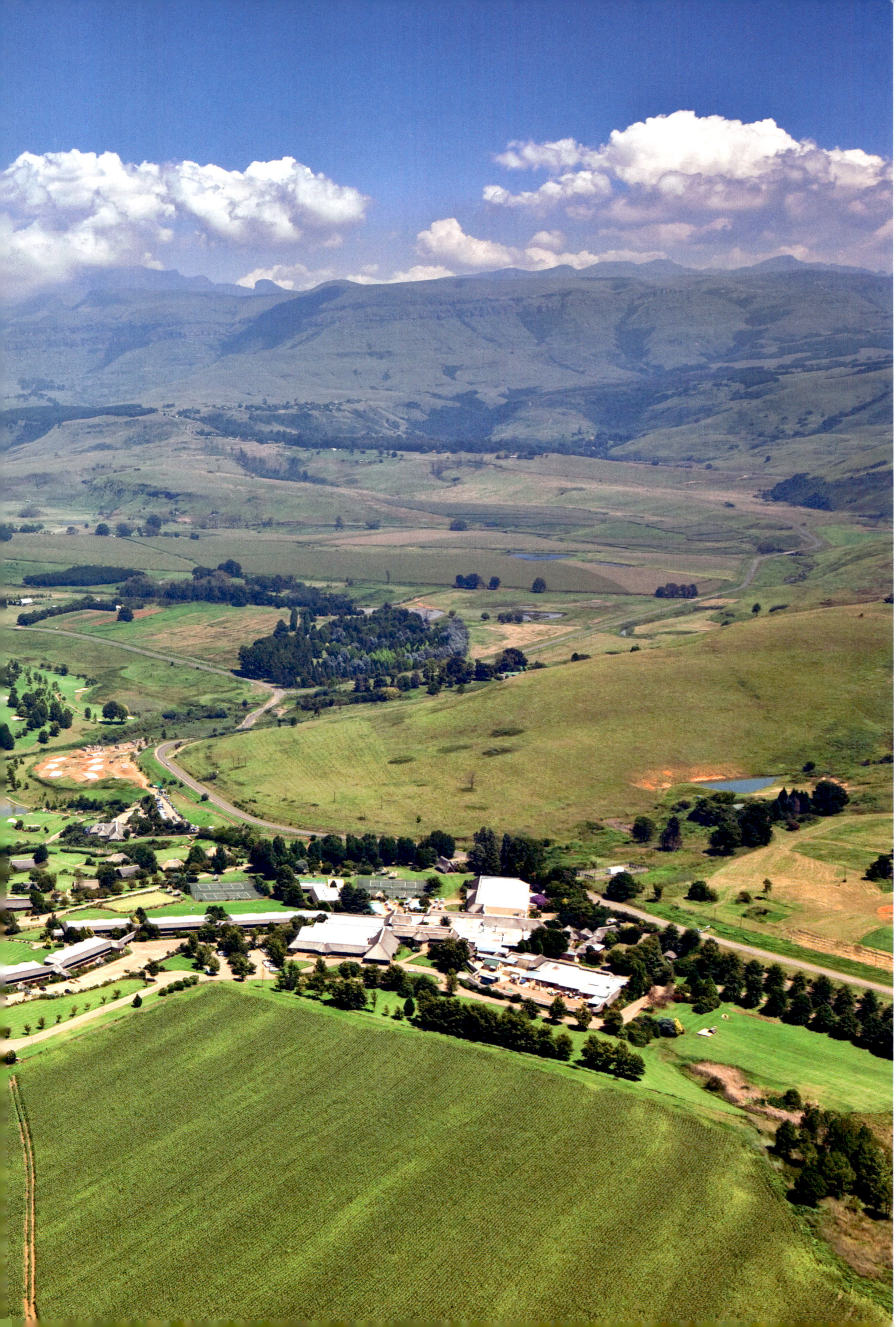

← Lodges and golf course Champagne Castle, Drakensberg

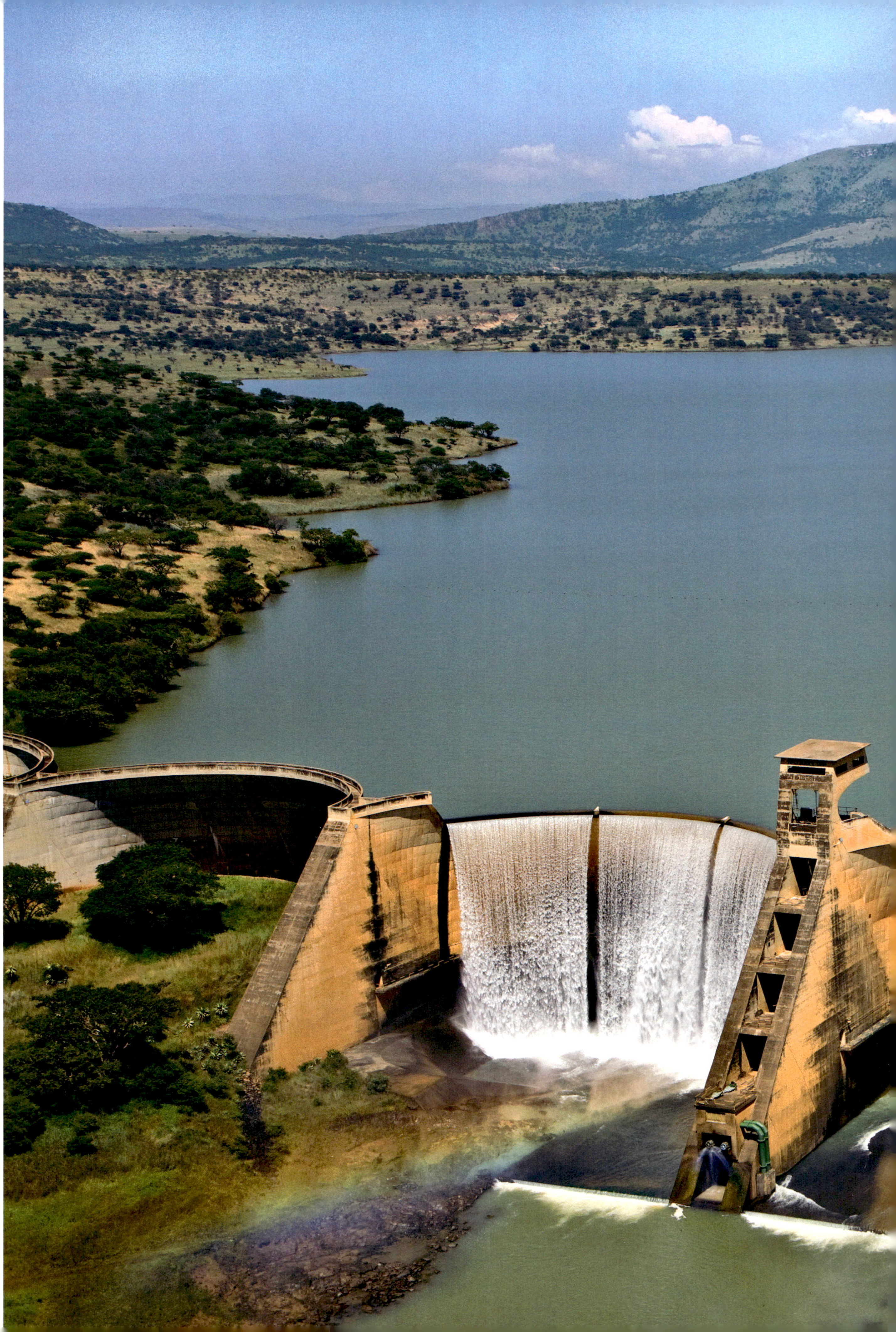

→ Wagendrift Dam,
Boesmans River

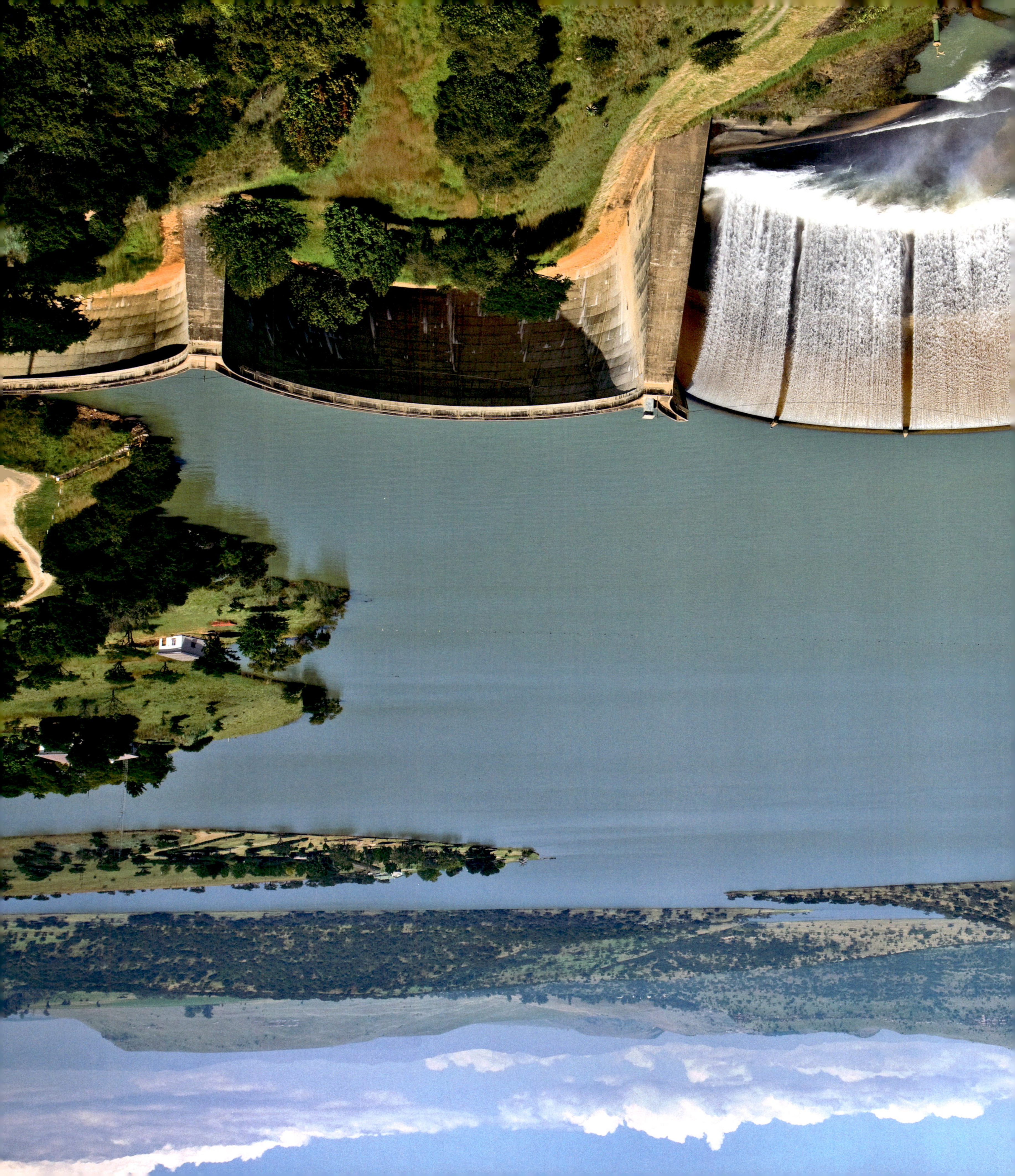

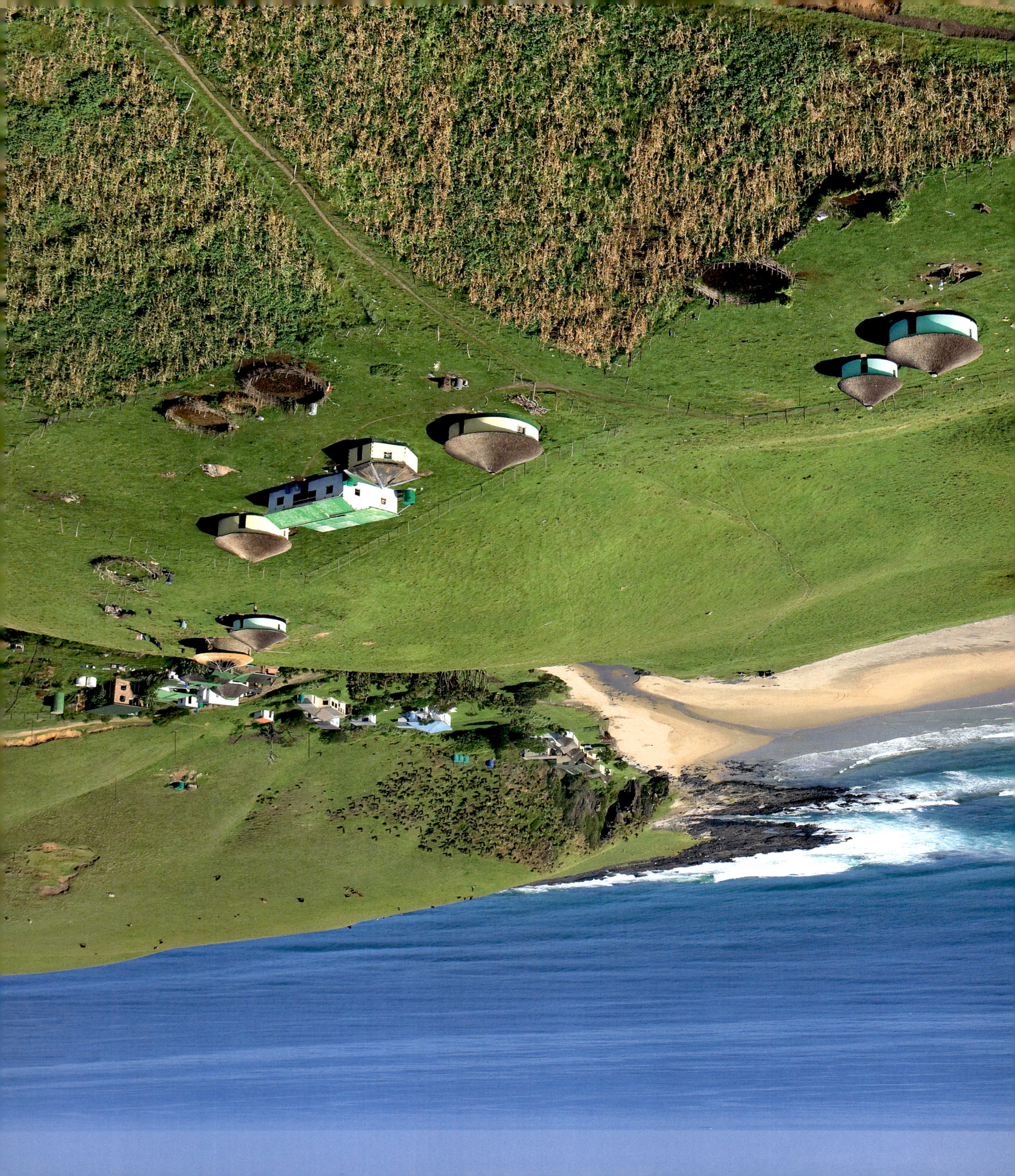

EASTERN CAPE

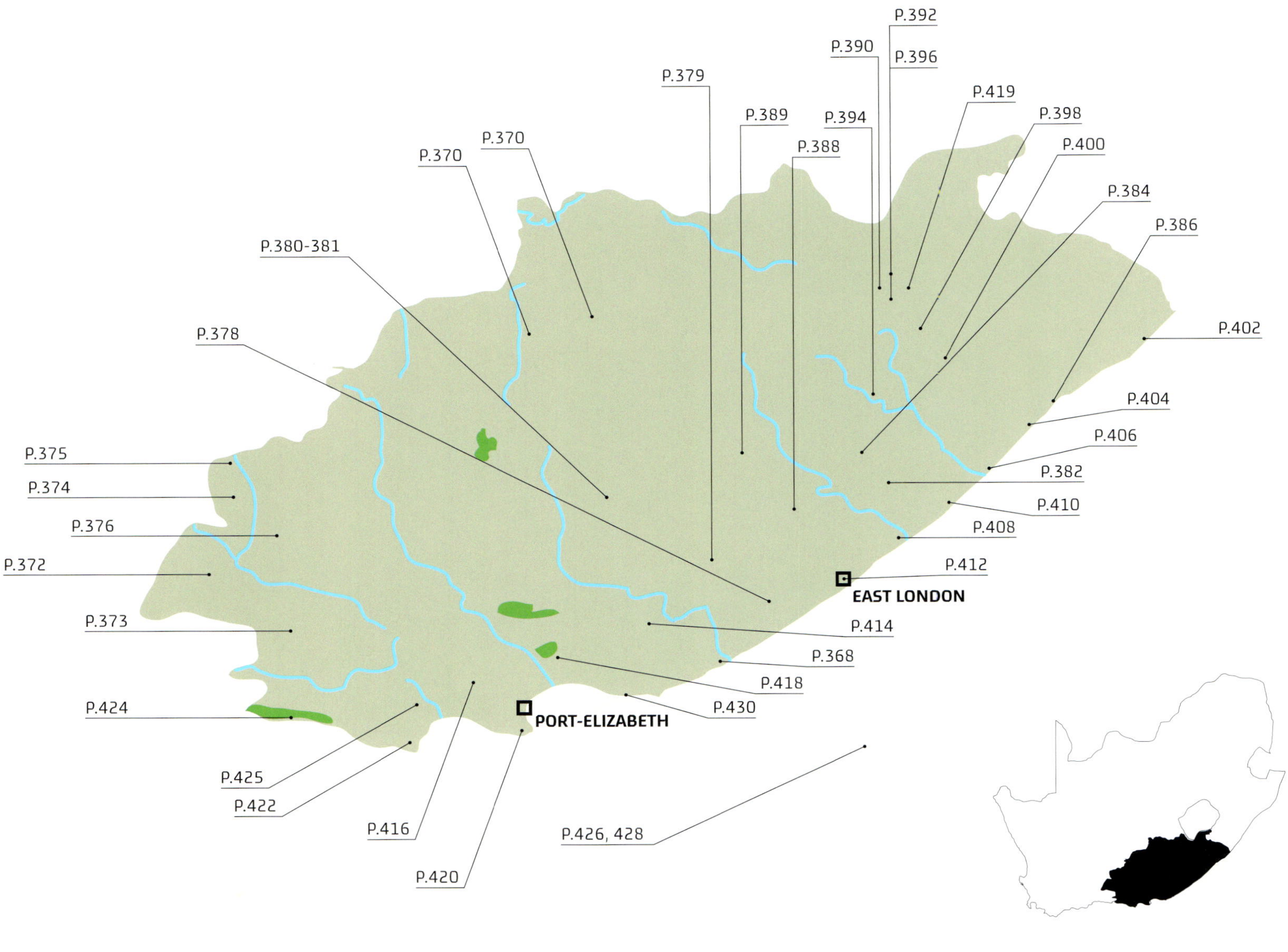

In the late 18th century, governor Joachim van Plettenberg went to the eastern border of what was then Cape Colony. Colonists were complaining about the behaviour of the Xhosa herders who were increasingly crossing the Great Fish River to find pastures for their livestock. Van Plettenberg signed an agreement with Xhosa chief Koba, who promised that his people would remain to the east of the river.
The agreement proved to have no value whatsoever, for the simple reason that Xhosa tradition did not permit even the king to enter into binding agreements on behalf of all his subjects. Decisions were never taken centrally by the government, but locally, and only after consultation between the local chief and the village council.

Traces of Mandela

European colonists long considered the Eastern Cape a wild country inhabited by a wild nation. Even missionaries in the 19th century were wary of working with the Xhosa. And indeed, even today, the Eastern Cape has something untamed about it. Anybody who has seen the capricious Wild Coast or the Baviaanskloof ('valley of the baboons') Nature Reserve will agree with that. But the uMlungu (foreigner) who visits the Eastern Cape will certainly not encounter a 'wild nation', but a people who are proud of their hospitality and ubuntu – the African philosophy that puts consensus and communal welfare before individualism.

In large parts of the Eastern Cape, tourism is still in its infancy. Partly because of that, the local nature and culture is still largely undiscovered even today. Take Ukhahlamba for instance, which even the people of Eastern Cape consider unspoiled. This area in the southern Drakensberg is sparsely populated and has, even now, an almost exclusively agrarian economy. With one major exception: since 1993, it has had a ski centre, Tiffendell, where, thanks to its high altitude (2700 metres) and the use of snow cannons, people can ski for at least 100 days a year.

Outside modern cities like East London and Port Elizabeth, also known as Africa's Watersport Capital, it's easy to imagine yourself in the past. There are small clumps of houses dotted here and there, often traditional rondawels, hidden among the green hills. Here, children still tend to herds of sheep and cows. And teenage boys, or Abakwetha, still undergo the three-month ritual which marks their passage to manhood. Former president and freedom fighter Nelson Mandela underwent these same rites of passage in his youth.

The Eastern Cape has honoured Nelson Rohihlahla Mandela not only by naming streets, squares and a university after him, but also a whole metropolis: the Nelson Mandela Bay Municipality, which includes Port Elizabeth and has more than one million inhabitants. Most traces of Mandela, however, are not to be found in the city, but in the Eastern Cape countryside: in Mvezo, the village where he was born, and in Qunu, where he grew up. Typical Eastern Cape villages where a visitor will feel he has returned to the past.

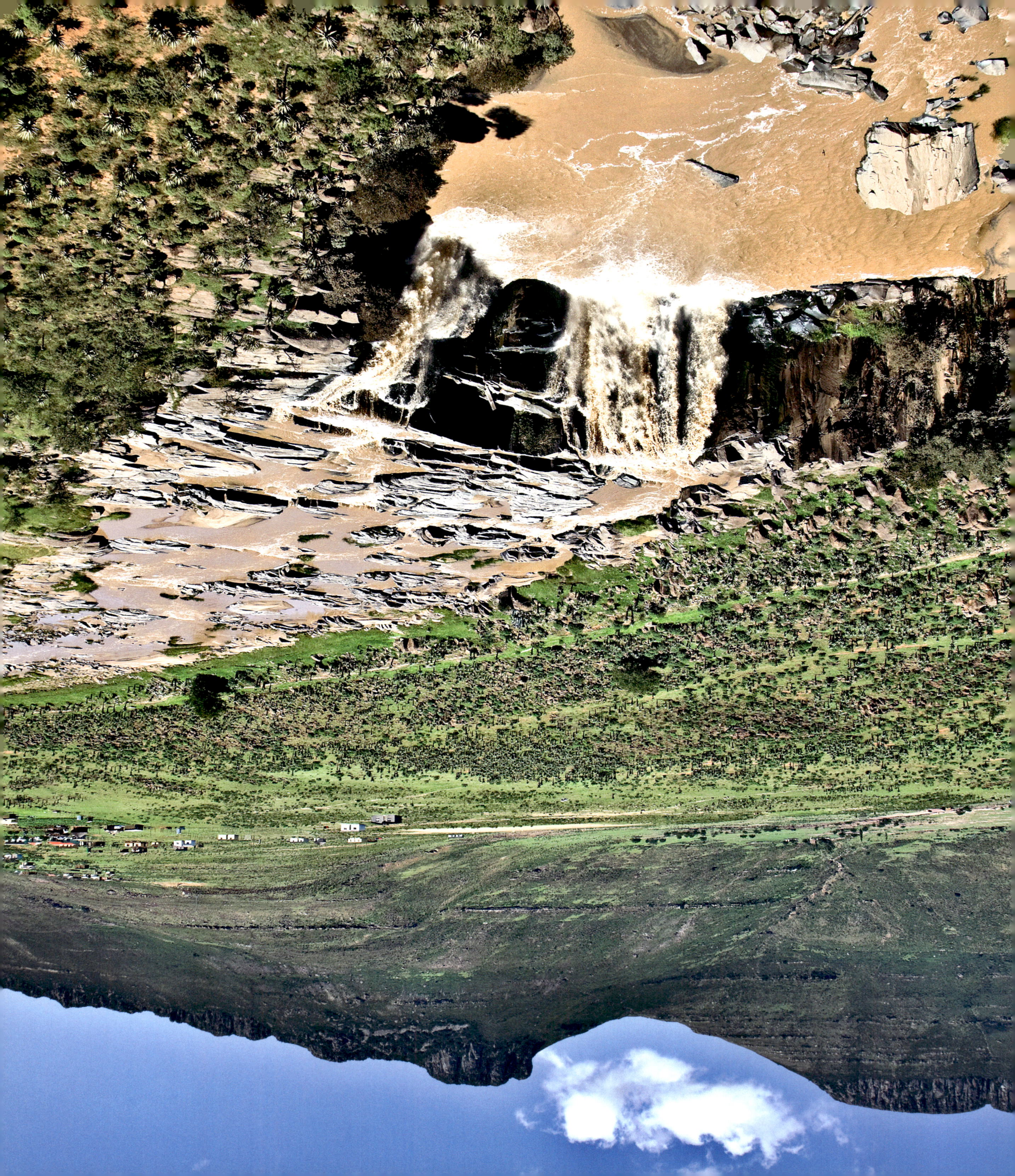

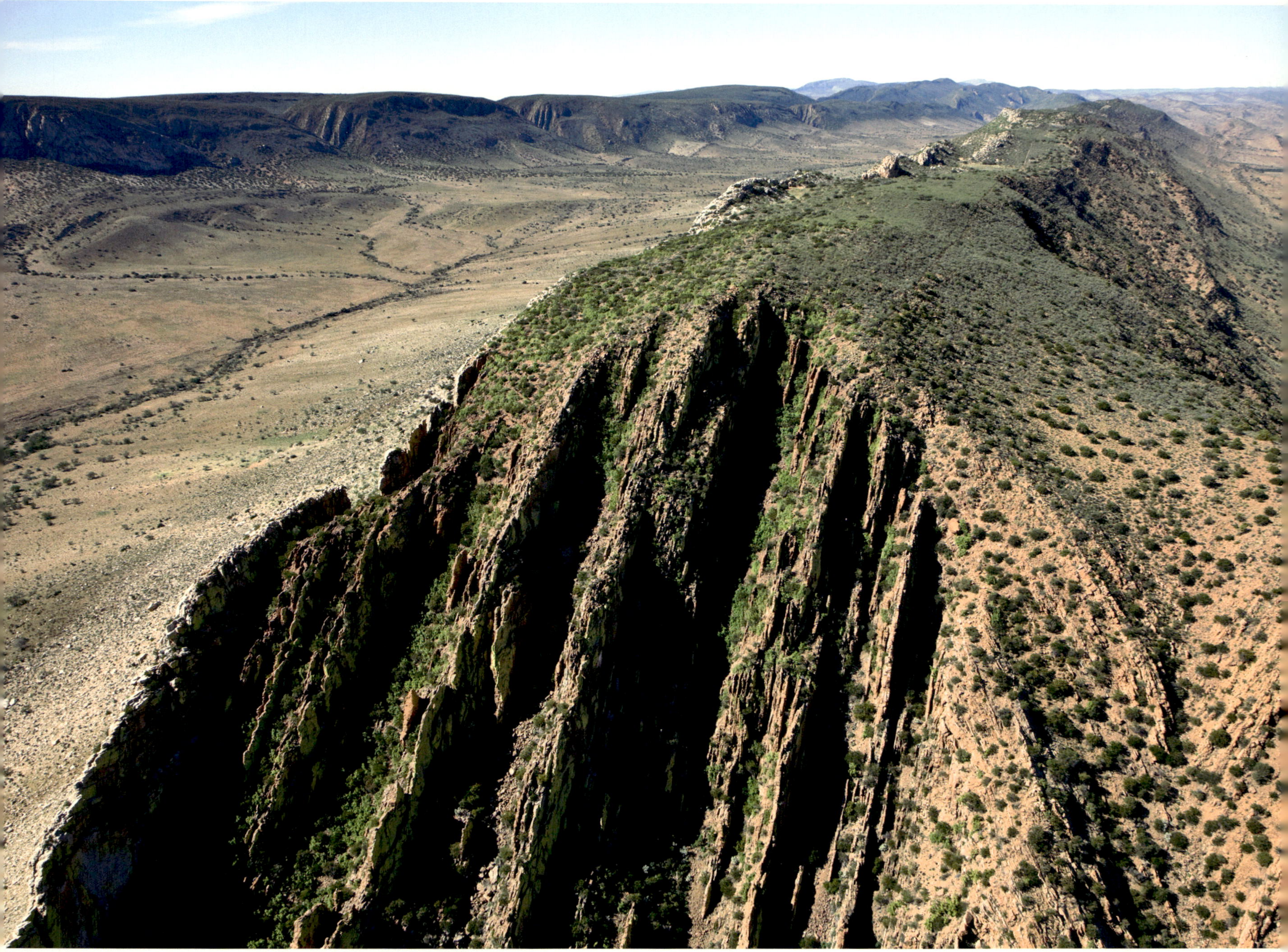

← Rock formations, Karee River
↓ Flying through the Baviaanskloof

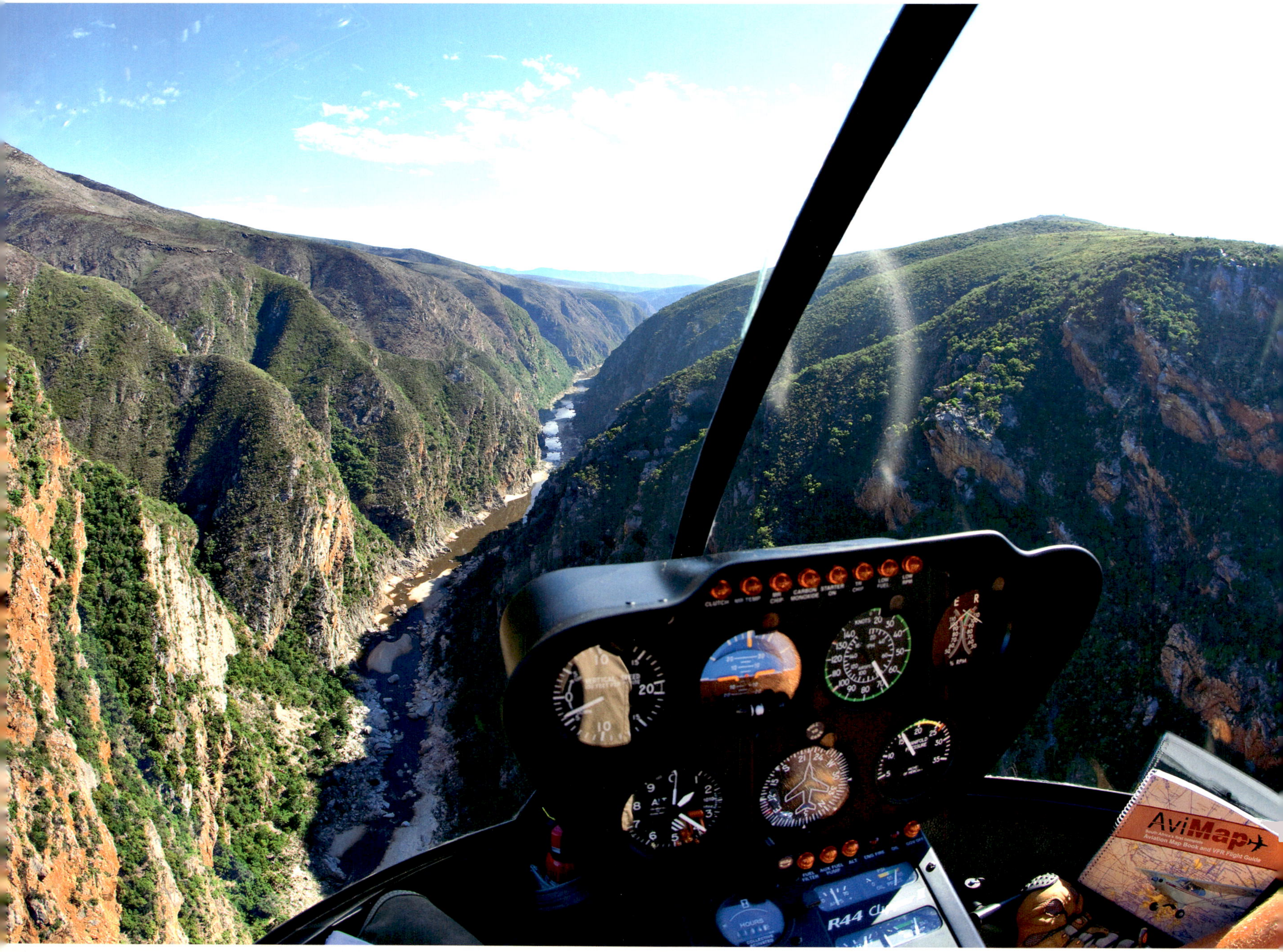

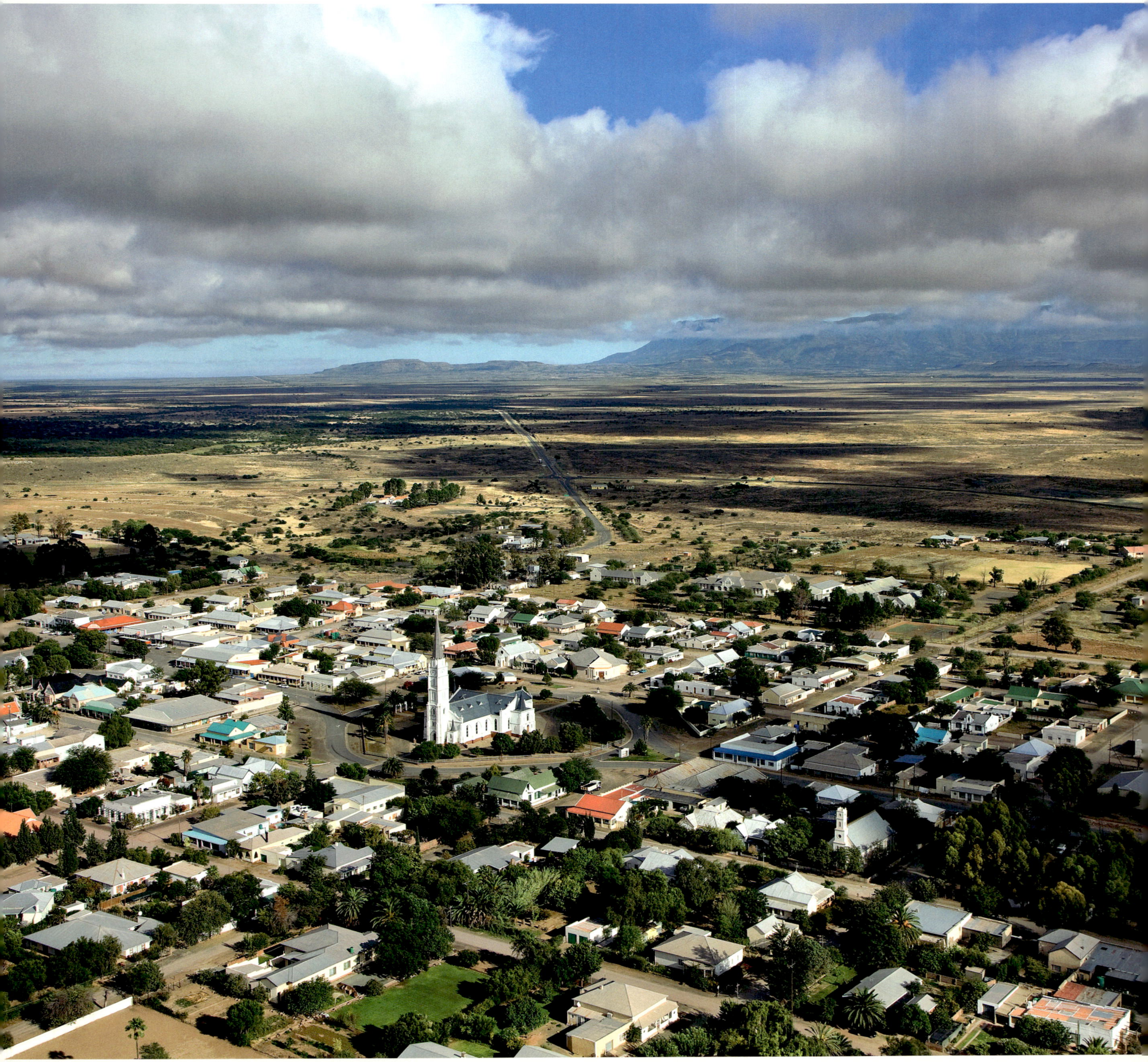

← Aberdeen
↓ National Park Camdeboo

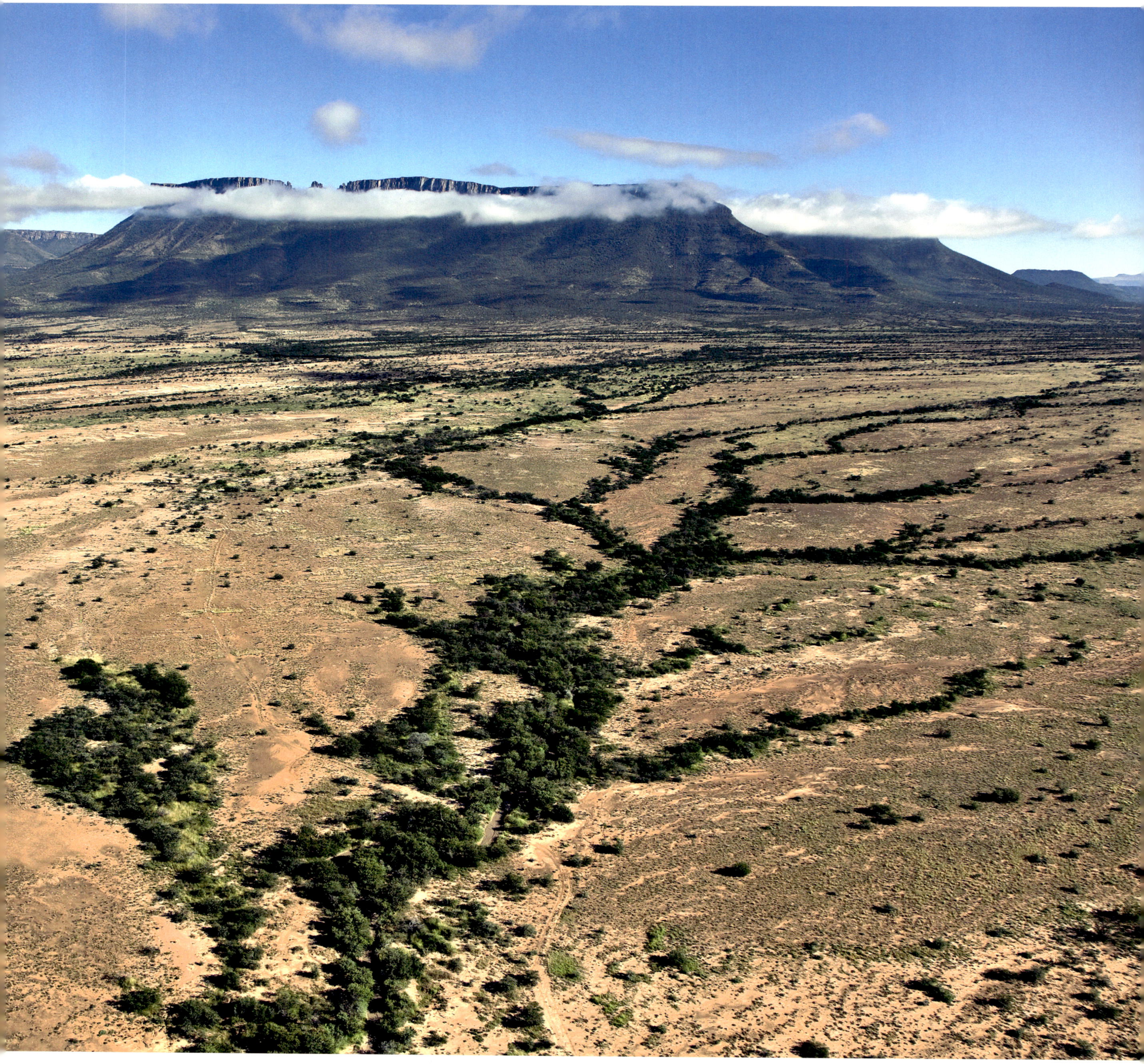

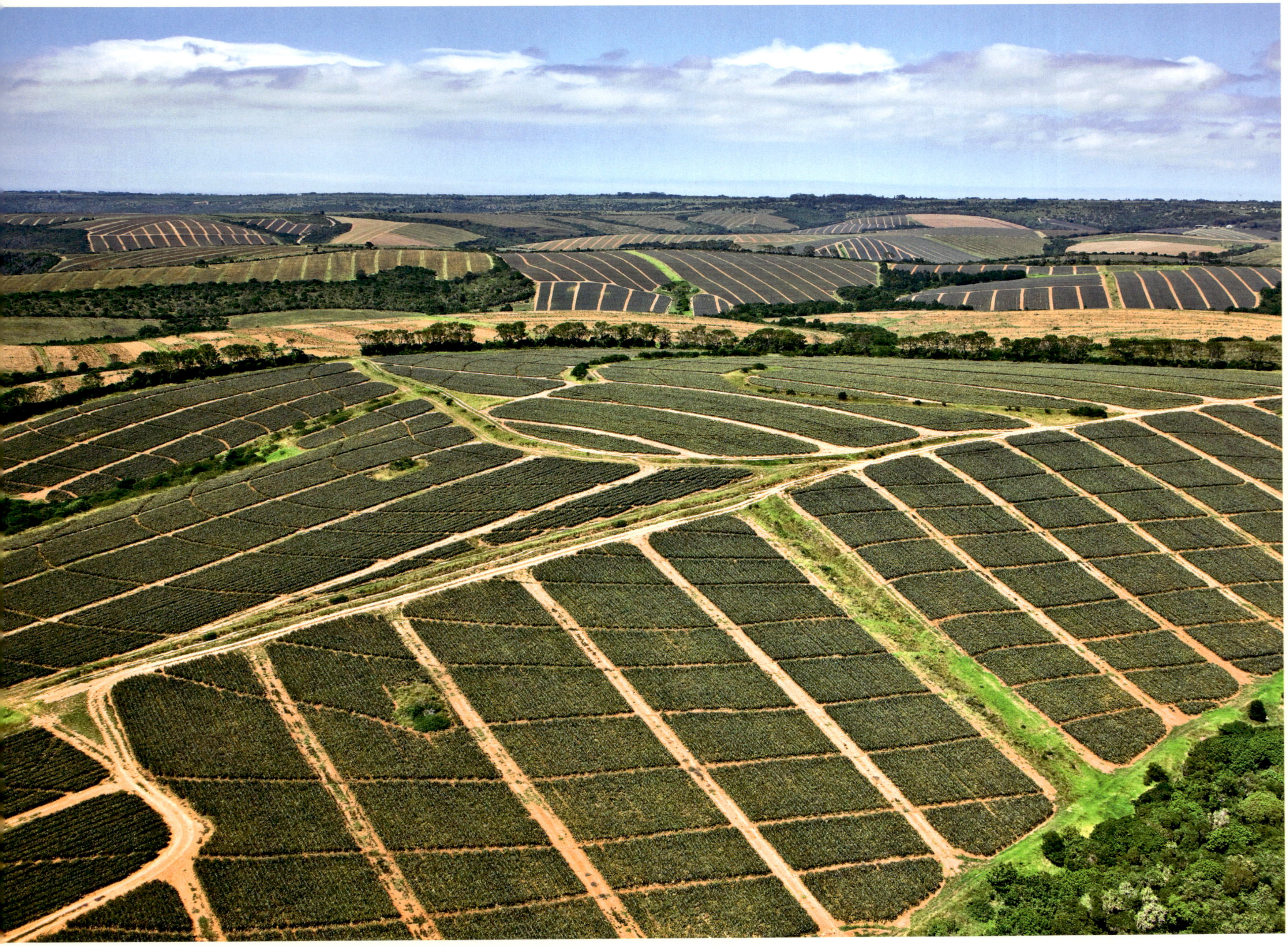

←↓ Pineapple plantations, Bathurst area

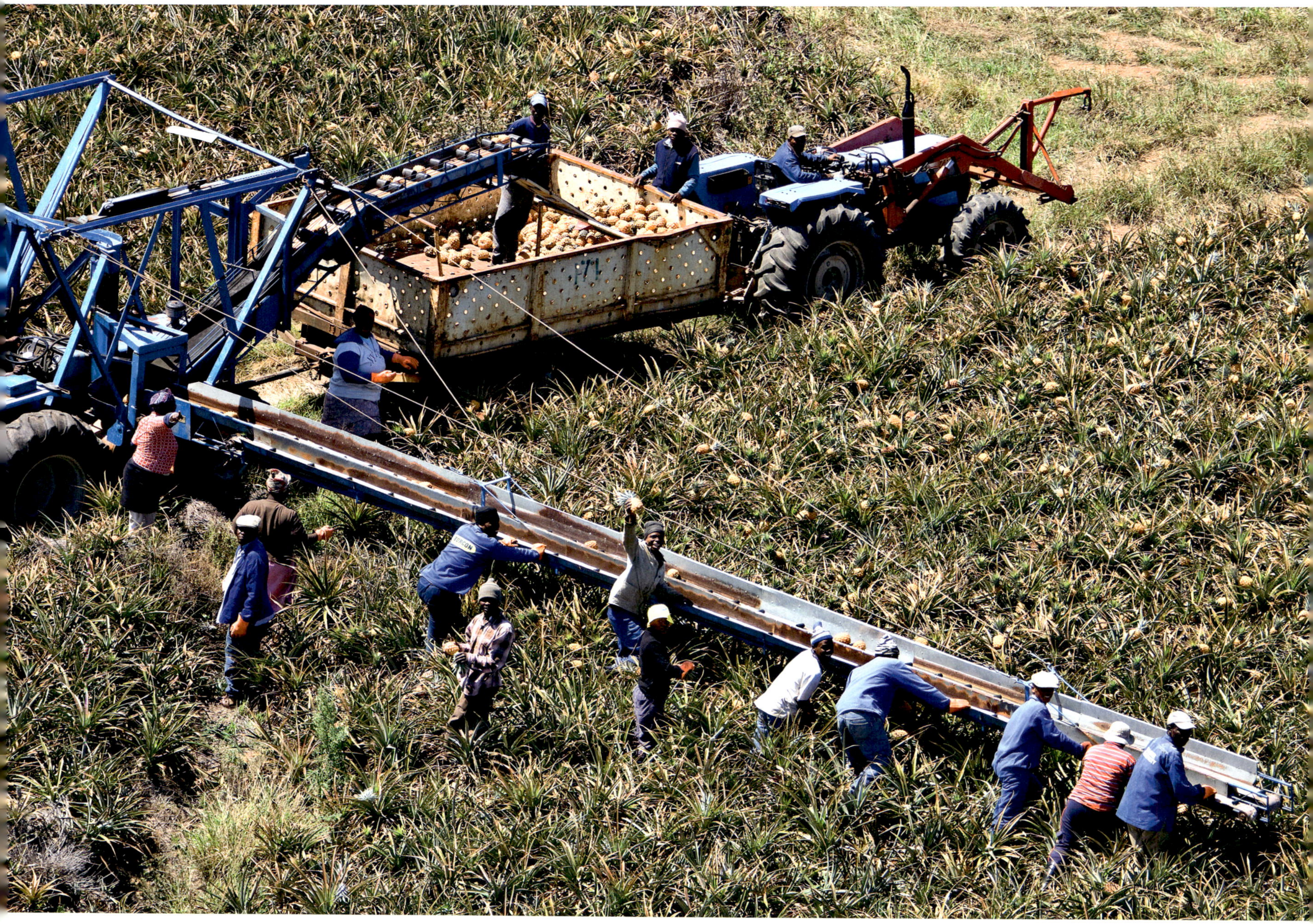

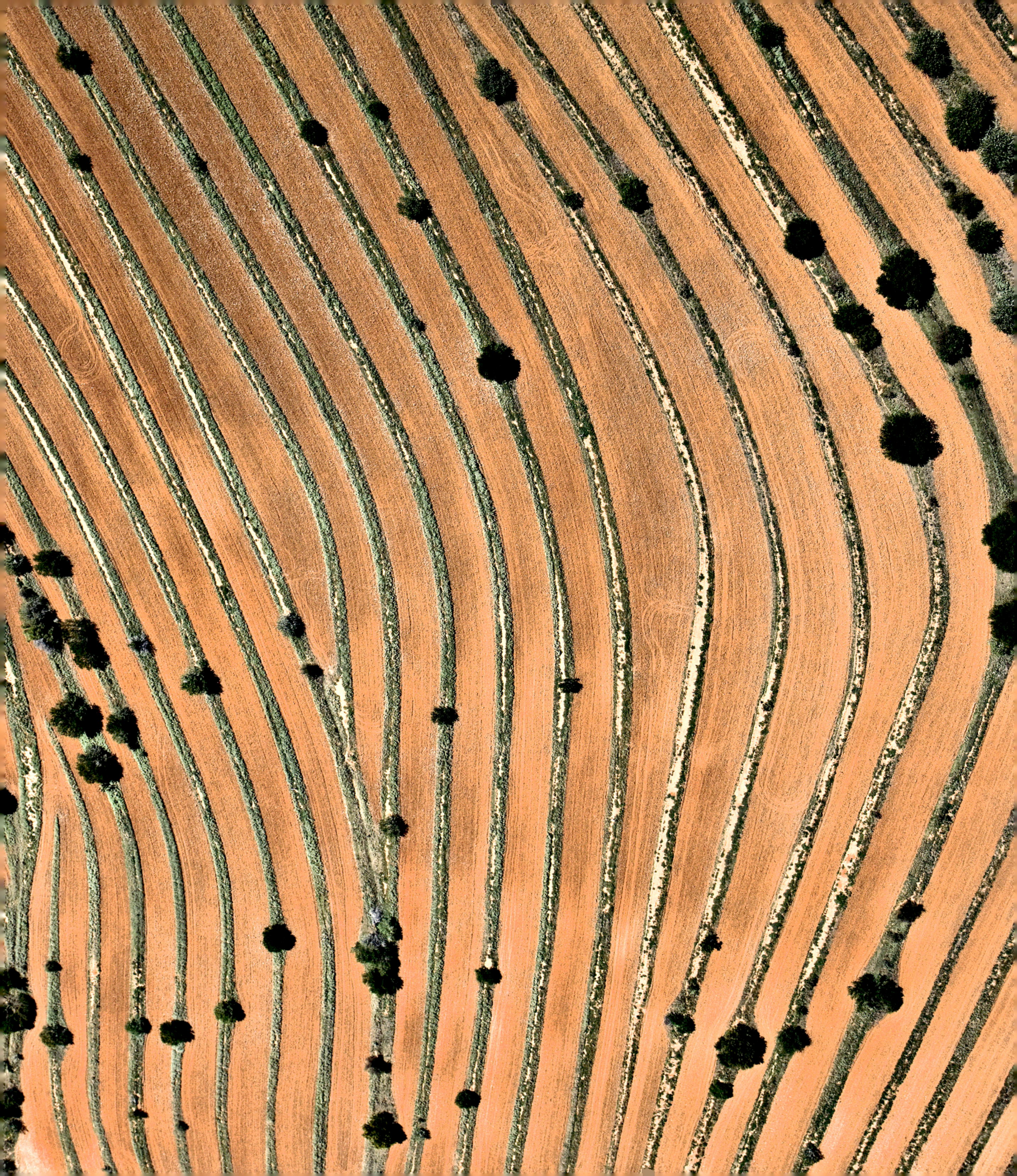

← Farmland

↓ Farm between Adelaide and Fort Beaufort

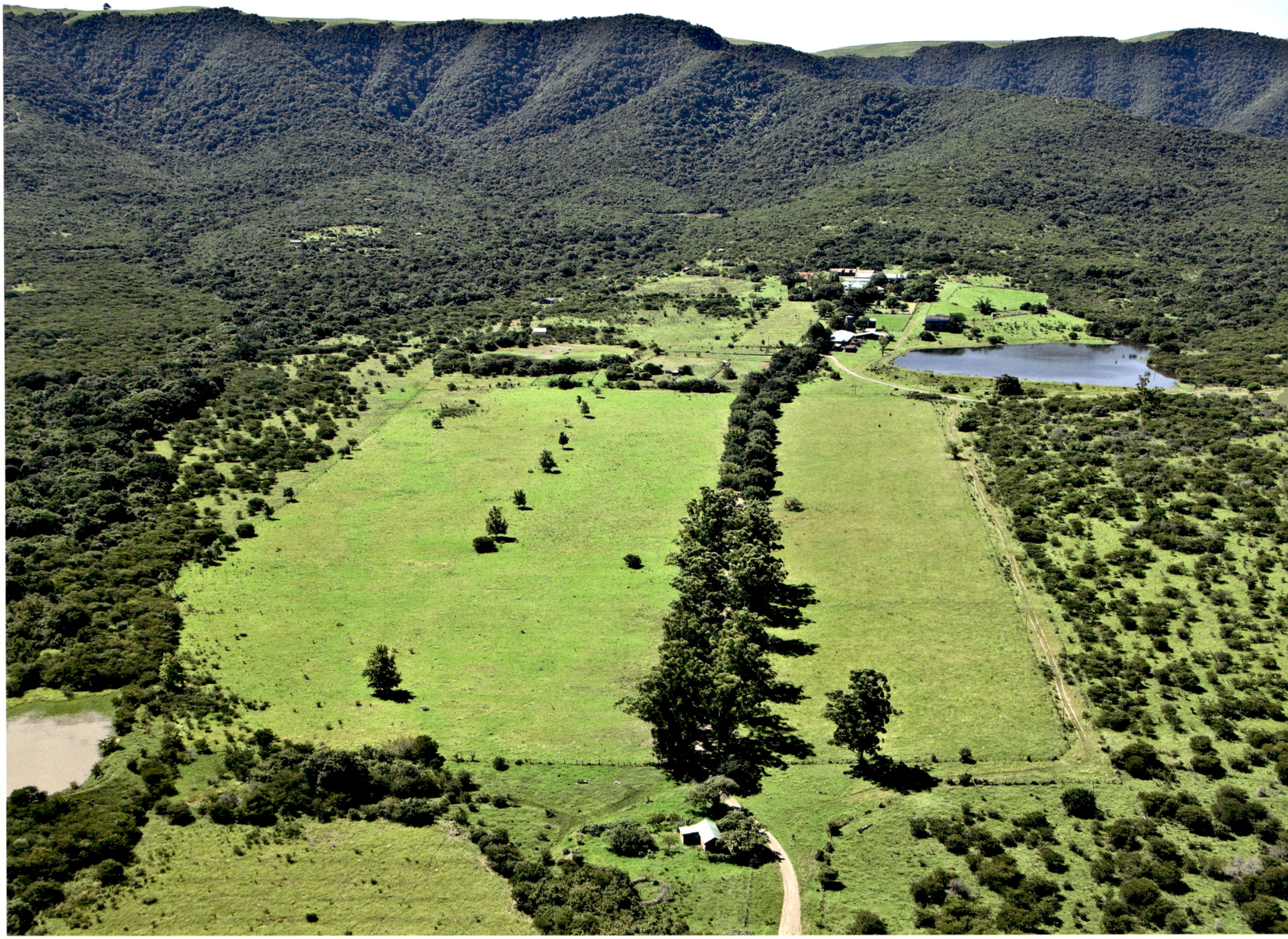

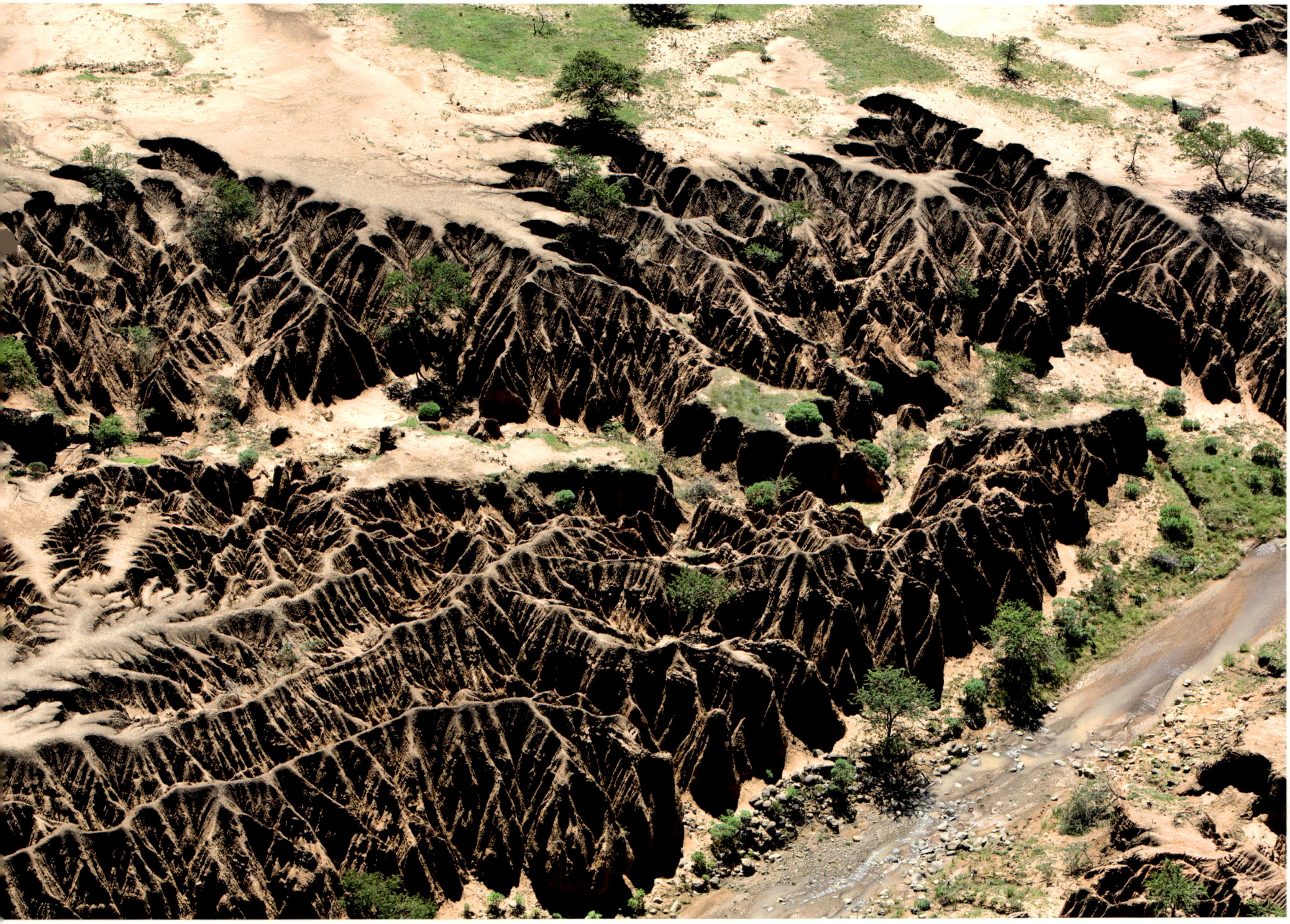

← Rock formation, Mtseko Stream
↓ Waterfall, White-Kei River

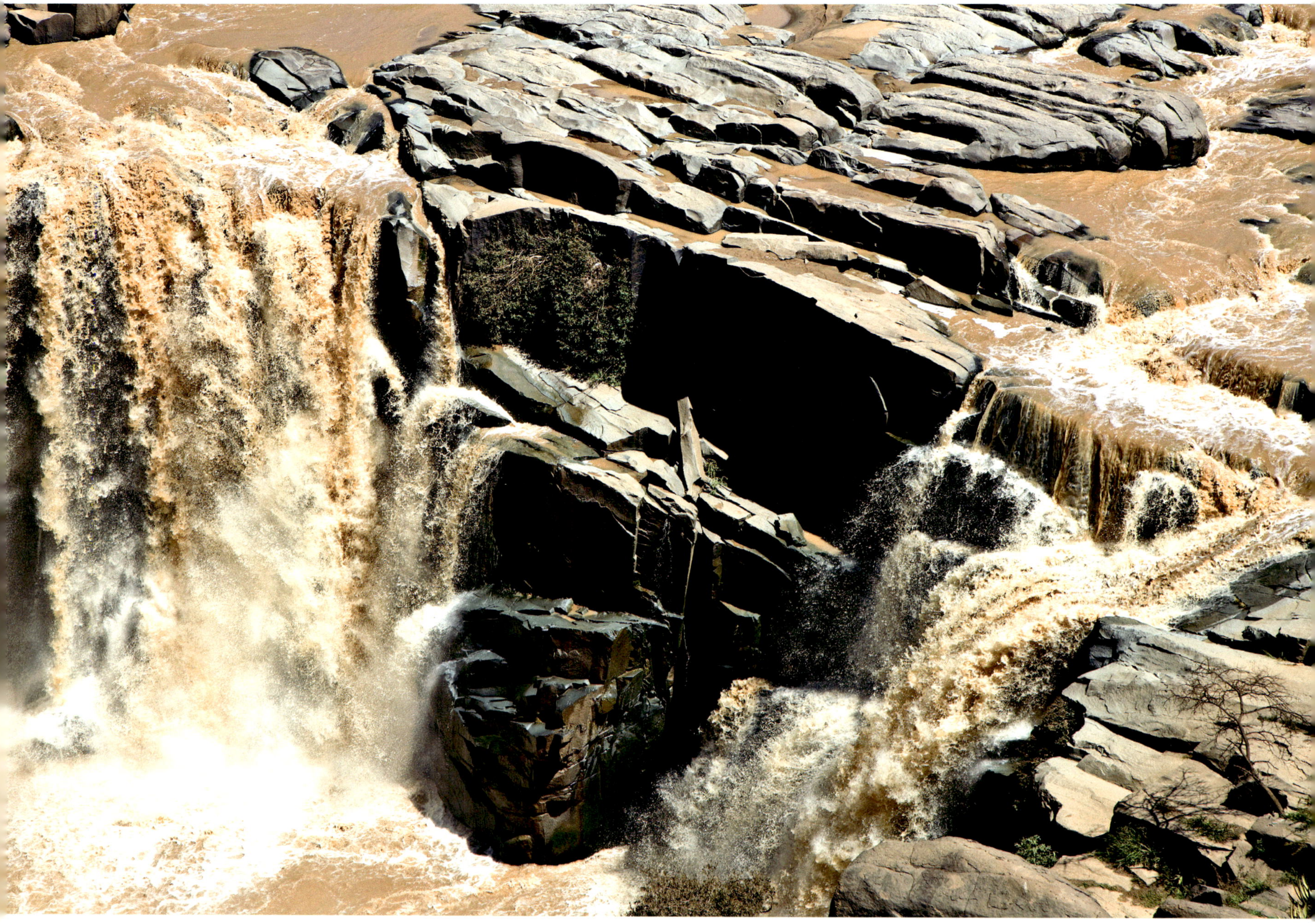

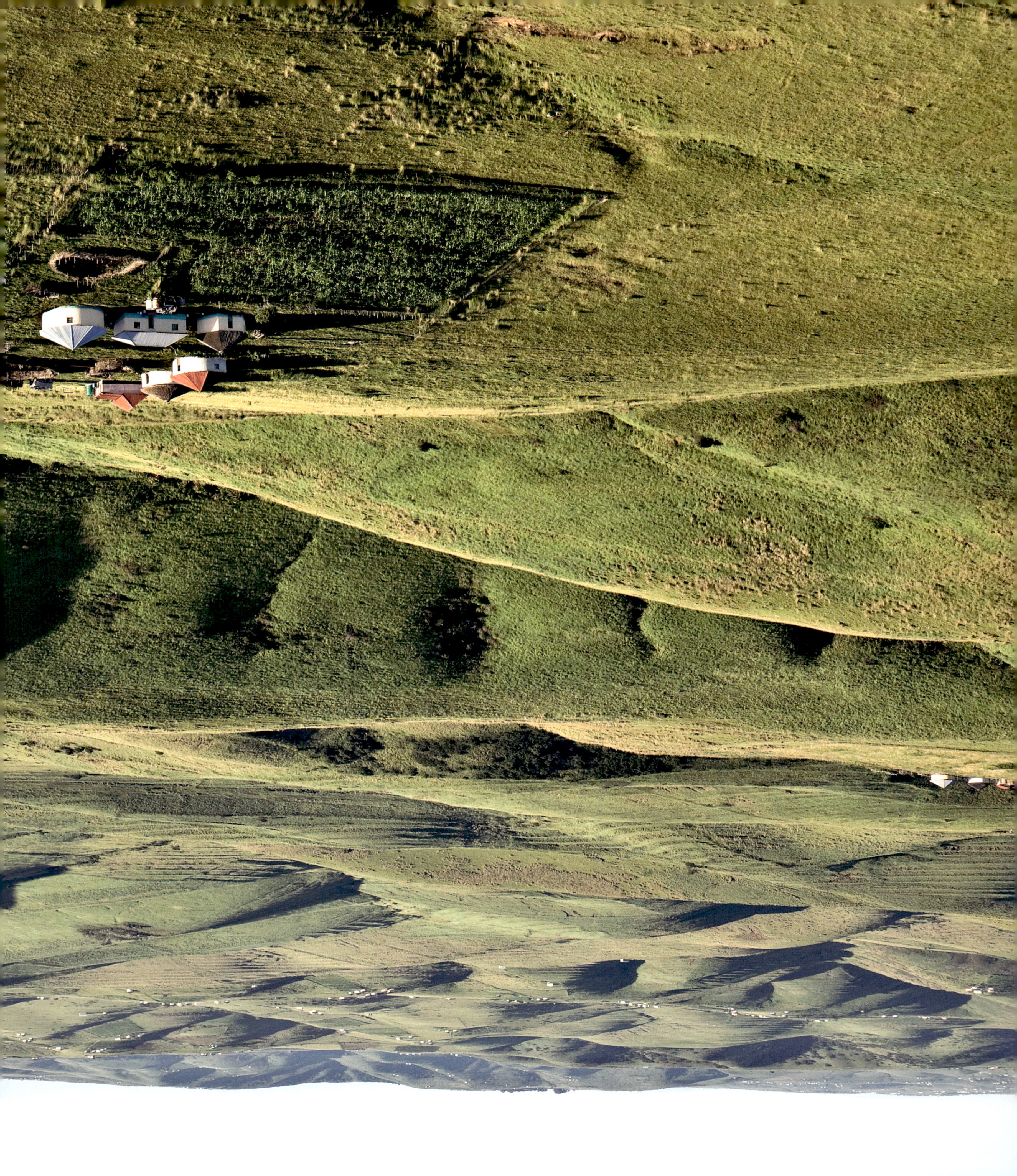

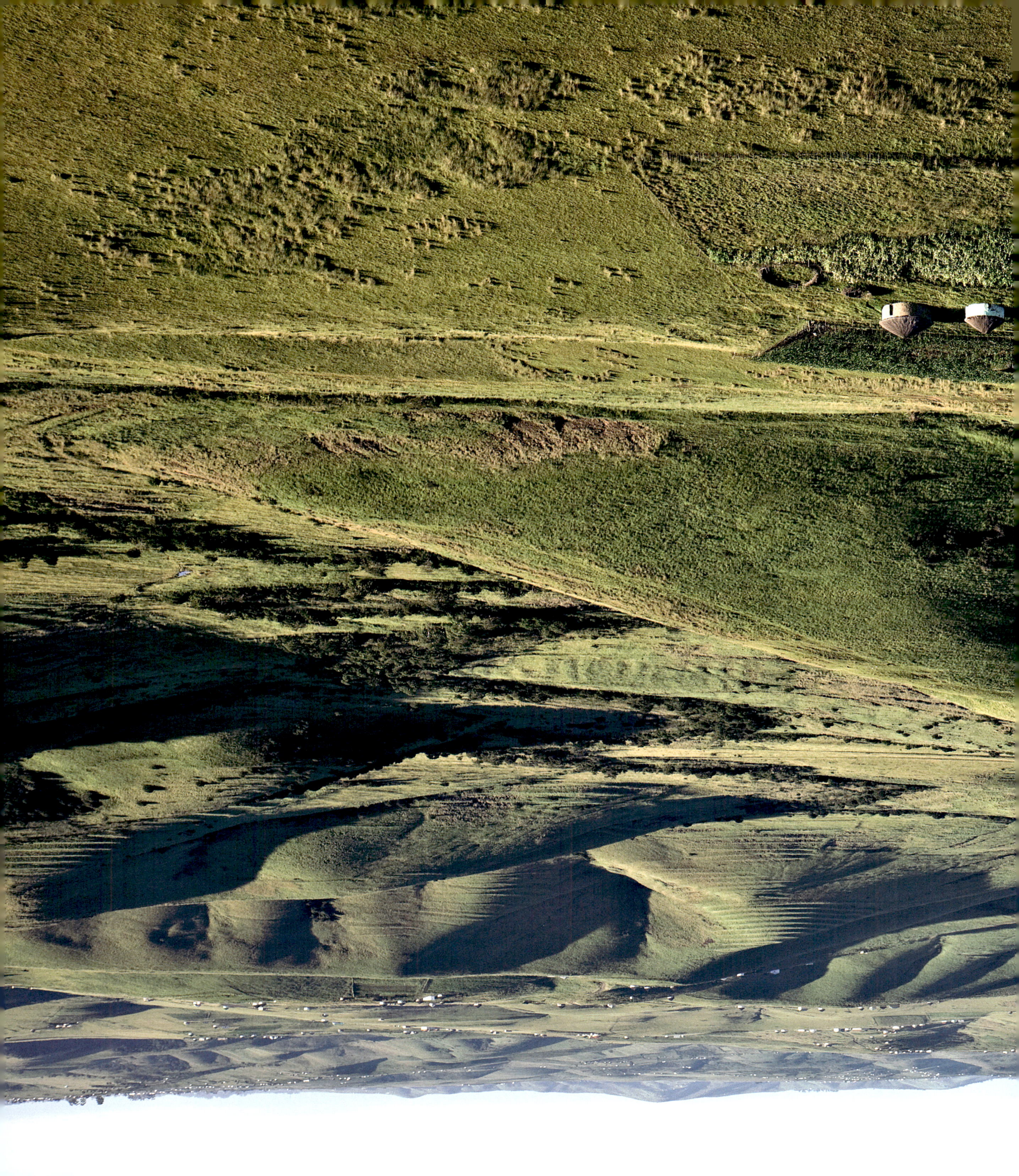

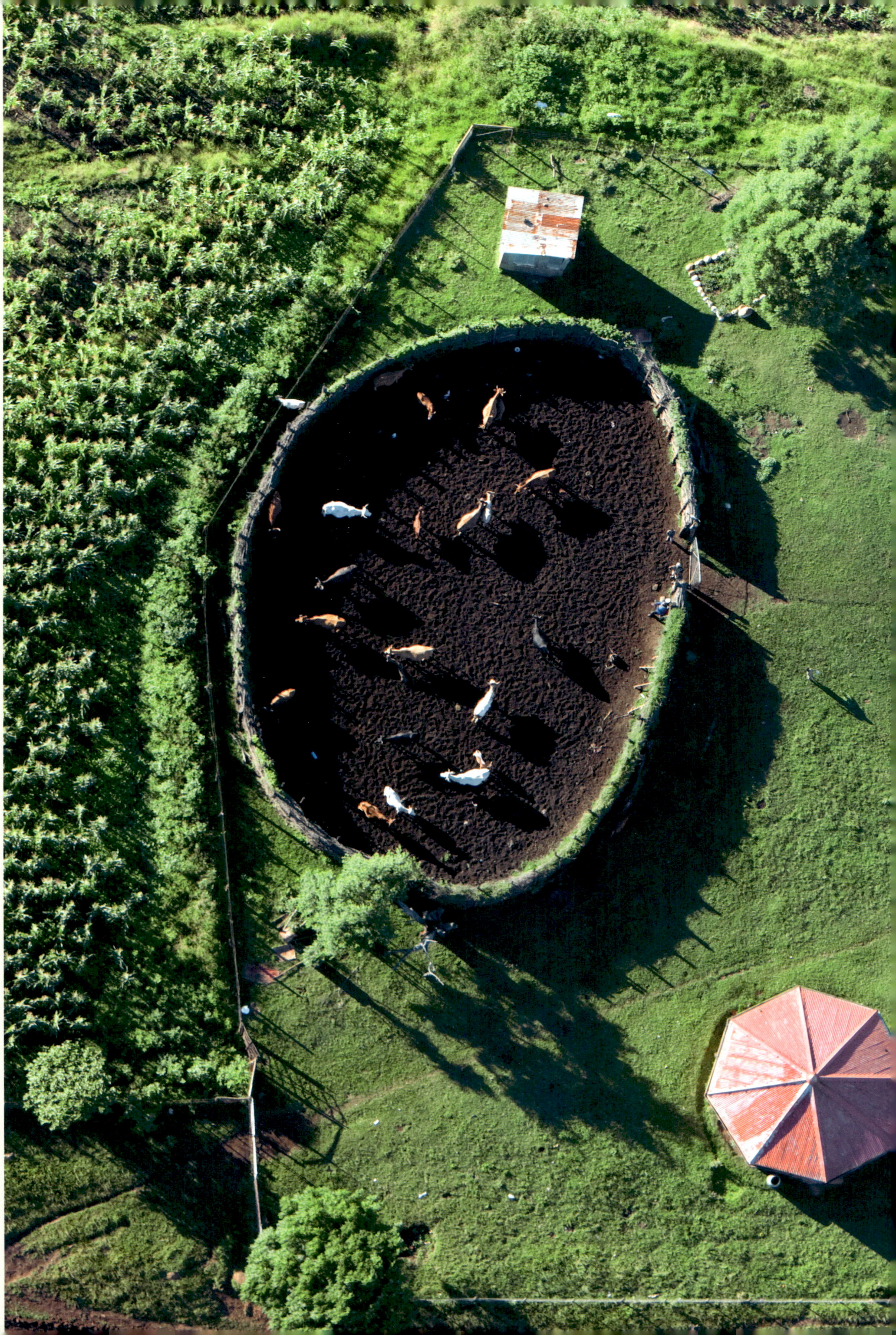

← Takazi, Transkei
→ Typical 'kraal', Hwantsana

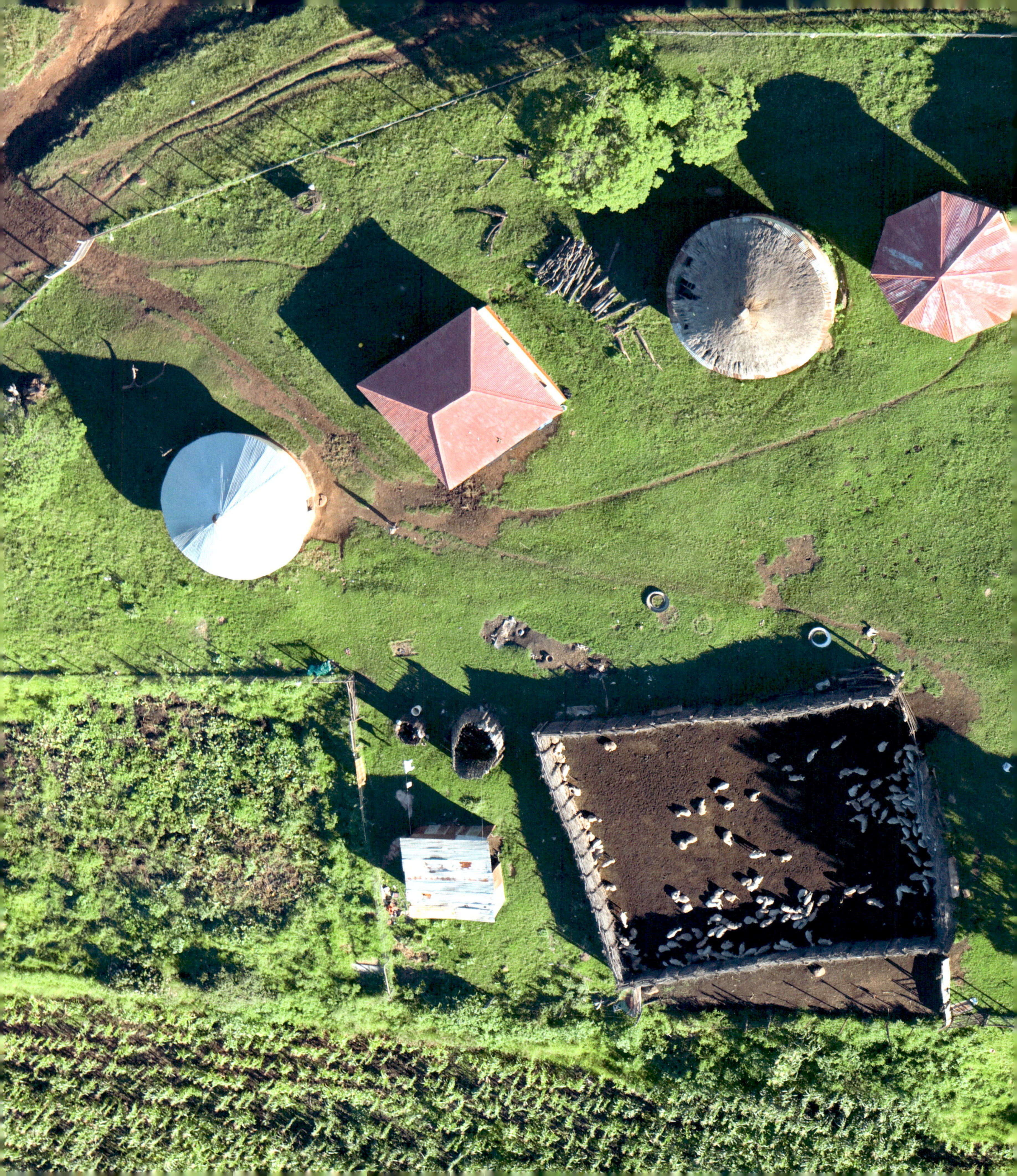

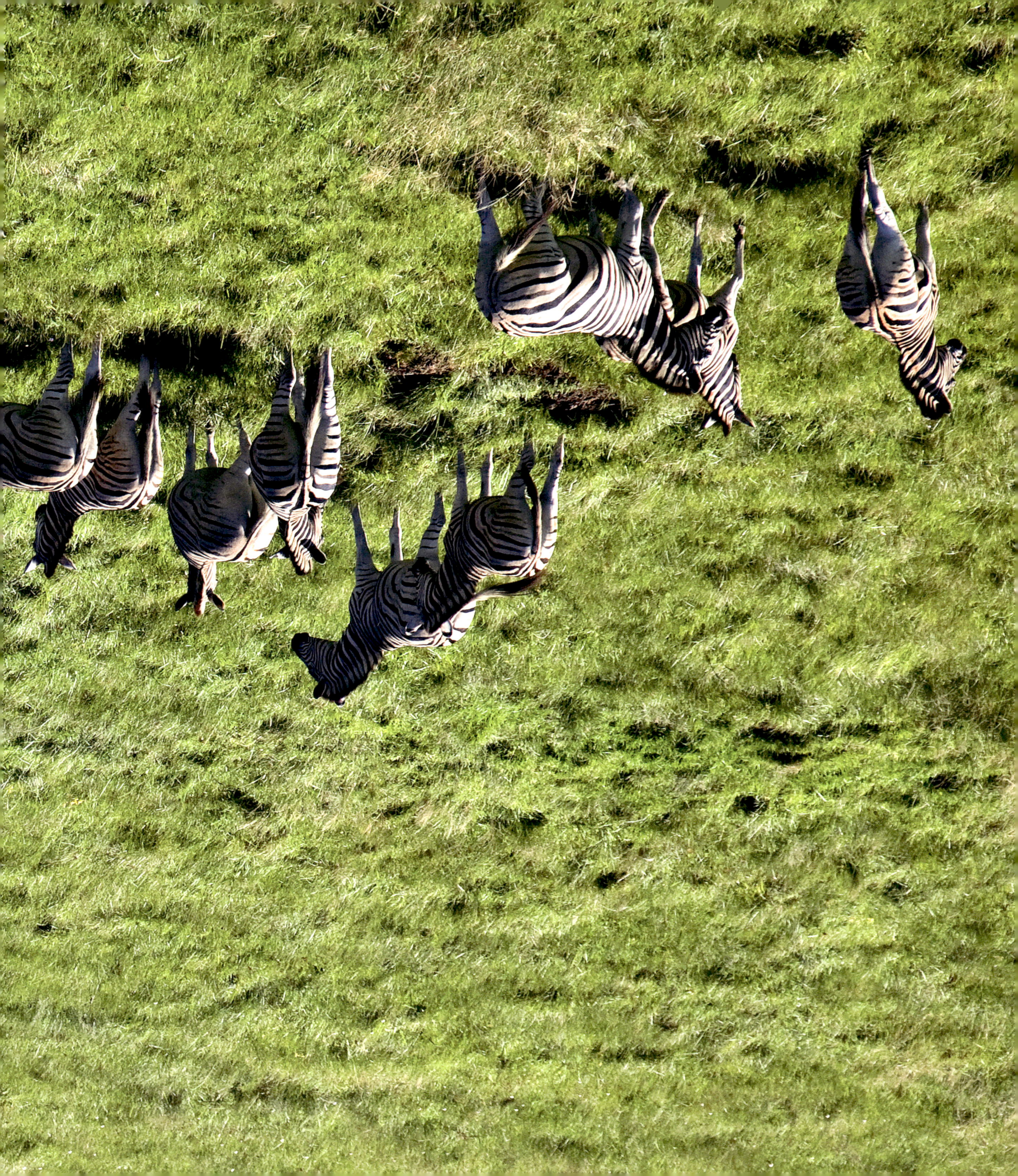

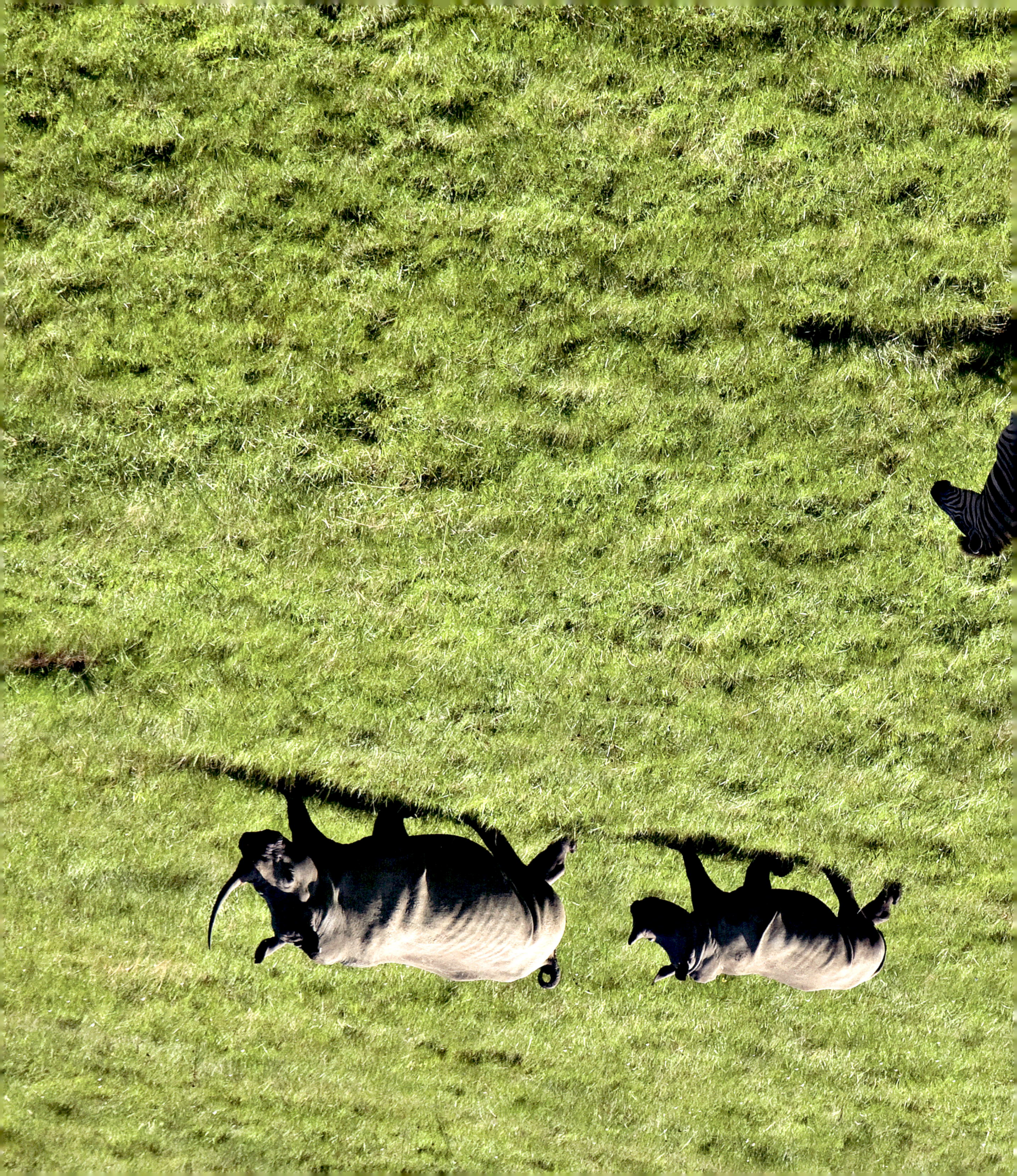

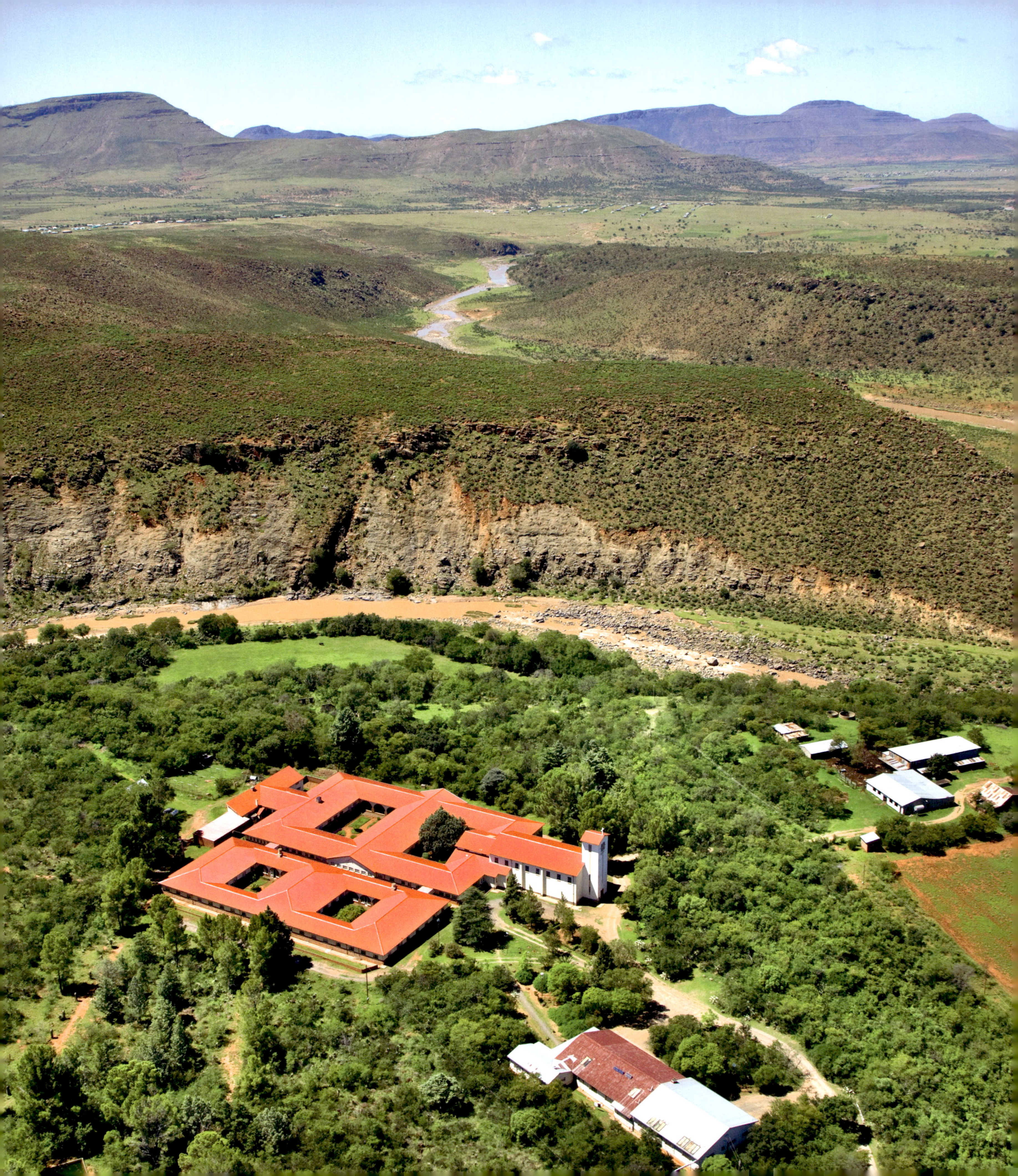

←← Rhinos and zebras, Wild Coast
← Ntaba Maria Mission, Transkei
↓ Queenstown

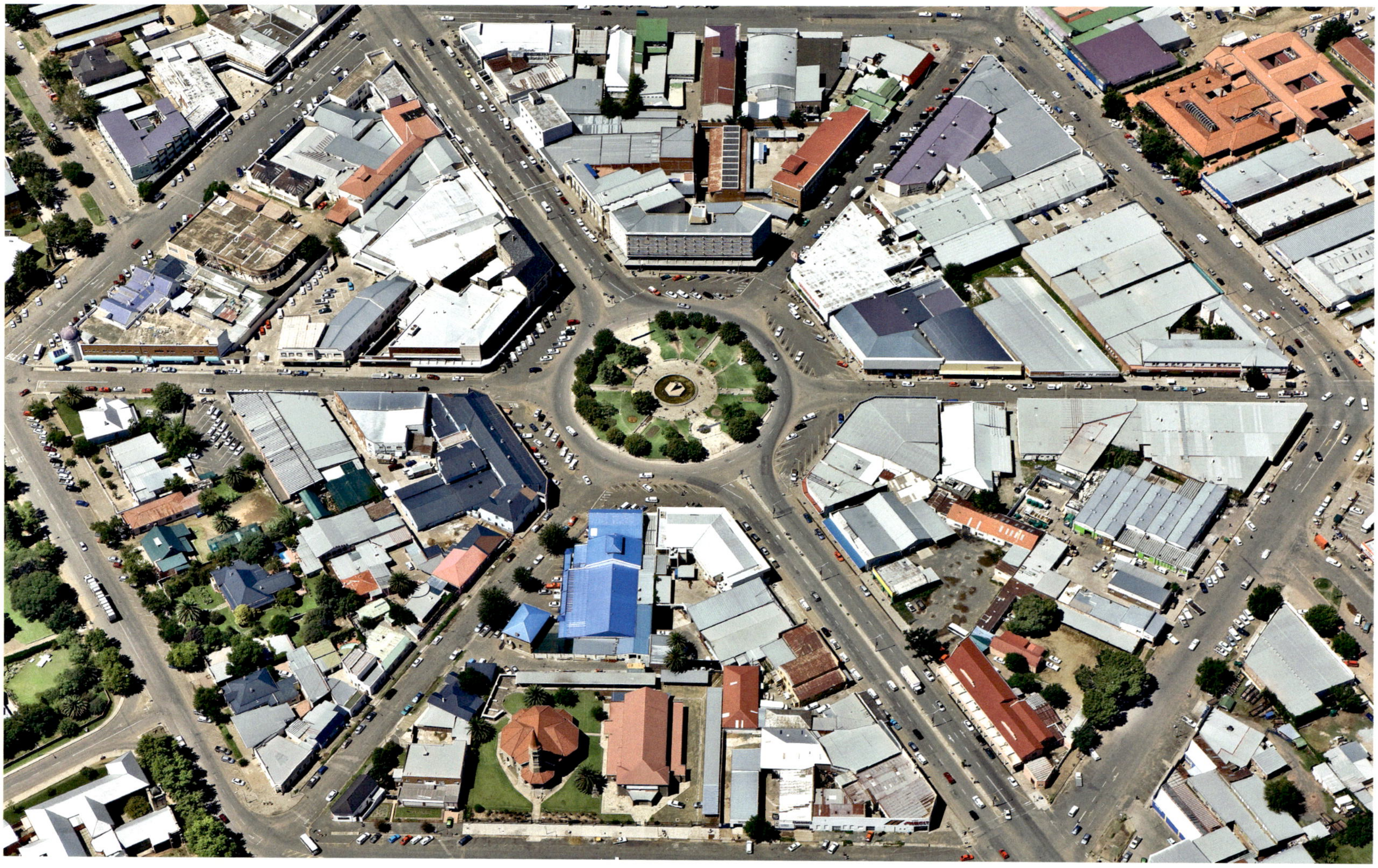

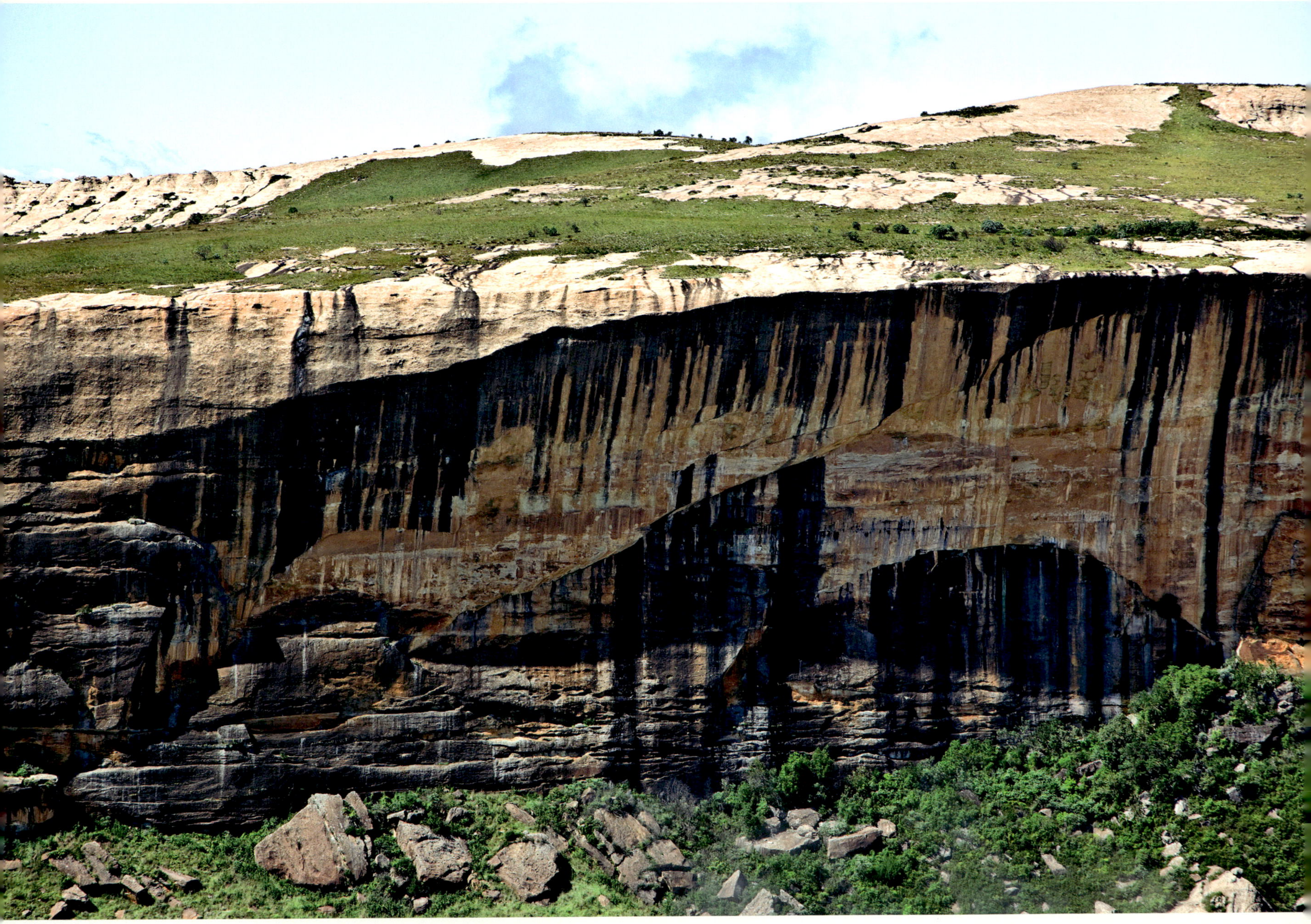

← Drakensberg, Transkei
↓ Slanghoek Valley, Transkei

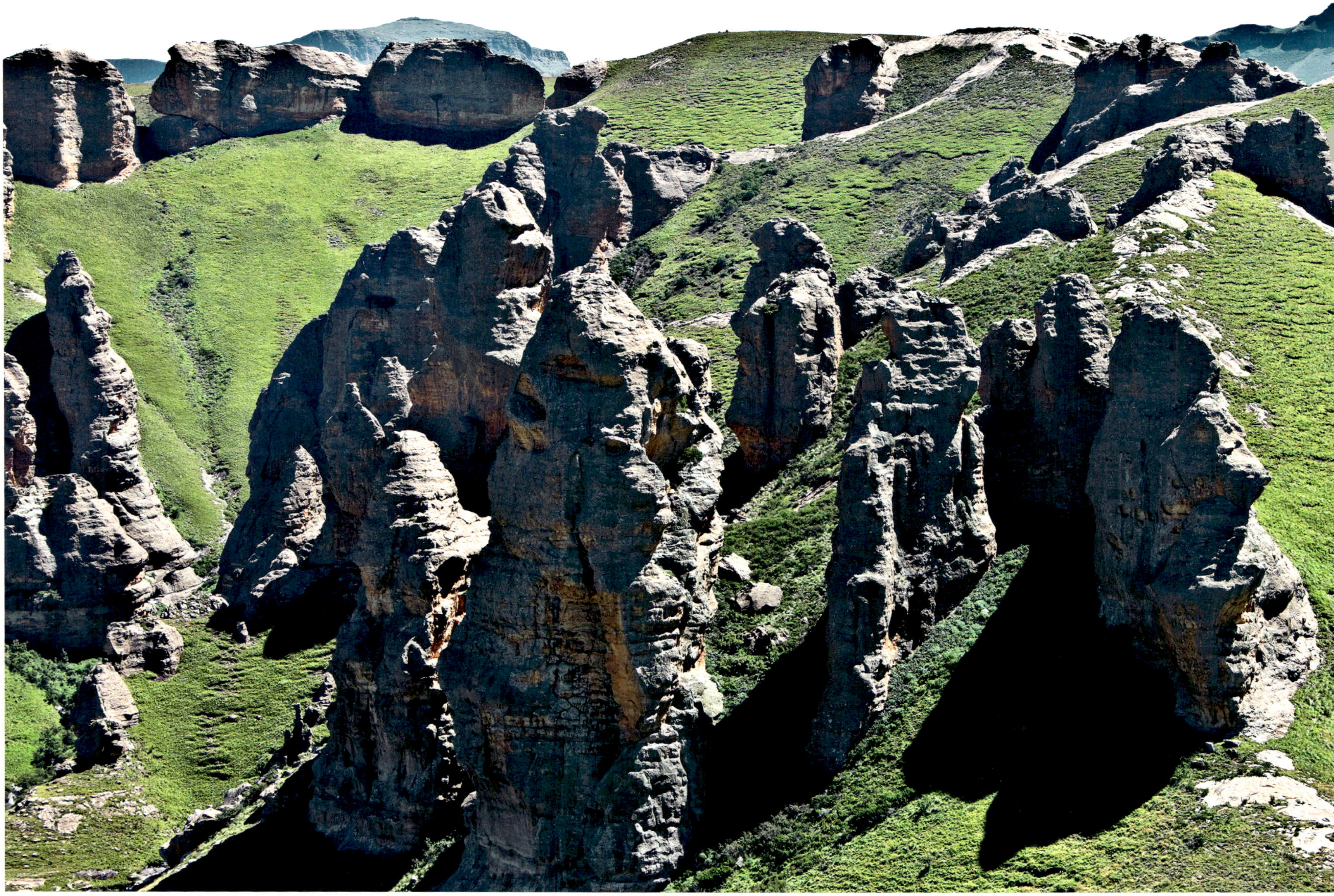

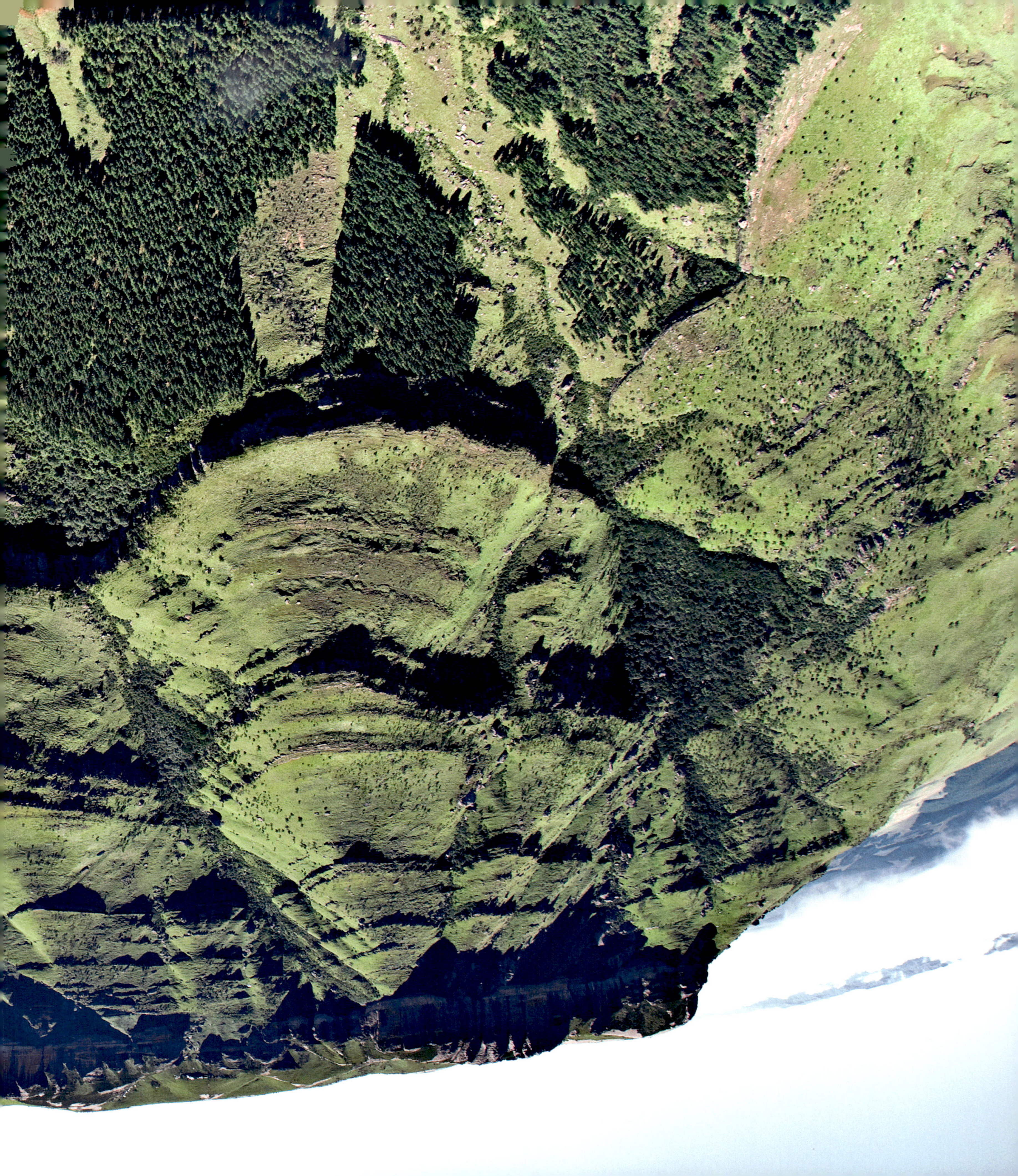

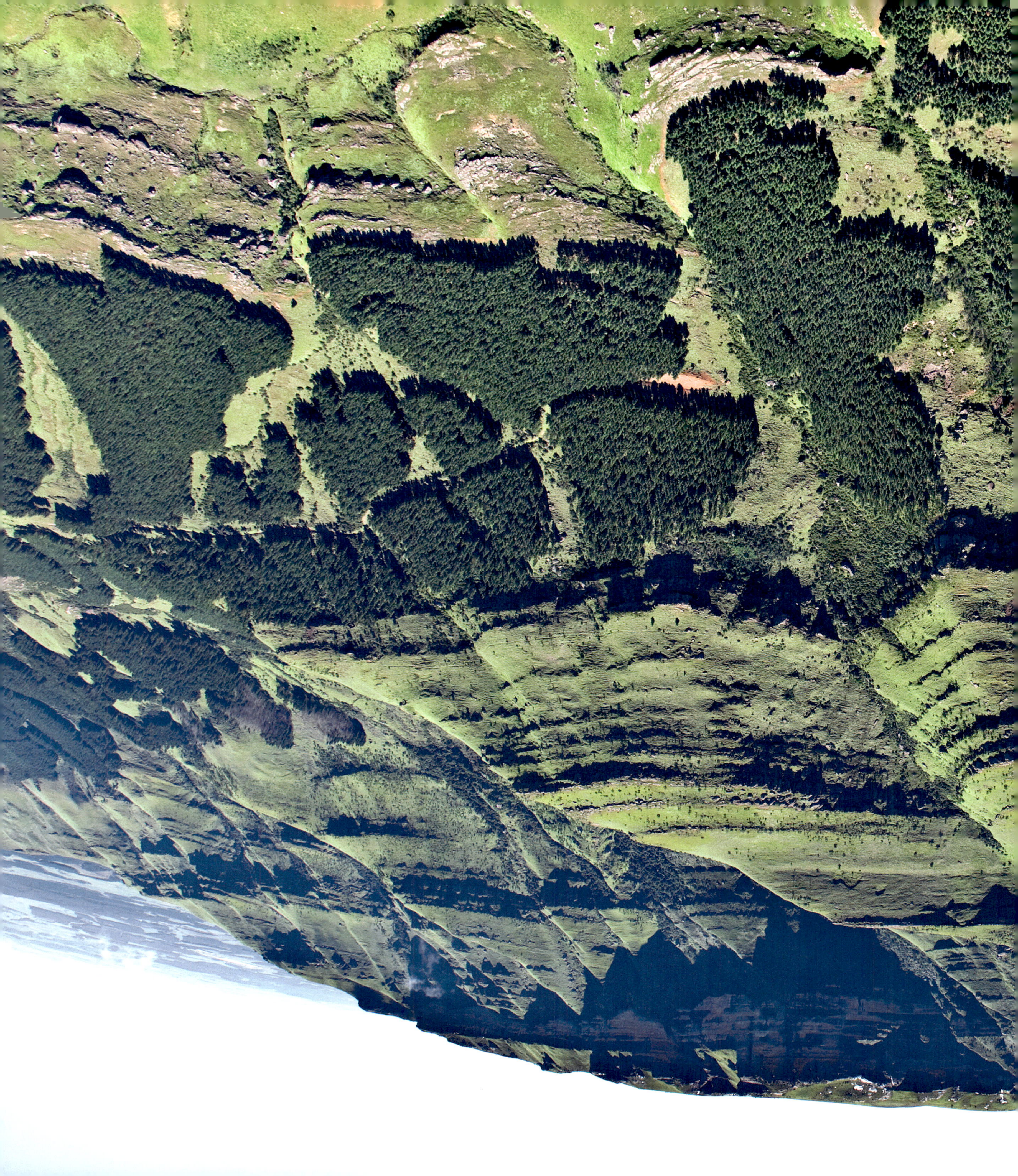

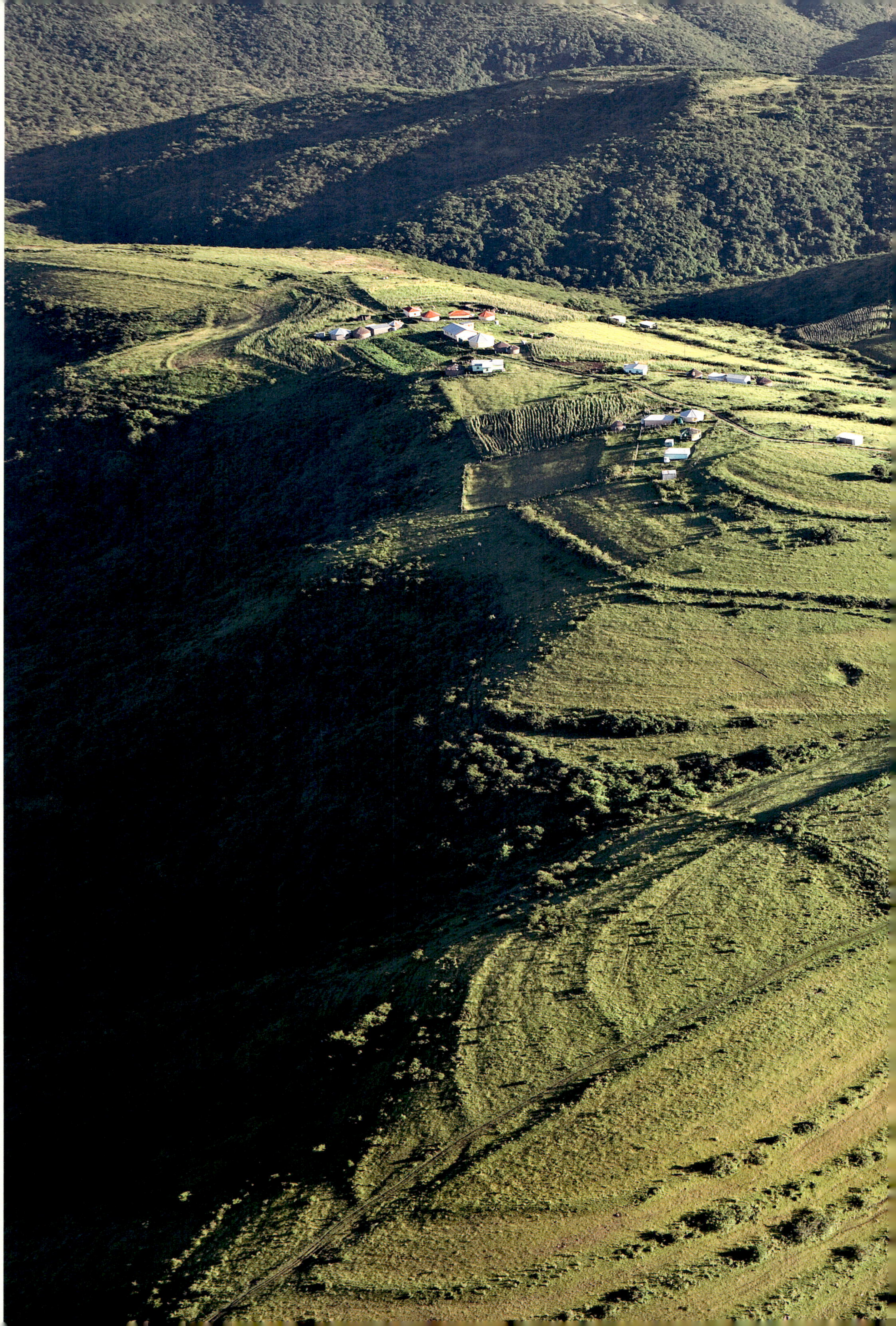

← Drakensberg, southern area near Ugie

→ The Valley of a Thousand Hills, eSigangala

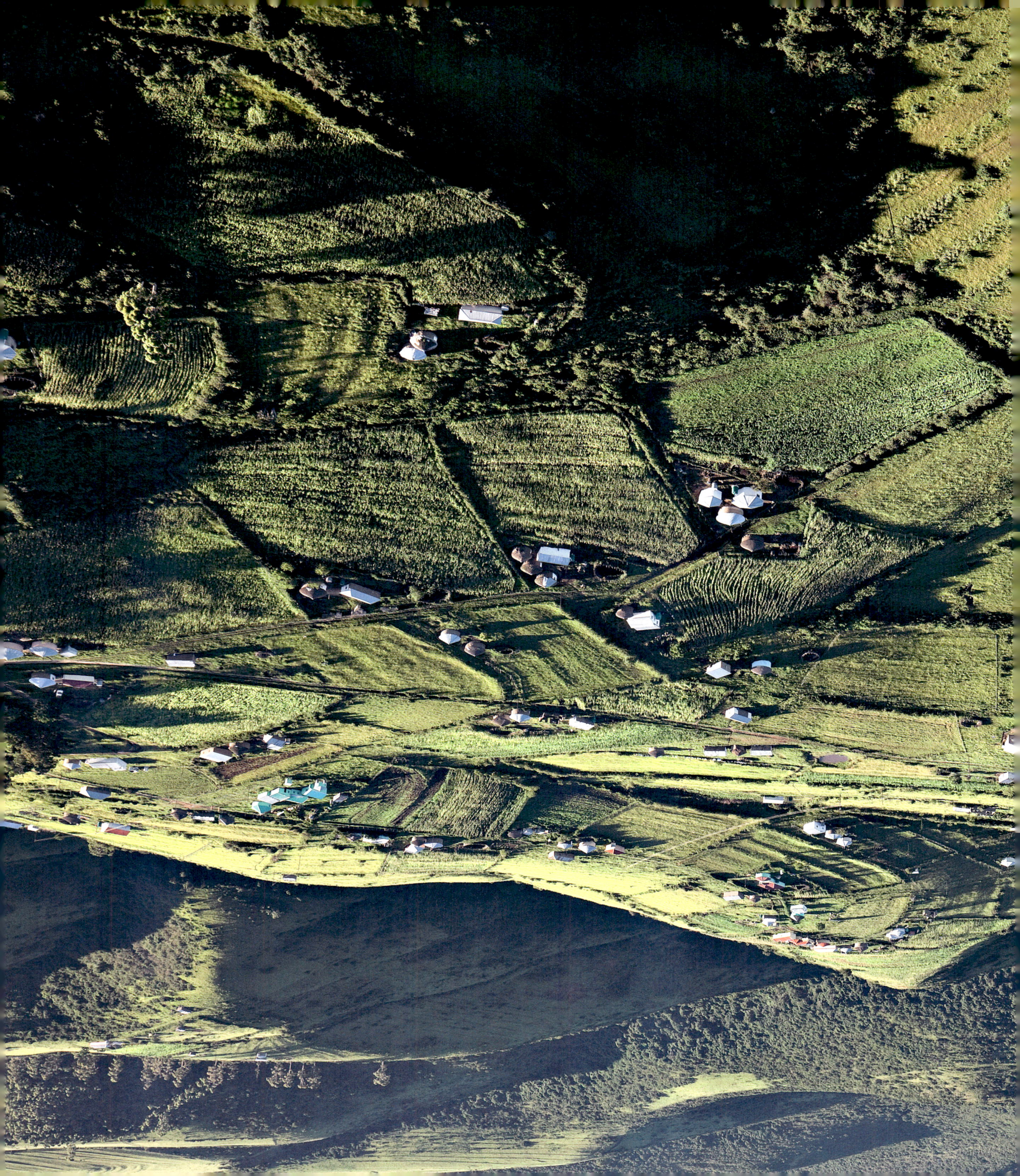

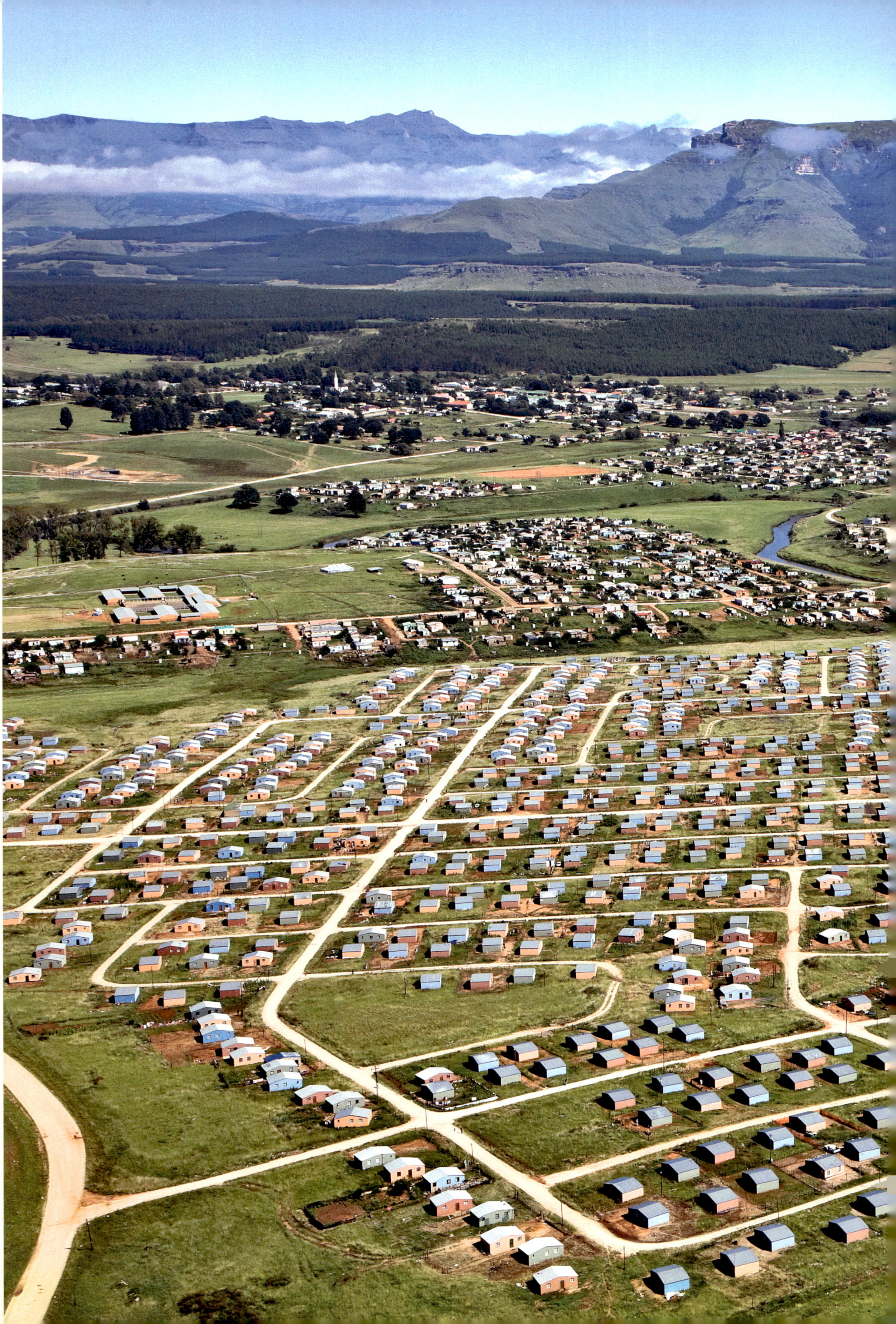

→ Ugie, Transkei

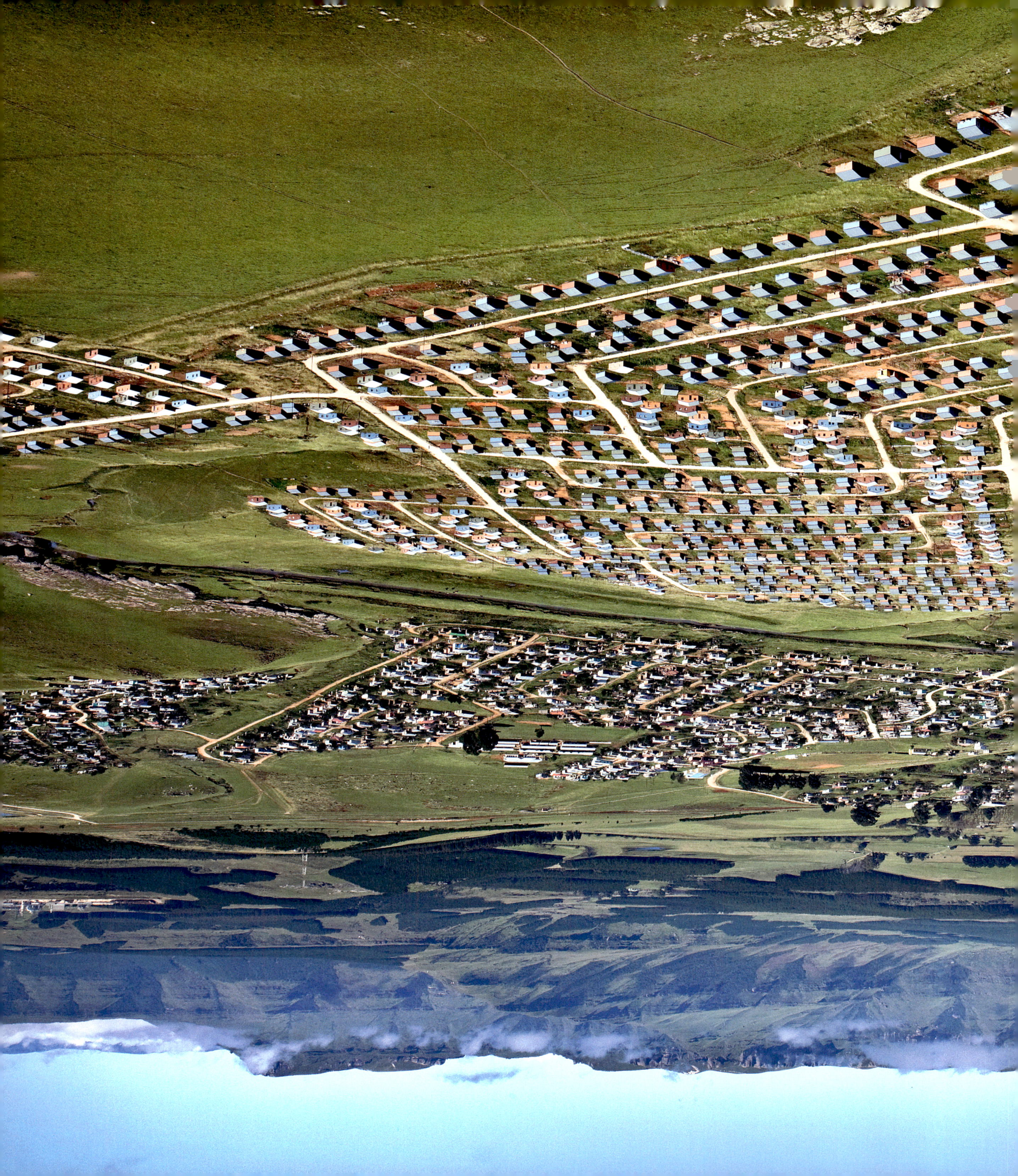

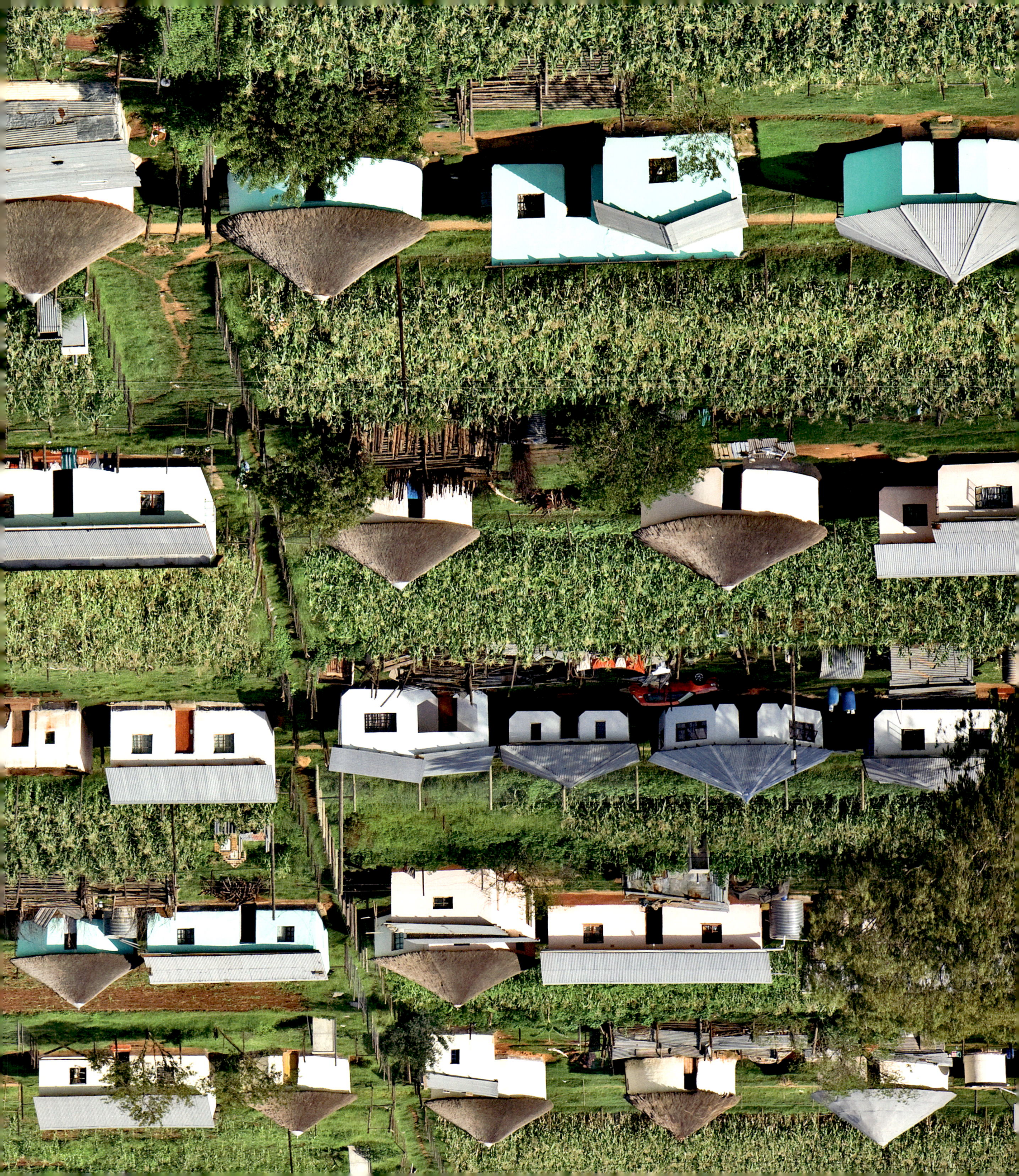

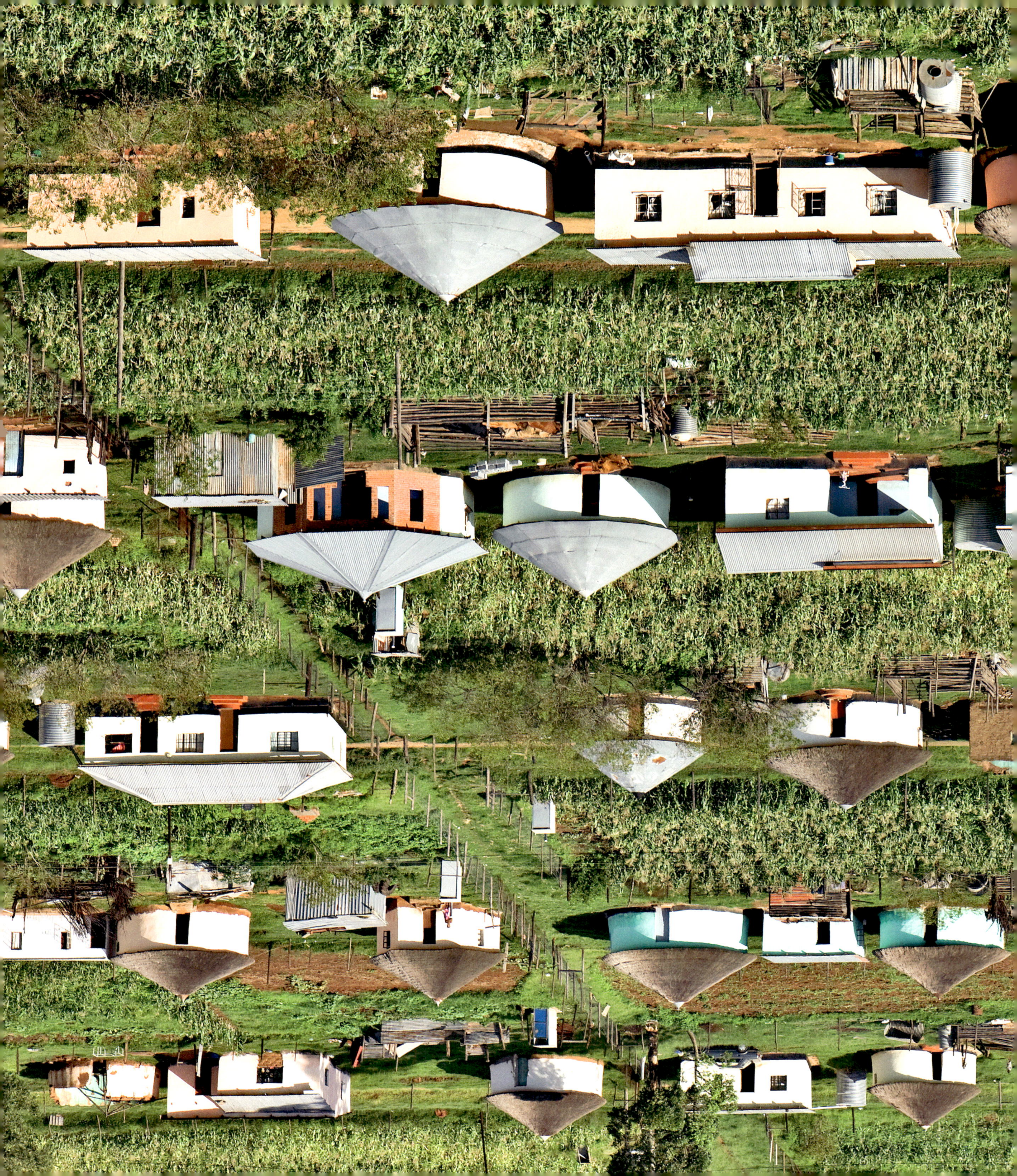

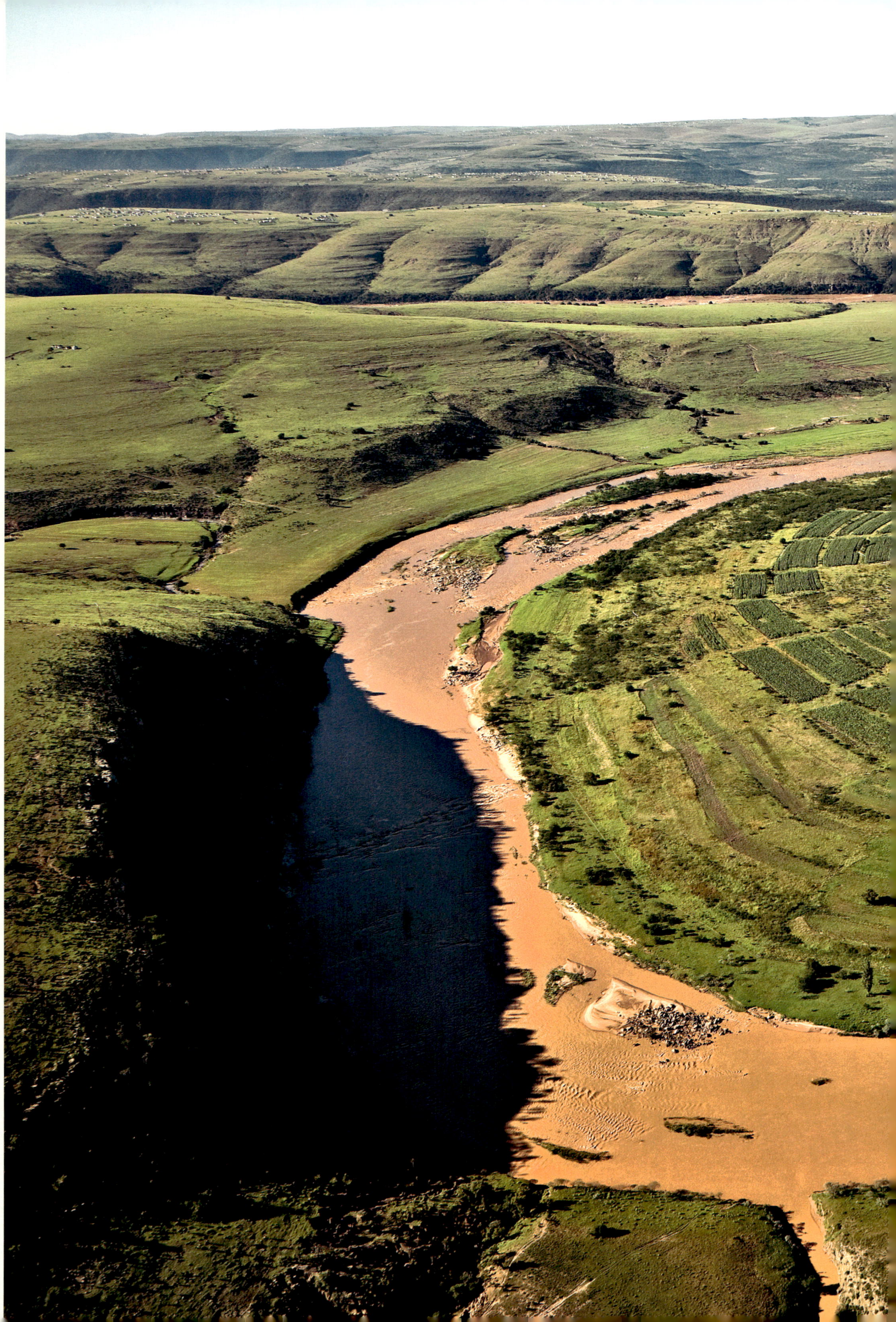

← Mthatha, Transkei
→ Ebashe River, Transkei

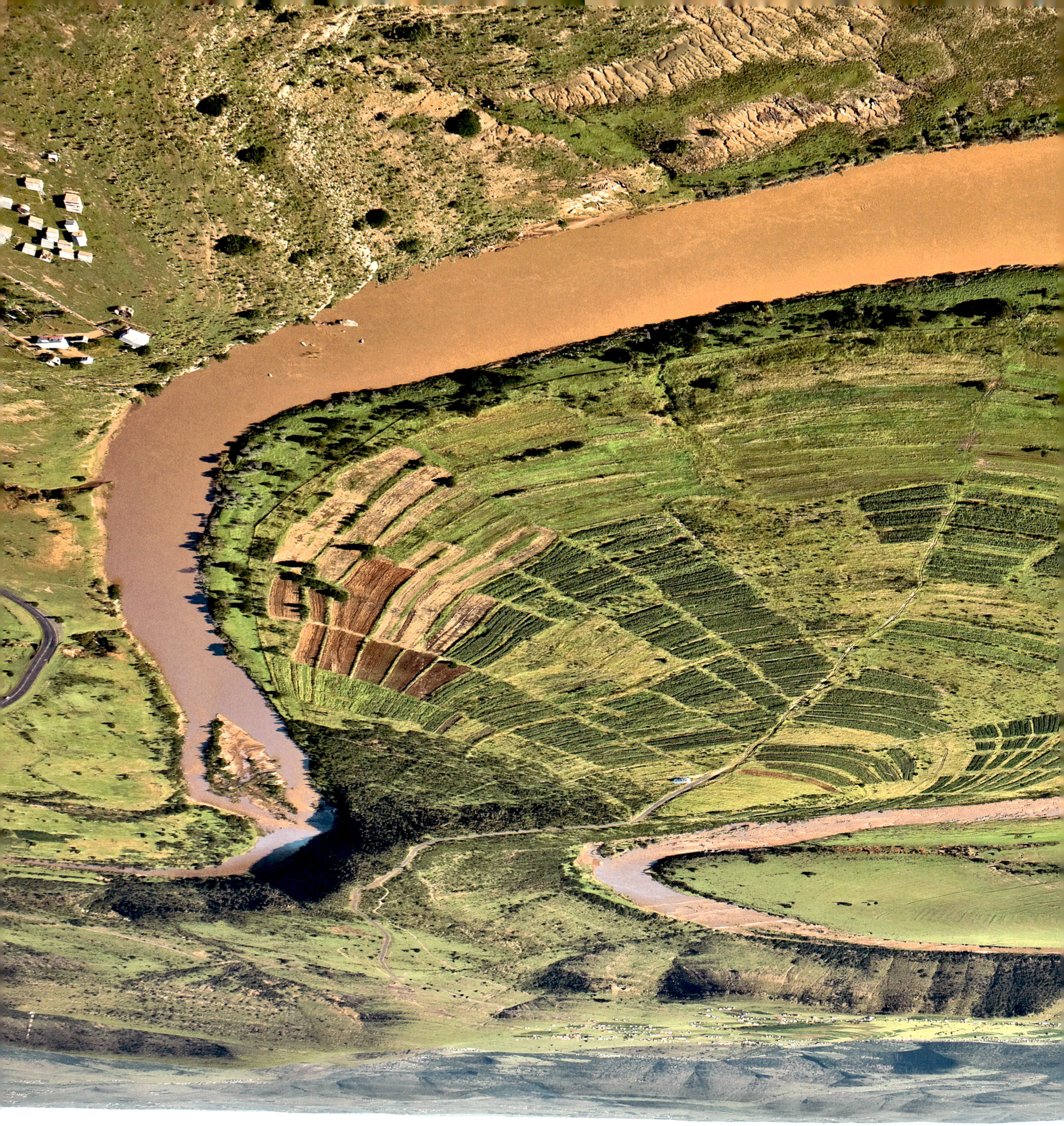

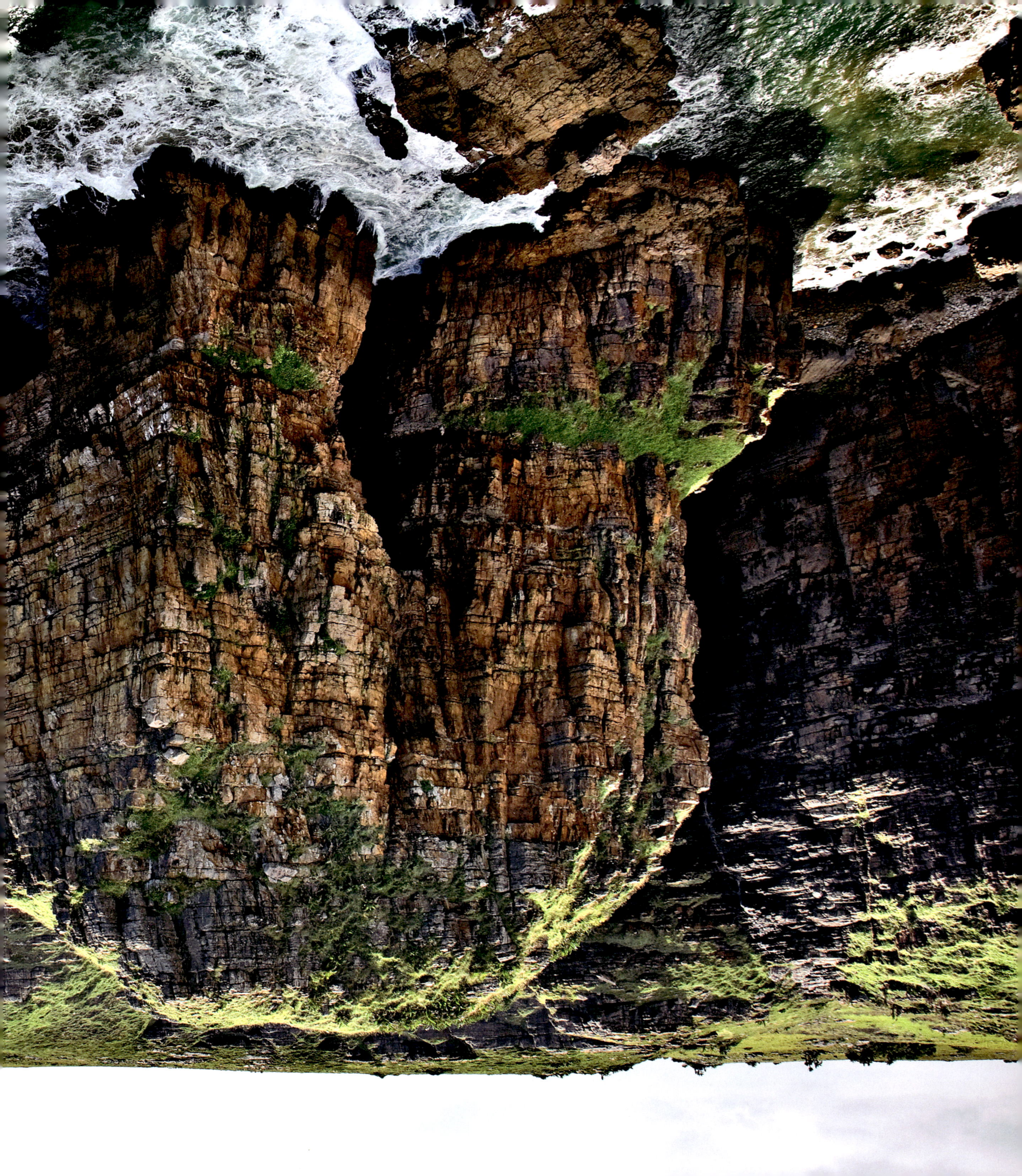

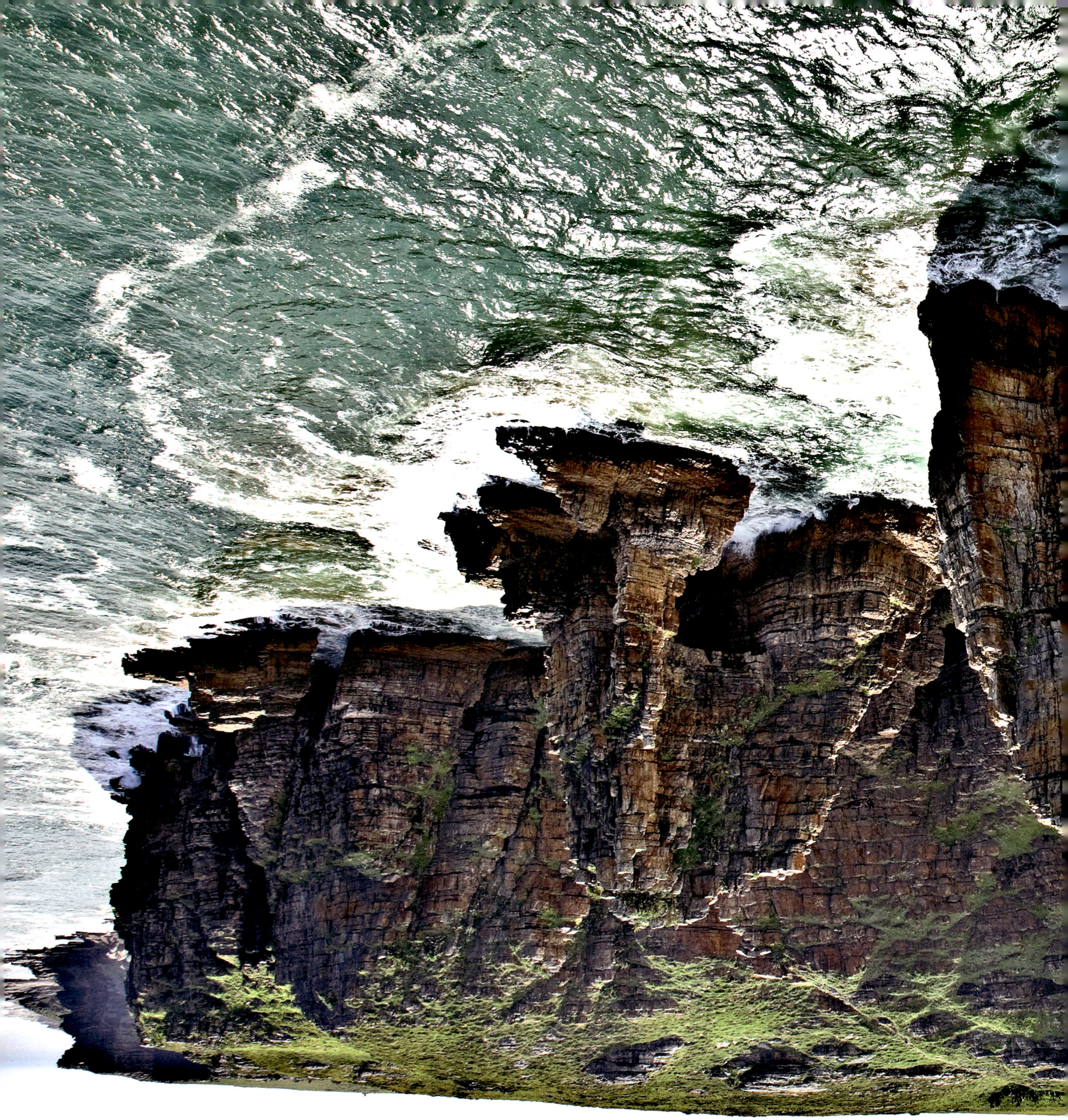

← Cathedral Rock, Wild Coast
↓→ Hole in the wall, Wild Coast

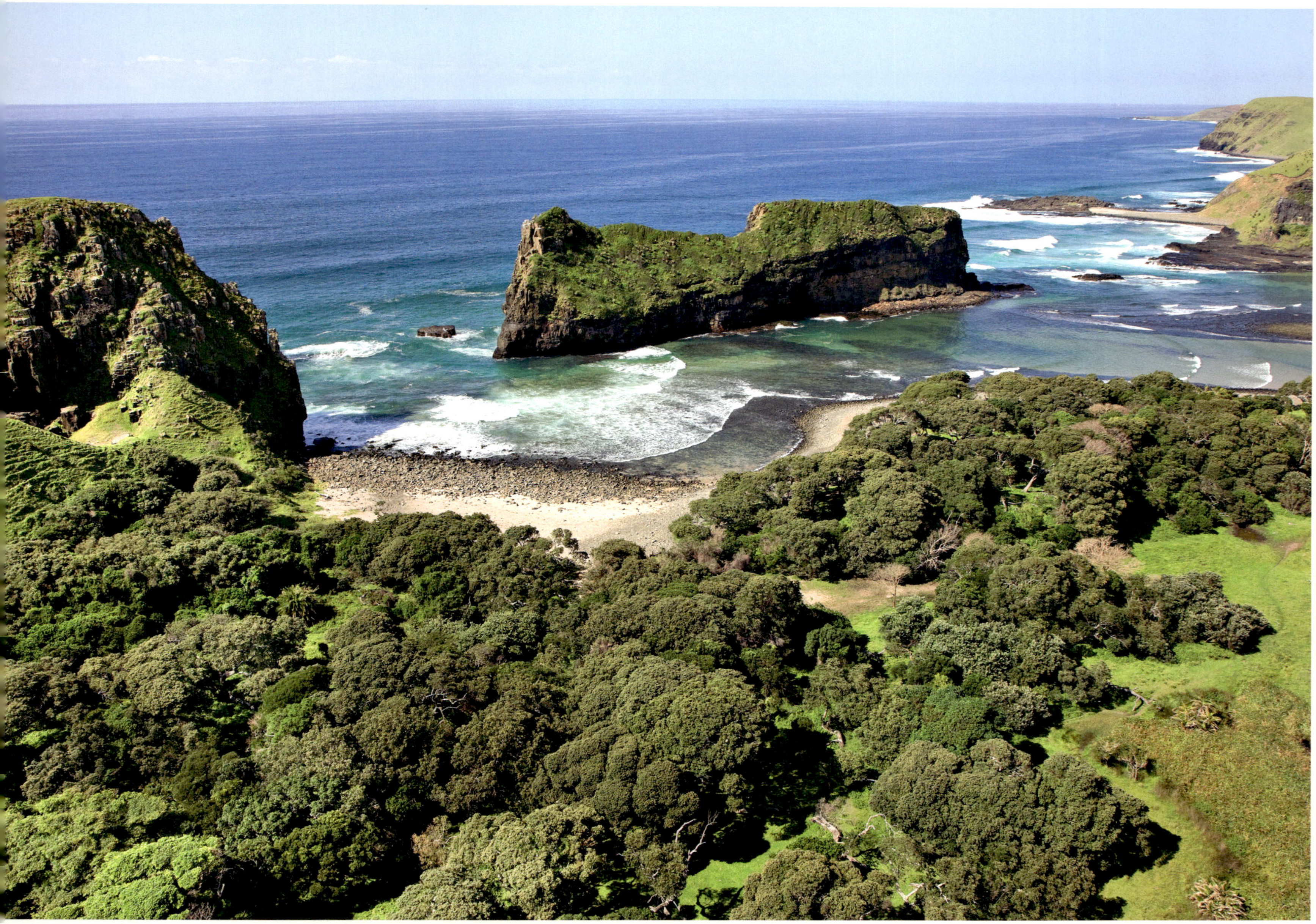

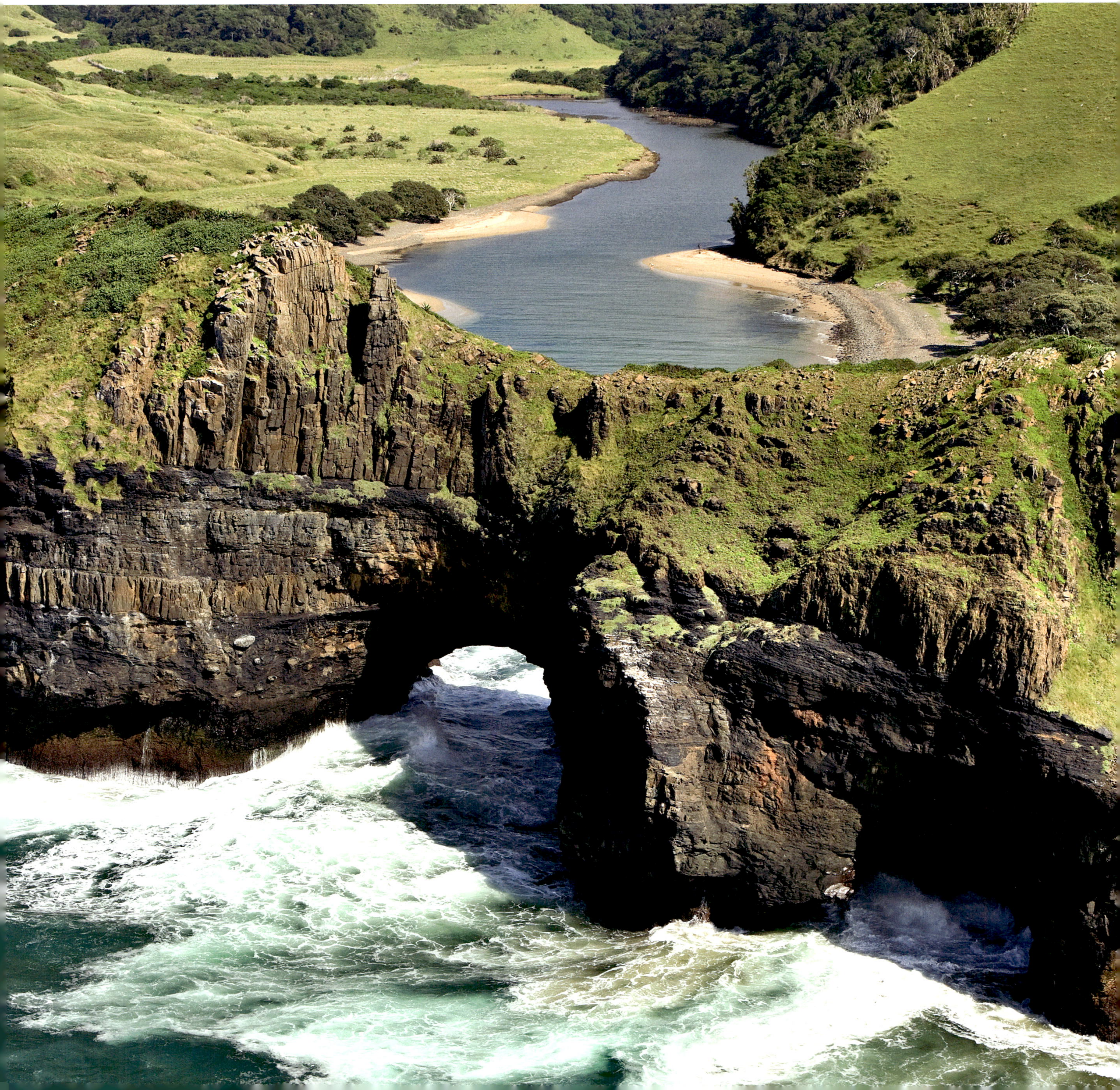

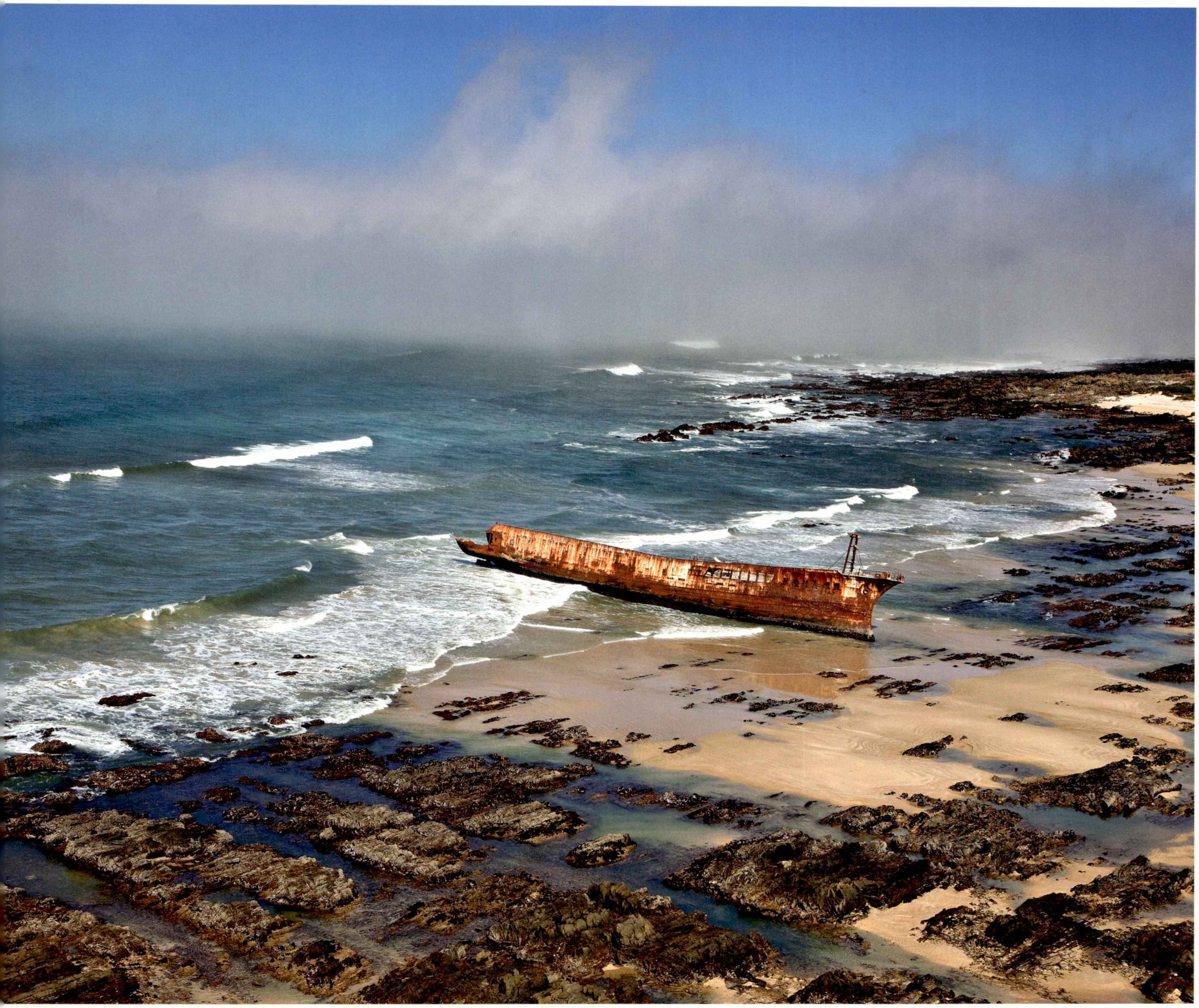

← One of the many wrecks along the coast

↓ Happy cows

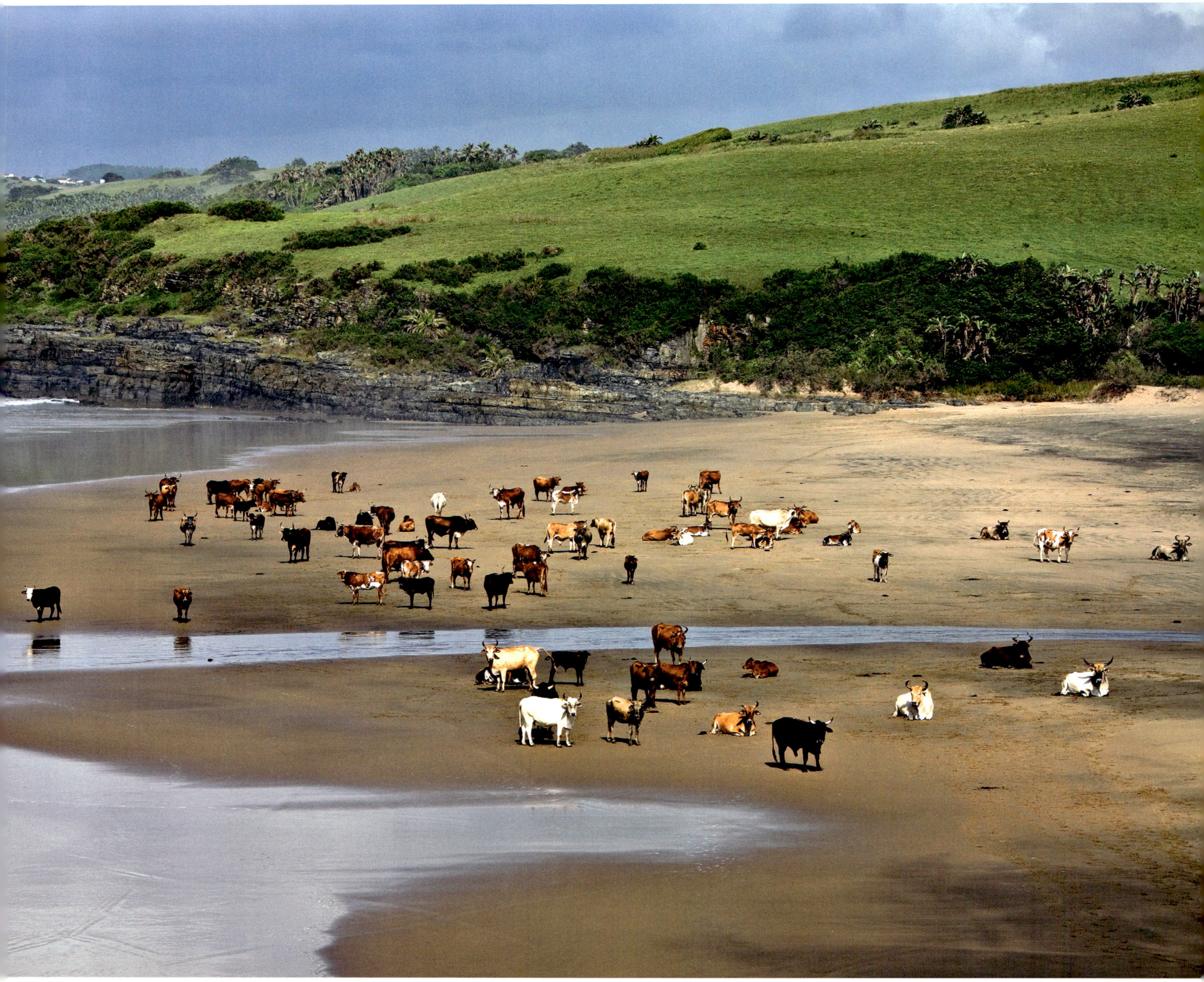

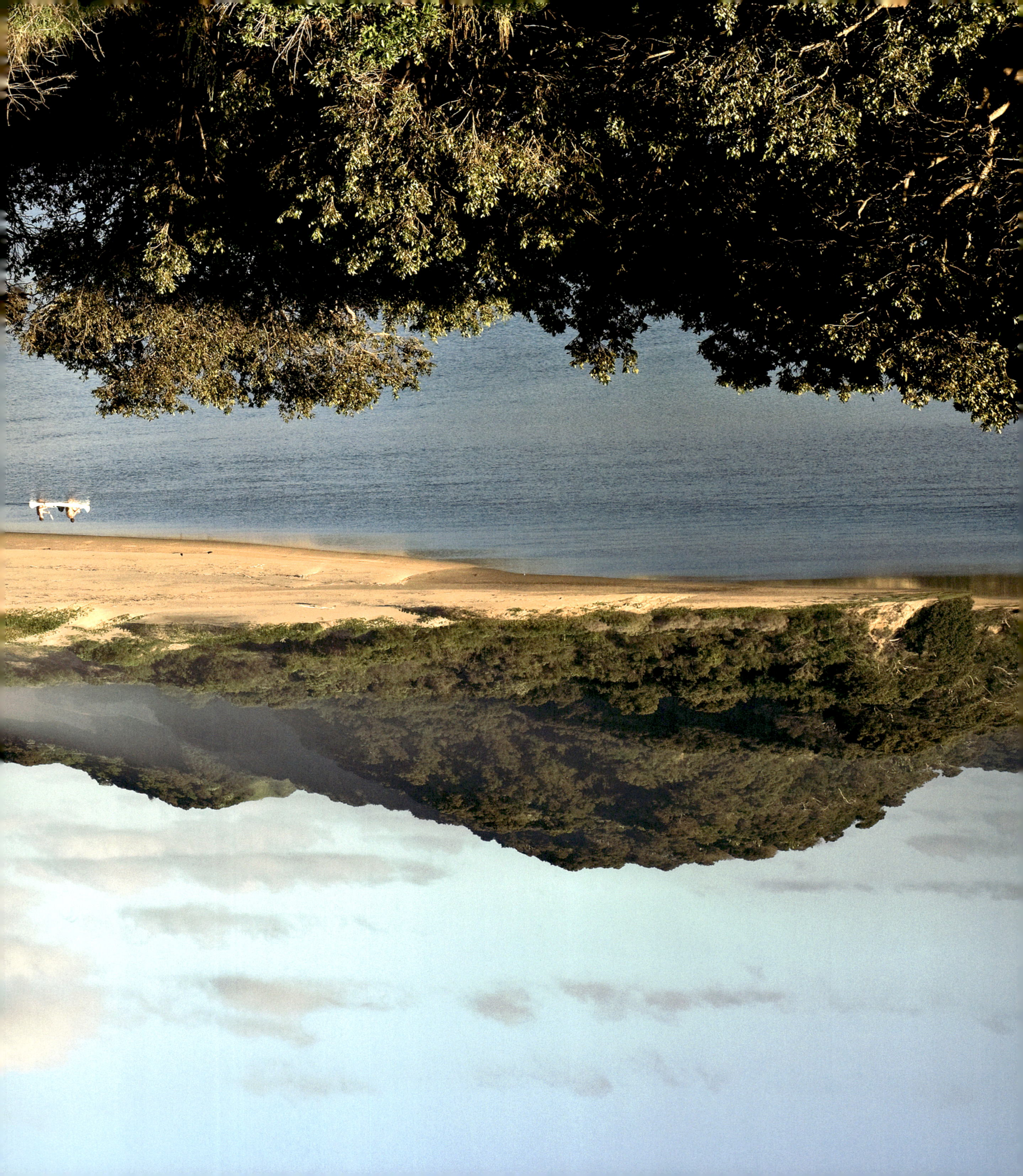

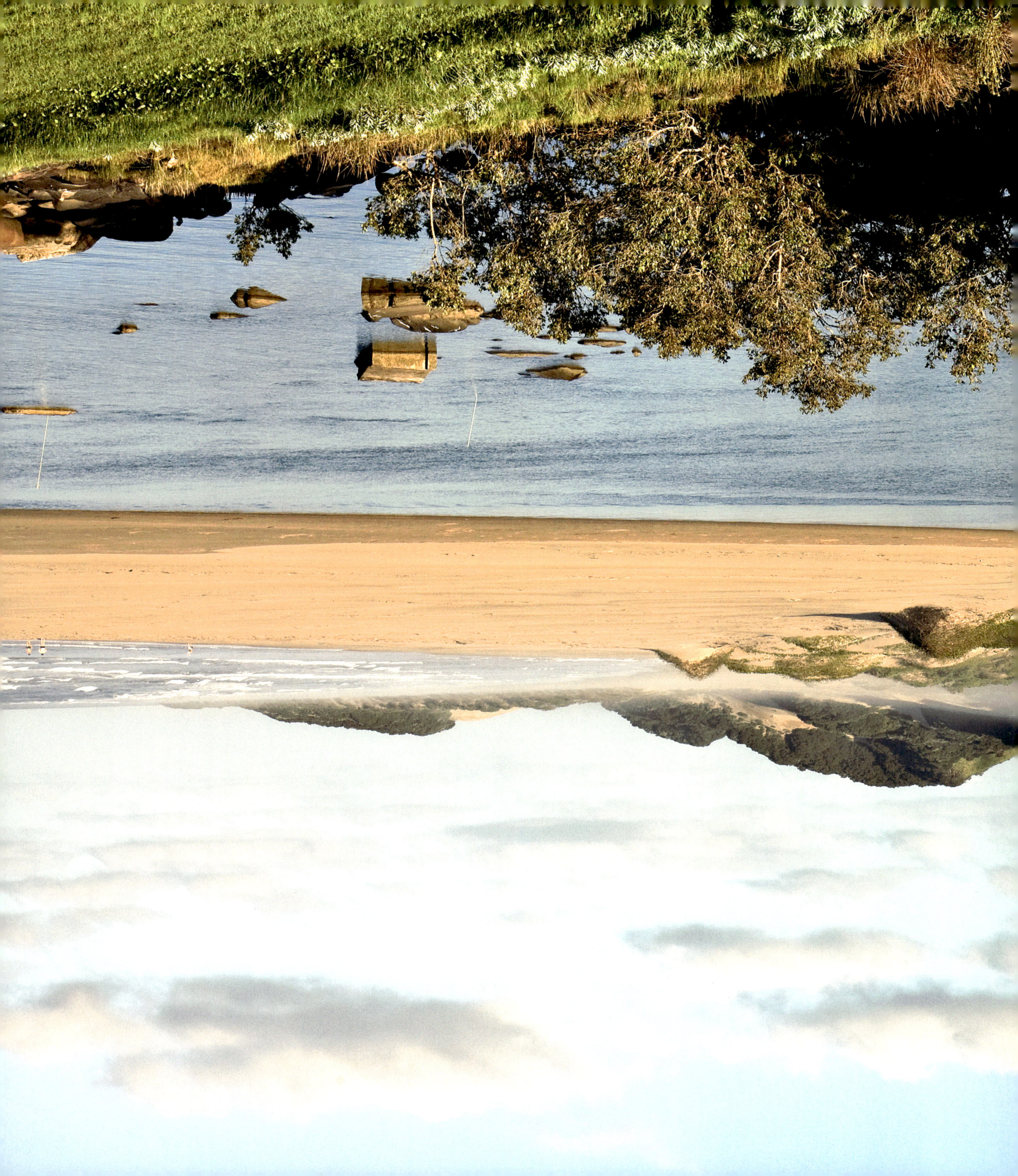

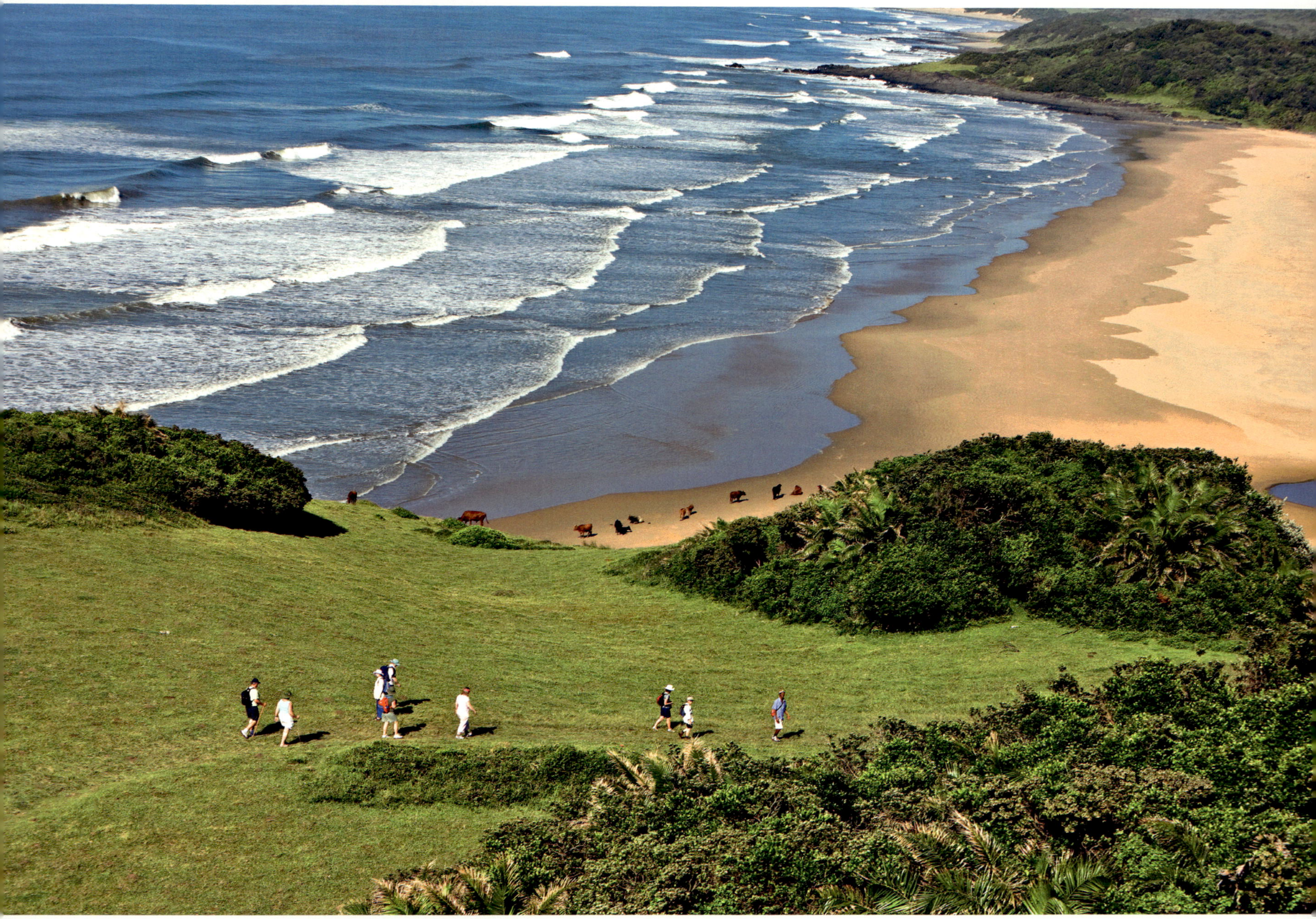

←← Wave crest at the mouth of Inxaxo River
← Wild Coast track
↓ Strong women carrying luggage

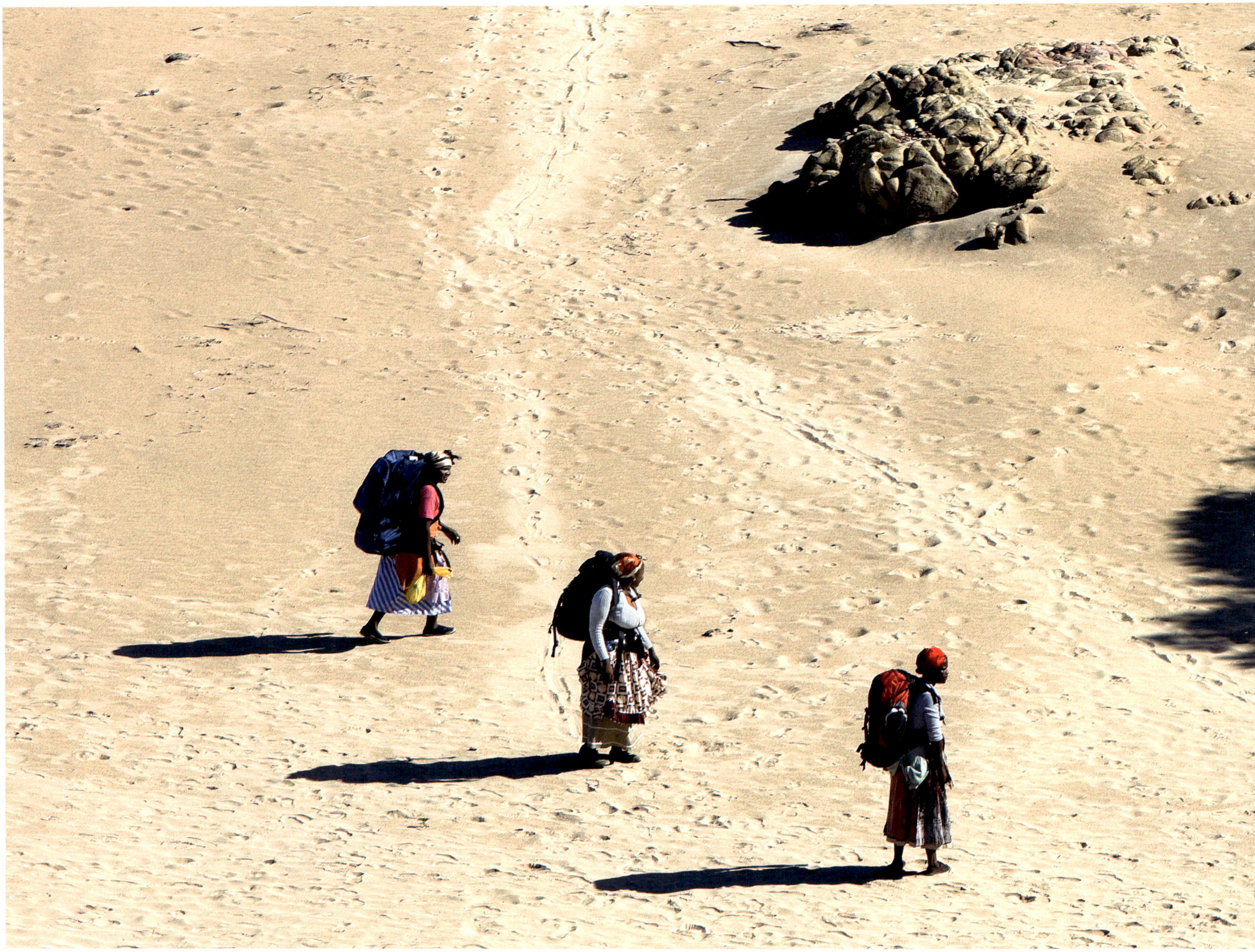

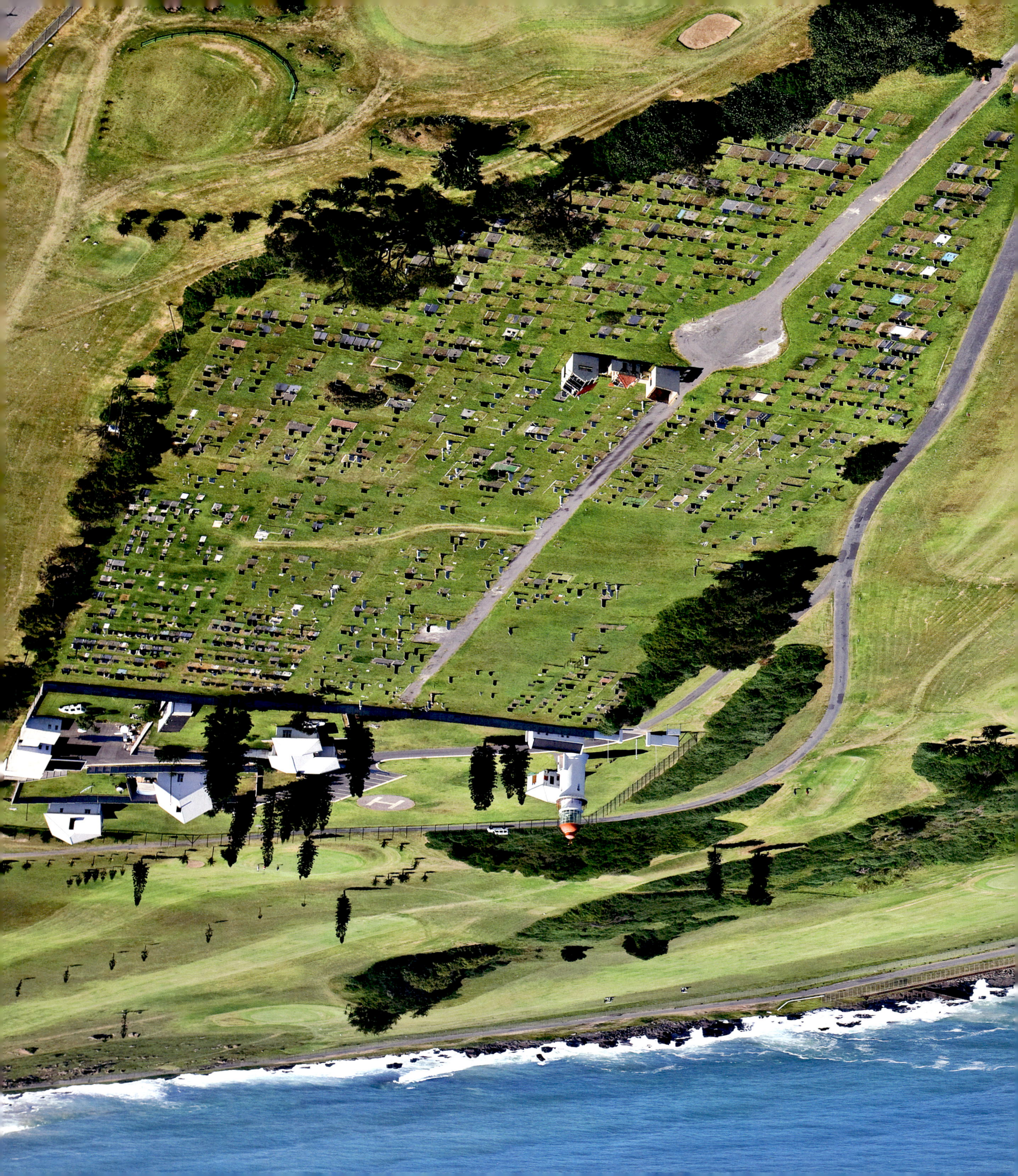

← Golf course, lighthouse and cemetery, East London

↓ East London

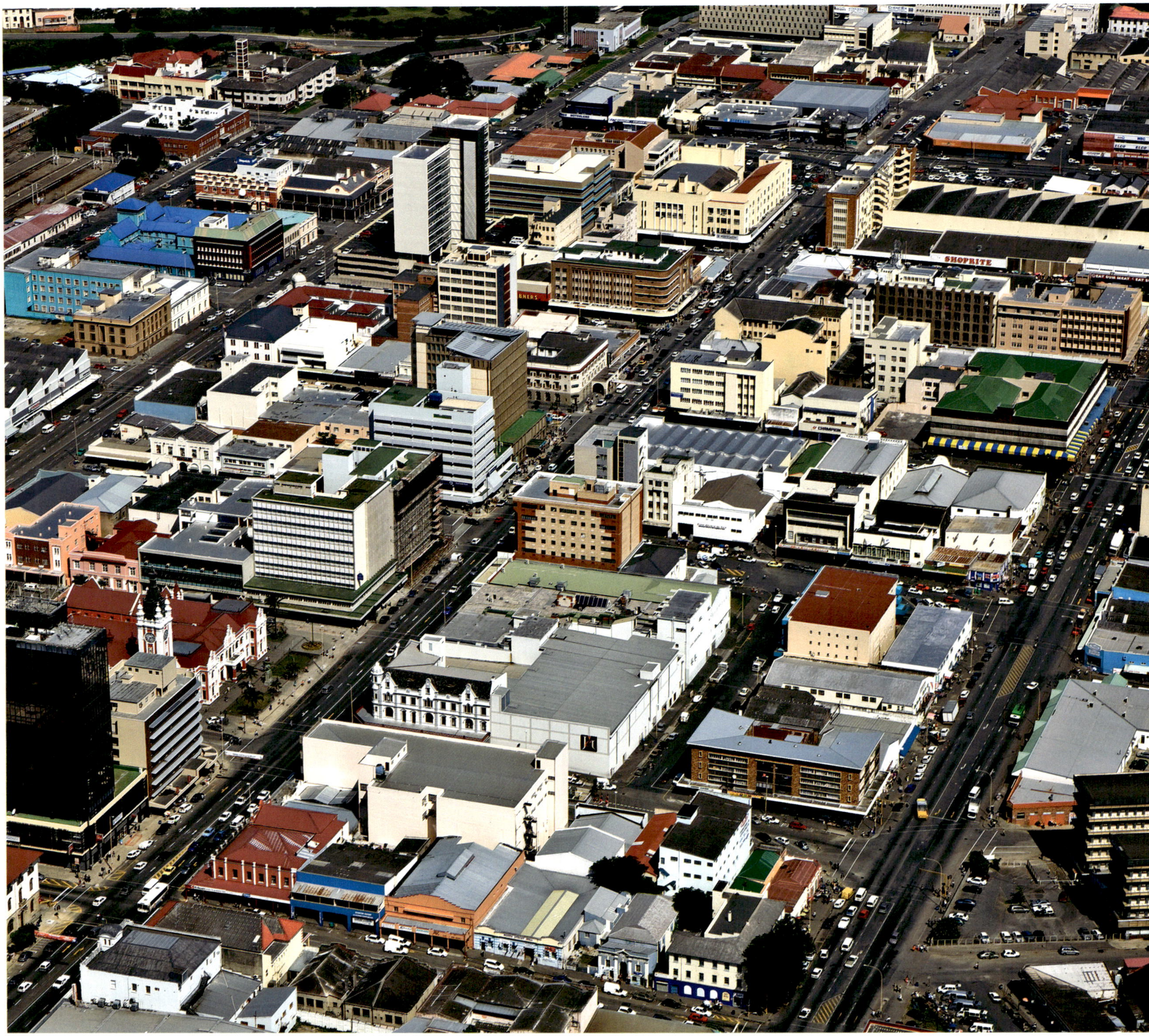

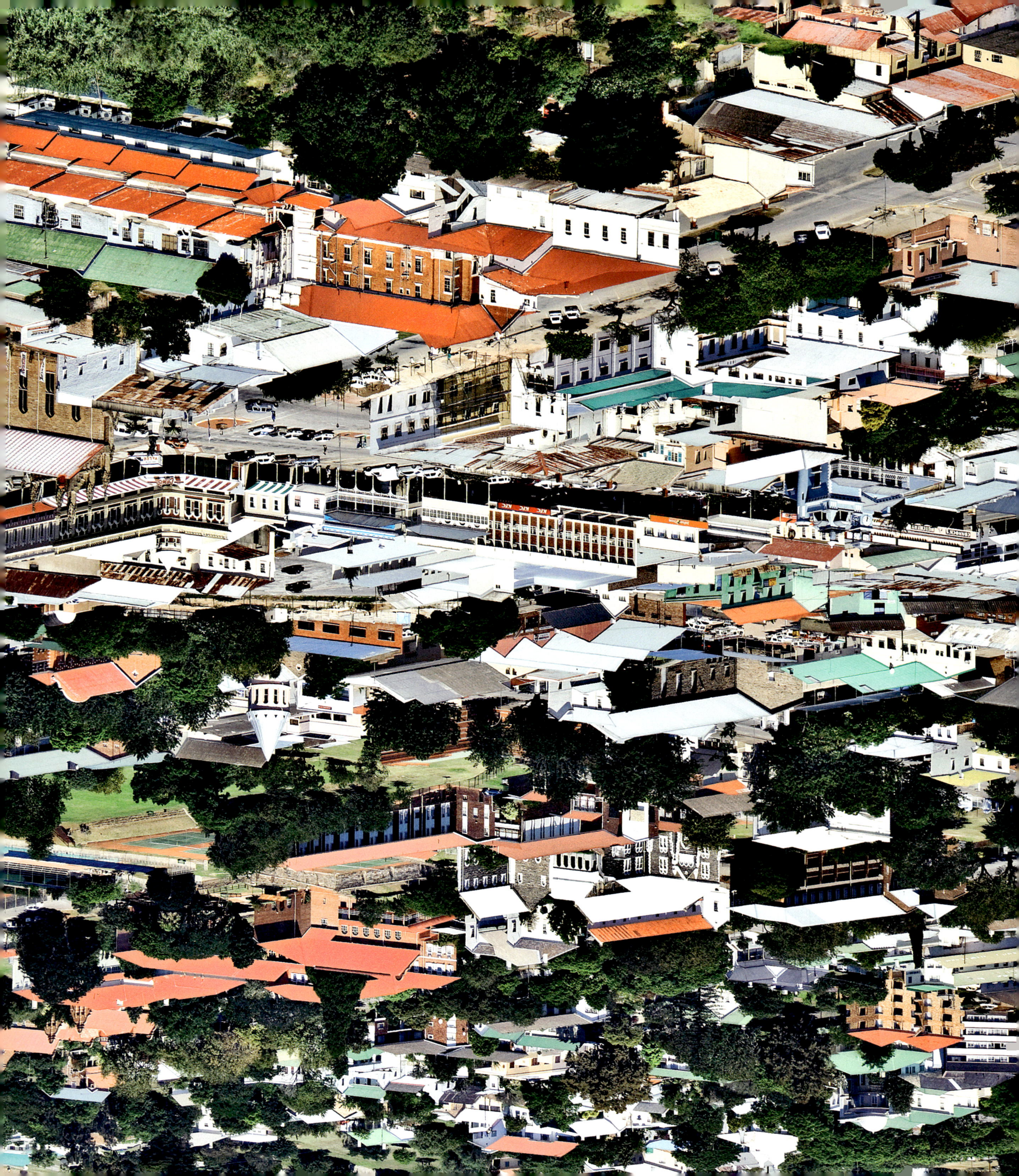

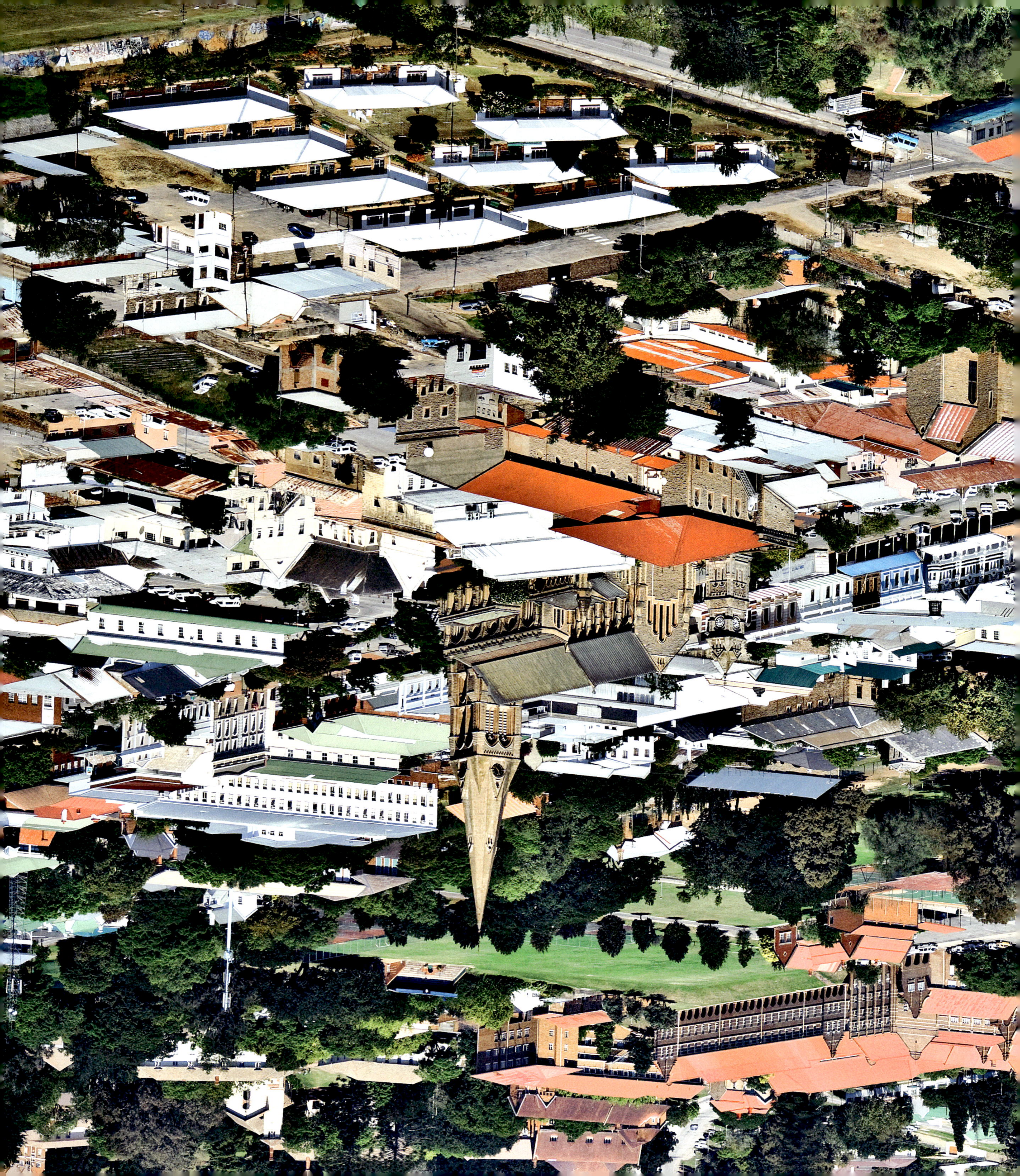

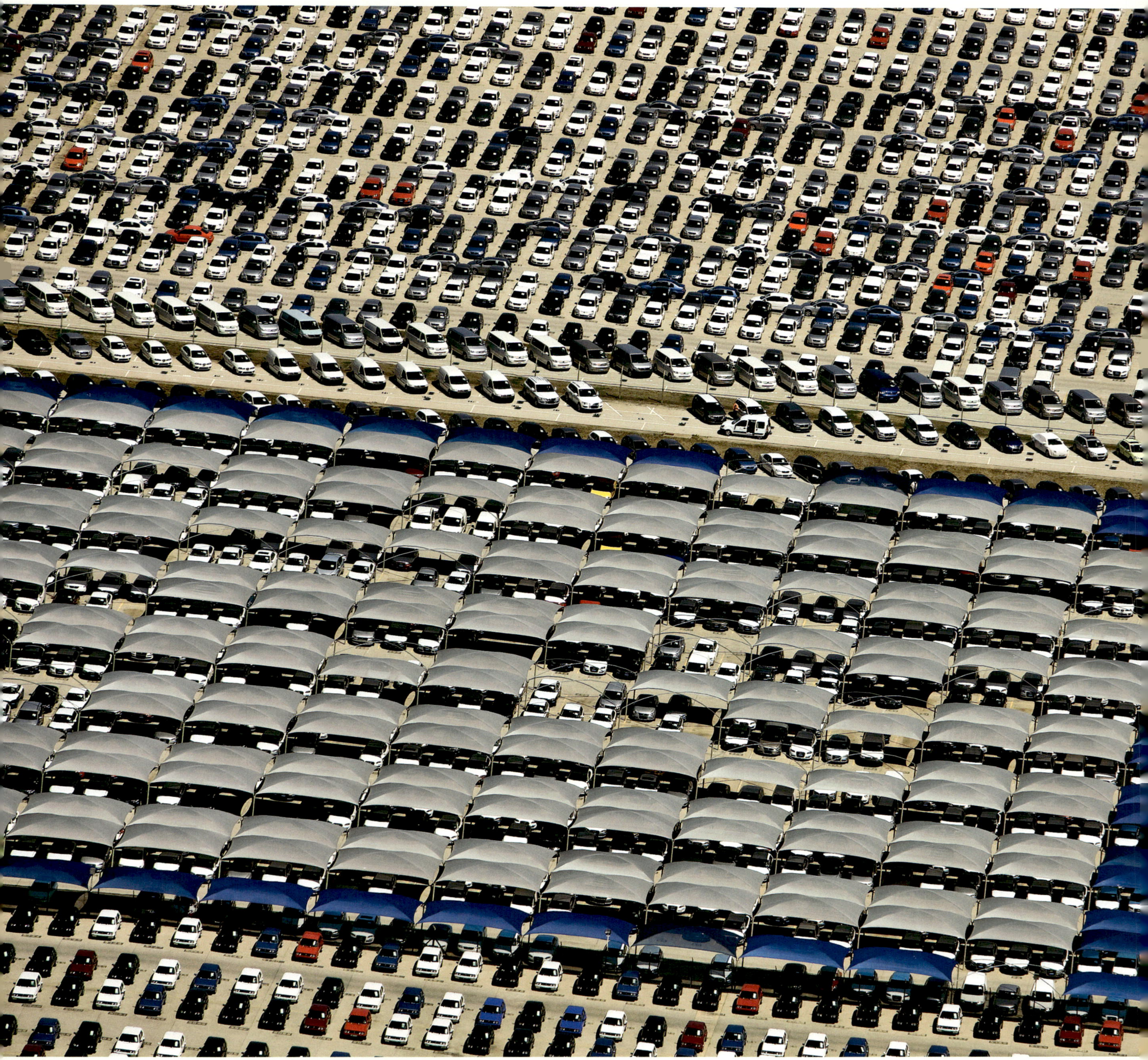

←← Grahamstown

←↓ Car and tire factories, Uitenhage

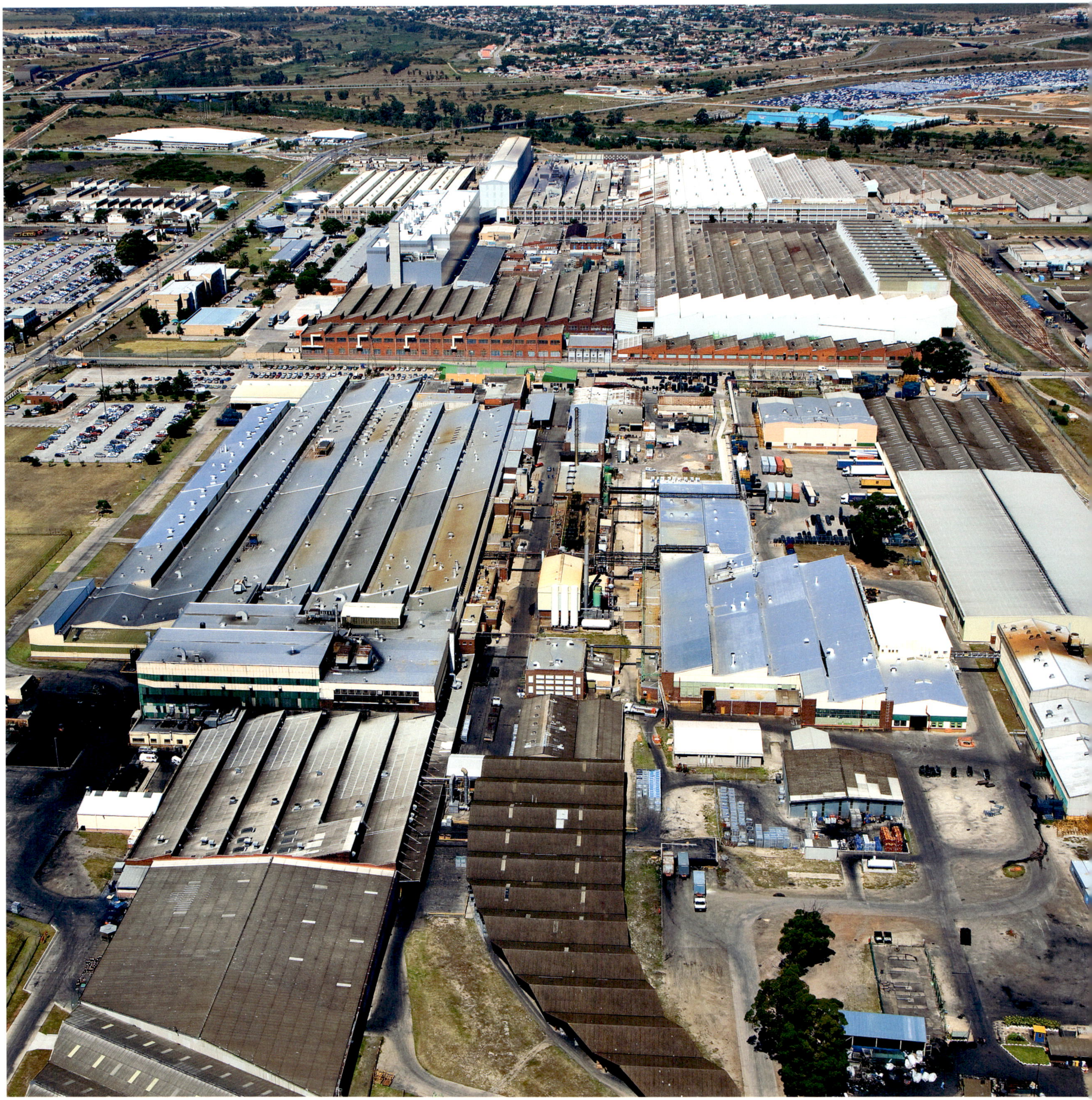

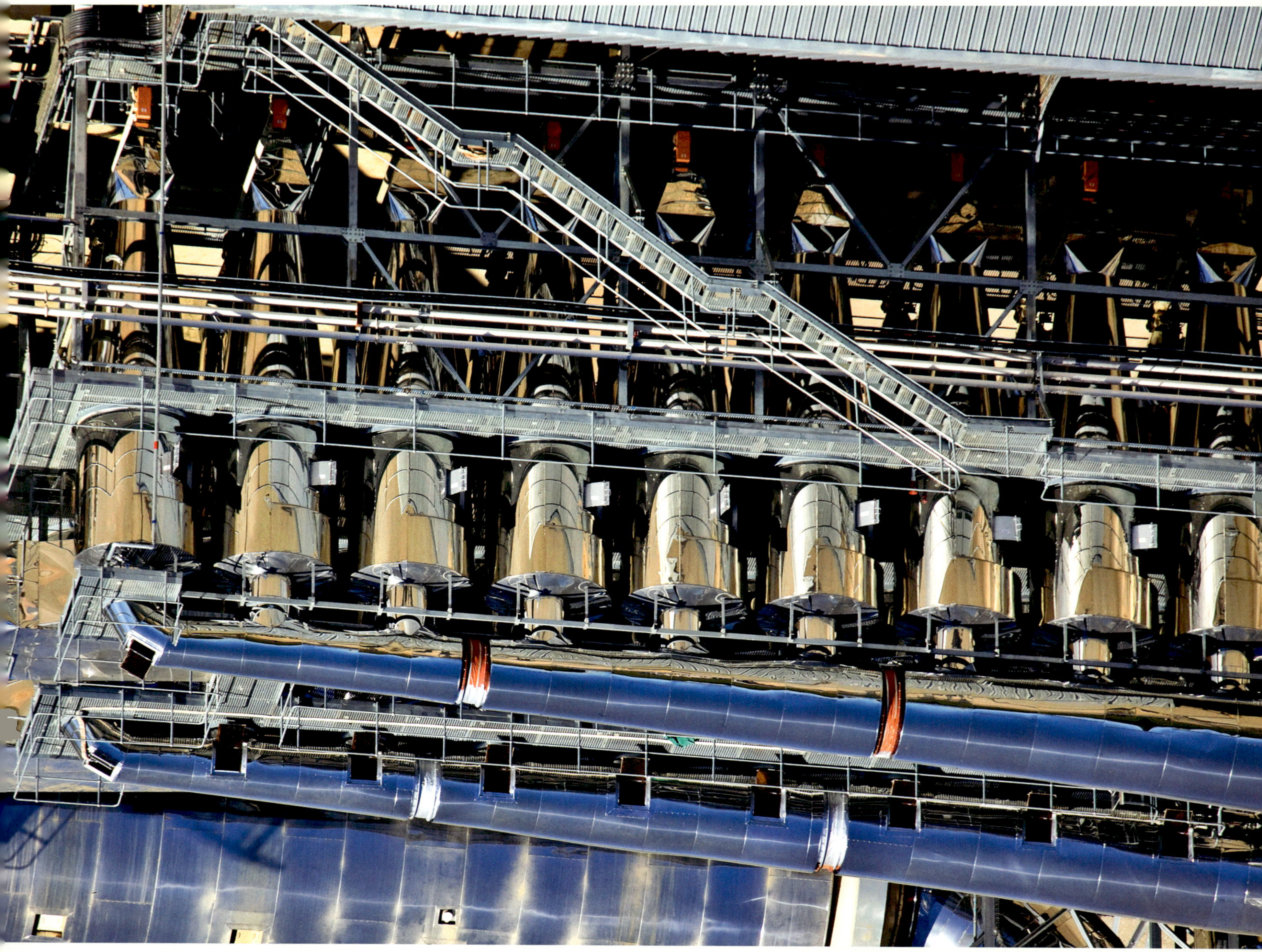

← Ultra-modern wood factory, Ugie

↓ Brick-making

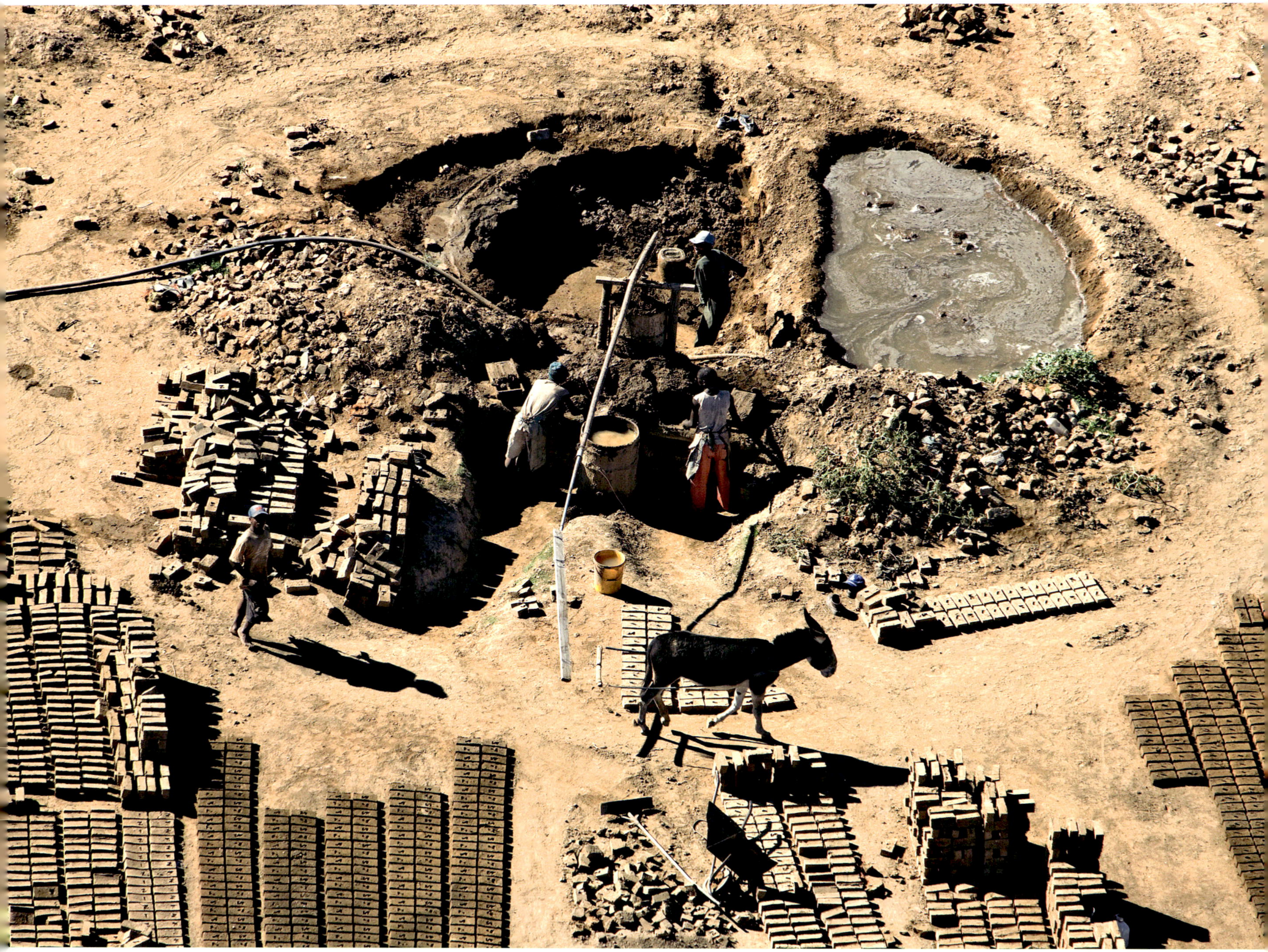

↓→ Port Elizabeth

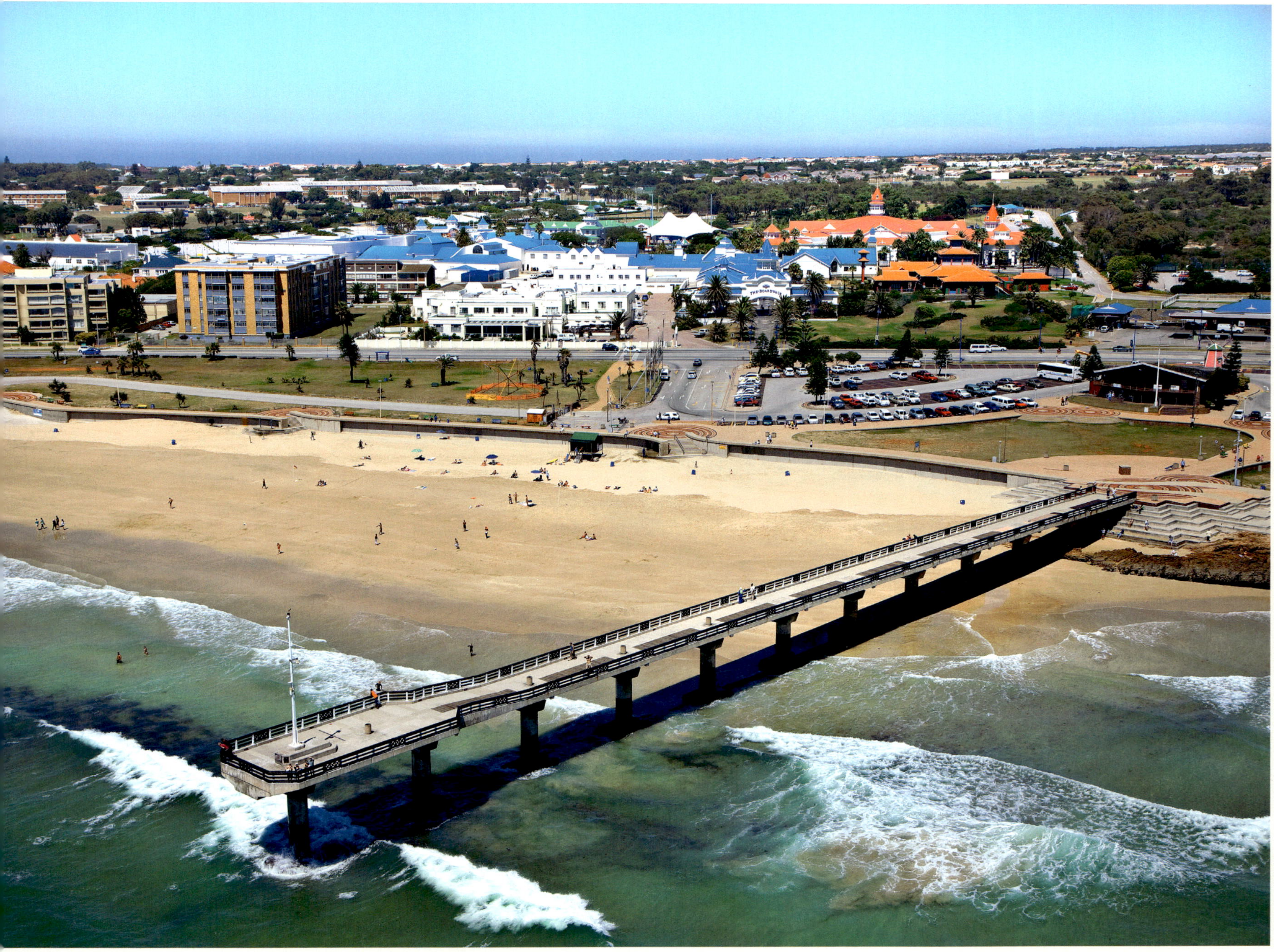

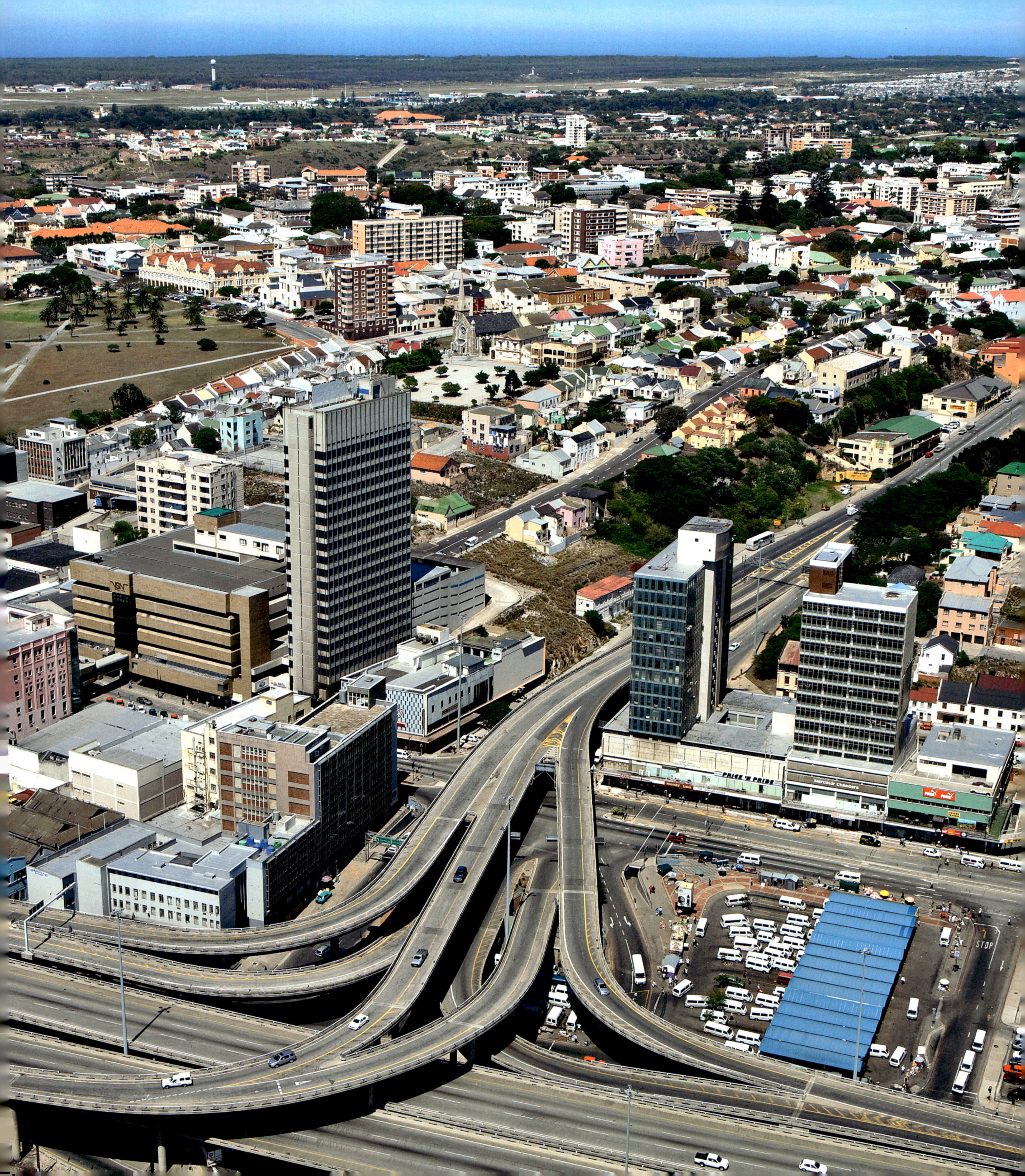

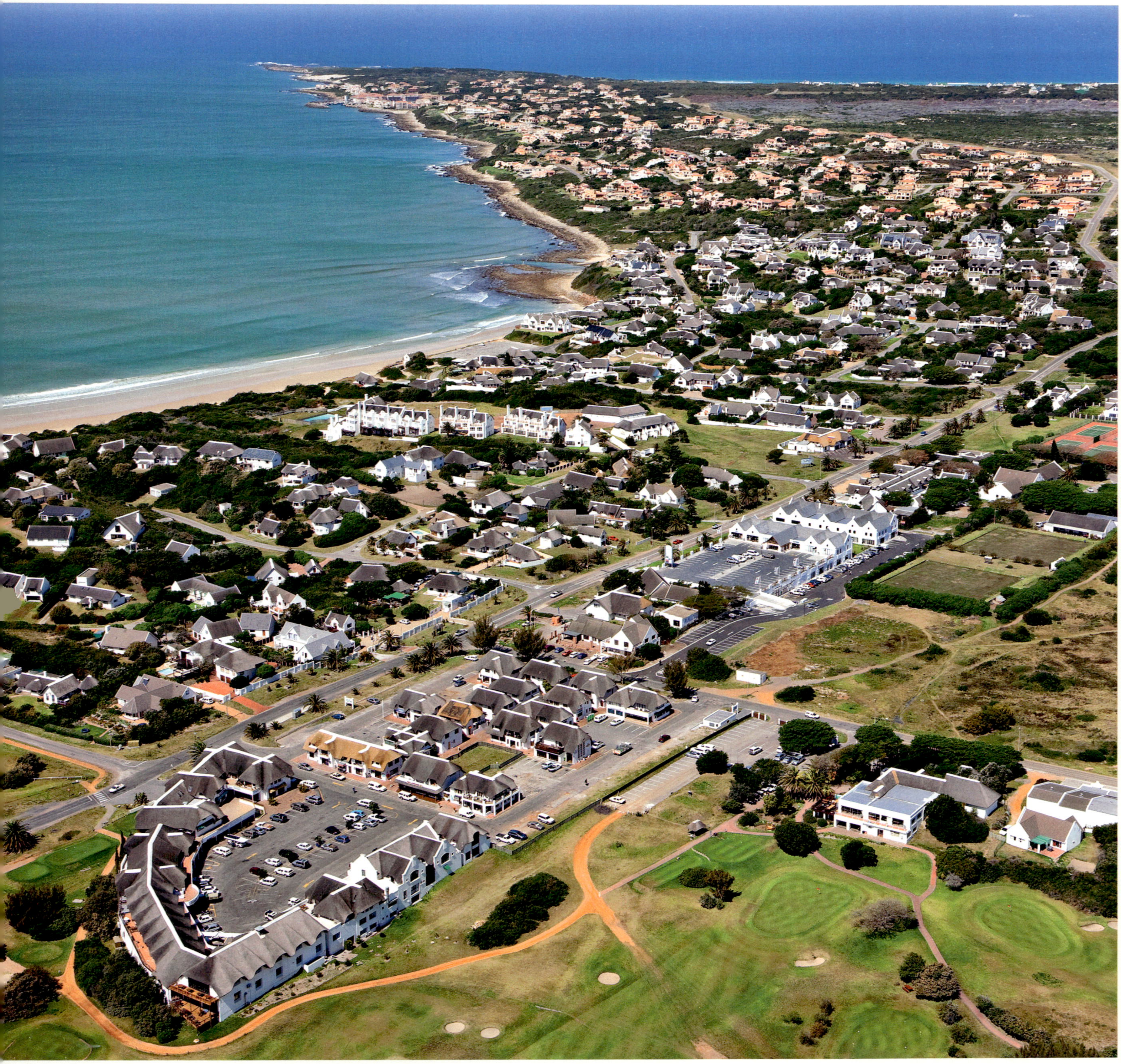

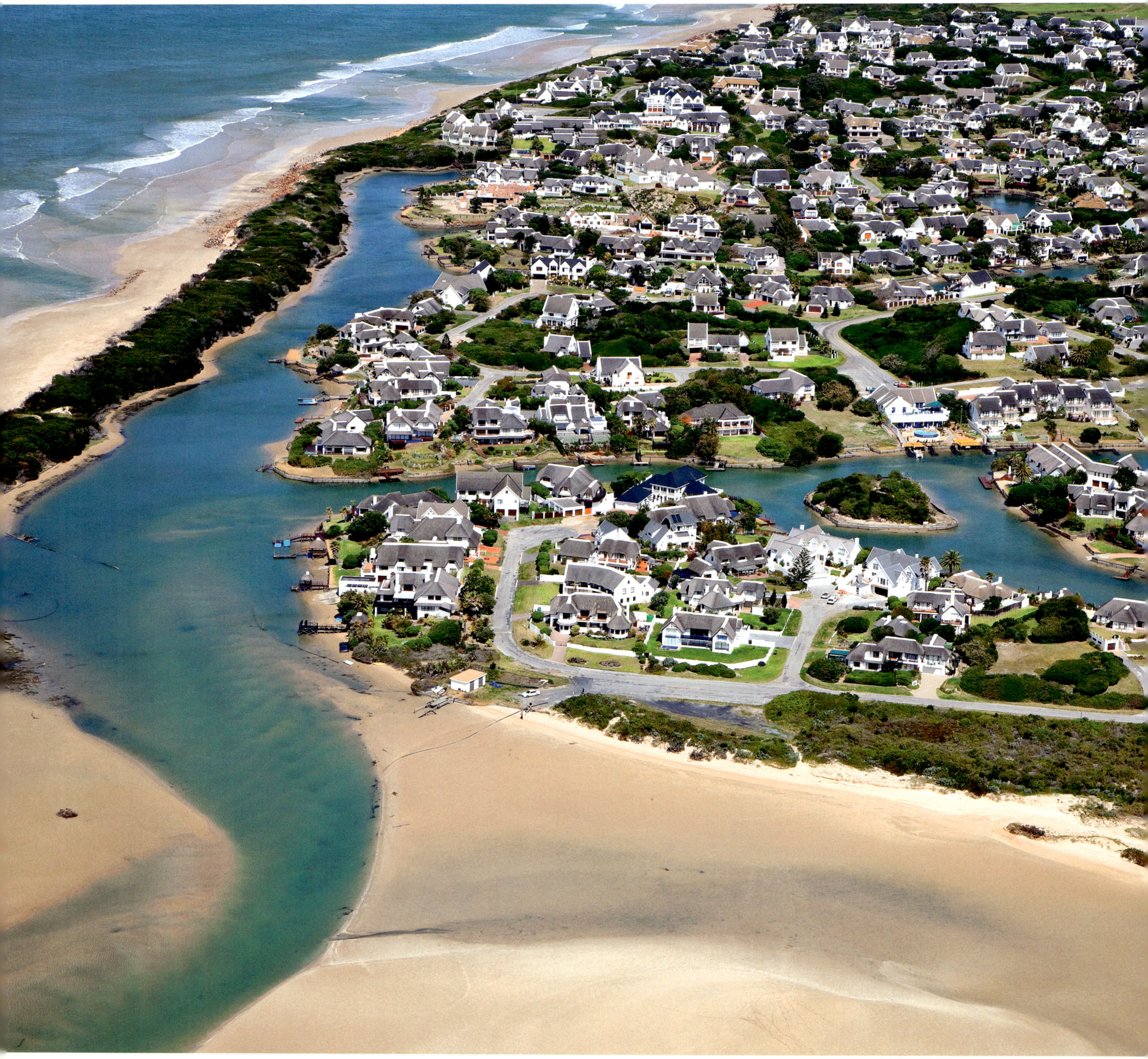

↓ Skuitbaai

→ Lonely house near Oyster Bay

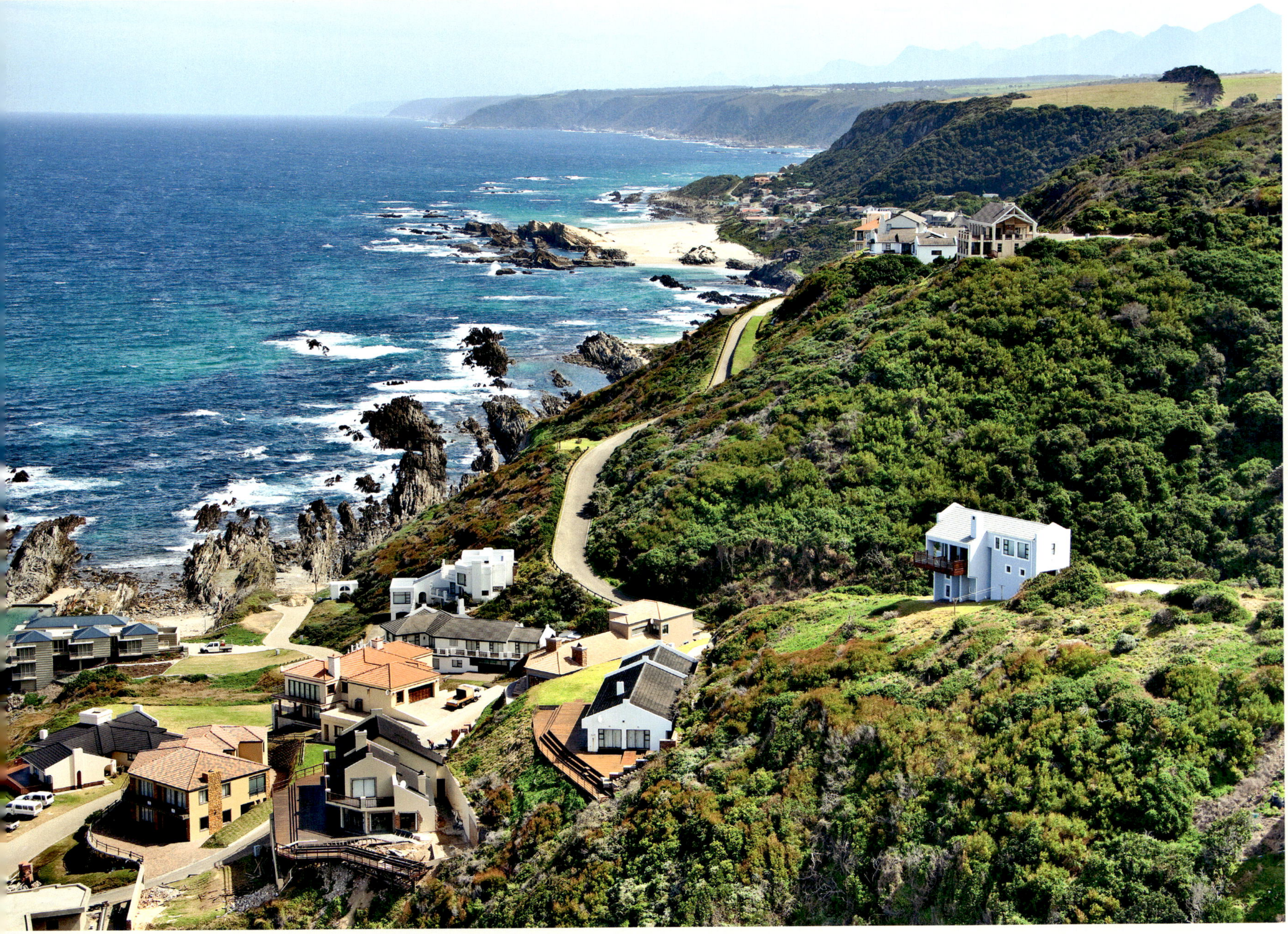

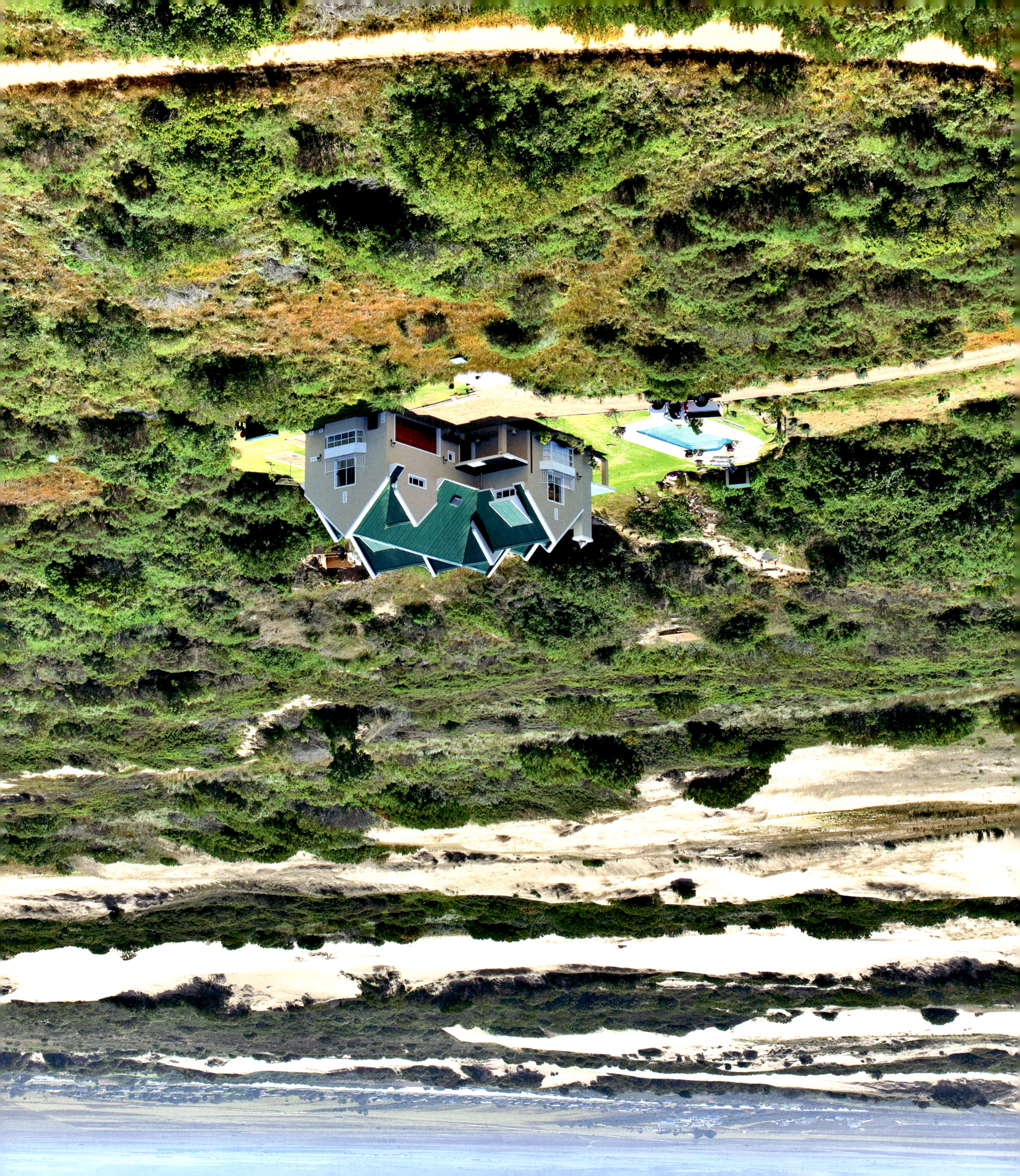

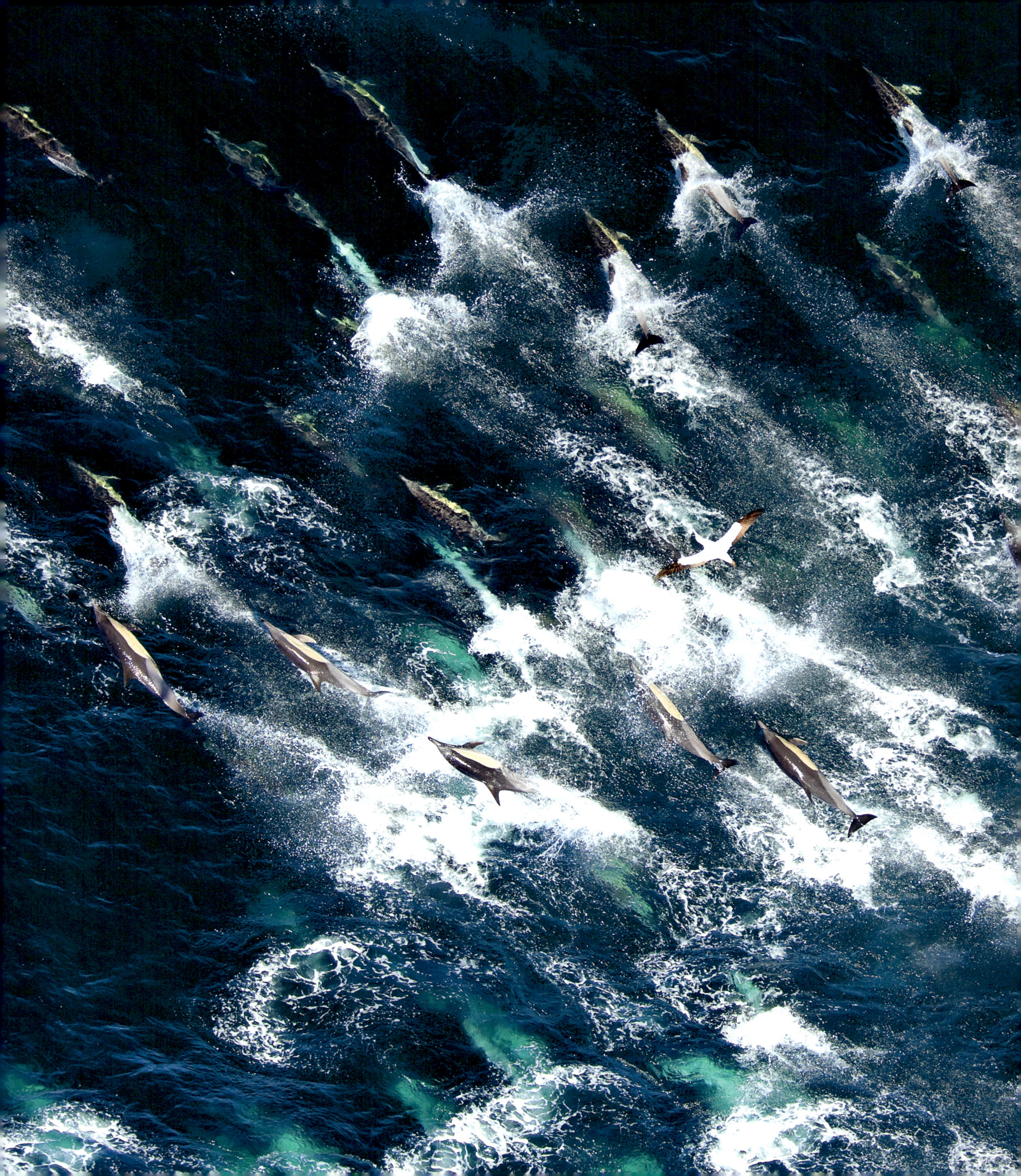

← Dolphins, Indian Ocean
↓ Diving seabirds
→ Hunting dolphins, Indian Ocean

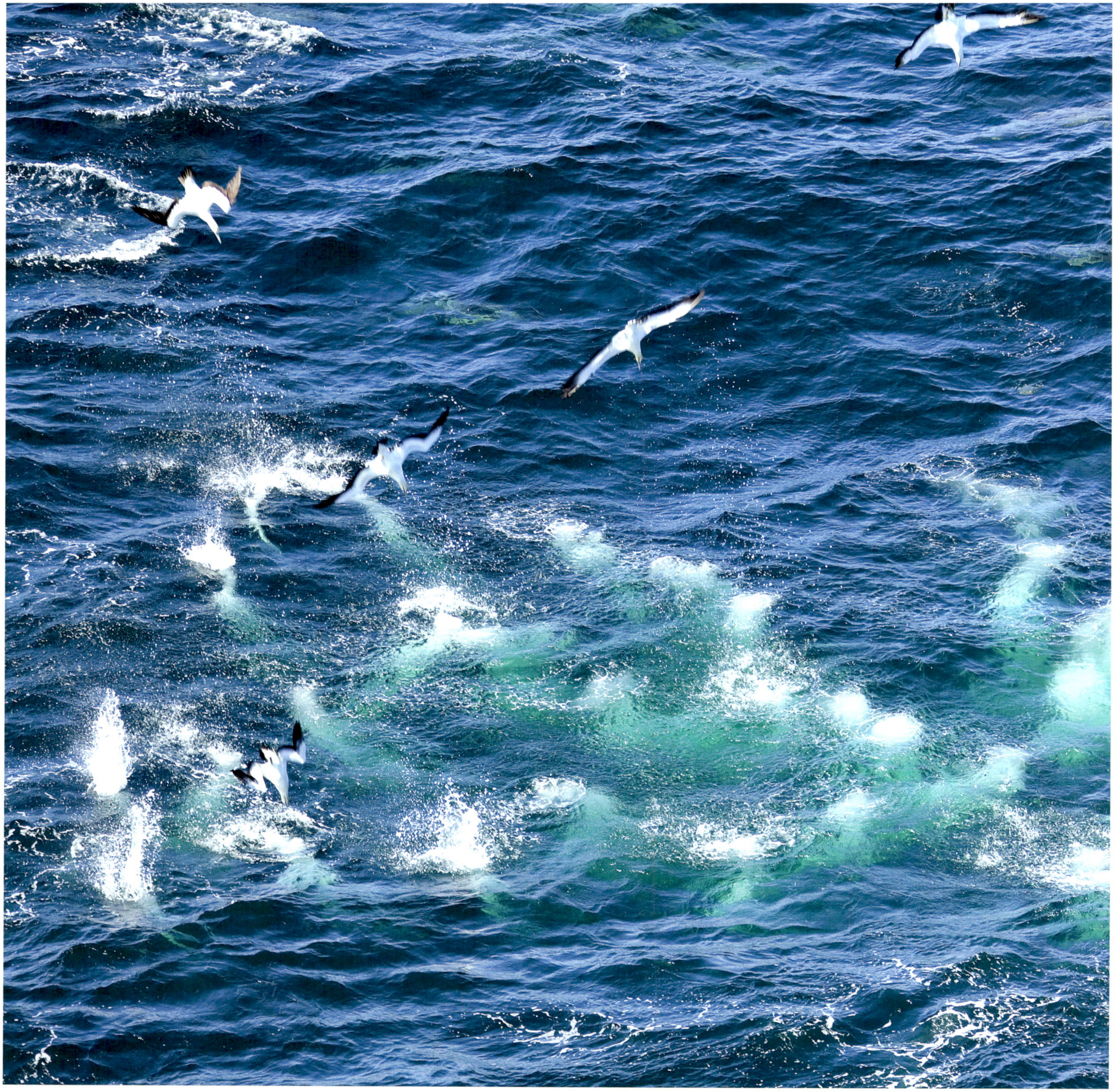

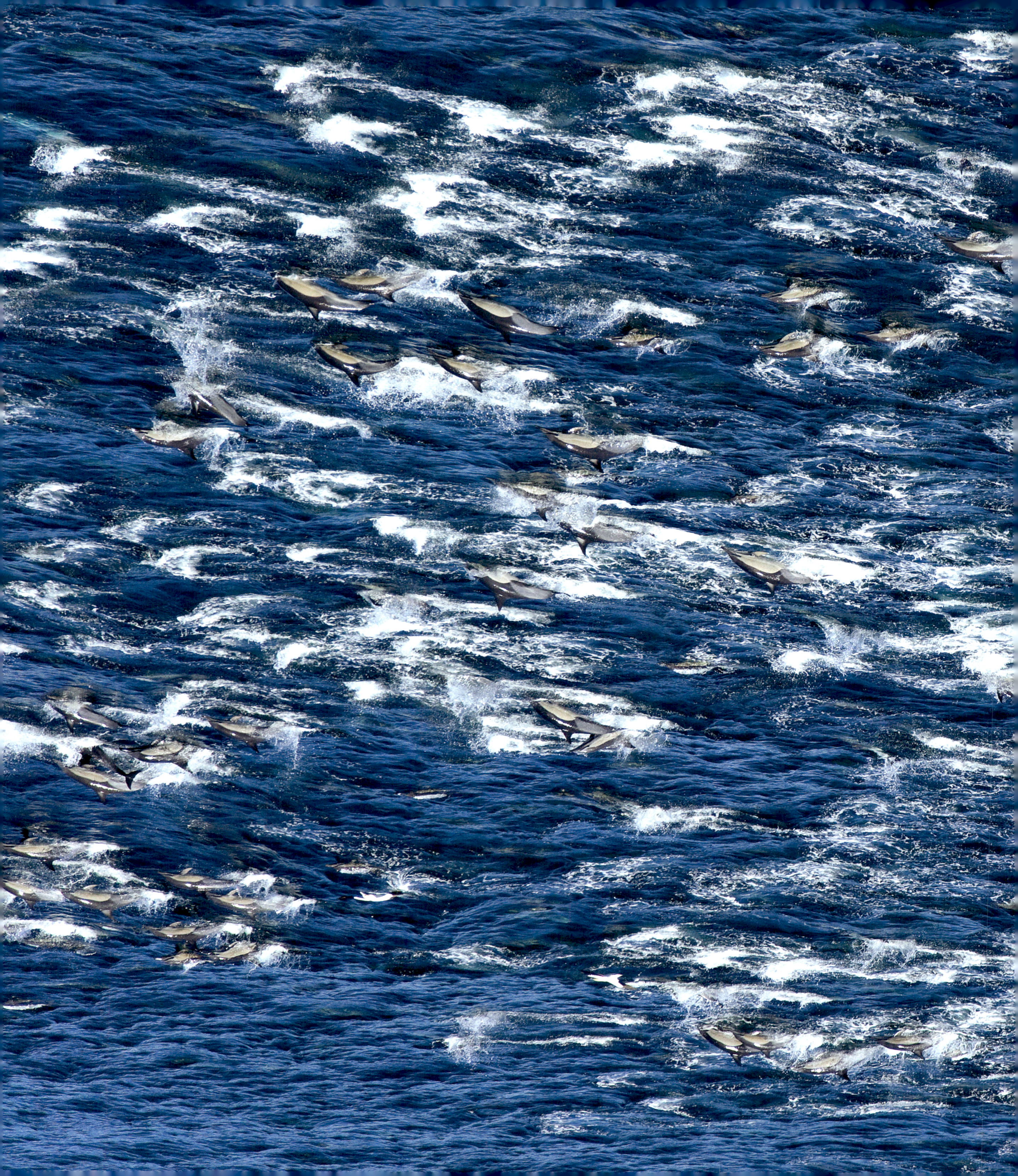

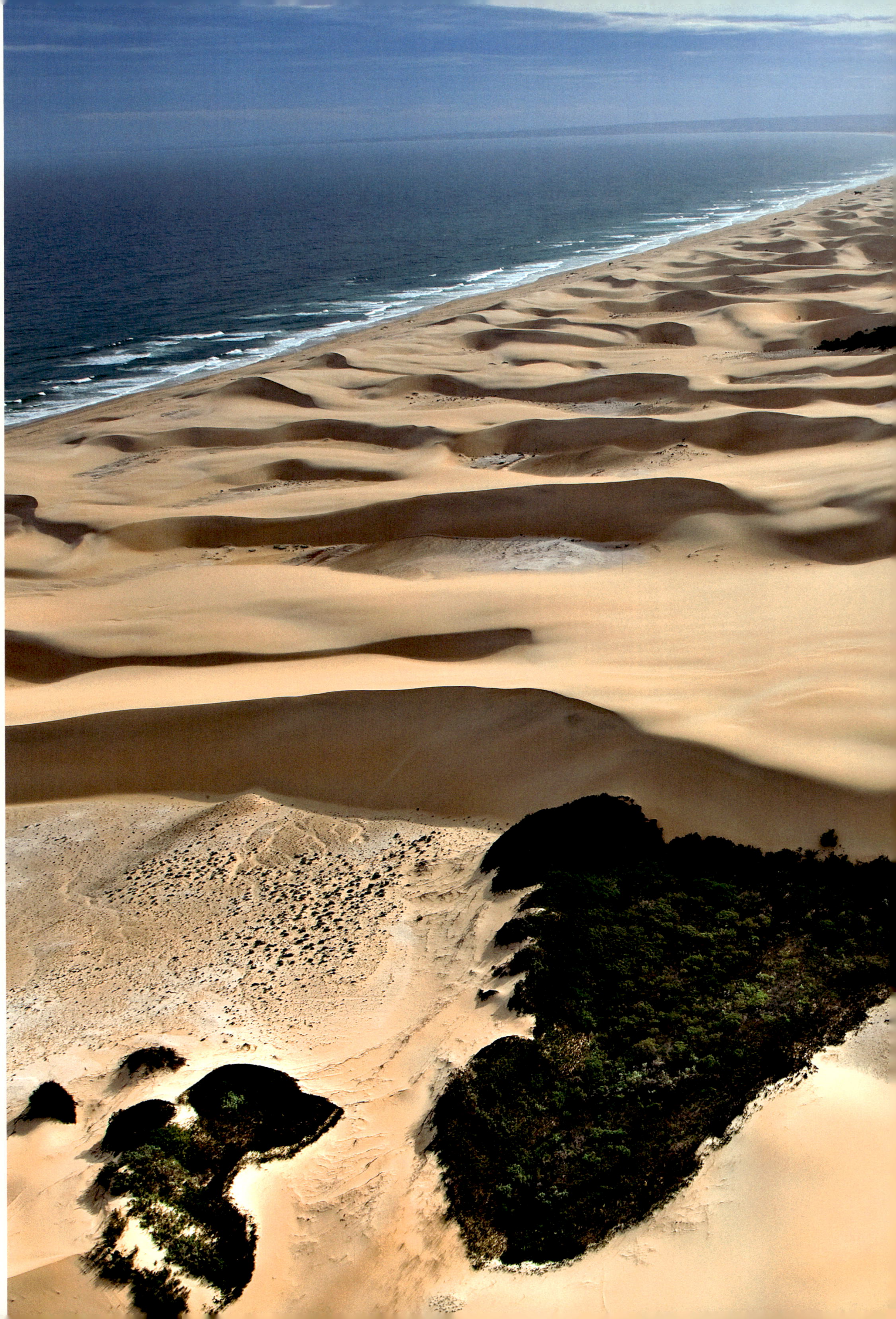

→ Woody Cape Nature Reserve

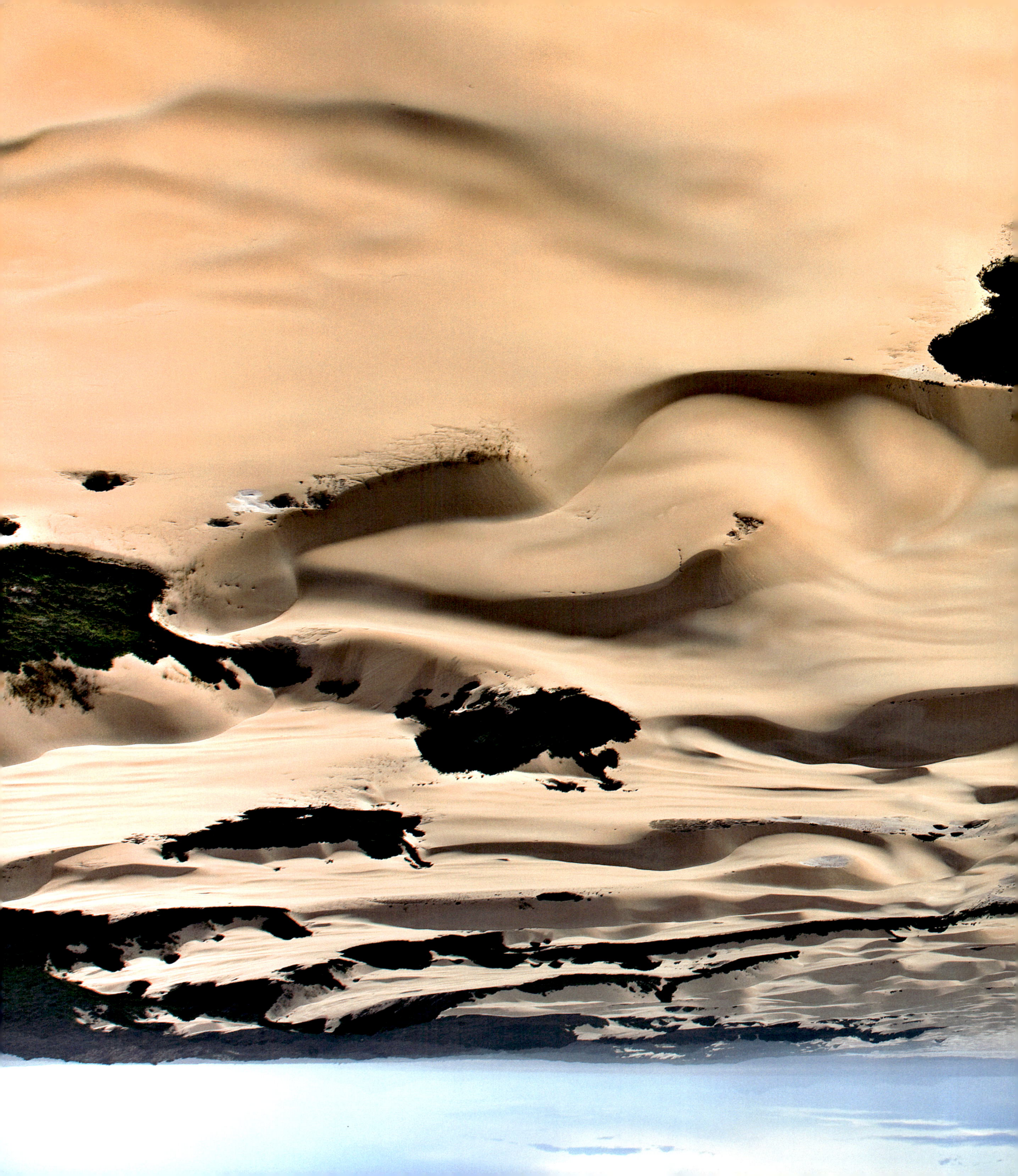

isbn 978 90 5594 704 1

Scriptum Publishers
Nieuwe Haven 151
3117 AA Schiedam
The Netherlands
info@scriptum.nl

© Photography
Karel Tomeï
(Karel Tomeï is a world-renowned Dutch photographer, best known for his abstract ground photography which he has elevated into a fine art. Karel Tomeï has won various international awards. In 2009 Queen Beatrix bestowed a knighthood in the Order of Oranje Nassau on Karel Tomeï for his photographic oeuvre. www.flyingcamera.nl)

© Text
Bart de Graaff
(Bart de Graaff is a historian, publicist and film scenarist. He studied at the Universities of Utrecht and Stellenbosch and is currently the editor of the Dutch Monthly Zuid-Afrika, which is published by the Netherlands-South African Association in Amsterdam.)

Frans Grotepass
(Frans Grotepass is a dental surgeon and a very experienced pilot who builds his own aircraft and has made countless flights for the International Committee of the Red Cross. He is not only a friend of Karel Thomeï, but, thanks to his considerable knowledge of South Africa and everything related to aviation, an adviser and a guide as well.)

Design and Layout
Maurice Blok, Mart Hulspas (LS, Rotterdam)
Technical support
Anthony de Kousemaeker
Translation
Jonathan Ellis
Interview Karel Tomeï
Peter de Lange
Lithography
Nederlof Repro
Print
DZS Grafik

visit us at:
www.scriptum.nl

Special thanks
Special thanks to Glen Brown, an excellent helicopter pilot and friend who, moreover, proved himself to be the most knowledgeble guide to South Africa I could have hoped for.

Special thanks to Karel's wife Monique, his biggest fan.

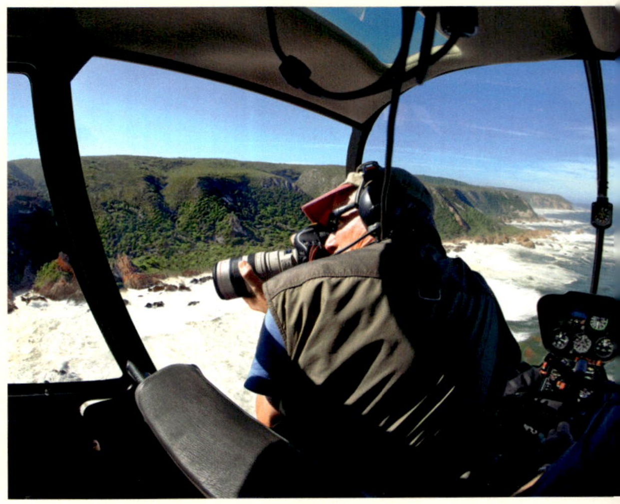

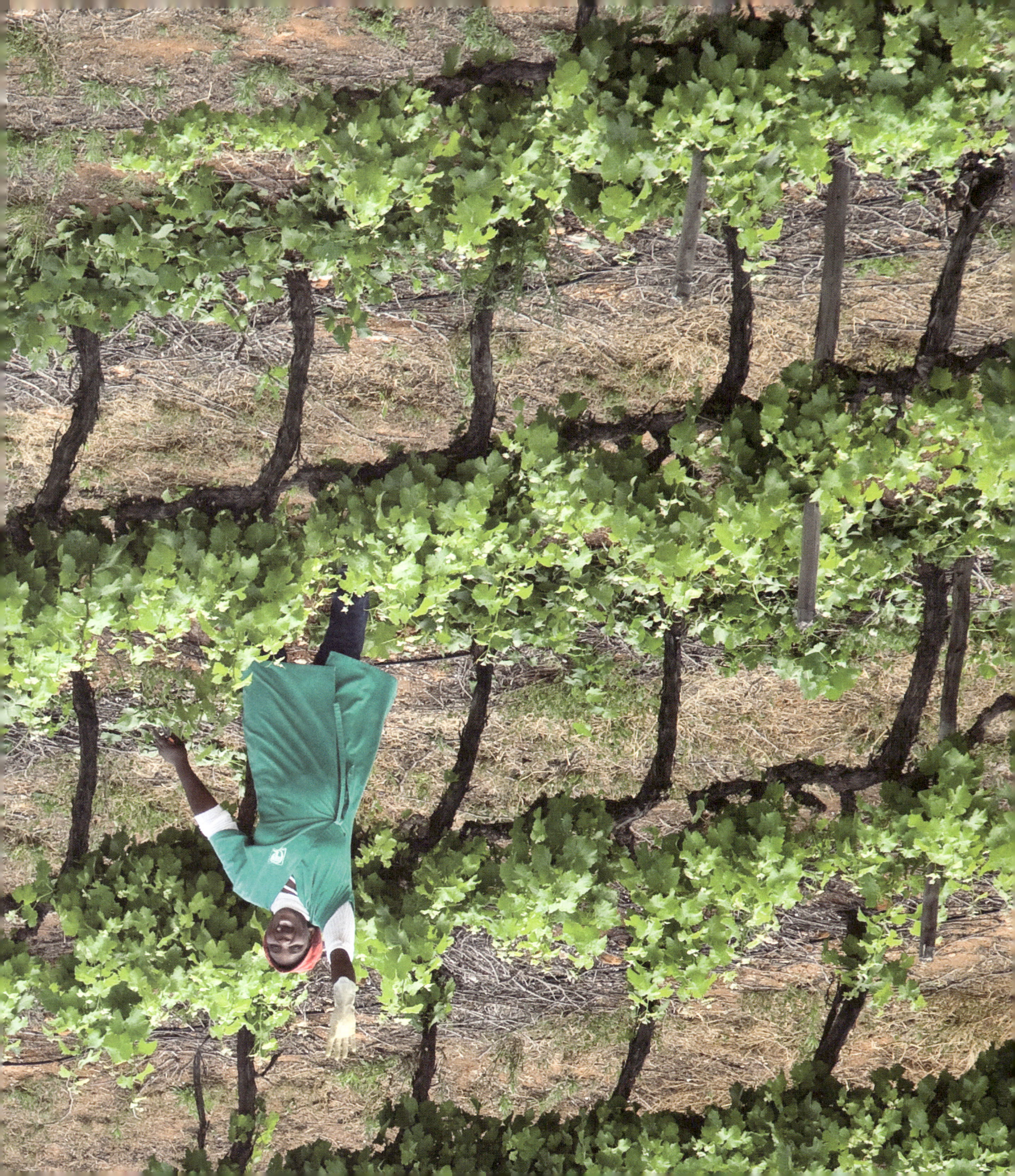